Marketing Tourism and Hospitali
and Cases

Richard George

Marketing Tourism and Hospitality

Concepts and Cases

Richard George
ICON College of Technology and Management/Falmouth University
London, UK

ISBN 978-3-030-64110-8   ISBN 978-3-030-64111-5   (eBook)
https://doi.org/10.1007/978-3-030-64111-5

© The Editor(s) (if applicable) and The Author(s), under exclusive license to Springer
Nature Switzerland AG 2021
This work is subject to copyright. All rights are solely and exclusively licensed by the Publisher, whether the whole or part of the material is concerned, specifically the rights of translation, reprinting, reuse of illustrations, recitation, broadcasting, reproduction on microfilms or in any other physical way, and transmission or information storage and retrieval, electronic adaptation, computer software, or by similar or dissimilar methodology now known or hereafter developed.
The use of general descriptive names, registered names, trademarks, service marks, etc. in this publication does not imply, even in the absence of a specific statement, that such names are exempt from the relevant protective laws and regulations and therefore free for general use.
The publisher, the authors, and the editors are safe to assume that the advice and information in this book are believed to be true and accurate at the date of publication. Neither the publisher nor the authors or the editors give a warranty, expressed or implied, with respect to the material contained herein or for any errors or omissions that may have been made. The publisher remains neutral with regard to jurisdictional claims in published maps and institutional affiliations.

This Palgrave Macmillan imprint is published by the registered company Springer Nature Switzerland AG
The registered company address is: Gewerbestrasse 11, 6330 Cham, Switzerland

Preface

Welcome to the *Marketing Tourism and Hospitality: Concepts and Cases*. Marketing is about strategically creating and maintaining a competitive advantage, producing a superior performance for a business and its customers. Although the fundamentals of marketing remain the same, tourism and hospitality marketers, managers and students have a responsibility to keep abreast of the dynamics of the industry. Information and communications technology has changed the way in which companies distribute their products and reach consumers. Social media marketing, digital marketing, health issues (such as COVID-19), safety and security of travellers, and social responsibility are important developments that have significantly changed the face of the tourism and hospitality industry. Tourism demand is always changing, and tourism trends are therefore important. The book retains the key principles of marketing applied in the international tourism and hospitality industry, with a particular focus on small businesses in the emerging markets.

The internet has undoubtedly changed the world in which we sell. It offers a new paradigm for the way in which consumers connect with brands and with each other. The online medium provides consumers with more choice, more influence, and more power. However, marketing on the internet does not necessarily mean throwing out the rule book on traditional marketing principles. Instead the internet provides a new environment in which to build on these principles. Profit is still revenue less cost. The internet does not change that.

The concept for this book emerged from my experience as a lecturer in tourism management in Cape Town, South Africa over 22 years ago. I found that there were no tourism and hospitality marketing textbooks that focused on developing countries, although many books that applied in an American or British context were available. I noticed that students (particularly those who had not had the opportunity to travel) found it difficult to relate to international examples used in these books.

The pedagogical features of this book are as follows:
- Each chapter includes a number of learning outcomes, which are stated at the beginning of the chapter to orientate the reader.
- Each chapter begins with a brief overview and introduction.
- Definitions and key concepts are clearly highlighted throughout the text.
- Short examples (Industry Insights) from the industry are given throughout the text for the application of marketing principles.
- Website links of organisations discussed in the text are supplied. Readers are encouraged to visit the web pages of these organisations for further information.
- Did-you-know snippets offer interesting information.
- An in-depth case study, including questions and activities, appears at the end of each chapter. The case studies have been selected to cover all sectors of the industry and offer readers the opportunity to apply theoretical knowledge to real-life situations.
- Each chapter includes references for further reading on core concepts.

━ A glossary of terms is included for quick reference.

This book is structured into five parts:

1. Part I: Understanding Marketing in the Tourism and Hospitality Industry
   In this part, the subject of tourism and hospitality marketing is introduced and the characteristics of tourism are discussed.
2. Part II. Understanding the Tourism and Hospitality Market
   This section describes the market in which tourism and hospitality businesses operate. It deals with consumer behaviour in tourism and hospitality marketing and marketing research.
3. Part III. Designing the Tourism and Hospitality Marketing Strategy
   This part explains the factors that influence the business environment in which organisations operate. It also covers market segmentation tourism and hospitality marketing planning
4. Part IV. Implementing the Tourism and Hospitality Marketing Mix
   This section discusses the implementation of various strategies of the marketing mix in marketing planning, including branding, pricing, tourism distribution, promoting and advertising, the promotions mix, and digital marketing.
5. Part V. Understanding Tourism and Hospitality Marketing Issues
   This part closes with a discussion on several issues, including internal marketing, relationship marketing, and destination marketing.

For students: *Marketing Tourism and Hospitality: Concepts and Cases* is written to meet the requirements of all travel, hospitality, and tourism courses as well as related industry courses. Marketing will have an important influence on your career, whether or not you are directly engaged in the field. Tourism and hospitality marketing offers a wide range of career opportunities.

For practitioners: Marketing is a very practical subject. This book aims to assist people who have not formally studied the subject or who may need to revisit the subject. You are encouraged to relate the principles to your business.

The role of the marketer is a crucial one in every tourism and hospitality organisation. People who work in the tourism and hospitality industry have to be consumer-oriented because they are part of the offering that the company is selling. Tourism and hospitality marketing is not just about selling a dream (a holiday). It is also about how to deal with consumers, solve problems and succeed in a growing industry.

Richard George
London, UK

Acknowledgements

Writing a book requires the acknowledgement of a number of people whose names never appear on the cover. I would like to recognise and thank the following people who assisted in the process of making this book a reality:

- The Palgrave team, including Liz Barlow, Sam Stocker, and Srishti Gupta.
- Stuart Bryan, Nazim Saleem, Alex Mawer, Tina Salimi, Rob Stokes, Dr. Chris Hattingh, Danielle Shaffer, Joseph Bird, Tanya Barben, Mayuri Rajani, Dr. Jonathan Wilson, and Rob Stokes for their continuous advice, support, and help.

Abbreviations

ABL	Above-the-line (promotions)	ATI	Automatic telephone interviewing
ABTA	Association of British Travel Agents (now known as the Travel Association) (abta.com)	ATINER	Athens Institute for Education and Research (atiner.gr/)
ACORN	A classification of residential neighbourhoods	ATLAS	Association for Tourism and Leisure Education (atlas-euro.org)
ADTCA	Abu Dhabi Tourism & Culture Authority (visitabudhabi.ae)	ATP	Autoridad de Turismo de Panamá (atp.gob.pa/)
AGM	Annual general meeting	ATTA	Adventure Travel Trade Association (adventuretravel.biz)
AHT	Articles in hospitality and tourism	AVE	Advertising value equivalent
AI	Artificial intelligence	B&B	Bed and breakfast
AIDA	Attention, interest, desire, and action	B2B	Business-to business
		B2C	Business-to-consumer
AIDS	Acquired immunodeficiency syndrome	BCG	Boston Consulting Group
AIOs	Activities, interests, and opinions	BHA	British Hospitality Association (bha.org.uk)
AJT	Athens journal of tourism	BOGOF	Buy-one-get-one-free
AMA	American Marketing Association (marketingpower.com)	BOS	Bristol online survey (onlinesurveys.ac.uk)
AONB	Area of outstanding natural beauty	BRICS	Brazil, Russia, India, China, and South Africa
AR	Augmented reality	BSP	Billing and settlement plan
ASI	Archaeological Survey of India (asi.nic.in/asi_aboutus.asp)	BT	Business tourism
		BTA	Bermuda Tourism Authority
ASA	Advertising Standards Authority (asa.org.uk)	BTL	Below-the-line (promotion)
ATA	African Travel Association (africa-travelassociation.org)	BTGS	Business tourism growth strategy
		C2B	Consumer-to-business
ATDI	Adventure tourism development index	C2C	Consumer-to-consumer

CAGR	Compound annual growth rate	CNTO	China National Tourism Office (cnto.org)
CAPI	Computer-assisted personal interviewing	COVID-19	Coronavirus 2019
CATI	Computer-assisted telephone interviewing	CPA	Consumer Protection Act (UK)
		CPT	Cost-per-thousand
CATS	Certified adventure travel specialists	CREST	Centre for Responsible Travel (responsibletravel.org)
CBD	Central business district	CRM	Customer relationship management
CBT	Community-based tourism	CRS	Central/computer reservation system
CECT	Chobe Enclave Conservation Trust	CS	Community survey
CEO	Chief executive officer	CSI	Corporate social investment
CFO	Chief financial officer		
CHR	Center for Hospitality Research (sha.cornell.edu/faculty-research/centers-institutes/chr/)	CSQ	Customer satisfaction questionnaire
		CSR	Corporate social responsibility
CIM	Chartered Institute of Marketing (cim.co.uk)	CSV	Creating shared value
CMS	Content management system	CTA	Corporate travel agency
CIP	Critical incident point	CTO	Community tourism organisation
CIPR	Chartered Institute of Public Relations (cipr.co.uk/)	CTR	Click-through-rate
		CVB	Convention and visitor bureau
CIRET	International Centre for Research and Study in Tourism (ciret-tourism.com)	DAB	Digital audio broadcasting
		DCMS	Department for Culture, Media & Sport (UK) (gov.uk/government/organisations/department-for-digital-culture-media-sport)
CLIA	Cruise Lines International Association (cruising.org)		
CMO	Chief marketing officer		
CMS	Content management system	DCB	Dublin Convention Bureau (dublinconventionbureau.com)
CNBS	China National Bureau of Statistics	DMAI	Destination Marketing Association International (destinationmarketing.org)
CNTB	Croatian National Tourist Board (croatia.hr/en-GB)		

DMC	Destination management company	ETC	European Travel Commission (etc-corporate.org)
DMO	Destination marketing/management organisation	ETOA	European Tour Operators Association (etoa.org)
DMS	Destination management system	EU	European Union
DMU	Decision-making unit	eWoM	Electronic word-of-mouth/eWord of mouth
DP	Destination positioning	FAQs	Frequently asked questions
DTV	Digital television	FFP	Frequent-flyer program
DRTV	Direct response television	FIFA	Fédération Internationale de Football Association (fifa.com)
DTCM	Department of Tourism and Commerce Marketing (Dubai) (dubaitourism.gov.ae/)	FIT	Fully independent traveller
DTP	Desktop publishing	FMCG	Fast-moving consumer goods
DRC	Democratic Republic of the Congo	FTT	Fair Trade Tourism (fairtrade.travel)
ECM	Emerging consumer market	GBCS	Great British Class Survey
ECPAT	End Child Prostitution, Child Pornography and Trafficking of Children for Sexual Purposes (ecpat.net)	GBTA	Global Business Travel Association (gbta.org)
		GDP	Gross domestic product
eCRM	Electronic customer relationship management	GDS	Global distribution system
		GEC	General Electric Company
EFL	English foreign language	GHG	Greenhouse gas
EMBRATUR	The Brazilian Tourist Board (visitbrazil.com)	GHS	General household survey
		GIS	Geographic information systems
EMC	Event management company	GMTI	Global Muslim travel index
EMIA	Export marketing and investment assistance	GNP	Gross national product
EPOS	Electronic point of sale	GNTO	Greek National Tourism Organisation (visitgreece.gr)

GPS	Global positioning system		explore/groups/ institute_for_dark_ tourism_research.php)
GSA	General sales agent		
GTO	Group travel organisers	IDTV	Interactive digital television
HI	Hostelling International (hihostels.com)	IGLTA	International Gay and Lesbian Travel Association (iglta.org)
HDE	Historically disadvantaged enterprises	IHCL	Indian Hotels Company Limited (ihcltata.com/)
HDI	Historically disadvantaged individuals	ICHG	InterContinental Hotels Group (ihgplc.com)
HRA	Heritage Railway Association (heritagerailways.com)	IGO	Intergovernmental organisation
HRM	Human resources management	IH&RA	International Hotel and Restaurant Association (ih-ra.com)
HTML	Hypertext mark-up language	IMC	Integrated marketing communication
IAB	Interactive Advertising Bureau (formerly the Digital Media and Marketing Association) (iabsa.net/)	IMC	International Marketing Council (South Africa) (imc.org.za)
IAT	International Academy for the study of Tourism (tourismscholars.org)	IMEX	Incentive Travel, Meetings and Events (imexexhibitions.com)
IATA	International Air Transport Association (iata.org)	IMM	Institute of Marketing Management (imm.ac.za)
IBA	International Backpacking Association (backpackingfun.com)	IMT	India Ministry of Tourism (tourism.gov.in)
		IMTs	Individual mass tourists
ICC	International conference/convention centre	IoT	Internet of things
		IPA	Importance-performance analysis
ICCA	International Congress and Convention Association (iccaworld.com)	IPS	International passenger survey
		IRL	In real life
		IS	Information systems
ICT	Information and communications technology	ISBA	Incorporated Society of British Advertisers (isba.org.uk)
IDTR	Institute for Dark Tourism Research (uclan.ac.uk/research/	ISES	International Special Events Society (ises.com)

ISIS	Islamic State of Iraq and Syria		Employment (mbie.govt.nz/)
ISP	Internet service provider	MCQ	Multiple-choice question
ISS	International space station	MCT	Ministry of Culture & Tourism, Turkey (ktb.gov.tr/)
ISTTE	International Society of Travel & Tourism Educators (istte.org)	MDP	Marketing decision problem
IT	Information technology	MDSS	Marketing decision support systems
ITB	International Tourismus Borse (itb-berlin.de)	MENA	Middle East North Africa
ITPs	Incentive travel planners	MERS	Middle East respiratory syndrome
ITM	Indonesian Tourism Ministry (indonesia.travel)	MIA	Meetings Industry Association (mia-uk.org/events/
ITO	Inbound tour operator	MICE	Meetings, incentives, conferences, and exhibitions
ITT	Institute of Travel & Tourism (itt.co.uk)	MIS	Marketing information system
IVF	In vitro fertilisation		
IVS	International visitor survey	MMS	Multi-media messaging service
JTB	Jordan Tourism Board (▶ www.visitjordan.com)	MNC	Multi-national corporation
		MOCAA	Museum of Contemporary Art Africa (zeitzmocaa.museum)
KPI	Key performance indicator		
LBS	Location-based marketing	MRS	Market Research Society (mrs.org.uk/)
LCC	Low-cost carrier	MS Excel	Microsoft Excel
LFS	Labour force survey	MSC	Mediterranean Shipping Company
LGBT	Lesbian, gay, bisexual, and transgender	MTPA	Mauritius Tourism Promotion Authority (tourism-mauritius.mu)
LRTI	Lodging, restaurant & tourism index	MTGS	Marketing tourism growth strategy
LSE	London Stock Exchange (london-stockexchange.com)	NASA	National Aeronautics and Space Administration (nasa.gov)
MAR	Mobile augmented reality	NBSC	National Bureau of Statistics of China (stats.gov.cn/english/)
MBIE	Ministry of Business Innovation &		

NEC	National Exhibition Centre (thenec.co.uk)	PDF	Portable document format
NGO	Non-governmental organisation	PESTLE	Political, economic, socio-cultural, technological, legal, and ecological
NHS	National heritage site		
NPA	National Parks Authority (national-parks.gov.uk)	PhD	Doctor of Philosophy
		PLC	Product life cycle
NPD	New offering development	PND	Portable navigation devices
NRS	National research survey	POD	Point of difference
		POI	Points of interest
NTO/A	National tourism organisation/agency	POP	Point of parity
		PoS	Point of sale
NTSS	National tourism sector strategy	PPC	Pay-per-click
		PPP	Public–private partnership
NVC	Non-verbal communication	PR	Public relations
NYCVB	New York Convention and Visitors Bureau (nycvb.com)	PRO	Public relations officer
		PSG	Paris St. Germain (en.psg.fr)
OECD	Organization for Economic Cooperation and Development (oecd.org)	PTA/O	Provincial tourism authority/organisation
OOHM	Out-of-home media	QCS	Quality customer service
OMTs	Organised mass tourists		
ONS	Office for National Statistics (ons.gov.uk)	QR	Quick response (code)
		QSR	Quick-service restaurant
ORM	Online reputation management	R&D	Research and development
OTA	Online travel agent		
OTO	Online tour operator	RAJAR	Radio Joint Audience Research (rajar.co.uk)
OTO	Outbound tour operator	RAMS	Radio audience measurement survey
PATA	Pacific Asia Travel Association (pata.org)	RDT	Rwanda Development Board (rdp.rw)
PCO	Professional conference organiser	RETOSA	Regional Tourism Organisation of Southern Africa (retosa.co.za)
PDF	Portable document format		
PDT	Philippines Department of Tourism (tourism.gov.ph)	ROAS	Return on ad spend
		ROI	Return/rate on investment

ROMI	Return on marketing investment	SMART	Specific, measurable, achievable, realistic, and time-bound goals
RoR	Rate-of-return		
RSA	Republic of South Africa	SMEs	Small and medium-sized enterprises
RTM	Responsible tourism management	SMERF	Social, military, educational, religious, and fraternal
RTO	Regional tourism organisation	SMM	Social media marketing
RTT	Reality Tours & Travel (Mumbai, India) (realitytoursandtravel.com)	SMMEs	Small, medium, and micro-enterprises
		SMS	Short message service
		SPSS	Statistical Package for the Social Sciences
SAA	South African Airways (flysaa.com)	ST	Space tourism
SADC	Southern African Development Community (sadc.int)	STA	Scottish Tourism Alliance (scottish-tourismalliance.co.uk)
		STO	Specialist tour operator
SARS	Severe acute respiratory syndrome	STO	Special tour operator (rates)
SAS	Statistical analysis software	STP	Segmentation, targeting, and positioning
SAT	South African Tourism (southafrica.net)	STU	Strategic research unit
SBU	Strategic business unit	SWOT	Strengths, weaknesses, opportunities, and threats
SDI	Spatial development initiative	SYTA	Student & Youth Travel association (syta.org)
SEM	Search engine marketing	TALC	Tourism area life cycle
SEM	Structural equation modelling	TEQ	Tourism and Events Queensland (teq.queensland.com/)
SEO	Search engine optimisation		
SERP	Search engine results page	TDI	Tourist destination image
SIT	Special interest tourism	TFDS	Total foreign direct spend
SITE	Society of Incentive Travel Executives (site-intl.org)	TFR	Total fertility rates
		THL	Through-the-line (promotion)
SLA	Service level agreement	TIC	Tourism information centre

TIM	Travel Industry Management (University of Hawaii) (tim.hawaii.edu/vision-mission-core)	VIC	Visitor information centre
		VNAT	Vietnam National Administration of Tourism (vietnam-tourism.com/)
TMC	Travel management company		
TNS	Taylor Nelson Sofres (tnsglobal.com)	VoD	Video on demand
		VR	Virtual reality
TQM	Total quality management	VRM	Visitor relationshoip marketing
TRINET	Tourism Research Information Network (tim.hawaii.edu/trinet)	VRML	Virtual reality modelling language
		VSO	Voluntary Service Overseas (vsointernational.org/)
TUI	Touristik Union International (tuigroup.com/en-en)	VTA	Virtual travel agency
		WAYN	Where are you now?
UAE	United Arab Emirates	WCTE	World Committee on Tourism Ethics (unwto.org/world-committee-tourism-ethics)
UCLan	University of Central Lancashire (uclan.ac.uk)		
		WEF	World Economic Forum (weforum.org)
UGC	User-generated content	WFR	Watching friends and relatives
UK	United Kingdom		
UNESCO	United Nations Educational, Scientific and Cultural Organization (en.unesco.org)	WHO	World Health Organization (who.int)
		WHS	World Heritage Site
		WoM	Word of mouth/mouse
		WTA	World travel awards
UNWTO	United Nations World Tourism Organization (▶ www.unwto.org/)	WTAAA	World Travel Agents Association Alliance (wtaaa.org)
		WTM	Wrld Travel Market (wtmlondon.com)
URL	Universal resource locator		
USP	Unique selling proposition/point	WTTC	World Travel and Tourism Council (wttc.org)
VAT	Value added tax	WWW	World wide web
VC	Video conferencing	WYSE	World Youth Student and Educational Travel Confederation (wysetc.org)
VDU	Visual display unit		
VE	VisitEngland (visitengland.com/)		
VFM	Value for money	YHA	Youth Hostels Association (yha.org.uk)
VFR	Visiting friends and relatives		

Contents

IV   Implementing the Tourism and Hospitality Marketing Mix

V   Understanding Tourism and Hospitality Marketing Issues

Understanding Marketing in the Tourism and Hospitality Industry

Contents

Tourism and Hospitality Marketing Principles

Contents

Electronic Supplementary Material The online version of this chapter (https://doi.org/10.1007/978-3-030-64111-5_1) contains supplementary material, which is available to authorized users.

Purpose

This chapter will provide you with the information, skills, and approaches necessary to understand some of the key issues and principles of tourism and hospitality marketing.

Learning Goals

After reading this chapter, you should be able to:

- Define the terms "tourism" and "hospitality"
- Explain the concepts "tourism marketing" and "marketing"
- Apply marketing to the field of tourism and hospitality
- Explain the core principles of tourism marketing
- Explore the reasons for studying tourism marketing
- Apply the principles of marketing to Warner Bros Studio Tour, London: The Making of Harry Potter.

Overview

In this chapter, we first define the terms "tourism" and "hospitality", and then we examine the concepts of marketing and tourism marketing. We consider how marketing applies to the field of tourism and hospitality, and briefly discuss the core principles of marketing, including information gathering, the marketing mix, marketing planning, and customer relationship management. Lastly, we look at some of the reasons for studying tourism and hospitality marketing.

The chapter's in-depth case study examines the concept of marketing orientation and its application to Warner Bros Studio Tour, London: The Making of Harry Potter.

1.1 Introduction

Have you ever used your smartphone to research a holiday destination, or booked and paid for an airline flight using the internet? Have you perhaps booked a dormitory bed at a backpacker's hostel via e-mail? Have you ever felt concerned about whether or not a tour operating company with which you were considering doing business was socially responsible? Have the brand names of tourism companies ever influenced your decision about which one to use or even which destination to visit? Many tourists think about these issues, and so these are the sorts of questions you need to consider when designing, pricing, distributing, and promoting tourism product offerings. This chapter aims to provide a thorough understanding of the core principles of tourism and hospitality marketing, which will be discussed in detail in later chapters.

1.2 Defining Tourism and Hospitality

The two main industries that make up the travel industry are tourism and hospitality. There is a considerable overlap between these two industries. Indeed, tourism can be described as an activity that is serviced by a number of industries, such as hospitality and transport (Horner & Swarbrooke, 2016: 4). A tourist visiting a destination, for instance, might get there by airplane, stay at a hotel, visit a number of attractions and restaurants, and hire a rental car.

 How would you define the terms "tourism" and "hospitality"? Write down your ideas, and then compare them with the definitions in this chapter.

1.2.1 Tourism

Over the last few decades, many academic writers have discussed the definition of **tourism**. Most define it as a recreational activity carried out in leisure time away from home over a limited period. However, this definition fails to determine how far a person has to travel and for how long that person has to be away from home in order to be labelled a tourist. In addition, the definition fails to take into account the business tourist, who may indeed be away from home for a limited period,

1

though for work, not leisure. Consequently, tourism researchers such as Middleton, Fyall, Morgan & Ranchhod (2009: 6) argue that marketers require definitions for their particular market segments. We discuss more accurate categories of tourist in ▶ Chaps. 3 and 7.

> *Tourism* is the term given to the activity that occurs when tourists travel. This encompasses everything from the planning of the trip, the travel to the place, the stay itself, the return, and the reminiscences about it afterwards. It includes the activities that the traveller undertakes as part of the trip, the purchases made, and the interactions that occur between host and guest (Mill & Morrison, 1992: 9).

This extensive definition acknowledges the importance of both the pre- and post-holiday experience as well as the experience that takes place at the destination. For many tourists, the holiday begins before leaving home and continues afterwards. For instance, the tourist may anticipate the holiday enthusiastically: "I can't wait to go on holiday. I'm so excited ..." In addition, he or she may have good memories after the holiday: "We had such a great time. It was sunny every day ..."

Tourism is defined by the United Nations World Tourism Organization (UNWTO) as "the activities of persons travelling to and staying in places outside their usual environment for not more than one consecutive year for leisure, business and other purposes not related to the exercise of an activity remunerated from within the place visited" (UNWTO, 2008). In its broadest sense, the tourism industry is the total of all businesses that directly provide products and services to facilitate business, leisure, and pleasure activities to people away from their home environment.

Most definitions of tourism reinforce the notion that tourism is concerned primarily with people who are:

- Outside normal routines of work and social commitments
- On a visit that is temporary and short term
- Required to travel to the destination (usually making use of some mode of transport)
- Usually engaged in activities that are associated with leisure and tourism
- Sometimes on business.

Visit this link to read more about the UNWTO: ▶ https://www.unwto.org/about-us

> According to the UNWTO, the business volume of tourism equals or even surpasses that of oil exports, food products or automobiles (UNWTO, 2017).

There are three locations of tourism:

1. It is not restricted to overnight stays. It includes excursionists (same-day visitors) or international excursionists (such as cruise ship passengers visiting a port and not staying overnight or people travelling intraregionally, for example, from Spain to France for shopping or trade purposes).
2. All tourism includes an element of travel, but all travel is not tourism. The definition excludes commuter travel, such as the travel of people on their way to neighbourhood shops, schools, and so on.
3. It is not restricted to people travelling for leisure. It includes travel for business as well as travel for social, religious, educational, sports, health, and most other purposes, provided that the destination of travel is outside the usual place of work and home.

The UNWO and other definitions of tourism include three principal locations for tourist activity within the industry:

1. Domestic tourism, which is concerned with people taking holidays, short breaks, and trips in their own country (See ◘ Images 1.1 and 1.2, and ▶ Industry Insight 1.1)
2. Outbound tourism, which is concerned with people leaving their usual country of residence to visit another country
3. Inbound tourism, which is concerned with people entering a country other than their own for holidays and trips.

A family from Manchester on a one-week holiday in London are domestic tourists. A tourist from the United Kingdom visiting Spain would be classified by the British government as an outbound tourist, but as inbound tourists by the government of Spain.

Tourism is classified as part of the services sector of an economy. It ranks alongside other components such as financial, entertainment, commercial, media, and professional services. Most developed and developing countries now have rapidly growing service economies, especially in tourism and the hospitality sector, which is the number one sector in the service industry.

Industry Insight 1.1

The Potential of Domestic Tourism

The reliance on domestic tourism varies significantly across continents, particularly in Asia. While India, China and the Philippines strongly rely on domestic tourism, Vietnam, Malaysia, and Thailand sit at the other end of the spectrum. Only 21% of travel and tourism spending in Thailand is attributed to domestic visitors with the remaining 79% coming from international tourists. Still, most of these countries attract a significant number of international visitors, not only because of their well-developed air infrastructure and availability of low-cost airlines but also due to good rail, land, or sea connectivity with other countries. Yet in certain cases, accommodation has been developed to satisfy international travellers' preferences and budgets, in turn limiting lower cost options and serving as a brake in the expansion of domestic travel. The coronavirus pandemic in 2020 led to many people having to forgo international/border travel for travel within their own country. It is likely that local travel will grow in the coming years, although there simply are not enough domestic tourists for the deficit of international tourists

Source: WTTC. (2018). 'Domestic tourism: Importance and economic impact'. Retrieved from ► https://www.wttc.org/-/media/files/reports/2018/domestic-tourism--importance--economic-impact-dec-18.pdf [12 June 2019].

◘ **Image 1.1** A domestic tourism campaign in South Africa. (Source: SA Tourism)

1

Image 1.2   Chinese tourists. (Source: Pexels.com)

1.2.2 Hospitality

The term "hospitality" is being used more and more in place of the phrase "hotel and catering" (or "accommodation, food and beverage services") because it can be expanded to cover all offerings to the consumer away from home, including travel, lodging, eating, conferences, entertainment, recreation, and gaming. At its simplest, the term "hospitality" refers to the sector in the tourism industry that provides food and shelter to tourists (Skripak, 2018: 334).

These three services (accommodation, meals and beverages) may be offered indepen-

dently or in combination. A bed & breakfast or guesthouse, for instance, may provide accommodation only or it may offer accommodation, meals, and beverages. We should note that different countries provide different definitions of what constitutes the 'hospitality sector'.

According to the British Hospitality Association (BHA), "the term 'hospitality' includes hotels, restaurants, food service management, fast food, coffee shops and pubs, bars, and nightclubs" (BHA, 2020). The (hospitality) industry also covers catering at conferences and meetings, hospitals, prisons, mines, school and university hostels, and company canteens. In fact, it includes every place that offers hospitality, whether they are in the business for profit or to provide a non-profit service to the people in their care" (BHA, 2020).

> The British Hospitality Association (BHA) is the private sector forum for the United Kingdom's hospitality sector representing over 700 businesses that employ over 3.2 million people (10% of the UK workforce) or 6% of all businesses. Source: BHA (2020). ► https://www.ukhospitality.org.uk/

In contrast, in India, its hospitality industry is defined as 'the business of providing catering, lodging and entertainment service and welcoming, receiving, hosting, or entertaining guests' (Ministry of Commerce & Industry, Government of India, 2019). So, the hospitality sector is mainly concerned with providing food, drink, and accommodation, but also promotes a warm and friendly experience that benefits consumers, whether it is at a hotel, leisure facility, restaurant, or any other tourism establishment.

This broader definition emphasises a more positive and consumer-friendly image. It focuses on developing a service culture in the industry. This means focusing on creating an atmosphere in which the successful delivery of the service to the consumer is the most important thing an organisation and its employees can achieve. It also implies that not all hospitality consumers are tourists. For instance, consumers visiting a local restaurant are not tourists.

❓ Why do you think definitions of hospitality vary in different countries and cultures?

1.2.2.1 Importance of the Hospitality Sector

Accommodation, the main component of the hospitality sector, plays an extremely important role in tourism. As we saw earlier, the term "tourism", by definition, implies a stay of more than 24 hours at a destination. With the exception of day visitors, all other forms of tourism involve overnight accommodation. Middleton and Clarke (2001: 387) define accommodation as "all establishments offering overnight accommodation on a commercial basis to all categories of visitor". This definition excludes visitors staying with friends and relatives (the visiting-friends-and-relatives or VFR market; see ► Chap. 3).

Accommodation provides a necessary facility that makes it possible, convenient, and comfortable to engage in the primary reason for travel. From a marketing perspective, locational convenience, high standards of comfort and efficiency, and value for money are primary features of the accommodation component of the destination product that need to be marketed. Many tourists make a decision based on their perceptions and expectations of the accommodation available at the destination.

❓ Before we look at a suggested definition of marketing, how would you define it? Write down what you think marketing entails, and then compare your definition with the definitions offered in this chapter. Browse the AMA website: ► www.ama.org

1.3 What is Marketing?

Many managers use the term "marketing" without knowing what it really means. They think of it as meaning good salespeople, effective advertising or getting people to spend money. While these descriptions are not totally incorrect, marketing is much more than this. **Marketing** is about customers (which could be individuals or organisations): how to find them, how to satisfy them, and how to keep them (Levitt, 1960). It is about first finding out what customers want (through marketing research, as illustrated in ► Industry Insight 1.2), then producing that product or service (a marketing-oriented approach). Today, in any business – be it tourism, hospitality, or banking – the consumer comes first. Marketing is customer or consumer centric. It is an ongoing interactive process and a philosophy.

1

Premier Inn Meets Business Travellers' Needs Through Marketing Research

The Premier Inn hotel chain was established by Whitbread as Travel Inn in 1987, to compete with Travelodge. Whitbread bought Premier Lodge in 2004 and merged it with Travel Inn to form the current business under the name "Premier Travel inn" which was then shortened to "Premier Inn". Premier Inn accounts for 70% of Whitbread's earnings. Over the past 30 years, Premier Inn has grown to become the UK's biggest hotel brand, with 785 hotels and more than 72,000 rooms. It is consistently rated the UKs best value hotel chain. With ever-changing market conditions and traveller requirements, Premier Inn commissioned a marketing research study into British business travellers to gather a detailed picture of individual requirements and regional variations. The study of 1000 respondents (who stay in a range of hotels from budget to full service) aimed to provide the company market intelligence into the business travel market and identify emerging trends to help their guests 'wake up wonderful!'. While some of the research findings confirmed what management at Premier Inn already knew (such as the reasons which business travellers rate as important when choosing which hotel to stay at such as quality and value for money), they are always striving to understand their business users better. According to Mark Fells, chief marketing officer (CMO) of the Premier Inn hotel group, one of the reasons for his success in the hospitality industry is that he has learnt that cleanliness and quality of service are more important than luxuries. Premier Inn plan now has five hotels in the Middle East and three in India, with further developments in the pipeline and a target for more international hotels.

Source: ► https://www.whitbread.co.uk/our-brands/premier-inn.html

---

> *Marketing* is the process by which firms create value for customers and build strong relationships in order to capture value from customers in return (Kotler & Armstrong, 2019: 5).

An important concept that can be extracted from the definition by Kotler and Armstrong (2019) in the box above is that of exchange. At its simplest, marketing can be explained as a process of exchange between two parties. It is the trade of something of value between consumers and producer organisations: consumers who choose to buy or use products and services, and the organisations that supply and sell these products and services. For instance, a person visiting a restaurant enjoys a dining experience, while the restaurant obtains money paid for the product and service.

The definition also focuses on the term "value". Consumer value is the difference between the benefits of a product or service and the cost of obtaining it. There is an imperative difference here between tourism marketing and that of marketing of physical goods. Wildlife enthusiasts, for instance, may pay a full month's salary for a two-week stay at a southern African game park or reserve. If the service is pleasing and they manage to see a variety of rare species, they will think of their stay as good consumer value. To them, the benefits of the product outweigh or at least equal its cost.

Marketing is also concerned with achieving goals. However, these goals are not just about making money. Although organisations such as *Trailfinders*, a UK-based travel company, might aim to increase their share of the travel market, other organisations such as the *National Trust* are not as profit-driven and also aim to conserve the natural environment. They are not concerned only with getting numbers through their gates.

❓ Access two tourism companies on the internet, such as two hotel groups or two online travel agencies (OTAs). Compare and contrast the two companies in terms of whether they:

- Satisfy consumers' needs and wants
- Create value for consumers
- Which company would entice you to purchase and why?

In terms of consumers, marketing is concerned with the following matters:

- Understanding the needs and wants of existing and potential buyers (why they buy)
- Which products and services buyers choose, when, how much, at what prices, and how often
- How buyers hear about the products and services
- Where they buy offerings (direct or through a retail intermediary)
- How buyers feel after purchasing and consuming the products and services.
- In terms of producer companies, marketing focuses on these issues:
- Which offerings to sell, especially new ones, and why
- At what price to supply these products and services
- How to communicate the products and services (type of media)
- When and where to make them available.

In essence, marketing is a holistic approach to presenting a product or service (offering).

? Questions

Think about needs and wants in the tourism and hospitality industry: your own needs and wants as well as those of other people.

- Are needs the same as wants?
- How are they different?
- Discuss whether holidaymakers actually need or want a holiday?

1.4 What is Tourism and Hospitality Marketing?

Tourism and hospitality marketing is a relatively new phenomenon that has developed during the last 20 years or so. The principles of marketing have features that can be applied to different industries, whether it is a motor car or a holiday that is being marketed. Thus, the principles are fundamentally the same, but they must be adjusted to suit the characteristics of tourism and hospitality (see ▶ Chap. 2).

The marketing principles include an understanding of the market, marketing research, marketing planning, and the marketing mix. The marketing mix in particular must be extended to suit the nature of tourism marketing. It is discussed at the end of this chapter. In addition, in the tourism industry, there should be greater emphasis on internal marketing and relationship marketing. We deal with these types of marketing in ▶ Chap. 13.

The major difference between marketing in tourism/hospitality and marketing in other service sectors is that the marketer is competing for the consumer's spare time and disposable income.

Overview

A survey of 11,144 adults in 19 countries commissioned by online travel agency (OTA) Expedia found that American employees not only have the fewest days' leave – about 14 days a year – but they tend to use only about ten of them. The French get the highest number of days' leave a year (30 days on average) and are happy to take full advantage of them. Employees in Japan and Thailand also use only 10 days off a year (Expedia, 2018).

Source: Expedia (2018). American vacation deprivation levels at a five-year high. [Online], Retrieved from: ▶ https://newsroom.expedia.com/2018-10-16-American-vacation-deprivation-levels-at-a-five-year-high#assets_all. Accessed 18 November 2019.

Tourism and hospitality marketing is the process through which a tourism and hospitality organisation first anticipates consumer needs, and then manages and satisfies those needs to achieve sales (Lumsdon, 1997: 2).

■ **Image 1.3**   Tourists don't always 'need' a holiday. (Source: Author's own photograph)

The definition by Lumsdon (1997) in the box above highlights the necessity for tourism and hospitality products and services to fulfil (or satisfy) the needs and wants of consumers. Human beings have a variety of complex needs, ranging from the need for food, clothing, and safety, to the need for self-expression, and a sense of belonging. Wants are linked with the way in which people communicate their needs; they are usually described in terms of objects that will satisfy needs. However, it could be argued that the marketing of tourism services and offerings is about fulfilling wants, not needs. People don't need a holiday; they usually want one (see ▶ Industry Insight 1.3 and ◘ Image 1.3). Holidays and leisure activities are considered non-essential items. This means that the task of tourism and hospitality marketers lies in creating value and promoting the desired experience so that consumers buy from them and not from their competitors (see ◘ Fig. 1.1).

Industry Insight 1.3

Needs or Wants?

Nalani Wakita, a travel agent from Mumbai, India, attempted to explain the difference between a need and a want. "I'd say that a need is an essential requirement, whereas a want has more to do with providing a luxury or fulfilling hopes and dreams. The travel industry aims to meet both needs and wants. For instance, this morning a business client telephoned in a panic and said, 'I need to catch a flight to Dubai in the UAE tomorrow morning. Can you find me a flight?'" Nalani added, "Shortly after, another client came into the agency, examined a brochure on Mauritius and declared, 'I want to book a holiday.'"

Source: Nalani Wakita, Sushant Travels, New Delhi, India

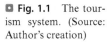

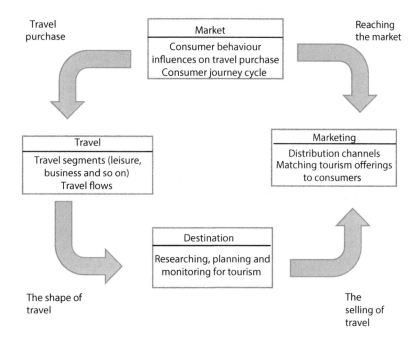

Fig. 1.1 The tourism system. (Source: Author's creation)

Travel purchase

Market
Consumer behaviour influences on travel purchase Consumer journey cycle

Reaching the market

Travel
Travel segments (leisure, business and so on)
Travel flows

Marketing
Distribution channels
Matching tourism offerings to consumers

Destination
Researching, planning and monitoring for tourism

The shape of travel

The selling of travel

Tourism and hospitality marketing involves finding out what tourists want (marketing research; see ▶ Chap. 4), developing suitable product-offerings (product development; see ▶ Chap. 8), telling people what is available (promotions; see ▶ Chap. 10), and providing instructions about where they can buy the offerings (place; see ▶ Chap. 9) so that they receive value (pricing; see ▶ Chap. 8) and the tourism organisation makes money.

To encourage the purchase of tourism products and services, and to ensure consumer satisfaction, a tourism marketer has to design and manage a service that offers value for money (VFM) to targeted consumers. To do this effectively, the marketer must also realise that the needs and wants of all consumers cannot be satisfied. The consumers that a business will target have to be chosen accurately. In addition, a successful marketer must be able to satisfy consumer needs in the rapidly changing business environment. The marketer has to confront the challenges of increasing competition as well as political and economic changes, and at the same time be more environmentally conscious than has been the case in the past.

1.5 Developing a Tourism Marketing Orientation

In today's competitive business environment, every business should have marketing as the basis of its operations. Having been exposed to a vast number of marketing communications, consumers are extremely sophisticated. It is thus better to regard marketing as an orientation or a management philosophy. The concept of **marketing orientation** is an outward-thinking approach that focuses on consumers' current and future needs to target consumers, and work on improved ways of communicating and delivering better value than competitors (Pike, 2018: 12). It can be applied to small- and medium-sized tourism and hospitality enterprises as well as large (multi-national) tourism and hospitality organisations and even tourist destinations. in essence, just about anything can be marketed: events, people, ideas, places, and of course, services such as tourism and hospitality. Tourism and hospitality marketers using a marketing orientation perspective always focus on the needs of

1

the individual consumer with a view to maintaining a long-term relationship (Kotler & Armstrong, 2019: 4).

Marketing orientation can be defined in three ways: as a process, as a philosophy, and as a relationship management activity.

1.5.1 Marketing as a Process

Marketing is not a means to an end. It is an ongoing process that starts by a business seeking to identify and understand the needs of consumers. As different consumers have different needs and wants, effective marketing targets particular types of consumers of the market.

1.5.2 Marketing as a Philosophy

To carry out the process of marketing, the marketer requires the support of other departments in the organisation, including the finance, sales, and human resources (HR) departments, and must work closely with them. Marketing is thus a company-wide responsibility. All staff must work in co-operation with each other to satisfy consumers' needs. As Drucker says, "Marketing is too important to be left to the marketing department. It is a philosophy, an approach to business that puts the consumer first" (1969: 6). Thus, marketing translates into a philosophy of thinking at every level in the organisation, from how the receptionist answers the telephone to how salespeople interact with clients and what the company business card looks like.

1.5.3 Marketing as a Relationship Management Activity

It is important that the marketing process does not end as soon as a sales transaction has occurred (e.g. a hotel room has been booked).

The organisation should aim to satisfy consumers so that they return. Marketers and all staff must work at building a relationship with valuable consumers as well as all of the other groups that affect the tourism organisation's success (stakeholders, the local community, destination marketing organisations [DMOs] and the travel trade or tourism intermediaries, including travel agencies and tour operators). Companies should develop retention programmes to focus marketing activity on enhancing **customer relationship management (CRM)** systems. Indeed, companies have been encouraged to undertake long-term interactive relationships (Gummesson, 1987). Good CRM creates customer satisfaction. In turn, satisfied customers remain loyal to the organisation and spread positive **word-of-mouth** (WoM) and e-WoM (e-word-of-mouth) influence about the tourism organisation and its products. Businesses In the tourism and hospitality Industry have been using CRM practices for decades: these include airlines' frequent flyer programs and hotel groups or car rental companies' reward programs (see ► Chap. 13.

> **Definition**
>
> **Customer relationship management** (CRM) enables companies to provide excellent real-time customer service through the effective use of individual account information (Kotler & Armstrong, 2019: 45).
>
> **Word-of-mouth** (WoM) influence is an unpaid form of promotion in which satisfied customers tell other people how much they like a business, product, or service (► https://www.entrepreneur.com/encyclopedia/word-of-mouth-advertising).

Marketing-oriented tourism organisations may demonstrate these characteristics:
- The organisation sees consumer needs as its first priority and is constantly concerned with understanding these needs.

Table 1.1 The evolution of marketing in non-service industries

Approximate dates	Marketing eras	Description
1920–1930	1. Production orientation	Focus on making products available, an inward-looking approach. Factories could not keep up with demand for goods. Customers' needs and wants were of secondary importance.
1930–1950	2. Sales orientation	Technology advanced. Demand for goods was satisfied. Emphasis of management shifted from production to securing sales. Focus was on exchange rather than on satisfying consumers needs and wants or building a long-term relationship.
1950–1960	3. Marketing orientation	Driven by research to understand consumer needs in a more competitive marketplace. A greater increase in competition. supply exceeded demand. Consumers had more choice than ever before. Businesses responded by adopting the marketing concept.
1970–Present	4. Societal marketing	This approach considers the wider needs and welfare of society rather than merely the individual consumer. This is the philosophy of utilitarianism.
1995–Present	5.Digital marketing (and social media marketing)	Power has shifted towards the consumer. This approach focuses on a customer-driven relationship. Electric word-of-mouth affects purchasing decisions.

Source: Adapted from Perreault and McCarthy (2006)

— Marketing research is an ongoing activity of the organisation (see ▶ Chap. 4).
— The organisation knows what consumers think of it.
— The organisation frequently reviews its strengths and weaknesses relative to competitors (see ▶ Chap. 5).
— The organisation frequently measures and evaluates its marketing activities.
— The organisation's policies reflect concern for consumer wants as well as society at large.

1.6 Evolution of Marketing

There are two opposing views (or trains of thought) of the evolution of marketing: by production orientation and by marketing orientation.

1.6.1 Evolution by Production Orientation

Several writers have identified either four or five key stages of the evolution of marketing in terms of the orientation of production (see Kotler & Armstrong, 2019; Perreault & McCarthy, 2006). These stages are outlined in ▢ Table 1.1 below:

1.6.2 Evolution by Marketing Thought

Vargo and Lusch (2004) proposed the evolution of marketing thought over three eras:
1. Nineteenth century. This era viewed marketing as based upon the exchange of the principle inherited from economics. It

1

focused on the unit of output and places goods in the centre of the stage.

2. 1970s and 1980s. A new paradigm emerged where services were viewed as different from goods. This type of thinking shifted marketing thought to a service-oriented perspective, with increased focus on service.

3. The 2000s. The concept of goods versus services was not very helpful; instead services were seen more as processes where the application of knowledge and skills are used for the benefit of another party.

The third approach – what has been described as the service-dominant approach – is particularly useful and applicable to tourism marketing (Shaw, Bailey & Williams, 2011).

1.7 Evolution of Marketing in the Tourism Industry

The tourism industry only began to flourish in the 1950s with the advent of the airline industry. This decade also saw the opening of *Disneyland*, a theme park in the United States, QSRs such as *McDonald's*, and the multinational hotel chain *Holiday Inn*.

During the last two decades, organisations have started to recognise their responsibility to society as well as the importance of satisfying the needs and wants of consumers. A good example in the tourism industry is a hotel that provides a non-smoking area or a QSR that uses environmentally-friendly packaging for its food and beverage items.

It has taken some time for many tourism and hospitality organisations – in developed countries as well as developing countries – to implement marketing-oriented skills and principles. Generally, there have been low standards of consumer service for many years.

However, this is now changing, mainly because of the increased number of international tourists visiting developing countries (emerging markets) who have high expectations of quality service delivery and the many American and other Western tourism franchises that have started doing business in such countries (such as *Holiday Inn, Starbucks, Hilton Hotels*, and *Costa Coffee* cafés).

The mid-1990s brought a new era of marketing in which the internet and other new technologies were adopted. Today, tourists research their stay, and book accommodation, travel, and visits to tourist attractions and restaurants online using the internet. Travel is the number one selling commodity online, with sales of more than US$560 billion (€508 billion) being logged on an annual basis (Statista, 2018). Gone are the days of telephoning around for bookings. Increasingly, consumers are using their netbooks and smartphones to make travel arrangements while they themselves are on the move. In doing so, travellers are increasingly referring to online review sites (or e-WoM) as a trusted source for decision-making information. The social networking site.

Facebook is replacing the traditional holiday postcard as a way of letting friends know that they are travelling. Similarly, on the product side, tourism and hospitality firms are utilising social networking platforms such as Facebook, Instagram, TikTok/Douyin, Flickr, Snapchat, and Twitter to communicate with consumers, and using video-sharing websites such as YouTube to tempt tourists with their product offerings. Most airlines no longer issue paper tickets; instead, tourists can download their tickets onto their smartphones, and then have them scanned at check-in points at airports. And the increase of 'big data' (very large sets of data that may be analysed computationally) enables tourism and hospitality businesses to track behaviour, target consumers, and to personalise their relationship with the consumer. Travel metasearch sites such as Kayak, Hipmunk, Trivago, and Skyscanner dominate advertising media in many countries. Over the last few years, *Trivago* has been one of the most visibly promoted travel sites in Europe and North America (see ▶ Industry Insight 1.4).

Industry Insight 1.4

Trivago

Trivago is a German technology company specialising in online products and services in the hotel, accommodation, and metasearch sectors. Founded in 2005, it is now owned by American travel company Expedia, which also owns ▶ Hotels.com, Orbitz, and Travelocity. Tourists can use the Trivago website to make hotel reservations, compare hotel prices, and book holiday packages. The Trivago website has a huge promotional presence, including television advertisements, magazine advertising, social media, and outdoor advertising. Its mission is to be "the traveller's first and independent source of information for finding the ideal hotel at the best rate". Trivago was the first hotel search engine in Germany; today it is one of the fastest-growing companies in Europe, operating in 60 regions around the world in 33 different languages. Anyone can access Trivago's fast and intuitive search, and compare over 1.8 million hotels from more than 180 online travel agents worldwide. The website's hotel information, pictures, ratings, reviews, filters, and other features are all available to help users find a hotel.

Source: Trivago. (2020). Retrieved from ▶ trivago.co.za [11 January 2020].

Today, there are more than 130 different kinds of marketing, including marketing tactics (such as loyalty marketing), marketing channels (for example, speed marketing; see ▶ Industry Insight 1.5), marketing styles (for example, **influencer marketing**; see ▶ Industry Insight 1.6) and marketing structures (that is, corporate marketing) as well as various other widely applicable aspects of marketing.

Tourism and hospitality businesses are increasingly utilising YouTube and Instagram travel influencers – through advertising – to

> **Definition**
>
> *Influencer marketing* (also known as "influence marketing" or "social media influencer") is the promotion and selling of products and services through people (influencers) who have a large base of followers on social media platforms (Vinerean, 2017).

help promote their products and brands (see ◼ Image 1.4 and ▶ Chap. 12 in-depth case study).

1

Industry Insight 1.5

"Speed Marketing" Creates Tourism Trade Connections at Indaba

Africa's Travel Indaba is the largest tourism marketing event on the African calendar and one of the top three "must visit" events of its kind on the global calendar. As in previous years, the 2019 Indaba included ever-popular speed-marketing sessions, where southern Africa's tourism trade and buyers created connections and business.

The hour-long speed-marketing sessions, one on each day of the show, took the form of four- to five-minute presentations and sales pitches from twenty tourism products to more than 200 international buyers. The sessions were fast, interactive, and highly effective. The organisations concerned showcased their tourism product offerings, supported by presentations and imagery. This gave buyers easy access to the South African tourism trade, enabling them to plan and impact positively on the bottom line of their businesses.

Source: Africa's Travel Indaba. 2019. Conversations, speed marketing, and a galaxy of stellar exhibits. Retrieved from ► https://www.indaba-southafrica.co.za/news/INDABA-2019-indaba-kicks-off.aspx [15 August 2019].

Industry Insight 1.6

Influencer Marketing: Social Media Driving Tourism

During the last few years, influencer marketing has become extremely popular as a form of social media marketing. Influencer marketing (or influence marketing) focuses on influential people rather than the target consumer market as a whole. It identifies the individuals that have influence over potential buyers, and then orients marketing activities around these influencers. Instagram more so than any other social media platform has created a wave of social media-driven tourism, particularly amongst millennials (also known as Generation Y, born between the early 1980s and the mid-1990s to early 2000s). Instagram has inspired and energised a new generation of travellers.

With this type of marketing, company and product brands partner with social media 'influencers' – people with a large following on one or more major social media platforms – to promote their offerings. These influencers may be celebrities (such as actors or professional sports people), personalities, activists, or bloggers; anyone with credibility and a large fan base. They may simply be popular figures within their social media platform of choice (for example, YouTube stars or Instagram models). Influencers have a major sway when it comes to fashion, brand loyalty, political beliefs, FMCGs, and even tourism.

Influencer marketing leverages off both the prior work of a social media influencer (in terms of building his or her own following on YouTube, Twitter, Instagram, Twitter, and so on) and the inherent power of each social media medium to reach a worldwide audience provided by the platform on which that person is active.

Travel is very personal and consumers are far more likely to trust a recommendation from someone they know than trust an advertisement. A restaurant, holiday resort, theme park, airline, hotel, or B&B can invite an influencer they know is important to their core target audience to write a review, make a quirky video, or share photographs from their experience on their personal blog or social accounts to help promote the product-offering brand.

One example of a successful influencer marketing campaign is when tourism officials in Wanaka, a resort town on New Zealand's South Island, hired a number of popular Instagram influencers to promote the picturesque town. Prior to the campaign, few international tourists knew the town existed. The result was a 14 per cent increase in the number of overseas visitors in the year following the campaign.

Source: Kinski, N. (2017). Upfluence. How influencer marketing can take your travel business to new heights. Retrieved from ► https://upfluence.com/influencer-marketing/influencer-marketing-travel-business [15 August 2018].

1

1.8 How Does Marketing Fit into the Subject Area of Tourism and Hospitality?

Marketing fits into the subject area of tourism and hospitality on two levels: at the individual business level and at the destination level.

1.8.1 At the Individual Business Level

All tourism organisations – no matter how small – conduct some kind of marketing activity. At the individual business level, the management of a company is involved with the marketing and functioning of the business. A small, family-run restaurant might carry out some advertising in a local newspaper as well as depend on some good positive reviews written by satisfied customers on its website. Large hotel groups (such as *Travelodge, Accor,* or *InterContinental Hotels Group*) and airlines (such as *Virgin Atlantic Airway* and *Emirates Airline*) have their own marketing departments that conduct a whole range of marketing activities. ❑ Figure 1.2 illustrates how marketing applies to tourism organisations. Businesses usually have four functional areas, namely: finance, marketing, human resource management (HRM), and operations management. All four functions (or departments) are interrelated. For instance, a promotional

❑ **Fig. 1.2** Marketing is an interrelated business function. (Source: Author's creation)

campaign needs to work to a budget, as set by the finance department or the chief financial officer (CFO). Successful tourism businesses have strong coordination between each function. For example, the marketing director/manager of a tour operator is dependent upon a budget (Finance department) and may require staff members to receive training (Human resources department).

1.8.1.1 Meeting Consumer Needs

If a tourism and hospitality organisation meets people's needs, it will attract and keep consumers. For example, parents who want time to themselves while on holiday might choose a hotel that provides a crèche or child-minding facilities.

1.8.1.2 Satisfying Consumers

A tourism and hospitality business must not only meet the needs of consumers, but must also do its utmost to guarantee satisfaction. This means fulfilling the desires of consumers by providing a quality product and service that are good value for money. The tourism marketer finds out what consumers like and dislike so that their specific needs and wants can be met. In addition, the tourism marketer should try to find out what consumers expect to ensure that they will be satisfied with the tourism service.

1.8.1.3 Generating Sales

All tourism and hospitality organisations need to generate sales to cover their running costs. These expenses include the cost of employing staff, of overheads (electricity, water, rent and so on), and of maintaining and updating equipment. Organisations may be privately run (commercial) businesses (a hotel, for instance), operated by the public sector (national parks or heritage sites such as the Archaeological Survey of India's Red Fort Complex in Delhi, for instance) or run by volunteers (*The National Trust* in the UK, for instance). The latter two categories are referred to as non-commercial operations. In the UK and internationally, growing recognition of the value of marketing in non-commercial operations has been a feature of the last decade.

1.8 · How Does Marketing Fit into the Subject Area of Tourism and Hospitality?

21

1

Tourism and hospitality organisations operate in the private, public, or voluntary sectors. Most tourism businesses belong to the private sector.

1. The main objective of private-sector organisations is to make a profit. This means that they strive to increase the amount of money remaining after all of the expenses of running the business have been paid. Effective marketing can generate more sales, which leads to a profit. Examples of private sector organisations include hotel groups and theme parks are profit oriented. The primary goal of private sector organisations is to increase their market share.

2. Public sector organisations are funded by the national government or local authorities. Publicly owned and voluntarily run tourism organisations may not need to make a profit, but they still have to conduct marketing activities to attract consumers, to try to break even (cover all of their costs), and to provide a service to the community. A local municipal swimming pool (or Lido) and VisitMalta (▶ visitmalta.com) (the national tourist organisation for Malta), for example, are both public sector (government-funded) organisations. Their aim is to provide a service to everyone, rather than merely making a profit. Tourism is often viewed as a vehicle for improving facilities and services for the local community. A museum, for instance, will most likely have the objective of providing education to all visitors.

3. Voluntary-sector organisations are often charities or trusts, which are funded mainly through their members, entrance fees to visitor attractions, fundraising, and donations These organisations use any profit they make to develop and improve facilities. The main objective of the *National Heritage Trust*, for example, is conservation. All money raised goes to covering costs and meeting this objective (see ◘ Table 1.2).

1.8.1.4 Informing Consumers

Another reason why tourism and hospitality organisations conduct marketing activities is to inform consumers. If people do not

◘ **Table 1.2** Examples of private, public, and voluntary sector tourism organisations

Private sector organisations	Public sector organisations	Voluntary sector organisations
TUI Disneyland Paris Holiday inn Virgin Trains PortAventura World (Spain) Hays Travel Airbnb	Museums Visitor information centres National gallery National tourism organisations Regional development organisations	The National Trust (UK) Tourism Concern The Travel Foundations Fair Trade in Tourism

Source: Author's creation

know about a facility, they will not use it. There are several ways in which tourism marketers can inform the general public. These include brochures, media advertisements, the internet, sales promotions, flyers, and coupons.

1.8.2 At the Local/Regional Destination Level

Marketing also fits into the field of tourism at the destination level. At the destination level, it is often an agency led by the public sector (for example, a DMO – see ◘ Fig. 1.1), either as a stand-alone agency or as part of a tourism department, that is responsible for tourism marketing. At the country level, for example, China National Tourism Association is the national tourism organisation (NTO) for China (see ▶ Industry Insight 1.7). At a city level, Cape Town Tourism is the DMO for the Mother City in South Africa (See ▶ Chap. 14 for a discussion on the role of NTOs and DMOs). Destination marketing (or place marketing) is about dressing-up and making a destination attractive to visitors and investors.

1

China National Tourism Association's Role

As the national tourism agency – China National Tourism Administration (CNTA) – is the government authority responsible for the development, promotion and regulation of tourism in China. CNTA's headquarters are in Beijing, with regional branches in various provinces. CNTA offices in each Chinese province report to the central office in Beijing. The agency has 19 overseas offices called "CNTOs" (China National Tourism Offices) that have the task of promoting tourism to China. There are offices in China's major tourism markets: London, Tokyo, Seoul, Sydney, Hong Kong, New York, Madrid, Los Angeles, and Paris.

CNTA launched a global tourism promotion campaign under the theme of "Beautiful China – 2017 Year of Silk Road Tourism". The advertising campaign aimed to attract an increasing number of tourists from different countries. The tourism campaign was released simultaneously in Beijing and more than 20 countries. CNTA intends to launch a series of marketing and promotional activities to promote China tourism in the coming years. The other popular themes of tourism promotion unveiled by CNTA and CNTO are – "China – Beyond Your Imagination" and "China – Like Never Before".

Source: ▶ http://www.chinatourism.ch/

❓ Questions

Think about times that you have used a tourism and hospitality organisation (such as a hotel, restaurant, or visitor attraction) and you were not satisfied with the product offerings provided.

− Were you unhappy because the service did not meet your needs?
− Was the facility unsatisfactory in other ways?
− Have you ever been so dissatisfied with a tourism and hospitality organisation that you would not go back?
− How could the tourism and hospitality organisation improve to meet your needs and wants?

1.9 The Main Principles of Marketing

The processes of effective tourism marketing include information gathering, marketing planning, the elements of the marketing mix, and promotional strategies.

1.9.1 Information Gathering

Knowledge about market trends, consumer segments, and consumer behaviour is mostly derived from marketing research activity. Gathering this information and research data is a vital process of marketing. The knowledge acquired is used to assist the organisation in making marketing decisions (see ▶ Chap. 4).

1.9.2 Marketing Planning

The marketing planning process is a systematic way of deciding on and communicating the goals and objectives of the organisation (Kotler, 2000). Marketing planning involves the organisation analysing its strengths and weaknesses in its current and prospective markets, identifying its aims and the opportunities it seeks to develop, and defining strategies to achieve its aims (see ▶ Chaps. 5 and 6).

1.9.3 Elements of the Marketing Mix

One of the most basic processes in marketing is the marketing mix. The marketing mix refers to the four main activities on which an organisation must focus its attention in order to achieve its marketing objectives. The traditional marketing mix, devised in 1960 by

◨ **Table 1.3** Summary of the marketing processes

Process	Description	Main chapter reference	Book part
Information gathering	Consumer behaviour, marketing research, and market segmentation	3, 4, and 7	II and III
Marketing planning	Trends in the external business environment and the marketing planning process	5 and 6	II
Understanding the marketing mix	The elements of the marketing mix	8, 9, 10, 11, and 12	IV
Promotional strategies	The communications mix and promotions mix strategies	10, 11, and 12	IV

Source: Author's creation

McCarthy (1960), consists of four variables that all begin with the letter P, hence the name "the four Ps": product, price, place, and promotion. These elements form the core decision areas that managers must manage to satisfy customer needs. These four Ps are located at the heart of a marketing plan. The theory of the marketing mix is that all of the elements are related to each other and can be controlled by the marketer to some extent. In this regard, the four Ps are sometimes referred to as controllable factors and represent the microenvironment of the company. Tourism marketers must also take into account uncontrollable factors such as the macroenvironment and the market. For example, the outbreak of the coronavirus pandemic in 2020 was an unforeseeable health issue that severely impacted on travel flows and tourism and hospitality businesses worldwide (see ► Chap. 6). The challenge for the tourism marketer is to use tools such as marketing research (see ► Chap. 4) to adapt the controllable aspects of marketing (the four Ps) within the uncontrollable elements of the marketplace.

Much of an organisation's marketing effort is made up of the design, implementation, and evaluation of the four Ps. When applied to the tourism and hospitality industry, these four marketing activities need to be manipulated. For example, promotion in the manufacturing industry refers to advertising, sales promotion, and so on. In the tourism industry, products and services are produced and consumed at the same time, so consumers are often part of the service production process. In addition, because services are intangible, consumers look for tangible cues to help them evaluate the service. Also, service providers such as receptionists and floor staff are involved in promoting the product or service (see ► Chaps. 2 and 13). These facts mean that tourism or services marketers have to extend the marketing mix to take into account three additional Ps: physical evidence, people, and process strategies (Booms & Bitner, 1981). See ► Chap. 2 for further discussion on the extended marketing mix.

1.9.4 Promotional Strategies

One of the main processes of marketing is to review the various promotional strategies used to achieve planned organisational goals and targets. The promotional mix consists of a blend of advertising (see ► Chap. 10), sales promotion, and personal selling, and public relations (► Chap. 11). In addition, digital marketing and social media are electronic promotional tools that are integrated to achieve marketing objectives (see ► Chap. 12).

◨ Table 1.3 provides a summary of the marketing processes.

1

1.10 Why Study Tourism Marketing?

Now that you understand the meaning of the terms "marketing" and "tourism marketing", and why it is important to adopt a marketing orientation philosophy, you may be asking, "Why should I study tourism marketing?" This is an important question, whether you are majoring in tourism, travel or hospitality management, or working for a travel and tourism or hospitality-related company. Here are several important reasons to study marketing:

- Marketing plays an important role in society.
- Marketing is important to all types of business.
- Marketing affects everyday life.
- Marketing offers career opportunities.
- Marketing is an important research topic.

These reasons are discussed in more detail below. Visit this link to read more about CSR:
► http://www.referenceforbusiness.com/management/Comp-De/Corporate-Social-Responsibility.html#ixzz4wmjoCQqQ

1.10.1 Marketing Plays an Important Role in Society

Marketing is a core element of modern societies that is still in its early stages of development. The marketing process will influence the tourism and hospitality industry to an increasing extent in the globally competitive conditions of the twenty-first century. It affects the allocation of goods and services that influence a nation's economy and stan-dard of living. Marketing helps the awareness and accelerates the growth of sales of products and services. An understanding of marketing assists in increasing consumer numbers to businesses and to entire destinations, which affects us all. Jobs are created, there is increased income to the local economy, and the local community may feel a sense of pride in living in a destination that is appreciated by visitors. Marketing is as relevant to domestic tourism as it is to international tourism (see ► Industry Insight 1.8).

During the so-called "information era" of the late twentieth century (Enright, 2002), which started in the early 1980s, companies began to acknowledge that they had a social responsibility in addition to their profit and customer-satisfaction objectives. Tourism and hospitality companies that implement a corporate social responsibility (CSR) approach operate in an environmentally and ethically responsible manner; and consider the long-term good of society as well as that of consumers (Carroll & Buchholtz, 2003). A company that uses such an approach is saying: "We are a good business and we are not selfish and we like to give something back to society".

> *Corporate social responsibility* means operating in an environmentally and ethically responsible manner; and considering the long-term good of society as well as that of consumers (Carroll & Buchholtz, 2003: 3).

Industry Insight 1.8

Responsible Tourism: G Adventures

G Adventures is a global adventure travel company, founded in Toronto, Canada. The organisation was founded as Gap Adventures by Bruce Poon Tip, who at the age of 22 after a backpacking trip to Asia. spotted a gap in the tourism industry for travellers looking for grassroots travel experiences, such as an alternative to holiday resorts and cruise ships. The name Gap Adventures has a double entendre, with the letters standing for "Great Adventure People" and 'bridging the gap' between backpacking and other forms of travel. Over the next two decades, Poon Tip led G Adventures to 40 per cent sales growth year-on-year, including during the global recession of 2008, when he declined an offer of $100 million to sell G Adventures. The company now has 28 offices worldwide offering 700 itineraries in more than 100 countries. Under Poon Tip's leadership, G Adventures has been named by *National Geographic Adventures Magazine* as a best 'Do It All Outfitter' on Earth and is a six-time recipient of the 'Top 10 Employers for Young People', a lifetime platinum recipient of the '50 Best Managed Companies' and for ten consecutive years was named as one of Canada's 'Fastest-growing companies' by *Profit* (magazine). Poon believes in the power of travel to be a force for good and is an authority on social entrepreneurship, 'quintuple bottom line' versus triple bottom-line and corporate social and environmental responsibility. The travel company now works with its non profit partner, the Planeterra Foundation, founded by Poon Tip in 2003, to support local communities through a community tourism business model. Working with small, locally owned companies and projects that offer support, empowerment and employment to women, Indigenous communities and at-risk youth, G Adventures also has a "ripple score" for each trip, evaluating what percentage of expenditure stays in the local economy. In India it supports 'Women on Wheels' (female-only chauffeurs) and in 2018 partnered with Wiwa Tours in Colombia, the region's first indigenous-run tour operator.

Source: ▶ https://www.gadventures.co.uk/

CSR is becoming extremely important in today's environmentally conscious marketplace. *McDonald's* sponsorship of Arches National Park near Moab, Utah in the United States is an example of CSR in action. McDonald's asserts that it is always ready to invest in the preservation of the environment, making the United States a better country for all its people. Similarly, *Abang Africa*, an inbound tourism company operating in southern Africa, has a CSR policy embedded into all of its business activities. It is also certified by Fair Trade Tourism (FTT), a non-profit organisation that promotes **responsible tourism** in Africa (see ▶ Industry Insight 1.9).

The CSR outward-looking approach lends itself to the increasingly important balancing of, firstly, business interests and long-term interests ("doing good is good for business!"), and secondly, responsible development and the growing concerns of the twenty-first century. For a number of tourism businesses, profit is not the only motive; organisations such as non-governmental organisations (NGOs) and voluntary organisations – for example The *National Trust* in the United Kingdom – has objectives of education, preserving and enhancing the environment, and creating jobs in communities.

It has been argued that the concept of CSR is no longer sufficient and as a result has been revised to take into account peoples' wider concerns for the environment. Porter and Kramer (2011) suggest a business's adopting a **creating shared value** (CSV) approach. The main difference between CSR and CSV is that CSV addresses social problems at scale while actually making a profit, so it is a business proposition. Traditional business does not always seek to address an unmet social need, which is not necessarily wrong, but then it is not shared value. Thus, CSR is about responsibility, while CSV is about creating value. This is what Porter and Kramer (2011) called "a reputation-driven social activity". By taking a CSV approach, companies share their values with stakeholders.

> *Creating shared value* (CSV) is a method of creating economic value, so it also adds value to society and addresses additional challenges (Porter & Kramer, 2011).

❓ Could corporate sponsorship turn your country's national parks into outdoor Disneylands?

1

Industry Insight 1.9

Fair Trade Tourism Path to Sustainable Tourism in South Africa

Fair Trade Tourism (FTT) officially launched its trademark in South Africa in 2002. The non-profit organisation encourages and promotes responsible tourism in southern Africa and worldwide. The aim of FTT is to make tourism more sustainable by ensuring that the people who contribute their land, resources, labour and knowledge to tourism are the ones who reap the benefits. The organisation awards its trademark to tourism organisations that meet the following criteria:

- Fair wages and working conditions
- Fair operations as well as fair purchasing and distribution of benefits

- Ethical business practices
- Respect for human rights, culture, and the environment.

Organisations receive the award for:
- Employing and buying locally
- Skills development
- Health and HIV/Aids awareness
- Environmental education
- Community support.

Source: Fair Trade Tourism. (2020). Certification. Retrieved from ▶ http://www.fairtrade.travel/home/ [12 January 2020].

1.10.2 Marketing is Important to all Types of Business

The main objectives of most organisations are survival, profits, and growth. Marketing functions contribute towards achieving these objectives. Marketing is equally relevant to both the private and public sectors of tourism and hospitality as well as to smaller businesses and multi-national corporations. In this sense, the adoption of the marketing approach is as relevant to provincial and local tourism agencies or organisations, museums, and national parks as it is to airlines, tour operators, B&Bs, or restaurants in the private sector. Marketing is, more than ever, the primary focus of management in the globally competitive conditions of twenty-first-century tourism and hospitality. It is crucial to the understanding of most businesses and it is important to an entire business, from the boardroom to the frontline staff.

The Chartered Institute of Marketing (CIM) represents the interests of the marketing industry offering numerous training courses and professional qualifications in the field of marketing. Visit the CIM website (▶ www.cim.co.uk). When was the association founded? What is its motto?

1.10.3 Marketing Affects Everyday Life

Marketing plays an important role in people's everyday lives. Whether you are conscious of it or not, you participate in marketing as a consumer in everyday life, whether you are queuing at a shop or supermarket, travelling to university or work by bus, or drinking coffee at a café. By observing your involvement in the decision-making process as a consumer, you will develop a better understanding of marketing and consumer needs and aspirations. Understanding marketing makes people better-informed consumers.

1.10.4 Marketing Offers Exciting Career Opportunities

Marketing will be a very important influence in your career, whether or not you are directly engaged in marketing practice. It offers a variety of opportunities in areas such as advertising, brand management, marketing / consumer research, sales, digital marketing, destination marketing, social media, pricing management, database management, and event marketing, Marketing opportunities exist in private-, public, and voluntary-sector

Image 1.5 Female chauffeur drivers in New Delhi. (Source: G Adventures and Women on Wheels)

tourism organisations, including hotels, theme parks, transport providers, tour operators and travel agencies, event management companies, airlines, museums, DMOs, national parks, and government tourism agencies.

1.10.5 Marketing is an Important and Growing Field of Study

Over the last decade, marketing has become an important component of any business course at all levels up to postgraduate level. It is an extremely diverse subject and no one person who has studied marketing can be expected to be an expert in all facets of the discipline. Marketing tasks, too, are extremely varied, requiring both management and creative skills. For instance, marketers need to be able to sell effectively, draw up an effective advertisement, carry out marketing research, and create an attention-grabbing website homepage. Marketing has also become an important research topic for tourism and hospitality management studies. Indeed, as Xiang and Petrick note, "Marketing is by far the most popular tourism/hospitality-related research topic, and includes areas such as des-

tination image, digital marketing and social media marketing and market segmentation" (2008: 235).

1.11 Responsible Tourism Marketing

Responsible tourism places the onus on individuals and businesses (tourists as well as destination managers) to act to deliver sustainable development (Lipman, Jiang, Vorster & DeLacy, 2014: 265). Green and environmental issues are putting pressure on individuals to travel less or by different means (this is referred to as a "modal shift") or by carbon offsetting (where individuals and organisations take responsibility and pay for the emissions produced from their activities). In the same way that travellers are increasingly choosing tour companies and accommodation providers based on their responsible tourism credentials (Frey & George, 2010), new websites allow travellers to choose flights from the airline with the lowest carbon footprint for their particular journey. The principles of responsible tourism should underpin everything to do with the business of tourism.

1

International travellers are beginning to realise that their visits to holiday destinations have an impact on local people and environments. Many of them want to ensure that their holidays make a positive contribution to local development. Thus, environmental considerations are increasingly playing an important role in the decision-making of tourists (Goodwin & Francis, 2003; Frey & George, 2010). A growing number of tourists want to interact with locals and experts (for example, sommeliers, artists, archaeologists, and marine biologists) who can take them inside a particular world. Holiday products should be environmentally sustainable, adhering to minimum standards of environmental practice.

Summary

Today, marketing plays an important role in all types of tourism organisations, and it is becoming more and more sophisticated. Tourism and hospitality marketers have to adapt their marketing activities accordingly. Demanding consumers are also putting pressure on the industry. Tourism marketers are realising the importance of digital marketing and customer relationship management, and are also showing greater concern for society and the environment, as reflected in the corporate social responsibility activities of many tourism companies.

In this chapter, we defined the terms "tourism" and "hospitality". We then looked at definitions of marketing and tourism and hospitality marketing as well as the evolution of marketing across all industries. We briefly discussed the core principles of tourism and hospitality marketing, including information gathering, marketing orientation, the marketing mix, marketing planning, and customer relationship management. We then considered some of the reasons for studying tourism and hospitality marketing. Lastly, we looked at the concept of responsible tourism marketing, which is becoming increasingly relevant as consumers are more discerning about the impact of travel on the environment.

❓ Review Questions

1. Value is one of the keywords in the definition of marketing. Explain the importance of value in the context of tourism and hospitality.

2. How is tourism marketing defined in this book?

3. Mathieson and Wall (1982) offer the following definition of tourism: "… the temporary movement of people to destinations outside their normal places of work and residence, the activities undertaken during their stay in those destinations, and the facilities created to cater to their needs." Critique this definition by referring to the more accepted definition of tourism offered by the United Nations World Tourism Organization (provided in the text).

4. "Marketing is the same as selling." To what extent do you agree with this statement?

5. Describe the rise in the importance of marketing in the tourism industry.

6. Read the section on the 'Elements of the marketing mix' and devise mixes for the following companies and their target consumers:
   (a) A student backpacker hostel
   (b) A luxury boutique hotel
   (c) A budget car hire company
   (d) A local independent café

7. Briefly explain the concept of responsible tourism marketing. Go online and find examples of tourism companies with a strong position on responsible marketing. What are the common characteristics among these organisations?

8. Describe the four main principles of tourism and hospitality marketing as outlined in this chapter.

9. Define and explain the concept of corporate social responsibility (CSR). Provide some examples of tourism and hospitality organisations in your country that use this approach.

10. Discuss why you should study tourism and hospitality marketing.

Warner Bros Studio Tour, London: The Making of Harry Potter

Objectives

- To apply the principles of marketing orientation to Warner Bros Studio Tour: The Making of Harry Potter.
- To understand Warner Bros Studio Tour, London: The Making of Harry Potter's marketing orientation.

Harry Potter's wand may now be in retirement, but the magical world of Hogwarts' sets, props and costumes are alive and well in a corner of Southeast England. Based in Leavesden in Hertfordshire, Warner Brothers acquired the film and media studio complex formerly known as "Leavesden Studios" in 2010. With a £100 million investment, Warner Brothers transformed the site into a film and literary tourist attraction known as the Warner Bros Studio Tour: The Making of Harry Potter.

The Making of Harry Potter Tour opened in early 2012, employing over 300 local residents and was an instant hit; attracting over 6000 visitors daily in spite of its location far from the main tourist trail of London. The rest of the complex continues to be a working film and media studio.

The attraction is promoted primarily as a filmmaking exhibition and aims to provide an authentic experience for visitors. Liz Thomas marketing manager/director explains more, "Warner Bros Studio Tour London is a unique opportunity to visit and experience the original sets, props, costumes, animatronics and special effects used in the eight Harry Potter films". Educational openings where students can learn about set design, movie graphic design and movie marketing are also provided as highlighted by Liz, "Our education programme brings film making to life in an interactive and inspiring way and gives students the opportunity to see first-hand the extraordinary artistry and talent involved in the film making process."

An informative approach and an emphasis on authenticity differs from the 'Wizarding World of Harry Potter' themed parks owned by Universal Parks and Resorts in Orlando, Hollywood, US and Osaka, Japan. These theme parks are inspired by and re-create popular Harry Potter locations with a purpose of entertaining visitors rather than educating.

During a Warner Bros Studio Tour, visitors are led by qualified teachers (guides), offering a three-hour walking tour. The tour starts in the Great Hall and moves into well-known sets such as Dumbledore's office, Hagrid's hut and the potion's classroom. Familiar props such as Hagrid's motorcycle and Platform 9¾ pop up along the way before reaching the iconic Hogwarts Express steam engine. The exhibition ends with a 1:24 scale model of Hogwarts as used during filming.

The Warner Bros Studio Tour makes full use of social media marketing. Its website has direct links to Facebook, Twitter, Instagram, Flickr, YouTube, and a TripAdvisor feed encourages visitors to post their reviews about their experiences. Visitors are encouraged to take photographs throughout the exhibition and are reminded to share their pictures and experiences during and after the visit on social media forums.

The Warner Bros Studio Tour: The Making of Harry Potter is an example of an outstanding experiential marketing experience. Visitors are immersed in the alchemy of the kingdom of Harry Potter and given a fantastical journey to remember.

Questions and Activities

1. Explain how Warner Bros Studio Tour, London: The Making of Harry Potter has demonstrated a marketing orientation philosophy.
2. Explain what other tourism organisations can learn from the marketing-orientated philosophy of Warner Bros Studio Tour, London: The Making of Harry Potter.
3. Assess Warner Bros Studio Tour, London: The Making of Harry Potter's philosophy and brand essence.
4. Go online to the Warner Bros Studio Tour, London: The Making of Harry Potter's official website (► wbstudiotour.co.uk/). Describe how the attraction attempts to satisfy the needs of its customers.

1

■ **Image 1.6**   Howart Express, Warner Bros Studio Tour, The Making of Harry Potter

References

Booms, B., & Bitner, M. (1981). Marketing strategies and organisation structures for service firms. In J. Donnelly & W. George (Eds.), *Marketing of services* (p. 48). Chicago: AMA Proceedings Series.

British Hospitality Association (BHA). (2020). About. Retrieved from https://www.ukhospitality.org.uk/page/About. (12 Oct 2020).

Carroll, A., & Buchholtz, A. (2003). *Business and society: Ethics and stakeholder management* (5th ed.). Australia: Thomson South-Western.

Drucker, P. F. (1969). *The practice of management*. London: Heinemann.

Enright, M. (2002). Marketing and conflicting states for its emergence: Hotchkiss, Bartels and the fifties school of alternative accounts. *Journal of Marketing Management, 18*, 445–461.

Expedia. (2018). *American vacation deprivation levels at a five-year high*. Retrieved from https://newsroom.expedia.com/2018-10-16-American-vacation-deprivation-levels-at-a-five-year-high#assets_all. (18 Nov 2019).

Frey, N., & George, R. (2010). Responsible tourism and the tourism industry: A demand and supply perspective. *Tourism Management., 31*(5), 621–628.

Goodwin, H., & Francis, J. (2003). Ethical and responsible tourism: Consumer trends in the UK. *Journal of Vacation Marketing, 9*(3).

Gummesson, E. (1987). The new marketing: Developing long-term relationships. *Long Range Planning, 20*(4), 10–20.

Horner, S., & Swarbrooke, J. (2016). *Consumer behaviour in tourism* (3rd ed.). Oxford, UK: Butterworth-Heinemann.

Kotler, P. (2000). *Marketing management: Analysis, planning, implementation and control* (10th ed.). London: Prentice Hall.

Kotler, P., & Armstrong, G. (2019). *Principles of marketing* (17th ed.). London: Pearson Education.

Levitt, T. (1960). Marketing myopia. *Harvard Business Review*. July/August.

Lipman, G., Jiang, M., Vorster, S., & DeLacy, T. (Eds.). (2014). *Green growth and travelism: Concept, policy and practice for sustainable tourism*. London: Routledge.

Lumsdon, L. (1997). *Tourism marketing*. London: International Thomson Press.

Mathieson, A., & Wall, G. (1982). *Tourism: Economic, physical, and social impacts*. New York: Longman.

McCarthy, E. J. (1960). *Basic marketing: A managerial approach*. Homewood, IL: Irwin.

Middleton, V., & Clarke, J. (2001). *Marketing in travel and tourism* (3rd ed.). Oxford, UK: Butterworth-Heinemann.

Middleton, V., Fyall, A., Morgan, M., & Ranchhod, A. (2009). *Marketing in travel and tourism* (4th ed.). Oxford, UK: Butterworth-Heinemann.

Mill, R. C., & Morrison, A. M. (1992). *The tourism system: An introductory text* (2nd ed.). London: Prentice Hall.

Ministry of Commerce & Industry, Government of India. (2019). *Retrieved from hotels and restaurants.* http://tourism.gov.in/hotels-restaurants. (13 May 2019).

Perreault, W. D., & McCarthy, E. J. (2006). *Essentials of marketing: A global managerial approach* (10th ed.). Boston: McGraw-Hill.

Pike, S. (2018). *Tourism marketing for small businesses.* Oxford, UK: Goodfellow Publishers.

Porter, M., & Kramer, M. (2011). Creating shared value. *Harvard Business Review, 89*(1/2), 62–77.

Shaw, G., Bailey, A., & Williams, A. (2011). Aspects of service-dominated logic and its implications for tourism management: Examples from the hotel industry. *Tourism Management, 32*, 207–214.

Skripak, S. (2018). *Fundamental of business* (2nd ed.). Virginia, USA: Virginia Tech Libraries.

Statista. (2018). *Online travel market – Statistics & facts.* Retrieved from https://www.statista.com/topics/2704/online-travel-market/. (14 Aug. 2018).

TripAdvisor. (2020). *Warner Bros. Studio tour London – The making of Harry Potter.* Available at: https://www.tripadvisor.co.uk/ShowUserReviews-g2691242-d2147749-r129360688-Warner_Bros_Studio_Tour_London_The_Making_of_Harry_Potter-Leavesden_Hertfordshi.html. Accessed 18 Jan 2020.

United Nations World Tourism Organization. (2008). *International Recommendations for Tourism Statistics 2008 (IRTS 2008).* Retrieved from http://statistics.unwto.org/en/content/conceptual-framework-tourism-statistics-international-recommendations-tourism-statistics-200. (11 Aug 2018).

United Nations World Tourism Organization. (2017). *Why tourism?* Retrieved from http://www2.unwto.org/content/why-tourism. (14 Aug 2018).

Vargo, S., & Lusch, R. (2004). Evolving to a new dominant logic for marketing. *Journal of Marketing, 68*(January), 1V17.

Vinerean, S. (2017). Importance of strategic social media marketing. *Journal of Marketing, 5*(1), 28–25.

VisitLondon. (2019). *Warner Bros. Studio tour London – The making of Harry Potter.* Available at: http://www.visitlondon.com/things-to-do/place/23035130-warner-bros-studio-tour-london-the-making-of-harry-potter#xdOLjgOTIZzmpduA.97. Accessed 18 Jan 2020.

Xiang, L., & Petrick, J. F. (2008). Tourism marketing in an era of paradigm shift. *Journal of Travel Research, 46*(3), 235–244.

Further Reading

Baines, P., Fill, C., Rosengren, S., & Antonetti, P. (2019). *Marketing* (5th ed.). Oxford, UK: Oxford University Press.

Kotler, P., & Armstrong, G. (2019). *Principles of marketing* (17th ed.). London: Pearson Education.

Characteristics of Tourism and Hospitality Marketing

Contents

Electronic Supplementary Material The online version of this chapter (https://doi.org/10.1007/978-3-030-64111-5_2) contains supplementary material, which is available to authorized users.

Purpose

This chapter will provide you with the information and skills necessary to understand the characteristics of tourism and hospitality marketing.

Learning Goals

After reading this chapter, you should be able to:

- Compare and contrast the difference between services marketing and manufacturing marketing
- Describe the four main characteristics that distinguish services offerings from manufacturing products
- Explain the implications of the characteristics of services marketing
- Understand the various marketing management approaches available to the tourism and hospitality marketer
- Apply the characteristics of tourism and hospitality marketing to low cost carrier Wizz Air.

Overview

In this Chapter, we build on the general principles of tourism marketing discussed in ▶ Chap. 1 by examining the unique characteristics of services marketing.

We begin by examining a philosophical question: is the marketing of tourism offerings fundamentally different from the marketing of manufacturing products? We discuss the implications of these differences on efforts to increase service quality.

Then we review the four special characteristics that make the marketing of these services different from the marketing of other products: intangibility, inseparability, variability, and perishability. We also look at a number of other features that are unique to the field of tourism.

Next, we look at the various marketing management strategies for tourism and hospitality businesses. Finally, we examine some of the marketing approaches, such as the extended marketing mix, to address the unique challenges facing the tourism and hospitality marketer.

The chapter's in-depth case study applies the principles and concepts discussed in this chapter to Hungarian low-cost airline, *Wizz Air*.

2.1 Introduction

Although manufacturing marketing and tourism and hospitality marketing are similar, there are distinct differences between them. The tourism industry is part of the services sector of a country's economy. It is different from the manufacturing, construction, and other primary industries, such as agriculture and mining. It is also different from other components of the services industry, such as the financial, retail, entertainment, and commercial sectors. Tourism marketing entails selling and promoting an intangible experience, unlike the marketing that is carried out in other industries, which involves a physical good (for example, in the car industry, the physical good being marketed is a car). This is why marketing approaches need to be adapted for tourism marketing.

Understanding the generic characteristics of tourism and hospitality offerings and the different marketing approaches helps us to explain the way in which decisions made by the tourism marketer lead to increased service effectiveness.

2.2 Tourism: Product, Service or Offering?

Most writers on tourism and hospitality marketing fail to distinguish between the terms "product" and "service". They refer to the tourism product, making it sound as though products and services are the same. Instead, we shall use the term "offering" because it describes the nature of tourism, as clarified by the characteristics discussed later, more accurately.

2

2.2.1 Service Marketing Versus Manufacturing Marketing

A wide range of manufactured products, from hair shampoo to television sets, have a strong element of intangibility, just like services, because the customer cannot try them out beforehand (Levitt, 1960). Likewise, on occasion, there is a tangible element when a consumer purchases a service. The consumer knows what to expect when visiting a restaurant that offers both products and services, for instance. We can see from the discussion in the next section, however, that there are many more differences than similarities between tourism offerings and manufactured products. As a result, there are implications for the tourism and hospitality marketer.

> The services industry is the part of the economy that creates services rather than tangible objects. The services sector includes banking, tourism, hospitality, leisure, retail, transport, food services, entertainment, and communications. The services industry is also known as the "tertiary sector of industry".

Services marketing did not develop at the same pace as marketing in the non-service industries, but has lagged behind by as much as 20 years. One of the main reasons for this lag in the development of services marketing is the historical tendency for technical and operations-oriented people to create and manage tourism and hospitality organisations. Few of these people had any formal training in marketing. They learnt it on the job. Manufacturers were creating marketing departments back in the 1950s, when tourism was in its infancy. Another reason for the delay involves the composition of the tourism industry: it is dominated by small businesses. Small-sized and family-run guesthouses, travel agencies, tour operators, car-hire companies, ground handlers, and tour operators outnum-

ber the larger chains and group businesses. Most small businesses cannot afford full-time marketing managers and have limited marketing budgets. Many of them regard marketing as a luxury that only the big firms can afford.

We can conclude that in many ways, marketing tourism and hospitality offerings can be more difficult than marketing products. Tourism and hospitality marketers can apply several strategies to increase their effectiveness.

2.3 Special Characteristics of Services

> » *Goods are produced. Services are performed.* (Rathmell 1974: 1)

Tourism and hospitality marketers need to be concerned with four generic characteristics that make the marketing of services offerings different from the marketing of manufactured products: intangibility, inseparability, variability, and perishability (see ◻ Table 2.1). We will discuss these characteristics, which are common to all service industries, as well as additional features that are specific to tourism.

2.3.1 Intangibility

Before a customer buys a car, he or she can inspect it. The customer can see the car, touch it and even take it for a test drive. The consumer can carry out an evaluation before deciding whether to buy it or not, as the car is tangible. The car can even be delivered to the consumer. Service offerings, in contrast, cannot be inspected or tested in advance and they cannot be brought to the consumer. They are intangible. They can be described as something that a consumer can buy, but that cannot be dropped on his or her foot! The tourism offering is an experience rather than a physical good (see ▶ Industry Insight 2.1). Consequently, an element of risk exists for consumers; they are unsure of exactly what they are purchasing.

Table 2.1 The differences between the characteristics of tourism and those of manufactured products

Offerings	Products	Example
Intangible	Tangible	The consumer cannot inspect the holiday before it is purchased, unlike the purchasing of a product such as a car.
Inseparable	Separable	Services are produced and consumed at the same time, and the service provider is part of the offering. Waiting staff are an inseparable part of the service offering. Products may be consumed independently.
Variable	Standardised	A restaurant meal experience is always unique. It exists only once and is never repeated exactly. Products are standardised.
Perishable	Non-perishable	A seat on a tour bus cannot be stored and saved for a later date, unlike a product, which can be stocked until demand occurs.

Source: Author's creation

Industry Insight 2.1

Blue Train Tourist Sees Red Over Yellow

Imagine booking the trip of a lifetime on the South Africa luxury safari train The Blue Train and discovering that the engine is … a different colour … Ian Crowhurst, a passenger on board The Blue Train, was so angry over what he described as a yellow locomotive that he lodged a complaint with the Advertising Standards Authority of South Africa (ASASA). In a ruling, however, ASASA said the locomotive on that trip was the only part of the five-star train that was not blue. The locomotive was supplied by Spoornet, which at that time had only yellow – not blue – locomotives available. "Should advertisers apply the complainant's logic, then the Green Truffle restaurant would be forced to sell only green truffles," ASASA said. A reasonable consumer would expect a predominantly blue train. "The service and experience offered by the respondent is what guests expect and get. The colour of the locomotive pulling the train is inconsequential."

Source: Staff writer. (2007). Blue Train Tourist Sees Red Over Yellow. *The Cape Times*, 19 August.

Intangibility indicates something that consumers cannot see, taste, feel, hear, or smell before they buy it. Since services cannot be evaluated or tested beforehand, consumers tend to rely on word-of-mouth recommendations from other people's experiences. When looking for a good value-for-money (VFM) restaurant, for instance, people will ask friends or people familiar with the town, such as a hotel receptionist or concierge, for their recommendation. Consumers may alternatively look for tangible elements in the offering itself (such as the cleanliness of a restaurant or the appearance of employees' uniforms) or in the offering's promotional material (a brochure, for instance). When purchasing a holiday, a prospective consumer can only imagine what the holiday will be like. For example, he or she may wonder if the rooms will be clean and how busy the resort will be. Consumers are helped by the tour operator's brochure as well as screen images from television and the internet.

So it seems that offerings such as a holiday are extremely intangible, while a restaurant meal is more tangible (a hybrid). There is a continuum or range of tangibility for all tourism offerings (see ■ Fig. 2.1).

In reality, then, most tourism offerings are a combination of tangible and intangible elements, so it makes little sense to refer to them as products or goods. For instance, a visitor attraction such as a museum is a mixture of goods (exhibits, café, souvenir shop, visitor centre and so on) offering a range of services (guided tours,

2

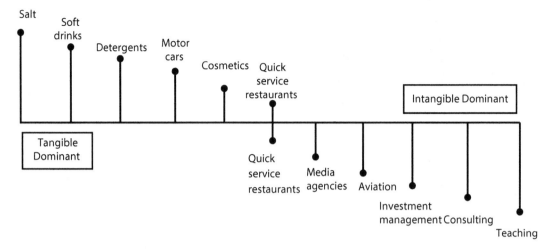

□ **Fig. 2.1**   Tangibility-intangibility continuum. (Source: Author's creation)

education and so on). Likewise, a holiday resort is a combination of facilities (hotels, swimming pool, restaurants, golf course, shops and so on) and services (housekeeping, reception desk, activities and so on). Although the offerings include tangible items such as food, beverages, and souvenirs, which consumers can often see beforehand, they cannot test or taste even these items in advance. Similarly, a fundamental part of the tourism offering lies in how it is delivered to the consumer. The consumer cannot experience this beforehand either.

The marketer has the task of promoting an intangible offering. The key challenge for tourism and hospitality marketers is, "How do we get consumers to take notice of our offering when they cannot see it?" Thus, the intangible benefits of the tourism offering (such as relaxation, education, entertainment or feeling superior) need to be communicated in an attempt to make the offering more tangible. ▶ Industry Insight 2.2 illustrates how several tourism companies such as hotels and travel agencies are using scents to promote holidays to remind customers of past trips in the hope of increasing holiday bookings. This concept is referred to as **olfactive marketing.** Smells are strongly associated with emotions and memories. For example, the distinctive smell of the seaside can send some people

Industry Insight 2.2

Smell of Success: Travel Agencies Use Virtual Reality Headsets and Smell Generators to Boost Package Holiday Sales

Travel agencies are adopting virtual reality experiences to entice customers to book package holidays. Hays Travel in the UK is one of the first to adopt virtual reality experiences using Samsung-powered headsets in its flagship stores. With immersive digital screens, virtual reality headsets and smell generators that can replicate the smell of sand and other holiday scents. Customers wearing a headset can virtually fly over New York, lie on a sun-lounger by a swimming pool in Mauritius, or visit a restau-

rant in Greece before spending money on a holiday.

Many leading travel agency chains in the United Kingdom are now using exotic smells to boost sales by recreating the memorable moments of previous travel experiences in the minds of potential customers. The aromas used included orange groves to evoke the Mediterranean, freshly mown grass for golf holidays, pina colada for romantic breaks and a sea-breeze scent for ocean cruises. One company rubbed coconut oil onto the backs of seats to promote Caribbean breaks, while another travel group considered using the smell of ice cream to appeal specifically to families. Similarly, Singapore airlines has created an aroma called 'Stefan Floridian waters' which has been used by flight attendants' perfume and in the hot towels served before take-off. It has become a distinctive scent of Singapore Airlines' brand,

The success of the strategy has been attributed to the fact that our sense of smell is directly connected to the parts of the brain responsible for processing emotions. Aromas go straight to the limbic system, which is the emotional control centre of your brain. When you smell something, it immediately triggers an emotion.

Source: The Future of the Travel Agent: Virtual reality, Digital Screens, and 'Smell Generators'. ▶ https://www.marketingweek.com/2015/07/07/the-future-of-the-travel-agent-virtual-reality-digital-screens-and-smell-generators/ [19 October 2018].

back to comforting memories of holidays in their childhood.

Another challenge facing tourism and hospitality marketers as a result of the intangibility of service offerings is pricing. It is difficult to measure the costs of a service that you cannot touch or use in advance. Tourism and hospitality pricing is problematic decision because of the variability of the product, the high degree of competition in certain tourism markets, and difficulties in accurately forecasting the level of demand (Meidan, 1989: 354). The relationship between price and quality is a complex construct that is multidimensional in nature, especially because of the duality in the effect of price: price can be an index of the amount of sacrifice the individual has to incur to consume the product, as well as of the level of quality that the individual might expect (Murphy and Pritchard, 1997).

2.3.2 Inseparability

A customer can assess a car purely upon its features (specifications, colour, sound and so on). Managers have time to plan these aspects and control quality to ensure that customer satisfaction is achieved. The circumstances under which a car is manufactured, how it is delivered and by whom are usually of little relevance to the customer. Services, on the other hand, are usually sold first, and are then created and consumed at the same time. For example, an airline seat cannot be provided until it has been purchased, and the flying experience is produced and consumed simul-taneously. Thus, the production and consumption of tourism offerings are **inseparable**.

> ┌ Definition ──────────────
>
> *Inseparability*, in the context of tourism, is defined as the condition that exists in instances where a service and the provision of that service occur at the same time, with both provider and consumer involved in the process of delivery (Zeithaml, Bitner, & Gremler, 2017: 412).

In addition, in most cases, service providers must be present for a service to be consumed. For example, to take advantage of an airline flight, both the customer and the transport operator must take the journey at the same time. As a result, the service providers (in this case, the airline staff) must be present in order for the transaction to take place. The consumers have a direct experience of the production of the service. In other words, the staff become part of the offering itself; the two are inseparable. The Servuction framework (see ▪ Fig. 2.2) demonstrates how consumers are an integral part of the service delivery process (Hoffman & Bateson, 2017). The term "servuction" was coined to designate the service production system (in other words, service production = servuction). According to the servuction framework, the elements of the service experience include the service's invisible organisation and system (aspects contributing to the service production beyond the customers' view). The framework

2

consists of these four factors, which directly influence customers' service experiences:
- **Servicescape** or physical setting (visible)
- Contact personnel/service providers (visible)
- Other customers (visible)
- Organisations and systems (invisible).

The **servicescape** is the physical environment in which services are delivered, and in which consumers and employees interact (Bitner, 1992). The visible elements include the servicescape (physical setting) in which the service is performed and other tangibles such as furnishings and business equipment. They also include the contact personnel (the employees who interact directly with the customer to provide the service), and both Customer A (the customer receiving the service) and Customer B (others who may be present in the visible area). The bundle of service benefits a customer receives increases out of the interaction with the contact staff (for example, their courtesy and competence) and the inanimate service environment (for example, comfort and décor). However, that interaction is greatly influenced by what happens in the invisible organisation and by other customers present at the service experience. For instance, actions that take place out of sight, such as

handling the reservation and cleaning the room, critically affect the quality of the ultimate service that a hotel's guest receives. Likewise, the number and character of other guests staying at the organisation may affect hotel experiences. Tourism establishments such as hotels and airlines serve multiple customers. Tourism managers must understand the many aspects of the invisible organisation and system in tourism services.

Tourism consumers are likely to be very concerned about the way in which the offering is delivered (in other words, the level of customer service). The seats on the aeroplane may be comfortable and the food may be exceptional, but if the flight attendant is rude or has a poor attitude, the consumer will notice. It also means that service providers as well as consumers are part of the offering. For example, a lively conversation with a fellow tourist during a tour may enhance a tourist's experience, while an unruly, intoxicated passenger on an airline flight may detract from a quality experience. Tourism organisations sometimes attempt to manage the behaviour of customers so that they can co-exist peacefully. For example, managers can target specific age segments to minimise potential conflicts between younger and older customers. Several airlines monitor and restrict the

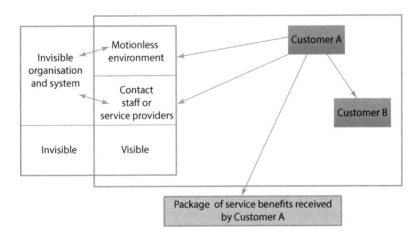

☐ **Fig. 2.2**   Servuction model. (Source: Adapted from Bateson (1995), p. 74)

amount of alcohol consumed by passengers. Train companies and restaurants now have quiet carriages or areas where the use of mobile phones is not allowed.

The task of satisfying consumers of services is much more difficult than it is for the manufacturer of a product in many ways. In tourism, everything must be right the first time, all the time. Any mistake can prove costly in terms of lost custom in the future. How tourism staff present themselves, what they say, what they don't say, how service oriented they are or how personable they are can determine whether the consumer purchases from the business again.

The inseparability of service production and consumption means that each and every service encounter is likely to be different, which contributes to the third generic characteristic of services: variability.

> A *service encounter* is an event that occurs when a customer interacts directly with a service (Zeithaml, Bitner & Gremler (2017).

2.3.3 Variability

Inspectors and robots can control and check the manufacturing process for cars and other products to ensure that these products are standardised. For example, one VW car is the same as any other when it comes off the production line. The two cars have the same shape, functions and engine, and so on.

Tourism and hospitality offerings are different. They always vary because humans produce them. For instance, the flight attendants are part of an airline's offering. Each attendant is fallible and cannot provide exactly the same levels of service as his or her colleagues. They are not machines! A passenger may receive outstanding service 1 day and average service another day from the same provider. Why? The flight attendant or service provider might just be having a bad day. Similarly, no two consumers are precisely the same. They have different demands, expectations, tastes, moods, percep-

tions, and emotions. Consequently, tourism offerings and experiences vary according to their situation. Indeed, no two services will be the same because services are performances (they happen in real time). Variability (or heterogeneity, as it is sometimes referred to) is one of the most visible differences between products and services. Heterogeneity – the variation in consistency between one service and another – is a fact of life for most tourism offerings.

Variability is perhaps the most challenging of the characteristics of a service. Ensuring consistent service is a major task. It is difficult to conduct quality-control checks, especially in labour-intensive services such as hospitality. Some organisations, particularly quick-service restaurants (QSRs) such as Nando's and coffee shop chains such as Costa Coffee, aim to offer consumers high consistency from one visit to the next as a result of standardised preparation procedures. The consumer receives the same offering whether he or she orders food from an outlet in London or one in Madrid. Another way to increase consistency is to merchandise the delivery process. Examples include vending machines that provide airline tickets or food and beverage items. Essentially, jobs are deskilled. Personnel are replaced with machines in order to reduce human variability. However, this is unrealistic, as people, not robots, are involved in the production, consumption, and delivery of most tourism offerings! The development of standards and employee-training programs is the key to ensuring consistent service.

 Discuss why inconsistency is considered a feature of restaurants in your country's hospitality sector.

2.3.4 Perishability

If a car in a showroom is not sold today, it can be sold tomorrow. It can also be stored and sold at a later date or resold. Once sold, it can even be returned to the manufacturer if the customer is not satisfied. Tourism offerings cannot be saved, stored, resold or returned. They are **perishable.** For example, a hotel

2

◘ Image 2.1   Empty seats/rooms equates to lost revenue in the hospitality sector. (Source: Unsplash)

room that is not sold today cannot be sold tomorrow. The room itself still exists, of course, but what is really being sold is time in the room on a particular day. If it is not booked for that day, the revenue from that room for that day is lost and cannot be recovered. Similarly, airlines and other transport operators that have a fixed number of seats face the same problem as hotels and guesthouses that have a fixed number of rooms: matching available demand to a perishable supply. For instance, once an aeroplane has taken off, the empty seats no longer exist and are not saleable. (In travel, this is known as "deadheading", in other words, making a trip without passengers.) If a hotel bed is not occupied on a particular night, that rental opportunity is lost and cannot be recovered.

> **Definition**
>
> *Perishability* describes offerings that cannot be saved, stored, resold or returned. (Kotler, Bowen, Makens, & Baloglu, 2017: 366).

The perishable nature of tourism offerings means that they are very often discounted, especially at the last minute. For instance, hotel rooms are usually discounted after 7 p.m. in a last-minute sale and airlines offer standby fares to fill empty seats at short notice in an effort to reduce the lost revenue accruing from unused supply (see ◘ Image 2.1).

We can see that one of the tasks for the marketer is to implement effective pricing strategies to manage the demand of tourism offerings. This applies particularly where the supply of a product offering is finite. We discuss pricing strategies in ▶ Chap. 8. Perishability is also closely associated with seasonality, which is discussed in the next section.

> Discuss this statement: "A hotel bed is not a can of soup that sits on a shelf until it is sold. Once the time has passed, the offering has expired."

2.4 Specific Features of Tourism Services

In addition to the four generic characteristics common to all services, there are several features that are unique to the tourism and hospitality industry: non-ownership, seasonality, fixed location, loyalty, high costs, distribution channels, the interdependence of tourism offerings, and the effect of external shocks and events.

2.4.1 Non-ownership

Non-ownership is considered to be the fifth characteristic of services. The importance of non-ownership as a service characteristic is underestimated. It was first introduced by Judd (1964) and Rathmell (1974), and has since been largely excluded from the literature. Besides the four main characteristics of services, most tourism offerings possess a non-ownership element.

When a car is purchased, the customer owns it from then on. In contrast, a consumer only has access to or temporary possession of a tourism offering. He or she does not usually receive ownership of anything tangible. For example, when a consumer hires a car, ownership is not transferred. In the same way, a hotel room is reserved for a period of time,

but is not actually owned by the consumer for that time. All that consumers take home are souvenirs and intangible memories of the experience. Since transfer of ownership is not involved, the task of building a relationship with consumers, of keeping their custom and of building brand loyalty, becomes more difficult in tourism marketing. Services cannot be owned. Consumers buy the right to use a product, service or offering. That is, customers buy the right to use a physical object such as a hotel room for a weekend or the right to use a rental car (Hoffman, Bateson, Wood & Kenyon, 2017: 27). They do not take the hotel or car home with them. They do, however, take away with them memories of the service and of how they felt during their stay (in other words, whether they had a memorable hotel or rental-car experience).

2.4.2 Seasonality

A common characteristic of tourism demand is that it fluctuates during different times of the year. According to Bull (1995: 4), "... tourism has one of the most highly seasonal patterns of demand for any product." Seasonality, therefore, plays a key role in determining when tourism companies (including destination marketing organisations, or DMOs) undertake marketing campaigns. A holiday resort, for example, might undertake marketing activities based on a seasonal quarter, say from September to November, after the school holidays. The resort might run numerous specials and direct marketing activities targeting regular visitors during this time.

Many destinations in the Caribbean, South east Asia, and Mediterranean are seasonal, based on school holiday patterns and climate. The main international markets for the United Kingdom include tourists from Western Europe (namely: Germany, France and Spain), and North America who tend to take holidays during their summer months of

2

Monthly distribution of the total number of arrivals and nights spent in tourist accommodation establishments, EU-28, 2018 (%)

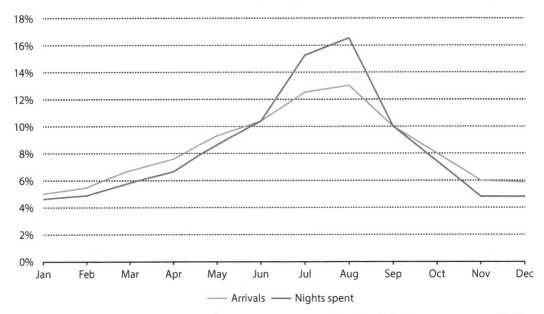

——— Arrivals ——— Nights spent

■ **Fig. 2.3** Seasonality of tourist accommodation in EU-28 countries (in 2018). (Source: Eurostat. (2019).
▶ https://ec.europa.eu/eurostat/web/products-eurostat-news/-/DDN-20200107-1)

■ **Image 2.2**   Cycling the Algarve. (Source: RG)

June to September. Most of the tourists from these countries therefore tend to visit during the United Kingdom's summer. Australia, another main market for the United Kingdom, however, tends to take their summer holidays in the European winter months of November and December. Consequently, many tourism businesses are at peak capacity for the same 2 months (July and August) when Britain's schools and businesses take holidays, and experience quieter periods during the off season, between October and April. The management of marketing is about the management of demand. A marketer's role can be to stabilise demand levels. Marketing strategies by DMOs aim to disperse tourist arrivals geographically and seasonally. This is done as a means of spreading the socio-economic benefits across the particular country and relieving the high demand on popular British visitor attractions at certain times of the year.

In Europe, the monthly accommodation statistics show a significant seasonal bias for arrivals and number of nights spent in tourist accommodation (see ■ Fig. 2.3). The 2018 statistics illustrate August was clearly the peak month for nights spent with 3.5 times higher number than in the slowest month (January). The two summer months, August and July, accounted for nearly one third (32%) of all nights spent in EU tourist accommodation in 2018. The period from June to September rep-resented more than half (52%) of all nights spent during the year.

Many destinations and their DMOs look at ways of combating seasonality. The Algarve in Portugal, for instance, have targeted new markets to increase tourist arrivals during its off-season (see ▶ Industry Insight 2.3).

Discuss this statement: "We are making it easier for visitors to travel beyond London and experience all of the world-class attrac-tions the United Kingdom has to offer, to make sure the benefits of this thriving indus-try are felt by the many and not the few." said Former Prime Minister, Theresa May,

Source: *The Telegraph,* 28 August, 2016 "Theresa May says Brexit can boost United Kingdom tourism as she encourages fami-lies to go on 'staycations'" *Source:* ▶ http://www.telegraph.co.uk/news/2016/08/25/theresa-may-says-brexit-can-boost-uk-tourism-as-she-encourages-f/

Industry Insight 2.3

New Tourism Products to Combat Seasonality in The Algarve

The Algarve, in Portugal's southernmost region, is known for its Mediterranean beaches and golf resorts. However, it faces strong com-petition from other European destinations, especially in the wintertime. Seasonality is, admittedly, one of the main challenges facing the Algarve's sustainability as a tourist desti-nation. Tourism authorities in the Algarve are now promoting cycling and walking activi-ties as ways of attracting tourists during the tourist off-season. The Algarve has cycling and pedestrian routes and tracks in loca-tions such as Ecovia do Litoral (Eurovelo), Via Algarviana, Rota Vicentina, and Rota do Guadiana. The region is ideal for such activi-ties: it has a mild climate, it is safe and there is a diverse landscape. At a European level, the demand for cycling tourism is growing and is already worth almost a billion euros in cycling trips annually.

In addition to a cycling tourism product, ANA Aeroportos de Portugal, in partner-ship with Turismo de Portugal and with the Associação de Turismo do Algarve (Algarve Tourism Association), have developed other initiatives to combat the effects of seasonal-ity at Faro Airport (also known as "Algarve Airport") such as increasing the number of lights to the region. Furthermore, Faro Airport has invested approximately 35 million Euros in a major remodelling of the passenger ter-minal. According to the Manager of ANA Aeroportos, Luís Vaz, "we are investing in Faro Airport because we believe in the future development of the region and in the capacity that we will have to overcome the challenge of seasonality together".

Source: ▶ http://www.routesonline.com/airports/8474/ana-aeroportos-de-portugal-faro-airport/news/254070/new-tourism-products-to-combat-seasonality-algarve-in-cycling-and-walking/

Hotels and restaurants also experience busy and slow periods depending on their location. For instance, a restaurant that is situated in a central business district (CBD) may have high rates of occupancy (as high as 80%) on weekdays and low rates of occupancy (as low as 20%, if it is even open) at weekends. Conversely, a restaurant situated in a city suburb may experience busy weekends and slow periods on weekdays. A number of hotels located in cities have adopted the strategy of offering rooms by the hour (see ▶ Industry Insight 2.4). Airlines also experience demand fluctuations depending on the time of day, the day of the week and whether it is a holiday period. For example, on a daily basis, seats on a scheduled flight may be 90% full at 7.30 a.m., while seats on the following flight at 10 a.m. may be only 45% full. This seasonality has implications for the prices and quantity of tourism offerings supplied between seasons (see ◻ Image 2.3). Tour operators, visitor attractions and charter airlines usually experience peak demand during school holiday periods.

Industry Insight 2.4

Hotel Rooms by the Hour

As its name suggests, Dayuse hotels allow consumers to rent a hotel room any time during the day, whether they want to rest between flights or take some time out during a busy work day. ▶ Dayuse-hotels.com rents out rooms for hours at a time in over 5000 selected 'partner' hotels in 25 countries around the world. The hotel booking company, which started in 2010, is an intermediary between hotels and consumers. Rooms can be reserved for different time slots for 3–7 hours at a time, depending on the hotel and its individual availability. Dayuse hotels can also be booked in the evenings up until 11 p.m. Prices are 30–70% less expensive than regular nightly rates, ranging from £53 (€62) to £175 (€204) for double rooms in three-, four- or five-star hotels. The intermediary has its headquarters in Paris, France.

Source: dayuse. (2019). Room by hour. Retrieved from ▶ https://www.dayuse.co.uk/pages/articles/room-by-hour [11 September 2019].

◻ **Image 2.3**   Theme parks such as Alton Towers use special offers to attract visitors during the off-season. (Source: Alton Towers Resort)

2.4.3 Fixed Location

Tourist destinations and tourism and hospitality businesses are fixed locations. This means that the role of communication and promotional methods such as advertising, digital marketing, social media marketing, and sales promotion are essential in order to bring the consumer to the locality.

2.4.4 Loyalty

Consumers may well – to some extent – be loyal to a particular hotel group brand (such as *Holiday Inn Express*), a local restaurant, a restaurant chain (such as *Nando's*) or an airline (such as *Emirates*). They tend to be loyal to restaurants and hotels that have met their needs. Some consumers enjoy visiting different destinations, while others may go to the same resort or hotel at a holiday destination every year for many years. A professional conference organiser (PCO) will be reluctant to change hotels if the hotel he or she has always used has been doing a good job in hosting conferences. Some consumers also remain loyal to a particular destination. Similarly, there are people who visit a destination only once. It is therefore impossible to generalise about whether or not consumers are loyal to a particular tourism product offering; it depends on availability (ease of purchase) and affordability (amount of disposable income).

2.4.5 High Costs

Tourism and hospitality businesses generally have high fixed costs of operation and relatively low variable costs. Fixed costs are costs that have to be paid in order for the business to operate, such as permanent staff wages, rent, heating, lighting, fuel and marketing expenditures. For instance, a hotel that operates at times with an occupancy rate of only 20% instead of 80% must still pay the rent and rates, permanent staff wages and so on. Variable costs are costs that depend upon the number of consumers that the organisation receives. These costs may include extra staff, maintenance or meals served. Variable costs fluctuate as the occupancy rate changes, but fixed costs still have to be covered. High fixed costs provide a challenging operating environment for tourism and hospitality businesses.

In addition, tourism and hospitality offerings usually represent a relatively high-cost purchase for the consumer. Going on holiday, purchasing an airline ticket, or staying at a hotel is expensive. Indeed, these purchases often represent the largest single outlay of expenditure for a consumer in a given year. Hence consumers tend to spend time making a decision and making comparisons with alternative offerings. This feature is important from a marketing perspective.

2.4.6 Distribution Channels

Various forms of transport physically move fast-moving consumer goods (FMCGs) to warehouses and retailers, and directly to customers. In contrast, there is no physical distribution in the tourism industry. Consumers have to travel to the tourism offering or destination. Part of the offering is the travel aspect of getting to the destination (the flight or other mode of transport). Thus, tourism consumers have to travel to the service factory to consume the service, rather than vice versa.

In most cases, distribution involves the many marketing intermediaries in the tourism industry. There is a great variety of distribution channels and a unique set of intermediaries in tourism and hospitality. Intermediaries are organisations such as travel agencies, sales representatives, call centres, tour operators, sales outlets and incentive travel planners that bring consumers and offerings together. These intermediaries play a vital role in the tourism indus-

2

try. The service of travel agents, (including online travel agencies – OTAs) for instance, is important to most tourists. Travel agents have a major influence on the satisfaction or dissatisfaction of tourists as they carry out a number of functions, such as providing advice on destinations and accommodation options, and handling bookings. (We will discuss travel agents and other intermediaries, and their role in tourism marketing, in ▶ Chap. 9). In the meetings industry, PCOs perform this function.

2.4.7 Interdependence of Tourism Offerings

Much of the tourism and hospitality industry is interdependent as most consumers use several different services and products, with multiple different owners when consuming their hospitality or tourism offering. A simple decision such as the purchase of a holiday in say France involves several complex processes.

– Firstly, deciding how to get there (by car, train, aeroplane or bus?) and which class of transport to use.
– Secondly, deciding which of the different visitor attractions (e.g Eiffel Tower, Notre Dame de Paris, Chomps-Elysees or the Louvre) as well as various amenities (different types of accommodation, restaurants, and so on) to choose from on arrival.
– Thirdly, deciding which of the different ways available to organise the holiday (package tour or independent travel?) to choose.

All of these offerings involved in the experience are interdependent (they rely on each other) and the processes are unique to the tourism industry. For example, a delayed flight can affect the outcome of a holiday. If something goes wrong, it has an effect on the experience. Waiting at the airport for 1 day will have a drastic effect on a 2-week holiday, for instance.

2.4.8 External Shocks and Events

The tourism and hospitality industry is particularly vulnerable to external shocks such as wars, disease, extreme weather conditions (for instance, cyclones, tornadoes, mudslides, typhoons, hurricanes and droughts), political elections and events, adverse publicity, terrorist attacks, transport accidents, pollution, earthquakes, volcanic eruptions, political events and strikes (for example, an airline can crew strike), electricity shortages, recessions and fluctuations in economic conditions (such as drastic changes in exchange rates). Even slight changes in the weather (e.g. unseasonal rain in coastal resorts in the summer or lack of snow in European ski resorts in the winter) can affect consumer demand for an offering.

These types of factors are often outside the control of marketers and managers, which makes it difficult for them to predict sales volumes. They also influence product quality and customer satisfaction, and are considered a major problem for the tourism industry in general.

During the last few years, the economic recession as well as political instability has had a major impact on the international tourism economy. These events have affected many individual tourism businesses reliant on international (inbound and outbound) tourism and tourists. Unexpected events of this nature also mean that many tourism offerings, such as hotel rooms and airline seats, are sometimes highly discounted because of perishability and the need to recover high fixed costs.

Between 2009 and 2014, the worldwide tourism industry was hit by the global economic downturn and the Eurozone debt crisis in 2011 as well as an outbreak of rare and unexpected diseases such as 2009 H1N1 influenza (swine flu) and the 2014–2016 Ebola outbreak which started in West Africa. In 2020/21, the world economy and the international travel, tourism, and hospitality industry was negatively affected by the outbreak of the coronavirus epidemic. The outbreak of the Coronavirus (COVID-19) pandemic had a considerable impact on people travelling worldwide with many eople being deterred and/or prohibited from travel between countries and within their own countries. Many international and national events (including sports, music, business meetings, and festivals) were postponed due to the virus. Airlines, cruise liners, hotels, restaurants, travel agents, holiday resorts, conference centres, visitor attractions, and destinations suffered a dramatic decrease in bookings during 2020/21 (see ▶ Chap. 6).

Intermittently, since 2011, political instability and civil wars in several countries in the Middle East and North Africa – in particular, Tunisia, Iran, Yemen, Iraq, Syria, and Libya – affected tourist arrivals in the region. Similarly, a spate of terrorist attacks in France, Belgium, and Germany in 2016 as well as in Manchester and London in the UK 2017 affected intraregional tourism in Europe. Disasters such as an erupting volcano in Manila in the Philippines in 2020, flooding and landslides in Mozambique in 2019 and an earthquake and tsunami In Indonesia in 2018, Typhoon Hagibis in Japan in 2019, Hurricane Irma in the United States and Hurricane Dorian in the Bahamas in 2019, and devastating bushfires (the worst on record) across Australia in 2020, and severe flooding in Venice, Italy in 2019 have demonstrated the incredible power of nature. In the past, tourism has shown resilience and emerged from crises.

Industry Insight 2.5

Devastating Floods Venice Tourism Industry

In November 2019, severe floods in Venice, Italy caused hundreds of millions of euros in damage. It was the worst flooding in the country in 50 years. Flood levels in the lagoon city reached 1.87 metres devastating streets, squares and landmark churches. St. Mark's crypt and mosaic floor were damaged, the baroque church of St. Moses and the city university were flooded. The city sits on thousands of wooden piles driven into mud, but rising sea levels and heavy cruise ship traffic have steadily eaten away at the surrounding marshes and mudbanks, causing the city to gradually sink.

Venice hotels reported a 35% cancellation for the month after the floods. Tourism is a $3.3-billion a-year business in Venice.

Source: The Guardian. (2019). 'An apocalypse happened': Venice counts cost of devastating floods Retrieved from ▶ https://www.theguardian.com/world/2019/nov/13/an-apocalypse-happened-venice-counts-cost-of-devastating-floods [21 November 2019]. *Source:* Momigliano, A. (2019). The flooding of Venice: What tourists need to know'. New York Times. Retrieved from: ▶ https://www.nytimes.com/2019/11/20/travel/venice-flooding.html [22 November 2019].

Sometimes a negative event can have a positive effect on a destination. For example, a youth football team was trapped in a mine in a cave in Thailand for two weeks in 2018. The event attracted worldwide attention. The twelve players and coach were eventually rescued and the way in which the world viewed Thailand changed for the better. The event helped boost Thailand's image and internationals tourist arrivals to the Southeast-Asian country are likely to increase.

2.5 Marketing Management Strategies for Tourism Businesses

The strategies that tourism marketers can apply to increase their effectiveness include tangibilising the offering, managing employees, managing perceived risk, managing supply and demand, and managing consistency. These strategies are discussed in more detail below.

2

2.5.1 Making the Offering Tangible

Consumers cannot see, sample or self-evaluate tourism offerings as a result of the intangible nature of these offerings. Consequently, mar-

keters must attempt to give consumers evidence of what it is they will get when buying these offerings. ▶ Industry Insight 2.6 shows how a contemporary arts museum in Cape Town, South Africa utilises an interactive website to make the offering more tangible to consumers.

Industry Insight 2.6

Using Online Tools to Make an Offering More Tangible

Tourism organisations use tangible promotional materials such as brochures, reports, videos and DVDs to help tangibilise an offering. The Zeit Museum of Contemporary Art Africa (MOCAA) in Cape Town has an interactive website – ▶ www.zeitzmoca.museum– to promote itself. The home page shows photographs of the museum and it has a YouTube video about the venue. There are links to a photo gal-

lery with numerous high-quality photos of exhibits. The virtual tour features 360-degree views from within the Museum. This allows a visitor to imagine what it would be like to visit the Museum. The Museum reinforces the tangibility of the experience by allowing users to download a brochure of the centre. All of these promotional materials help the Zeit MOCAA make its service offering more tangible and thus more likely to attract customers.

Source: ▶ www.zeitzmoca.museum

❓ Discuss the physical evidence provided by a hotel or restaurant in your community to help it tangibilise its offerings.

Consumers usually rely on certain tangible cues when deciding what to purchase. These include physical evidence and personal touches. Both of these elements must be apparent to potential consumers on site as well as in advertising and promotional materials.

The physical surroundings of the tourism organisation can provide tangible evidence of what consumers can expect to receive when purchasing a tourism offering. The marketer must manage the physical elements to the last detail. The car park must be well kept, there should be no misspellings or missing letters on signage, and the greening (indoor and outdoor plants) and décor must be well maintained. In addition, the marketer must ensure that the lighting and employee uniforms are in line with the organisation's image. Slogans and logos are other examples of tangible cues that can be used in tourism marketing. For instance, *Premier Inn's* slogan ("A good night's

sleep guaranteed") and its logo (a half-moon – see logo/picture below) both emphasise security and shelter.

Tourism and hospitality organisations can provide personal touches as a way of giving that little bit of extra-special service. Hotels can provide small distinctive touches such as turning down the bed while guests are out for the evening. This is a way of saying, "While you were out, we didn't stop working to make you happy."

2.5.2 Managing Employees

As a result of the inseparable nature of tourism offerings, employees are part of the product itself. Staff should be friendly, polite and well-motivated. They must be well trained in the importance of marketing orientation. The task of training and motivating employees to provide service excellence is called "internal marketing". Well-prepared organisations implement internal marketing programs in their operations. We will discuss this further in ▶ Chap. 13.

2.5.3 Managing Perceived Risk

The high risk that people perceive when purchasing tourism offerings increases loyalty to organisations and destinations. Prospective tourism consumers often feel hesitant because they cannot evaluate the offering concretely beforehand. Tourism marketers can provide innovative ways for consumers to sample their services.

One of the ways in which marketers can encourage consumers to purchase is to offer familiarisation trips. Hotels and resorts can invite meeting and conference organisers for lunch. Tour operators can offer free trips to travel agents and accommodation managers. Airlines often arrange complimentary flights for travel agents or other important tourism role players. DMOs host familiarisation trips so that travel writers, inbound tour operators, and travel agency consultants can visit the destination (see ▶ Chap. 14). Familiarisation trips (also called "fam trips" or "educationals") reduce the intangibility of an offering by allowing intermediaries to gain experience of it in the hope that they will recommend the offering to consumers.

To overcome the problem of intangibility, tour operators, travel agents, DMOs, conference centres, holiday resorts, restaurants, cafés, and hotels record their features on video and share content (such as visitors' holiday photos and videos) and make these available online (on their official website as well as various social media platforms such as YouTube, Instagram, LinkedIn, and Facebook) for viewing by potential consumers, who can download video clips and view a photo gallery. The advantage of videos is that they provide a more interactive and in-depth image of a destination than a holiday brochure. This takes away some of the uncertainty the consumer may have when booking and purchasing tourism and hospitality offerings.

2.5.4 Managing Supply and Demand

To minimise the effects of perishability, tourism marketers need to synchronise supply and demand. Marketers can do this by altering opening and closing hours or the number of staff. Opening hours can be extended during peak periods or decreased during quieter periods. Extra part-time staff can be employed at busy times or full-time staff can work overtime. In addition, staff members who possess a number of skills can do different types of work. For instance, a receptionist might be required to work the floor of a hotel's restaurant during a busy period. The consumer can also be involved in the offering delivery. For instance, a restaurant can provide a buffet service. A hotel that has the necessary technology can enable guests to enter their rooms using a swipe card, thus eliminating the need to request a room key at reception. Similarly, most airlines allow passengers to check in online prior to arriving at the airport. Although they are giving travellers convenient tools and increased options when it comes to checking in, the airlines are also outsourcing the check-in process to their travellers. As more travellers elect to check themselves in, staff costs for airlines can be reduced. The travellers are doing the job for free. In some cases, low-cost carriers charge customers more if they do not make use of self-service options.

Marketers can use aspects of the marketing mix to increase, create or reduce demand for the tourism offering. Various forms of promotional technique can be used to increase demand during quieter periods. VisitGreece, Greece's NTO (national tourism organisation), introduced an initiative to attract international and domestic tourists during its so-called "secret season" between the months of October and April, which is traditionally a quiet time for the Greek tourism industry and especially lesser known destinations.

Demand can also be increased by lowering the price of the offering. For example, Avis *Rent-a-Car* may offer discounted weekend rates, a resort hotel such as *Sands* in Cornwall may offer special rates on weekdays or the *Legoland* in Windsor may reduce ticket prices during the low period between October and March.

Marketers can also take advantage of times when demand exceeds capacity. They

2

know that on holidays like New Year's Eve, more people than usual want to go out. Thus, they can anticipate that they will sell more or perhaps not even have enough of what they are selling to meet this demand. For example, a restaurant may offer meals and entertainment at higher prices than usual and still fill all of its tables (its capacity).

2.5.5 Managing Consistency

The fact that tourism and hospitality offerings are variable makes the marketer's task of ensuring consistent service a challenging one. In the tourism industry, this means that consumer expectations must be met without any unwanted surprises (Kotler et al., 2017: 40). For instance, a hotel must keep its promise of delivering breakfast to a room at 7.00 a.m. in order to provide a consistent service.

Ways of creating consistency and reducing variability include recruiting the right employees and continuous staff training (see ► Chap. 13), standardising the service delivery process through service blueprinting and careful monitoring of consumer feedback (see ► Chap. 4). With increased technology in recent years, the use of ticketing and vending machines has standardised offerings and also reduced staffing costs.

However, fluctuating demand can still affect consistency. For example, if a coach full of tourists arrives at a guesthouse without a booking, the staffing capacity of the guest-house will be stretched no matter how well it is managed.

2.6 Services Marketing Triangle

Bitner's (1995) services marketing triangle (see ◘ Fig. 2.4) suggests that there are three types of marketing – all of which revolve around making and keeping promises to consumers – that must be carried out for a service marketing organisation to succeed.

The left side of the triangle suggests the important role of internal marketing (treating employees in the same way as external consumers) so that the organisation will be successful in delivering its promises to consumers. Employees must be enabled – recruited, trained, and rewarded for good service – so that promises are kept.

The right side of the triangle indicates the external marketing activities that the organisation should conduct truthful communications. These activities raise consumer expectations and a promise is made to consumers that these expectations will be met. The Package Travel Regulation (PTR), which became effective in July 2018 in the UK, states that consumers have the right to expect that the holiday they booked and paid for matches the description given to them when they bought it (see ► Industry Insight 2.7). Besides the traditional elements of marketing (such as advertising, digital marketing, social media, sales promotions, and public relations), the organisation's mission statement,

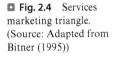

◘ **Fig. 2.4** Services marketing triangle. (Source: Adapted from Bitner (1995))

Organisation

Internal marketing: "Supporting the promise"

External marketing: "Setting the promise"

Employeess

Consumers

Interactive marketing: "Delivering the promise"

physical evidence and its employees are included here.

The actual service delivery takes place at the bottom of the triangle. This is known as "interactive marketing". It is where the organisation's employees interact directly with consumers and where the promise is delivered. It is also where service promises are most often kept or broken by employees. It is critical to deliver on the brand promise - whatever you are saying though marketing - make sure it really exists; make sure you deliver what is promised.

All three marketing activities are interlinked, and are essential for building and maintaining relationships. A complete marketing effort requires the support of all three sides of the services marketing triangle.

❓ Discuss the philosophy proposed in this statement: "It's better to under offer and over deliver."

2.7 Tourism Marketing Management Approaches

As we can see from the characteristics discussed above and the services marketing triangle, the differences between tourism offerings and manufacturing products mean that they cannot be marketed in exactly the same way. While the general marketing principles and theories remain the same, the way in which they are applied should be different. Thus, the tourism marketer is required to implement various marketing approaches, including the following:

- Use of the extended marketing mix
- Greater significance of word-of-mouth communication
- More use of emotional appeals in promotions
- Stronger emphasis on personal selling
- Increased importance of relationships with suppliers, carriers, and intermediaries.

These marketing approaches are discussed in more detail below.

2.7.1 Use of the Extended Marketing Mix

Most marketing textbooks identify the four Ps (product, price, place, and promotion) as the components of the marketing mix. Service marketers generally consider this concept to be unnecessarily restrictive (Morrison, 2010: 56; Payne, McDonald & Frow, 2011: 28; Lumsdon, 1997: 138). Zeithaml, Bitner & Gremler (2017: 31) suggested an extended marketing mix consisting of additional variables that services marketers can use to communicate with and satisfy their customers.

Although the extended marketing mix was originally introduced by Zeithaml, Bitner & Gremler (2017: 270), some authors have since developed their own variations. Morrison, for instance, recommended that packaging, programming, people, and partnership (2010: 291) be added to the traditional mix. As with the components of the original mix, the components of the extended mix are interrelated and can also be controlled by the tourism marketer. Any or all of them can influence consumer buying decisions as well as consumer levels of satisfaction.

Three extra Ps are added to the list for the marketing of tourism offerings: people, physical evidence and processes. The people component includes the firm's staff (their appearance, how friendly they are and so on), the customers and other consumers in the tourism service environment. The physical evidence is the environment in which the service is delivered. It includes tangible aspects or cues such as signage, décor, noise level, staff uniform, and equipment. Lastly, the process refers to the actual procedures or the flow of activities by which the tourism service is delivered. It includes the service time and the waiting time (see ▶ Industry Insight 2.7).

The components of all seven Ps of the extended marketing mix are controllable and are interrelated (Booms & Bitner, 1981). An adjustment in one component impacts on the others. The extended mix is more appropriate for the tourism and hospitality industry and offers more flexibility. Its elements need to be considered when marketers develop a marketing programme (see ◖ Table 2.2).

◻ Table 2.2   7Ps applied to a low-cost airline

Product	Price	Place	Promotion	People	Physical evidence	Process
No-frills	Differences depending on size of seat, leg room, type of carrier, purchasing method	Via mobile apps and internet	internet	Check-in staff	Colour scheme	Self-service via mobile phone or internet
Basic service			Billboards	Baggage handling staff	Food and snacks	
Ancillary services			Press	Customer service	In-flight magazine	
			Sponsorship	Airline crew	Airline loyalty card	

Source: Author's creation

Industry Insight 2.7

Jumeirah Beach Hotel, Dubai, UAE: People, Physical Evidence and Processes

Jumeirah Beach Hotel in Dubai, UAE has received numerous international awards, including being named the Middle East's Leading Family Hotel in 2018 at the World Travel Market (WTM). Jumeirah Beach Hotel is part of the Jumeirah Group consisting of numerous hotels and resorts in cities across the Middle East region: Dubai, Abu Dhabi, Bahrain, Kuwait, and Oman, as well as in Europe: Frankfurt, London, and Mallorca, and in Asia-Pacific: Bali, Guangzhou, Maldives, Nanjing, and Shanghai. The components of Jumeirah 's extended marketing mix all strongly reinforce its position as one of the world's premier game reserves.

- People: A highly structured approach to staff recruitment, training and development is the starting point. People are hired to work at Jumeirah Beach Hotel for their attitudes, people skills and personal attributes. A high degree of Dubai-styled hospitality is present so that guests feel that they are in a welcoming home-from-home environment.
- Physical evidence: All of the tangible elements linked with the hotels further reinforce its position as a premier hotel and resort group. All employees are dressed immaculately in uniforms, and the landscaping and indoor plants are of the highest quality. All stationery (in other words, e-mail signatures, letterheads, writing paper and envelopes), signage and anything else that bears the Jumeirah logo are done in gold-leaf lettering. The rooms and suites are all elegantly designed with balconies that have exquisite views. All of the rooms have white or cream-coloured finishes, floor-to-ceiling mirrors, hand-woven rugs, and contemporary furniture. A theme approach is taken to the furnishings. All of the interior décor has a bright minimalistic and modern feel.
- Process: The service delivery at Jumeirah Beach Hotel also confirms its position as one of the Middle East's best hotels. The hotel focuses on upmarket leisure travellers and is concerned with meeting their needs. Thus, its processes are highly customised to the individual and employees are empowered to provide non-standard service when needed. The Jumeirah Beach Hotel offers chauffeur airport collection and drop-off services.

Source: Based on information on the website of Jumeirah Beach Hotel. (2019). Book the Safari That Makes a Difference ... [Online], Available: ► https://www.jumeirah.com/Stay/Dubai/Jumeirah-Beach-Hotel?utm_source=google&utm_medium=google%20places&utm_campaign=hotel Accessed 2 June 2019.

2.7.2 Greater Significance of Word-of-Mouth Communication

Since tourism product-offerings are intangible and the opportunities to test them prior to purchase are limited, the consumer frequently relies on the recommendations of others to a greater extent than is the case with manufactured products. These recommendations and this advice from friends, relatives, business associates, peers and opinion leaders are a powerful source of communication. (These influencers are called "reference groups", as discussed in ▶ Chap. 3.) Certain influencers are more powerful than others. For instance, a local radio talk-show host talking about a favourable experience at a local restaurant is likely to benefit that restaurant greatly. These sources of information or referral communications are what consumers use to gather information about tourism offerings and destinations. Sometimes this is called "word-of-mouth" (WoM) advertising or electronic word-of-mouth (eWoM). WoM marketing is considered to be one of the oldest forms of commercial communication and is gaining in popularity. However, the term is misleading as no formal

paid advertising takes place. Furthermore, WoM marketing can only be controlled (indirectly) to a certain extent. Organisations do not always have control over how their brands are presented. WoM marketing is not the sort of marketing that can be switched on and off by remote control. Instead, the organisation relies on people talking to each other, which is in fact more powerful than advertising or any other form of promotion. The expansion of the internet, particularly social networking, means that the power of personal recommendation has exploded and digital "word-of-mouth" can play a powerful role in a person's decision to buy a product. People value and listen to the opinion of others who have actually experienced a product or service through the social network connection. Finally, word-of-mouth marketing is no longer merely one-to-one conversation. In today's digital age, the influence of word-of-mouth marketing operates on a one-to-many basis. Travel and tourism product reviews are posted online, and opinions are disseminated through social networks such as *TripAdvisor* and *Wikitravel*. Many tourism companies also post edited testimonials on their websites. Some consumers even create websites or blogs to praise or pun-

2

ish brands. For instance, ► hellopeter.com is a well-known website that consumers can use to report good or bad service received from a company. Consumers can submit their views about the service they received at any organisation in the form of a report posted on the website. In turn, the service provider is able to respond to the customer. The aim of this consumer rating site is to increase service levels of organisations. Marketing researchers use the term eWOM (electronic word-of-mouth), which is defined as "any positive or negative statement made by potential, actual or former customers about a product or company, which is made available to a multitude of people and institutions via the internet" (López & Sicilia, 2014).

It has been suggested that WoM marketing is the primary factor behind 20–50% of all purchasing decisions (Bughin, Doogan & Vetvik, 2010: 18). Its influence is greatest when consumers are buying a product (such as a netbook or a digital camera) for the first time or when products (such as travel, for example) are relatively expensive. Prospective tourists tend to carry out more research, seek more opinions and deliberate longer than they would otherwise.

Word-of-mouth marketing has more credibility than other forms of promotion and is considered to be the most potent form of marketing communication. ◘ Figure 2.5 shows that 90% of respondents trusted recommendations from people they know "com-

pletely" or "somewhat". Potential travellers are more likely to take advice from friends who have experienced an offering or destination than from a person such as a travel agent who has a vested interest in promoting the offering.

A consumer is likely to recommend a tourism and hospitality offering only if he or she has experienced a consistent, VFM quality experience. Research shows that there is a positive relationship between service quality and behavioural intentions, and that there is a positive and significant relationship between a customer's perceptions of service quality and his or her willingness to recommend the firm or destination to others (Zeithaml, Bitner & Gremler, 2017: 75). WoM information can be spread from one person to another face-to-face, by e-mail and by SMS (or text messaging) as well as via blogs (such as Wikitravel), micro blogs (for example, Twitter), consumer rating websites (for example, ► which.co.uk) and online communities (for example, *TripAdvisor*, ► WAYN.com and Dopplr). Viral marketing, where consumers forward a marketing message or a special offer to their friends, has become a very effective way of triggering WoM publicity (see ► Chap. 12). Indeed, social networking is an ideal platform for mass WoM marketing (see ◘ Fig. 2.5).

The spread of positive WoM information via consumers is paramount to most successful tourism organisations. In his book *Purple Cow*, Seth Godin refers to WoM recommen-

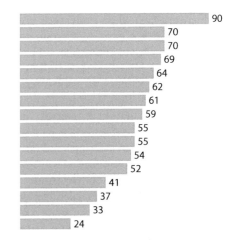

◘ **Fig. 2.5** Degree of trust. (Source: ► https://www.marketingcharts.com/television-36767)

Recommendation from friends	90
Consumer opinions posted online	70
Brand websites	70
Editorial content	69
Brand sponsorships	64
TV	62
Newspaper	61
Magazines	59
Billboard advertising	55
Radio	55
Email sign ups	54
Adverts in the cinema	52
Search engine results	41
Online video adverts	37
Online banner adverts	33
Mobile text advertising	24

dations as "sneezing". He says, "Sneezers are the experts that tell all their colleagues or friends or admirers about a product or service on which they have a perceived authority." (2008: 31). (The title of the book – *Purple Cow* – is a reference to what Godin calls the new P of marketing: making products and services remarkable, worth noticing and worth being talked about.) This is also referred to as the "wow factor", meaning a feature that leaves the consumer impressed or overawed, creating a favourable and memorable impression. Thus, we can conclude that WoM advertising is generated by having a remarkable product offering.

Firms can also formalise this advertising by encouraging consumers to "tell a friend" (for example, by "liking" a Facebook page), and by incorporating testimonials from satisfied clients or customers into advertisements, brochures, and other promotional materials. The spreading of positive word-of-mouth information is becoming increasingly important in a society in which we as consumers are exposed to as many as 1700 marketing messages during a 24-hour period, of which we might retain only eight! (Traupel, 2017: 1).

Social media trends are just one of the influences that marketers need to monitor.

2.7.3 More Use of Emotional Appeals in Promotions

The intangibility of tourism and hospitality offerings means that they require a unique promotional treatment. Consumers tend to respond to emotional appeals when they purchase travel products. Marketers sometimes do this by using a symbol that they hope will appeal emotionally to consumers to give a promotional campaign a distinctive personality. For instance, European tour operator TUI, uses the symbol of a smile and a dot alongside the red "TUI" to emphasise happy consumers. Similarly, Travelodge uses a picture of a person lying in a bed at night-time as a symbol and its slogan is "Sleep tight", which suggests security, hospitality, and warmth.

Tourism/hospitality is a people industry. People deliver and receive services. Thus, emotional bonding is more likely to occur. Interactions between service providers and consumers (known as "service encounters") generate emotions and personal feelings, which in turn influence consumer behaviour. Consumers also buy tourism offerings to match their self-images. People who value themselves and their status go on a cruise, go on a golf getaway holiday, stay at a *Ritz-Carlton* resort, or travel on *Golden Eagle Danube Express*, for example.

2.7.4 Stronger Emphasis on Personal Selling

The inseparable nature of services dictates that an organisation's frontline staff (receptionists, travel consultants and so on) should capitalise on the promotional tool of personal selling. Staff members need to be trained in the personal selling techniques (such as up-selling and cross-selling) covered in ▶ Chap. 11. All frontline staff, for instance, should know the prices of all of the company's products and services, the firm's website address, its Twitter address and even the company's slogan. It is also important that consumers be able to identify frontline employees. This can be achieved by the use of well-designed and attractive uniforms.

2.7.5 Importance of Relationships with Suppliers, Carriers, and Intermediaries

An effective relationship marketing program can have a profound effect on the marketing of tourism offerings. Marketers should focus on their relationships with consumers – internal and external – as well as their relationships with other organisations within the industry. A tourism and hospitality marketer should build relationships with suppliers such as visitor attractions (natural, built and cultural), accommodation providers (hotels, guesthouses or B&Bs), ground transportation (car-hire companies as well as taxi and bus operators),

2

carriers (airlines, railway companies, coach operators and cruise liners), intermediaries (tour operators, travel agents, DMOs, PCOs and tourism information centres [TICs]), and other destination stakeholders, including the host community as well as local, provincial and national government. The objective of relationship marketing with these groups is to develop co-operation between all parties who can impact on the ultimate satisfaction of the consumer (see ▶ Chap. 13). All of these tourism organisations are interdependent. If a hotel or guesthouse is unable to honour a reservation, this will reflect badly on the travel agent and tour operator who made the reservation. Similarly, if a tourist receives poor service at a visitor attraction, the consumer is likely to develop a negative impression of the destination. These supplier members play an important role in delivering vital service quality.

Summary

In this chapter, we explained the main differences between manufactured products and tourism offerings. Service offerings are intangible, inseparable, variable, and perishable. In addition, tourism and hospitality offerings have their own unique features. These differences and features mean that the tourism marketer is confronted with a number of challenges. One of these challenges is to deliver a quality offering of a consistent standard.

We also looked at the concept of the services marketing triangle and various marketing approaches, including the extended marketing mix. These are all tools with which tourism and hospitality marketers can address the unique challenges of the tourism and hospitality industry.

? Review Questions

1. Define services marketing.
2. Explain the following terms and provide examples of each:
   (a) Products
   (b) Goods
   (c) Services
3. Should tourism and other services be marketed in exactly the same way as manufactured products? Explain your answer.
4. Explain what is meant by inseparability. Why might its existence pose problems to tourism and hospitality organisations? Discuss various methods by which its impact may be reduced.
5. Why are airline seats considered highly perishable?
6. Briefly describe the components of the extended marketing mix? Apply the mix to a small local tourism and hospitality organisation with which you are familiar.
7. Explain why a service provider (a waitress or waiter, for example) is considered to be part of the offering.
8. Define the term "service encounter".
9. Compare internal and interactive marketing. Give an example of how a specific tourism and hospitality company might use these concepts to increase the effectiveness of its services.
10. Visit the website of an international hotel group (e.g. Accor, Travelodge) or holiday resort (e.g. Club Med., Sandals Resorts). Describe what the website does to make the offering tangible for the consumer. Explain how the website relates to the characteristic of perishability, for example, any special offers at some of its properties.

In-depth Case Study 2: Tourism Services Marketing Whizz Air: Making a Service Tangible Whizzing Through the Sky

Objectives

- To understand the importance of service excellence to a tourism and hospitality organisation
- To examine the characteristics of a marketing applied to a tourism and hospitality organisation.

As an airplane soars through the sky, the passengers on board are enclosed in a generally static experience. There are no breaks in the journey, roadside attractions, or opportunities to change the itinerary as the flight progresses. When it comes to overseas transportation, airlines must transport, serve, and entertain passengers who are essentially captive in a giant tin cylinder. The biggest carriers with the biggest budgets have traditionally been able to focus on creating memorable customer experiences; but in recent times, some low-cost carriers have followed in the slipstream. One such airline carrier is the Hungarian company Wizz Air.

The majority of successful low-cost carriers in Europe are mainly British, Irish or from other Western European countries (Dobruszkes, 2006). Bucking this trend, Wizz Air is one of the first Central- and Eastern European-based low-cost airlines to start operating in the European market, linking Western and Eastern European destinations. Wizz Air's main contribution to the low-cost carrier (LCC) phenomenon has been through its innovative approach on fares and bundles and offering a range of services to suit the needs of business travellers and leisure travellers: individuals, couples, groups and families.

Wizz Air started in 2003 and by 2004 took off for real as their first flight left Katowice, Poland. Fast forward 13 years and Wizz Air has a dominant position in the air space of Eastern Europe, offering over 500 routes, flying 77 aircraft from 28 bases in the following countries: Poland, Hungary, Bulgaria, Moldova, Romania, Ukraine, Czech Republic, Serbia, Lithuania, Macedonia, Latvia, Bosnia and Herzegovina, Georgia, and Slovakia (Wizz Air, 2019).

By 2015, Wizz Air had become Central and Eastern Europe's largest low-cost airline, employing over 3000 people, leading to being floated on the London Stock Exchange (LSE). Following the floatation in 2015, Wizz Air was reborn with a full brand rejuvenation and new aircraft livery in line with more progressive traveller requirements such as seat allocation, priority boarding and enhanced fare system.

Wizz Air is now seeking to climb to the heights of the world's best airlines and garner its reputation for excellent customer service: from ensuring passengers receive impeccable service from the moment tickets are booked through to touch down at the final destination.

The low-cost airlines' phenomenon initially broke with such traditional perceptions of what good customer care or the flying experience should be as they became known as "discount", "no-frills" or "budget" airlines. Pacific Southwest in the US in the 1970s launched the rise of the low-cost carriers, Ryanair in 1985, and EasyJet in 1995 were notable European leaders. The de-regulation of the air transport market in 1987 in the US and the 1990s and 2000s for the EU resulted in further expansion in the low-cost airline market (Dobruszkes, 2006).

According to the European Travel Network, 'An airline is recognised as a low-cost carrier if at least 75 per cent of its seats are sold at their lowest published fares or if it offers a very good deal' (Van der Zwan, 2006). Some of the characteristics of low-cost airlines include:

- No free food or beverages are offered; they must be paid on-board or pre-booked and paid before the flight.
- They fly to secondary airports; sometimes hours outside the city, far from the city centre.
- Short-haul and point -to- point.
- Often criticised for their service quality.
- Fast turnaround time at airports (often less than 25 minutes).

Wizz Air conforms to many of the aforementioned characteristics of a low-cost carrier: a simple service model, ticketless travel, cost and time efficient secondary airports, single class all-leather seat configuration, and catering on demand for an additional cost. Wizz Air promotes its service quality as: 'A value-orientated airline focusing on innovation all along the way of the customer journey. Our aim is to make flying affordable for the citizens of Central Eastern Europe, as well as to provide a new travel experience to all travellers in the EU.'

A prominent area where Whizz Air differs from most other low-cost carriers is its flexible menu of fares offered through three different bundle options (Wizz Air, 2019):
- Basic – Aimed at travellers who like to select the specific services they deem important, such as a small cabin bag and online check-in.
- Wizz Go – A bundle of four popular and proven services; seat selection, large cabin bag, 23 kg checked-in bag and online check-in.
- Wizz Plus – Includes extra services at a discount price, providing the most comfortable passenger experience. This includes premium seat selection with extra legroom seats, option to change flight date without charge, airport or on-line check in, priority boarding and the option to bring an extra small personal item on board along with a large cabin bag.

Wizz Air also offers a range of convenience options including Security Fast Track or Exclusive Lounge; Wizz Discount Club; Privilege Pass; Priority Boarding; Wizz Flex; On-time Guarantee; Wizz for Families and a Wizz Account. (Wizz Air, 2019).

In addition, Wizz Air also offers partner services including:
- 'Complete Savings', which is an online membership programme for British residents, offering access to discounts and cashback opportunities from leading retailers and service providers.
- Hotels.
- Car Hire.
- Airport Parking.
- Airport Transfer.
- Wizz Credit Card.

The Wizz Air website covers all the travel requirements for travellers, resulting in customers able to book and tailor their experiences in a straightforward manner. Wizz Air operates a call centre servicing all cancellations and customer issues.

Environmental issues appear to have been a factor for Whizz Air in a recent order of new aircrafts with advanced systems and engines that will reduce the company's carbon footprint.

Wizz Air is a low-cost carrier which has been operating a business model above the level of many of its competitors. Offering many extra services and price ranges on top of the basic services and low-cost has helped Wizz Air rise to the number one low-cost airline in central and Eastern Europe and challenge Ryanair and EasyJet in Western Europe. With its relaunch in 2015, Wizz Air's more vibrant, fresh, and sophisticated outlook aims to raise the company to the level of Europe's major low-cost airlines.

Questions and Activities

1. One of the underlying frameworks discussed in the text is the services marketing triangle. Discuss each of the three sides of the services marketing triangle in the context of Wizz Air.
2. Discuss the physical evidence provided by ▶ wizzair.com to help it tangibilise its product-offerings.
3. How does Wizz Air manage variability?
4. Using the information on the Wizz Air website (▶ wizzair.com), briefly explain how you would describe this low-cost airline. Identify and list the tangible elements the website conveys.

References

Booms, B., & Bitner, M. (1981). Marketing strategies and organisation structures for service firms. In J. Donnelly & W. George (Eds.), *Marketing of services* (p. 48). Chicago: AMA Proceedings Series.

Bateson, J. E. G. (1995). *Managing services marketing* (4th ed.). London: Dryden Press.

Bitner, M. J. (1992). The impact of physical surroundings on customers and employees. *Journal of Marketing, 56*(2), 57–71.

Bitner, M. J. (1995). Building service relationships: It's all about the promise. *Journal of the Academy of Marketing Science, 23*(4), 246–251.

Bughin, J., Doogan, J. & Vetvik. O.J. (2010). *A new way to measure word of mouth marketing*. Retrieved from: http://www.mckinseyquarterly.com/A_new_way_to_measure_word-of-mouth_marketing_2567. (4 Mar 2014).

Bull, A. (1995). *The economics of travel and tourism* (2nd ed.). Melbourne, Australia: Longman.

Dobruszkes, F. (2006). An analysis of European low-cost airlines and their networks. *Journal of Transport Geography, 14*(4), 249–264.

Godin, S. (2008). *Purple cow*. London: Penguin.

Hoffman, K. D., Bateson, J. E. G., Wood, E. H., & Kenyon, A. K. (2017). *Services marketing: Concepts, strategies and cases* (5th ed.). London: South-Western.

Judd, R. C. (1964). The case for refining services. *Journal of Marketing*, January,, 58–59.

Kotler, P., Bowen, J., Makens, J., & Baloglu, S. (2017). *Marketing for hospitality and tourism* (7th ed.). Upper Saddle River, NJ: Prentice Hall.

Levitt, T. (1960). Marketing myopia. *Harvard Business Review*, July/August,, 45–56.

López, M., & Sicilia, M. (2014). Determinants of E-WOM influence: The role of consumers' internet experience. *Journal of Theoretical and Applied Electronic Commerce Research, 9*(1), 28–43.

Lumsdon, L. (1997). *Tourism marketing*. London: International Thomson Press.

Meidan, A. (1989). *Pricing in tourism*. New York: Prentice-Hall.

Morrison, A. M. (2010). *Hospitality and travel marketing* (4th ed.). New York: Delmar Publishers.

Murphy, P., & Pritchard, M. (1997). Destination price-value perceptions: An examination of origin and seasonal influences. *Journal of Travel Research, 35*(3), 16–22.

Payne, A., McDonald, M., & Frow, P. (2011). *Marketing plans for services: A complete guide* (3rd ed.). New York: Wiley.

Rathmell, J. M. (1974). *Marketing in the service sector*. Cambridge, MA: Winthrop.

Traupel, L. (2017). *Marketing to today's distracted consumer*. Retrieved from http://www.marcommwise.com/article.phtml?id=517. (14 Apr 2017).

Wizz Air. (2019). *Information and service* [Online]. Available: https://wizzair.com/en-gb/information-and-services/about-us/company-information#. Accessed 13 June 2019.

Zeithaml, V., Bitner, M., & Gremler, D. (2017). *Services marketing: Integrating customer focus across the firm* (7th ed.). New York: McGraw-Hill.

Zwan, J. van der. (2006). *Low Cost Carriers - Europa*. Thesis at Utrecht University, Human Geography and Planning.

Further Reading

Hoffman, K. D., Bateson, J. E. G., Wood, E. H., & Kenyon, A. K. (2017). *Services marketing: Concepts, strategies and cases* (5th ed.). London: South-Western.

Zeithaml, V., Bitner, M., & Gremler, D. (2017). *Services marketing: Integrating customer focus across the firm* (7th ed.). New York: McGraw-Hill.

Understanding the Tourism and Hospitality Market

Contents

Tourism and Hospitality Consumer Behaviour

Contents

Electronic Supplementary Material The online version of this chapter (https://doi.org/10.1007/978-3-030-64111-5_3) contains supplementary material, which is available to authorized users.

3

Purpose

This chapter will give you the information needed to understand consumer behaviour in the context of buying tourism products.

🌐 Learning Goals

After reading this chapter, you should be able to:

- Understand why the buying process of tourists is unique
- Recognise the importance of understanding consumer behaviour and what motivates consumers to purchase tourism products
- Outline the four factors affecting consumer behaviour
- Become familiar with the consumer journey cycle as applied to the purchasing of a holiday
- Briefly describe the various tourism consumer markets
- Explain how tourism consumers are grouped together (the typologies used to classify tourists)
- Apply the principles of consumer behaviour to Halal tourism in South East Asia.

Overview

How do consumers make their travel choices? By answering this question, tourism marketers determine who to target, and how and why consumers choose to shop for, buy and consume the products that have been designed to meet their needs. In this chapter, we try to understand how and why consumers make their choices among tourism products and who the consumers are, all of which is crucial to effective marketing.

We begin with a discussion of the personal, psychological, cultural, and social factors that strongly influence consumers, causing them to behave the way they do when choosing to buy tourism and hospitality products. We summarise the various roles that consumers might play in the decision-making process. Next, we introduce the consumer journey cycle to show how consumers pass through a series of stages when purchasing holidays and tourism and hospitality products. We conclude with a discussion of the consumers who make their final purchasing decisions: the various consumer markets (from adventure tourism to volunteer tourism) and tourist typologies.

The chapter's case study applies the principles of consumer behaviour to the Halal tourism market in South East Asia.

3.1 Introduction

The last time you went on holiday, did you make the decision on your own, or did you ask friends or family for recommendations? Did you spend more time deciding where to go than you would have spent if you had been going out for a meal at a restaurant? What were your reasons for going on holiday? Did you gather information about the holiday destination online? Why did you choose that particular destination? These are the types of complex decision-making processes that all consumers go through when purchasing tourism products. The study of consumer behaviour focuses on how individuals make decisions to spend their available resources (time, money and effort) on consumption-related items (Schiffman & Kanuk, 2018: 6).

Consumer behaviour is defined by Blackwell, Miniard and Engel (2006: 37) as "those activities directly involved in obtaining, consuming, and disposing of products and services including the decision processes that precedes and follows these actions". This definition highlights the importance of the psychological process that consumers go through during the pre-purchase, purchase, and post – purchase stages. Consumer behaviour is primarily linking the consumer decision-making process to their consumption choice and experience. Tourism marketers need to have an understanding of why their particular products are purchased or rejected as well as knowledge about the motivations affecting choices. Through marketing research (see ▶ Chap. 4) marketers can find out about consumer behaviour and help predict what people will do. They can then influence choices through information, branding, promotional activities and making other decisions about the marketing mix. **Consumer behaviour** – why and how consumers make decisions – lies at the heart of marketing theory (Hyde & Lawson, 2003). Consumer behaviour is one of the most explored topics in tourism marketing, interchangeably denoted by the terms 'traveller behaviour', 'tourist behaviour', or 'guest behaviour'. Consumer behaviour acts as an origin for every tourism and hospitality marketing activity.

> *Consumer behaviour* is the behaviour that consumers display in searching for, purchasing, using, evaluating, and disposing of products and services that they expect will satisfy their needs (Schiffman & Kanuk, 2018: 19).

Travel is not the same today as it was ten or even five years ago: the way people travel, how much they spend and where they go has changed. Travellers are also not the same as they were several years ago. Tourists nowadays are all bloggers and publishers sharing their holiday experiences with friends on social media sites such as Facebook, TikTok (Douyin), Renren, Twitter, Instagram, Snapchat, YouTube, and WeChat. The value of friends' recommendations and experiences is particularly important. Indeed, travel photographs are the most posted pictorial items on Facebook.

Tourism marketers need to understand what motivates consumers to purchase tourism products. In addition, they need to understand the process that consumers go through when they decide to buy a tourism offering. Finally, marketers need to comprehend how tourism consumers are grouped together. There are three key areas of consumer behaviour:
- The factors affecting consumer behaviour
- The consumer journey cycle (decision-making process)
- The various consumer markets and tourist typologies.

3.2 Why is the Buying Process of Tourists Unique?

The purchasing decision relating to a tourism offering differs from the purchasing decision relating to a traditional product in many ways. Some of these ways are described below.

3.2.1 No Tangible Assets

When evaluating an offering, the prospective consumer has to make a choice from a number of similar alternatives without being able to inspect the purchase beforehand because of the intangible nature of tourism products. For instance, prospective holidaymakers have a wide selection of destinations from which to choose, but these destinations cannot be examined like a motor car or television is before it is bought (see ► Chap. 2).

3.2.2 Expenditure is Substantial

Tourist holiday expenditure is often substantial. There are large monetary outlays. Consumers usually spend more on their annual holidays (especially overseas holidays) than on most other consumer purchases (perhaps with the exception of buying a home or car).

3.2.3 Purchases are not Usually Spontaneous

Most tourism purchases are carefully planned. Leisure tourists consider a choice of destinations, types of accommodation, modes of travel and a range of tourist activities. Seldom does a consumer wake up one morning and say, "Right, I'm going on an overseas holiday tomorrow!" Business travel, however, is an exception, as sometimes business people are required to attend a meeting or event at short notice.

3

3.2.4 Consumers Visit the Site of Production

Tourists visit the destination – the site of production – to consume the holiday. This is different from the purchasing of manufactured goods, where in most cases, consumers buy from a retail outlet, or the product is delivered to their home or workplace after they have purchased it off the internet.

3.2.5 Increasingly People Need a Holiday

In today's fast-paced, time-precious and technology-driven world, people – increasingly need to take time out and go on holiday. Prospective travellers anticipate their holidays.

3.2.6 Prospective Travellers Anticipate Their Holidays

» *Flaubert believed that anticipation was the purest form of pleasure...and the most reliable.* (Julian Barnes)

Consumers usually anticipate their holidays and for many, a destination or holiday resort is nothing like they imagined. A prospective tourist might conjure up mental images of an island while reading a holiday brochure. These images might be of a golden beach lined with palm trees against a setting sun, a hotel room with wooden floors, and a view through white wooden shutter doors, and a clear azure blue sky. These mental images may bear little or no resemblance to the actual holiday destination. Increasingly, when anticipating their holiday, consumers refer to travel blogs and social media sites such as Facebook (for holiday photograph postings) or speak to friends and relatives who have experienced the holiday destination.

Consumer behaviour in tourism is a fascinating but complex subject to study, particularly in the tourism field (Cohen, Prayag &

Moital, 2014). No two people are exactly alike. Even people with the same background or level of education are completely different. They may have some things in common (for example, studying the same university course), but they may have quite different attitudes and opinions. For example, although all of the tourists in a group on a slum tourism in Mumbai, India are interested in cultural tourism, the group may include a retired bank manager, a schoolteacher and a computer technician, and their ages might range from 22 to 75. While they have some common interests, they may be completely different in other ways.

Studying consumer behaviour helps tourism marketers understand consumers' minds better and provides a clearer picture as to how tourists make decisions relating to the consumption of product products.

3.3 Factors Affecting Consumer Behaviour

There are a range of both external and internal factors influencing consumers' travel behaviour. External factors include the main macroenvironmental forces as well as the tourist destination's attributes (see ▶ Chap. 14). The external factors are analysed by using the PESTLE model: political, economic, socio-demographic, technological forces, legal, and ecological (see ▶ Chap. 6).

There is a complex array of internal influences affecting consumer travel behaviour; these can be categorised into four types of factors:

1. Personal factors
2. Psychological factors
3. Cultural factors
4. Social factors.

It is evident that buying decisions are not made in isolation. Each of the four types of factor involves its own complex series of factors that affect individual consumer decisions about tourism products, as outlined in ▢ Fig. 3.1.

These four factors are discussed below.

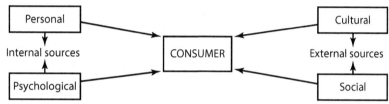

Fig. 3.1 Factors affecting consumer behaviour. (Source: Author's creation)

Table 3.1 The life cycle model

Stage	Characteristics	Consumer behavior
At-home singles	Under 35 years, single people, still live with their parents and have no children	Adventure tourism (Africa/South America/Southeast Asia), volunteer tourism, fast food; youth tourism holidays
Starting-out singles	Under 35 years, left home, unmarried without children; fashion conscious; low financial commitments	Similar to at-home singles
Mature singles (e.g. bachelors)	Mostly between 35 and 49 years, unmarried and without children	Long-haul holidays, dine out frequently
Young couples	Up to 49 years old, married couples without children	Package holidays, holiday resorts, dine out frequently
New parents	Married with children under the age of twelve years	Family package holidays, children or visiting friends and relatives; family restaurant meals or fast food
Mature parents	Married with at least one child over the age of thirteen years	Luxury holidays, upmarket restaurants, spas
Golden nests	Over 50 years old, married without dependent children	Luxury holidays, upmarket dining out, museums
Left alones	Over 50 years old, unmarried and without dependent children	Similar to golden nests

Source: Author's creation

3.3.1 Personal Factors

Consumers' tourism buying decisions are influenced by personal factors such as age and life stage, lifestyle, personality, and self-image.

3.3.1.1 Age and Life Stage

There are differences in travel preferences between different age groups (Horner and Swarbrooke (2016: 78)). Consumers in their early 20s tend to desire different holidays, modes of travel, and accommodation options to consumers aged over 55 years of age. Another powerful factor influencing consumer behaviour in tourism is the family life cycle stage (i.e. pre-family, family and empty nesters) that the consumer is currently in. Holiday resorts such as Butlin's and Center Parcs, for instance, have been successful at targeting families with their family entertainment and facilities (such as baby gyms for infants and a teen's lounge) as well as special offers for families. Several airlines have introduced seating areas designated for parents who are accompanied by their children on their aircraft in recent years. Bachelors are more likely to go on long-haul holidays; as they are less restricted in their holiday choices, and spend more time and money on holidays.

The characteristics of a typical life cycle model used by tourism marketers are outlined in Table 3.1.

3

As consumers progress through the early stages of the model, their lives become more hectic and their time becomes more limited. As a result, convenience, flexibility, and accessibility become increasingly important. Marketers can provide information to help them make decisions as well as offer online services and faster transactions. It is perhaps only when consumers progress towards the end of the life cycle that they have more disposable income and the discretionary time required to travel. This segment of the market is known as the "grey tourism" (or "senior tourism") market. It is characterised by travellers aged 60 years old and over. The grey market (or "grey gappers" or "silver tourists") tend to travel to several destinations and generally have considerable amounts of "silver dollars" to spend (Patterson & Balderas, 2018).

3.3.1.2 Lifestyle

Lifestyle refers to a person's pattern of living as expressed in his or her activities, interests, and opinions. and services (Tanner & Raymond, 2012: 178). People who share the same culture or social class, or belong to the same reference group, may nevertheless live quite differently. Psychographics, which is a method of studying people's lifestyles, attempts to measure people's activities, interests, and opinions (AIOs) (Vyncke, 2002). Activities (for example, work, hobbies, holidays, shopping, sports and recreational activities, entertainment, and social events) and interests (for example, home, job, community, food and media) are the things that people spend time doing, whereas opinions (about politics, religion, economics, future events, education, products and culture, for example) are beliefs that people have about a variety of subjects.

3.3.1.3 Personality and Self-image

An individual's distinct personality influences his or her travel and tourism buying behaviour. Whether a person is adventurous or cautious, sociable or a loner, confident or shy most definitely affects the type of holiday purchased. Personality can be useful in analysing

consumer behaviour. For example, tourism marketers have found that backpackers (or youth travellers) tend to be highly sociable, thus backpacking hostels create environments where consumers can relax and socialise with like-minded travellers. For example, *Matchbox: The Concept Hostel,* which opened in Singapore in 2013, backpackers sleep in pod-style dormitories. The hostel has a bar and lounge as well as a balcony for guests to mix and socialise (see ▶ Chap. 10).

Marketers have discovered that personality is associated with self-image or self-concept. This concept is based on how consumers like to see themselves and the idea that our possessions reflect our identities (Grubb & Stern, 1971). ("We are what we have."). For instance, consumers who perceive themselves as shy and introverted are unlikely to pursue a trans-African overland trip or book a holiday with *Contiki Tours.* However, the relationship between personality types and holiday behaviour is debatable. It could also be argued that the very reason the introverted consumer might take a holiday of this nature is to meet more people and become more outgoing.

3.3.2 Psychological Factors

Psychological factors relate to four characteristics of the individual that influence his or her decisions to purchase tourism products: perceptions, learning, attitudes, and motivation.

3.3.2.1 Perceptions

Tourist buying behaviour is influenced by his or her perceptions (Pike, 2018: 40). **Perception** is a function of motivation, learning and attitudes, and is especially related to previous (travel) experience. It refers to the way in which consumers interpret messages via their senses – sight, hearing, taste, touch and smell – to make a decision when buying a tourism offering. As a result of the intangible nature of tourism products (they cannot be seen or tested beforehand), consumers have to make decisions based on how they perceive products.

> *Perception* (from the Latin *perceptio*) is the organisation, identification, and interpretation of sensory information in order to represent and understand the presented information or the environment (Schacter, Gilbert & Wegner, 2011).

❓ Think about the last holiday you purchased. Draw a simple model (a series of boxes) to illustrate the process that you went through to reach the decision and the factors that you took into account. Compare your model with the models of your classmates. Identify the similarities and differences.

Consumers are exposed to hundreds of marketing messages and stimuli every day. Digital marketing experts estimate that most Americans are exposed to around 4 000 to 10 000 advertisements each day (Simpson, 2017). They cannot pay attention to them all. They block out most of these messages through selective attention. Consequently, marketers must attempt to attract the attention of consumers. This is one reason why hotels and airlines change their décor, furnishing and layout (the physical evidence) regularly. Consumers tend to notice products and features that are unusual and stand out.

3.3.2.2 Learning

Learning refers to the process by which individuals acquire the purchase and consumption knowledge and experience that they apply to future related behaviour (Schiffman & Kanuk, 2018: 202). When people consume a tourism product offering, they learn about it. In addition, people gain experience through a variety of other sources, such as listening to others. The consumer builds up a mental inventory of products and good or bad experiences. For example, an individual may have experienced a very good package holiday in Mauritius through *TUI*. This information (type of holiday and destination) is stored and recalled, and then taken into account when the person selects a holiday in the future.

Cognitive learning acknowledges that consumers influence the outcome in an active way, so that the learning process is not always easy for a marketer to manage. There are five elements of cognitive learning (Dollard & Miller, 1950):

1. *Drive* (motivation) is the strong internal stimulus derived from a consumer's need or goal. The impulse to learn can be driven by the desire to maximise the benefits of the purchase (Sethna & Blythe: 2016: 282).
2. *Cue.* A cue is the internal motive which encourages learning, and is weaker than a drive. It is external and is specific.
3. Response. This is how consumers react to drive and cue. This may result in a purchase.
4. *Reinforcement.* The aim of this is to get consumers to associate the offering with certain benefits (for example, health benefits from taking a holiday).
5. *Retention.* This is the stability of the learned material over a period of time (i.e. how well it is remembered). For example, advertising jingles have extremely high retention.

Cognitive learning usually involves reasoning. People need to think about what they are seeing or hearing in order to remember the information. Due to the nature of tourism where consumers generally have high involvement with the offering (Cooper & Hall, 2019: 101) – the information is processed and absorbed much more effectively because they are thinking about the product much more (Krugman, 1965). Nevertheless, given the ubiquity of budget airlines and hotels it could also be argued that tourism has become more transactional, and therefore consumers are less involved in such offerings.

3.3.2.3 Attitudes

An attitude is an evaluation of the object, or level of liking (Pike, 2018: 41). People have feelings and thoughts about a range of subjects such as religion, politics, food, clothes, sport and so on. Attitudes put people into a frame of mind for liking or disliking something. Indeed, purchasing behaviour is strongly influenced by attitudes towards a given brand, product or service (Blackwell et al., 2006: 7). Attitudes extend to knowledge of products (travel destinations) as well as to people and events. Nowhere is this more evident than in the hospitality industry: if consumers have a negative experience at a resort, hotel, or restaurant, it is likely that they will develop a negative attitude that will deter them from returning. Similarly, consumers may reject going to a holiday destination that is overcrowded with polluted beaches, is unfriendly and inhospitable, is environmentally irresponsible, or is unethical. Tourists are increasingly concerned about ethical consumption (Cohen, Prayag & Moital, 2014).

The tricomponent attitude model consists of three parts: cognition, affect, and conation (Rosenberg & Hovland, 1960). The cognitive part captures a consumer's knowledge and perceptions that are acquired by a combination of direct experience with the attitude-object and related information (see ■ Fig. 3.2). Using an example such as Disneyland Paris, the cognitive component reflects the person's knowledge of various theme parks, hotels, prices, and activities, as well as his or her beliefs about *Disneyland*. A consumer's emotions or feelings about an offering constitute the affective component of an attitude. A person's positive feelings about Disneyland advertisements might lead him/her to conclude that visiting *Disneyland Paris* will be a positive and pleasant experience. Conation, the last part of the tricomponent attitude model, is concerned with the likelihood or tendency that an individual will

undertake a specific action or behave in a particular way with regard to the attitude-object. In the case of visiting *Disneyland Paris*, this component reflects a person's intention to visit the resort in the foreseeable future.

❓ Questions

In groups, apply the tricomponent attitude model to one of the following:
— Club Med holidays
— Responsible tourism
— Mass tourism and all-inclusive resort holidays
— The promotion of sex tourism
— Cruise-ship holidays
— Slum tours.

3.3.2.4 Motivation

Understanding why consumers choose particular products and destinations is complex. Motivation is a state of arousal of a drive or need that impels people to activity in pursuit of goals (Seaton & Bennett, 1996: 66). The term is an overused term in the tourism industry. The reason for travel should not be confused with the motivation for travel (Pike, 2018: 44). For instance, "to visit friends or family" does not represent motivation for travel. There is a wide range of factors that motivate consumers to buy tourism offerings. One of the reasons for a lack of understanding of tourism motivation is that it can be difficult for consumers to recall and articulate what motivated their recognition of the need for travel (Pike, 2018: 44). The theory behind this definition is that once a person's goals have been achieved, his or her needs subside

■ **Fig. 3.2** Attitudes model. (Source: Adapted from Rosenberg and Hovland (1960))

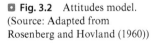

Attitudes:
Evaluative statements or judgements concerning products, people or events

Cognitive factor
The *opinion or belief* sector of an attitude

Affective factor
The *emotional or feeling* sector of an attitude

Behavioural factor
An intention to *act in* certain way towards someone or something.

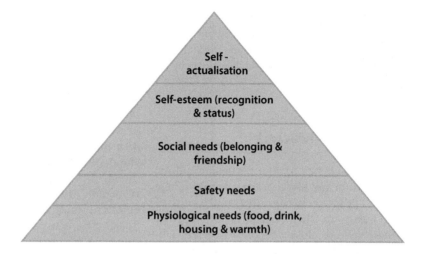

Fig. 3.3 Maslow's (1954) hierarchy model. (Source: Adapted from Maslow (1954))

and the individual returns to a state of normality before new needs arise. One of the most common theories of motivation used in marketing is that of Maslow (1954: 80–106), who proposed a hierarchy of individual needs expressed as a pyramid (see **Fig. 3.3**).

At the base of the pyramid are the basic physical needs – for food, water, rest, and shelter – that are necessary for survival. Maslow (1954) argued that these needs, along with the next layer of security and safety needs, must be satisfied on a reasonably regular basis before people will focus on social needs or the need for self-esteem and status. For example, if consumers perceive that a hotel chain provides a sufficient guarantee of food, shelter, and security, these physical and safety needs are no longer significant to them. The implication for the marketer in this case would be to appeal to consumers with higher-level needs, such as status. The most sophisticated level of needs is the need for self-development (self-actualisation in Maslow's terms). Self-development means an individual's striving for personal fulfilment of his or her potential. According to Middleton, Fyall, Morgan & Ranchhod (2009: 62), people who are likely to travel are most likely also in a position to focus on their own self-development, which many people associate with quality of life.

There have been several attempts at categorising tourism motivations. For instance, Horner and Swarbrooke (2016: 58) proposed six categories of travel motives (excluding business travel), given in **Table 3.2**.

Table 3.2 Typology model

Emotional	Personal
Nostalgia (e.g. visiting place of birth) Romance Escapism	Visiting friends and relatives Making new friends
Physical	**Cultural**
Relaxation Suntan Exercise and health Sex	Sightseeing Experiencing new cultures
Status	**Personal development**
Exclusivity Fashionability	Increased knowledge Learning a new skill

Source: Adapted from Horner and Swarbrooke (2016)

Pearce (1993) suggested that travel behaviour reflects a hierarchy of travel motives. He argued that individuals have a travel career ladder where they "… start at different levels [as with a career at work], they are likely to change levels during their life cycle and they can be prevented from moving by money, health and other people [in other words, family]. They may also retire from their travel career or not take holidays at all and therefore not be part of the system" (Pearce, 1993: 115). According to Pearce, individuals learn, progress, and change as tourists. They have different motivating patterns at different stages of their life cycles.

3

The Maslow Hotel in Johannesburg (see Image 3.1) is named after the psychologist who devised the model of the hierarchy of needs.

3.3.3 Cultural Factors

All consumers belong to a particular culture, ethnic group and social grade category. These cultural factors help consumers make sense of and relate to their environment. Specific behaviours are closely linked to certain cultures, but not to others.

3.3.3.1 Culture and Ethnic Groups

Culture is the sum total of learnt beliefs, values and customs that serve to direct the consumer behaviour of members of a particular society (Schiffman & Kanuk, 2018: 481). Culture is made up of what a group has in common and what distinguishes it from other groups. A group expresses its culture through language, food, clothing, art, religion, and architecture. Many of these components are passed on from generation to generation. Culture has an important role in the industry of tourism.

Culture determines how people communicate, how people express their feelings (for instance, the British are sometimes seen as being quite reserved when compared to their American counterparts) and how people socialise (for example, over a barbeque or taking part in or watching outdoor sporting events). Similarly, in certain cultures, but not in others, holidays are viewed as rights and necessities for relieving stress ("going on holiday, take a break from work").

An example of the importance of culture is how businesses are increasingly interested in marketing offerings to ethnic groups within a particular population. Many countries in Europe have large ethnic populations. Similarly, the United States has a significant Hispanic, Black American, and Latino population (Baines, Fill, Rosengren & Antonetti,

2019: 74). These groups when sizable and profitable enough represent marketing opportunities.

3.3.3.2 Social Grade

Consumers' buying behaviour is strongly influenced by the social grade to which they belong or aspire to belong (or not!) (Horner & Swarbrooke, 2016: 63). The social grade (or class) of consumers determines how much money they make and also how they spend it (Coleman, 1983). A typical class structure entails an upper, middle, and lower class. Social class is usually determined by occupation level, education, lifestyle and income.

❓ *Is taking a holiday a luxury only for those with the means to travel?*

3.3.4 Social Factors

Consumers and their decisions are strongly influenced by the people they interact with, either directly or through observation. The main social factors include reference groups and family.

3.3.4.1 Reference Groups

A reference group is a group of people who influence an individual's buying behaviour (Sethna & Blythe, 2016: 340). People make decisions (for example, where to go on holiday) based on their current reference groups (or groups they aspire to join or groups from which they wish to disassociate themselves) (Kotler & Keller, 2016: 223). Reference groups influence a large part of people's purchasing behaviour. These groups may include family and friends, music and television celebrities, a social club, the workplace, social networking sites (such as Instagram, TikTok, YouTube, Twitter, and Snapchat), a university or a church (see ▢ Fig. 3.4). They help consumers attach meaning to tourism products and services. Although the size of the reference group may vary, marketers need to understand which reference groups are influencing their consumers and how to capitalise on this influence.

◘ **Image 3.1** The Maslow Hotel in Johannesburg, South Africa. (Source: The Maslow Hotel)

3

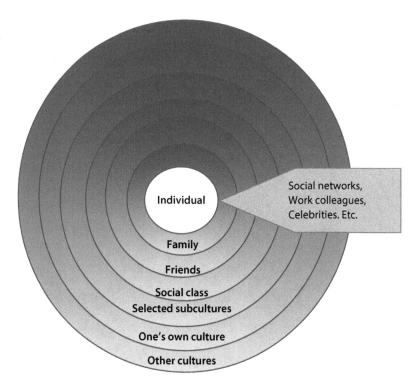

□ **Fig. 3.4** Reference groups. (Source: Author's creation)

In the tourism and hospitality industry, consumers are more strongly influenced by word-of-mouth (including on-line reviews and product ratings) input from members of reference groups than by advertising or other promotional activities (Jalilv & Samiei, 2012). This is especially true when the person making the recommendation has experienced the tourism offering. Consumers also tend to trust the opinions of family and colleagues (Baines et al., 2019: 71). For instance, a family member who recommends a holiday destination or a restaurant that he or she has recently visited has a strong influence on another family member's buying decision. In this case, the family acts as a purchasing unit (this is also known as "shared decision-making"). These family members are known as "shared motivators". Each family member fulfils a special role within the group. In essence, consumers balance others' needs and preferences against their own. Research shows that shared decision- making is most prevalent in emerging markets, where it is partly a function of

limited disposable income for families (Sudhir et al., 2015).

Over the last decade, the social network sites such as Instagram, Facebook, Snapchat, and Twitter have enabled like-minded consumers to share information about their travel and hospitality experiences. The credibility and mass of this information source has overtaken that of traditional marketing communications in the tourism industry (Pike, 2018: 39). Facebook's "Like" button and Instagram posts and 'Instagram Stories' act out as a form of peer pressure advertising, encouraging friends to try to buy various products. Social media influencers (defined as a user on social media who has established credibility in a specific industry) have had a significant impact on travel buying as they have access to a large audience ('followers') and can persuade others by virtue of their authenticity and reach (see □ Image 3.2). Tourism and hospitality businesses and brands are increasingly utilising travel influencers to help promote their brands.

3

Social media has helped develop the trend of "smoasting", which means using social media to boast of holiday fun. Tourism – people travelling to sell or donate their organs to patients in need – is on the rise around the world.

3.3.4.2 Family

One of the most influential reference groups is the family, as consumers generally interact closely with their families. Research has shown that children strongly influence the purchase of tourism products. For instance, children may see a television commercial for *Disneyland Paris* and insist that their parents take them there for a holiday or a day trip. Multi-generational travel – parents, children and grandparents involved in holiday decision-making – has become one of the fastest-growing segments of the tourism industry. Travelling with kids, parents and grandparents has been a trend for the last few years. For example, when planning a traditional family holiday, the decision-maker or requester may be the child and the grand-

parents may pay for the holiday. In the last few years, there has been a growing trend for parents to holiday with older age children. So-called "genervacations" are particularly popular with children at university and those in their late-20s and early-30s. With many multi-generational travel blogs and influential families active across social media platforms such as Instagram and YouTube, there will continue to be resorts and travel brands catering to an all-ages family travel experience — from the services they offer to the campaigns they push in the digital marketing space. Tourism companies have to find ways of attracting all of these consumers as well as families in general (▶ Industry Insight 3.1).

There are many individual factors influencing consumer behaviour. Consumer choice is the result of a complex interplay between the personal, psychological, cultural, and social factors discussed above. While the tourism and hospitality marketer cannot control these factors directly, they can help the marketer to understand consumer reactions and behaviour better. Marketing research (see ▶ Chap. 4) reveals how consumers think and why they behave as they do.

Industry Insight 3.1

TUI Introduces Its Family Life Holidays

TUI Family Life, a subsidiary of TUI, offers a range of family holiday packages and target families through their kids' clubs and entertainment programmes. They can arrange holidays for every family member. All of the 'Family Life' resorts offer teenagers their own zone – 'the Hangout' – where they can connect

to Wi-Fi and make new friends, while adults can relax by the pool or the spa, or grab some quiet time in a café. There are Baby Clubs that host children from new-born up to 3 years old and family-friendly food and a kids' buffet on offer.

Source: ▶ http://www.tui.co.uk/holidays/family-life

TUI BLUE | FOR FAMILIES

◻ **Image 3.3** 'TUI Blue for Families' logo. (Source: TUI Travel Group)

3.4 The Consumer Journey Cycle

> » "He [Flaubert] didn't really like travel, of course. He liked the idea of travel, and the memory of travel, but not travel itself". Julian Barnes (2009).

In the last section, we discussed the reasons why consumers choose to purchase tourism products. It is also necessary to consider how these choices are made. This is achieved by examining the stages that the consumer goes through before and after making a purchase. This process is similar to the process of purchasing manufactured products in that a consumer moves through a number of stages leading up to the purchase. However, as a result of the diversity and interdependent characteristics of tourism (as described in ► Chap. 2), the process of buying holidays is more complex; differing widely by individual, by trip and by time of year. Travel decision-making involves multiple decisions about the various elements of the holiday itinerary, some of which are made prior to the arrival, while others are made while at the destination (Choi, Lehto, Morrison & Jang, 2012). In the age of information overload, consumers are spoilt for choice; making a purchase decision is becoming a much more complex process; consumers do not always follow rationale decision-making. In addition, travellers do not always make planned decisions, especially repeat visitors and frequent travellers (Pike, 2020, 46).

A consumer persona is a fictive person that represents the main characteristics of a market segment. In marketing, consumer personas aim to provide a factual profile of a specific customer who is representative of a broader segment.

❓ Questions

Consumer persona. Think about Jack Walsh for a moment. Jack, aged 25, is a junior accountant who rents an upmarket apartment in the trendy suburb of Shoreditch in east London, UK. Jack earns in the region of £2000 (€2300) per month and is entitled to 5 weeks paid annual holiday. What type of holiday could he go on? Should he visit an overseas, regional, or local destination? Should he travel independently, go on a Contiki Tours Holiday or on a Club Med holiday? Should he go on a cultural holiday in Belize, Central America or an adventure holiday in Canada? How about a beach holiday in Mozambique or a sun, sea, and sand holiday closer to home? For that matter, why should he go on holiday at all when he can spend the money on a new Smart LED television?

No marketing manager has the answers to all of these questions. However, the more marketers find out about what sort of consumers choose particular products and what needs they look to fulfil from going on holiday, the better they will know how to communicate with consumers, who to target and how to persuade them to stay at their hotel, go on a tour, use an airline, or visit an attraction or destination.

3.4.1 The Stages in the Consumer Journey Cycle

The consumer journey cycle (or decision-making process) is based on the assumption that consumers move through a series of push and pull factors or a process of stages before and after purchasing an offering (see ◘ Fig. 3.5). As you can see, the six-stage journey is influenced by social and personal factors, as explained in the preceding section.

The six stages of the consumer journey cycle are discussed below.

3.4.1.1 Stage 1: Awareness (Needs and Wants Recognition)

The consumer journey cycle begins the first moment the consumer recognises a desire for a holiday. For instance, a person might claim, "I need a break, I need a holiday."

3

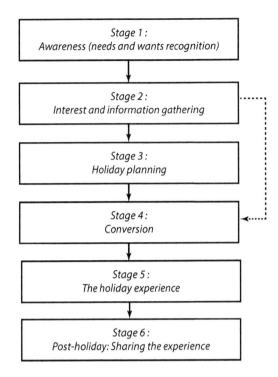

Stage 1:
Awareness (needs and wants recognition)

Stage 2:
Interest and information gathering

Stage 3:
Holiday planning

Stage 4:
Conversion

Stage 5:
The holiday experience

Stage 6:
Post-holiday: Sharing the experience

◻ **Fig. 3.5**   The consumer journey cycle. (Source: Author's creation)

Reasons for and against that desire are weighed against time and money available ("What can I afford?"). Consumers are not always aware of their needs. When they are aware of their needs, the tourism marketer has to convince them to buy the product offering. Otherwise, the marketer has to help them recognise the need for a holiday or tourism product. For example, a marketer can use promotions to make prospective consumers desire a holiday. A "winter in the sun" travel brochure portraying the contrast between a sandy beach fringed by a turquoise sea and a frantic office, for example, might influence consumers to yearn to get away. Consumers Visitors in this phase consume inspirational content with no conversion goal, like hero videos, travel vlogs on YouTube, Instagram Stories, documentaries on TV. Awareness might also be initi-

ated by word-of-mouth recommendations, through information searches such as browsing travel review sites or travel blogs on the internet, consumer-generated content (such as Instagram, Facebook, and Pinterest), or through works of art (paintings of Provence in France by Vincent van Gogh, for example), literature (romantic poems about the Lake District in England by William Wordsworth (see ▶ Industry Insight 3.2) or a book, such as *The Girl with the Dragon Tattoo*, set in Stockholm, Sweden, for example, a television series, such as Chernobyl (set in Ukraine), or movies, for example, the *Lord of the Rings* trilogy (set in New Zealand).

Industry Insight 3.2

Paris' Literary Holiday Breaks

France's capital city is booming with literary history. Literary tourists can follow in the footsteps of legendary authors, from Ernest Hemingway and James Joyce to F. Scott Fitzgerald and Gertrude Stein. A typical literary tour will pass by iconic Parisian addresses such as the Café de Flore, Brasserie Lipp and Les Deux Magots.

Components of literary tourism holidays in Paris include:

- Literary-inspired weekend
- Explore Paris's literary hotspots
- Walk in the footsteps of literary greats
- Literary-inspired places to stay

3.4.1.2 Stage 2: Interest and Information Gathering

When consumers are motivated to act, they become decision makers (Pike, 2018: 46). Decisions need to be made about where to go, when to go, how to get to the destination, where to stay, and what to do at the destination. These decisions take place in the mind, in what Pike called the consumer's "black box" (Pike, 2018: 46).

Consumers are already aware of the destination and start thinking about it in a more active way, looking for specific information on what you can see and do at the destination. In this stage travel brands should try to reach consumers through social media like Facebook, Pinterest (image, hacks, hints, check lists…), Instagram (stories and TV). In this stage promotional efforts should play a role in search engine optimisation (SEO), PR and traditional media, and blog content.

The search for information used to plan holiday travel is likely to take longer and to involve the use of more information sources than the search for information about most other consumer products (Fodness & Murray, 1998: 108). Potential consumers surf the internet for low-cost flights. Research shows that some travellers begin their planning process based on the availability of air tickets on sale rather than the destination features (Keshavarzian & Wu, 2017). They consult travel agents for information, study brochures and advertisements, watch television travel programmes and channels such as the *National Geographic* Channel or the *Discovery Channel,* refer to the opinions of fellow travellers on social media sites (such as Snapchat), and surf travel sites (for example, travel review sites and blogs such as ► Couchsurfing.com, ► travelblog. org, Wikitravel, and ► TripAdvisor.com) (see ► Industry Insight 3.3) on the internet.

Industry Insight 3.3

TripAdvisor

TripAdvisor, Inc. is an American travel website company providing reviews of travel-related content. It also includes interactive travel forums. TripAdvisor was an early adopter of user-generated content. The website services are free to users, who provide most of the content, and the website is supported by an advertising business model. Founded in 2000, the travel reviews website sends out 80 million e-mails weekly, and 453 million reviews are posted on the site. TripAdvisor is the largest social travel website in the world with over 320 million reviewers and approximately 500 million reviews of accommodation outlets, visitor attractions, restaurants, and other tourism-related businesses. destinations. In addition, TripAdvisor has a function on its website (mobile and desktop versions) and a mobile app that allows users to order food from more than 20,000 restaurant partners of Deliveroo.

Source: Smith, C. (2019). DMR. 35 amazing TripAdvisor statistics and facts (March 2019). Retrieved from ► https://expandedramblings. com/index.php/tripadvisor-statistics/ [21 April 2019].

TripAdvisor, which was founded in 2000, receives more than 40 million visitors every month. The average number of user contributions to the website per minute is 270 (Smith, 2018).

Most travellers look for reviews in the beginning of the holiday planning process as a means to help them narrow down choices. Positive reviews increase confidence and help reduce risk.

Consumers are increasingly making use of mobile travel apps on their mobile phones to search for good deals on flights as well as holiday destinations by price, length of flight, season, and place. Travellers access the internet and apps via their smartphones, laptops, tablets, iPods, and at cafés. They also study maps, buy and refer to travel guidebooks such as the Lonely Planet series, and talk to friends, relatives, and other members of their reference groups.

Travel agents in the tourist-generating region are considered a credible and reliable information source. Research has shown that tourists show a preference for booking holidays through travel agents because of the element of human interaction. In addition, travel agents are able to give expert advice and can offer considerable value to the consumer (Seabra, Abrates & Lages, 2007: 16). Likewise, destination marketing organisations (DMOs) in the destination region play an important role in disseminating information (for example, via a website or via social media) to prospective visitors. The consumer assesses the benefits of the product offering as presented by the marketing messages, but may well gather more information before making an actual buying decision. For instance, an individual may read about a destination in promotional literature, but will consult a travel agent for more information.

3.4.1.3 Stage 3: Holiday Planning

The third stage of the cycle is the planning, the phase in which consumers have already chosen the destination of their travel and start to plan their trip by consulting prices and options. The channels used in this phase are a DMO's official website (App if available), OTAs, and social media platforms. It is important for the DMO to curate content on the official tourism website, integrating it with trip planner options in order to provide any possible information to the visitor and help them plan their trip.

This is often a very exciting part of the decision-making process for consumers. It is at this stage that potential holidaymakers anticipate the holiday. It is the dream phase of the decision-making process. According to

Kelly (1955), experience shapes anticipation and expectations. Kelly proposed that travel experience is derived from the act of construing (interpreting) a series of events, and not by merely being a participant in those events or being exposed to them (1955: 124). Experience consists of five phases: anticipation, investment, encounter, confirmation or disconfirmation, and revision.

A consumer decision is the result of a mental process in which one alternative is specifically selected from a set of available options (Moutinho, 1987). The consumer determines a set of choice criteria based on price (customers often use price as an indication of quality; price is the main consumer influence), convenience, travel distance, location, amenities including accommodation, activities specific to their interests, attractions (for example, wildlife, heritage, beach, and so on), the weather and the season, past experience of the destination, health and safety issues, visitor taxes and levies (for example, visa costs, and hotel and airport taxes), recommendations, returns on foreign exchange, and so on. The consumer ranks the alternatives in order of preference, taking into account the information available when making these decisions.

❓ Countries such as Bhutan in Southeast Asia have extremely high tourist taxes (US$250). Do you think high visitor taxes and levies deter people from visiting a tourist destination? Do you think Bhutan only wants to attract up-market international tourists?

3.4.1.4 Stage 4: Conversion

The fourth stage is conversion. This is the most crucial moment for any travel brand, it is the turning point from inspiration to purchase. In this phase consumers are ready to pay for transport, accommodation, experiences, attraction tickets, etc. and they are committing to their plan. The channels used at this point are OTAs, booking tools – including the ones in the DMO's website – TripAdvisor, ▶ Booking.com, Airbnb and any other website with integrated booking tools.

Bookings are then made and confirmed. Most consumers book holidays in advance (sometimes weeks or months beforehand), while some book at the last minute, usually on the internet. From a marketing management perspective, it is important that the booking process be made as easy as possible (taking a "booking fast and holiday slow" strategy). Consumer preferences (such as allocation of rooms and dietary needs) can be found out after payment. Following up the booking is also paramount. Overseas clients can be sent weather reports, photos of new developments (for example, snaps of a new-born leopard at a game reserve), and information about issues such as malaria prophylaxis in malaria-affected areas to keep them interested and informed. It is important to keep time differences in mind when dealing with overseas markets such as the United States. Round-the-clock telephone contact may be required during the booking period.

Increasingly, consumers are using the internet when making purchasing decisions, whether they are shopping for a specific brand of backpack or a holiday. Microsoft's Bing is a type of search platform, for instance, that helps consumers to make decisions on what to buy and where to travel. Bing provides online shoppers with a list of prices, locations where products can be purchased, and product ratings.

3.4.1.5 Stage 5: The Holiday Experience

The consumer actually experiences the holiday by visiting the destination. At this stage, the decision-making process is usually repeated a number of times (with a spiralling effect within the tourism industry as tourists make additional purchases [such as visiting attractions, eating at restaurants, and participating in tourist activities]). For example, a tourist on holiday may make decisions to purchase hotel accommodation, tours, special activities, meals, or car rental: in other words, anything that was not arranged in advance. Consumers usually take various factors that were used in the pre-purchase evaluation, such as price, previous experience, convenience, travel distance, and rec-

ommendations, into account when making purchasing decisions.

The experience provided in the destination has a direct impact on WoM and what is happening online – what people are saying about their destination experience. DMOs need to tap into those conversations. At a product-offering level, this is in the form of hotel and restaurant online reviews – these have a critical and direct impact on whether someone makes a decision to book or not or purchase or not. It does not matter how good the marketing is, if the experience does not match the marketing promises made people will not book or purchase. WoM ambassadors and influencers are critical and key for telling new consumers about the holiday experience.

3.4.1.6 Stage 6: Post-Holiday: Sharing the Experience

The last stage of the cycle is sharing the holiday experience. Travellers have completed their holiday and have returned home. In this stage they share their experience with family, friends, peers, and online readers. They post photographs and videos and write reviews and posts about their trip. They possibly are already thinking about going back to the destination in the future. The channels used in this phase are social media, travel blogs and review platforms. Often, the importance of this stage of the decision-making process is underestimated.

Research suggests that there is a strong association between consumers' perceptions of service quality and the likelihood that they will return to a destination or recommend a holiday destination (Baker & Crompton, 2000; Petrick, 2004). Tourism and hospitality businesses at the destination play an important role in service delivery. The 2018 FIFA World Cup™ tournament hosted in Brazil is a good example of an event that provided visitors with an experience that exceeded their expectations. As a result, it is likely that many soccer tourists will return to Brazil as holidaymakers, and will recommend the country as a holiday destination to their friends and colleagues (Swart & George, 2018).

The first-time consumer consumes on a trial basis. If the destination or hotel satisfies the consumer, he or she will come back. In the 1970s, psychologists from Israel Danny Kahneman and Amos Tversky devised the "peak end rule" theory to economics. Their research found that our minds trick us in into believing things that simply are not true. For example, if we enjoy the last day of a holiday, then we tend to significantly over-rate how the entire experience was (Kahnerman & Tversky, 1999).

Although the consumer journey cycle is a useful model for examining buying decisions, the process is not always as straightforward as it appears. Firstly, the prospective buyer can withdraw at any stage prior to the actual purchase. For example, if the need for a holiday diminishes, the process will suddenly come to an end. Secondly, it is not uncommon for some stages in the process to be skipped. For instance, a satisfied regular visitor to a destination is likely to skip the third stage, holiday planning. And thirdly, information touch points change at each stage of the consumer journey cycle (for example, in the initial stages, consumers consult with travel agents and surf the internet, whereas during consumption (the holiday experience), tourists consult with concierges, and make use of travel apps and social media platforms to log and share their experience.

? With the aid of a diagram, describe the process that a 25-year-old single professional man living in New York might go through in deciding whether or not to go on holiday to the Cayman Island, Mexico. Use the information from this chapter to assist you.

In the first two sections of this chapter, we examined the factors that influence why consumers behave the way they do when buying tourism products and how they make buying decisions. In the next two sections, we will discuss who the actual consumers making these final purchase decisions are. This involves looking at two areas: the diverse consumer markets that make up the international tourism industry and the various typologies of tourism consumers. Having information about these two areas can help the marketer in a number of ways.

3.5 Consumer Markets in Tourism

The tourism market is extremely diverse and can be divided into many segments, all of which share similar consumer behaviour patterns. Several of these market segments are sometimes also referred to as "niches". A niche is a market segment, usually with a well-defined product that can be tailored to meet the interests of the consumer. It is a group of consumers within a larger target market who have similar lifestyle characteristics and identifiable tastes. Numerous forms of niche tourism (also known as "adjectival tourism" or "speciality travel") have emerged over the last decade, each with its own adjective. Many of these terms have come into common use by the tourism industry as well as by academics. Other terms used for forms of niche tourism are relatively obscure or new concepts that may or may not become popular and more mainstream. Niche tourism opposes the homogenous and undifferentiated mass tourism product. From its impact in the world – ranging from space tourism to gastronomic tourism – it could be said that "even the most extreme corners of the human imagination can be catered for in a packaged way" (Stone, 2005: 19).

? How many different types of tourism can you think of? Make a list and then cross-check them with the list in the text below.

The following list gives an A–Z of some tourism niche markets:
- Aboriginal, accessible, accidental, active, activist, activity, adoption, adventure, affinity, agri-, alternative, ancestry/ancestral, archaeological, architectural, Arctic and Antarctic, armchair, art, astro, atomic, avitourism
- Backpacking, battlefields, beach, beer, benefit, bicycle, birding, birth, black, bookstore, Brexit, bucket list, Buddhist, budget, building tourism

■ **Table 3.3** Various niche tourism markets

Dark tourism	Dark tourism (the name was coined in the 1990s by Lennon & Foley [2000]) involves travel to macabre sites of suffering, death, and disaster. Examples of dark tourism include Robben Island and District Six in Cape Town, the London Dungeon, Ground Zero in New York, Auschwitz-Birkenau in Poland, the Killing Fields of Cambodia, and the Fukushima nuclear power plant in Japan. Dark tourism (also known as "thanatourism" or "grief tourism") is growing in popularity (Stone, 2018: 22). In 2012, Dr Philip Stone of the Institute for Dark Tourism Research (IDTR) opened the world's first academic centre into the subject, saying that such places make people face their own mortality and can often help us to understand how a particular society felt about death. IDTR researchers say they want to examine why people feel compelled to visit sites like Auschwitz or Ground Zero. Source: Current issues in dark tourism research. (2018). *Institute for Dark Tourism Research.* Retrieved from dark-tourism.org.uk/ [21 August 2018].
Dooms-day tourism	Doomsday tourism, which is also known as "tourism of doom" or "last chance tourism", is believed to be on the increase. With global warming and climate change beginning to take effect, the tune has changed to "top ten sites to see before they die". This has led to the concept of doomsday tourism, which is the rush to see some of the world's most endangered tourist attractions before they are lost forever. Kilimanjaro is one such example, as its glacial ice is predicted to disappear by 2030. Other examples include the melting glaciers of Patagonia and the coral of the Great Barrier Reef. The danger is that in their rush to see these sites, tourists may unwittingly be contributing to their demise by encouraging irresponsible tourism practices. Source: Oskin, B. (2013). Kilimanjaro's shrinking glaciers could vanish by 2030. Retrieved from ► https://www.livescience.com/41930-kilimanjaro-glaciers-shrinking.html [14 September 2018].
Edutour-ism	Edutourism is defined as "purposeful learning and travel" (Ritchie, 2003).Edutourism is an important sector in the global tourism industry. Many English Foreign Language (EFL) centres can be regarded as part of the tourism industry since they act as inbound tour operators, sourcing clients through agents and various promotional activities, and arranging their flights. Most EFL centres offer English and tourism packages, consisting of English language courses, accommodation, and sightseeing tours. Source: Wells, J. (2016). The role of edu-tourism in bridging racial divides in South Africa. In M. Kozak & N. Kozak (Eds).*Tourism and Hospitality Management*. Bingley, U.K.: Emerald Group Publishing, pp. 251–263.
Slum tourism	Slum tourism is a type of tourism that involves visiting impoverished areas. The concept was coined back in the Victorian era (the 1880s), when wealthy citizens visited poor areas in London's East End to observe the conditions in which poor people lived. Slum tourism emerged in developing countries in the 1990s in the inner-city slums of India, the crowded favelas of Brazil, and the bustling townships of South Africa. These tours combine history with social issues and are usually frequented by western tourists. The tourism industry is embracing the concept; other countries where slum tourism is on the rise are Kenya, Egypt, Mexico, and Indonesia. Source: George, R. & Booyens, I. (2014). Township Tourism Demand: Tourists' Perceptions of Safety and Security. *Urban Forum*, 2(3), 49.

Source: Author's creation

- Camper, camping, cannabis, carnival, casino, cemetery, charity, cheese, Christian, city, clubbing, coastal, coffee, conflict, congress, cosmetic, creative, cruise, culinary, cultural, cycling tourism
- Dark (see ■ Table 3.3), dark sky, debaucherism, deep ocean, dental, desert, diaspora, disabled, disaster, divorce, doom or doomsday (see ■ Table 3.3), Dracula, drought, drive-through, drug tourism
- Eco-, education, elephant back, elephant, elite,energy, epicurean, ethical, ethnic, ethno, euthanasia, extreme sports tourism
- Faith, family, farm, fashion, Favela, fertility, film (or film-induced), fishing, food, football, fright, tourism

3

- Gambling, gaming, garden, gastronomy, gay, genealogy, genocide, geo-, ghetto, golf, green, grey, grief, guerrilla tourism
- Hair transplant, Halal (see ◘ Table 3.3), health, hedonistic, heritage, hobby, holistic, Holy Grail, homestay, hooligan, hunting tourism
- Inclusive, indigenous, industrial, Islamic, island, intelligent tourism
- Jazz, jungle tourism
- Knitting tourism
- Lake, LGBT (lesbian, gay, bisexual and transgender), language, life-seeing, lighthouse, literary, lunar, luxury tourism
- Marine, marijuana, medical, memory, military, moon, moral, motor car, mountain, music, mystical tourism
- Nature-based (see ◘ Image 3.4), naturist, nautical, Ninja, nostalgia, nudist tourism
- Off-beat, over tourism
- Package, paleo, para-normal, park, party, peace, perpetual, photographic, pilgrim, pink, polar, pop culture, post-disaster, pot, poverty, property tourism
- Railway, recession, rehab, religious (see ◘ Image 3.5), research, residential, resort, river, road, romance, roots, rural tourism
- Sacred, scenic, scuba-diving,, self-guided, senior, sex, sharia, shark, shock, shopping, silver, slum (see ◘ Table 3.3), smart, smoking, social, spa, space, spiritual, sport, sport-fishing, stem cell, stopover, struggle, suicide, surfing, sustainable tourism
- Tea, TEFL, thanatourism, thermal, tiger, toddler, tombstone, torture, township, tragedy, trail, train, transplant, transport, tribal tourism
- Under-, underwater, urban tourism
- Veteran, visiting-friends-and-family, village, volcano, volunteer (see ◘ Image 3.6), virtual tourism
- War, water, wedding, wellness, whiskey, wilderness, wildlife, wine, writer tourism
- Yachting, yoga, yourism, youth tourism
- Zombie, zoo tourism

■ **Image 3.5** Religious tourism. (Source: Unsplash)

■ **Image 3.6** Voluntourism. (Source: Unsplash)

The niche tourism market of transplant tourism – people travelling to sell or donate their organs to patients in need – is on the rise around the world.

Niche markets are important to a nation's tourism and hospitality industry as they contribute to the government's objectives of increasing tourists' length of stay and spend, widening geographical distribution, increasing volumes, and reducing seasonality in the sector. Niche markets offer huge potential and opportunity. They are more sustainable, less damaging, and more capable of delivering to high-spending tourists than mass tourist markets (Robinson & Novelli, 2005).

There is a dearth of research on the various niche markets (Robinson & Novelli, 2005). More research is required into the various tourism markets to gather marketing intelligence (in other words, to estimate the size of the various niches from a demand or supply perspective as well as to gain a greater understanding of their characteristics and motivations).

Some of the consumer market segments that make up the international tourism industry are discussed in the ◘ Table 3.4.

◘ **Table 3.4**   Various tourism consumer markets

Consumer market	Definition
Adventure tourism	A heavy emphasis on outdoor pursuits, usually encompassing high levels of risk, adrenaline rushes, excitement, and personal challenge (Page, 2019: 144). (See ► Industry Insight 3.4).
Backpacking tourism	Also called the "youth travel" market. Backpackers tend to be young travellers who take extended holidays or working holidays. They seek destinations that are off the beaten track, mixing with local communities, and taking part in safaris and adventure tourist activities.
Business tourism	The provision of facilities and services to the millions of delegates who attend meetings, congresses, exhibitions, business events, incentive travel, and corporate hospitality (ICCA, 2017).
Cultural tourism	The "movements of persons essentially for cultural motivations such as study tours, performing arts and cultural tours, travel to festivals and other events, visits to sites and monuments, travel to study nature, folklore or art, and pilgrimages" (UNWTO, 2021).
Family tourism	A form of travel involving any combination of family members travelling together, regardless of age or type of travel (Amster, 2013)
Gay tourism	Gay tourism (also known as the "lesbian, gay, bisexual and transgender" or "LGBT" market) is a form of niche tourism marketed to gay people who are open about their sexual orientation and who wish to travel to gay tourism destinations in order to participate to some extent in the gay life of that area (Pritchard et al., 2000).
Health tourism	The activities of tourists who actively seek to improve their health and/or their well-being as part of their visit (Voigt et al., 2010: 4).
Hedonistic tourism	(or debaucherism tourism or pleasure-seeking tourism) involves people going on holiday to seek pleasurable activities such as partying.
Medical tourism	Involves people who travel to another country specifically to consult medical specialists or undergo elective procedures, including cosmetic, cardiac and dental surgery, organ transplants and joint replacements.
Religious tourism	Also called "faith tourism "or "spiritual tourism", refers to travel that is undertaken solely or predominantly for pilgrimage, missionary or leisure (fellowship) purposes (Stausberg, 2011).

◻ Table 3.4 (continued)

Consumer market	Definition
Shopping tourism	Involves travel to a destination with the explicit aim of buying goods that are not available, difficult to find or extremely expensive in the tourist's own country (Wessely, 2002: 4)
Special interest tourism	Special interest tourists are motivated by the desire to go on holiday and take part in a current interest or develop a new interest in a new or familiar location (Horner & Swarbrooke, 2016: 43). ▶ Industry Insight 3.5 discusses wildlife tourism.
Sport tourism	Travel to participate in or attendance at a pre-determined sports activity (Turco et al., 2011: 4).
Volunteer tourism	The engagement in volunteer work as a tourist (Alexander, 2012: 119).

Source: Author's creation

Industry Insight 3.4

New Zealand – A Mecca for Adventure Tourism

New Zealand is one of the most popular adventure tourism destinations worldwide. The country's 8700 (14,000 km miles) of coastline and numerous mountain ranges make it ideal for adventure tourism. Certain areas of New Zealand are promoted as being particularly suitable for adventure tourism.

Milford Track in the Fiordland National Park on the South Island, for example, has gained a reputation amongst adrenaline junkies. The country is very popular for adventure tourism activities including skydiving, bungee jumping, hiking ('tramping'), jet boating, rafting, caving, canyoning, zip lining, and off-road driving.

▶ www.activeadventures.com/new-zealand

Industry Insight 3.5

Wildlife Tourism

Wildlife tourism comes in many forms, including going on safari, viewing marine wildlife, and photographing wildlife such as birds. Wildlife tourism is an important part of the tourism industries in many countries including many African and South American countries, Australia, India, Canada, Indonesia, Bangladesh, Malaysia, Sri Lanka, and the Maldives. For these countries, wildlife is the major product that is promoted to international tourists.

Wildlife holidays range from luxury, coach and lodge-based trips to overland tours on trucks and accommodation in tents. Trips can vary from a two- to three-day extension of a general holiday to a two-week specialist safari. Examples of popular international wildlife destinations include India (tigers, wild elephants, bison, boar and deer), Borneo (orangutans and gibbons), Australia (dolphins and sharks), US (bears, moose and wolves), Uganda (lions, elephants and hippos), Oman (mountain goats and gazelles), and New Zealand (whales, dolphins).

Source: ▶ https://www.worldbank.org/en/news/feature/2018/03/01/growing-wildlife-based-tourism-sustainably-a-new-report-and-qa *[23 August 2018]*.

3

3.6 Consumer Typologies in Tourism

Tourism marketers can group tourists together on the basis of shared characteristics so that consumer behaviour can be both understood and predicted. This has resulted in a number of typologies of tourists and their behaviour. A **typology** is a classification that subdivides a group into subgroups that share similar characteristics, needs and wants (Horner & Swarbrooke, 2016: 49). Several tourist typologies, which were originally developed by researchers, have been adopted by practitioners and marketers. They are important to the tourism marketer for the following reasons:

- They assist marketers to make decisions on the marketing mix.
- They increase the marketer's knowledge of consumer behaviour in tourism.
- They help the marketer predict future trends in tourism.
- They contribute to the basis of market segmentation techniques (discussed in ► Chap. 7).

> A *typology* is a classification that subdivides a group into subgroups that share similar characteristics (Horner & Swarbrooke, 2016: 61).

3.6.1 Tourist or Traveller?

» *The traveller sees what he sees, the tourist sees what he has come to see. G.K. Chesterton (2003)*

Before discussing various typologies, it is important first to attempt to distinguish between travellers and tourists. Over the decades of research in tourism marketing, there has been much debate over whether consumers are tourists or travellers. Generally, a tourist is someone who buys an organised holiday from a tour operator, while a traveller is a person who makes his or her own travel-ling arrangements. As Sharpley notes, "Travellers make their own choices; tourists have their decisions made for them" (2008: 100). However, tourists often want to make their own decisions about how and where to travel.

Thus, the term "traveller" is applied to a person who is travelling for an extended period of time (for example, a backpacker) and the term "tourist" is used to describe a person who purchases a mass tourism product involving a means of transport and use of accommodation, and who purchases souvenirs, visits attractions and/or hires the services of tourist guides.

In this section, we will look at some of the typologies that various researchers have formulated to group tourists together so that marketers can understand and predict their behaviour.

3.6.2 Cohen (1972)

One of the earliest efforts to distinguish between different types of tourist was made by Cohen (1972). He classified tourists into four types (organised mass tourists, individual mass tourists, explorers and drifters) based on their motivation and the type of experience they seek. These four classifications are discussed below.

3.6.2.1 Organised Mass Tourists (OMTs)

Organised mass tourists buy a package tour to a popular holiday destination and travel in what is referred to as an environmental bubble. They stay in hotels, ride in air-conditioned buses and adhere to a fixed tour itinerary. Once at the destination, these tourists duplicate the main elements of their home environment and spend most of their time at their hotel (see ► Industry Insight 3.6). They are not particularly interested in local architecture, landscapes or culture, and go to a destination because they are certain that they will meet some of their compatriots there.

□ **Image 3.7** Mass tourism. (Source: Unsplash)

Industry Insight 3.6

The English Abroad

Here's an account of English holidaymakers abroad extracted from Michel Houllebecq's Lanzarote: "They [the English] gather in small groups and head for unlikely islands absent from Continental holiday brochures – Malta, Madeira or, indeed, Lanzarote. Once there, they duplicate the principal elements of their home environment right there. When asked to explain their choice of destination, they give answers that are evasive and tautological: 'I came because I came here last year.' It is appar-ent that the Englishman is not motivated by a keen appetite for discovery. In the early eve-ning, after a short trip to the beach, he is to be found drinking cocktails. The presence of the English at a resort, therefore, is no guide to the intrinsic interest of the destination, its splen-dour or its possible tourist potential. The Englishman goes to a particular destination purely because he is certain that he will meet other Englishmen there."

Source: Houellebecq, M. (2004). Lanzarote. London: Vintage Random House, p.13.

3.6.2.2 Individual Mass Tourists (IMTs)

Individual mass tourists are similar to organ-ised mass tourists, although they have a little more flexibility and freedom. Their holidays are not entirely pre-planned. They occasion-ally step outside the environmental bubble to experience some novelty. For example, indi-vidual mass tourists may take a fly-drive holi-day or a fly-cruise holiday and stay on the beaten track, yet they are able to drive to and visit local tourist attractions. They are more spontaneous in their decision-making than organised mass tourists.

3.6.2.3 Explorers

Explorers arrange their own holidays, consciously making an effort to avoid other tourists by getting off the beaten track. They attempt to meet local people, eat in local restaurants, and even try to speak the local language. They are less dependent on the tourism industry than organised mass tourists and individual mass tourists. However, explorers still require some security and comfort, and usually stay in accommodation used by other travellers.

3.6.2.4 Drifters

Drifters immerse themselves in the local community. They are at the opposite extreme from organised mass tourists since they have no planned travel itinerary and avoid contact with the tourism industry. Drifters, for the most part, have escaped from the environmental bubble. They seek novelty at all costs, even at the cost of danger and discomfort.

Cohen further subdivided these types of tourists into two groups. He categorised organised mass tourists and individual mass tourists as institutionalised tourists. These tourists are controlled by and catered to by the mass tourism industry. Explorers and drifters are non-institutionalised tourists who have little or no contact with the tourism industry. According to Cohen (1972: 178), non-institutionalised tourists are the pioneers of the tourism industry. They explore new destinations and pave the way for mass tourists.

However, it could be argued that institutionalised and non-institutionalised tourists are not entirely distinct from each other nowadays. For example, explorers may make use of travel review websites such as Wikitravel, blogs or specialist travel guidebooks (for example, books from the *Lonely Planet* or *Rough Guides* series) that are also used by mass tourists in order to make decisions regarding mode of transport and accommodation venues. Some criticisms of Cohen's classification are that it does not take into account the increasing diversity of holidays undertaken (for example, eco-tourism, business tourism and so on) and the different destinations chosen by tourists. It can also be

debated that Cohen's drifter is not a feasible categorisation. As the world is getting smaller and more homogenous, and as information and communication technology (ICT) continues to advance, it becomes less likely that any individual can fully escape his or her home environment.

> ❓ Read the account in ► Industry Insight 3.6. Where would you place this type of tourist on Cohen's (1972) continuum of familiarity to novelty? What are some of the popular international mass tourism destinations at present?

3.6.3 Plog

Plog (1984) linked personality traits to tourist behaviour. His work involved research on behalf of seventeen airline companies in the USA to find out if an understanding of travel motivation could help them expand their businesses. Plog (2002) categorised tourists into two opposite types: Venturers and dependables.

3.6.3.1 Venturers

Venturers are adventurous and outgoing. Their inquisitive personalities and their interest in travel and adventure mean that they prefer exotic destinations and unstructured holidays rather than packaged tours, and more involvement with local cultures. For example, travelling around South and Central American countries Peru and Bolivia. Allocentrics are synonymous with Cohen's (1972) explorer and drifter type ('non-institutionalised') tourists.

3.6.3.2 Dependables

Dependables are inward-looking, inhibited, less adventurous travellers who prefer familiar, "more touristy" holiday destinations. They are more aligned with Cohen's 'institutionalised tourists'. For example, British tourists holidaying in popular European destinations the Algarve, Ibiza, and the Canary Islands.

Plog's midcentrics are tourists who do not fall into either category, but share some elements of both venturers and dependables. Midcentrics, according to Plog (2002), actu-

▣ **Table 3.5** Personality and travel-related characteristic of venturers and dependables

Venturers	Dependables
Use their own judgement	Look for the opinions others
Travel more	Travel less
Adventurous	Non-adventurous
Seek off-the-beaten-track destinations	visit well-known tourist spots
Prefer less-developed locations	Like well-organised travel itineraries
Stay for longer periods	Stay for shorter periods
Travel more frequently	Travel less frequently
Prefer local guesthouses and restaurants	Like branded tried-and-trusted accommodation and conventional meals
Buy locally made arts and crafts	Like buying souvenirs and trinkets
Avoid crowds	Enjoy crowds

Source: Adapted from Plog (1995)

ally make up the majority of the population. They go to known destinations, but do not go for adventure or exploration tourism.

▣ Table 3.5 provides a more detailed list of the characteristics and tourism behaviour attributed to these categories of tourist.

Criticisms of this model include the fact that Plog (1995) attempted to link tourist types with specific destinations. However, destinations change over time. For example, as a resort is discovered and attracts an increasing number of visitors, it will evolve from an allocentric to a psychocentric destination. In addition, tourists change over time. For instance, mass tourists to popular destinations (psychocentric tourists) gain confidence after a number of overseas trips and become more adventurous. Similarly, young adults may be allocentric for a period in their life cycles and more mid-centric during their full nest stage. Nevertheless, Plog's (1995) model is useful to tourism marketers as it reinforces the importance of promoting the aspect of the holiday (adventure or mass tourism) to the market at which it is aimed. It is also helpful as it encourages marketers to think about the types of product that should be offered to meet different consumers' needs.

Summary

It is important for tourism marketers and researchers to try to understand how and why consumers make their decisions to buy tourism offerings. In this chapter, we have explored the complex and diverse factors that influence tourism consumer behaviour. These range from internal factors such as perception and personality to external factors such as lifestyle and culture. Research into tourism consumer behaviour is still in its primary stages and many of the principles have been adopted from traditional marketing theory. However, it is apparent that prospective tourism consumers are greatly influenced by word-of-mouth recommendations from friends and colleagues.

We have also examined the various tourism typologies that academics and marketers use in an attempt to group tourists together based on shared characteristics. By identifying groups that share similar characteristics, the tourism marketer knows who can and should be targeted so that marketing activities can be designed accordingly. However, in reality, tourist consumer behaviour is complex. Tourists are irrational and unpredictable. One year, a tourist may take an ecotourism holiday in Belize, Central America, for example, and then the same tourist may take a mass tourism holiday at a holiday resort in Tenerife, Spain the following year.

As individuals become more sophisticated in their holiday behaviour, research must become more sophisticated to explain this behaviour. Researchers must consider aspects such as travellers' perceptions of destinations and visitor attractions, how they make decisions, their sources of travel information, and the likelihood that they will return to or recommend a destination. All of this information is useful to tourism destination marketers.

3

◘ Image 3.8   Halal tourism Indonesia logo

❓ Review Questions

1. Briefly explain why it is important for a tourism and hospitality marketer to understand the behaviour of consumers.
2. Explain why marketing researchers have found it problematic to understand what motivates people to go on holiday.
3. Contrast needs and wants in the context of holiday consumer behaviour.
4. Describe what is meant by a reference group. Using examples, discuss the extent of reference groups' influence on tourism consumer behaviour.
5. Explain the role that the family plays in the consumer journey cycle when choosing a holiday destination.
6. Do consumers always follow rational consumer journey cycle approaches when purchasing products such as holidays? Why or why not?
7. Justify why the post-purchase behaviour stage is included in the consumer journey cycle.
8. Identify the factors that might motivate a tourist to travel to a range of different holiday destinations.
9. Briefly describe some current trends in tourism consumer behaviour.
10. Discuss some of the limitations of tourist typologies for tourism marketers.

In-depth Case Study 3: Tourism and Hospitality Consumer Behaviour: Halal Tourism in South East Asia

Objectives

- To apply the principles of consumer behaviour to the case study
- To examine the international Halal tourism market.

Promotional activities for tourism tend to feature white Westerners holidaying: pictured bronzing on the beach, refuelling in restaurants, or spending in shops. It can appear that non-white Westerners either don't travel or are not seen as attractive and adventurous tourists. Such a pro-Western bias is an exotic fantasy world as illustrated by Muslims, who have a strong travelling heritage and a rich tradition in absorbing new cultures and adding their own flavours.

The word 'Halal' is Arabic and means 'permissible for all Muslims' and covers all activities of daily life in accordance to the Islamic Sharia law (▶ www.muslimbreak.com). Halal tourism essentially deals with a Muslim-orientated tour, designed to address Muslim traveller's needs, where the tourists abide by Sharia laws as facilitated by the hosts (Mohsin, et al., 2016). It is also important to acknowledge that Halal tourism takes place within a context of recreational, leisure, and social purposes and Islamic people travel for the same reasons that many people wish to travel (Smith,

2017). Experiencing different cultures and histories is aligned to Islam as it is believed such travel enables Muslims to appreciate the wonder of the world as created by God (Ryan, 2016).

According to the 2019 Global Muslim Travel Index (GMTI), the number of international Muslim travellers in 2018 was 140 million, an increase of 10% over the previous year. This figure that is expected to grow to 156 million by 2020, represents more than 10% of tourists worldwide. By 2026, the Halal travel sector's contribution to the global economy is expected to jump 35% to US$300 billion, up from US$220 billion in 2020 (Mastercard, 2019). Thus, there are huge returns for Halal-friendly destinations and products. Three of the most popular countries for Halal tourism are Turkey, Malaysia, and Indonesia. The Muslim travel market is one of the fastest-growing tourism sectors in the world, but despite its huge potential, remains relatively untapped.

The United Nations World Tourism Organization (UNWTO) states that Turkey is attracting a growing number of visitors from the Middle East; tourist arrivals from this region increased from 2.1 million in 2011 to 4.5 million in 2018 (Ahval, 2019). It is projected that over the next few years there will be strong growth in visitors from Middle Eastern countries. Muslim-friendly beach resorts are emerging as a high growth sector and Turkey is the most established market for such resorts (Wazir, 2017). Turkey as a destination has the added appeal to attract both non-Muslim as well as travellers of the Muslim faith. Ufuk Secgin, Chief Marketing Officer (CMO) for ▶ www. HalalBooking.com, says Halal tourists interpret Islamic rules in varying ways. What is common is they usually want a beach holiday and indoor and outdoor pools. They want women-only and men-only spa facilities. But while they want Halal food and a no-alcohol policy, they don't want segregation in restaurants (Wazir, 2017).

Currently, Malaysia is the tourist destination of choice for Muslim travellers; over one quarter of all international tourists visiting the country are of Muslim faith (Samori et al., 2016). Malaysia has actively pursued the Halal tourist market, particularly from the Middle East. Malaysia offers a welcoming cultural milieu as well as alluring scenic and climatic conditions such as desert-like landscapes associated with the Middle East (Samori et al., 2016). The Malaysian government is committed to a programme of tourism promotions aimed at the lucrative Middle East market; including a 'Feel at Home' campaign, which involved upgrading street signage in Arabic, multi-language tourist information brochures and restaurant menus and employment of Arab speaking staff in the hospitality and retail sectors (Samori et al., 2016).

With a population of 263 million, 90% of whom are Muslim, Indonesia is the most populous Muslim nation in the world (Jaelani, 2017). Indonesia's tourism sector is the country's biggest foreign exchange earner and the Indonesian Tourism Ministry (ITM) aims to reach a target of a minimum of 400,000 Muslim tourists from the Middle East over the coming years (Jaelani, 2017). The ITM recently appointed a 'Halal tourism development acceleration team' to target the high spending Middle Eastern travellers. To help promote Indonesia's intent on growing their Halal tourism sector, the ITM launched a new destination brand and logo in 2016, using the Garuda (a large legendary bird-like creature), which is the national symbol of Indonesia.

Halal tourism practices and activities are affected by the political environment in the Middle East and globally. International tourist arrivals to Turkey, Egypt, Tunisia, Algeria, Iran, and Lebanon have suffered in recent years due to a plethora of terrorism incidents and political instability affecting the region. However, these countries, along with Muslim countries (or 'Muslim-majority') such as Malaysia, have benefited from an increase in demand from tourists travelling from Middle Eastern countries including Yemen, Syria, Iraq, and Libya (Battour & Ismail, 2016).

A 2019 Global Muslim Travel Index (GMTI) study tracked the health and growth of Muslim-friendly travel destinations in four

3

■ Image 3.9   Halal tourism – Case study Photograph of vlogger/influencer Huda Khalid surfing in Bali, Indonesia. (Source: Jonathan A. J. Wilson)

strategic areas – access, communications, environment and services. The GMTI (2019) is now the leading study providing insights and data to help countries, the travel industry and investors gauge the development of travel sectors while benchmarking a country's progress in catering to Muslim travellers.

A challenge for tourism professionals is to create a single, global Halal certification system, which will encourage the expansion of the Halal tourism industry (▶ www.muslimbreak. com). The number of Shariah-compliant hotels is growing in Muslim-majority and Muslim-minority countries, where services are in accordance with Islamic teachings such as offering Halal food, alcohol-free beverages, and prayer rooms (Battour & Ismail, 2016). Nevertheless, there are a limited number of Shariah-compliant and Halal resorts in Muslim-minority countries. That said, hotels that do not cater primarily for Muslim guests tend not to apply for Halal certification as they are concerned that such practices are unattractive to non-Muslim (Western) tourists. However, such businesses can still attract and cater for Halal tourists by adhering to certain practices such as refraining from storing alcoholic products in guest rooms and providing separate swimming and spa areas for male and female guests (Battour & Ismail, 2016).

The growth in Halal tourism has generally come from Muslims visiting Islamic countries. The numbers of non-Muslim travellers to Muslim-majority countries have tended to fluctuate due to socio-political factors and the media-led threat of extreme Islamic activity. Muslim nations have identified that Muslims tend to be less sensitive about avoiding Muslim-majority countries as holiday destinations. Muslim-minority countries are increasingly developing Halal-friendly products and services. Thus, there is a case that Muslims should be targeted more frequently and in a way that clearly shows their faith-based decisions are linked to and influence holidaymaking.

☐ **Image 3.10** The Garuda, the national symbol of Indonesia, and the one used by the national airline. (Source: Wilson (2018))

Questions and Activities

1. Discuss the reasons for a growth of interest in Halal-friendly products and services.
2. What are the main problems in analysing the motivations of individuals and groups who consume Halal tourism holidays such?
3. How could non-Muslim (Muslim-minority) countries such as Spain and Thailand and organisations such as holiday resorts and hotels cater for Halal tourists?
4. Discuss whether Halal tourism is likely to alienate Muslim tourists from general tourism activities, or otherwise, to alienate non-Muslim visitors in certain tourist destinations.

References

Alexander, Z. (2012). The impact of a volunteer tourism experience in South Africa on the tourist: The influence of age, gender, project type and length of stay. *Tourism Management Perspectives, 4.*

Ahval. (2019). *Turkey risk loss of culture with embrace of Arab tourists* [Online]. Retrieved from: https://ahvalnews.com/turkey-tourism/turkey-risks-loss-culture-embrace-arab-tourists-independent. Accessed 5 Jan 2020.

Amster, R. (2013). *Booking family travel is hot opportunity for agents* [Online]. Retrieved from: www.travelmarketreport.com/articles/Booming-Family-Travel-is-Hot-Opportunity-for-Agents. Accessed 5 Oct 2013.

Baines, P., Fill, C., Rosengren, S., & Antonetti, P. (2019). *Marketing* (5th ed.). Oxford, UK: Oxford University Press.

Baker, D., & Crompton, J. (2000). Quality, satisfaction and behavioral intentions. *Annals of Tourism Research, 27*(3), 785–804.

Barnes, J. (2009). *Flaubert's parrot*. London: Vintage.

Battour, M., & Ismail, M. (2016). Halal tourism: Concepts, practices, challenges and future. *Tourism Management Perspectives, 19*, 150–154.

Blackwell, R., Miniard, P., & Engel, J. (2006). *Consumer behavior* (10th ed.). Cincinnati, OH: Thomson, South Western.

Chesterton, G. K. (2013). *The Temple of silence and other stories*. London: Miniature Masterpieces.

Choi, S., Lehto, C., Morrison, A. M., & Jang, S. (2012). Structure of travel planning processes and information use patterns. *Journal of Travel Research, 51*(1), 26–40.

Cohen, E. (1972). Towards a sociology of international tourism. *Social Research, 39*(1).

Cohen, S., Prayag, G., & Moital, M. (2014). Consumer behaviour in tourism: Concepts, influences and opportunities. *Current Issues in Tourism, 17*(10), 872–909.

Coleman, R. (1983). The continuing significance of social class to marketing. *Journal of Consumer Research, 10*(3), 265–280.

Cooper, C., & Hall, M. (2019). *Contemporary tourism: An international approach* (4th ed.). Oxford, UK: Goodfellow Publishers.

3

Dollard, J., & Miller, N. E. (1950). *Personality and psychotherapy*. New York: McGraw-Hill.

Fodness, D., & Murray, B. (1998). A typology of tourist information search strategies. *Journal of Travel Research, 37*(2).

George, R., & Booyens, I. (2014). Township tourism demand: Tourists' perceptions of safety and security. *Urban Forum, 2*(3), 48–63.

Global Muslim Travel Index, GMTI. (2019). *Halal travel development goals' as industry moves into 'new phase'*. Available at: www.crescentrating.com/reports/global-muslim-travel-index-2019.html. Accessed 26 April 2019.

Grubb, E., & Stern, B. (1971). Self-concept and significant others. *Journal of Marketing Research, 8*(3), 382–385.

Horner, S., & Swarbrooke, J. (2016). *Consumer behaviour in tourism* (3rd ed.). Oxford, UK: Butterworth-Heinemann.

Hyde, K., & Lawson, R. (2003). The nature of independent travel. *Journal of Travel Research, 42*(1), 13–23.

International Congress and Convention Association (ICCA). (2017). [Online], Available: http://www.iccaworld.com/aeps/aeitem.cfm?aeid=107 Accessed 15 April 2017.

Jaelani, A. (2017). Halal tourism industry in Indonesia: Potential and prospects. *International Review of Management and Marketing, 7*(3), 25–34.

Jalilv, R., & Samiei, N. (2012). The impact of electronic word of mouth on a tourism destination choice: Testing the theory of planned behavior (TPB). *Internet Research, 22*(5), 591–612.

Kahneman, D., & Tversky, A. (1999). Evaluation by moments: Past and future. In D. Kahneman & A. Tversky (Eds.), *Choices, values, and frames* (pp. 2–23). New York: Cambridge University Press.

Keshavarzian, P., & Wu, C. L. (2017). A qualitative research on travellers' destination choice behaviour. *International Journal of Tourism Research, 19*(1), 546–556.

Kelly, G. A. (1955). *The Psychology of personal constructs*. London: Routledge.

Kotler, P., & Keller, K. L. (2016). *Marketing management* (15th ed.). London: Pearson Education.

Krugman, H. E. (1965). The impact of television advertising: Learning without involvement. *Public Opinion Quarterly, 29(Fall)*, 349–56.

Lennon, J., & Foley, M. (2000). *Dark tourism: The attraction of death and disaster*. London: Continuum.

Maslow, A. H. (1954). *Motivation and personality*. New York: Harper and Row.

Mastercard. (2019). *Press Release*. https://newsroom.mastercard.com/asia-pacific/press-releases/mastercard-crescentrating-global-muslim-travel-index-gmti-2019-indonesia-and-malaysia-take-the-top-positions-in-the-fast-growing-muslim-travel-market/

Middleton, V., Fyall, A., Morgan, M., & Ranchhod, A. (2009). *Marketing in Travel and Tourism* (4th ed.). Oxford, UK: Butterworth-Heinemann.

Mohsin, A., Ramli, N., & Alkhulayfi, B. (2016). Halal tourism: Emerging opportunities. *Tourism Management Perspectives, 19*, 137–143.

Moutinho, L. (1987). Consumer behaviour in tourism. *European Journal of Marketing, 21*(10), 1–44.

Page, S. J. (2019). *Tourism management* (6th ed.). Oxford: Routledge.

Patterson, I., & Balderas, A. (2018). Continuing and emerging trends of senior tourism: A review of the literature. *Journal of Population Aging, 11*, 213–216.

Pearce, P.L. (1993). The fundamentals of tourist motivation. In Pearce D & Butler R, Tourism Research: Critique and Challenges. London: Routledge.

Petrick, J. (2004). The roles of quality, value and satisfaction in predicting cruise passengers' behavioural intentions. *Journal of Travel Research, 42*(1), 397–407.

Pike, S. (2020). *Destination marketing essentials* (3rd ed.). Abingdon, UK\Oxford, UK: Routledge.

Pike, S. (2018). *Tourism marketing for small businesses*. Oxford, UK: Goodfellow Publishers.

Plog, S. C. (1984). Why destination areas rise and fall in popularity. *Cornell Hotel and Restaurant Quarterly, 14*(4).

Plog, S. C. (1995). *Vacation places rated*. Redondo Beach, CA: Fielding Worldwide.

Plog, S. C. (2002). The power of psychographics and the concept of venturesomeness. *Journal of Travel Research, 40*(February).

Pritchard, A., Morgan, N., Sedgley, D., Khan, E., & Jenkins, A. (2000). Sexuality and holiday choices: Conversations with gay and lesbian tourists. *Leisure Studies, 19*(4), 267–282.

Ritchie, B. (2003). *Managing educational tourism*. Clevedon, UK: Channel View Publications.

Rosenberg, M., & Hovland, C. (1960). Cognitive, affective and behavioral components of attitude. In M. Rosenberg (Ed.), *Attitude of organization and change*. New Haven, CN: Yale University Press.

Robinson, M., & Novelli, M. (2005). *Niche tourism: Contemporary issues, trends, and cases*. Oxford, UK: Butterworth-Heinemann.

Ryan, C. (2016). Halal tourism. *Tourism Management Perspectives, 19*, 121–123.

Samori, Z., Salleh, N., & Khalid, M. (2016). Current trends on halal tourism: Cases on selected Asian countries. *Tourism Management Perspectives, 19*, 131–136.

Schacter, D., Gilbert, D., & Wegner, D. (2011). *Psychology* (2nd ed.). New York: Worth Publishers.

Schiffman, L. G., & Kanuk, L. L. (2018). *Consumer behavior* (12th ed.). Upper Saddle River, NJ: Prentice-Hall.

Seabra, C., Abrates, J., & Lages, L. (2007). The impact of using non-media information sources on the future use of mass media information sources: The mediating role of expectations fulfilment. *Tourism Management, 10*(1).

Seaton, A. V., & Bennett, M. M. (1996). *Marketing tourism products*. London: ITP.

Sethna, Z., & Blythe, J. (2016). *Consumer behavior* (3rd ed.). Thousand Oaks, CA: SAGE Publishing.

Sharpley, R. (2008). *Tourism, tourists and society* (4th ed.). Huntingdon, Cambridge: ELM Publications.

Simpson, J. (2017). Finding brand success in a digital world. *Forbes*. Retrieved from https://www.forbes.com/sites/forbesagencycouncil/2017/08/25/finding-brand-success-in-the-digital-world/#74036bc626e2. Accessed 7 May 2019.

Smith, L. (2017). Hajj 2017: *Two million Muslim pilgrims from all over the world head to Mecca*. Retrieved from https://www.independent.co.uk/news/world/middle-east/hajj-2017-muslim-pilgrimage-mecca-islam-pilgrims-saudi-arabia-a7917851.html [14 June 2018].

Smith, C. (2018). *38 amazing TripAdvisor statistics and facts*. Retrieved from http://expandedramblings.com/index.php/tripadvisor-statistics/ [14 September 2018].

Stausberg, M. (2011). *Religion and tourism: Crossroads, destinations, and encounters*. London: Routledge.

Stone, P. (2005). Niche tourism: Contemporary issues, trends and cases. *Journal of Vacation Marketing, 11*.

Stone, P. (Ed.). (2018). *The Palgrave handbook of dark tourism studies*. Basingstoke, Hampshire: Palgrave Macmillan.

Swart, K., & George, R. (2018). The 2014 FIFA World Cup™: Tourists' satisfaction levels and likelihood of repeat visitation to Rio de Janeiro. *Journal of Destination Marketing & Management, 21*(3).

Sudhir, K., Priester, J., Shum, M., Atkin, D., Foster, A., Iyer, G. (2015). Research opportunities in emerging markets: An inter-disciplinary perspective from marketing, economics, and psychology. *Customer Needs and Solutions, 2*(4), 264–276.

Tanner, J., & Raymond, M. (2012). *Marketing principles*. Creative Commons: Flat World Knowledge.

Turco, D. M., Riley, R., & Swart, K. (2011). *Sport tourism* (2nd ed.). Morgantown, WV: Fitness Information Technology.

United Nations World Tourism Organization. (UNWTO). (2021). Tourism and culture. Madrid: United Nations World Tourism Organization and WYSE Travel Confederation. Retrieved from https://www.unwto.org/tourism-and-culture. Accessed 24 Jan 2021.

Voigt, C., Laing, J., Wray, M., Brown, G., Howat, G., Weiler, B. (2010). *Health tourism in Australia: Supply, demand and opportunities*. Gold Coast, QLD: CRC for Sustainable Tourism Pty Ltd..

Vyncke, P. (2002). Lifestyle segmentation from attitudes, interests, and opinions to values, aesthetic styles, life visions, and media preferences. *European Journal of Communication, 17*(4), 445–463.

Wazir, B. (2017). *Halal holidays boost Muslim tourists to Turkey*. www.ft.com/content/21c0f6d0-864b-11e7-8bb1-5ba57d47eff7. Accessed 7 Nov 2017.

Wessely, A. (2002). Travelling people, travelling objects. *Journal of Cultural Studies, 16*(1).

Wilson, J. A. (2018). *Halal branding*. London: Claritas Books.

Further Reading

Horner, S., & Swarbrooke, J. (2016). *Consumer behaviour in tourism* (3rd ed.). Oxford, UK: Butterworth-Heinemann.

Kumar Dixit, S. (Ed.). (2017). *The Routledge handbook of consumer behaviour in hospitality and tourism*. Oxford, UK: Routledge.

Pearce, P. (Ed.). (2019). *Tourist behaviour: The essential companion*. Cheltenham, UK: Edward Elgar Publishing.

Schiffman, L. G., & Kanuk, L. L. (2018). *Consumer behavior* (12th ed.). Upper Saddle River, NJ: Prentice-Hall.

Tourism and Hospitality Marketing Research

Contents

Electronic Supplementary Material The online version of this chapter (https://doi.org/10.1007/978-3-030-64111-5_4) contains supplementary material, which is available to authorized users.

Purpose

This chapter will provide you with an understanding of the role of marketing research in tourism and hospitality marketing.

Learning Goals

After reading this chapter, you should be able to:

- Understand why tourism organisations need to undertake marketing research
- Contrast the different types of research used in tourism and hospitality
- Become familiar with the stages of marketing research process
- Identify sources of secondary data collection in tourism and hospitality marketing research
- Compare and contrast the various types of survey contact methods
- Explain the importance of questionnaire layout, structure, and presentation
- Produce a well-structured marketing research report
- Apply the principles of the marketing research process to East Coast Rentals.

Overview

We begin this chapter with a discussion of the importance of research to the tourism and hospitality marketer. We provide a definition of marketing research, and an explanation of the differences between marketing research and market research. We then discuss the reasons for doing marketing research and outline different types of marketing research commonly used in tourism.

We cover the seven steps involved in the process of conducting a marketing research project:

1. Identifying the research problem and defining the research objectives
2. Investigating the available sources and resources
3. Devising the research plan
4. Conducting qualitative and quantitative research
5. Analysing and interpreting the data
6. Presenting the findings and recommendations to the client in a clear manner
7. Following up with the client to maintain a relationship and to ensure the sustainability of the recommendations.

The case study considers the marketing research activities carried out by *East Coast Rentals*, a small car-rental company based in Australia.

4.1 Introduction

Tourism and hospitality marketers need to be able to make effective marketing decisions. These decisions may be about entering a new market (and the timing of that decision), developing or promoting a new product offering, or choosing the best platforms and distribution channels to promote product offerings. Marketers also need to be aware of trends and predictions so that their offerings are up to date with what customers require. Finally, marketers need to possess information about their consumers (consumer behaviour). All this information can only be found through marketing research.

There are many research methods available to the marketing researcher. These methods enable an organisation to get closer to its consumers and help it to understand the markets in which it operates. The practice of marketing research is about an organisation paying attention to its customers.

Marketing research today is at a crossroads, with new discoveries about how people think and why they behave as they do affecting the core of marketing research activity. Digitalisation had led to an overwhelming amount of information available to marketers: **big data**, social media networks (for example, TripAdvisor, Facebook, Tik Tok, Twitter, Instagram, and Snapchat), mobile access to information, and travel websites have transformed the marketing research sector and have created a completely new field of research for tourism marketers and companies (■ Table 4.1).

◘ **Table 4.1**   Marketing research concepts and definitions

Concept	Source	Definition
Big data	McAfee and Brynjolfsson (2012)	The systematic gathering and interpretation of high-volume, high-velocity, and high-variety information using cost-effective innovative forms of information processing to enable insight and decision-making.
Marketing information system	Jobber and Ellis-Chadwick (2016)	A is a structure of people, equipment and procedures to gather, sort, analyse, evaluate and distribute needed, timely and accurate information to marketing decision-makers
Marketing intelligence	Kotler and Armstrong (2019)	The systematic collection and analysis of publicly available information about competitors and development in the marketing environment
Market research		Research into consumer preferences, and the expectations and patterns of behaviour of competitors and other stakeholders,
Marketing research	Babin and Zikmund (2016)	The systematic and objective collection, analysis, and interpretation of data collected for decision-making about marketing problems of all kinds, using recognised scientific methods

Source: Author's creation

4.2   What is Marketing Research?

Better research, better decisions.

Marketing research is the term used for the whole range of information intelligence gathering and analysis. It is applicable at every stage of the marketing planning process (see ◘ Table 4.2).

❓ Visit the MRS website (▶ www.mre.org.uk).

Marketing research includes all types of research undertaken to assist the marketer in examining all the components of the tourism marketing mix: offerings, distribution (place), price, promotion, people, physical evidence, and process. ◘ Figure 4.1 shows the interdependent nature of the marketing mix and marketing research. It illustrates how information is gathered from consumers and analysed, and then how the mix is adjusted accordingly for future marketing decisions. Research also helps marketers understand the marketplace in which they work: its tourism suppliers, tour operators, travel agencies, competitors, and consumers.

Research can be defined as having three functions:

1. The descriptive function involves the process of finding out things to list, report on, and describe (the "who", "what", "how", and "where" of consumer behaviour).
2. The diagnostic function involves the process of explaining ("why").
3. The predictive function combines the first two kinds of research to suggest a course of action (that is, how to use the research).

Descriptive research is commonly used in tourism and hospitality marketing research (especially consumer behaviour); organisations and destinations need to find out who goes where, when they go, how they get there, what they thought of the offering, and other basic information about consumer behaviour. Another reason why descriptive research is common in the industry is that levels of participation in tourism activities change over time as markets change. For instance, over the last decade or so, cruise holidays have become more attractive to a younger and technologically savvy audience (Mody, 2018). Descriptive research, however, cannot be used to address the "why" questions (for example, "Why do you think the service is unsatisfactory?"). Experimental research (for example, causal research) is used to measure relationships between variables (see page 125), and is therefore used to address the "why" questions. This

Table 4.2 Marketing research and the tourism marketing planning process

	Stages in the tourism marketing planning process	Uses of marketing research
Planning and research	1. Where are we now?	Research for planning and analysis to profile market segment
	2. Where would we like to be?	Research for strategy selection
Imple-mentation	3. How do we get there?	Research to guide the seven Ps
Control	4. How do we make sure we get there?	Research for monitoring the marketing plan
Evaluation	5. How do we know if we got there?	Evaluation research

Source: Author's creation

type of research is rarely used for small tourism/hospitality businesses due to the high level of complexity involved.

❓ Visit this website: ▶ https://research-methodology.net.

4.3 Marketing Research Versus Market Research

Marketers are increasingly seeking to understand why tourism and hospitality consumers behave in a particular way and how they make purchasing decisions. For example, what makes a consumer choose a particular tourist destination, organisation or event? How long would a visitor stay at a tourist attraction? Would the introduction of a buffet-style breakfast instead of a full breakfast increase or reduce the satisfaction of hotel guests? This type of research into consumer preferences, and the expectations and patterns of behaviour of competitors and other stakeholders, is known as "**market research**". Market research is applied research, which is undertaken to answer specific questions.

Marketing research consists of all of the research that helps the tourism marketer in making marketing decisions (including secondary research and competitor analysis). Market research is therefore a subset of the more all-embracing term "marketing research".

4.4 Why Do Marketing Research?

Many marketers make the error of focusing heavily on the marketing mix and, in doing so, neglect marketing research. The marketing mix must be adapted to suit consumers. Research should therefore be viewed as a fundamental part

Fig. 4.1 Marketing research in tourism and hospitality marketing mix. (Source: Author's creation)

of marketing planning. In addition, unless marketers carry out research to find out what their consumers' needs and wants are, they cannot be sure that the tourism offering will appeal to them.

Unfortunately, businesses often regard marketing research as an optional extra and an unnecessary cost, rather than the foundation of sound marketing and product development strategies and, as such, an investment in the future. All tourism and hospitality organisations, however small, should carry out research. The belief held by many smaller firms is that marketing research is a luxury that is affordable only by larger travel corporations. This is a dangerous, misleading notion. Just like larger companies, small tourism organisations require market information. Start-up tourism businesses, for example, need information about their industry sector, competitors and potential consumers. Similarly, existing small businesses need to track consumer needs, reactions to new product-offerings and customer retention rates. Indeed, the latter – customer relationship research – is a growth area in tourism marketing research. Many of the marketing research techniques discussed later in this chapter can be used by small tourism organisations in a fairly unstructured manner and at little or no expense (see ▶ Industry Insight 4.1).

Industry Insight 4.1

Small Tourism Businesses Need to Conduct Marketing Research Too

Marketing research – surveys, interviews, experiments and secondary research – can all be used by small to medium enterprises (SMEs), even those with small budgets. A B&B owner can monitor competitor advertising by collecting advertisements from local newspapers. He or she can visit their competitors to gain more insight. The B&B owner can also conduct informal surveys on current guests using small convenience samples. A B&B owner might make random telephone calls during quiet hours to interview guests about what they thought of their stay at the B&B. The owner might decide to experiment by advertising different prices to various markets. A small museum can carry out informal focus groups (where small groups discuss a topic of interest) and learn what visitors think about new exhibits. Secondary research sources such as government data (for example, statistics collected by a national tourism organisation or a private research company such as Mintel), trade journals, and research conducted by university students and academics should also be utilised (◻ Image 4.1).

◻ **Image 4.1** Even small tourism and hospitality businesses need to carry out marketing research. (Source: Unsplash)

There are many other reasons why tourism organisations need to undertake marketing research and gather **marketing intelligence**. Some tourism firms have a very systematic approach and see it as a vital and integral component of their marketing plan. Other organisations use it on an *ad hoc* and piece-meal basis (usually as a result of limited resources) to achieve a particular objective in one or a number of difficult situations (for example, when a hotel's bed occupancy rates are falling). Marketing research is used at the core of any feasibility study. Consultants and developers undertake marketing research to assess the potential of resorts, or to evaluate specific sites for the development of hotels, visitor attractions, or retail complexes (Lumsdon, 1997: 123).

The five main reasons for doing marketing research are to:

1. help make marketing decisions and reduce risks
2. plan and solve problems
3. assist the marketer in forecasting
4. develop knowledge of past and potential consumers
5. obtain information about competitors.

These reasons are discussed below.

4.4.1 Making Decisions and Reducing Risks

Marketing research cannot ensure the right decisions, but it can reduce the degree of risk and uncertainty when marketers and managers make decisions. It helps them reduce the risk of making the wrong decision. For example, marketing research can help to reduce the risk of pricing an offering too high or entering it into an unprofitable market (such as a very niche market).

4.4.2 Planning and Solving Problems

Marketing research is vital for planning. It allows organisations to identify and solve problems (for example, why visitor numbers to a museum are dropping). Ultimately, it allows organisations to increase their efficiency.

When used for planning, marketing research deals mainly with the identification of opportunities. It considers questions such as the following:

- What types of consumers buy our tourism product offerings? (social class, age, and gender)
- Where are they from? (catchment area)
- How much do they earn? (socio-economic characteristics)
- How many of them are there?
- What do they think of our facility or service? (consumer satisfaction evaluation)

Marketing research should be used at every stage of the marketing planning process (that is, internal and external situation analysis, setting goals and defining objectives, strategic decisions, implementation, and monitoring) (see ◻ Table 4.2).

When it is used for problem-solving, marketing research focuses on short- or long-term decisions that tourism organisations (including destination marketing organisations) must make regarding elements of the marketing mix (the four Ps).

Marketing research plays an important role in achieving satisfactory profits by promoting an understanding of how to satisfy consumer needs and wants. In addition, marketing research is carried out on competitors, suppliers, and stakeholders (including government tourism policymakers).

4

4.4.3 Assisting with Forecasting

Marketers need to be aware of trends, changes, and forecasts relating to their product offerings and markets. Marketing research allows a marketer to develop a market forecasting system based on a marketing information system (MIS). A marketing research information system is the way in which a company gathers, uses and disseminates research in the marketing context (Jobber & Ellis-Chadwick 2016). Domestic and international tourism markets are constantly changing.

Similarly, by using social media analytical tools and searching the latest posts, tourism marketers can gain insight into emerging trends and track conversation in real time.

Over the last decade, single travellers, women travellers, and older travellers ("Grey Gappers") have all become more significant. Through research, marketers can keep up with these trends, and improve their forecasting and future planning (see ► Industry Insight 4.2).

Industry Insight 4.2

Google Trends

Google Trends allows marketers to access data behind emerging trends from instantly. It does so by providing data on the search terms people use in the Google search engine and locates research geographically, offering information about anywhere in the world, down to the smallest town. In essence, it tells us what people's preferences are, including their holiday preferences. For example, on the Google Trends site, you can type in "Sport tourism" and obtain results concerning levels of interest in the topic over a period of time (for anywhere from the last hour to the last year). In addition, you can obtain results for related topics such as "Sport tourist" and "Sports and Olympic museum".

Visit this website: ► https://trends.google.com/trends/?geo=ZA.

4.4.4 Developing Knowledge About Consumers

One of the most important reasons for conducting marketing research is that it helps the tourism and hospitality organisation in gathering detailed knowledge about its consumers, including new, existing, potential, and lapsed consumers (see ► Industry Insight 4.3). It provides the manager with information on how the organisation is meeting consumer needs and wants, and helps to determine the organisation's position in the marketplace. It can be used to measure customer retention rates ("relationship marketing") through satisfaction surveys and recommendation rates (see ► Chap. 13). This research data can then be used to develop consumer profiles.

Research into India's Medical Tourism Sector

There are many reasons tourists visit India: the culture, the food, or the weather. But in recent years, another factor drawing visitors is health care. According to the India Ministry of Tourism (IMT) its medical tourism industry is growing rapidly. The country's medical tourism USPs are its state-of-the-art facilities, highly skilled doctors, low-cost treatment, and traditional practices such as yoga.

India's 'e-tourist visa' regime has been expanded to include medical visits as well. Medical and medical attendant visas have been introduced to ease the travel process of medical tourists. The maximum duration of stay in India under the e-medical visa is a longer duration of six months. Research shows that the global medical tourism market is expected to reach $143 billion by 2025 (In 2017, it was estimated to be worth around $53 billion). Other leading medical tourism destinations include Malaysia, Singapore, Thailand, Turkey, and the USA. There are, however, several challenges facing the global medical tourism industry, namely: quality issues and continuity of care. There is no quality assurance between countries, thus, if something goes wrong, there is no way for legal redress, whether there's malpractice or serious complications following a procedure. In addition, as it is largely private-sector practice, there is no international governing body or quality assurance. That said, for most health tourists cost savings out way the drawbacks. In India, the savings can start from 65% and go up to 90% with patients receiving quality care. In Taiwan, Thailand, Mexico, and Turkey patients can save between 40% to 65% on procedures and treatments.

CNN Health. (2019). The global medical tourism market was valued at $53,768 million in 2017, and is estimated to reach at $143,461 million by 2025, registering a CAGR of 12.9% from 2018 to 2025. Retrieved from ▶ https://www.prnewswire.com/news-releases/the-global-medical-tourism-market-was-valued-at-53-768-million-in-2017--and-is-estimated-to-reach-at-143-461-million-by-2025--registering-a-cagr-of-12-9-from-2018-to-2025--300870675.html [27 January 2020].

Research into what a typical British seaside two-week' holiday for families looks like was carried out based on a study of 2000 respondents. The research, carried out in 2016, found that on average eight ice creams are eaten per person, four picnics are taken, and two trips are undertaken to local visitor attractions during a typical holiday. In addition, holidaymakers build on average five sandcastles, take 81 photographs, and make three holiday-related Facebook statuses. And finally, two days on average are spent indoors due to rain!

Source: Staff writer. (2016). 'Life's a beach'. The Independent. Tuesday 12 July, p.2.

4.5 The Marketing Research Process

Marketing research activities usually follow a systematic process, meaning that the procedures followed in each stage (or step) of the research process are methodologically sound, well-documented, and, as far as possible, planned in advance (Malhotra, Birks & Nunan, 2017). This process consists of five stages, as outlined in ▫ Fig. 4.2, beginning with identifying the marketing decision problem (MDP). These stages include identifying the research problem and defining research objectives, investigating the available sources (secondary research), devising

4

Stage 1
Identify the marketing decision problem

↓

Stage 2
Investigate the available sources

↓

Stage 3
Devise the research plan and gather primary data

↓

Stage 4
Analyse and interpret the data

↓

Stage 5
Present the findings to the manager/CEO

Fig. 4.2 Stages in the research process. (Source: Author's creation)

the research plan (primary research), analysing and interpreting the data, and presenting the findings.

4.5.1 Stage 1: Identify the Marketing Decision Problem and Set or Define the Objectives

A marketing decision problem (MDP) is a statement that identifies the purpose of the research. Before gathering information, it is necessary to identify the marketing problem to be researched and to draw up a research brief (or proposal). A research brief is a formal document prepared by a marketer that outlines the research problem to be investigated (Baines, Fill, Rosengen & Antonetti, 2019: 95). The stage of defining the MDP and setting the research objectives is often the most difficult in the research project process. Getting the MDP and objectives right is criti-

cal to the success of the research project because they lay the foundation for the remaining stages of the marketing research process (Pike, 2018).

It is important that the decision-maker (for example, the marketing director) work closely with the marketing researcher to identify management problems that exist. Decision-makers in tourism and hospitality organisations best understand the marketing problem for which information is needed and the researcher best understands how to obtain relevant information (the appropriate methodology to use) in order to solve the MDP (see ▶ Industry Insight 4.4). Identification of a research problem does not always imply that there is a major threat facing the company (Baines et al., 2019: 97).

The MDP should be written as a problem statement. This is important because it directs the entire research process. Some situations require only a simple problem statement, while others lend themselves to a detailed statement of the purpose of the research project (in other words, what the project hopes to achieve). An example of a research problem is: "To what extent are environmental factors influencing visitation to the National Marine Aquarium?"

Once the researcher has identified the MDP, he or she should formulate a series of research objectives (which also be expressed as research questions). Careful and clear definition of research objectives is a key requirement for accurate and beneficial marketing research outcomes (Parasuraman, Grewal & Krishnan, 2007). If realised during the research process, these objectives will ensure that the research addresses the problem statement. They will also serve as criteria for assessing the relevance of the questionnaire and the various sets of scale items (statements

Industry Insight 4.4

The Commodore Hotel's Marketing Decision Problem

In some cases, the research problem must be reidentified. For example, the manager of The Commodore, a hotel in Jerusalem, Israel, notices that the number of bookings is declining. The problem is interpreted as ineffectual advertising. The manager consults a researcher, who in turn investigates the company's advertising campaign. The researcher identifies the research problem: "To determine to what extent hotel bookings are being influenced by various marketing factors." The researcher then devises a questionnaire that is used in interviews with consumers, sales representatives, tour operators and others. It is revealed that sales have declined as a result of a new competitor that offers cheaper rooms. This information makes it clear to the researcher that an investigation into the hotel's advertising campaign will not solve the problem. Subsequently, the problem is reidentified, in conjunction with the manager, as concerning competitive pricing strategies.

that measure responses), known as "constructs", or other research instruments to be used in the primary research stage of the process. A construct is an operational instrument that measures a concept or tests a metric. For instance, the research instrument SERVQUAL has 22 scale items (see ► Chap. 13 for a detailed discussion of this service quality tool).

If we use the research problem formulated above ("To what extent are environmental factors influencing visitation to the National Marine Aquarium?"), the research aim (the goal you're trying to achieve) would be:

- "To examine the main external factors affecting visitor numbers to the National Marine Aquarium".

The research objectives (4 to 6) would then follow:

- To research the academic literature on visitor attraction management, pricing strategies, and macroenviromental factors.
- To analyse the extent to which exchange rates affect visitor numbers to the National Marine Aquarium.
- To assess the extent to which perceptions of safety and security of the city are affecting visitation to the National Marine Aquarium.
- To evaluate the extent to which seasonality affects visitation to the National Marine Museum.
- To determine the extent to which an advertising campaign affects the relationship between pricing and visitation to the National Marine Aquarium.
- To make recommendations to the National Marine Aquarium regarding factors affecting future marketing activity.

Research objectives should be measurable and specific. One of the main reasons for researchers not carrying out research effectively is a report brief/proposal that is too broad. For instance, the manager of a tourism and hospitality organisation may decide to track consumer awareness of the organisation's advertising. This is a broad statement that requires one or more specific research objectives, such as finding out what percentage of a survey's respondents noticed a specific newspaper advertisement.

By deciding on research objectives (which can be written in the form of questions), the researcher is able to determine which research method to use and what questions to ask. The first objective should relate to the academic literature to be examined, the next few objectives should relate to the discussion/evaluation (questions covered in the research), and the last objective relates to a recommendation to the organisation based on the research findings.

The scope of the research should be defined. Typically, the client discusses the scope with the researcher. The scope reports when and where to concentrate the marketing research efforts, and what they should be concentrated on. For example, a research study into the market's perceptions of inbound tour operators might include the following scope:

- Geographical (local, state/provincial or international)
- Industry or trade sector (accommodation, transport, or government)
- Consumers (local, international, domestic, state/provincial or repeat visitors)
- Timing (biannual or longitudinal) of research or data involving information about an individual or group
- Focus group or in-depth interviews with relevant role-players.

When devising a research problem or question, ask yourself: "Can I find this out?" In other words, is the research achievable? (Can you access data? Is there literature on the topic?). You should then ask yourself, "How good is my research topic?" It is important to have a good research topic that inspires and interests you. If you answer "Yes" to most of these questions, then you should have a good "researchable" topic:

- Do I know something about the subject already?
- Does the topic interest me?
- Does the topic inspire me?
- Do I have a good title in mind?
- Does it make a contribution to my field?
- Is it evident that the proposed research falls into an area that would be recognised as belonging to my subject discipline?

- Is there a pre-existing body of research literature on the topic that I can draw upon?
- Is there an established theoretical framework to which I can refer?
- Are there established research methods that I can draw upon?
- Does the topic lend itself to interesting argument and debate?

? Research title:

? *"An investigation into the travel behaviour of Chinese college students".*

? With reference to this research title, write a research aim and four or five research objectives.

? Visit this research dissertation advice website:
  - ▶ https://gradcoach.com/

4.5.1.1 Types of Marketing Research

There are several types of marketing research (see ◘ Table 4.2). Thus, the marketing researcher must consider carefully what type of research is required. This research requirement can be specified according to the following three types of research, which we discuss in this section:

1. Methodology: Quantitative and qualitative
2. Objectives: Exploratory, descriptive, and causal
3. Source: Primary and secondary

- **Methodology: Quantitative and Qualitative Research**

The difference between quantitative and qualitative research is that quantitative research data is in the form of numbers, whereas qualitative research data is not in numbers (Punch, 2014). Therefore, quantitative research means studies to which numerical estimates can be attached. Quantitative research enables the researcher to ascertain how many respondents agree or disagree with a particular statement, but it is not likely to provide insight into why respondents have answered as they have.

Quantitative research (also known as "quant research") includes facts and figures, factual information on the characteristics of the market (in other words, consumers' socio-demographic details) and the destination (that is, visitor numbers and their spending patterns), and statistics on the performance of the organisation (sales figures and market share). For example, a manager of a visitor attraction may wish to know the number of people using the facility and how much visitors are spending in the gift shop. This type of hard data usually gives some indication of the respondents' motivations. Quantitative research is usually based on structured questionnaires in which every respondent is asked the same questions. It is descriptive in nature, rather than analytical.

Qualitative research, on the other hand, tends to focus on the interpretation of words rather than numbers (Walle, 1997). It is designed to interpret data, rather than simply providing data. Qualitative research collects, analyses, and interprets data that cannot be meaningfully quantified or summarised in the form of numbers (Parasuraman, Grewal & Krishnan, 2007: 178). Qualitative research (also known as "qual research") is mainly concerned with the perceptions, attitudes, and opinions of consumers about organisations, their competitors, and their product offerings (Aaker et al., 2016: 189). This type of exploratory research using small samples attempts to find out what is in a consumer's mind. Lewis, Chambers and Chacko point out that the purpose of qualitative research is usually "to provide information for developing further quantitative research" (1995: 171). The most popular examples include in-depth interviews, focus groups, and projective techniques. Research into backpacking tourism, for instance, might involve conducting qualitative research (in-depth interviews and focus groups) with tourism industry stakeholders such as a representative from the tourism government, the CEO of a backpacking tourism association, a backpacker hostel manager, and a backpacker.

Most qualitative research, which is more in-depth than quantitative research, involves open-ended research in which small samples of targeted individuals are asked to express their views. Generally, qualitative research includes questions that start with "What do you think ...?", "Explain ...", "Why ..." or "Describe ...". This type of research may be conducted on a one-to-one basis or in a focus group situation. For example, in-depth interviews may be conducted with tourism role players to explore their experiences or the feelings that they hold about a current issue in the tourism industry (examples of such issues could include accessibility, pricing set by local tourism businesses, or safety and security). This type of qualitative data can then be used to identify items to be included in a questionnaire.

Quantitative and qualitative research can be combined. This is called "**triangulation**" or "mixed method" research. Triangulation research involves combining several research methods to study one thing. Although triangulation is more complex and resource intensive, the quantitative and qualitative approaches can complement each other to provide deeper insight into the research problem.

> *Triangulation research* is an attempt to map out, or explain more fully, the richness and complexity of human behaviour by studying it from more than one standpoint (Cohen & Manion, 1986: 254).

- ■ **Objectives: Exploratory, Descriptive, and Causal Research**

There are three types of marketing research objectives: exploratory, descriptive, and causal (Baines et al., 2019: 103). **Exploratory research** seeks to develop initial insights and to provide direction for any further research that is needed (Parasuraman, Grewal & Krishnan, 2007: 56). It is an investigation into a problem or situation which provides insight to the researcher and it is used when little is known about a particular management problem and it needs to be explored further (Baines et al., 2019: 103). It clarifies vague situations. Exploratory research is invaluable for the following reasons:

— It serves to shed some light on the nature of a vague situation (in other words, to gather information that will help define the research problem).
— It identifies any specific objectives or data that need to be addressed through additional research.
— It facilitates the discovery of ideas that may be potential business opportunities.
— It can be used to describe the size and composition of the market.

Exploratory research draws on many types of empirical techniques (for example, in-depth interviews, focus groups, pilot studies, surveys, and feasibility studies) and non-empirical techniques (such as secondary data sources and content analysis). (Refer to ◘ Table 4.3). When conducting exploratory research, the researcher ought to be willing to change his or her direction as a result of the discovery of new data or new insights (Saunders, Lewis & Thornhill, 2020: 624).

Descriptive research enables the marketing researcher to describe the tourism phenomenon under investigation. It does not attempt to explain the reasons for the phenomenon (Finn, Elliott-White & Walton, 2000). This type of research generates data describing the characteristics of objects, people, groups, organisations, or environments. In tourism, descriptive research contributes to the development of tourist profiles (for example, socio-demographic profiles), tourist flows and patterns (including information such as statistics on duration of stay, purpose of travel, type of accommodation used, activities engaged in, and expenditure), descriptions of travel experiences, and consumer behaviour (for example, steps in decision-making and consumer typologies). Descriptive research may be developed using quantitative research, qualitative research, or a combination of both methods.

Causal research is usually generated from either exploratory or descriptive research. This type of research is unambiguously linked to the use of a quantitative methodology. It involves the use of variables and the construction of hypotheses to support or reject causal relationships between two or more variables (Jennings, 2010: 18). A tourism marketing researcher, for instance, may consider the following hypothesis: "High admission fees will decrease visitation to the tourist attraction in the off season." Based on this example, the independent variable will be admission fees and the dependent variable will be visitation rates. The researcher would execute the data collection and employ multi-variate statistical

◘ **Table 4.3**   Types of marketing research used in tourism

	Quali-tative	Quanti-tative	Pri-mary	Sec-ond-ary	Examples
Exploratory research	✓		✓		Interviews, focus groups, experiments, and content analysis
Descriptive research	✓	✓	✓	✓	Segmentation, surveys, and secondary data (for example, a theme park's visitor satisfaction survey)
Causal research		✓	✓	✓	Surveys, longitudinal studies, and secondary data (for example, UNWTO, WTTC, or a country's NTO statistics)

Source: Author's creation

techniques such as t-tests and analysis of variance, also called "ANOVA" (for exploring the differences between groups in the sample), and factor analysis (for analysing the interrelationships among variables) to prove or disprove the expected relationship between the two variables (Aaker et al., 2016). If the hypothesis is supported, the data might be used to adjust pricing strategies to increase visitation during the off season. If the hypothesis is rejected, more research may be necessary to determine additional factors that have a negative influence on visitation rates during the off season (such as the weather, people going on holiday, or other events taking place).

Other advanced statistical research techniques include cluster analysis for segmenting a population, exploratory factor analysis for reducing a long list of attributes to a reduced set of common themes, regression analysis, and structural equation modelling (SEM) (for testing the statistical relationships between independent variables and dependent variables).

■ Source: Primary and Secondary Research

Primary research (sometimes referred to as field research) consists of information generated by new research (Bryman, Bell & Harley, 2018: 232). It includes techniques such as surveys, interviews, and observations. It is information collected for the specific purpose at hand. Primary research yields data that fall into two categories: quantitative data and qualitative data (Aaker et al., 2016). Such research is specifically commissioned by an organisation to contribute to its marketing decisions. It requires the gathering of data that is not available from any other secondary or desk source. A survey commissioned by a hotel group to study the current attitudes of business guests towards its own and other hotels competing in the same market is an example of primary research.

Secondary data (sometimes referred to as desk research or documents-and-desk research) yields information that is collected for purposes other than solving the problem at hand. In this sense, the researcher becomes the secondary user of the data (Aaker et al., 2016: 110). All published sources – including government sources, trade association statistics, company annual reports, and commercial companies' market surveys – are classified as secondary data. The United Nations World Tourism Organization (UNWTO), for example, compiles annual reports of statistics on international tourist flows between countries, which regions and countries tourists travel to, tourist-generating countries, foreign tourist expenditure, and so on.

4.5.2 Stage 2: Investigate the Available Sources (Secondary Data or Desk Research)

Once the marketing research problem has been identified and the research objectives or questions have been decided on, the next stage of the marketing research process involves reviewing existing sources of information – both internally and externally – to find out what, if anything, is already known about the problem. This allows the researcher to determine whether primary data (new data collection) is required or not. Primary data collection is invariably costly and time consuming, so it is important to check if the information is not already available (Aaker et al., 2016: 160).

The data that already exists is known as "desk research" or "secondary research" data. A large amount of relevant information may be found in the organisation's existing records (or may have been researched by a competitor). These sources of information are known as "internal databases". They consist of electronic collections of consumer market information obtained from data sources within the organisation network. Information in the database can be derived from many sources. Online reviews such as *TripAdvisor* (based on a rating of 1 to 5 stars), guest history information, bookings, reservations, previous consumer surveys, comment cards, customer databases,, enquiries, conversion percentages (percentage of enquiries to reservations), usage and sales figures or staff debriefs are all examples of internal secondary data. Guest history records enable accommodation marketers to identify repeat guests and their individual needs and preferences. For example, if a guest requests an espresso coffee during one stay, a notation added to the guest's file will ensure that the same coffee is received during all future visits. Listening to and speaking with guests is a powerful source of information and an excellent way to find out what guests think.

The ability to make better use of customer databases is becoming increasingly important. This has arisen partly as organisations have been forced to clean-up their databases because of consumer protection legislation and have realised its potential. Tourism marketers can readily use information in their databases to identify marketing opportunities and problems. The internal data should be analysed to establish whether the research objectives could be realised using only this information. However, it may well be that additional research outside the organisation is required. These external sources of secondary data range from free or inexpensive information (e.g. searching the internet) to relatively expensive reports and publications (e.g. from private consulting companies).

4.5.2.1 The Potential of Secondary Data in Tourism Research

There are several possible tourism research projects that researchers can conduct using secondary data analysis:

- Examining trends over time
- Exploring statistical relationships
- Mapping areas of a region/country
- Making international comparisons.

4.5.2.2 Secondary Data for Tourism and Hospitality

In today's media age, the volume of secondary data available is overwhelming. Tourism and hospitality researchers need to familiarise themselves with the data that is relevant to their research. Most of the data available is quantitative or numerical in nature (such as details of tourist numbers, accommodation occupancy rates, city or country rankings, average tourist spend, contribution to gross domestic product, and so on). Sources of secondary data include academic journals, international bodies, government sources, and commercial sources; as described in ▢ Table 4.4.

Industry Insight 4.5

Tourism Research Information Network (TRINET).

TRINET is an e-mail distribution list that connects members of the international tourism research and education community. Its purpose is to promote an open exchange of ideas, information, and opinions that are relevant to tourism scholarship, including theory, research, education, policy development, and operational matters. Postings are primarily of an intellectual and scholarly nature. TRINET does not accept postings that are purely commercial. Announcements that promote communication, research, education, and scholarship, such as conference announcements, new books, announcements of academic positions, and the availability of funding and scholarship awards, fit the spirit and mission of TRINET.

Source: University of Hawai'i at Mānoa School of Travel Industry Management. (2019) Retrieved from ▶ https://tim.hawaii.edu/about-values-vision-mission-accreditation/trinet/ [3 May 2019].

Table 4.4 Secondary data in tourism and hospitality

Type of secondary data	Description and examples
Refereed academic journals (peer-reviewed)	An academic journal is a periodic publication through which academic research is written by experts and evaluated by other experts (peers) to assess its quality and suitability, and then communicated to wider audiences. Academic journals and books are core sources of secondary data for students and other researchers wishing to access research outcomes in all aspects of tourism and hospitality research. They are most useful for the literature review stage of the research process. Articles in academic journals have the advantage of having undergone a rigorous reviewing process, which increases the quality and objectivity of the published results. Several tourism, hospitality and marketing journals are referred to throughout this textbook.
Academic books and e-books	Academic books on tourism and hospitality management have proliferated since the early 1990s and are an invaluable resource for researchers. Tourism researchers can use e-mail alerts to look for a research topic or gather information (see ▶ Industry Insight 4.5). An e-mail is sent to the researcher when an issue of a journal that he or she is interested in is published. Researchers can also be sent an e-mail alert when articles with certain keywords or written by certain authors are published. Researchers can set up an e-mail alert service with the main journal publishers such as Sage or Elsevier. They can then customise their research results according to areas of interest and receive alerts when relevant articles are cited.
International tourism and hospitality bodies	International governing bodies put together data from central government organisations and national data services. The two most important sources for international tourism statistics are the United Nations World Tourism Organization (UNWTO) and the World Travel and Tourism Council (WTTC). The Organization for Economic Cooperation and Development (OECD) publishes various travel and tourism titles, and the World Economic Forum (WEF) and the International Air Transport Association (IATA) produce various reports which can be found on their websites.
Internet/ online search engines	The internet is an important source of secondary research information, especially as many of the organisations' publications discussed in this section are available online as a more accessible alternative to hard copy. Industry Insight ▶ 4.6 illustrates how a search engine can be utilised to gather literature pertaining to a research subject area. Tourism researchers can also use ResearchGate, a social networking site for scientists and researchers to share papers, ask and answer questions, and find collaborators. The website has over 150 million publications and 15e million members (researchers).
Online databases	There are numerous online databases available to researchers, including EBSCO (▶ ebsco. com) and Cornell University's Hospitality and Tourism Index (▶ johnson.library.cornell. edu/databases/), a bibliographic database covering English language hospitality and tourism journals and trade magazines since the early 1960s.
Government official statistics and public records	Most governments hold more marketing data than other external secondary data sources since they have access under the law to types of data that are impossible for private organisations or individuals to obtain. For example, in the UK, the Office for National Statistics (ONS) provides socio-economic and demographic statistics (referred to as census data). Tourist figures can also be accessed, including the migration of domestic and international tourists, tourist arrivals, hotel occupancy, purpose of visit, mode of travel, where tourists come from, and how much money they spend. Similarly, the UK's DMO VisitBritain undertakes quarterly surveys of the country's inbound tourist arrivals markets. VisitBritain also conducts monthly exit surveys at major land exit points and airports in the country. This research includes findings on international tourists' purpose of visit, travel arrangements, places visited, expenditure, and perceptions of facilities, service levels, and perceptions of safety, as well as overall evaluations of visits.

(continued)

◫ **Table 4.4** (continued)

Type of secondary data	Description and examples
Commercial sources of data	Commercial organisations generate data on areas such as market trends, tourist satisfaction, employment, and expenditure on tourism. However, given the commercial nature of this data, it is very often confidential (referred to as commercial confidentiality) or expensive to access. Tourism reports from commercial research organisations can cost thousands of pounds/dollars. The issue of commercial confidentiality can be tackled by approaching the organisation and emphasising the limited circulation of the research (for example, by stating that the research project will stay within the confines of your university). Large tourism and hospitality organisations such as airlines and major hotel groups have their own research departments and publish annual reports that contain valuable statistical information. (These annual reports are usually available to the public and will be posted to you on request.)
Trade journals, magazines, and newspapers	Trade journals/magazines provide a mix of news items and insights into practice. Trade journals are useful for providing news of recent events as well as tourism and hospitality industry trends and perspectives. Travel trade publications include magazines and newsletters published by various industry organisations as well as government agencies. However, as a source of data, they have the disadvantage of being unscientific and journalistic in orientation. These sources are particularly useful for providing research topic ideas and research problems. Trade journals are not as widely available in university libraries as academic journals; most trade associations, however, will have an associated website.
Theses	Theses are a good source of information when compiling a major research project such as a Masters or PhD. Unfortunately, they can be difficult to locate as well as to access as there may well be only one hard copy at the awarding institution. EThOS is a thesis service which aims to maximise the visibility and availability of the UK's doctoral research theses.
Miscellaneous sources of data	Numerous universities publish research and statistics on their local areas. Examples include the University of The University of Hawai'i at Mānoa School of Travel Industry Management (TIM) Cornell University's Hospitality Database, Articles in Hospitality and Tourism (AHT) (formerly by the University of Surrey and Oxford Brookes), and the Lodging, Restaurant & Tourism Index (LRTI) (formerly by Purdue University). The Hong Kong Polytechnic University houses the International Academy for the Study of Tourism. And the Athens Institute for Education and Research (ATINER) has a Tourism Research Unit which hosts an annual conference and publishes a journal (the Athens Journal of Tourism (AJT). The Cornell Hotel School houses the Center for Hospitality Research (CHR) offers a wide variety of accessible reports aimed at providing specific approaches for addressing hospitality industry issues. The Centre International de Recherches d'Etudes Touristiques (CIRET), an organisation based in France, has created a website consisting of a worldwide directory of academic institutions (850 in 120 countries) and individual researchers (more than 5 400). The 2020 database has computerised in excess of 175 000 documents relating to tourism, leisure, recreation and hospitality, including books, journal papers (with refereed articles from over 180 journals) and reports.

Source: Author's creation

Google Scholar focuses on ▶ scientific and hard-research academic material that has been subjected to scrutiny by scientists and scholars. Example content includes graduate theses, business publications, tourism research, and explanations of economics and world politics.

Source: ▶ https://www.lifewire.com/best-search-engines-2483352

Undertaking an Online Search Using a Search Engine

BA (Hons) Tourism Management student Amahle Madlala decided she wanted to look at dark tourism as her research topic. Her research aim was to look at slum tourism, and how and why consumers make decisions to visit such places. Amahle had already accumulated a number of tourism, leisure management, and sociology journals from ResearchGate and several other databases. However, she decided to search the internet using a general search engine. Amahle's first search, (she typed in "dark tourism") resulted in over 2,670,000 sites and displayed the first ten. Of these, the ninth appeared to be potentially the most useful as it referred to the Institute for Dark Tourism Research (IDTR) based at the University of Central Lancashire (UCLan). She clicked on this link and accessed the home page for the Institute. Eventually, through a series of a few more links, she accessed a number of publications written by researchers associated with the Institute (◻ Image 4.2).

The Institute for Dark Tourism Research (IDTR), based at the University of Central Lancashire, England, is a world-leading academic centre for dark tourism scholarship, research and teaching.

◻ **Image 4.2** UCLan's Institute for Dark Tourism Research's homepage. (Source: Dr. Philip Stone, Director, IDTR, UCLan)

❓ Visit these websites to identify the experts in your field: ► *https://www.google.com/scholar* (Google Scholar), ► *www.academia.net* (Academia.edu, and ► *www.researchgate.net* (ResearchGate).

❓ Browse this website, which monitors web traffic and ranks the most popular sites: ► www.jupiterresearch.com. Compile a list of the top five most popular websites.

❓ Visit these tourism journal and marketing websites:

━ ► http://www.travelweekly.co.uk/
━ ► www.travelbulletin.co.uk
━ ► www.traveldailymedia.com/uk/
━ ► www.marketingweek.com

4.5.3 Stage 3: Devise the Research Plan and Gather Primary Data (Field Research)

After all of the available sources of secondary data have been assessed, a plan must be devised to identify what additional information is required and how to collect it (a meth-

4

odology). The researcher should then conduct primary research. As we have already mentioned, this involves collecting new research information.

We shall first look at various qualitative techniques for gathering primary research data, including interviews, focus groups, and content analysis.

4.5.3.1 Qualitative Research

Very rarely is enough known about a marketing problem for the researcher to be able to proceed into the field to carry out a quantifiable study. Qualitative research is therefore carried out to obtain a basic feel for the problem before the researcher proceeds to the analytical part of the study. Qualitative research methods include open-end (also called "open-ended") questions and are less structured than standard questionnaires. The number of respondents is generally small and therefore findings are not necessarily representative of the entire population. Qualitative methods are, however, excellent for gaining customer insights and perspectives. Today, qualitative research makes use of online bulletin boards, chat rooms, social media, and other devices. The five most widely used qualitative research methods in tourism marketing are individual in-depth interviews, focus groups, observational methods, content analysis, and experiments. These research methods are discussed below.

■ **Individual In-Depth Interviews**

In-depth interviews (also called "depth interviews") are usually conducted face-to-face with the respondent as it is easier for the researcher to detect non-verbal communication (NVC) or body language. The subject matter of the interview is explored in detail (Aaker et al., 2016: 192). Individual (one-on-one) **in-depth interviews** are underrated and should be considered more often by tourism and hospitality marketing researchers. They are useful for the following reasons:

- They can be used in situations where the limited number of subjects (for example, a business's employees) renders quantitative research methods inappropriate.

- Familiarity and flexibility. An interview is a conversation and thus not a completely alien or bizarre way to collect data from someone. They are flexible because they allow you to change the wording and order of the questions that you ask to make sure you obtain the most detail and Information from each person.

- In-depth interviews are particularly useful for gaining information in consumer markets about new product development, product offering benefits, and decision-making.

- They can be used to explore a topic as a preliminary stage in devising a more formal questionnaire.

> An *in-depth interview* is a qualitative data collection method that enables an interviewer to talk to the interviewee one-to-one in order to uncover a consumer's underlying attitudes and/or motivations (Aaker et al., 2016).

In-depth (individual) interviews are seen as the main alternative to focus groups. In-depth interviews, however, avoid responses that are influenced by other people. They have a number of advantages and limitations (see ▢ Table 4.5).

The success of this research method depends entirely on the interviewee and on the expertise of the interviewer since interpretation is critical. In addition, respondents need to be carefully selected to provide representation. Consumers and busy industry role players are often difficult and costly (if travel is involved) to recruit for interviews.

In-depth interviews may be either non-directive or semi-structured (Aaker et al., 2016: 193). In non-directive interviews, the respondent is given complete autonomy to respond to the topic of interest. Interviews, which last between one and two hours, can also be recorded (with the permission of the respondent) so that every word is taped and later transcribed. In semi-structured inter-

Table 4.5 Advantages and disadvantages of in-depth interviews

Advantages	Disadvantages
Flexibility – allow to change wording and order of questions	Lack of replicability – not asking the same questions to all respondents
Familiarity – respondents are used to having an Informal conversation	Researcher must be skilled and well-trained and be a good interviewer
High awareness	Time consuming and interviewer fatigue
In-depth probing	Small sample size
Presence of non-verbal feedback	Can be subjective (due to interviewer presence)
No group pressure	Participants must be carefully chosen to avoid bias

Source: Author's creation

views (also called "focused individual interviews"), the interview covers a list of topics or subareas. This type of interview is more demanding than non-directive interviews and requires more skill as the interviewer must decide how much time to allocate to each question area. Semi-structured interviews are effective with executives and thought leaders. Semi-structured interviews do have a structure based around creating a question (an interview) guide which lists the main elements that need to be addressed during the interview. The content of the interview guide should be based on your research questions/objectives and the guide should be memorised. You should start with easy questions - asking the respondent basic questions about their opinions on the topic or their general experience. Test the Interview guide with a friend or colleague In order to gain feedback and practice your Interviewing skills.

Interviews need to be succinct. They are typically fifteen minutes to three-quarters of an hour long (although they may last as long as two-and-a-half hours).

> *Projective techniques* or what-if techniques get subjects to respond to hypothetical or projected situations.

■ **Focus Groups**

A **focus group** is a qualitative technique for interviewing. The principal difference between a focus group and an individual in-depth interview is that in a focus group, the main line of communication is between the respondents themselves rather than between an interviewer and a respondent. Focus groups have been widely used in marketing research since the late 1980s. By definition, a focus group interview is a meeting of between six and ten people, led by a moderator, who meet for 90–120 minutes to discuss ideas, feelings, and experiences related to a specific topic (Cooper & Schindler, 2014: 230). The group may consist of current or past clients. Open-end questions are used to prompt participants to discuss a topic such as the introduction of a new product offering (a hotel, destination, or food item on a menu, for example) freely. They are used to gain insight into a particular destination market. Open-end questions are used when, for example, the members of a focus group are shown a draft brochure and asked their opinion of a destination that a tour operator is intending to offer to its customers. The moderator guides the discussion in order to probe attitudes to a particular tourism offering more deeply (see ► Industry Insight 4.7). It is important that the moderator ensure that the group remains objective and that their egos or other factors do not taint or swing their opinions. The group discussion is often video recorded so that it can be studied later to observe the participants' interest and buying behaviour. In addition, participants usually receive an incentive for their time (such as a gift or a cash amount).

> A *focus group* is a research method in which the researcher acts as a facilitator to obtain the views of six to ten people about a particular topic.

4

Industry Insight 4.7

Professional Focus Group Moderator

Mary Olsen is a professional focus group moderator specialising in the hospitality sector. She has moderated many focus group sessions for companies such as British Airways as well as the hotel chains Travelodge and Holiday Inn. For the hotel chains, the group focused on a needs analysis, looking at business and leisure travellers' expectations of hotels in the UK. Olsen points out, "In the hospitality industry, focus groups centre mostly on needs analysis, whether it be service excellence or how consumers perceive the offering."

Source: Based on an interview with Mary Olsen, focus group moderator.

According to Aaker et al. (2016: 200) and Babin and Zikmund (2016: 99), the following factors are necessary to ensure the success of a focus group:
- Careful recruitment of respondents to ensure a reasonably representative sample
- Provision of an inviting venue and incentivisation of focus group attendance by making the event more enjoyable (for example, offering cheese and wine to respondents)
- Preparation of a comprehensive interview (or discussion) guide that has been edited and checked by academics and practitioners to ensure that the objectives of research are met.
- Use of a professional moderator to facilitate discussion
- Recording of the discussion to be used for future analysis and reference
- Provision of a small thank you gift for respondents as a token of appreciation.

Industry Insight 4.8

Rural Tourism Focus Group Research

Research was carried out into rural tourism in Botswana. The study utilised focus groups to investigate the perceptions of stakeholders on the opportunities that would be created for the poor by opening up Botswana's forest reserves for eco-tourism. Tourism now ranks second after mining in its contribution to Botswana's GDP. Research data was collected using mixed methods involving in-depth interviews with government departments, traditional leaders, quasi-government organisations, and the Hospitality and Tourism Association of Botswana. In addition, several focus group discussions were held with village development committees as well as members of the Chobe Enclave Conservation Trust (CECT) and the Kasane, Lesoma, and Pandamatenga Trust (KALEPA). The study found that opening up forest reserves for eco-tourism has the potential to alleviate poverty among the disadvantaged groups living adjacent to these reserves through direct effects (employment, and small- and medium-sized enterprises [SMEs]), secondary effects (linkages and partnerships), and dynamic effects (sustainable livelihoods). The study concluded by cautioning that whilst pro-poor tourism may yield short- and medium-term benefits, in keeping with sustainability objectives, participants in the programme need to be mindful of forestry encroachment and come up with strategies to ensure the sustainability of the Botswana forest reserves.

Source: Manwa, H. & Manwa, F. (2014). Poverty alleviation through pro-poor tourism: The role of Botswana forest reserves. Sustainability 2014, 6.

Virtual focus groups have become a commonly used research tool in the tourism and hospitality industry in recent years. Focus group interviews can be conducted online, in which case they are referred to as 'online chat sessions'. They enable respondents to speak as well as type in responses to a guided online discussion. They are effective for bringing together participants from anywhere in the world to discuss an issue or experience, or to provide product feedback. They are also useful when travel and contact is not possible such as during an endemic (as was the case in 2020 during the Coronavirus outbreak). They are a cost-saving and time-saving research tool in that travel is not required. However, they lack the personalisation that traditional face-to-face focus groups offer.

■ Content Analysis

Content analysis is also a form of human observation. Content analysis describes a variety of techniques that are used to examine and measure the meaning of communicated material systematically by classifying and evaluating selected words, themes, or images (Wheeler, 1994: 581). It is a qualitative means of analysing non-statistical written material. The unit of analysis may be any of the following:

- Words (different words or types of words in the message)
- Characters (individuals or objects)
- Themes (propositions)
- Space and time measures
- Topics (subject of the message) (Malhotra, Birks & Nunan, 2017).

Content analysis is primarily used for the study and interpretation of communication content. It can be applied to items such as newspaper articles and advertisements, television, and radio programmes or advertisements, books, letters and diaries (Finn et al., 2000: 135). In the context of tourism research, material such as tour operators' holiday brochures, destination promotional brochures and posters, the travel pages in newspapers, holiday postcards and travel blog sites (see ▶ Industry Insight 4.9) could be analysed. For example, content analysis is increasingly being used in tourist destination image (TDI) research, in which destination marketers seek to examine the images portrayed in holiday brochures (see ▶ Chap. 14).

Industry Insight 4.9

Content Analysis of Travel Blog Sites

Research by Pan, MacLaurin, and Crotts analysed visitor opinions posted on leading travel blog sites to gain an understanding of the consumer destination experience. Travel blogs on Charleston, South Carolina, United States, were collected through the three most popular travel blog sites and three blog search engines. Blogs were analysed using content analysis to ascertain what bloggers were communicating about their travel experiences. Study findings revealed that major strengths of the destination were its attractions, historic charm, Southern hospitality, beaches, and water activities. Major weaknesses included poor weather, inadequate infrastructure, and too many fast-service restaurants. Qualitative results demonstrated that travel blogs are an inexpensive way of gathering rich, authentic, and unsolicited customer feedback. As information technology advances, travel blogs are increasingly being used as a cost-effective method for destination marketers to assess their service quality and improve travellers' overall experiences.

Source: Pan, B., MacLaurin, T. & Crotts, J.C. (2007). Travel Blogs and the Implications for Destination Marketing. Journal of Travel Research, 46(1), 34.

An example of content analysis is a marketing researcher recording the number and type of gay images that appear in Australian travel guidebooks on the city of Sydney. This could also involve analysing the images that appear in tourism advertisements of the city of Sydney and classifying the context in which Sydney is mentioned (for example, a researcher might find 54 references to gay nightlife (bars and clubs), 28 references to gay beaches, and 21 references to gay accommodation). Content analysis provides a good indication of the destination's development trend and changing image, which could be useful in testing the validity of Butler's (1980) tourism area life cycle (TALC) model (see ▶ Chap. 14).

4.5.3.2 Quantitative Research

The purpose of quantitative research is to measure the situation or phenomenon and generalise the results to the wide population (that is, to infer that the findings from the research sample can be applied to a wider population with a moderate level of confidence (Pike & Larkin, 2010). The three main quantitative methods used in tourism are observation, experiments, and surveys.

■ Observation

Observational methods are another widely used exploratory research technique. Researchers using this method collect primary data by observing the actions of people and their buying behaviour. No interviews are involved, although an interview may be used as a follow-up activity to obtain additional information. Examples of this method include counting foot traffic, such as in along a high street where an up-market restaurant is located, observing (and counting) vehicle movement past an advertising billboard, and counting the number of unoccupied spaces in the car park at different times of the day or week to determine a visitor attraction's usage rate. Other applications include the following:

— Recording the average length of time that visitors to a theme park have to wait in a queue before gaining entry and noting their body language
— Counting and observing the behaviour of a number of people who attend a festival
— Following a tour group to observe the behaviour and spatial distribution of the group
— Observing guests at a hotel's new self-service restaurant, and then asking them if they prefer this style of service.
— Observational methods may be useful in situations where a questionnaire or interview might be inappropriate, for example, evaluating competitors' offerings, including internet websites, brochures, menus, price lists, and point-of-sale promotions.
— Information can be gathered through direct human observation or through mechanical observation (including the use of video cameras to record patterns of consumer behaviour).

Human observation includes, for instance, a travel agency or hotel sending an observer who pretends to be a customer, known as a" mystery shopper", to a branch or hotel to provide feedback on customer service. Mystery shopping is a technique used to explore the customer relationship in hospitality, tourism, and retail businesses (Miller, Hudson & Turner, 2005). It is a process for measuring service quality with feedback that is understandable to all members of staff. A mystery shopping programme can be used as "an assessment tool for evaluating and improving consumer service" (Erstad, 1998: 34).

A wide range of businesses use ethnographic research. This involves sending trained observers to watch and interact with consumers in their natural habitat. **Ethnographic research** allows researchers to gather information and acquire a rich understanding of consumers that is not obtainable from more traditional research methods such as questionnaires and focus groups. It allows researchers to gain insights into the thoughts of consumers. Ethnographers directly observe the population they are studying (Lamb, Hair & McDaniel, 2012).

Ethnographic research or the study of human and behaviour, is the observation of behaviour and physical setting (Lamb, Hair & McDaniel, 2012).Observational methods have various advantages. They can provide information that people are normally unwilling or unable to provide. Consumers (or employees) are usually unaware that they are being observed, so they presumably behave in their usual fashion (unself-conscious behaviour). Thus, observational methods result in unbiased data.

Observation can show how consumers or employees behave, but it cannot tell researchers why they behave in a certain way. Researchers cannot deduce the motives, attitudes, or opinions of consumers. In addition, the idea of personal observation raises some ethical questions about how and when it is acceptable to spy on paying guests. On the other hand, such observation could be seen as a logical extension of the concept of managing by walking about. Ideally, observational methods should be used to accompany other research methods, such as individual interviews and surveys.

- **Experiments**

Experiments are most effective for gathering causal information (Armstrong et al., 2009). Experiments are usually carried out in a laboratory setting where the researcher has complete control over the environment. Mechanical devices are able to measure subjects' physical responses. For example, advertisers use eye cameras to study viewers' eye movements while they are being shown an advertisement. Researchers observe the point on which their eyes focus first and how long they linger on any given component of the advertisement. Facial imaging software, pupil dilation and eye tracking are other examples of advanced experimental methodologies that are increasingly being used by marketers. However, there are other methods of experimentation that can be carried out away from the laboratory. For example, a travel agent may decide to experiment by moving brochures in a display around to see how this affects selection (Holloway, 2004: 83).

An example of experimenting with promotional activities could be launching a new promotion in one region of the country, and then comparing results against another region or city, where standard promotional activities have been taking place. Measuring the difference in sales can indicate how successful the new campaign has been and what its potential is for widespread usage. These methods are often referred to as "test marketing". Experiments can help the marketer to determine the correct marketing mix for the launch of a new tourism offering. For example, identical rooms of a new hotel may be priced lower in a town than in the centre of a country's capital city. The method is effective in helping establish if there is a **causal relationship** between two variables, in other words, if a change in one variable produces a change in another. In this example, marketers are comparing the price variables or differences.

A *causal relationship* means that a change in one variable produces a change in another variable (Fraenkel, Wallen, Hyun, 2011: 376).

Experimental methods, partic-ularly test marketing in a laboratory set-ting, are expensive and time consuming. Test marketing is also difficult to keep secret from competitors, who may unin-tentionally disrupt the experiment by adjusting the marketing mix (for example, price, distribution, and promotion) of their similar or competing offerings.

❓ Discuss the following statement by John Sculley, President of PepsiCo (1977–1983) and CEO of Apple (1983–1993): "No great marketing decisions have ever been made on qualitative data."

❓ Perhaps if Sculley had made use of qualitative research, Pepsi would have been able to take a larger percentage of the Cola market.

Unfortunately, Pepsi-Cola has never been able to achieve the success of Coca-Cola (except for a short period after the Britney Spears advertisements).

■ Surveys

In this section, we look at the role of various survey contact methods. A survey contact method is a medium of data collection in which respondents are contacted in one or more various ways (for example, by post, via the internet, or by mobile phone) (Malhotra, Birks & Nunan, 2017).

The survey method is one of the most commonly used methods in tourism marketing research projects (Brunt, 1997: 4). The purpose of a survey is to obtain reliable and valid data on the subject being researched. The survey method involves gathering descriptive information by interviewing the sample members (Bryman, 2016: 233). It invariably consists of a questionnaire, which is a series of questions designed to help solve the problems (that is, the research statement and objec-

tives) that the researcher is investigating (Brunt, 1997: 7) (see ◘ Image 4.3). The survey questions are usually put to respondents via survey (postal, in-house, internet, or mobile) over the telephone, or during the course of a personal interview, or. The choice of survey method is influenced by the availability of time, money, access to respondents, trained personnel, and facilities. Some of these survey contact methods have associated advantages and disadvantages (see ◘ Table 4.6).

The six survey contact methods are discussed in more detail below.

■ ■ Postal Surveys

This method involves posting a questionnaire to potential respondents and having them return the completed form by mail (a stamped, self-addressed envelope is usually included). Postal surveys (sometimes referred to as mail surveys or mail questionnaires) are particularly useful in covering a large geographical area and may include the whole of a state, county or province or even the entire country.

◘ **Image 4.3** A questionnaire - devised for the purposes of a survey or statistical study. (Source: Unsplash)

⬛ **Table 4.6** A comparison of survey contact methods

Criteria	Postal survey	In-house survey	internet survey	Mobile survey	Telephone survey	Personal interview
Cost	Moderate to high	Low	Low	High	Moderate	High
Response time	Slow	Fast	Fast	Very fast	Fast	Very fast
Ability to reach geographically dispersed segments	High	Very low	Very high	Very low	Medium	Very low
Length of questionnaire	Long (between four and twelve pages)	Short (five to ten minutes)	Long (between four and twelve pages)	Short (five to ten minutes)	Short (five to ten minutes)	Medium (ten minutes to half an hour)
Questionnaire complexity	Simple to moderate	Simple only	Simple to moderate	Simple to moderate	Simple only	Simple to complex
Respondent anonymity	Possible	Possible	Possible	Not possible	Not possible	Not possible
Rapport with respondents	None	Moderate	None	Moderate to high	Moderate	High
Potential for interviewer bias	None	None	None	Medium to low	Moderate	High
Need for trained interviewer	None	None	None	Very high	High	Very high
Response rate	Low	Low	Moderate	Moderate	Moderate	High

Source: Adapted from Baines, P., Fill, C., Rosengren, S. and Antonetti, P. (2019). *Marketing*, 5th edn. Oxford: Oxford University Press, p. 105; Aaker, D., Kumar, V., Leone, R. and Day, G. (2016). *Marketing Research*, 12th edn. New York: John Wiley & Sons, p. 444

Postal surveys require quite a complex procedure: identifying respondents and their physical postal addresses, mailing them the questionnaire, waiting for the responses, and making up a mail interview package. This consists of an outgoing envelope, a covering letter, a questionnaire, a return envelope, and an incentive.

■■ **In-House Surveys**

These are surveys provided for consumers to complete when they are on the premises of tourism organisations. Examples of in-house surveys are the customer comment cards found on restaurant tables and survey forms on board planes (see ⬛ Image 4.4), in visitor attractions, at car rental outlets, and in hotel rooms. These types of surveys are usually used to determine consumer satisfaction regarding service and quality of offering.

❓ Obtain an in-house survey from a tourism organisation (for example, a hotel, a quick-service restaurant [QSR], a visitor attraction, or a transport provider). Produce a report in which you:

— Critically evaluate the content, layout and design of the survey
— Develop a new in-house survey for your chosen organisation.

4

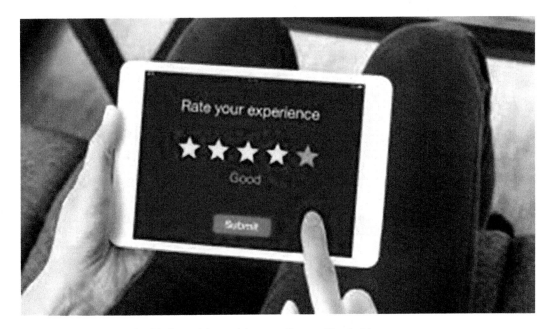

■ **Image 4.4**   An example of in-house (electronic) survey. (Source: Unsplash)

■ ■ Online Surveys

Internet technology is changing the role of marketing survey research. Online surveys (internet surveys, survey software, web-based surveys, or eSurveys) are surveys sent electronically via the internet or e-mail. Advantages of online survey generators are that they make it easy to set up a basic survey. The generated surveys are of high quality. In addition, they are fast and inexpensive. No interviewers are involved in web-based surveys, eliminating interviewer bias or error. Internet surveys allow the researcher to have much more control over data quality than other survey contact methods. With this type of survey, the questionnaire is posted on a secure website where clients and researchers can view responses simultaneously as soon as any respondent has answered the questions. This allows for immediate review and analysis of responses.

Online surveys are easy for participants to access and complete online. They are also professional in appearance. SurveyMonkey (see ■ Image 4.5) is one example of a survey soft-

ware program (a survey generator) that allows researchers to set up a survey questionnaire on the SurveyMonkey website (▶ surveymonkey. co.uk). Research assistants can then download the questionnaire to their smartphones and, while conducting an interview, enter survey responses into their smartphones. When the interview is finished, the researcher automatically sends the survey responses to SurveyMonkey. This greatly shortens and simplifies the task of analysing survey data. SurveyMonkey is free for surveys of ten questions or fewer. Another example of a popular online survey generator is the Bristol Online Survey (BOS), which makes it easy to set up both basic and more advanced surveys. The BOS, however, requires a subscription to use. As with SurveyMonkey, participants access the eSurvey via an internet link and complete it online. It also records responses automatically, and provides the researcher with an overview and analysis of the responses. Other popular online survey platforms (or survey generators) include Google Forms, SurveyGizmo, and Zoho Survey.

Choose from our most popular plans

Get an individual plan with features that fit your needs, or create a team instead!

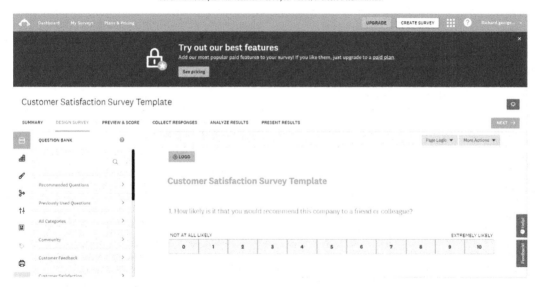

□ **Image 4.5** SurveyMonkey's (a survey generator) homepage

How to compile a Google Forms survey:
1. Navigate to ▶ www.docs.google.com/forms/ or click on Forms in Google, or access from Google Drive
2. Choose a blank or template form
3. Tap on Untitled form and give the survey name
4. Choose a colour code, a theme or upload a photo for background
5. Tap on Untitled Question and give the question a title
6. Choose type of question (MCQ, multiple question, short answer, drop-down, etc.)
7. Example, click Multiple choice
8. Provide options for answers (e.g. Option 1) (questions and options can be moved around and duplicated)
9. Images and videos can be uploaded
10. Add sections
11. Click the side menu icons to add to your survey.
12. Click the Required switch to make a question mandatory.
13. Preview the survey (Form)
14. Send out survey (via e-mail) or e-mail link to survey, embed URL address into your website

View summary of responses.

■ ■ Mobile Surveys

Mobile surveys (including hand-held computers) are growing in popularity, perhaps because they are short and quick. Mobile surveys generate large samples and use simple automatic response questions. They are more likely to elicit truthful responses than cumbersome traditional surveys. Many consumers now use smartphones, which are becoming more affordable, increasing representativity.

❓ Conduct a survey (personal interview or face-to-face interview) to research a special interest tourism (SIT) market (for example, adventure tourism, edutourism, health tourism or cycling tourism) in your country. Interview tourists in this market to establish their demographic characteristics (age, gender, social class, and level of education) and their buying behaviour (reason for participating, frequency of usage and how much they spend). Produce a report detailing your methodology and findings and outline the implications of your results (in other words, state recommendations) for your country's national tourism organisation.

■ ■ Telephone Surveys

In a telephone survey (or telephone interview), the respondent is contacted by telephone or mobile phone and the interview is completed at that time.

A large percentage of telephone interviews are conducted with the aid of computers. Most commercial survey organisations carrying out telephone interviewing utilise **computer-assisted telephone interviewing (CATI)**. The questions that comprise an interview schedule appear on a computer (laptop) screen. As the researcher asks each question, he or she inputs the responses, and then proceeds to the next question.

> *Computer-assisted telephone interviewing* (CATI) is a technique for survey data collection in which the respondent uses a computer to complete the survey questionnaire without an interviewer administering it to the respondent (Lavrakas, 2015).

■ ■ Personal (Face-to-Face) Interviews

There are three types of personal or face-to-face interview: door-to-door, intercept, and executive interviewing. Personal interviews involve interviewing people in their homes (door-to-door), in a public place such as in the street, at an airport, at an event, at a visitor attraction, at a shopping centre (intercept) or in their offices (executive). An intercept interview is a popular research method in tourism. For instance, the Dublin Convention Centre utiises this technique to interview several thousand delegates each year. Interviewing is carried out at different locations in the centre and at different times of the day. After the interviews, delegates are given souvenirs as a form of reward.

■ Sampling Plan

In order to carry out any one of the qualitative interviews (that is, in-depth interviews and focus group interviews) and survey contact methods discussed above, the researcher needs to select who is going to be interviewed or surveyed. It is virtually impossible to interview all of the people concerned, so a sample has to be chosen. A sample is a segment of the population selected for marketing research to represent the population as a whole.

Marketers in search of data often find that it is practical to gather information from sample groups of people rather than a whole research population. It is sufficient to collect data from a sample if the reactions of the people surveyed represent the entire group. For instance, a researcher might interview a sample of 500 international tourists about their holiday experiences in a particular country rather than all of the hundreds of thousands of international tourists who arrive in the country every month.

The sampling process involves six decisions or stages, which we look at below.

- Stage 1: Who is to be interviewed/surveyed? (Defining the target unit or 'sampling population'). This is the first decision. It is very important that marketers choose the right people when undertaking a survey or interview. The result of a sampling study is no better than the sample on which it is based. A balanced and complete picture of the market is required. An unbalanced sample will give a distorted picture. Choosing a balanced sample is not always as straightforward as it appears. Should all international tourists to the UK be interviewed, for example, or only those who have come on business? Should tourists who are visiting friends and relatives be interviewed, or tourists who are visiting the country for religious or educational reasons?

- Stage 2: Can a sampling frame be drawn? Researchers attempt to obtain sampling frames (listings, databases, directories or rosters of all the known cases in a population) from which the sample will be chosen. Examples of sampling frames include a tour operator's database and a destination marketing organisation's membership list. It is important that the sample of respondents contribute to the research objectives. If an organisation targets business travellers, it would be a waste of time to interview holidaymakers. Other groups and tourist stakeholders, such as destination marketing organisations, travel agents, inbound tour operators and hotel managers, will need to be interviewed.

- Stage 3: How many people should be surveyed? (Determining the sample size). Thirdly, the sample size (the number of subjects included in a sample) should be determined. This is perhaps the most difficult aspect of sampling. In general, larger sample populations are more accurate than smaller ones. However, it is not neces-

sary to sample the entire target market or a large portion to obtain reliable results.

- Stage 4: How should the people in the sample be chosen? (Selecting the sampling procedure). There are several approaches that can be followed when choosing a sample. Time and costs are factors that researchers should consider when deciding on the sampling approach. Sample members might be chosen at random from the entire population. For instance, a researcher might randomly (by chance) select international tourists on arrival at the airport. The tourism researcher might select people from whom it is the easiest to obtain information, for example, tourists who are staying nearby (a convenience sample) or a specified number of participants (a quota sample) from one of the targeted demographic groups (for example, students, single travellers, or females over 55). If a sampling frame (see stage 3 above) is being used, then the researcher can make use of probability sampling (or random sampling). This means that everyone (name or thing) in the sampling frame has an equal chance of being surveyed. (In other words, every person on a travel agent, a tour operator, or a destination marketing organisation's database is equally likely to be chosen if that database is the sampling frame.) The test of the random sample is this: "Does every name or thing in the whole group have an equal chance of being in the sample?" Where a sampling frame does not exist, non-probability sampling is used. In non-probability sampling, all elements do not have an equal chance of being selected. (This is the case in, for example, a survey conducted at an airport, at a shopping mall, at a visitor attraction, or on the street). This type of research sampling is not random as such. Non-probability sampling techniques are common in emerging markets as a result of time and financial constraints as well as the problem of obtaining respondents. If market research is being conducted at a visitor attraction or event, pre-determined entry and exit points provide suitable points for obtaining a fair sample. Probability sampling is the preferred sampling method in tourism research, as it is more precise than other methods and can also be used for more advanced statistical analysis techniques. For instance, inferential statistics – values calculated from a sample used to estimate the same value for a population – should be used only for probability samples.

> In *non-probability sampling*, the sample is selected in such a way that the chance of any member of a unit within the population or universe being selected is unknown (Bryman, Bell & Harley, 2018: 222).

— Stage 5: When will the survey be carried out? (Deciding on timing). The researcher has to decide on timing, in other words, when the survey method will be administered. Example ▶ 4.10 illustrates the tim-

ing considerations for New Zealand's tourism research department, which carries out visitor surveys during the off season and during peak periods. A visitor attraction survey carried out during peak season will reflect mainly tourists who are visiting a destination for leisure reasons, whereas a survey conducted during the off season is most likely to be completed by other types of tourists, such as tourists who are visiting friends and relatives or tourists who are arriving for business reasons. Therefore, researchers desiring information on all three types of tourist should conduct surveys during both busy and quieter periods, on different days of the week and at different times of the year, to provide more representative and reliable results. More defined results can be gained during specific time periods.

— Stage 6: Drawing the sample and collecting the data. The last stage in the sampling process is implementation. During this stage, the sample is chosen and surveyed.

Industry Insight 4.10

New Zealand's International Visitor Survey
New Zealand's government department the Ministry of Business Innovation & Employment (MBIE) conducts research on international tourists visiting the country. The Ministry undertakes tourism projections and produces a range of useful tourism data tools and publications. The International Visitor Survey (IVS) measures the travel patterns and expenditure of international visitors to New Zealand. Data includes expenditure, places visited, activities/attractions, accommodation and transport. The survey is carried out four times a year, at quarterly intervals. In this way, differences in

market composition, purposes of travel, length of stay, expenditure patterns and so on, which may be associated with different seasons, can be identified. Foreign tourists departing from the NZ's international airports are asked to complete a questionnaire while they wait in departure lounges to board their flights. The objective of the survey is to determine foreign visitors' travel patterns and opinions about the country's infrastructure and facilities.

Retrieved from: ▶ http://www.mbie.govt.nz/info-services/sectors-industries/tourism/tourism-research-data/ivs *[Online], Accessed 29 March 2017.*

The sampling process has a direct impact on the validity of the results of the study. Thus, if the survey method is the primary research technique for data collection, careful consideration must be given to the technique administered (see ▢ Table 4.7) and the sample size chosen.

❷ A Spanish holiday resort company, Club La Santa, has approached you to do some research into repositioning the company. It currently attracts the family market (quire up-market and exclusive) and would like to target new markets. The chain's holiday resorts are located in coastal areas around

Table 4.7 Types of samples	
Probability sample	**Non-probability sample**
Simple random sample: Every member of the population has a known and equal chance of selection.	Convenience sample: The researcher selects the easiest population members from which to obtain information.
Stratified random sample: The population is divided into mutually exclusive groups (such as age groups) and random samples are drawn from each group.	Judgment sample: The researcher uses his or her judgment to select population members who are good prospects for accurate information.
Cluster (area) sample: The population is divided into mutually exclusive groups (such as blocks) and the researcher draws a sample of the groups to interview.	Quota sample: The researcher finds and interviews a prescribed number of people in each of several categories.

Source: Author's creation

the country and offer self-catering accommodation facilities, including caravan parks and chalets. Each resort offers conference facilities, a playground, family entertainment, indoor and outdoor sports activities, a spa and a swimming pool. The resort group may consider offering new facilities and products. Design a research plan to solve management's problem.

- ■ **Questionnaire Design**

After the researcher has decided on the sample, the design of the questionnaire needs to be determined. A questionnaire is a series of questions put to respondents to address the identified research objectives. There are numerous ways to ask questions. Open-end questions allow subjects to answer in their own words. These types of questions enable the researcher to find out what people think about a product, organisation or destination, but do not reveal how many people think in a certain way. An example of an open-end question is: "What is your opinion of the service offered by Sea View Hotel?" Closed-end questions include all possible answers, from which respondents make their choices. Closed questions are easier to process answers and are easy for interviewers and/or respondents to complete. **Likert scale** or rating, ranking, scale, filter (or screening) and category are all examples of closed-end questions. ■ Table 4.8 provides some examples of both open-end and closed-end questions used in questionnaires.

> A *Likert scale* is a questionnaire scale (usually a five- or seven-point scale) asking respondents to indicate how much they agree or disagree with a statement, approve or disapprove of it, or believe it to be true or false (Allen & Seaman, 2007).

All six survey contact methods –postal surveys, in-house surveys, internet (web-based) surveys, mobile (computer interactive) surveys, and telephone surveys, personal (one-to-one) interviews,– normally require a questionnaire. One of the keys to getting quality research information (data) is a well-designed questionnaire that is well organised and professional. The people being questioned are more likely to co-operate if they feel that the questionnaire is interesting, important, and easy to complete (Morgan, 1996: 59). Furthermore, a well-organised questionnaire makes analysis later on in the research process easier. Some of the guidelines recommended for effective questionnaire design are discussed in ■ Table 4.9 below.

Ethics in research is about following good moral principles. As an academic researcher, you should aim to bring integrity to your work, and should respect the welfare, rights, and safety of all potential stakeholders. Design and implement a short survey questionnaire to identify the main market segments using a tourism organisation. Once you have completed the survey, discuss with the rest of the group how your questionnaire

4

■ **Table 4.8** Types of survey questions

Name	Description	Example
Closed-end questions		
Dichotomous	A question with two possible answers	Is this your first visit to the Warrior Toy Museum? Yes/No
Multiple choice	A question with three or more answers	With whom are you travelling during this visit to the Warrior Toy Museum? No one / Children only / Spouse / Friend / Spouse and children / As part of a tour group
Likert scale	A scale showing the respondent's extent of agreement or disagreement with a statement	Rate the service you received here today at the Warrior Toy Museum café, on a scale of 1–5 (1 = excellent; 5 = poor). Circle the rating that best applies

Under the Likert scale example:

	1	2	3	4	5
The availability of staff	1	2	3	4	5
The welcome you received	1	2	3	4	5
How quickly you were served	1	2	3	4	5
Value for money	1	2	3	4	5
The quality of food	1	2	3	4	5

Name	Description	Example
Semantic differential	A continuum of bi-polar (opposite) attitudes (feelings)	The Warrior Toy Museum is: Interesting _____ Boring / Modern _____ Old-fashioned / Inexpensive _____ Expensive
Rating scale	A scale that rates an attribute from "poor" to "excellent"	The Warrior Toy Museum is: [tick box] Excellent (1) / [tick box] Very good (2) / [tick box] Good (3) / [tick box] Fair (4) / [tick box] Poor (5)
Importance scale	A scale that rates the importance of an attribute	To me, service at a museum is: The Warrior Toy Museum is: [tick box] Extremely important (1) / [tick box] Very important (2) / [tick box] Quite important (3) / [tick box] Not very important (4) / [tick box] Not at all important (5)
Open-end questions		
Unstructured	A question that respondents can answer in any way	What is your opinion of the Warrior Toy Museum?

▫ Table 4.8 (continued)

Name	Description	Example
Word association	Words are presented, one at time, and the survey respondent mentions the first word that comes to mind	What is the first word that comes to mind when you hear these words? Toy _____ Museum _____ Warrior _____
Sentence completion	An incomplete sentence is presented, and survey respondents complete the sentence	When I decide to go to a museum, the most important consideration is _____ _____

Source: Author's creation

could have been improved. For example, did all of the respondents understand the questions?

■ **Customer Satisfaction Questionnaires**

Researching customer satisfaction has become increasingly important in the tourism industry as organisations seek to achieve competitive advantage. Customer satisfaction and quality have become buzzwords, but they are rarely defined. Quality is about the product or service offered, while satisfaction is concerned with how consumers perceive these offerings and whether or not they think that their needs have been met effectively (Horner & Swarbrooke, 2004: 290).

Researching customer needs involves identifying the benefits that customers expect in a service (see ▶ Industry Insight 4.11). It is advisable to carry out some qualitative research techniques before devising a customer satisfaction questionnaire (CSQ). Unfortunately, many companies do superficial research, often developing surveys on the basis of intuition or company direction rather than through customer probing.

Customer Survey Reveals Southern Fails on Passenger Satisfaction

A survey shows that Southern railway failed to hit satisfaction targets in punctuality, delays, helpfulness of staff, station upkeep, overcrowding, passenger information and seating. Only 53 per cent of passengers were satisfied with punctuality compared with a minimum target of 72 per cent. A mere 25 per cent thought the company dealt well with delays; set against a target of 35 per cent. Southern, which operates between London and the south coast, face management issues such as staff shortages and strikes.

Source: Paton, Graeme. (2016). The Times. 'Southern fails on passenger satisfaction'. Saturday 13 August, p. 6.

4

| Table 4.9 | Effective questionnaire design guidelines |

Guidelines	Description
Relevance	The questions that you will ask in your self-completion questionnaire or structured interview should always be geared to answering your research objectives. Thus, you should ask questions that relate to your research objectives; there is little point in asking questions that do not relate to your research questions.
Length	Avoid consumer or respondent fatigue by making sure that the questionnaire is not too long. Ensure that individual questions are short, simple and to the point.
Question purpose and wording of questions	Avoid making assumptions (for example, the question, "How many overseas holidays have you been on over the last year?" assumes that the respondent actually has been on an overseas holiday in the last year. Use simple words and plain, everyday language in questions. Avoid technical terms (for example, an instruction such as, "Answer the following quantitative questions" may confuse respondents). Avoid jargon or shorthand. Respondents might not understand acronyms, trade jargon, and words commonly used by tourism practitioners and researchers (for example, "Are you a member of your local DMO?"). Avoid hypothetical questions. It is difficult for respondents to answer questions on imaginary situations (for example, "If you had £/€10 000 to spend on an overseas holiday …?"). Although it is important to make questions as specific and succinct as possible, there may be occasions when it is advisable to lengthen the questions by adding memory cues. For example, a researcher could refer to specific time periods by asking questions such as, "How many times have you been on holiday in the last twelve months?" Avoid double-barrelled questions and estimates. (Double-barrelled questions are ones that in fact ask about two things.) Every question should focus on a single issue. The words "and" and "or" often indicate a double-barrelled question and should not be used. Do not use ambiguous, leading, or assumptive language. Words such as "often", "recently", "frequently", "regularly", and "usually" can be interpreted differently by different respondents and need qualifying (for example, "How many times per year do you usually go on a domestic holiday?"). Think about how the survey will be administered. This will determine the framing of the questions (for example, open-end questions usually result in poor responses in self-completion questionnaires). Ask yourself whether a respondent will be able to answer a question. Does he or she have the information you want? Think about the possible answers at the same time as thinking about the questions. Do not rely too much on stretching respondents' memories to the extent that some of the answers are likely to be inaccurate (for example, "How much money did you spend whilst on this holiday?")

◼ Table 4.9 (continued)

Guidelines	Description
Layout/ question sequence	Include a date or a reference number. Include a questionnaire title. Include an introduction (also referred to as the boiler plate) at the start of the questionnaire or in a separate cover letter. the introduction briefly stating the purpose of the questionnaire, how long it should take (be honest with the respondent on approximately how long the survey will take to complete) and if the respondent must answer all questions. Include information about the importance of the research. State that the information that the respondent provides will remain confidential and explain how the results will be used. This information should be phrased so as to capture the respondent's interest. People are more likely to co-operate if they feel that the questionnaire has a legitimate purpose. Use the funnel approach. First ask general questions and then zoom in on specific details. If possible, the first question should stimulate the respondent's interest. It should be simple, but interesting. You may need to ask a screening (or filter) question (for example, "Are you an international visitor?") at the start of the questionnaire or section to determine whether a respondent qualifies to answer the questionnaire or the particular section. Provide explanations and instructions on how the respondent should answer questions, for example, "Tick one box only", "Answer all questions", "In this section, you will be asked to provide details about your holiday" or "Please skip this question if you answered 'Yes' to the previous question." Use emboldening or italicisation to differentiate these instructions from the text. Provide enough space for a respondent to answer an open-end question. All questions on a particular topic should be grouped together (these are called "constructs"). Place personal (demographic) questions concerning age and nationality, for example, at the end of the questionnaire so that respondents do not become defensive. Try to avoid questions that are too personal, such as, "Are you married?" or "What is your income?" (unless this information is essential for the research). If appropriate, supply "Don't know", "No opinion", and "Other" options. Provide closure by ending the questionnaire with a sentence such as, "Thank you for taking the time to complete this survey." After the questionnaire has been constructed, carry out a pre-test as part of a pilot study. Test out the questionnaire on a few respondents and see if it works before using it on a large scale. A pre-test is the presentation of a questionnaire in a pilot study to a representative sample of the respondent population. It may provide useful and important information about whether the research questionnaire is likely to achieve the results that the researcher hopes to achieve. For online surveys, the e-mail page must include a web link to the online questionnaire. In addition, computer screens look different from paper questionnaires. The horizontal width of questions should be limited to fewer than 70 characters.

(continued)

◻ **Table 4.9** (continued)

Guidelines	Description
Ethics	Get permission to carry out the questionnaire, especially for personal one-to-one interviews. Most visitor attractions and commercial organisations (such as shopping malls or airports) do not allow surveys to be conducted without management's permission. Assure respondents of confidentiality and anonymity. Confidentiality is about protecting the individual from harm when the results are made public. For example, personal details of respondents should be kept secret and not released to a third party by researchers. Research for selling purposes is not always ethical. An example of this is if respondents answer a few questions on a questionnaire, and then suddenly become eligible to purchase a specific offering. This type of research can harm the reputation of the research organisation as well as the particular tourism organisation. Avoid erosion of privacy. Some people refuse to respond to requests for information from marketing research organisations and individual researchers. Highlight that this research will be used for academic purposes only. Emerging technology can create ethical dilemmas. For example, the use of a cookie (a mechanism for remembering details of a single website visit and facts about the consumer) that records details about consumer behaviour may not be ethical. Make sure that you get approval from the ethics committee of your college or university. This is important especially at higher levels of study or when vulnerable participants are involved in the study.
General design	Make effective use of white space so that the questionnaire is clear and easy to read. Questions and response options should be laid out in a standard format. Make sure that the typeface is large enough to read. Where appropriate, there should be ample space to write in open-end comments. Ensure that questions flow easily from one to another and are grouped into topics (constructs) in a logical sequence.

Source: Author's creation

Although questionnaires are used to measure consumer satisfaction in the tourism industry worldwide, there are various problems associated with CSQs:

- Response rates are often very low as questionnaires are left in hotel rooms or on reception desks at visitor attractions, with no real incentive for customers to complete them.
- Many questionnaires seem to focus on numerical scales of satisfaction (1, 2, 3, and so on), or on various pictures of smiling or scowling faces. The problem with this technique is that it does not tell the organisation why the consumer is satisfied or dissatisfied, or with what.
- On the whole, consumers rarely find out what action has been taken as a result of completed questionnaires about satisfaction.
- Often opportunities are not taken to ask regular consumers if they think the product or service is getting better or worse. This could be useful information, given the importance of consumer retention.
- Certain questions may raise doubts in the mind of the consumer about the quality of the product or service. If a hotel, for instance, asks if the guest's room was clean, it may make consumers think that the hotel does not set extremely high standards.
- Relatively few questionnaires seem to be interested in finding out how consumers rate the organisation against competitors or the industry average.
- The results of CSQs are usually not distributed on a regular basis to staff so that they can see how they are performing.

One of the major problems with CSQs is the wording of the actual questions (for example, a hotel asking a guest if the television worked or not, or a tour operator asking about the weather). Before designing CSQs, organisations need to learn more about what really satisfies or dissatisfies their consumers, and then focus on things that they can actually control.

There are a number of research and consumer feedback methods for monitoring customer service satisfaction. The SERVQUAL model is a technique used by larger tourism organisations to measure service quality (see ▶ Chap. 13). Longitudinal research studies help researchers see how expectations of the same respondents increase over time and enable them to keep ahead of those expectations. However, longitudinal research is rarely used by small and medium-sized tourism businesses due to time and resource constraints (Pike & Larkin, 2010).

4.5.4 Stage 4: Analyse and Interpret the Data

Once the secondary and primary research has been completed, the next stage of the research process is to analyse and interpret the data that has been collected. The value of the research is determined by the results. Many techniques are used.

Computers have made it possible for researchers to process large amounts of data rapidly and inexpensively. The information obtained can be analysed using computer software packages such as statistical analysis software (SAS) or Statistical Package for the Social Sciences (SPSS), or a spreadsheet package such as Microsoft Excel (MS Excel). Statistical software licenses can be expensive. Thus, Microsoft Excel (MS Excel) is an ideal option for small tourism businesses. Classes and online courses on how to use these statistical packages are available. For instance, "SPSS for Beginners 1: Introduction" – a tutorial instructional video – is available on YouTube. For a detailed discussion on using spreadsheets and MS Excel for data analysis, see Burns and Bush (2012). Online survey software using SurveyMonkey or Google Forms has built-in analysis which generates visual charts (bar charts, pie charts, diagrams, graphs) automatically as responses are entered and for final review (for report 'write-up').

Qualitative data either requires human analysis (in other words, transcribing interview recordings, and extracting key themes, 'categorising', or 'coding') or the use of software tools such as NVivo, which is used to analyse transcripts of individual interviews and focus groups. Categorising and generating' idea blocks' is one of the most frequently used techniques for analysing interview responses and content If a computer-assisted personal interviewing (CAPI) method is used, analysis can occur while the interviews are being conducted.

An exhaustive discussion on measuring statistical associations and inferential statistics is beyond the scope of this book. For a detailed account of research statistical techniques, see Finn et al. (2000).

It is important that the manager and researcher work closely together when interpreting the research data and results. The researcher's ability to extract important information, and then to identify key relationships and patterns, is what transforms data into useful information. Marketers or managers do not want to receive reams of computer printouts. They want findings, figures, and diagrams to help solve the problem.

4.5.5 Stage 5: Present the Findings to the Manager/CEO

Marketing research projects should be designed with the end-user (audience) in mind, as is the case with all marketing communications. In other words, researchers need to ask themselves, "Who am I writing the report for and what do they require from me?" In the case of a report submitted to a client

4

organisation, the user is likely to be a manager. The client is unlikely to want to read a lengthy literature review or chapters on academic theory. The general rules for report writing can be summed up as follows:

- Tell the reader what you are going to say (introduction).
- Say it (the main body of report).
- Remind the reader about what you have said (conclusion).

Most research projects require that the report be written (typed). In addition, an oral presentation to management might be required.

Reports are often accompanied by pie charts, graphs, tables, and other graphics that display relevant information. A general rule is that the reader should still be able to make sense of the results if the figures, graphs, and tables are extracted from the report. Furthermore, it is not always necessary to depict all of the findings in diagram form. For instance, basic male/female findings do not require a pie chart and should merely be recorded in writing (for example, "Of the respondents, 42% were male and 58% were female").

The report should begin with an executive summary containing the key findings, recommendations for action, and their implications for the organisation. It may be useful to include answers to open-end questions derived from interviews and surveys. It is important to follow up with the client in order to ensure the sustainability of the recommendations and to maintain the relationship.

If you are writing a research dissertation as part of a university or college course, your supervisor or lecturer should provide you with guidelines on the sections to be included. ◻ Table 4.10 gives a suggested structure for a research report and some guidelines for writing a good report.

4.6 Common Marketing Research Errors

Several of the shortfalls that can occur during a marketing research project are described below.

4.6.1 Problem Definition

This refers to an error made during the first step of the marketing research process when the marketing researcher misinterprets, misunderstands, or does not define the issue or marketing decision problem (MDP) and related information needed properly.

4.6.2 Lack of Qualitative Information

Research studies often lack qualitative information. For example, researchers carry out surveys and interviews without conducting sufficient qualitative research to help devise the content of the survey or interview questions.

4.6.3 Using Only Secondary Resources

Relying on the published work of other researchers will not provide a full picture; researchers can miss out on other factors relevant to the study. Using secondary data is important to use as a place to begin the study (to 'see what exists already').

4.6.4 Improper Use of Statistical Analysis

When this error occurs, analysis is performed incorrectly. For example, far greater information can be mined from the results through additional statistical analysis such as cross-tabulation, cluster analysis, factor analysis and multiple regression than when simple frequency reporting (that is, straight number percentage reporting) is executed.

4.6.5 Failure to Have a Sample That is Representative of the Population

Ideally, a sample should be representative of the target population, otherwise the study

◘ Table 4.10 Suggested structure for a research report

Section	Guidelines
Title or title page	Use a short, precise, attention-grabbing title. It should not be over fanciful or wordy. It should be clear so that the reader is in no doubt what the research is about. It should contain a question, implicitly or explicitly, that the research will address. Include a subtitle (to clarify the nature of the report), the names of the authors, and the date of completion. A dissertation requires the name of the university and the supervisor.
Executive summary or abstract	An executive summary is a brief summary of the results of a project commissioned by the client. It highlights the major findings, conclusions, and recommendations. An abstract is a summary of the entire research study. The abstract should stand alone. It should include concise details about the objectives of the research, how the study was carried out, how many respondents there were, key findings, and recommendations. This is a difficult section to write well. It takes the form of a miniature report and is typically 200–300 words in length.
Table of contents	Include the titles and the page numbers of all of the section headings and main subheadings. (See the Contents page of this book for an example.) The table of contents requires a separate page or pages.
List of illustrations	List all of the tables, figures, graphs, maps, and other illustrations that have been used in the report. Include the figure number, title, and page number.
Acknowledgements	Acknowledge any assistance provided during the course of the research (from a supervisor, librarian, friends, family, interviewees, and so on).
Introduction	State the reasons for choosing the topic, the aims of the research, and the scope and limitations of the research investigation. Give any relevant background information. Define key concepts and terms used in the project.
Literature review	This is a synthesis of what has been studied or written on a subject, topic, or area to date through evaluation and analysis. Identify the particular areas of the topic on which the research has focused. Highlight any gaps (missing arguments) in the research knowledge. Identify any improved methods for researching the subject (that is, the future directions that the subject should take). State how the intended research will build on or depart from previous and current research (in other words, what contribution the research will make in the field).
Research methodology	Give a detailed account and evaluation of the research instrument used, why it was chosen, pre-testing of the questionnaire, sampling (size, response rate, selection method, composition, and so on), and an analysis of questionnaires. Justify the research approach/method and its associated methodology. (For example, explain that the researcher has chosen to administer a personal one-to-one survey because he or she does not have the necessary resources, such as time and interviewers, to conduct interviews.). Discuss sampling and study limitations Justify each step or activity in the methodology, explaining how it contributes to the research objectives and the research question.
Results and discussion	Include appropriate extracts of interviews, reporting, and discussion of results. Only use results that are important. Make use of diagrams, tables, graphs, and so on where appropriate. Do not use a pie chart for displaying two variables (for example, yes/no, male/female).

(continued)

▣ Table 4.10 (continued)	
Section	**Guidelines**
Conclusions and recommendations	Summarise key findings. Do a comparison with the existing literature. Determine if the objectives have been met and if the research added to the body of knowledge on the topic. Make recommendations for further research. Do not introduce any new material in this section. All findings should appear in the main body of the report.
List of references	Include a list of all information sources used at the end of the report. This gives the work credibility and allows readers to track material used.
Appendices or transcripts	Reference material in the text so that readers refer to it. Include appropriate material such as a copy of the questionnaire, interview schedule, and transcriptions, if used.

Source: Author's creation

cannot claim that it has included important subgroups that reflect the target population.

4.6.6 Misuse of Research Findings

Research studies can be powerful persuasion tools for marketers. However, manipulation of samples, incorrect choice of wording in a survey, or misrepresentation of findings can distort research conclusions. When findings are misused, consumers are misled. Marketers are discredited in the process.

4.6.7 Sampling Error

Sampling errors occur when a population sample is used to explain the behaviour of the total population.

4.6.8 Questioning Error

This occurs when the interviewer leads the respondent improperly in any way as a result of personal bias or any other improper delivery of interview questions.

4.6.9 Problems with Interpretation

Results can be interpreted in several ways. When data is interpreted incorrectly, it can be confusing and have exaggerated effects in graphical illustrations. For example, inferences based on improper tests of statistical significance or incorrect reports of estimates can change the graphical representation of data.

4.6.10 Results are Based on a Snapshot at One Point in Time

Most research studies take place in a snapshot at one point in time, and results may well be different if research is carried out at another time. Longitudinal studies that involve multiple surveys of the same respondents over time are rare due to resource and time constraints.

Summary
Marketing research plays a crucial role in tourism and hospitality marketing. It enables the marketer to conduct research

into the marketing mix, to understand the market better, and to measure levels of consumer satisfaction. Furthermore, it minimises risk when managers make marketing management decisions.

The tourism and hospitality marketer should undertake research at every level of the marketing planning process. The marketer must decide how much information can be obtained from reviewing secondary data. This data can provide a great deal of information without the need for expensive, time-consuming primary research. Primary research, when undertaken, should be carefully planned and should provide the marketer with relevant, unbiased data that will be of use to the organisation. Research must be analysed, interpreted, and made accessible to all of the key players, who should use it to benefit the organisation.

? Review Questions

1. List the three keywords used in the definition of marketing research used in this book.

2. Explain why tourism and hospitality organisations should conduct marketing research.

3. Why is it just as important for small tourism/hospitality companies to conduct market research as it is for larger companies?

4. How would you decide whether to use quantitative research or qualitative research in the research design? Provide examples of how each research type could be utilised by a small tourism business such as a local tour operating company.

5. What is the aim of exploratory research?

6. Differentiate between secondary and primary data.

7. What are focus groups? How are they used to help with marketing decisions?

8. Explain why it is important to pre-test survey questionnaires as part of a pilot study.

9. Compare and contrast probability sampling with non-probability sampling. Why is it difficult to obtain a probability sample in tourism?

10. Outline the main items of information that should be included in a research brief?

In-Depth Case Study 4: Measuring Consumer Satisfaction: East Coast Car Rentals

Objectives
- to understand the concept of marketing research
- to understand the importance of consumer satisfaction research

When Olivia Root checked her e-mails, she noticed one from East Coast Car Rentals. Her initial response was worry. She had rented a car from the company recently whilst on holiday in Sydney. Several thoughts crossed her mind: "I've probably damaged the car", "Maybe I left something in the boot", "I forgot to refill it with fuel". Olivia anxiously opened the e-mail and was relieved to find it was a thank you from East Coast Car Rentals for using their company and a polite request to complete a survey regarding his experience of using the organisation in order that the company could further improve its cus-

tomer service. The survey consisted of one page with six questions (see below).

East Coast Car Rentals was established in 1979 and has been providing cars to hire for Australians and international tourists for nearly forty years. The company has offices and depots in Australia's major cities, as well as at airport locations around Queensland, New South Wales, Victoria, South Australia, and Tasmania.

East Coast Car Rentals provide a wide range of vehicle styles: small compact cars, intermediate and larger cars, 8-seater Minivans, 12-seater Minibus, and a 1-Tonne van. The car rental company's slogan is 'Pay less, get more' and is regarded as providing low-cost rates for more price sensitive consumers. East Coast Car Rentals also provide an express loyalty membership scheme, which provides a range of exclusive benefits for previous customers. The car rental company competes for business in the airport market, providing vehicles for people travelling for business or pleasure. The company also provides short and long term rental for the local market for those without their own transport.

In order to gauge and then respond to customer experiences, East Coast Car Rentals introduced a customer feedback survey. The surveys are e-mailed to customers one week after completion of a car rental. On average about 30% of the surveys are returned. According to Brad Williams, the survey has resulted in "receiving much valuable information from customers about our performance and business". Brad states that as a result of the surveys' responses, "We have implemented many changes in our procedures. One of the most recent is that we have simplified our waiver options, a direct result of comments saying they were a little complicated".

Customer feedback options can also be found on the East Coast Car Rental website. The first of these is an online suggestion box for customers to share their views to enhance service delivery. Secondly, the company has online testimonials from customers for potential new customers to review. The testimonials are both qualitative by sharing a written review and quantitative by giving a rating from 1 to 5 stars. "It appears that a significant proportion of the business is derived from personal recommendations" says Brad.

East Coast Car Rentals is an excellent example of a tourism company applying the principles of marketing research to establish how satisfied their customers are.

Case interview: Brad Williams, Managing Director, East Coast Car Rentals.

4.6.10.1 Consumer Satisfaction Survey

Please answer all questions. Tick one box only for each question.

1. For what reason did you rent this car?

	Business	Leisure/ holiday	Car being repaired	Car was stolen	Some other reason
	☐	☐	☐	☐	☐

	Completely satisfied	Somewhat satisfied	Neither/ nor	Somewhat dissatisfied	Completely dissatisfied
2. How satisfied were you with your recent car rental from East Coast Car Rentals?	☐	☐	☐	☐	☐

	Yes	No
3. Did you receive any problems during the rental process?	☐	☐

4. What, if anything could East Coast Car Rentals have done better?_____

_____

_____

5. How would you rate the...	Excellent	Good	Fair	Poor	N/A
* timeliness with which you collected at the start of the rental/dropped off afterwards?	☐	☐	☐	☐	☐
* East Coast Car Rentals employee who handled your paperwork					
at the START of the rental?	☐	☐	☐	☐	☐
at the END of the rental?	☐	☐	☐	☐	☐
* mechanical condition of the car	☐	☐	☐	☐	☐
* cleanliness of the car interior	☐	☐	☐	☐	☐
* cleanliness of the car exterior	☐	☐	☐	☐	☐

6. How many times in total have you rented a car from East Coast Car Rentals in the last year?	Excellent	Good	Fair	Poor	N/A
	☐	☐	☐	☐	☐

4.6.10.2 **Questions and activities**

1. Analyse East Coast Car Rentals' consumer satisfaction survey (below). What information is it trying to gather?
2. What are its research objectives?
3. What are the advantages and disadvantages of e-mailed surveys?
4. Using the e-mailed survey below, along with the chapter information, construct a cover letter and an electronic (e-mail) or internet survey for a tourism organisation such as an airline, tour operator, travel agency, or hotel.
5. What are some of the problems associated with consumer satisfaction research?
6. What other research methods could East Coast Car Rentals use to monitor customer service satisfaction?

References

Aaker, D., Kumar, V., Leone, R., & Day, G. (2016). *Marketing research* (12th ed.). New York: Wiley.

Allen, I., & Seaman, C. (2007). Likert scales and data analyses. *Quality Progress, 40*(7), 64–65.

Armstrong, G., Kotler, P., Harker, M., & Brennan, R. (2009). *Marketing: An introduction.* Harlow, Essex: Pearson.

Babin, B. J., & Zikmund, W. (2016). *Essentials of marketing research* (6th ed.). Ohio: Cengage Learning.

Baines, P., Fill, C., Rosengren, S., & Antonetti, P. (2019). *Marketing* (5th ed.). Oxford: Oxford University Press.

Brunt, P. (1997). *Market research in travel and tourism.* Oxford: Butterworth-Heinemann.

Bryman, A. (2016). *Social research methods* (5th ed.). Oxford: Oxford University Press.

Bryman, A., Bell, E., & Harley, B. (2018). *Business research methods* (5th ed.). Oxford: Oxford University Press.

Butler, R. W. (1980). The concept of a tourist area life-cycle of evolution: Implications for management resources. *Canadian Geographer, XXIV*(1), 5.

Cohen, L., & Manion, L. (1986). *Research methods in education.* London: Croom Helm.

Cooper, D., & Schindler, P. (2014). *Business research methods* (12th ed.). Harlow: Prentice-Hall.

Erstad, M. (1998). Mystery shopping programs and human resource management. *International Journal of Contemporary Hospitality Management, 10*(1), 34.

Finn, M., Elliott-White, M., & Walton, M. (2000). *Tourism and leisure research methods.* Essex: Longman.

Fraenkel, J., Wallen, N., & Hyun, H. (2011). *How to design and evaluate research in education* (8th ed.). New York: McGraw-Hill.

Horner, S., & Swarbrooke, J. (2004). *International cases in tourism management.* Amsterdam: Elsevier Butterworth-Heinemann.

Jennings, G. (2010). *Tourism research* (2nd ed.). Queensland: Wiley.

Jobber, D., & Ellis-Chadwick, F. (2016). *Principles and practice of marketing* (8th ed.). New York: McGraw-Hill.

Kotler, P., & Armstrong, G. (2019). *Principles of marketing* (17th ed.). London: Pearson Education.

Lamb, C., Hair, J., & McDaniel, C. (2012). *Essentials of marketing research* (7th ed.). Boston, MA: Cengage.

Lavrakas, P. (2015). *Encyclopedia of survey research methods* (2nd ed.). London: Sage.

Lewis, R., Chambers, R., & Chacko, H. (1995). *Marketing: leadership in hospitality.* New York: Van Nostrand Reinhold.

Lumsdon, L. (1997). *Tourism marketing.* London: International Thomson Press.

Malhotra, N. K., Birks, D., & Nunan, D. (2017). *Marketing research: An applied approach* (5th ed.). London: Prentice-Hall.

Miller, G., Hudson, S., & Turner, R. (2005). Applying the mystery shopping technique: The case of Lunn Poly. In B. W. Ritchie & C. Palmer (Eds.), *Tourism research methods: Integrating theory and practice.* Wallingford, Oxfordshire: CABI.

Mody, S. (2018). Cruise lines are trying to win over millennials – with trampolines and sky bikes. *CNBC News.* Retrieved from https://www.cnbc.com/2018/07/24/cruise-lines-are-attempting-to-win-over-millennials%2D%2D-will-it-work.html [8 May 2019].

Morgan, M. (1996). *Marketing for leisure and tourism.* Hemel Hempstead: Prentice-Hall.

Parasuraman, A., Grewal, D., & Krishnan, R. (2007). *Marketing research* (2nd ed.). Boston: Houghton Mifflin Company.

Pike, S. (2018). *Tourism marketing for small businesses.* Oxford: Goodfellow Publishers Ltd..

Pike, S., & Larkin, I. (2010). Longitudinal evaluations of student satisfaction with a postgraduate unit using Importance-Performance Analysis. *Journal of Teaching in Travel & Tourism, 10*(3), 215–231.

Punch, K. F. (2014). *Introduction to social research: Quantitative and qualitative approaches* (3rd ed.). London: Sage Publications.

Saunders, M., Lewis, P., & Thornhill, A. (2020). *Research methods for business students* (8th ed.). Harlow, Essex: Pearson.

Wheeler, B. (1994). Content Analysis. In S. Witt & L. Moutinho (Eds.), *Tourism marketing and management handbook*. New York: Prentice-Hall.

Further Reading

Brunt, P., Horner, S., & Semley, N. (2017). *Research methods in tourism, hospitality, and events management*. London: Routledge.

Saunders, M., Lewis, P., & Thornhill, A. (2020). *Research methods for business students* (8th ed.). Harlow, Essex: Pearson.

Veal, A. J. (2017). *Research methods for leisure and tourism: A practical guide* (4th ed.). Upper Saddle River, New Jersey: Prentice-Hall.

4

Designing the Tourism and Hospitality Marketing Strategy

Contents

Tourism and Hospitality Marketing Planning

Contents

Electronic Supplementary Material The online version of this chapter (https://doi.org/10.1007/978-3-030-64111-5_5) contains supplementary material, which is available to authorized users.

Purpose

This chapter will give you the understanding and tools necessary to negotiate some of the key issues in tourism and hospitality marketing planning.

🏵 Learning Goals

After reading this chapter, you should be able to:

- Define the terms "marketing planning", "strategies", and "tactics"
- Understand the nature, scope, and importance of planning in marketing
- Compare the differences between strategic and tactical marketing planning
- Explain what is meant by an organisation's mission statement
- Become familiar with the strategic marketing planning process
- Identify and describe the contents of a marketing plan
- Apply the principles of marketing planning to Marine Dynamics Shark Tours.

Overview

In Part II, the principles of tourism marketing that we examined in Part I are applied to the process of gathering information to be used for marketing decision-making. In this chapter, we examine how marketers can apply the functions of marketing planning to the marketing activities of tourism organisations.

We begin with a definition of marketing planning as well as an explanation of why planning is important to both the tourism marketer and the organisation. We then discuss the differences between a firm's strategic marketing and its tactical marketing.

Following that, we focus on the four stages of the marketing planning process: analysis, planning, implementation, and monitoring. We concentrate on the planning process and the development of longer-term strategic plans. We briefly discuss the short-term tactical marketing plan itself. A large part of the rest of this book is devoted to developing tactical marketing plans (that is, tourism marketing mix strategies).

Within the stages of this process, we introduce various strategic analysis tools, such as the strengths, weaknesses, opportunities, and threats (SWOT) analysis, and the Boston Consulting Group (BCG) and General Electric Company (GEC) grids. We then discuss several techniques for making strategic choices, including Porter's generic strategies, the price/quality matrix, and the Ansoff matrix. Finally, we outline the elements necessary to construct a marketing plan.

The chapter's case study examines the marketing strategy of *Marine Dynamics Shark Tours* in South Africa.

▪ Introduction

Every tourism organisation conducts marketing activities, whether consciously or not. A local guesthouse owner, for example, has to make decisions about which services to offer and how to promote the guesthouse. The owner may check past records to see who regular consumers are, ask guests how they heard about the establishment, read local newspapers, and scan the internet to see what other businesses are advertising. These are all marketing activities. Some organisations choose to make these types of decisions on the spur of the moment. Other organisations prefer to think out and carefully coordinate an approach to marketing. Organisations that take the latter approach are essentially carrying out marketing planning and are more likely to be successful than organisations that make spur-of-the-moment decisions.

Marketing planning is the process of developing marketing plans, which can be strategic or tactical. The term "marketing plan" is generally used in the tourism industry to mean a tactical marketing plan, which is a detailed short-term plan covering a period of 1–3 years. Strategic marketing plans are generally less detailed and cover a period of 3–5 years. Just as it is vital to all business activities, careful planning with identified aims and objectives is a key component of tourism management. Knowing

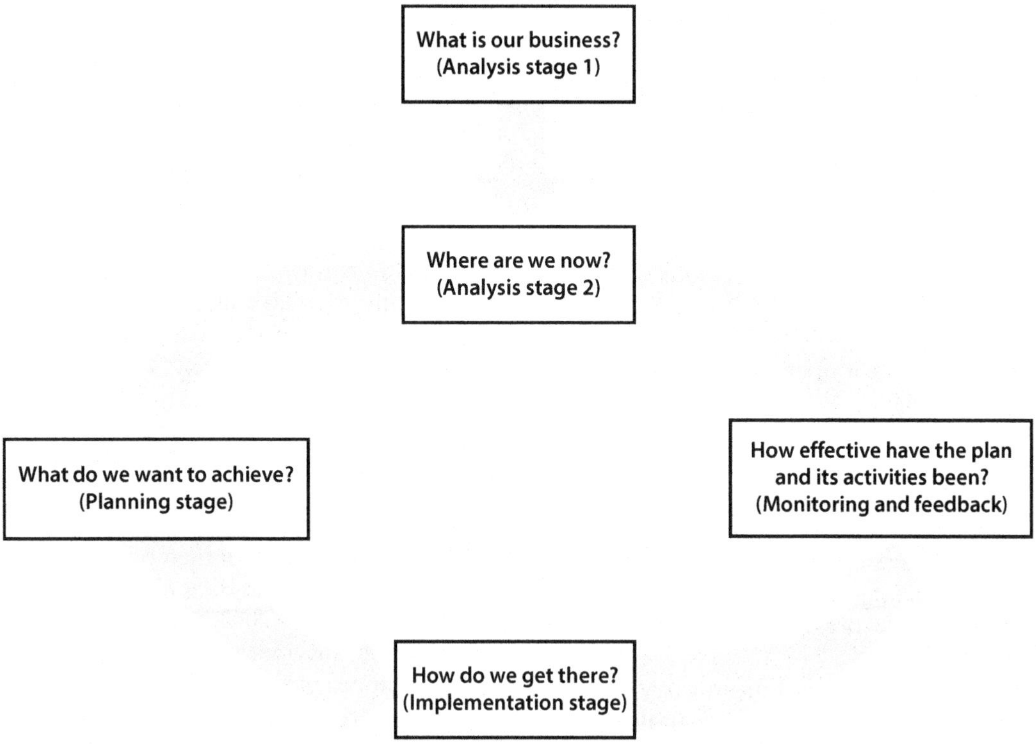

```
┌─────────────────────────┐
│   What is our business? │
│   (Analysis stage 1)    │
└─────────────────────────┘


┌─────────────────────────┐
│   Where are we now?     │
│   (Analysis stage 2)    │
└─────────────────────────┘


┌──────────────────────────┐          ┌──────────────────────────────┐
│ What do we want to achieve? │       │ How effective have the plan    │
│   (Planning stage)       │          │ and its activities been?       │
└──────────────────────────┘          │ (Monitoring and feedback)      │
                                       └──────────────────────────────┘


          ┌──────────────────────────┐
          │   How do we get there?   │
          │  (Implementation stage)  │
          └──────────────────────────┘
```

◘ Fig. 5.1 The marketing planning process. (Source: Author's creation)

about and understanding the internal and external factors that affect a business or will affect it in the future are crucial requirements of a successfully planned marketing campaign.

Marketing planning consists of a systematic process that includes the stages of analysis, planning, implementation, and monitoring (Kotler, 2000). The marketing planning process is shown in ◘ Fig. 5.1. These stages might be expressed as follows:

- Analysis: Where are we now?
- Planning: Where do we want to be?
- Implementation: How do we get there? (What decisions do we make to get there?)
- Monitoring: How successful are we?

These four questions help to explain three concepts in marketing planning (Davidson, 1997: 109):

Vision, goals, and objectives

- Strategies (chosen routes for achieving goals)
- Plans (action programmes for moving along the route and evaluating achievement against targets).

5.1 What is Marketing Planning?

Marketing planning is the process by an organisation analysing its strengths and weaknesses in its current and prospective markets, identifies its aims and the opportunities it seeks to develop, and defines strategies to achieve its aims" (Middleton, Fyall, Morgan, & Ranchhod, 2009: 211). Marketing planning results in marketing plans. Marketing should be planned in a systematic (step-by-step) way if it is to be implemented effectively. First marketers must understand the components of this planning, and then they must be able to use them effectively.

5.2   Why Plan Marketing?

In terms of the tourism marketer, marketing planning:
- Ensures that the marketer targets the right markets and segments
- Makes sure that the marketing is cost effective
- Encourages marketers to look at individual offerings.

In terms of the tourism organisation, marketing planning:
- Causes the organisation to identify and concentrate on its objectives
- Helps to shape the corporate mission statement
- Encourages the organisation to concentrate on internal strengths and weaknesses
- Forces the organisation to plan for the future
- Helps the organisation to carry out marketing on a day-to-day basis (not on an ad-hoc - as and when needed - basis)
- Encourages the organisation to look at who its competitors are.

5.3   The Differences Between Strategies and Tactics

It is important to know the difference between the two marketing planning terms "strategies" and "tactics" because they clarify two specific areas of the marketing planning process, as discussed in the next section.

While strategies and tactics may seem to overlap at times, the basic difference is that tactics actually map out how strategies are going to work. For example, an outbound tour-operating company's strategy might be to raise consumer awareness of its offerings over the next 3 years. The company's tactics might include promoting a special cruise package to several countries along the coast of Africa through television, newspaper and online advertising. Its tactics might also include an advertising campaign focused on making the company name a household word.

The definitions of strategic and tactical marketing planning are given below. Marketers must remember that these elements of planning work together in practice and the lines may not always be drawn so clearly. What is important is to make sure that the planning process addresses where an organisation wants to go as well as how it will get there.

5.3.1   Strategic Marketing Planning

Strategies relate to how tourism and hospitality marketers seek to meet their objectives and usually refer to an organisation's main lines of direction (Evans, 2003: 134). Strategies include statements that explain how things are made to happen over a given time-frame (usually over a period of 3–5 years). Strategic marketing plans are general, with few details of the firm's marketing activities. Strategic marketing planning has a greater emphasis on analysing the external environment, opportunities, and challenges facing the organisation in the medium and long terms. Strategies are not tactical (or action) plans.

5.3.2   Tactical Marketing Planning

Tactical marketing planning follows strategic plans, is more detailed and specific, and covers a shorter timescale (1–3 years). It includes what the organisation is actually going to do to achieve its overall strategy (Tribe, 2016). Tactics set out how strategies are going to work in detail by specifying what is going to happen, who will make it happen, and by when it will happen. The tactical marketing plan includes an in-depth analysis of the tourism marketing mix (the seven Ps), detailed budgets, and timetables.

5.4 The Marketing Planning Process

The marketing planning process is what leads to a marketing plan. It is a systematic way of incorporating marketing into a tourism and hospitality organisation. Planning is a series of steps, but it is also more than that. It involves an understanding of the human aspect of an organisation. All departments and key employees should be involved in the formulation of a plan if it is to be successful. They bring the ... and they are the p... plan. It is mor... in making a ... when the pla... must watch ... processes in ... be a result of ...

— Insufficie... which co... support ... (CEO) o...
— Confusi... over planning terms.
— Unexpe... external events or unpredicted macroenvironmental occurrences that mi... affect the organisation's per-

formance negatively (e.g. COVID-19 in 2020);

— Too much detail, irrelevant data/facts, or information given in the early stages of the planning process, which results in so-called "paralysis analysis", when ideas are so overwhelming that people cannot imagine putting plans into action;

— Varying company and managerial acceptance, when members of the management team demonstrate different levels of acceptance of the plan; and

— Disgruntled employees who have been left ... ...nning process and may feel ... ...ds plans, especially when the ... ...ft solely to one individual.

... add that there is no one right ... ("one-plan-fits-all") for any ... ...sm and hospitality organisa- ... ...isations differ in terms of size, ...perations, and the levels of ... ...e people involved in the plan-...

... an organisation to have a mar- ... has to go through a series of ... ...es that take the form of ques- ... ...n in ● Fig. 5.2.

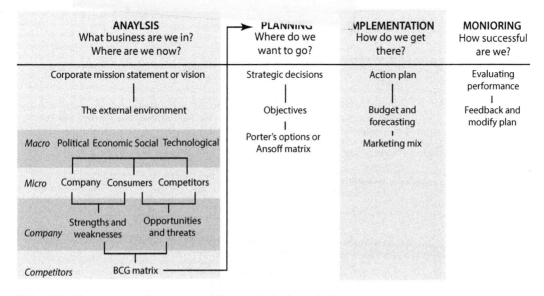

ANAYLSIS What business are we in? Where are we now?	PLANNING Where do we want to go?	IMPLEMENTATION How do we get there?	MONIORING How successful are we?
Corporate mission statement or vision │ The external environment	Strategic decisions │ Objectives │ Porter's options or Ansoff matrix	Action plan │ Budget and forecasting │ Marketing mix	Evaluating performance │ Feedback and modify plan

Macro Political Economic Social Technological

Micro Company Consumers Competitors

Company Strengths and weaknesses   Opportunities and threats

Competitors BCG matrix

● **Fig. 5.2** The marketing planning stages. (Source: Author's creation)

5.4.1 Analysis: I (What is Our Business?)

The analysis stage of marketing planning consists of devising a mission statement.

5.4.1.1 Mission Statements

Before any planning takes place, it is important that the organisation have a clear understanding of what business it is actually in. The staff at the tourism and hospitality organisation must agree on its overall mission statement. This mission statement must reflect the aims and scope of the organisation. A mission statement should describe what the business wants to achieve and should also identify its user groups. Thus, it is usually expressed in terms of the benefits that the organisation offers consumers, stakeholders, and employees (Kotler, 2000: 212). It is also a guide (an 'invisible hand') that helps employees know the purpose of the organisation. a company's missions statement is usually found on its official website (often in the "About us" link), in its promotional literature, company, report, and on the wall of premises. Some organisations combine the two e.g. "Our Vision and Mission" and the terms are used interchangeably. The difference between a mission and a vision is that a mission looks at the present; whereas a mission looks to the future.

More specifically, a mission statement should:

- Be broad
- Focus on markets
- Provide inspiration (to consumers, staff, and stakeholders).

The marketing plan should be designed to fulfil this mission. Extracts from several mission statements are provided in ◘ Table 5.1.

◘ **Table 5.1** The mission statements of a selection of international tourism and hospitality organisations

Organisation	Mission statement
African Eagle	"As an incoming operator, we are in the business of arranging tour packages on behalf of wholesale tour operators and retail travel agents – they are our clients." Source: African Eagle. (2018). Retrieved from ► https://www.africaneagle.com/missionstatement.aspx [18 September 2019].
Skyline India Travels	"To become the leading tour operator in Varanasi, by relying on a well-motivated workforce, applying appropriate technology, and providing maximum satisfaction to the customer." Source: Retrieved from ► https://skylines.co.in/visionandmission.php [20 November 2019]
Contiki	"To be the best cost/quality youth tour operator in the world ..." Source: Retrieved from ► https://www.contiki.com/uk/en/about/contiki-cares [20 November 2019]
Ocean View Hotel	"Ocean View Hotel is in business to satisfy guests' needs by operating a hotel that provides: L Individuality and first-class facilities L Location and convenience L Guest service of an excellent standard L Value for money."
Happy Cow Café, Bucharest, Romania	"To serve the best cup of coffee you've ever had while supporting fair trade coffee practices in Costa Rica."

◻ Table 5.1 (continued)

Organisation	Mission statement
Tanzania National Parks	"To sustainably conserve National Parks through innovative approaches for maximisation of ecosystem services and optimising tourism development for human benefits" Source: retrieved from ► https://www.tanzaniaparks.go.tz/pages/mission-and-vision [28 November 2019]
Nova Car Rental (Croatia)	"Our mission is to complete our customers' rent a car needs in Croatia and, in doing so, exceed their expectations for service, quality and value." Source: Retrieved from ► https://www.rentacarsplit.net/index.php/mission-statement [28 November 2019]

Source: Author's creation

Industry Insight 5.1

Skyline India Travel's Missions Statement

Skyline India Travel Ltd. is a travel agency located in Varanasi, north-east India. The company started in 1994 offering a range of travel management services. The agency is approved by IATA as well as the Ministry of Tourism, India.

Skyline India Travel's vision and mission are as follows.

Mission

"Our vision is to become the leading travel operator in Varanasi, by relying on a well-motivated workforce, applying appropriate technology, and providing maximum satisfaction to the customer."

Mission

"Our mission is to provide high quality services in the tourism and hospitality industry, timely and efficiently; through:
– Prompt service delivery
– Regular training of staff
– Competitive pricing of services
– Progressive programs & strategies aimed at motivating our employees to produce their best."

"Marketing myopia" is the term used to describe management's failure to recognise the scope of its business (Levitt, 1960). On the one hand, defining the scope of the business too narrowly can lead to lost opportunities. Defining the business too broadly, however, can lead to suboptimal use of resources as the organisation gets involved in business in which it should not be involved. The company's mission statement should provide a direction for the company for the next 10–20 years.

The mission statement of the *Ocean View Hotel* provides direction for each of the four Ps:
– Product (individuality, first-class facilities)
– Price (value for money)
– Place (location and convenience)
– Promotion (conveys the message that the customer can enjoy individuality, excellent service, and first-class facilities).

❓ Find three examples of mission statements, or visions, for tourism organisations (use the internet as a research tool). For each example, try to find at least three facts about the company from the statement. Critically evaluate each statement in terms of its clarity. Does it inspire its staff? Does it express the benefits it offers consumers?

5.4.2 Analysis: II (Where Are We Now?)

Once an organisation has defined its mission statement, its marketing planners can address the question of how to achieve results that will lead to the organisation's success. This stage of the strategic planning process aims to understand the current situation by asking, "Where are we now?" or, in other words, "Where are we in the industry and in the marketplace that we occupy?" Answering these questions requires an analysis of the organisation, its markets, and the external forces that influence them (Morgan, 1996: 38).

While the future situation is of foremost concern in forward planning, analysis of the past and present situations can be most helpful to the marketing planner in forecasting that situation. Managers want some context or some sense of where the organisation is now. An analysis of the current situation (sometimes called a 'marketing audit') highlights the performance gap that may exist between the present situation, and the desired goals and objectives. This situational analysis should take place at a number of levels:

- The whole organisation
- The individual strategic business units (SBUs)
- The individual offerings.

In addition, the analysis of the current situation can be divided into two main areas:

1. Internal or microenvironmental factors (affecting the organisation, its competitors, and its consumers)
2. External or macroenvironmental factors (the trends on a national, regional, or global scale).

One of the most popular tools used by the marketing planner to help with the analysis of the current situation is the SWOT analysis.

While a SWOT analysis is widely used by tourism businesses, you can carry out one on yourself. It may provide useful insights that enable you to identify your strengths and weaknesses, and the opportunities and threats you face, so you can plan for career success.

5.4.2.1 SWOT Analysis

A SWOT analysis (or matrix) is perhaps the most widely used tool in marketing planning. The SWOT analysis was created by Humphreys in the 1960s when he conducted research on the Fortune 500 companies in the USA (Humphreys, 2005). It is a useful tool for examining the micro and macro factors affecting the whole organisation. The firm should appraise itself critically in terms of how it compares with competitors, how it is seen by its consumers, and what resources and capabilities it has to deal with a changing market. A SWOT analysis considers the following aspects of an organisation's offerings in the business environment:

- Strengths
- Weaknesses
- Opportunities
- Threats.

Some of the strengths and weaknesses (micro-environmental or internal factors) of an organisation can be influenced or changed. However, the opportunities for an organisation and the threats to an organisation (macroenvironmental or external factors) cannot be changed.

Marketing planners should not merely list every factor they can think of, but should use only those factors that are relevant and significant to a particular organisation. In addition, the SWOT analysis is not an end in itself, but a means of deciding on priorities for action. Its completion should be followed by recommendations on how to exploit the organisation's strengths, repair its weaknesses, capitalise on opportunities, and avoid threats. Here are some examples of criteria that could be used to conduct a SWOT analysis of a tourism organisation's marketing activities.

- Strengths and weaknesses (internal)
- What is your location?
- What are your current offerings (service levels and products)?
- What are your current markets?
- Do you have the right staff well-trained, experienced)?
- What is your company's image? (How do your consumers perceive your company/brand?)
- Strength of goodwill in the community
- How do you fare with competitors?
- How effective is your marketing?
- How effective is your management and organisational (e.g. top-down) structure?

- Opportunities and threats (external)
- What is happening in the macroenvironment (political, economic, socio-demographic, technological, legal, and ecological forces)?
- What are the trends in the marketplace?
- What are the trends of product-offerings?
- Where are your competitors going? What are their strategies?

Table 5.2 shows an example of the implementation of a SWOT analysis for a boutique hotel in Romania that has recently entered the market.

Prepare a SWOT analysis for a small tourism business with which you are familiar (for example, a restaurant or tourist attraction in your province). Use the criteria given above as a guideline.

There are many different approaches to analysing an organisation's current situation. Some of the tools that are used as part of a SWOT analysis are described below.

- Internal analysis (strengths and weaknesses)

Strengths and weaknesses are associated with the internal resources and capabilities of the firm, as perceived by consumers (Piercy, 2002). The following tools can be used to analyse the strengths and weaknesses of an organisation:

Table 5.2 A SWOT analysis for a boutique hotel, Bucharest, Romania

Internal

Strengths	Weaknesses
Oldest four-star property in Bucharest Location of eight UNESCO World Heritage Sites Hotel is a cultural attraction in itself Use of information and technology facilities	High maintenance High staffing costs Low international awareness Need to re-adapt to fast-changing market demands No air conditioning in public spaces Limited size of the superior rooms

External

Opportunities:	Threats:
Dynamic city for international events Nearby operation of low-cost airlines Close proximity of several world-class vineyards	Five other boutique hotels in proximity Lack of promotions as a luxury destination Hotel has reached its maturity stage in its lifecycle Instability of the economic environment

Source: Author's creation

- STP (segmentation, targeting and positioning) is used as part of the competitor analysis (see ▶ Chap. 7).
- PLC (product life cycle) or TALC (tourism area life cycle) are used to predict the development path of a tourism product or destination (see ▶ Chaps. 8 and 14 respectively).
- The BCG (Boston Consulting Group) and GEC (General Electric Company) matrices are tools for analysing the organisation's SBUs in comparison to its major competitors.

- External analysis (opportunities and threats)

Opportunities and threats are external forces that have the potential to influence the performance of a firm or product offering (Baines,

Fill, Rosengren, & Antonetti, 2019: 176). The PESTLE analysis is effective for examining the current macro trends in the market (see ▶ Chap. 6).

5.4.2.2 The BCG Growth Share Matrix

The BCG growth share matrix (sometimes referred to as the "Boston Box") is a tool used to help the marketing planner analyse the product portfolio of an organization (Henderson, 1970). As with other models used in marketing analysis, the BCG growth share matrix is a simplifying tool. This tool is based on the idea that an organisation is made up of individual tourism offerings or SBUs. An SBU is a single business or a collection of related businesses that can be planned for separately from the rest of the company (Kotler & Armstrong, 2019: 62). A travel agency might have a number of SBUs: safaris, winter sun holidays, long-haul holidays and sports holidays, for example. All of the SBUs are plotted into the matrix, usually represented as circles (where the size of the circle relates to volume of sales). The BCG matrix assesses offerings against the product offerings of the organisation's largest competitor (in terms of market share and market growth). For instance, Go Travel's winter sun holidays might be compared to Flight Centre's winter sun holidays.

■ Figure 5.3 shows the BCG growth share matrix applied to an imaginary travel agency and its top competitor. The vertical axis on the grid indicates the growth rate of the market in which the agency operates. The horizontal axis, market share, refers to the SBU's market share relative to that of its largest competitor. If the SBU is plotted on the centre axis, it has the same share of the market as the competitor. If, however, it is plotted towards the high area, it has x times that of its competitor. For example, sports holidays with a share of 20% of the market where the next-biggest competitor has a market share of 10% would have a relative share of 2 (2×), whereas four-day safaris with a market share of 15% and a biggest competitor that also has a market share of 15% would equate to a relative share of one. (The cut-off point between high and low market share is one, so high-market-share SBUs in the BCG analysis are market leaders.)

The BCG suggests that an organisation's individual offerings can be divided into four groups:

– Stars are the market leaders in a growing market. A star is often a new tourism offering that has been introduced to the market. The organisation must spend money on these types of strategic business unit to keep up with the high market growth and fight off competitors.

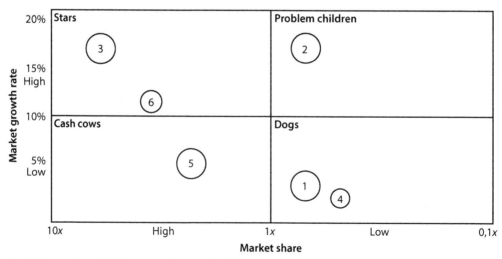

Key: 1 Safaris (1–3 days) 2 Safaris (4+ days) 3 Sports holidays 4 Long-haul holidays 5 Township tours 6 Winter-sun holidays

■ **Fig. 5.3** BCG. (Source: Adapted from Henderson (1970). *The Product Portfolio Matrix.* Boston: The Boston Consulting Group.)

- Cash cows are the leaders in a mature market in which growth rates have slowed. Cash cows produce a lot of revenue for the organisation, and are used to support the stars, problem children and dogs.
- Dogs have a weak market share in low-growth markets. It usually costs the organisation a substantial amount of money to keep them running. Therefore, the organisation should consider selling them off (divesting).
- Problem children (or question marks) are offerings that operate in high-growth markets, but have a low relative market share. They are a problem because they require a lot of investment. The marketer has to decide whether to continue spending money on these offerings to increase market share or to withdraw them from the market.

In a balanced product portfolio, a new product enters the matrix in the problem child or question mark phase, after which it should move to the star phase, then to the cash cow phase (where the product must remain for as long as possible) and eventually to the dog phase. It could also happen that a new product moves directly from the question mark phase to the dog phase. Tourism marketers should always strive to maintain a balanced product portfolio over the long term. Such a portfolio consists of enough cash cows to provide for the cash needs of question marks, and to finance future stars and new products in development.

The BCG growth share matrix can then be evaluated to determine the appropriate strategies for the SBUs: which ones to sell off (divest) and which ones to develop or where to invest resources. A key point of the BCG growth share matrix is that market share and market growth provide approximations of the organisation's ability to generate cash (Evans et al., 2003: 144).

The BCG matrix offers a way of assessing product offerings in terms of their market share and market growth, and helps an organisation plan its portfolio. It helps to identify which offerings to push or drop and when. However, it does have limitations. One of the

major limitations of the BCG matrix is that extensive information is needed to apply to the matrix. This information might be both difficult and time consuming to obtain. Some tourism marketers feel that the effort is not worthwhile. Additional limitations of the BCG matrix when used in tourism marketing planning include the following:

- It does not tell an organisation what the overall market share is. It only shows how the organisation is doing against its major competitor.
- It requires the organisation to find the data for each particular SBU and to have similar data for the offerings of the organisation's nearest competitor.
- It does not take account of the dynamics of the market. Some markets change rapidly (for example, restaurant markets), while others move slowly (for example, national parks).
- The matrix is less meaningful than when used in some other industries because there are many competitors in the tourism industry (for example, multi-national hotel companies), which is not the case in industries such as the manufacturing industry (for example, household detergents).
- It does not take account of the interrelationships between offerings, which are vital in building strategy. Some offerings might be complementary or supportive (such as a hotel's swimming pool or conference centre).

The BCG growth share matrix can be a useful analytical tool in giving some insight into potential strategy options in tourism organisations, especially medium-sized and larger organisations. It is particularly helpful during the marketing audit stage of marketing planning. When using the BCG matrix, the marketing planner needs to examine competition at regional, national and international levels. For example, the BCG matrix could be used to compare Alton Towers in Staffordshire, UK with its national competitor (Thorpe Park in Surrey, UK) or its international competitor (Disneyland, Paris, in France). Marketers should use this tool alongside other strategic tools such as the Ansoff matrix (see the section on the planning stage later in this chapter).

5.4.2.3 General Electric Company (GEC) Grid

Another portfolio analytical tool used by marketers is the GEC (or GE McKinsey) grid or matrix, which takes into account a greater number of factors than the BCG matrix. The GEC grid (or matrix) is usually applied to strategic business units such as subsidiaries of a holding company. The GEC matrix could be applied to an organisation such as *TUI Group*, which has numerous subsidiaries operating directly and indirectly in the United Kingdom and European tourism industry. Examples are tour operators such as *First Choice, Robinson Holidays*, and airline *TUI Airways*. The GEC grid rates market attractiveness as high, medium or low (McKinsey & Company, 2008). It rates competitive strengths as strong, medium or weak and is divided into nine cells, as shown in ◻ Fig. 5.4.

The SBUs are placed in the appropriate cell according to market attractiveness criteria (for example, market growth, strength of competition, profitability, and legal regulation factors) and competitive strength factors (for example, brand image, technological capability, distribution channel links, and financial strength factors). These variables are given a weighting to establish their importance. Cells in the upper-left area of the grid (A, D, and B cells) indicate strong SBUs in which the organisation could invest. The three cells from the bottom left to the top right (G, E, and C) indicate SBUs that are medium in attractiveness. The three cells at the lower right (H, I, and F)

indicate SBUs that are low in overall attractiveness. Organisations in these cells generally have a weak competitive position and a small market share in a static or declining market. Marketers would perhaps consider divesting or minimising investment in SBUs in these cells.

5.4.2.4 PESTLE Analysis

The PESTLE analysis (the acronyms STEEPLE, PEST, and STEP are used in some texts) involves an examination of the external (macroenvironmental) factors that may affect an organisation or destination. These macroenvironmental factors (sometimes called "forces") affect all tourism and hospitality businesses. They are similar to the opportunities and threats of the SWOT analysis, and are out of the marketing planner's control. However, it may be possible to influence some of them through methods such as lobbying the local government. They include political, economic, socio-demographic, technological, legal, and ecological factors (PESTLE). Although we cover these factors in detail in ▶ Chap. 6, it is useful to consider them in the context of marketing planning (see ◻ Table 5.3 below).

> *Competitive advantage* is the prolonged benefit of implementing some unique value-creating strategy not simultaneously being implemented by any current or potential competitors along with the company's inability to duplicate the benefits of this strategy (Hoffman, 2000: 6).

◻ **Fig. 5.4** GEC (GE McKinsey) matrix. (Source: Adapted from McKinsey and Company (2008))

	Competition strength		
High	Strong	Medium	Weak
A	B		D
D	E		F
G	H		I
Low			

Market attractiveness

◻ Table 5.3 PESTLE analysis

Factor	Description
Political	The political environment is important to tourism organisations since it is here that changes in laws, regulation, and policy occur (Hall & Jenkins, 1995). The marketing planner should focus on the political environment in the market or markets in which the organisation operates or hopes to operate. In some cases, there may be political unrest and instability in receiving countries, which could affect the organisation (particularly tour operators and travel agencies). On a more local level, there are also legal factors to consider, such as government legislation affecting the organisation's business activity (for example, accommodation licences) or local government policies in areas such as sustainable development and health initiatives.
Economic	Economic influences can affect almost all of an individual organisation's marketing activities. Economic factors such as consumer spending levels, unemployment levels, exchange rates, and inflation rates should be analysed. Further afield, global economic trends should be assessed along with the levels of income and other economic factors in the organisation's consumer-generating market or markets.
Socio-demographic	Socio-demographic factors are major influences in the marketing activities of tourism organisations. The marketing planner should assess factors that include the following: The market's interest in responsible tourism (there might be a trend towards environmentally friendly destinations, hotels, tour operators, and resorts) Changes in lifestyles and fashions, perhaps towards healthy eating and fitness Demographic shifts towards an ageing population Changes in types of holiday from international to domestic ('staycation') holidays, shorter holidays and airline flights,
Technological	The increasing number of mobile phones and smartphones, tablet computers, iPads, and laptops worldwide has meant that prospective consumers can be targeted directly via their mobile phones, e-mail, or social media platforms. The development of new technologies such as 5th Generation ('5G') wireless technology, recognition technology (e.g. for hotel check-in), apps, AI, AR, internet of Things (IoT) (Inter-connectivity of devices), VR, big data, and robotics has created more possibilities for marketing. Advancements in information and communications technology (ICT) (in particular digital marketing) are leading to changes in business processes and service standards. An increase in home-based entertainment (led by new technology such as digital television and computer games) may reduce consumers' spending on tourism product offerings.
Legal	The tourism industry is affected by legislation and regulations that affect business. Tourist and hospitality (or "bed") taxes provide a useful source of income for national and local governments. Laws regarding landing taxes, gaming licences, health regulations, and visas all affect the travel and tourism and hospitality industry. In 2020, many countries brought in new legislation as a result of the COVID-19 pandemic, for example, social distancing measures in restaurants, face masks to be worn by passengers on public transport, no crowds on beaches, and in parks and other tourist spaces.
Ecological	The environment, natural disasters, global warming, climate change, erosion, CO_2 pollution, and pollution all affect an organisation's marketing activities. In recent years, more attention has been paid to environmental issues. Natural disasters, over which the organisation has no control, can seriously impact upon business and a destination's tourism and hospitality industry. Public health issues such as hygiene and sanitation, infectious diseases, and viruses (e.g. COVID-19).

Source: Author's creation

5

5.4.2.5 Competitor Analysis

Regular analysis of major competitors is an important part of marketing planning. Competitor analysis aims to establish the nature of the competition in the tourism industry and should indicate the tourism organisation's **competitive advantages.** Horner and Swarbrooke (2005: 156) suggest that the following factors should be considered when undertaking a competitor analysis:

- The market share and turnover of major competitors
- The geographical area that is covered by competitors
- The key strengths and weaknesses of competitors
- Marketing methods and activities
- Regional, national, and international links of competitors
- Price structures of the competition.

A competitor analysis involves a relatively detailed examination of a tourism organisation's existing and potential competitors. It enables the organisation to formulate a strategy in the light of an assessment of key rivals. Porter (1980) outlines a framework for competitor analysis by deploying a two-stage response profile of competitor organisations. The first section details questions about the motives of competitors. The second section asks questions about the current and future activities of competitors. The detailed issues that need to be addressed within the response profile include:

- Product lines
- Prices
- Quality
- Differentiation
- Advertising
- Market segmentation
- Marketing practices
- Growth and prospects
- Points of parity (POP)
- Points of difference (POD).

A competitive analysis, as with all aspects of marketing planning, should be ongoing and not a one-off activity. Porter's (1980) five forces model is one of the most widely used tools for analysing the nature and structure of competition within an industry. Porter (1980) identified five factors that determine the level of competition and therefore profitability within the tourism industry (see ◘ Fig. 5.5). Understanding these forces helps tourism marketers in developing the competitive strategy of their firm. These five forces are as follows:

New entrants (the threat of potential entrants to the tourism industry and markets)

- Suppliers (the power of suppliers to businesses in the tourism industry)
- Buyers (the power of buyers or customers)
- Substitutes (the power of substitute products)
- Competitive rivalry (rivalry among businesses in the industry).

Porter's (1980) five forces model allows a tourism business to identify the major forces that are present in the tourist sector. This can be related to the critical factors that were identified in the PESTLE analysis discussed in the previous section. By determining the relative power of each of these competitive forces, a tourism firm can identify how to position itself to take advantage of opportunities and overcome threats. Strategies may then be designed to exploit the competitive forces at work within the industry. The five forces model is flexible, and can be applied to individual business and SBUs as well as to visitor attractions and tourist destinations. Given that the nature of the competitive environment is one that is constantly changing, the model should be applied on a regular basis in order to detect changes before competitors and allow for an early adjustment of strategy.

5.4.3 Planning Stage (What Do We Want to Achieve?)

After marketing planners have evaluated how the organisation's current situation affects its marketing activity, they look at "where the organisation wants to be", evaluating and setting marketing goals, objectives, and strategic options (Kotler, 2000).

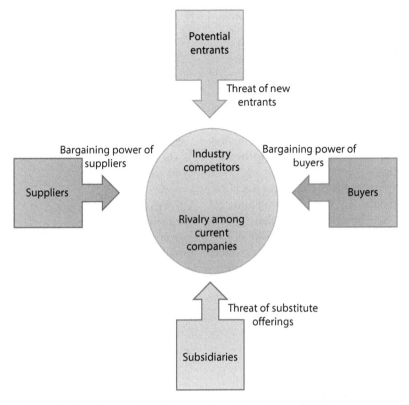

Fig. 5.5 Porter's (1979) Five Forces model. (Source: Adapted from: Porter (1979))

5.4.3.1 Setting Marketing Goals

According to the Chartered Management Institute (CMI), goals are defined as "the organisation's primary intended accomplishments" (CMI, 2017). Goals provide target areas for achievements. They are less specific than objectives. For example, a hotel might set a goal of becoming a market leader in a particular city. Goals, however, need objectives to act as yardsticks when an organisation is trying to evaluate its progress.

5.4.3.2 Setting Marketing Objectives

Objectives are defined as "the specific aims that the marketing manager accomplishes to achieve organisational goals" (CMI, 2017). Objectives are statements of "where we want our organisation to go" (O'Hanlon, 1972: 21). Without them, it is not possible to know if a campaign is effective or not. Objectives provide a blueprint or road map for the company's marketer. They also provide a way of justifying marketing spend. Objectives are more specific than goals. They should be real-istic and need to be compatible with the organisation itself. Thus, the first guideline in setting marketing objectives is to make sure that they will help in enabling the overall business objectives to be met. Each marketing objective should correlate to a specific business objective. An organisation's marketing objectives are usually set within a given timeframe and state what is to be achieved. For instance, the objectives of a hotel might be to increase market share of the international leisure tourist market by 20% by a specific date (for example, June 2023).

Before it became a popular tourist destination, Dubai made its money from oil. Prior to the discovery of oil, fishing, farming, and pearl diving were the Emirate's main trades. In the early twentieth century, there were 300 pearl diving dhows (traditional sailing boats) based in Dubai Creek, with more than 7000 sailors on board.

? Analyse Skyline India Travels' objectives in ▶ Industry Insight 5.4. Discuss whether each objective follows the criteria in the SMART concept (see below).

It is essential that objectives be set before a marketing campaign is launched. Objectives need to reflect the aspirations of the organisation. At the same time, they need to be realistic so that the organisation can improve its market position.

Marketing objectives should also be launched against an established point or benchmark. Benchmarking is critical for the setting and reviewing of any marketing objective. It provides some specifics against which the company can build and measure the effectiveness of a campaign. Sources of benchmarking information include sales figures, visitor numbers, and telephone responses to print media advertisements. A benchmark could even be the number of hits received on a company website compared to a similar period 18 months ago.

The SMART concept is used as the basic criteria for setting objectives. According to this framework, objectives should be:

- Specific: Objectives should be clear and easy to understand throughout the organisation. The more specific the goal-setting, the more credible the company's goals will be perceived to be by colleagues, management, and other departments.
- Measurable: Each objective should be capable of being measured (in other words, targets should be tangible). Objectives that are not measurable are not worth the paper they are written on. They should also not be too lofty (for example, "become well-known in the tourism industry" or "break even within twelve months").
- Achievable: Objectives should be achievable within the limits set by trends and the constraints of the organisation's market position. They should express possible goals, not impossible dreams.
- Realistic: Objectives should be attainable. They should not be too easy to achieve, but at the same time, they should not be larger than life. They should be set against time and budget constraints.

- Time-constrained: Each objective should have a specific timeframe. This timeframe will vary depending on the type of business the company is in, the product offering being marketed, and the nature of the objective. Without a timeline, there is no point in an objective. Sometimes the nature of the marketing objective (for example, repositioning a brand) means that it should be measured over a longer period of time.

An organisation's marketing plan should be designed to achieve objectives. If the organisation is attempting to expand, it might use growth strategies to achieve this objective. Organisations must be prepared to accept that they may have to give up some things to achieve other objectives. For example, a tourism organisation might have to give up short-term profits in order to increase its market share (perhaps by spending money on an advertising campaign).

It is possible to connect an organisation's objectives to its mission statement. This is illustrated by the fictitious organisation in ▶ Industry Insight 5.2.

Industry Insight 5.2

Mad Monkey's Mission Statement and Objectives

Mission statement   To be the leading international backpacker hostel in Johannesburg.

Objectives
- To achieve an increase in 8% of sales within 12 months
- To increase profits by 15% within 12 months
- To increase current market share by 10% within 12 months.

5.4.3.3 Setting Strategic Options or Choices

Marketing objectives are essential and should be taken seriously. One of the biggest mistakes that many tourism marketers make is to set retro-objectives. These are objectives that are set after the fact (Hefer, 2010). In other management disciplines such as finance or human resources, objective setting is automatic. Tourism marketers also need to extend their organisations by setting challenging goals rather than setting objectives that are too easy to achieve.

Once goals and objectives have been set, marketing planners must decide on appropriate strategies to meet these objectives. Marketing planners should examine each objective closely and draw up strategic options. For example, if one of the objectives of a low-cost airline is to increase market share by 10% over a twelve-month period, this can be achieved in several ways. It may be possible to achieve this objective by charging a lower price, by offering something different, or by focusing on a new market, for example.

Porter's generic strategies and the Ansoff matrix are two strategic tools that are used extensively in tourism marketing. The two aspects of strategic formulation include competition strategy and strategic direction. Porter's generic strategies framework is used for competitive strategy, while the Ansoff matrix is used for strategic development (or growth).

5.4.3.4 Porter's Generic Strategies

Porter (1980, 1985) was an early analyst who asserted that once an organisation has evaluated its marketing situation, it can choose from one of three alternative strategies: cost leadership, differentiation, or focus (see ◘ Fig. 5.6).

■ **Cost leadership strategy**

The cost leadership strategy is the least sophisticated of the three strategies. It is used when an organisation aims to reduce costs to undercut competitors, and can be used by both large and small tourism organisations. Large organisations can benefit from their mass purchasing power and economies of scale. Large airline companies (for example, *Emirates Airlines*), tour operators (for example, *TUI*) and travel agencies (for example, *Hays Travel*) can reduce prices to undercut their competition. Small and medium-sized tourism organisations (for example, backpacker hostels, B&Bs and boutique hotels) can maintain strict control of their overheads and minimise costs.

SpiceJet, a no-frills or low-cost airline operating in India, provides an example of an organisation that uses less expensive resource inputs. *SpiceJet* has removed additional product features, leading to reduced staffing and other costs (such as the costs of entertainment and meals).

The benefits of a cost leadership strategy are as follows:
- It allows the organisation the possibility of increasing both sales and market share by being the lowest-cost producer.
- It can be particularly profitable in a market where consumers are price sensitive (for example, youth travellers).
- The organisation can earn higher profits by charging a lower price than competitors.

◘ **Fig. 5.6** Porter's 3 generic strategies. (Source: Adapted from Porter (1985))

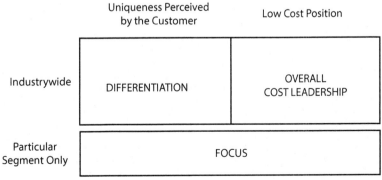

The problem with this strategy, however, is that consumers usually want value for money, not just a low price, when purchasing tourism offerings. In recent years, the tourism industry has become more sophisticated and marketers have generally moved away from pricing strategies to other strategies (Porter, 1985).

■ Differentiation strategy

This is a far more commonly used strategy in tourism marketing planning. A differentiation strategy is based upon an organisation creating consumer perceptions that an offering is superior in some way to the offerings provided by competitors so that a premium price can be charged (Porter, 1985).

Differentiation can be achieved in the following ways:

— Creating a product that stands out from the products of competitors by virtue of technology or design. For example, the tour operator *Audley Travel* offers superior quality compared to competitors.
— Offering a very high standard of service delivery. For example, an upmarket private game reserve in South Africa such as Sabi Sabi differentiates by offering a very high level of service.
— Creating a strong brand name through advertising, design, innovation, frequent-flyer programs (FFPs) and so on. For example, *Qantas'* development of its FFP creates loyalty for its brand among passengers.

❓ Think of some initiatives that are just not done in the tourism industry. It could be an airline instituting a dress code for passengers or an airline giving away a free airline ticket to the best-dressed person on the plane. Do you think these are risky or clever marketing strategies?

■ Focus strategy

A focus strategy is aimed at a segment of the market rather than the whole market. Within a specific market segment, the marketer can utilise either a differentiation strategy or a cost leadership strategy.

Smaller tourism organisations that have fewer resources than large ones, but a good understanding of their target markets, often use this market-focus approach. For instance, a travel agency might focus on birdwatchers and a hotel might focus on business executives. Each organisation would provide facilities and services to attract their target segments, such as tours guided by bird experts or a business centre. The main benefit of this strategy is that it allows for specialisation and greater knowledge of the segment being served.

Poon (1993) argued that there are difficulties in applying Porter's (1980) analysis to tourism. Poon identified the following four key strategic principles for effective tourism:

1. Putting customers first
2. Quality leadership
3. Product innovation
4. Strengthening the organisation's strategic position in the value chain.

Tribe (2016) reworked Porter's typology of strategies using the variable of perceived quality and price (see ◻ Fig. 5.7).

— A hybrid strategy seeks to provide high-quality offerings at low prices. This is difficult to achieve because adding extra consumer value adds costs and forces up prices.
— A differentiation strategy offers product quality and uniqueness. This is usually achieved through innovation, design, attention to quality, and advertising.

◻ **Fig. 5.7** Price/quality model. (Source: Adapted from Tribe (2016))

Perceived quality	Low Price	High Price
High	Hybrid-based	Differentiation-based
Low	Price-based	Zone X

- Some tourism organisations seek to gain a competitive advantage by offering the lowest prices in the industry (a price-based strategy). For example, a limited-service (budget) hotel (for instance, *Ibis Hotels*) offers a basic no-frills accommodation facility.
- Zone X (high prices and low quality) is generally a failure route except where an organisation is a monopoly (for example, the *British Rail* on certain routes) or where consumers lack information about a market.

❓ Consider the following businesses in your nearest city and how they differentiate their offering from that of competitors:
  - A local tour-operating business
  - A hotel in the central business district.

❓ How difficult would it be for competitors to copy your business idea? Provide an example of a market segment on which the organisation might focus.

In the tourism and hospitality industry, reputation goes a long way towards differentiation, particularly in the case of accommodation establishments. Most hotels and guesthouses provide similar tangible offerings (a room with a bed, for example), but the offerings are made different by less tangible elements such as the view from the room window, the warm hospitality of the owners or the overall experience. *Westin Grand Hotels*, for instance, provide shuttle services to and from visitor attractions and shopping centres. Airlines are another good example. They all use the same aircraft, fly the same routes and offer the same in-flight entertainment. However, each airline attempts to differentiate itself from its competitors by creating a strong brand name to develop consumer loyalty, through providing superior service or something unique (see ▶ Industry Insight 5.3). Likewise, a travel agency might specialise in particular types of holidays, such as sailing, birdwatching, or sporting holidays. Similarly, a restaurant might offer superior service and food to develop a competitive advantage.

Industry Insight 5.3

Emirates First-Class Suites Are Top-of-the-Class

Today, airlines attempt to gain a competitive edge by offering exceedingly high quality in their first-class suites. Emirates" Boeing 777 first-class suites were inspired by Mercedes Benz S-Class. The suites feature zero-gravity seats, virtual windows, and active noise-cancelling headphones. The virtual windows are a feature on the otherwise windowless cabin suites along the middle aisle, and project a high-definition view of the outside using real-time cameras mounted on the aircraft. The NASA-inspired zero-gravity seat features a "buttery-soft" leather and a lounging position that Emirates says removes any pressure from the elbows, back, and neck so that travelers can achieve maximum comfort. Safari binoculars are available in the side suites for customers who want to look out outside their windows and there is an entertainment system featuring 4500 channels and a wireless remote, a full HD LCD TV, and custom-controlled mood lighting and climate control, allowing passengers to adjust the cabin's temperature to anywhere between 18 and 26 °C. Customers who fly in these game-changing, fully enclosed private suites receive a complimentary chauffeur service that uses Mercedes Benz S-Class cars.

To summarise, there are many different strategies for developing a competitive edge. The tourism marketing planner needs to ask the following questions:

- Why should anyone buy my offering instead of a competitor's?
- What makes my offering different from or superior to those of my competitors?
- What are the benefits to my consumers?

◻ **Fig. 5.8** Ansofff matrix. (Source: Adapted from Ansoff (1988))

	Tourism offerings	
	Existing	New
Existing	Market penetration	Offering development
Markets		
New	Market development	Diversification

❓ What competitive advantage does Raffles Hotel in Singapore have over other luxury hotels in Southeast Asia? Visit this website:
▶ www.raffles.com/singapore

5.4.3.5 Ansoff's Matrix

One of the most commonly used tools for analysing the possible strategic directions that an organisation can follow is the product market matrix devised by Ansoff (1965). The Ansoff product market matrix (sometimes referred to as the growth vector matrix) illustrates where generic strategies can be deployed (see ◻ Fig. 5.8). Note that the matrix is related to the amount of risk that marketing planners are prepared to take. Developing new product-offerings or entering new markets presents a level of risk since a large proportion of new product-offerings fail. Ansoff (1988) noted that organisations face four broad options: market penetration, market development, product development, and diversification. The product market matrix helps organisations decide what course of action should be taken given current performance. ◻ Table 5.4 summarises the four strategic directions or options.

◻ **Table 5.4** The Ansoff (1988) matrix strategic options: Description and examples

Strategy	Description	Example
Market penetration	Selling more of the organisation's current offerings in an existing market (see ▶ Industry Insight 5.4). This is the lowest-risk option for the marketing planner.	A quick-service restaurant (QSR) chain such as *Nando's*, might encourage consumers to buy more frequently or it could attempt to attract consumers from one of its competitors, such as *KFC*, by offering special promotions.
Market development	Looking for new markets for an organisation's offerings.	A city hotel chain might target new markets such as leisure (holiday and weekend getaway) tourists. The Vietnam National Administration of Tourism (VNAT) has been aggressively marketing war tourism as part of its marketing plan.
Product development	Developing new products/offerings for the organisation's existing markets (see ▶ Industry Insight 5.5).	Hotels might pursue this strategy; while continuing to concentrate on their core products such as rooms, food, service, and business facilities, they could develop leisure facilities (such as a gym) to become more attractive to the business market. *Pizza Express* has attempted to target families more welcome by providing children's menus and play areas, and large flat-screen television sets.

◼ **Table 5.4** (continued)

Strategy	Description	Example
Diversification	Developing and selling new products in new markets. This is the most dynamic and risky of Ansoff's strategies. It is an appropriate strategy in the following situations: Current products and markets no longer provide financial returns. The organisation has underutilised resources. The organisation wants to spread risks. The organisation wishes to broaden its portfolio of business interests across more than one offering or market segment.	Pier 70 in San Francisco, California, USA. Once an old fishing harbour, Pier 70 has been revamped into retail shops, restaurants, and hotels, and is now one of San Francisco's most visited tourist attractions. Similarly, the Virgin (Group) brand provides an excellent example of this high-risk, high-return strategy. By launching *Virgin Cola*, *Virgin Airlines*, *Virgin Media*, *Virgin Holidays*, and *Virgin Money*, *Richard Branson* successfully penetrated new markets with new products.

Source: Author's creation

Industry Insight 5.4

PREMIER INN: Market Penetration

Founder and managing director of Premier Hotels & Resorts, Samuel Nassimov, has been described as a visionary who built an empire of sixteen outstanding properties from nothing. From a humble forty bedrooms, the group's portfolio has grown to encompass a number of hotels and resorts throughout South Africa. Offering almost 2000 bedrooms and employment opportunities to more than 1500 passionate members of staff, Premier Hotels & Resorts has a proven, long standing reputation for delivering superior results.

Source: (n.a.). (2017). Hospitality marketing maven joins Premier Hotels & Resorts. Retrieved from ▶ http://www.leadershiponline.co.za/articles/premier-hotels-resorts-23147.html [12 September 2018].

The War Remnants Museum in Ho Chi Minh City, Vietnam is ranked among the top 25 best museums in the world by tourism website TripAdvisor.

Industry Insight 5.5

Designer Airship Designed for Military to Be Luxury Liner of the Sky

The world's largest airship, Airlander 10, was intended to become a luxury liner of the sky. The airship, which is 92 m long (the length of a football pitch and the height of six double-decker buses), was originally designed for military use by the United States Navy. However, the military project was terminated due to financial cutbacks. The airship was then redeveloped by British company Hybrid Air Vehicles (HAV). The 48-seater Airlander 10 was described as "a Gucci cruise liner that can fly over the Grand Canyon, the Serengeti, or the Pyramids".

There is no internal structure in the Airlander; it maintains its shape due to the pressure stabilisation of the helium inside the hull. According to HAV, the airship can stay airborne for up to 5 days at a time. At the end of its second test flight in August 2016, however, the nose of the airship crashed into the ground. The airship is currently being rebuilt after it was damaged when it broke away from its moorings in November 2017.

5.4.4 Implementation Stage (How Do We Get There?)

Once strategies have been selected, the next stage of the process involves asking the question, "How do we get there?" It is concerned with putting the plan into action (see ▶ Industry Insight 5.6). This means actually doing things based on the strategy for the whole time period the plan covers. It is the application of the tactical plans based on each component of the marketing mix: product, price, place, and promotion. The implementation stage of marketing planning is all about the development and management of the marketing mix. The marketing mix has been simplified into the well-known four Ps (Product, price, promotion, and place). We will examine in closer detail in Part IV (Implementing the strategies of the marketing mix). In addition, financial indicators are described in detail, such as the required budgets (for promotional tools, marketing research, product development, and other elements of the marketing mix) as well as the predicted expenses, revenues, cash flow, and profit (see ▶ Sect. 5.5.1.7 below).

Industry Insight 5.6

Philippines Tourism's Performance Plan

In February 2017, the Philippines Department of Tourism (PDoT) compiled a tourism performance plan and a strategy plan with a vision for 2025. Its performance report shows how the country performed in the international tourism marketplace. It showed that Korea is the main source market of international tourists with 1,4 million arrivals. Korean tourists constitute almost one-quarter of the country's arrivals. The United States of America was the second top market with a total of 869,463 visitor arrivals. The Chinese market was in third spot in 2016 with total arrivals of 675,663. Japan finished fourth with 535,238 arrivals; Australia followed with 251,098 arrivals. Among the top 12 markets, China posted the highest growth of 37% followed by Taiwan with 29% increase.

Source: ▶ http://www.tourism.gov.ph/Pages/IndustryPerformance.aspx

---

5.4.5 Monitoring and Feedback (How Effective Have the Plan and Its Activities Been?)

The last stage in the marketing planning process is the issue of monitoring. Monitoring answers the question, "How successful were we?" The marketing planning campaign needs to be monitored and assessed so that any problems can be identified and remedied. Usually this involves a systematic review of all aspects of the marketing plan against targets. The monitoring should be carried out on a regular basis, usually monthly or quarterly, so as to ensure prompt attention and action in areas where the results fall behind targets set. One of the easiest and most widely used methods to evaluate marketing planning performance is to analyse the numbers: were the organisation's sales objectives met? In simple terms: "Did the ad' get people to show up?"

A company needs to set key performance indicators (KPIs) and measure performance. A marketers can set KPIs to measure success as a standalone social campaign or as part of a multi-channel campaign.

Sales figures/data is easily accessible to the marketing planner and is an accurate method of analysing how consumers respond to adjustments made to the marketing mix. For instance, results are clear when there is an increase in the number of guests coming to a hotel after a recent advertising campaign. Analysis of sales or bookings on a regular basis allows a marketer to adjust the plan accordingly in the short term and to reallocate resources where necessary. However, marketers must also take coincidental factors into account, positive or negative WoM, a news item, a rapid change in exchange rates, a natural disaster or external unforeseeable event (e.g. a transport strike). If a holiday weekend (with favourable weather) occurs at the same time as a promotion, it could simply be the holiday and not the promotion that caused higher sales. (We will discuss this further in ► Chap. 11).

Digital marketing is the most measurable of the promotions mix tools. It is important to assign KPIs, as they are the metrics you will track to understand whether or not your campaign is meeting your business goals. If your objective is in fact direct conversion, you can also measure this by clicks and conversions, or app downloads if this is your KPI. If your objective is to generate leads for your business, you can track signups and app downloads as your KPIs. Finally, if your objective is to increase brand affinity, this can be indicated through social engagements, follower growth, content views, signups, and app downloads.

A log-file analyser programme can be used to analyse all the traffic to a company's website, time spent on each page and the website in general, favourite pages, requests for a brochure, and other useful stats. With most social media platforms, for example, on Facebook Business Page - a designated 'administrator' automatically has access to the site's analytics tool. Similarly Instagram uses 'Instagram Insights', which can show you when your audience is on Instagram, which of your posts are most popular, and your account's impressions and reach.

Another monitoring method is gathering consumer feedback (e.g. using online consumer ratings and reviews) as part of the marketing research process (see ► Chap. 4).

As we emphasised earlier, effective planning depends on the entire tourism organisation being involved in the whole process. Once the data is gathered and evaluated, it is time for the marketing team to return to the beginning of the tactical or strategic marketing planning process and start all over again although with more data to use.

5.5 The Marketing Plan

Fail to plan, plan to fail.

The marketing process can be considered as the "analysis, planning, implementation and control" of marketing (Kotler, 2000: 3), whereas the marketing plan is the accepted output in written format. It is the essence of purposeful marketing management. Burke and Resnick (2000: 114) describe the marketing plan as a company's road map that shows how the company intends to reach its marketing objectives: "Like a road map, a well-conceived marketing plan can prevent an organisation from taking wrong turns, wandering into blind alleys, and going down dead-end streets." Ferrell, Lucas, and Luck (1994: 144) described a marketing plan as a blueprint according to which the marketing activities of a small to medium enterprise (SME) are structured.

In the tourism industry, marketing planning documents appear in many forms and sizes. For most hotel groups, airlines, visitor attractions, and destinations, the planning format might well take a formal approach and is often embodied in a marketing plan. The marketing plan is the central management tool for approaching and achieving integrated marketing planning. It outlines objectives and goals as well as every aspect of future marketing activity.

Briggs (2001: 47) emphasised the importance of a marketing plan by stating that it is an effort to co-ordinate all marketing activities in order to make the process more effective and to save money. A well-devised marketing plan is the cornerstone of a marketer's skills. O'Hanlon (1972: 45) suggested that a marketing plan serves the following purposes within any tourism organisation:

— It examines the major facts in the marketing situation under consideration.
— It identifies the problems and opportunities inherent in the particular marketing situation.
— It establishes specific long- and short-range corporate objectives for the tourism offering.
— It proposes a long-range strategy to solve problems and to capitalise
— on opportunities.
— It recommends specific selling, advertising, and promotional tactics to carry out short-range strategy and to accomplish the objectives set for the next twelve-month period.

The marketing planning process is ongoing, but the marketing plan covers different timescales. A tactical marketing plan is usually carried out annually, and strategic plans usually span between 3 and 5 years (see ◘ Table 5.5). A corporate marketing plan, in contrast, covers five or more years. Tactical and strategic marketing plans should be cross-referenced with the corporate marketing plan, in which scenarios of where the organisation wishes to be in the longer term are outlined.

▶ Industry Insight 5.7 details Guyana's Tourism Action Plan (TAP) to grow tourism over the next several years.

◘ **Table 5.5** A comparison of strategic and yearly marketing plans

Strategic marketing plan (between 3 and 5 years)	Tactical marketing plan (1 year)
Situation analysis Macro Micro External Internal	Summary of situation analysis SWOT
Forecasts	Target segments and positioning
SWOT analysis	Product [Objectives] Strategies Tactics
Target segments	Price [Objectives] Strategies Tactics
Positioning statement	Place [Objectives] Strategies Tactics
Marketing objectives	Promotion [Objectives] Strategies Tactics
Marketing strategies Product Price Place Promotion	Monitoring, evaluation, and control, including budget
Evaluation and control, including budget	

Source: Author's creation

Industry Insight 5.7

Guyana's Tourism Action Plan 2020–2025

Mission National Tourism Policy: To raise the profile of Guyana as a tourism destination that emphasizes the development of a sustainable, and essentially, though not exclusively, nature-based product that exceeds visitor expectation while making a substantial contribution to the national economy and to the enhancement of the quality of life of all Guyanese. Guyana Tourism Authority: To develop and promote sustainable tourism in Guyana through collaboration to maximise local socio-economic and conservation outcomes and improve the visitors' experience. Department of Tourism: To elaborate the Policy Framework and define the strategic directions as would support the development of sustainable tourism and diversify the product profile of Destination Guyana. Vision 2025 National Tourism Policy: To be recognised internationally, by the year 2025, as a leading sustainable destination. Guyana Tourism Authority: To be recognised locally and internationally as a premier destination for protecting its natural and cultural heritage, providing authentic experiences, and benefitting residents.

Source: ▶ https://www.guyanatourism.com/wp-content/uploads/2018/12/Guyana-National-Tourism-Strategic-Action-Plan-Draft.pdf

The marketing planning process is on-going, but the marketing plan covers different timescales. A tactical marketing plan is usually carried out annually, and strategic plans usually span between 3 and 5 years (see ◪ Table 5.5). A corporate marketing plan, in contrast, covers five or more years. Tactical and strategic marketing plans should be cross-referenced with the corporate marketing plan, in which scenarios of where the organisation wishes to be in the longer term are outlined. For instance, an airline company such as *British Airways* might prepare a corporate plan stating its main intentions in a global setting over the next 20 years. From this, both tactical and strategic marketing plans should flow. Linking corporate and marketing plans ensures that the direction of the organisation is followed.

In this book, a marketing plan (also known as a "tactical plan") is a blueprint to be used to guide a tourism organisation's marketing activities for a period of 1 year. A marketing plan sets out how an organisation will achieve its strategic objectives. It is the central management tool for approaching and achieving integrated marketing planning. It is usually document typed in MS Word (so that it can be modified) consisting of detailed objectives, overall goals and ways of meeting them, broken down into very specific tasks, and covering every aspect of future marketing activity. There should be a tight fit between the tactics in the marketing plan, and the organisation's objectives and strategic marketing plan.

As mentioned earlier, large tourism and hospitality organisations may devise marketing plans for specific brands, key market segments or product offerings, for example, the Beach holidays, Ski holidays, Weddings, Accessible holidays, or City Breaks that *TUI Travel* offers. The form of an integrated communications campaign on a shared message (for example, Durban Africa's "Beyond the Beach" or Cybele's "Inspiration for the mind, body, and soul").

As mentioned earlier, large tourism organisations may devise marketing plans for specific brands, key market segments or product offerings, for example, the cruises, city breaks, family holidays, weddings, villa holidays, long-haul holidays, or luxury holidays that *TUI Travel* offers. Furthermore, some tactical plans may take the form of an integrated communications campaign on a shared message (for example, Durban Tourism's "Beyond the Beach" or British tour operator *Combadi's* "Inspiration for the mind, body and soul").

5.5.1 The Structure of the Marketing Plan

The eight components of a marketing plan, which are described below, largely parallel the structure of the strategic marketing planning process. It should be noted that the development of a marketing plan does not include company objectives or company strategies. A marketing plan is essentially developed for marketing a single product or brand.

5.5.1.1 Executive Summary

This is an abbreviated summary of the main points of the plan for management to review quickly. The summary includes the most important conclusions from the SWOT analysis, the goals included in the plan, the chosen strategies, and the financial expectations. The main aim of the executive summary is to provide top management with insight into the plan without having to study the entire document. It is one of the last elements to be prepared in a tourism marketing plan because it is not possible to summarise the plan before all parts of it have been finalised.

5.5.1.2 Introduction and Background

This part serves as a general introduction to the marketing plan and as a framework for decision-making. The first item is a description of the company mission and the company objectives as well as the SBU objectives. The market that is specifically applicable to the offering or brand has to be defined. Without this definition, it is not clear what the plan refers to. Some background information about the offering, brand or company should also be included in this part of the marketing plan. Lastly, a conclusion summarising the basic problem should be provided.

5.5.1.3 Situation Analysis

A thorough situation analysis forms the basis for well-thought-out objectives and strategies. The situation analysis begins with an internal analysis, including a review of the company's results. It starts with the external analysis and then includes a customer analysis, a description of STP, identifying USPs, product positioning (see ▶ Chap. 7), and a product life cycle analysis (see ▶ Chap. 8). The next step is an overview of the whole industry as well as carrying out a competitor analysis.

5.5.1.4 SWOT Analysis

The SWOT and PESTLE analyses form a summarising description of the situation analysis and provide a starting point for strategies (as described in this chapter as well as in ▶ Chap. 6).

5.5.1.5 Marketing Objectives

The results that need to be achieved in terms of sales, turnover, and market share are an important reason why a particular strategy is chosen. Objectives are often formulated for a one-to-three year period.

5.5.1.6 Marketing Strategy

This section includes the blend of marketing mix ("the 7Ps") components (as described in ◘ Table 5.6.

5.5.1.7 Implementation: Decisions, Finance, and Control

Decisions need to be made regarding the marketing mix components. The plans should be translated into what will be done, who will do it and when it will be done. A detailed development and assignment of responsibilities is important for good implementation. Four questions should be answered:

- What exactly is going to happen?
- When will it happen?
- Who will do it?
- How much will it cost?

Detailed financial indicators are described: the required budgets (for sales promotions, marketing research, product development, and other elements of the marketing mix) as well as the predicted expenses, revenues, cash flow, and profit. Various methods exist to assess and set the marketing campaign budget (Kotler & Armstrong, 2019: 475):

- *Objective-and-task method*: This is a bottom-up approach in which all marketing tasks are determined, and then costed accordingly. The objective-and-task method (or task-based zero method) is popular because it is based on facts, experience, and personal judgement. However, this method can be frustrating for marketing and advertising agencies when the client does not provide a clear indication of the budget limit.
- *Percentage-of-turnover method:* In this case, the marketing budget is based on a fixed percentage of the estimated sales (or turnover) for the year. The risk involved

Table 5.6 Marketing mix "strategies"

Plan	Description
Product-offering	This is an analysis of the product-offering range and product life cycle implications, including plans for branding and new offering development (see ► Chap. 8).
Pricing	The pricing plan should include various pricing strategies to reflect ways in which the organisation sets prices as a signal to markets (see ► Chap. 8).
Communications or promotions	This plan outlines how each tool in the promotions mix (advertising, sales promotions, digital marketing, direct marketing, PR, personal selling, printed literature, and sponsorship) will be used. It is often the largest section of the tourism marketing plan (see ► Chaps. 10, 11, and 12).
Distribution	This plan outlines how the product-offering will be made available. It reviews the range of direct and indirect intermediaries such as travel agencies, the internet, and direct selling (see ► Chap. 9).
Physical evidence	This plan sets out the design of the organisation, including the physical layout, signage, and employee dress code. These are all important factors to consider for gaining a competitive edge.
Relationship marketing	This plan includes a discussion of how the organisation can use various relationship marketing strategies to retain consumers (see ► Chap. 13).

Source: Author's creation

is that the marketing budget declines when sales decline, while a bigger budget may actually be needed to increase sales. Benchmarks for allocating the figure range between 3% and 10% of the revenue figure. The main problem with this method is that it does not take into account a drop in revenue owing to a recession, loss of market share or other external event.

— *Share-of-voice method:* Here products and brands are assessed as to what share of voice they have in the marketplace. This is worked out according to the value (based on cost) of the exposure they receive during monthly periods in promotional material, including advertisements in print, on television and radio, out-of-home, in cinemas, on flyers and on the internet. A tool called "AdEX" measures advertising expenditure in different categories based on media owners' standard rate cards.

— *Competitive parity method:* This method is based on the concept that the budget is set according to the budgets of major competitors. The major disadvantages are that it may be difficult to obtain this information as well as the fact that competitors may budget in an incorrect way.

Marketing control procedures should be implemented to ensure that planned performances as set out in the marketing plan correspond with actual performances (Pitt, 2013: 331). For example, results need to be evaluated against objectives and the implementation of the decisions made must be checked.

5.5.1.8 Appendices

Appendices might include items such as additional data on the market, a timetable and schedule of activities, and references.

Table 5.7 summarises the eight components of the market plan as we have discussed them above.

5

▪ **Table 5.7** Contents of the marketing plan for a tourism offering or brand

Component	Number of pages
1. Executive summary	1–2
2. Introduction and background Company objectives and strategic business unit objectives Market definition	2–3
3. Situation analysis Company mission statement Internal analysis Customer analysis Industry analysis Competitor analysis STP Target audiences Product offering positioning PLC	6–10
4. SWOT analysis The strengths and weaknesses of the company The opportunities and threats facing it (key issues that the plan must cope with)	2–3
5. Marketing objectives What the plan aims to achieve, for example, sales volume or market share.	1
6. Marketing strategy Objectives for marketing mix components Strategies and tactics for marketing mix components	6–10
7. Implementation and marketing control Decisions regarding the marketing mix elements Financial indicators Marketing control	1
8. Appendices Any additional market data Timetable and schedule of activities References	10

Source: Author's creation

Summary

Planning basically means deciding now what to do later. The strategic marketing planning process consists of analysis, planning, imple- mentation, and monitoring. The marketing planning process is not completed until the plan has been put into action and is being monitored on an ongoing basis. The action-oriented components of a tactical marketing plan are born out of the strategic planning process. The term "marketing plan" is widely used in the tourism industry to mean a short-term tactical plan (1–3 years). A strategic marketing plan is different in that it covers 3–5 years or more. Although we have not yet discussed the role of marketing research in the planning process, it should be used as the basis of the decisions made at every stage. For instance, it is all very well to decide to develop a new offering, but research is required to be sure there is indeed a demand from the marketplace. We looked at marketing research in the previous chapter (► Chap. 4).

❓ Review Questions

1. Why is marketing planning important to a tourism organisation?
2. What is the difference between strategic planning and tactical planning?
3. Describe Levitt's (1960) concept of marketing myopia. Provide examples of international tourism companies that have suffered from marketing myopia.
4. Distinguish between goals and objectives. What are your goals after completing your studies? What objectives have you set? Discuss.
5. What are the key elements of the strategic planning process?
6. What is the name of the strategy of developing new product offerings for existing markets?
7. Why is a situational analysis so important in the marketing planning process?
8. In which two ways does Porter (1980) propose that companies can differentiate themselves from competitors? Use examples of several tourism organisations to illustrate your answer.
9. What is a product portfolio analysis and why is it useful?
10. List the core parts of a marketing plan.

In-Depth Case Study 5: Tourism Marketing Planning: Marine Dynamics Shark Tours

Objectives

- To understand the marketing planning process
- To apply the principles of marketing planning to the case study.

Sharks are usually best viewed from a distance, but tour operator Marine Dynamics offer consumers an up-close viewing experience of Great White sharks from the boat deck, and for the adventurous, an even closer and more thrilling experience from the actual cage.

Marine Dynamics specialise in Great White shark cage diving trips from Gansbaai, a seaside village located 170 km south-east of Cape Town. Gansbaai is renowned worldwide for its high concentration of Great White sharks found in "Shark Alley", a channel flowing between Dyer Island and the Cape fur seal colony of Geyser Rock.

The ethos of Marine Dynamics has been shaped by the values and motives of the owner, Wilfred Chivell, an avid marine conservationist who recognised that marine conservation had been neglected. In 2000, Chivell established Dyer Island Cruises, a whale-watching company that eventually became the main sponsors of his marine conservation initiative: The Dyer Island Conservation Trust. Chivell then went on to purchase Marine Dynamics in 2005. Both Dyer Island Cruises and Marine Dynamics fund the Dyer Island Conservation Trust and, in turn, the Trust contributes to research that helps to conserve the marine life that is needed for the survival of the businesses. Chivell feels that a close relationship between the two marine tourism businesses and the Trust is necessary. The platform of Marine Dynamics is financial and operational and many of the staff do much for the Trust without impacting the finances of the Trust.

■ Vision and mission statement

The vision statement defines Marine Dynamics' long-term aim and provides a guideline as to how shark tours can be a tool for conservation. The vision of the strategy is, "To change peo-ple's perceptions about sharks from fear to awe." The mission statement of the strategy is, "To offer adventure and education in a quality shark cage diving experience," and it provides detail on how Marine Dynamics can deliver the vision. The mission provides a connection to Marine Dynamics' marketing strategy.

Goals

As well as being a commercial entity, Marine Dynamics' goals are guided by the owner's conservation ethos. Marine Dynamics aims to:

- Change consumers' perceptions about sharks and shark cage diving
- Give people the opportunity to support shark research and conservation
- Lead by example in the shark cage diving industry
- Conduct research on sharks
- Lobby for stricter conservation laws and affect legislation.

■ ■ Situational analysis

A situational analysis entailed a three-stage process: a macro analysis, a micro analysis, and a SWOT analysis.

■ Macroenvironmental analysis

The macroenvironmental scan provided information on how shifting attitudes towards wildlife as well as lifestyle changes are affecting the demand for shark tours. The viewing of wildlife is an increasingly popular activity worldwide, largely fuelled by the many wildlife programmes on television as well as photographs and videos of wildlife available online. There appears to be a strong interest in sharks, particularly the powerful and mysterious Great White, around which so many myths exist.

Worldwide, there has also been an increase in both adventure tourism and adventure activities. Bungee jumping is one such adventurous activity, but it can hold mass appeal as a result of possible factors such as the fact that the risk is minimal, and no specialist skills are required. Bungee jumping tends to appeal to a younger market, such as backpackers, and is extremely high on the bucket lists of tourists' top ten things to do in South Africa. However, a growing number of tourists are looking to make responsible tourism choices. They seek tourism products that promote conservation and biodiversity, and wish to support conservation projects directly. In addition, volunteer and intern programmes are an important part of Marine Dynamics' model as they support tourism and conservation work.

- **Microenvironmental analysis**

A micro analysis assessed Marine Dynamics' consumers, leadership and staff, competition, and how the media plays a role in Marine Dynamics' success. The microenvironmental analysis revealed that Marine Dynamics' clientele were originally backpackers and adventure tourists, but the market has expanded to include families and people of all ages. The common factor among both its historic and present clientele is an interest in sharks.

The market has also expanded geographically. Marine Dynamics currently attracts tourists from all over the world; 2016 market research showed that tourists came from 85 countries, including the United Kingdom, the United States, and several European countries.

Marine Dynamics has strong leadership. Wilfred Chivell's altruistic goals drive the company and inspire staff. Staff members are motivated to improve their performance through incentives, training, and scope for growth within the company. They also feel a strong sense of pride in working for a reputable company that is active in conservation.

The media plays an important role in creating exposure for Marine Dynamics and enhancing the company's reputation. Features on television documentaries (for example, *National Geographic* has shot footage of shark-cage-diving assisted by Marine Dynamics) and public relations activities (including photo shoots with high-profile celebrities such as Microsoft founder Bill Gates) are other channels through which the company has been promoted. The German car manufacturer Volkswagen sponsors and assists the Trust financially, which helps with credibility and promotion in the German market.

Marine Dynamics is one of eight shark cage diving operators based in Gansbaai. Tours are homogenous and operators are differentiated by price, service quality, and brand reputation. Marine Dynamics' tours are slightly more expensive than those of competitors, but offer a value-added product with good service quality. Every trip has a marine biologist on board educating clients of white sharks and other species.

- ■ **SWOT analysis**

A SWOT analysis assessed Marine Dynamics' value-added service as shown in ☐ Table 5.8.

- ■ **Market segmentation, targeting, and positioning**

Market segmentation was a two-part process. The first part involved identifying South Africa's key international source markets and the second involved identifying niche markets. The selected target markets are nature and adventure tourists from the United Kingdom, the United States, Germany, the Netherlands, and several other European countries. The common denominator among all of the targeted segments is an interest in adventure tourist activities and in particular, Great White sharks.

Based on the fascination of many consumers for Great White sharks, Marine Dynamics opted for subjective positioning or positioning based on the emotional benefits offered to guests. Its slogan is "Your Choice Makes a Difference" and its motto is "Discover and Protect". By going on a tour with Marine Dynamics, guests support shark research and conservation, which can promote a feeling of self-worth. This is also a point of difference as no other shark cage diving operator in Gansbaai has a dedicated research boat supporting its partnership with a research facility and conservation initiative.

Strategic options

Marine Dynamics can use both Porter's generic strategies and the Ansoff matrix to

◘ Table 5.8 A SWOT analysis for Marine Dynamics

Strengths

Good facilities, including a restaurant and dedicated briefing rooms (licensed business premise, unlike many other operators)
Aligned with the Dyer Island Conservation Trust
Experts and researchers accompanying each trip can answer questions
Purpose-built boat can accommodate large groups of people, and is safe and stable
Comprehensive third-party insurance
Strong and inspiring leadership
Good brand image and reputation
Dedicated, passionate, and competent staff
Certified by Fair Trade Tourism (FTT)
Effective marketing in target countries
Part of a collection of products that offer visitors a well-rounded experience
Ownership of several complementary marine tourism companies along the supply chain
Marine volunteer programme attracts hundreds of paying volunteers every year, who assist in carrying out duties and bring revenue to the area.

Weaknesses

Lack of spend on marketing research
Marginally more expensive than competitors
Reliant on Wilfred's leadership.

Opportunities

Further market development both geographically as well as beyond the adventure and backpacker tourist markets
Expanding the use of existing facilities to create a market for marine conferences
Further publicity from nature shows and exposure online.

Threats

Permits have to be renewed every 5 years
Bad weather
Seasonality
Unpredictable shark behaviour
Negative reputation of the shark cage diving industry created by poor service quality
Groups objecting to chumming (luring sharks with chum).

Source: Author's creation

guide its competition strategy and its strategic direction respectively.

Using Porter's (1985) generic strategies, Marine Dynamics is well positioned to adopt a differentiation strategy based on its strong brand name. The brand name can be enhanced by emphasising its high level of service and Marine Dynamics' contribution to conservation. The superiority of the company's boat and facilities in comparison to its competitors will further strengthen the brand name.

This differentiation strategy can then be deployed in the Ansoff product market matrix to determine areas of growth. Shark cage diving is a fledgling adventure activity and there is a strong latent demand. Marine Dynamics can take advantage of its brand name, and engage in market penetration and market development by growing market share within existing markets in Europe and the United States, and moving into expanding markets such as India and China.

5

■■ Marketing mix components

Marine Dynamics makes use of the following components of the marketing mix:

- Pricing strategy: Marine Dynamics has adopted a premium pricing strategy in which its high tour price reflects the quality of its product.
- Communications strategy: Marine Dynamics utilises several traditional promotional tools to communicate messages to consumers and intermediaries. Public relations and advertising in trade and consumer publications that cater to target markets are mostly likely to be effective. The company also attends trade shows abroad in order to build and maintain relationships with agents. It focuses on those shows that are appropriate to its target markets: World Youth Student and Educational Travel Confederation (WYSTC) for backpackers, volunteer tourists, and adventure tourists, and World Travel Market (WTM) for the English market. It also attends Indaba. It goes on road shows in target countries to network with agents, and has representation in the United Kingdom and South America. Marketing collateral is distributed at shows as well as through accommodation establishments and visitor information centres in the area. Continued sponsorship of the Dyer Island Conservation Trust and other conservation initiatives is also recommended. TripAdvisor and other online reviews are increasingly important online tools that the company needs to include in a digital marketing strategy. It has a company website with a facility through which tourists can make bookings or enquiries. The company employs a search engine marketing strategy that involves paying for a good position on the result pages of relevant search engines. Social media is used to attract and maintain interest in the company. Facebook is used to share photos, outstanding video footage is uploaded to YouTube, happenings and updates are recorded in a blog, and Marine Dynamics also utilises Twitter. Film footage of trips is also made available for download, making it accessible to guests and easy for them to share online. The company employs an online community manager dedicated to managing digital content.
- Distribution strategy: The distribution strategy of Marine Dynamics includes both direct selling and indirect selling through intermediaries. Direct bookings are made possible via telephone and the company website. Indirect sales are made through agents in source countries, accommodation establishments in the area, tour operators, and destination management companies (DMCs).

■■ Monitoring and feedback

Assessing sales data is a simple tool for monitoring the effectiveness of a strategy. Marine Dynamics uses the number of trips made within a timeframe and compares it to targets or benchmarks it against the data of previous years. However, given the threat that the weather poses, sales data may not be an accurate reflection of the strategy's success.

Considering Marine Dynamics' mission to offer a quality service, feedback from guests is a better method of assessing the effectiveness of the strategy. Marine Dynamics currently uses basic customer service feedback tools, complaints, and reviews (including a guest comment book and TripAdvisor) as a means of gauging guest satisfaction.

Nature tourists and adventure tourists from South Africa's key source markets were identified as the company's target markets. The opportunity for growth exists through market penetration of existing markets or developing new markets in India and China, countries from which there has been an increase of foreign tourist arrivals in South Africa.

As noted above, Marine Dynamics' tours are priced at a premium to reflect the quality of its offerings. Direct sales are facilitated via the corporate website, but the company also relies on the use of intermediaries located in the source markets.

Traditional promotional tools that are used to communicate the value proposition to the target market include advertising in trade publications, public relations, attendance at trade shows, and sponsorship of marine conservation. Marine Dynamics adopts a comprehensive marketing strategy involving attending travel trade shows, direct marketing techniques, and a corporate website, and uses social media channels such as Facebook and YouTube to attract attention online. In addition, it uses market research to monitor and obtain a better understanding of target markets and the effectiveness of marketing activities.

Shark cage diving is an increasingly popular activity in a competitive industry that has little scope for differentiation. Marine Dynamics offers a superior product in terms of brand name, service quality, and facilities. In addition, the brand name is given further credibility by the company's contribution to research and conservation.

Source: Based on an interview with Brenda du Toit, marketing and sales manager of Marine Dynamics.

Case Study Questions and Activities

1. What are the unique selling points (USPs) of Marine Dynamics?
2. Explain how Marine Dynamics could target domestic tourists.
3. Identify the main target markets of Marine Dynamics?
4. Explain what other promotional tools the company could utilise.
5. Define marine tourism (in your own words).
6. Critique the slogan and motto of Marine Dynamics. Discuss how these brand elements position the company in the marketplace.
7. Go online to the website of Marine Dynamics (► http://www.sharkwatchsa.com). Critique the domain name of the website.
8. What are the advantages of this domain name (► http://www.sharkwatchsa.com) for Marine Dynamics from the perspective of search engine optimisation (SEO)?

References

Ansoff, H. I. (1965). *Corporate strategy: Business policy for growth and expansion*. New York: McGraw-Hill.

Ansoff, H. I. (1988). *The new corporate strategy*. New York: John Wiley & Sons.

Baines, P., Fill, C., Rosengren, S., & Antonetti, P. (2019). *Marketing* (5th ed.). Oxford, UK: Oxford University Press.

Briggs, S. (2001). *Successful web marketing for the tourism and leisure sectors* (2nd ed.). London: Kogan Page Ltd..

Burke, J. F., & Resnick, B. P. (2000). *Marketing and selling the travel product* (2nd ed.). Vancouver, Canada: Delmar Thomson Learning.

Chartered Management Institute (CMI). (2017). *Setting SMART objectives checklist 231*. Retrieved from https://www.managers.org.uk/~/media/Files/Campus%20CMI/Checklists%20PDP/Setting%20SMART%20objectives.ashx [18 August 2018].

Davidson, H. (1997). *Even more offensive marketing* (2nd ed.). London: Penguin.

Evans, N. (2003). *Strategic management for travel and tourism* (2nd ed.). Oxford, UK: Butterworth-Heinemann.

Ferrell, O. C., Lucas, G. H., & Luck, D. (1994). *Strategic marketing management: Text and cases*. New York: International Thomson Publishing.

Hall, C., & Jenkins, J. (1995). *Tourism and public policy*. London: Routledge.

Hefer, D. (2010). *From witblits to vuvuzelas: Marketing in the new South Africa*. Cape Town, South Africa: Zebra Press.

Henderson, B. (1970). *The product portfolio matrix*. Boston: The Boston Consulting Group.

Hoffman, N. (2000). An examination of the sustainable competitive advantage concept: Past, present, and future. *Academy of Marketing* Science *Review*, (4) pp. 45–56.

Horner, S., & Swarbrooke, J. (2005). *Leisure marketing: A global perspective*. Oxford, UK: Butterworth-Heinemann.

Humphreys, A. (2005). SWOT analysis for management consulting. *SRO Alumni Newsletter*, 1.

Kotler, P. (2000). *Marketing management: Analysis, planning, implementation and control* (10th ed.). London: Prentice Hall.

Kotler, P., & Armstrong, G. (2019). *Principles of marketing* (17th ed.). London: Pearson Education.

Levitt, T. (1960). Marketing Myopia. *Harvard Business Review.* July/August, pp. 45–56.

McKinsey & Company. (2008). *Enduring ideas: The GE-McKinsey nine-box matrix.* The McKinsey Quarterly, September.

Middleton, V., Fyall, A., Morgan, M., & Ranchhod, A. (2009). *Marketing in travel and tourism* (4th ed.). Oxford, UK: Butterworth-Heinemann.

Morgan, M. (1996). *Marketing for leisure and tourism.* Hemel Hempstead, UK: Prentice Hall.

O'Hanlon, J. (1972). Making the marketing plan. *Marketing.* June.

Piercy, N. (2002). *Market-led strategic change: Transforming the process of going to market.* Oxford, UK: Butterworth-Heinemann.

Pitt, L. F. (2013). *Marketing for managers* (3rd ed.). Cape Town, South Africa: Juta & Co, Ltd..

Poon, A. (1993). *Tourism technology and competitive strategies.* Oxford, UK: CAB International.

Porter, M. E. (1979). How competitive forces shape strategy. *Harvard Business Review, 57*(2), 137–145.

Porter, M. E. (1980). *Competitive strategy: Techniques for analyzing industries and competitors.* New York: Free Press.

Porter, M. E. (1985). *Competitive advantage.* New York: Free Press.

Tribe, J. (2016). *Strategy for tourism* (2nd ed.). Oxford, UK: Goodfellow.

Further Reading

Baines, P., Fill, C., Rosengren, S., & Antonetti, P. (2019). *Marketing* (5th ed.). Oxford, UK: Oxford University Press.

Porter, M. E. (1985). *Competitive advantage.* New York: Free Press.

The Tourism and Hospitality Marketing Environment

Contents

Electronic Supplementary Material The online version of this chapter (https://doi.org/10.1007/978-3-030-64111-5_6) contains supplementary material, which is available to authorized users.

Purpose

This chapter will provide you with the knowledge necessary to understand the business environment in which tourism and hospitality marketers and their organisations operate.

Learning Goals

After reading this chapter, you should be able to:

- Describe the three core marketing environments: external, performance, and internal
- Understand how to analyse the performance and internal business environments
- Explain how the PESTLE tool is used for analysing the external business environment
- Apply the PESTLE analysis to a tourism and hospitality business
- Critically analyse the main global, regional, national tourism flows and statistics
- Discuss how a tourism and hospitality marketer can respond to these environmental factors
- Apply a business analysis to MSC Cruises.

Overview

Marketing does not exist in a vacuum, but rather in a changing and complex business environment. To understand marketing, we must first understand the environment in which tourism and hospitality marketing operates.

An important task for the marketer is to analyse and make sense of the environment in which the tourism and hospitality organisation operates so that effective marketing decisions can be made.

We begin with a review of the internal environment. Here tourism and hospitality organisations have a much stronger degree of influence. The internal environment consists of the company itself as well as its resources, its processes, and the policies it uses to achieve its goals.

We then examine the performance environment, which concerns the consumers, suppliers, intermediaries, and competitors.

Next, we cover the external environment that affects all individual tourism and hospitality organisations, including political, economic, socio-demographic, technological, ecological (natural), and legal factors. We then examine the fundamental national, regional, and global tourist flows. All of these factors have significant implications for the tourism marketer. They affect not only the way in which an organisation conducts its marketing, offers its products, and runs its operations, but also the market's demand for tourism and hospitality products. However, organisations have very limited influence on these conditions. This examination of the external environment forms the basis of two analyses that help a marketer to understand the current situation in which an organisation finds itself: the SWOT (strengths, weaknesses, opportunities, and threats) analysis and the PESTLE (political, economic, socio-demographic, technological forces, legal, and ecological) analysis. These analyses equip the marketer for action related to strategic marketing planning (discussed in ▶ Chap. 5). Finally, we consider environmental scanning as a method for responding to these factors.

The chapter's case study analyses the business environment in which a cruise liner company, *MSC Cruises*, operates.

6.1 Introduction

All tourism and hospitality organisations internationally operate within a dynamic business environment consisting of many factors that the marketer should consider when making decisions.

Some of these factors are external to the organisation and thus largely out of the marketer's control. The tourism marketer, for example, cannot change the cultural, legal or political environments within which the organisation operates. Similarly, although marketers may be able to influence their customers or suppliers, they do not have complete control over them. In ▶ Chap. 1, we referred to these as uncontrollable factors. Factors that are external to the organisation are known as "macroenvironmental factors".

Factors within an organisation are generally controllable by the marketer. These are known as "internal environmental" factors. They can also be called "microenvironmental" or "performance" factors.

The external, performance, and internal factors are interrelated. For example, the relationship between an organisation and its intermediaries (performance factor) is affected by interest rates, which are an economic factor (external environmental factor).

An analysis of the current business environment is crucial for success as marketers must be able to understand (and even predict) factors that might play a key role in strategic marketing planning. The marketer must also be concerned with the macroenvironmental factors within tourist-generating countries. For example, economic influences such as exchange and employment rates in Germany affect German tourist demand to the United States.

In addition, marketers need to be aware of the trends in the tourism and hospitality industry and the marketplace, both locally and globally. This examination of the business environment forms the basis for conducting both a SWOT analysis and a PESTLE analysis (see ▶ Chap. 5). These analyses, which are also known as "environmental analyses", are discussed in more detail later in this chapter.

> The *internal environment* concerns the resources, processes, and policies an organisation manages to achieve its goals (Baines, Fill, Rosengren & Antonetti, 2019: 153).

6.2 Analysing the Internal Environment

A marketer's task is to develop and promote attractive tourism and hospitality offerings to target markets. The degree of success will be affected by factors within the organisation's **internal environment**. The internal environment consists of those factors that are within the immediate business environment of the organisation. These include the organisation's product offerings as well as human, marketing, and financial resources, as shown in ◘ Fig. 6.1.

Within an organisation itself, a number of aspects that are largely controllable by the marketer affect the organisation's marketing activities. These aspects include the following:

- The organisation's tourism offerings and the markets at which they are targeted, for example, the quality and price of a hotel room usually determine its target market
- The role of other departments in the organisation and how the marketing department fits in; the marketer must work closely with management as well as the finance, accounts, sales, human resources, and other departments
- The corporate culture of the organisation, for example, whether an organisation has either a bureaucratic or an entrepreneurial culture
- How the organisation functions, in other words, what kind of organisation it is.
- Various publics also influence an organisation's marketing activities. These publics may include any organisation – such as shareholders, government, media, local publics, political bodies, or pressure groups – with an interest in the tourism and hospitality organisation achieving its objectives.
- Marketing services agencies that assist tourism and hospitality organisations compile and implement their marketing strategies. These include marketing research, media, advertising, and marketing consulting companies. These companies vary in quality, service, creativity, and price.

The Boston Consulting Group (BCG) matrix (a portfolio analysis) and the SWOT analysis are two analytical tools used for analysing an organisation's internal environment. Wed discuss these in ▶ Chap. 5.

6

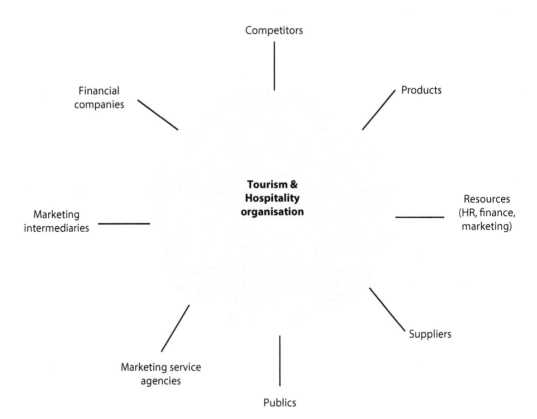

□ Fig. 6.1   The micro- and performance environmental factors. (Source: Author's creation)

6.3 Analysing the Performance Environment

The performance environment (also known as the "microenvironment") includes those organisations that influence an organisation's operational performance, either directly or indirectly (Baines et al., 2019: 144). The performance environment includes competitors as well as suppliers and intermediaries or distributors.

6.3.1 Competitors

An understanding of competition is vital in tourism planning. A company such as a tour operator needs to understand the nature and scope of the competition it faces from other tour operating companies.

Marketers must accept that they face direct and indirect competitors as well as the threat of new competition. They must be aware of what competitors are doing and make the

necessary marketing decisions to respond to competitors' strategies when the time comes.

It is vital that tourism companies understand their competitors. Noble, Sinha, & Kumar (2002) found that organisations who pay more attention to their competitors generally perform better than those who do not. To undertake an analysis of a company's competitors, six key questions should be answered:

1. Who are the company's main competitors?
2. What share of the market do these competitors have?
3. What are their strengths and weaknesses?
4. What are their strategic goals?
5. Which strategies are they following?
6. How are they likely to respond?

Anything that competes for consumers' time and disposable income (the amount of money left over when all necessary expenses have been met) may be viewed as competition. In recent years, the buying habits of consumers in most developed and developing countries have changed (Deloitte Insights, 2019). Many consumers spend money on smartphones, gym contracts, going to football matches, online shopping, gambling, cars and houses. All of these items should be considered competitors to a tourism and hospitality organisation. Economists use the term "cross-elasticity of demand" (the extent to which a change in the price of a holiday leads to a change in consumer demand) to explain this extremely important factor, which is too readily overlooked in the tourism industry.

There are several types of competitor:

Direct competitors are all of the organisations that provide similar tourism offerings to the same consumer at a similar price. For example, *My Travel* is in direct competition with *Hays Travel* in the United Kingdom's travel agency sector of the tourism industry.

— Substitute competitors are alternative offerings that perform essentially the same function as far as the consumer is concerned. At almost every level, non-essential travel competes with various substitute products. A potential leisure traveller may choose to buy a television set, an art course, or a kayak instead of a holiday. Similarly, as a substitute for staying in a hotel, for example, a consumer could choose to stay in an Airbnb apartment, at a campsite, at a holiday resort, or in a B&B.

— Indirect competitors provide alternative offerings. Indirect competitors to a theme park or a holiday resort, for instance, include other forms of leisure activities on which time and money can be spent, such as tickets to the theatre, gardening, or an outing to the cinema.

As we noted in ▶ Chap. 1, to be successful, a tourism and hospitality company must satisfy the needs and wants of consumers better than its competitors do. The marketer must not only adapt to the needs and wants of consumers, but also to the marketing strategies of its competitors. This is most evident when one organisation introduces a strategy, only to find it copied by its competitors shortly afterwards. Some organisations seek to gain an advantage by competing on price (airlines frequently have price wars, as discussed in ▶ Chap. 8). Other organisations do so by providing something different. For example, a quick-service restaurant (QSR) may add vegetarian dishes to its menu. Organisations that are unaware of what their competitors are doing are less likely to be successful.

In addition to existing competitors, new competitors are a constant threat to an organisation. If a Lebanese restaurant in Paris, France for example, is always overcrowded at weekends, a businessperson may see the opportunity to enter the market and open a competing restaurant.

Finally, organisations do not only compete for consumers. They also compete for control of the intermediaries who help them promote, sell, and distribute their offerings to consumers. For instance, hotels may depend on tour operators to send them consumers. Tour operators depend on hotels to give them cheaper rates so that they can attract consumers with better deals. A larger tour operator can offer a hotel more business. In return, larger operators get better rates on block bookings for rooms and are able to pass on these savings to consumers. A smaller tour operator or a smaller hotel may have to focus on other things to make good deals with intermediaries. Within the travel (trade) industry in particular, there is a great deal of vertical and horizontal competition. Travel agents compete with other travel agents as well as with the internet and with tour operators that are encroaching onto the retail sector by selling directly to end-consumers.

The competitive environment within an industry should be reviewed to identify the major competitive forces, as this helps assess their impact on an organisation's present and future competitive forces (Porter, 1980). We discuss Porter's (1980) five forces model in the next chapter. (see ◘ Fig. 6.2).

6.3.2 The Suppliers

Tourism organisations rely on a number of suppliers to satisfy their consumers. The relationship between the organisation and suppliers has become closer and more important

6

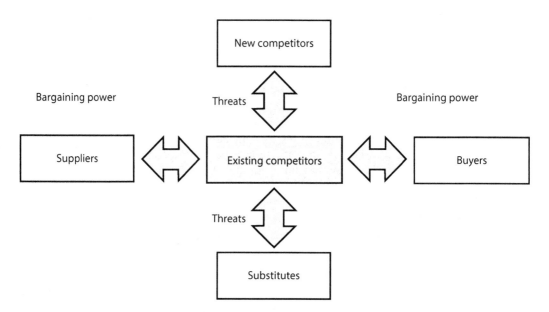

🔲 **Fig. 6.2**   Major competitive forces in the company's environment. (Source: Author's creation)

during the last few years because consumers are demanding higher-quality offerings. The quality of an organisation's offerings depends largely on the goods and services provided by its suppliers. A hotel, for example, relies on food and drink suppliers, a local laundry service, and perhaps a local security company.

The supplier networks and chains in the tourism industry are extraordinarily complex. A network can involve hundreds of suppliers. An airline, for example, relies on caterers, cleaning staff, training, and recruitment organisations, uniform suppliers, engineers and maintenance crew, and manufacturers of engines, parts, and interiors, to name only a few suppliers. In addition, at the other end of the airline industry distribution chain, there is the airline manufacturing market, which consists of a small number of customers: national airlines and low-cost airlines. In such an instance, the suppliers have a strong bargaining advantage.

An individual organisation can also act as a producer and a supplier at the same time. An airline may be viewed as a producer when it sells tickets directly to consumers and as a supplier when it provides holiday packages to tour operators or consumers.

6.3.3 Marketing Intermediaries

Marketing intermediaries are independent companies that promote, sell, and distribute offerings to consumers. They operate between an organisation and its markets, and between an organisation and its suppliers. Thus, they are sometimes referred to as distribution channels or middlemen. In the tourism industry, examples of intermediaries include travel agents (e.g. *Flight Centre, STA Travel*) online travel agencies (OTAs) (e.g. *Expedia, Trivago,* and *Travelocity*), tour operators (e.g. *Saga Holidays, TUI Travel*), destination marketing companies (DMCs), hotel representatives, and food and beverage suppliers. OTAs for example, combine airfares with hotel rooms creating value for customers. The complex relationship between an organisation and its intermediaries can significantly affect its marketing activities. Many tourism organisations use a range of intermediaries to market their offerings to prospective consumers. For example, *British Airways* (BA) relies on many travel agencies, OTAs, and tour operators to promote its flights. Word-of-mouth (WoM) recommendations, social media, and the internet can substitute for these intermediaries, and are becoming more important as tourism and hospitality organisations seek to cut out the costs of middlemen and sell directly to consumers. We will look more closely at the role of intermediaries in ▸ Chap. 9.

6.4 Analysing the External Environment

The **external environment** (or macroenvironment) consists of the societal and global (external) factors that affect a tourism organisation. These factors not only affect external influences on the organisation (such as its competitors), but also impact on the internal environment (for instance, the resources). These elements tend not to have an immediate impact on the performance of the organisation, although they might do so in the long term. The external environment is sometimes referred to as the far or remote environment because it tends to exert forces from outside the organisation's control. To help us make sense of the external environment, we can use the acronym PESTLE. PESTLE stands for the political, economic, socio-demographic, technological, legal, and ecological factors that impact on an organisation (see ▪ Fig. 6.3). This is the one of the most useful frameworks for analysing the external environment (we were introduced to this tool in ▸ Chap. 5).

The external environment consists of political, economic, socio-demographic, technological, legal, and ecological factors that influence an organisation (Aguilar, 1967). Although we use the PESTLE analysis in this book, it is not the only framework that is used to analyse the external business environment. Other frameworks include the PLEETS, PESTEL, SPELIT, SPENT, STEEPL, and STEEPLE analyses. These tools should be considered as checklists that enable tourism marketers to identify the salient and significant forces in the external business environment.

Changes in the external environment can be of vital importance to an organisation. They can bring about the birth or death of an entire industry, make markets expand or contract, determine the level of competitiveness within an industry (Evans, 2019: 156).

▪ **Fig. 6.3** The external (macro-) environment. (Source: Author's creation)

This suggests that the level of risk attached to the external environment is potentially high. As mentioned earlier, an understanding of the current business environment is an essential prerequisite for marketing planning (see ▶ Chap. 5).

> *Marketing planning* is a systematic process involving the assessment of marketing opportunities and resources, the determination of marketing objectives, and the development of a plan for implementation and control (Kotler, 2000).

These external (macro-) environmental factors are subject to continual change. The task of the tourism marketer is to anticipate, review and adapt to these forces continually. For instance, an organisation could adapt to technological changes by installing the latest computer software or a hotel could adapt to the growing number of women business travellers by providing facilities for them. Some of these forces bring opportunities, such as a growing international tourism market from China, for example. Some of them bring threats to an organisation. An example is socio-demographic factors. For instance, high levels of crime in a region may deter international tourists. These external factors are, however, largely beyond the marketer's control. For example, the national tourism organisation Mauritius Tourism Promotion Authority (MTPA) has no control over natural disasters such as a widespread flooding that would most probably affect tourist arrivals to the Indian Ocean Island. Similarly, when a Dubai-based inbound tour operator deals with the North American travel market, which is affected by a fear of international travel as a result of war and political instability in North Africa and the Middle East, this fear is beyond the organisation's control. Nevertheless, an organisation may be able to exert some influence over some of the factors. For example, through organisation and industry sector lobbying, a marketer may have some influence on the political and legal forces in its business environment. The outbreak of the Coronavirus (COVID-19) pandemic in 2020 had a devastating impact on people's lives, with millions of people all around the world falling ill, thousands of people dying, and disrupting peoples' work and education routines as well as travel plans. All tourism and hospitality businesses - most notably airlines, hotels, restaurants, bars, cruise liners, holiday resorts, visitor attractions, and tour operators - were affected and led to thousands of job losses. During this period, role-players around the world such as tourism and hospitality trade associations lobbied their respective governments to announce COVID-19 post-lockdown re-opening dates and relax social distancing measures to make holidaying and dining possible.

Marketing planners must also be aware of macroenvironmental factors in their tourist-generating regions, which are the countries or regions where their target markets originate. For example, the economic variations (in other words, changes in exchange rates and prices) in France concern individual Mauritian businesses since this is a major international market for the Mauritian tourism and hospitality industry.

The macroenvironmental factors that affect an individual organisation, market demand and the tourism and hospitality industry exist at four levels:

- *Local* (for instance, at a local or destination level, perceived high crime rates in cities such as Manchezter affect operations)
- *National* (for example, on a national scale, the interest rate, which affects all British citizens, is a significant factor for all of the tourism Mauritius organisations operating in the United Kingdom)
- *Regional* (for instance, at a regional or western European level, terrorist incidents in a neighbouring country could affect tourism demand at a national level)
- *Global* or international (for example, on a global or international scale, an outbreak of a natural disease such as a virus could affect the demand for world travel and ultimately affect tourism organisations throughout Europe and the rest of the world).

In the next section, we will discuss the external environmental factors predominantly in the context of the UK. We will do this by applying the PESTLE analysis. While each country or region in Europe, or in the world for that matter, has its own unique patterns, the underlying factors are the same.

6.4.1 Political Environment

The political environment relates to the interaction between business, society, and government (Baines et al. 2019: 130). An assessment of the political environment is important because tourism companies can identify signals concerning potential legal and regulatory changes in the tourism and hospitality industries, and have a chance to impede, influence, and alter that legislation. In most instances, the political environment is uncontrollable, although there are situations when an organ-

isation or industry coalition can influence legislation in its own favour.

The political environment affects the marketing decisions of tourism companies and impacts on the business environment at different levels. Tourism is dependent on the freedom of people to travel both internationally and domestically. Government plays a key role in influencing other external business factors such as the economy, which in turn affects the tourism industry. For instance, in the short-term, UK domestic tourism as well as inbound tourism both benefited largely due to the fall in the value of the British sterling against major currencies following the referendum to leave the EU making it more expensive for British citizens to holiday in Europe; although making the UK a more affordable destination for foreign visitors to the UK (Calder, 2016) (see ▶ Industry Insight 6.1).

Industry Insight 6.1

EU Referendum: Impacts on the UK Tourism Industry

In June 2016, a referendum was held as to whether the United Kingdom should remain in or leave the European Union (EU). The British population – through a referendum - voted to leave the EU. Departure from the EU officially took place on the 31st January 2020. The impacts on tourism in the UK and tourism flows between the UK and the EU (as well as between Northern Ireland and Ireland) are uncertain as they will depend upon what the future relationship and agreements the UK have with the EU and what policies subsequent United Kingdom governments adopt in response to the UK being outside the EU.

The UK and the EU tourism industries are highly interdependent with very high levels of travel and expenditure in both directions. When the UK leave the EU):

- The ease of access to the British visitors is likely to fall, although the level of this reduction would depend on the new relationship negotiated with the EU. However,

any significant reduction in accessibility or cost associated with travel to the EU for British residents will benefit the British domestic tourism industry.

- The availability of skilled workers for the tourism and hospitality industry would be severely impacted if freedom of movement for EU citizens was removed. This would have implications for business costs and the quality of service provided to customers.

- The main EU outbound tourism markets rank the UK relatively poorly in terms of perceived welcome. This perception is likely to be reinforced now that the UK has left the EU, impacting on their desire to visit the UK.

- Business travel to the UK is likely to be reduced as companies put investment decisions on hold until there is certainty regarding the UK's relationship with the EU.

Source: Tourism Alliance, EU Referendum. May (2016). Calder, S. 2016. Sunday June 5. The Independent. 'How Brexit will affect British Tourism'.

Factors such as the government's attitude towards business activity may have an impact on an organisation's future plans. For example, the government's involvement in international airline routes and the deregulation of the airlines in the United Kingdom has allowed for greater competition within the domestic airline industry.

Political risk and its potential in the destination country are of great importance to the tourism industry, since the perception of terrorism and political instability may result in a drop in consumer demand. In this regard, outbound tour operators are in a particularly vulnerable position since they cannot assure the safety of their clients in countries or regions beset by political unrest. In recent years, several countries (for example, Spain, Germany, France, Belgium, the United Kingdom, the Ukraine, Turkey, and the United States), and regions in Southeast Asia (such as Thailand), in Africa (Zimbabwe, Somalia, Niger, Tunisia, and Egypt), and the Middle East (for instance, Lebanon, Syria, and Libya) have experienced terrorist attacks and periods of political instability. A significant number of countries are (approximately 60), at the time of writing, deemed off limits by the British Foreign Office (BFO). These include Syria, Iran, Afghanistan, Libya, Lebanon, South Sudan, and Yemen.

Terrorist bombings (such as those that took place in New York and Washington, D.C. in the United States in September 2001, and more recently in Paris in 2015, in Brussels and Istanbul in 2016, in Manchester and London in the United Kingdom, and in Barcelona in 2017) impact negatively on world travel and tourism. Political instability in several countries (for example, Yemen, Iraq, Pakistan, and the Ukraine) have impacted on tourist arrivals to their respective regions. Tourists have been taken hostage, and visitor attractions, tourist areas (including beaches, as in the terrorist attacks at a holiday resort in Tunisia in 2015, which resulted in 38 foreign tourists being killed), nightclubs, hotels, and public transport networks are seen as soft targets by terrorist groups. It is therefore necessary to monitor the political situation in a destination country closely, as the political risks can be significant.

Political change in Eastern Europe has allowed the region to open its doors to inbound and outbound travel. Consequently, Eastern Europeans are now an emerging tourism market for long-haul foreign destinations such as Brazil, South Africa, and Argentina. Similarly, countries in central Asia such as Mongolia have benefited from tourism after a relaxation of political barriers has made it more accessible to tourists. Southern African countries Zimbabwe and Mozambique have both benefited from international inbound tourism arrivals in recent years, following several decades of political instability. In addition, Far Eastern countries such as China have changed their attitudes towards tourism in recent years and have joined the potential growth-generating markets.

The political environment affects the marketing decisions of tourism companies and impacts on the business environment at different levels. Forces to monitor include effects of upcoming local and national elections on consumer confidence; change of government; governmental travel advisories; and threats of terrorism.

Political risk and its potential in the destination country are of great importance to the tourism industry, since the perception of terrorism and political instability may result in a drop in consumer demand. In this regard, outbound tour operators are in a particularly vulnerable position since they cannot assure the safety of their clients in countries or regions beset by political unrest. In recent years, several countries (for example, Spain, Germany, France, Belgium, the UK, the Ukraine, Turkey, and the United States) as well as countries and regions in Southeast Asia (such as Thailand), in Africa (Zimbabwe, Somalia, Niger, Tunisia, and Egypt), and the Middle East (for instance, Iran, Lebanon, Syria, and Libya) have experienced terrorist attacks and periods of political instability (see ► Industry Insight 6.2).

❓ Visit the BFO's website (► https://www. gov.uk/foreign-travel-advice) for advice on countries deemed unsafe. Which countries are currently high-risk?

Africa: The New Battleground for Terrorism

In 2017, a series of bombings which killed more than 350 people in Mogadishu, Somalia, and more recent terror attacks in several countries in Africa highlight the continent as a new battleground for terrorism. Somalia, Tunisia, Niger, and Egypt have been hit by a wave of returning Islamic State fighters as they are being driven out of the Middle East. The Islamic State of Iraq and Syria (ISIS) has expanded into other states such as Niger, Burkina Faso, and Nigeria. In addition, al-Qaeda is looking to secure its future by expanding operations and alliances in the sub-Saharan region, analysts say.

Source: Burke, J. (2017). Moga as they lose ground in Mideast. ishu truck bomb: 500 casualties in Somalia's worst terrorist attack. Retrieved from ► https://www.theguardian.com/world/2017/oct/15/truck-bomb-mogadishu-kills-people-somalia [11 September 2018]. Wirtschafter, J. (2017). Africa becomes the new battleground for ISI and Al-Qaeda. USA Today ► https://eu.usatoday.com/story/news/world/2017/10/25/africa-becomes-new-battleground-isis-and-al-qaeda-they-lose-ground-mideast/796148001/ [18 October 2018].

Terrorist bombings (such as those that took place in New York and Washington, D.C. in the United States in September 2001, and more recently in Paris in 2015, in Brussels and Istanbul in 2016, in Manchester and London in the UK, and in Barcelona in 2017, and more recently in Sri Lanka in 2019) impact negatively on world travel and tourism. Political instability in several countries (for example, Yemen, Iraq, Pakistan, and the Ukraine) have impacted on tourist arrivals to their respective regions. Tourists have been taken hostage, and visitor attractions, tourist areas (including beaches, as in the terrorist attacks at a holiday resort in Tunisia in 2015, which resulted in 38 foreign tourists being killed), nightclubs, hotels, and public transport networks are seen as soft targets by terrorist groups. It is therefore necessary to monitor the political situation in a destination country closely, as the political risks can be significant.

Political change in Eastern Europe has allowed the region to open its doors to inbound and outbound travel. Consequently, Eastern Europeans are now an emerging tourism market for long-haul foreign destinations such as South Africa, Brazil, and Argentina. Similarly, countries in central Asia such as Mongolia have benefited from tourism after a relaxation of political barriers has made it more accessible to tourists. In addition, Far Eastern countries such as China have changed their attitudes towards tourism in recent years and have joined the potential growth-generating markets. Several African countries Angola, Libya, Mozambique, Rwanda, and Zimbabwe have benefitted from international inbound tourism arrivals in recent years, following several decades of political instability and wars (UNWTO, 2018).

6.4.2 Economic Environment

Tourism marketers should be aware of the economic environment in which a tourism organisation operates. It has a significant effect on the organisation's marketing programme and influences the volume of demand generated. Interest rates, employment rates, exchange rates, wealth distribution, and comparative prices are all factors that marketers should take into account. These economic variables in the countries where potential tourists live are particularly important factors that influence consumer purchasing power and spending patterns (for example, demand for travel). These factors also affect production costs and competitiveness in the business environment. They have a much faster and more immediate effect than gradually changing demographic factors.

There are local, national, regional, and global components of the economic environment. Changes in local and regional economies can have a very direct influence on a tourism organisation. Global economic patterns and trends should also receive attention.

6.4.2.1 Interest Rates
Interest rates affect the way British citizens spend their money. This has an impact on market demand as well as investment in new tourism offerings such as restaurants, hotels, and other tourist attractions at a national level. Low- and middle-income earners have less disposable income after paying higher home-loan and hire-purchase instalments. Inevitably this decreases the demand for holidays and other leisure consumption.. During high inflationary periods, consumers are more price sensitive and compare prices to seek value-for-money destinations among tourism offerings.

On a global scale, people in countries with developed economies (such as the United States and Germany) have more disposable income and are most likely to take advantage of tourism offerings. Clearly, there is a direct relationship between the performance of a country's economy and the demand for leisure holidays.

6.4.2.2 Employment Rates
The rate of unemployment obviously affects demand because unemployed people are unable to afford tourism offerings. On the flip side, the tourism industry is a good creator of jobs, creating primary or direct employment in organisations such as restaurants, attractions and lodges. It also generates secondary employment, with indirect creation of jobs in areas such as construction and manufacturing.

In its annual analysis quantifying the global economic and employment impact of travel and tourism in 185 countries and 25 regions, the World Travel & Tourism Council's (WTTC) research reveals that the sector accounted for 10.3% of global GDP and 330 million jobs, or 10% of total employment in 2019 (WTTC, 2019).

6.4.2.3 Exchange Rates
Currency exchange rates play an important role in the tourism business environment especially for tourism companies operating in foreign markets (see ▶ Industry Insight 6.2). In recent years, the value of the British pound sterling has weakened against major international currencies (such as the $US and Euro). At mid-2020, it was trading at $1.27 against the US dollar.) When the British pound is weak against major currencies it is more expensive for UK citizens to go on overseas holidays. However, foreign tourists from such countries benefit as they receive a better exchange rate for their currency. In addition, such a situation may, however, provide opportunities for the British domestic tourism market to prosper. The UK is still a relatively expensive tourist destination, particularly for travellers from developing countries and emerging markets (i.e. Brazil, India, and China, and South Africa), who do not benefit from the exchange rate. Some internationally owned airlines and hotels have attempted to price their offerings in United States dollars, although this is generally frowned upon by domestic tourists and locals. Currency devaluation can have a significant effect on tourism demand.

Overview
As a result of the global economic recession in 2007/2008, two new words were accepted into the Oxford English Dictionary (OED):
— Staycation (a stay-at-home holiday)
— Glamping (glamorous camping) (see ▶ Industry Insight 6.3).

Industry Insight 6.3

Weak Pound Boosts British Domestic Tourism

According to a survey carried out by hotel company Travelodge, over half (55%) of all Britons holidayed at home during 2017 because of the weaker pound. Domestic tourism in 2017 gave the British economy a boost of over £17-billion ($24-billion/€19-billion). The 'holiday index' study found that 53 per cent or respondents stated that their favourite domestic holiday destination was a trip to the seaside. Cornwall, and Devon were popular among study respondents as were north Wales, Blackpool, and the Isle of Wight. Thirty-four per cent (a third) or respondents visited rural destinations such as the Lake District and Scottish Highlands, with more than 27 per cent opting for city breaks to the likes of London, Oxford, Bath, and York. The study has been carried out on over 3000 British during the last seven years.

Source: ▶ http://www.hospitalityandcatering-news.com/2017/06/travelodges-annual-holiday-index-u-k-britons-top-holiday-destination-summer/

6.4.2.4 Inflation

Inflation drives consumer prices higher in a particular country; the price of goods and services might become more expensive, triggering a decrease in sales. Typically, during a recession, consumers tend to purchase less goods and increase their savings. Prices then fall in an attempt to stimulate demand. However, prices may also increase during a recession. It is thus important to understand the wider general economic trends and an organisation's marketplace. ▶ Industry Insight 6.4 describes how the global economic recession boosted domestic tourism in the UK (and for many countries). Annual wage increases in the tourism and hospitality sector will depend on the supply of labour in the sector. In recent years in the United Kingdom, there has been an oversupply (especially in lower skilled jobs) largely due to the influx of migrants from Europe. This has resulted in a stabilisation of wages. However, this may change as a result of Brexit, the United Kingdom leaving Europe) and changes in laws regarding EU nationals working in the United Kingdom.

Industry Insight 6.4

Global Economic Recession Hits Leisure and Corporate Travel, but Boost Domestic Tourism and Staycations

The global economic recession, following the Coronavirus pandemic in 2020, affected tourism worldwide. The global economic crisis was characterised by a credit crunch, economic disarray, and increasing unemployment. Long-haul leisure destinations and business travel suffered. India, for example, suffered a 85% drop in inbound holiday tourist arrivals from the two most-affected countries: the UK and USA. In response, India's Ministry of Tourism used its "Incredible India" campaign to target new markets Worldwide, corporates also tightened the strings on business travel as conferences were either cancelled or became smaller and less lavish. As a result of both fear of the pandemic and economic conditions, consumers altered their travel behaviour and changed their travel plans. Consumers continued to travel, but they travelled differently. They spent less, booked last-minute holidays, travelled locally, and took shorter breaks (known as "snack holidays") and staycations (stay-at-home holidays during which consumers take short trips from their homes to visit local attractions). Self-catering, boating, camping, glamping (glamorous camping) and caravanning holidays were all popular activities during the recession.

Source: ▶ https://m.economictimes.com/industry/services/travel/indian-tourism-industry-hit-by-us-recession/articleshow/3047534.cms

---

6.4.2.5 Taxation

The taxation of tourism is a controversial and topical issue. On the one hand, governments raise revenue from tourism to provide and maintain the necessary infrastructure and sustain the economic benefits from this industry. On the other hand, businesses argue against these taxations on the basis that they slow down growth rates and they reduce the potential for creating and sustaining employment (see ▶ Industry Insight 6.5).

6

Tourist Tax Proposed for the City of Edinburgh, Scotland

The possible introduction of a "tourist tax" – which could take the form of an extra levy on top of hotel room rates – has been proposed by Edinburgh councillors for several years, but the idea has never got off the ground due to opposition from tourism agencies. A tourist tax could bring in £10 million ($14 million/€11,5 million) and that it could have potential benefits such as promoting the Scottish capital city. It could also be used to create new events during the off-season.

Marketing Edinburgh, the city's destination marketing organisation, believes that the tourist tax should not be restricted to hotels only, but could include visitor attractions, transport, bars and restaurants around Edinburgh. The Scottish Tourism Alliance (STA), the main voice of the country's tourism industry, has campaigned against the introduction of a levy in the past, arguing that it would discourage tourists from visiting.

Source: Green, C. (2016). News. The Independent. 'Tourist tax for Edinburgh would raise city's profile'. Wednesday 29 June, p.2 2.

Overview

Venice's gondolas are set to become even more costly after the Italian taxman ruled that boat transport should be subject to VAT. Previously tax-exempt, gondoliers must now pay 5% on takings. The current price of a 40-minute ride is €80 (£68/$97).

Source: Anon. (2016). Taking off. Briefing. The Sunday Times. 'Gondoliers taxed'. Sunday 11 December, p. 2.

❓ Discuss the pros and cons of introducing tourist taxation to a city.

6.4.3 Socio-demographic Environment

The socio-demographic environment is made up of social, cultural, and demographic factors. It comprises the attitudes, values, and norms of society. Tourism companies need to recognise the changes in the socio-demographic environment and adapt or change their offerings. Marketers face the complex task of responding to these rapidly changing factors. We will begin our discussion of the socio-demographic aspects that impact significantly on the tourism consumer markets in both receiving and generating countries by considering the social and cultural factors of fashion and tastes,

changes in lifestyle, the role of women in society, and crime and prostitution. We will then discuss demographic factors – another uncontrollable variable in the external environment – including the main population characteristics: age and race structure, geographic location, family life cycle, and education. Demographic changes – for example, a rise or fall in population, or a decline in a particular age group – should be understood and taken into account when marketers plan long-term objectives, as these important factors influence demand for tourism. The size and structure of a population change constantly and have an impact on the demand for tourism.

6.4.3.1 Fashion and Tastes

Tourism is a great example of a fashion product. A newly opened stylish boutique hotel with themed décor in a metropolitan area can be the flavour of the month, but destinations, like clothes, enjoy cycles of popularity, and go in and out of fashion. Visiting an exotic destination such as the Seychelles is seen by some consumers as a status symbol because of its exclusivity and exotic faraway location, and it soon becomes the "flavour-of-the month" holiday destination.

In addition, destinations and organisations labelled "responsible tourism", "ecotourism", or "sustainable tourism" have become increasingly fashionable in recent years. Consumers are, however, seldom loyal in their tourism demands. In fact, they are more often fickle and will opt for restaurants or destinations that are currently in fashion. Marketers can exploit these opportunities, but a word of caution is required. When an organisation claims to follow a fashion such as responsible tourism, it must be sincere, not merely using the fashion as a marketing tool. For example, marketers who claim that their organisations are environmentally friendly have an ethical responsibility to "practise what they preach" and ensure that their organisation does indeed act in an environmentally responsible manner. If not, this marketing tool will become useless when consumers find out the truth and lose faith in the organisation. In fact, such an organisation will suffer in general if consumers no longer trust it.

6.4.3.2 Changes in Lifestyle

Lifestyles are forever changing, and, over time, consumers shift their preferences. Recent social trends towards healthier lifestyles have led to an increase in sporting holidays, restaurants that provide healthier menus (for example, major brands such as *McDonalds* and *Nando's*), and hotels with more sports and leisure facilities. The dietary habits and lifestyles of many British citizens have changed during the last few years. There has been a growing interest in consuming vegetarian foods as well as in taking part in health and fitness activities. New boutique hotels and lifestyle concepts have emerged to appeal to the millennial generation as well as customers who are aware of the environment and their own health. Examples include *Moxy Hotels* by *Marriott International* (see ▶ Chap. 7 case study) and *Element* by *Westin Hotels and Resorts*. The latter positions itself as an eco-friendly concept, and its slogan reads: where guests can "eat well, sleep well, move well, feel well, work well and play well" (Westin Hotels & Resorts, 2021).

6.4.3.3 The Role of Women in Society

Another factor that has altered the attitudes and values of society has been the changing role of women in many countries. Today, many women in the UK and other developed countries in particular work outside the home and attain managerial positions, making them discerning consumers with particular needs. Marketers of travel agencies can target these businesswomen, as can hotels and restaurants, by providing facilities such as hairdryers, good security, full-length mirrors, and healthy menus. The *Sofitel Le Grand Ducal* (Accor Hotels group), Luxembourg, for instance, is considered 'women-friendly' because of its low-risk location, 24/7 manned reception, on-site secure parking, room service delivered by female staff, as well as for its high-powered hair dryers and Hermes toiletries (Sofitel, 2019). Similarly, The *Peninsula Hotel* in New in York, has a designated female wing and desks that turn into vanity tables. In addition, the rooms have dedicated dressing rooms with nail dryers and Hermes toiletries (▶ http://www.peninsula.com/en/PenCities?property=new%20york).

6.4.3.4 Crime and Prostitution

Various countries such as Brazil and South Africa have high crime rates (George, 2003: 575) and have thus acquired a somewhat tarnished image as a holiday destination. Several criminal incidents involving tourists have occurred and subsequent media attention in the various markets may well have deterred people from visiting Brazil and South Africa.

As for prostitution, social values are culturally based and are not universal. So, for example, organised prostitution in Thailand is tolerated and is a tourist attraction in its own right, whereas it is viewed as a social problem in the United Kingdom and most other European countries. Tourism might not cause prostitution, but it does contribute to it. The social impact of this may be horrific, particularly with the spread of HIV/Aids (Sharpley, 2008: 198).

Destination marketers must try to change negative perceptions that people may have about the region they are marketing. This is often hard to do because the media in tourist-generating countries have created negative images (see ▶ Chap. 14 – Destination marketing). Careful public relations techniques are required (see ▶ Chap. 11) along with integrated efforts by police, tourism stakeholders and the communities at the destinations. A stakeholder is defined as "any group or individual who can affect or is affected by the achievement of an organisation's objectives" (Freeman, 1984: 46). Marketers also need to promote safety and security within their organisations, although with caution, in order to avoid frightening away consumers.

6.4.3.5 Age and Race Structure

At a national level, the age and race structure of the population is important to an organisation in terms of both target markets and the recruitment of employees. People in Western and developed countries are undoubtedly living longer, which increases the size of the population and in turn increases the demand for leisure and tourism activities. Since mid-2005, the British population aged 65 and over has increased by 21%, and the population aged 85 and over has increased by 31% (ONS, 2018). This rise in proportion of the population indicates that the United Kingdom has an ageing population. This is due to both the existing age structure of the population, where people born in the 1960s' baby boom are entering older ages, as well as the population living longer. This has significant implications for the tourism and hospitality marketer, as the older population and retired market (the 'grey tourism' or 'silver' tourism market) represent a large market for cruises, coach travel and niche tourism holidays (such as health tourism and medical tourism, which are discussed in ▶ Chap. 3).

People in the retired market are often free from family commitments, and have the time and the money for travel. People in their fifties who have retired represent an attractive target for tour operators. In developed countries, there is an increasing number of active, relatively affluent people over the age of 55 who are retired or near retirement. Tourism marketers need to find ways to attract this expanding mature market. These trends have led to the increased provision of niche (or specialised) tourism offerings. One such example is the tour operator *Saga Holidays* (who cater for the over 55 s travel market) and coach tours for retired people (see ▶ Chap. 7).

Developing countries (especially those in Latin America and in Africa), however, are characterised by younger populations, with significant numbers of young adults and those in the 18–24 age group (IPOS, 2018). These trends have led to the increased provision of niche (or specialised) tourism offerings. For example, businesses and markets targeting people in the 18–35 age group such as youth tour operators, short-break holidays, and live concert on-board cruise liners (see ▶ Chap. 3). The young Asian traveller market is a relatively untapped market and is now being targeted by various tourism organisations. (see ▶ Industry Insight 6.6).

Industry Insight 6.6

The Pacific Asia Travel Association Targets Youth Travellers

The Pacific Asia Travel Association (PATA) launched a new study focussing on the way young people from North-east and South-east Asia experience travel, and how the future expected increase in outbound travel from Asia can be managed to ensure that both large and small destinations can benefit from growth. Following the Association's report on Millennial travel trends: 'The Rise of the Young Asian Traveller', an additional study aimed to understand the implications of future outbound tourism growth from Asia. The study involved research gathered from an online survey on the travel trends of young consumers in the Asia Pacific region. "As young people travel further and more frequently, they gain confidence to discover the hidden corners of the places they visit, spending with local businesses and gaining an authentic experience of the lifestyle of local people," said Rajiv Kapoor, head of marketing and cross border Asia Pacific.

Source: ▶ http://www.travelweekly-asia.com/Marketing/PATA-targets-young-travellers-in-new-study

6.4.3.6 Population

China and India are the two most populated countries. Both of these developing countries have a huge and increasing middle class. India has an estimated 250 middle class consumers, and thus represent great potential for overseas travel (Popescu, 2018). Tourists from China participated in over 149,7 million overseas trips in 2018: accounting for a fifth of all sales by international tourists (UN-WTO, 2019). According to the UN Population Division (2017), by 2050 India's population is set to reach around 1,6 billion, China's is set to reach 1,3 billion and the United States is set to reach almost 400 million, and the United Kingdom is set to reach 75 million (▶ ons.gov.uk).

Several countries such as Russia and China are forecast to experience a decrease in populations. These changes will have a significant effect on the International tourism flows between countries, in particular the likes of China which is forecast to have a growing outbound tourism market (UNWTO, 2016: 11).

6.4.3.7 Education

The influence of education is an important determinant of travel. In general, the higher the level of education people achieve, the greater the amount of travelling they undertake. Education is linked to factors such as income, social class, and household composition. Having a tertiary education – particularly a degree – increases one's chances of getting a job.

In developed countries, there is a trend for students to experience overseas travel as part of their education. 'Gap years', during which students take a year off before or after college or university, have become popular and almost a 'rite of passage' for many graduates.

> **Overview**
>
> South Korea has the highest projected life expectancy for men and women. South Koreans girls born in 2030 can expect to live until the age of 90,8 and boys born in 2030 can expect to live to 84.
>
> The Economist, 2019. Pocket World in Figures 2019. London: Economist Books.

6.4.4 Technological Environment

The impact of technology on people's lives has increased dramatically during the last few decades. Nowhere has this been more evident in recent years than in the travel and tourism industry. One of the most significant changes is from social media platforms. Consumers are increasingly researching, booking, and paying for travel services using their smartphones. Individuals are using their smartphone as a boarding pass for airlines, paying for services such as coffee by scanning a bar code from the smartphone or smartwatch, registering at a hotel, using it as a key access to their hotel, and using it as a boarding pass when checking-in for a flight. Similarly, technological advances in the hospitality sector enable guest services such as check-in (using facial recognition devices) room service, valet parking, spa services, and dining room reservations to be accessed from guests' smartphones and tablets. Mobile phones can even be used by authorities to track tourists' whereabouts.

The development of new technologies (or 'tech trends") such as 5th Generation ('5G') wireless technology, recognition technology (e.g. for hotel check-In), apps, AR, Internet of Things (IoT) (Internet-based interconnectivity between everyday devices), VR, big data, artificial intelligence (AI), robotics, and new geographic information systems (GISs) has created more possibilities for marketing (see ◘ Table 6.1). In airports, meanwhile, luggage cases can be installed with sensors that will alert passengers when they pass by. Advancements in information and communications technology (ICT) (in particular digital marketing) are leading to changes in business processes and service standards. An increase in home-based entertainment (led by new technology such as digital television and computer games) may reduce consumers' spending on tourism product offerings. Product-offerings are increasingly being promoted and distributed on the internet, accessible to consumers anytime of the day almost anywhere via their smartphones and tablets.

□ Table 6.1 Tech trends in the tourism and hospitality industry

Tech trend	Example in tourism and hospitality industry
IoT	Used in hotel rooms to provide guests with a device that connects to everything from the lights to the heaters and air conditioning, allowing all to be controlled from one place.
Recognition technology	Recognition technology is already being used in some hotels to allow access to rooms via fingerprints, or to allow for semi-contactless check-outs. However, in the future, it is hoped that this technology may be able to allow for customers to pay for meals in the hotel restaurant simply by walking through the exit.
Big data	Used by tourism companies to improve personalisation, using the information they gather to make specific adjustments to their offerings. Hotel owners use big data for revenue management purposes, using historic occupancy rates and other past trends to better anticipate levels of demand. When demand is predictable, pricing and promotional strategies can also be optimised.
Robotics	Robots are also utilised in airports to detect concealed weapons, while some manufacturers are also using robotics to create luggage cases that intelligently follow passengers.
Artificial intelligence (AI)	Used for customer service purposes, with 'chatbots' possessing the ability to deliver rapid response times to consumer problems or queries. Hotels and travel companies make use of AI to sort through data accurately and continuously. It will be able to draw conclusions about business performance or trends associated with customer satisfaction, and even intelligently manage stock.
Augmented reality (AR)	AR involves augmenting a person's real surroundings, rather than replacing them. One of the major plus points of this particular technological trend is that it is cheaper than VR, with users requiring only a smartphone or tablet device which has access to the internet. Used to enhance the customer experience, providing customers with valuable information or even pure entertainment. For instance, apps can allow for photographs to be augmented through filters and effects.
VR	Hotels use VR to showcase their rooms, reception areas, and local visitor attractions on their website in order to increase awareness and encourage bookings, Interactive virtual maps or VR hotel tours/360 video tours to present a hotel upfront.

Source: Author's creation

Technology has enabled and improved security in holiday resorts, conference centres, and hotels as well as at events. It has also impacted on consumer research: tourism and hospitality businesses develop databases (and big data) of customer profiles and customer buying behaviour to assist in effective direct and digital marketing.

It is important for tourism and hospitality marketers to understand and anticipate changes in the technological environment. Because tourists are involved in the delivery process, technology changes often mean that staff need training in how to use the new technology.

Chester Card Machines Tap Tourists for Donations

In July 2017, the Roman city of Chester installed "Oyster-style" card readers on its Roman walls so that tourists can donate and contribute towards the upkeep and maintenance of the walls. The sandstone walls built almost 1900 years ago as part of Chester's defences, cost £600,000 (€855,000) a year to maintain and protect (Anon, 2016). The two-mile circuit of Grade 1-listed walls attracts over 2,5 million tourists to the north-west British city each year. The card payment hotspots - like Transport for London's Oyster system - are located at the historic Roman Amphitheatre, Newgate Tower and King Charles Tower.

Tourists are being asked to consider donating a minimum of £2 (€2.3/$2.8) by tapping their bank card against one of the machines. The ancient Chester Walls are one of the city's most recognised and visited tourist attractions. As a result, the Council have explored ways to enable them to maintain the significant levels of investment needed to ensure they are well-maintained and safe for the 2.5 million people that walk and enjoy them each year. Chester was founded as a "castrum" or Roman fort with the name Deva Victrix in the reign of the Emperor Vespasian in 79 AD. Chester was one of the last cities in England to fall to the Normans but when it did, William the Conqueror ordered the construction of a castle, to dominate the town and the nearby Welsh border. The Romans began building them between 70 AD and 80 AD as a defensive structure to protect the city and fortress.

Source: Anon. (2016). The Times. News, 'Chester card machines tap tourists for donations' Monday 8 August, p. 11.

6.4.5 Legal Environment

The legal environment covers every aspect of an organisation's business. Codes of practice in advertising and transparency of pricing have been enacted in most countries. However, advertising standards differ around the world. In the United Kingdom, advertising is self-regulated, i.e. by the advertising industry itself. In other countries, advertising is restricted by legislation. In the United Kingdom, advertising is overseen by the Advertising Standards Authority (ASA). ASA applies codes of practice in advertising and upholds advertising standards for consumers, business, and the general public. Such self-regulating agencies operate in other countries (e.g. the Advertising Standards Council in India, and the Bureau de Vérification de la Publicité in France). In the European Union, the European Advertising Standards Alliance oversees both statutory and self-regulatory provision in most European countries and even in non-European countries such as Russia, the United States, Canada, Turkey and New Zealand. See ▶ Chap. 11 for a discussion on advertising.

Transportation can be affected by external regulations as well as actions by the transport company's staff. For example, regulations may determine the number of flights, the routes that can be flown, and the number of seats on an aircraft, while the staff of a public transport company (such as a team of air traffic controllers) may decide to take industrial action (strike), affecting the accessibility of tourism offerings .

On a local level, tourism and hospitality marketers are affected by legislation and regulation. Destinations and businesses are affected by visa requirements and border controls, government deregulation, health and safety, funding of the destination marketing organisation (DMO), and employment legislation. ▶ Industry Insight 6.8 illustrates the impact of the increased cost of visas in Egypt is likely to impact on tourist numbers from the UK.

6

Egypt Doubling the Cost of Visas

Egypt has started charging tourists more than double the amount they pay for a visa to enter the country. The cost of a single-entry visa increased from $25 (£20 /€23) to $60 (£48/€55) from July 2017. Multiple-entry visas cost $70 (#54). The increases were tabled at a time when the country's tourism sector was still struggling to regain normality after a series of terrorist incidents, including the bombing of a Russian passenger aircraft in 2015. The October 2015 plane crash prompted Russia to suspend all air links with Egypt and the British Government to halt flights to Sharm el-Sheikh, a popular Red Sea resort in the Sinai from which the doomed Russian aircraft took off. For a couple of years since the attacks the UK Foreign Office has warned tourists to avoid Sharm el-Sheikh. Other tourist destinations such as Greece, Spain, and Italy popular with Western European tourists have benefited from political uncertainty in North Africa and countries in the Middle Eastern region.

Source: ▶ http://www.msn.com/en-gb/travel/news/one-million-fewer-britons-are-visiting-egypt-so-why-is-it-doubling-the-cost-of-visas/ar-AAnw9LX?li=AA5afI&ocid=spartanntp

6.4.6 Ecological Environment

The marketer must also be aware of the natural environment in which the tourism organisation operates. The natural environment involves the natural resources that are needed as inputs by marketers or that are affected by marketing activities (Kotler & Armstrong, 2019: 95). The various stakeholders in the industry should be concerned with these factors and should respond by attempting to support the positives while minimising the negatives. The natural environment of a country is, after all, very often the main attraction to domestic and international tourists. The natural environment includes the environment itself as well as health issues, natural disasters, and wildlife accidents (see ▶ Industry Insight 6.9).

6.4.6.1 The Environment

On a local and national level, environmental issues represent both opportunities and threats to the tourism industry. The opportunities relate to the fact that many consumers will pay more for an environmentally friendly offering and will remain loyal to, say, a hotel group that recycles or participates in environmentally responsible activities. However, the tourism industry also poses a threat to the natural environment. For example, tourist aircraft generate carbon emissions (CO_2) and air and noise pollution, and the construction of hotels, resorts, and attractions generates various negative or undesirable environmental impacts. These impacts depend on the type of development, the environmental characteristics of the area, and the extent to which proper planning and management are conducted.

Tourism places enormous stress on local land use, and can lead to soil erosion, increased pollution, natural habitat loss, and more pressure on endangered species. These effects can gradually destroy the environmental resources on which tourism itself depends. According to Hall (2010) the main global environmental issues judged likely to affect consumer behaviour and cause a threat to tourism and hospitality businesses are outlined below.

1. *Biodiversity*

Biodiversity is essentially every living thing and ecosystem that makes up the environment; from trees to microorganisms, everything plays an important role in the maintenance of the planet. However, with the increase in global warming, pollution and deforestation, biodiversity is in danger. Billions of species are going or have gone extinct all over the world. Reducing our meat intake, particularly red meat, as well as making sustainable choices can help to keep the planet running more efficiently.

2. *Depletion and pollution of water*

Lack of water prevents populations from reaching their potential. During the 2018 holiday season, Cape Town, South Africa suffered from a severe drought, which impacted negatively on the city's tourism industry (see ► Industry Insight 6.9). Some tourist facilities, destinations, and resorts (such as swimming pools and golf courses) consume large amounts of water. Pollution of water such as an abundance of plastic waste and toxic chemicals entering waterways causes damage to this most valuable resource the planet has to offer. By educating people on the causes and effects of water pollution, we can work together to undo the damage humans have caused. Laws also need to change to make pollution stricter, consistently across international borders.

3. *Deforestation*

Many of the Earth's natural resources are becoming scarce as a result of excessive human needs and wants. In particular, deforestation is threatening the forests of the Amazon and the African bush. Plants and trees provide oxygen, food, water and medicine for every-

one, all around the world. To help combat this issue hotels and hospitality businesses can purchase more recycled and organic products, limiting the amount of paper and cardboard they consume.

4. *Pollution*

Pollution is one of the primary causes of many of the other environmental concerns, including climate change and biodiversity. The seven key types of pollution: air, water, soil, noise, radioactive, light and thermal are affecting our environment. All types of pollution and environmental concerns are interrelated and influence one another.

5. *Climate Change*

The Earth is warming-up more than it would do naturally as a result of human activities, including the use of chlorofluorocarbons (CFCs). Greenhouses gases are the main cause of climate change, trapping in the sun's heat and warming the surface of the earth. The rise in global sea levels is shrinking the land, causing mass floods and extreme weather incidents across the world. Examples of the consequences of global warming include an increased frequency of serious storms such as typhoons or hurricanes, which affect tourism resorts, and a rise in sea levels, which affects low-lying countries such as Mauritius.

Industry Insight 6.9

Drought Hits the Western Cape's Tourism Industry

Tourist numbers to Cape Town decreased as a result of one of the worst droughts ever in the region. While no official data was available to quantify the impact of the severe water restrictions in the city, there was no doubt that the tourism industry was affected. Several tourism

businesses reported a drop in bookings, despite ongoing messages that the city was open for business. Hoteliers complained that it was virtually impossible to enforce the 50-litres-per-person-per-day restriction on guests. Initiatives to curb water usage included removing bath plugs, fitting showers with water-limiting devices and buckets, encouraging shorter showers, and washing linen and towels less frequently. At the same time, the price of water significantly increased, with some accommodation owners saying there were increased costs of around 450%.

Sisa Ntshona, CEO of SA Tourism, said that Cape Town is not alone in dealing with drought. Cities all around the world, from Los Angeles to São Paulo to Jakarta, are all facing the same problem. "This is the new norm," he said. "Even if it rains tomorrow, we can never go back to the old way of consuming water."

Source: Venter, L. (2018). JAMMS: Cape drought hits tourism, Joburg meeting to engage trade. Daily Southern and East African Tourism Update. Retrieved from ▶ http://www.tourismupdate.co.za/article/176997/JAMMS-Cape-drought-hits-tourism-Joburg-meeting-to-engage-trade [16 August 2018].

6.4.6.2 Health and Safety Issues

On a global level, particularly in developing countries, public health issues such as viruses and diseases will continue to threaten tourism and hospitality offerings and destinations. Over the last few years, most countries around the world and their tourism and hospitality companies (such as resorts and cruise liners), and international sporting events were negatively affected by an outbreak of the Coronavirus in 2020 (see ▶ Industry Insight 6.10).

Industry Insight 6.10

"Closed for Business": Coronavirus Pandemic Hits Global Tourism

During the first few months of 2020, China was hit by a public health crisis when a new strain of coronavirus, from the family of viruses that gave rise to severe acute respiratory syndrome (SARS). The government of China asked citizens not to leave the city of Wuhan, where the outbreak originally occurred. A coronavirus (called COVID-19) was confirmed and swept the world as soon after the majority of countries were affected. During 2020, tens of thousands of people died and millions of people contracted the virus. This led the World Health Organization (WHO) to announce the virus a pandemic and declare the outbreak a global health emergency. Many major cruise liners and international airlines went into administration and announced job losses after struggling to raise funds, and travel bookings dropped off due to the pandemic, which was considered the worst for over one hundred years since the Spanish Flu pandemic which killed over 50 million people worldwide. Iconic tourist attractions including the Eiffel Tower, Disneyland, all theme parks and zoos, National Trust parks, entertainment venues, and gardens were forced to close their doors. German-based tour company TUI suspended hotel bookings, package holidays and cruises for several months. Most hotels, pubs, restaurants, and cafes in all affected countries suffered a significant decrease in footfall. Closures of restaurants caused a ripple-effect among related industries such as food production, alcohol, wine, and beer-production, food and beverage shipping, fishing, and farming. Global sporting events such as the London

Marathon 2020, Tokyo 2020 Olympic Games, Euro 2020, and all festivals were postponed or cancelled. This was the biggest macro environmental impact since the 9'-11 terrorist attacks with airports and international borders being forced to close resulting in hundreds of thousands of redundancies in the transport, tourism, and hospitality industries. International travel between Europe, which became the epicentre of the virus - was prohibited. In Europe, the UK, Italy, Belgium, and Spain were particularly affected. Outside of Europe, the United States, Brazil, Russia, Peru, South Africa, Iran, Mexico, and India were particularly affected. Tourism dependent nations in Europe such as Spain, Greece, Cyprus, Croatia, Italy, and Portugal suffered badly with international travel being cancelled during most of 2020. For instance, hotels, apartments, and restaurants in the Spanish resort town of Benidorm were empty during the 2020 summer season. This was a similar pattern in all tourist resorts around the world. Anybody that was able to travel was forced to 'self-quarantine' and isolate for up to two weeks following a holiday in countries experiencing high infection rates. A wide range of measures were implemented in destinations and businesses worldwide in order to attempt to sustain business. Safety and hygiene products, the promotion of domestic tourism, combined with measures such as travel corridors/bubbles, temperature testing at hotels, resorts, and airports, and mandatory wearing of face masks and 'social distancing' measures when using public transport and in social and public settings were implemented. A number of countries implemented a number of initiatives to boost travel and tourism, these included travel vouchers, hospitality tax deductions, travel subsidies, and social programmes. Japan, for instance, introduced a 'Go To' campaign, which included travel expenses paid by the Japanese government to stimulate domestic tourism demand within the country.

Over the last couple of decades, the international travel and tourism industry has been affected by global health issues including severe acute respiratory syndrome (SARS), Middle East respiratory syndrome (MERS), and Ebola but not to the extent and severity of COVID-19. The pandemic outbreak led to a re-think in consumer behaviour and the way consumers travel: people were forced to live locally and had to limit their travel to shorter travel, trips closer to home or proximity travel, travel by car, shorter holidays (one-week holidays and not two-weeks), staycations, and confined to inter-state/province/county travel. Travel trends emerged such as 'localism', driving to local attractions, day trips, cycling holidays, self-catering holidays, camping, nature holidays, and increased demand for boutique hotels and B&Bs in small towns and in the countryside. Business travel, which airlines rely on, were particularly affected..The pandemic highlighted the inter-connected impact of macroenvironmental factors affecting the global economy. COVID-19 was an example of an unforeseen global health crisis that severely impacted on the international travel and tourism industry in 2020 and beyond. However, history shows the tourism and industry is resilient and will eventually recover, but to what extent it will recover remains to be seen (◘ Image 6.1).

6

◩ **Image 6.1** The 2020 Coronavirus pandemic decimated the tourism and hospitality sectors worldwide. (Source: Unsplash)

6.4.6.3 **Natural Disasters**

Natural disasters occur throughout the world and have a dramatic impact on the lives of the people who are directly affected as well as on people planning to visit the area. Natural disasters include crises such as earthquakes, hurricanes, floods, tornadoes, typhoons, avalanches, tsunamis, cyclones, fires, and volcanic eruptions. The occurrence of a natural disaster at any destination affects its popularity. An example is the December 2004 Asian tsunami, which devastated parts of Southeast Asia and was one of the worst natural disasters in history.

Similarly, during 2019 and 2020 Australia experienced horrific wildfires destroying millions of acres of bush and thousands of homes. Mozambique, Malawi, and Zimbabwe were affected by a cyclone in 2019 which resulted in over one thousand casualties. Many areas in both regions were declared disaster zones. Flooding creates further problems, including mud and landslides. The Bahamas, Cuba, eastern Florida, and the Florida Keys were hit by severe hurricanes in September 2017, resulting in catastrophic damage to homes and tourism businesses.

Damage to infrastructure such as roads and bridges limits access to destinations affected by natural disasters. In addition, many of these disasters occur without warning and have a devastating effect on a region's tourism industry when widely reported on television or in newspapers. Thus. natural disasters, along with their associated media exposure (which includes newspaper reports and images, and shocking scenes on television and on social media and the internet) combine to reduce the numbers of visitors to the affected region.

In certain cases, a shortage of natural resources impacts on the tourism business environment. Most cities in developed and developing countries, from time-to-time, experience power failures impacting transport services and service providers such as local restaurants and hotels. Such inconveniences affected businesses in the region and resulted in a loss of hundreds of thousands of pounds to the economy.

Industry Insight 6.11

Thailand Floods Results in Deaths and Causes Havoc to Tourists

The Thai holiday islands of Koh Samui and Koh PhaNgan in southern Thailand were affected after severe flooding and heavy rains left 18 people dead and hundreds of villages partially submerged in December 2016. The torrential rain, which lasted for two days, turned roads into rivers and caused structural damage to over 1500 schools in the region Anon (2017). Armed forces had to be mobilised across the region to help evacuate flood victims, distribute aid, and provide temporary shelter for victims. Army helicopters were also deployed to deliver food to families trapped inside their homes. The months of December and January are traditionally the high season for tourists who flock to the Thai island resorts. As a result of the disaster, hundreds of tourists had their flights delayed, while train and bus services on the mainland were also suspended.

Source: Anon. (2017). At least 18 dead in Thailand floods. The Guardian. Available: ▶ https://www.theguardian.com/world/2017/jan/08/at-least-18-dead-from-flooding-in-thailand-and-malaysia. Accessed 1 June 2017.

❓ Discuss the PESTLE analysis as it might apply to tourism in your country or region.

6.5 **Global and Regional Flows**

Understanding where international tourists prefer to travel to is also important to the tourism marketer. Here we examine trends from at a global level.

6.5.1 **Global Flows**

International tourist arrivals (overnight visitors) decreased by −74% during 2020 (UNWTO,

2021:1). This represents 1.1 billion fewer international tourist arrivals in January–December 2021 compared to 2019, which translates into US$ 1.2 trillion lost in international tourism receipts (export receipts), and up to 120 million jobs at risk, worldwide, under the impact of the COVID-19 pandemic and resulting economic crisis (UNWTO, 2021: 1). In the previous year 2019, the number of international tourist arrivals had increased by 3,9% to reach a total of 1,4 billion, according to the latest UNWTO world tourism statistics (see ◘ Table 6.2). Some 51 million additional tourists (overnight visitors) travelled internationally in 2019 compared to 2018 (UNWTO, 2020). Based on these statistics, more than half of this total number (745 million) travelled to Europe (see ◘ Table 6.2), and more than two-thirds of international travellers went to just 20 countries.

The UNWTO's *Tourism Towards 2030* report is UNWTO's long-term outlook over the two decades from 2010 to 2030 . According to the *Tourism Towards 2030* report, the number of International tourist arrivals worldwide is expected to increase by an average of 3,3% per year over the period 2010 to 2030 (UNWTO, 2016: 14). At the projected rate of growth, international tourist arrivals worldwide are expected to reach 1,8 billion by 2030 (UNWTO, 2016: 7). This projection will be dependent on the global tourism industry's rate of recovery following the COVID-19 pandemic in 2020. ◘ Table 6.3 shows the growth of international tourism receipts by region from 1960 to 2019. Europe appears to dominate in terms of international tourism receipts. Africa and the Middle East have grown rapidly in terms of both international visitor arrivals and tourism receipts since 1960. International tourism receipts throughout 2020 are likely to reflect record lows due to the COVID-19 pandemic.

6.5.2 Regional Flows

In 2019, Africa received 73,1 million tourist arrivals, accounting for almost 5% of global arrivals (Morocco held first position in the region, with almost 12,9 million tourists arriving in 2019, with an increase of 5,2% over the previous year (UNWTO, 2020: 16). South Africa occupied second place in the continent, with 10,2 million tourist arrivals in 2019 (a decrease of 2,1% over 2018) (UNWTO, 2020: 11). The United Arab Emirates (UAE) rose several places in the Middle Eastern rankings in 2019, with 16,7 million tourist arrivals (+5,1% over 2018) (UNWTO, 2020: 1).

With 82,6 million international arrivals in 2019, France remained the top global tourism destination (see ◘ Table 6.4) (UNWTO, 2020: 6). The country hosted approximately more than three million more international arrivals than the United States. Thailand, China, and Mexico all featured among the top ten of world tourist destinations (UNWTO, 2020: 6).

Although the United States was second in the league of top international arrivals (79,3 million), it was the leading global tourism earner (US$214 billion) in 2019, followed by Spain ($79,7 billion), and Thailand ($60,5; climbing three places) (UNWTO, 2020: 12). This highlights the fact that the United States attracts a greater share of higher-spending long-haul tourists than its European competitors, which rely much more on short-haul (interregional) tourism. Completing the top ten in international tourism receipts was the Chinese Special Administrative Region, Macau (in tenth position with $39,5 billion), and Japan, which made it into the top ten with $46,1 billion, an increase of 8% over 2018 (see ◘ Table 6.5). Total international tourism receipts grew to US$1478 billion in 2019, corresponding to an increase in real terms of 3,6% over 2018 (UNWTO, 2020: 14). The top three spenders on international tourism in 2019 were China (US$255 billion), the United States (S$152 billion), and Germany (S$93,1 billion) (see ◘ Table 6.6).

Table 6.2 International tourist arrivals (millions), 1970–2020*

	1970	1980	1990	1995	2000	2005	2010	2017	2018	2019	Change (%) '19/'18	% +/– 2020 YTD	% +/– 2020 Q1
World	162,0	277,0	526,0	527,0	674,0	809,0	956,0	1333,0	1409,0	1460,0	3,6	–55,6	–22,8
Europe	1154,0	177,3	261,5	303,5	386,6	489,0	489,3	673,0	710,0	745,2	4,0	–57,9	–18,1
Northern Europe			29,8	36,4	44,8	59,9	57,0	78,4	78,9	80,2	2,0	–54,3	–16,9
Western Europe			108,6	112,2	139,7	142,6	154,4	192,7	200,4	204,8	2,3	–52,0	–10,7
Central/Eastern Europe			33,9	60,0	69,4	87,8	98,1	134,6	141,4	156,1	4,8	–54,3	–16,1
Southern/Med' Europe			90,3	102,7	140,8	157,3	176,9	267,52	289,4	304,1	5,4	–65,5	–26,1
Asia and the Pacific	8,7	22,8	55,8	82,4	110,5	155,3	208,2	324	347,7	360,7	3,7	–60,0	–34,9
Northeast Asia			26,4	41,3	58,3	87,5	111,5	159,5	169,2	170,6	0,8	–64,7	–39,7
Southeast Asia			21,2	28,8	36,9	49,3	69,9	120,5	128,7	137,4	6,8	–58,0	–33,6
Oceania			5,2	8,1	9,2	10,5	11,6	16,6	17,0	17,5	2,4	–51,3	–25,3
South Asia			3,1	4,2	6,1	8,0	11,5	27,5	32,8	35,2	7,4	–47,4	–22,1
Americas	31,1	71,0	92,8	109,0	128,2	132,5	150,4	207	215,7	219,4	1,6	–47,5	–16,2
North America			71,7	80,7	91,5	89,2	99,2	135.7	142,2	146,4	3,0	–47,8	–14,3
Caribbean			11,4	14,0	17,1	18,8	20,0	18,9	25,7	26,7	3,6	–49,8	–20,9
Central America			1,9	2,6	4,3	6,3	7,9	11.1	10,8	10,9	0,8	–45,6	–17,1
South America			7,7	11,7	15,3	18,2	23,6	35,1	37,0	35,3	–4,8	–44,9	–18,3
Middle East	3,0	7,0	9,6	13,7	24,1	36,3	58,2	57,7	60,5	61,4	2,1	–51,6	–20,2
Africa	5,4	7,2	14,8	20,1	27,9	34,6	49,9	62,7	67,1	73,1	6,4	–47,3	–13,6
North Africa			8,4	7,3	10,2	13,9	18,8	21,7	23,9	26,1	8,5	–52,9	–17,5
Sub-Saharan Africa			6,4	12,8	17,7	23,3	31,0	41,1	43,3	46,9	5,2	–44,4	–11,8

Source: Adapted from UNWTO (2020), p. 6
ªJan – May, 2020

6

Table 6.3 International tourism receipts by region (US$ billions), 1960–2019

	1960	1970	1980	1990	1995	2000	2005	2010	2015	2016	2017	2018	2019
World total	7	18	105	271	415	495	706	975	1260	1245	1346	1457	1010
Europe	4	11	62	143	212	232	318	422	451	468	519	570	573
Asia & Pacific	0,2	1,2	11	46	81	90	141	254	418	370	396	436	443
Middle East	0,1	0,4	4	5	11	18	28	52	54	59	68	74	82
Americas	2,5	5	25	69	96	131	145	215	304	314	326	338	342
Africa	0,2	0,5	3,4	6,0	9	11	22	30	33	35	36	38	38

Source: UNWTO (2020), p. 14

◻ Table 6.4 World's top ten international tourist destinations in 2018 and 2019

Tourism destination rank	Country	International tourist arrivals 2018 (million)	International tourist arrivals 2019 (million)	Change (%) '19/'18
1	France	89,4	82,6	–2,2
2	Spain	82,8	83,7	1,1
3	United States	79,7	79,3	–0,6
4	China	62,9	65,7	4,5
5	Italy	61,6	64,5	4,8
6	Turkey	45,8	51,2	11,9
7	Mexico	41,3	45,0	9,0
8	Thailand	38,2	39,8	4,2
9	Germany	38,9	39,6	1,8
10	United Kingdom	36,3	37,5	3,2
	World	1409	1460	3,9

Source: UNWTO (2020), p. 15

6.6 Environmental Scanning

In order to adapt to the changes in the business marketing environment, the internal and external factors described in this chapter should be analysed continually. A SWOT analysis – used in the marketing planning stage – aims to highlight the environmental factors that have either a positive or a negative impact on a tourism organisation. This then enables the marketer to determine the appropriate strategic action. A SWOT analysis forms part of a marketing audit. A marketing audit examines the organisation's strengths and weaknesses, and their potential impact on performance as well as on customer and supplier relations. A marketing strategy audit identifies opportunities and threats as well as their probability and potential impact on the organisation (Burgess & Bothma, 2011: 27).

As part of this analysis, the marketer should:

— Identify both positive and negative influences
— Control those influences that can be controlled

— Use those influences that can contribute to competitive advantage
— Overcome or defend against potentially damaging influences.

In addition, marketers need to analyse links between the internal, performance, and external environments. For example, technological advancements can help organisations to gain an advantage over competitors. Tourism marketers also need to be on the lookout for information concerning the business environment.

Activities associated with environmental scanning include making use of external sources of information such as conferences, secondary data from government departments (such as the Office for National Statistics (ONS) [► ons.gov.uk], and the Brazil Ministry of Tourism [► http://www.turismo.gov.br/]), consulting firms (for example, Grant Thornton [► granthornton.com], research agencies (for example, KANTAR TNS [► tnsglobal.com]), economic indicators (these can be sourced from the media, for example, television, newspapers, books, or journals), consumers, and the com-

☐ **Table 6.5** World's top ten tourism earners, 2019

Tourism earning rank	Country	International tourism receipts 2019 (billion US$)	Change (%) '19/'18
1	United States	214,1	−0,3
2	Spain	79,7	3,2
3	France	63,8	1,9
4	Thailand	60,5	3,2
5	United Kingdom	50,4	8,5
6	Italy	49,6	6,2
7	Japan	46,1	8,0
8	Australia	45,7	−2,9
9	Germany	41,6	2,2
10	Macau (China)	39,5	−2,7
	World	1478	0,7

Source: UNWTO (2020), p. 17

☐ **Table 6.6** World's top ten spenders on international tourism, 2019

Tourism spending rank	Country	International tourism expenditure 2016 (billion US$)	Change (%) '19/'18
1	China	254,6	−4,2
2	United States	152,3	5,4
3	Germany	93,1	2,9
4	United Kingdom	63,6	7,5
5	France	40,5	11,5
6	Russian Federation	29,1	5,5
7	Australia	26,6	4,8
8	Canada	25,0	5,1
9	Korea (ROK) Australia	24,9	−8,1
10	Italy	24,2	6,31

Source: UNWTO (2020)

petition. Internal sources include a company's own records (sales figures and so on), research reports, and experienced employees.

Ginter and Duncan (1990) listed the following activities as components of macroenvironmental analysis:

— Scanning macroenvironments for warning signs and possible environmental changes that will affect the organisation
— Monitoring environments for specific trends and patterns
— Forecasting future directions of environmental changes
— Assessing current and future trends in terms of the effect such changes could have on the organisation.
— The benefits of an environmental scan include the following:
— Increased managerial awareness of environmental influences
— The ability of management to focus attention on influences and strategic change
— Improved decision-making
— The ability to anticipate opportunities and threats, and to devise appropriate responses.

6.6.1 Environmental Approaches

According to Walker, Mullins and Boyd (2010: 101), there are three basic approaches to environmental scanning. These approaches are outlined below.

6.6.1.1 The Irregular Approach

This consists of *ad hoc* studies (studies that are done as and when they are needed) carried out only when specific events that may affect the tourism organisation arise. For the tourism industry, for example, this could cover a report on the growing problem of crime or HIV/Aids and its economic effects on tourism businesses.

6.6.1.2 The Regular Approach

This involves periodically updated studies of particular events of special interest. This approach enables the organisation to be informed regularly on selected issues so that it can take action before a crisis occurs.

6.6.1.3 The Continuous Approach

This involves regularly monitoring a variety of environmental components and provides inputs to the standard marketing planning process.

The decision as to which of these three environmental approaches is suitable for a specific tourism business depends on the organisation's potential vulnerability to environmental factors and the strength of its resources. An organisation's vulnerability depends to a large extent on the complexity and stability of its environment. As we discussed in ▶ Chap. 2, the tourism industry operates in a complex and dynamic environment that is highly susceptible to external events. Consequently, it requires a more complete scanning system than an organisation operating in a less complex and more stable environment.

Summary

This chapter highlighted the fact that we live in a rapidly changing world. Successful tourism marketers must attempt to anticipate and respond to the changes, and adjust their marketing strategies accordingly. The marketer can control some of the internal environmental factors (that is, the company's resources, its processes, and its policies) and performance environmental factors (that is the consumers, suppliers, intermediaries, and competitors) to which the organisation is subject.

However, external macroenvironmental factors, which often affect the whole tourism industry, cannot be controlled. They are unpredictable and volatile, changing all the time. In this chapter we used a PESTLE analysis as part of an external environmental audit used by tourism organisations. The marketer should be concerned with specific factors in tourist-generating countries, such as the demographics of the target market. A marketer should also examine trends in developed countries, which are the leaders in leisure activities and technology.

Tourism and hospitality marketers and practitioners should be aware of the scope of the tourism industry throughout the world. Some are concerned with local or national markets. For others, global trends are of significance. Sufficient information enables marketers and practitioners to construct an analysis of the business environment in which they work. This plays a key role in strategic marketing planning, which we will discuss in the next chapter.

❓ Review Questions

1. Briefly describe the six main microenvironmental factors in the tourism business environment.
2. Explain why marketers should be concerned with the macroenvironmental factors in the tourist-generating country?
3. Justify why should tourism and hospitality marketers be concerned with the macroenvironment if they have little or no control over it?
4. Briefly explain Porter's (1980) 'Five Forces' model.
5. Explain how the changes in the political environment affect a tourism and hospitality company's marketing strategy?
6. How might the ecological environment threaten a tourism and hospitality organisation's marketing strategy?
7. Compare statistics in ▣ Tables 6.4, 6.5, and 6.6. What patterns do you notice in terms of the top destinations and earners?
8. Carry out an audit of the top three international tourist destinations (see

Table 6.4) in terms of their political, economic, socio-demographic, technological, legal, and ecological environments.

9. Why is it problematic to obtain data on domestic tourism? How do tourism authorities do this (for example,

in terms of number of trips, spend, and VFR)? Apply your resident country as an example in your answer.

10. Describe the tools that can be implemented to carry out an audit of the macroenvironmental factors that impact a tourism and hospitality business?

In-depth Case Study 6: The Business Environment of MSC Cruises

Objectives

- To understand the business environment in which tourism organisations operate
- To demonstrate how the various environmental factors, affect a tourism organisation's marketing activity.

Cruising to the Top

It is rare to find an area of contemporary living which thrives on a slower pace and attitude to life, but the recent revival of the cruise-liner industry offers a touristic alternative to high speed travel and lifestyle. The renewal of the cruise-liner industry was highlighted by the launch of the *Queen Mary 2* in 2004 a year after Concorde was decommissioned and offering the opposite to supersonic transatlantic travel. Built at a cost of £460 million (€532-million/$656-million), the *Queen Mary 2* (see Image 6.2) is the largest and most expensive cruise-liner ever built and showcased that the more sedate nature of cruise holidays is back in vogue (Jivanda, 2014).

Cruise tourism is defined as travelling for leisure to various destinations on a ship with the intention of experiencing a country's beauty and culture (Teye & Paris, 2011). The global cruise market has now become one of the fastest-growing sectors of the tourism and hospitality industry. According to the Cruise Lines International Association (CLIA), more than thirty-two million people worldwide took a cruise holiday in 2018, with an average spend (at each port city) of US$376 (approximately £288/€453) per passenger (CLIA, 2019). Although North America now accounts for almost 70% of all cruise passengers, this dominance is expected to decline as other markets

mature (CLIA, 2019). Additional major markets for cruise tourism include the United Kingdom, Germany, Italy, Russia, Japan, and Australia. The popularity of cruising worldwide is set to continue as the CLIA forecast cruise-ship capacity to grow over the next ten years (CLIA, 2019).

MSC Cruises which is one of the largest privately-owned cruise-liner companies in the world, is a brand market leader in Europe, South America, and southern Africa. MSC Cruises is primarily known for the warm Italian exceptional service aboard its fleet of luxury cruise ships. MSC Cruises (Italian: MSC Crociere) is a Swiss-based European company with deep Mediterranean roots employing over 30,000 staff globally and selling cruise holidays in 69 countries around the world (MSC Cruises, 2020). MSC stands for Merchant Shipping Company. Through provision of cruise destinations in the Mediterranean and the Caribbean, and its seasonal itineraries include Northern Europe, the Atlantic Ocean, South America, southern Africa, China, Dubai, Abu Dhabi, and Qatar, they have single handedly mastered the art of being "Truly Italian". The company, which has been in operation since 1957, has a portfolio of 17 cruise ships featuring a host of cutting-edge innovations and the latest technologies.

These "floating cities" have acres of deck, offering almost every entertainment facility imaginable such as cinemas, bowling alleys, outdoor family activities, night clubs, and casinos. On some of the fleet's ships passengers can experience thrills of F1 simulators and 4D cinemas. MSC ships offer a world of distinctive culinary opportunities at several specialty restaurants that provide a variety of international

☐ **Image 6.2** *Queen Mary 2* cruise liner. (Source: ▶ https://www.freeimages.com/photo/queen-mary-2-3-1512218 Source: Unsplash)

dining options from authentic Asian dishes and succulent steaks to chef's table experiences. Passengers can enjoy fun new experiences around the clock on an MSC Cruises' ship, from enriching indoor and outdoor activities during the day to night-time entertainment.

The MSC Cruises fleet was born of a €6bn investment programme in 2003 and after successful completion of the first investment phase, the Company launched a €11.6 billion (U$13,7 billion) plan that will see the fleet expand to 25 ships by 2027. Furthermore, MSC Group's Cruises division is investing an additional €2 billion in a new luxury cruise brand comprising four super-yacht ships, launching one per year between 2023 and 2026. MSC Cruises is the first global cruise line brand to develop an investment plan of such length and magnitude. By 2027, MSC Cruises intends to welcome 5,5 million passengers annually, tripling its global capacity as well as add eight

cruise ships in the contemporary segment and a further four in the luxury segment to its' fleet. Research has shown that the average ages and incomes of cruise passengers have decreased dramatically since the mid-1970s. Cruise ships are now perceived as floating 'all-inclusive' resorts with a full range of accommodation options, and many dining, recreation, and entertainment facilities, therefore appealing to a wider demographic than ever before. A 2019 CLIA study reported the following trends in the cruise travel industry:

- Unprecedented on-board experiences and amenities - from Broadway productions and designer shops to zip lining, golf, and bumper cars.
- Overnight stays at ports-of-call are increasing.
- Intergenerational cruising is increasing in popularity as cruise amenities designed to satisfy every age from teens to seniors.

- More volunteer cruising options available in the coming years.
- Cruise ships designed to appeal to passenger's cultures and pay homage to ports-of-calls.

MSC Cruises has been quick to spot new target markets and respond to emerging trends. Most of the company's fleet has a significant volume of group business, including shipboard conventions and meetings, as well as incentive trips. MSC Cruises has fly-cruise packages enabling consumers to board at any destination on a ship's itinerary. The company's global reputation and ongoing success is demonstrated as in 2019 they were named 'World's Leading Cruise Line' and 'North America's Leading Cruise Line'; for two and three years in a row respectively by the World Travel Awards (WTA). MSC Cruises was also nominated as 'Europe's leading Cruise Line' and 'Caribbean's Leading Cruise Line' by the WTA.

Over the last decade, the growth of the cruise-line sector has been boosted by several worldwide business environmental factors. A world population that is ageing has led to more people purchasing cruise holidays as the older generation tends to have more time and more to spend on holidays. In addition, an increasing number of people in certain segments of the market have more discretionary income, allowing them to book cruise holidays. Technological advancements have improved ship design, which in turn has increased passengers' comfort and safety, making cruise holidays more attractive. Technology has also improved onboard communications for passengers such as the availability of mobile and internet facilities. Other factors that have contributed to the growth of the cruise-line industry have been the increasing popularity of the all-inclusive holidays that cruise liners now offer as well as the way in which cruise liners have developed partnerships with travel agencies.

However, the cruise-liner industry has not been immune to several macro environmental factors impacting the sector over the last 20 years or so. The September 11, 2001 terrorist attacks ('9/11') reduced tourism flows and impacted various sectors of the travel industry, most notably air travel and cruise tourism. The worldwide economic recession from 2007 to 2009 further reduced demand for luxury international cruise travel. Then the cruise industry suffered an additional setback when the 114,000-ton Costa Concordia capsized off the coast of Italy in 2012, resulting in numerous casualties. The incident damaged the image of cruising and brought into question the safety of modern cruise-liners. More tellingly, a series of terrorist attacks and general political instability during the period 2013 to 2018 in the Middle East, North Africa and parts of Europe caused a drop-off in demand for international cruises, especially from the North American market. The United Kingdom referendum in 2016, which resulted in the UK leaving the European Union (EU) in January 2020, led to a weaker pound and damaged the UK cruise travel market. Notwithstanding, by far the most significant external business environmental factor was the outbreak of the coronavirus (COVID-19) pandemic in March 2020, which greatly negatively impacted on cruise travel; perhaps more so than any other occurrence in the last century The coronavirus pandemic virtually decimated the global travel and tourism industry. Anxiety associated with the virus's spread, along with mobility and travel restrictions in many countries, placed the travel and tourism industry in a precarious economic position. Millions of people around the world lost their jobs in the travel and tourism industry. The breadth and depth of stifled demand for travel also brought unforeseen consequences to tourists, destinations, communities, and tourism industry stakeholders.

All cruise-liner companies, including MSC Cruises, were forced to cancel all bookings for the remaining nine months of 2020. According to Allan Foggitt, director of sales and marketing of MSC Cruises speaking in mid-2020 said the economic effects of the crisis would be felt far beyond the cruise lines and workers. "It has a trickle-down effect to everybody around us, even furniture companies that sell to cruise ships or whatever, everyone's going to cut back and do different things," he said. When things

■ **Image 6.3** MSC Cruises' logo

finally return to normal, Foggitt, said, cruise-liners will be offering attractive deals to entice customers back. "I always say there's a price for fear. Right now they may say, 'I don't want to go, I'm a little fearful of this Covid-19', but once the rates start dropping the same people that said no are like, 'Oh, for that price, yes I'll book it.' Added Foggitt: "As a true comparison, when 9/11 happened, everything stopped, the world stopped moving almost. I worked at a cruise line call centre and the phone stopped ringing. As soon as the rates were lowered those same people were calling back. It will turn around. That is the great thing about the cruise industry, it's flexible".

It all adds up to the biggest challenge facing the cruise companies since 9/11, experts assert, threatening the survival of smaller players. Until the coronavirus outbreak, growth in the North American cruise industry was steady, with more than 14,2 million passengers expected to travel in 2020 and 19 new cruise ships making their maiden voyages, according to the CLIA. This never materialised. Virtually all of the world's ocean and river cruise lines suspended global operations due to the COVID-19 pandemic.

MSC Cruises provides an excellent example of an externally oriented tourism organisation that has both introduced innovative ways of operating and taken advantage of new opportunities created by the business environment. It is likely that the industry will eventually rebound strongly once the coronavirus crisis passes after

very deep discounting, but images of passengers being stuck at sea on coronavirus-infected ships and confined to tiny cabins will take time to fade (■ Image 6.3).

Case Study Questions

1. Outline the business environmental factors that have impacted the cruise-line industry worldwide.
2. Discuss the extent to which MSC Cruises controls the impact of these factors?
3. Explain why the 2020 coronavirus had such a devastating impact on the world cruise tourism sector.
4. Discuss what measures international cruise liners such as MSC Cruises could take to respond to the coronavirus and make cruising a safe touristic experience .
5. Go online to the website of MSC Cruises (► msccruises.co.uk). Compare what it offers with cruises offered by international cruise-ship operators such as Cunard (► cunard.com) and Carnival (► carnival.com), NCL (► www.ncl.com) and Fred.Olsen Cruise Lines (► fredolsencruises.com) (■ Image 6.4).

Queen Mary 2 is the largest and most expensive ocean liner ever built. She also remains the longest, tallest and widest ocean liner as well as being the most famous and fastest passenger ship in operation today.

6

◘ Image 6.4   MSC Cruise liner (Source: MSC Cruises)

References

Aguilar, F. (1967). *Scanning the Business Environment*. New York, NY: McGraw-Hill.

Baines, P., Fill, C., Rosengren, S., & Antonetti, P. (2019). *Marketing* (5th ed.). Oxford: Oxford University Press.

Burgess, S., & Bothma, C. (2011). *International Marketing* (2nd ed.). Cape Town: Oxford University Press.

Cruise Lines International Association. (2019). *CLIA releases 2020 state of the cruise industry outlook report*. Retrieved from: https://cruising.org/news-and-research/press-room/2019/december/clia-releases-2020-state-of-the-cruise-industry-outlook-report [22 January 2020].

Deloitte Insights. (2019). The consumer is changing but perhaps not how you think. *Deloitte Review, 25*(July).

Evans, N. (2019). *Strategic management for travel and tourism*. Oxford: Butterworth-Heinemann.

Freeman, R. E. (1984). *Strategic management: A stakeholder approach*. Boston, MA: Pitman.

George, R. (2003). Tourists' perceptions of safety and security while visiting Cape Town. *Tourism Management, 24*(5).

Ginter, P., & Duncan, J. (1990). Macroenvironmental analysis for strategic management. *Long Range Planning, 23*(6).

Hall, C. M. (2010). Tourism and biodiversity: more significant than climate change? *Journal of Heritage Tourism, 5*(4).

IPOS. (2018). *Countries that have a younger population are more optimistic about 2018 than countries with an ageing population*. Retrieved from https://www.ipsos.com/en/countries-have-a-younger-population-are-more-optimistic-about-2018-countries-aging-population [12 April 2018].

Jivanda, T. (2014). Queen Mary 2, the largest and most expensive ocean liner ever built celebrates tenth birthday. *The Independent*. Retrieved from https://www.independent.co.uk/news/pictures/queen-mary-2-the-largest-and-most-expensive-ocean-liner-ever-built-celebrates-tenth-birthday-9175906.html [7 May 2020].

Kotler, P. (2000). *Marketing management: Analysis, planning, implementation and control* (10th ed.). London: Prentice Hall.

Kotler, P., & Armstrong, G. (2019). *Principles of marketing* (17th ed.). London: Pearson Education.

MSC Cruises. (2020). *About MSC Cruises* [Online] Available at: https://www.msccruises.com/en-gl/About-MSC.aspx

Noble, C. H., Sinha, R. K., & Kumar, A. (2002). Market orientation and alternative strategic orientations: A longitudinal assessment of performance implications. *Journal of Marketing, 66*(4), 25–40.

Office for National Statistics. (2018). Living longer: How our population is changing and why it matters. *ONS*. Retrieved from https://www.ons.gov.uk/peoplepopulationandcommunity/birthsdeathsandmarriages/ageing/articles/livinglongerhowourpopulationischangingandwhyitmatters/2018 [21 November 2020].

Popescu, A. (2018). *Tourism in India is booming. So why is everyone so worried?* Retrieved from: https://www.bloomberg.com/news/articles/2018-07-06/tourism-in-india-is-booming-so-why-is-everyone-so-worried [23 August 2018].

Porter, M. E. (1980). *Competitive strategy: Techniques for analyzing industries and competitors*. New York, NY: Free Press.

Sharpley, R. (2008). *Tourism, Tourists and Society* (4th ed.). Huntingdon, Cambridge: ELM Publications.

Sofitel. (2019). Retrieved from https://sofitel.accorhotels.com/gb/hotel-5555-sofitel-luxembourg-le-grand-ducal/index.shtml# [23 November 2018].

Teye, V., & Paris, C. (2011). Cruise line industry and Caribbean tourism: Guests' motivations, activities, and destination preference. *Tourism Review International, 14*(1), 17–28.

The Economist. (2019). *Pocket World in Figures 2019*. London: Economist Books.

United Nations World Tourism Organization (UNWTO). (2016). *UNWTO tourism towards 2030*. Retrieved from http://mkt.unwto.org/barometer/january-2016-volume-14-advance-release [11 November 2016]

United Nations World Tourism Organization (UNWTO). (2018). *UNWTO tourism highlights* (2018th ed.). Retrieved from https://www.e-unwto.org/doi/pdf/10.18111/9789284419876 [19 September 2018].

United Nations World Tourism Organization (UNWTO). (2019). *UNWTO tourism highlights* (2019th ed.). Retrieved from https://www.e-unwto.org/doi/pdf/10.18111/9789284421152 [2 November 2019].

United Nations World Tourism Organization (UNWTO). (2020). *World tourism barometer, 18*(4) July 2020. Retrieved from https://www.e-unwto.org/doi/epdf/10.18111/wtobarometereng.2020.18.1.4 [5 August 2020].

UNWTO. (2020). *Tourism highlights* (2019 ed., p. 15). Retrieved from https://www.e-unwto.org/doi/pdf/10.18111/9789284419029 [12 May 20120].

United Nations World Tourism Organization (UNWTO). (2021). UNWTO *tourism data dashboard*. Retrieved from https://www.unwto.org/unwto-tourism-dashboard [12 February 2021].

Walker, O., Mullins, J., & Boyd, H. (2010). *Marketing Strategy: A Decision-focused Approach* (8th ed.). London: McGraw-Hill Irwin.

Westin Hotels & Resorts (2021). Retrieved from https://westin.marriott.com/ [26 January 2021].

World Travel & Tourism Council (WTTC). (2019). *Travel & tourism economic impact 20209: World*. London: WTTC. Retrieved from https://wttc.org/Research/Economic-Impact [29 May 2020].

Further Reading

Baines, P., Fill, C., Rosengren, S., & Antonetti, P. (2019). *Marketing* (5th ed.). Oxford: Oxford University Press.

United Nations World Tourism Organization (UNWTO). (2021). *UNWTO tourism highlights, 2020 edition*. Madrid: UNWTO.

Market Segmentation, Targeting, and Positioning

Contents

Electronic Supplementary Material The online version of this chapter (https://doi.org/10.1007/978-3-030-64111-5_7) contains supplementary material, which is available to authorized users.

7

Purpose

This chapter will help you understand market segmentation as well as how tourism and hospitality marketers can position their offerings to gain a competitive advantage in the marketplace.

Learning Goals

After reading this chapter, you should be able to:

- Understand that tourism and hospitality consumers are not all the same and that they have different requirements that need to be satisfied
- Define the terms "market", "market segmentation", "market targeting", and "market positioning"
- Describe the advantages and disadvantages of market segmentation
- Explain how tourism and hospitality marketers can identify attractive target market segments
- Describe how and why tourism and hospitality companies undertake positioning their products.
- Apply the principles of market segmentation, positioning, and targeting to Marriott's Moxy Hotels.

Overview

In this chapter, we examine the tourism markets and how they can best be defined so that an organisation can target them effectively.

We begin with an explanation of market segmentation, which is essential for designing and implementing a marketing mix (▶ Chaps. 8, 9, 10, 11, and 12). We consider how tourism and hospitality companies decide on which market segments to focus their marketing efforts. We discuss the criteria used by the marketer to ensure effective segmentation: using demographic, psychological, and behavioural criteria.

This brings us to the process of target marketing and the different approaches that a tourism and hospitality organisation can take. We conclude by discussing market positioning and how companies can position their offerings to gain a competitive advantage.

The chapter's in-depth case study examines these principles in the context of *Moxy Hotels*, designed to capture the millennial traveller market, and owned by *Marriott Hotels International* group.

7.1 Introduction

Segmentation, targeting and positioning (STP) make up a series of steps that are interrelated. The first step, segmentation, involves dividing the market into groups (segments or clusters) of consumers who share similar needs (actual and desired), wants, characteristics, and/or behavioural patterns (Weaver & Lawton, 2002: 173). By segmenting a market, marketers obtain knowledge of the actual or potential consumers and thus discover particular subgroups whose members will be most profitable to focus their marketing efforts on (Pride et al., 2017: 200). For example, *iExplore*, an online adventure travel company, might satisfy the needs of various international consumers and businesses that want to travel or organise travel to exotic natural destinations such as Alaska, Antarctica or the Galapagos Islands. The second step, market targeting, refers to the way in which a marketer evaluates the attractiveness of each market segment and selects one or more segments on which to focus. *iExplore*, selects internet users, inbound tour operators and corporate groups as potential customers to target for its southern African destination packages and offerings. The last step involves a tourism organisation positioning its offerings and marketing mix to meet the expectations of its current or potential consumers. *iExplore's* slogan is: "The number one ranked website for adventure travel", which attempts to position the company in the marketplace as an online adventure travel portal. ◧ Figure 7.1 shows the relationship between these three steps.

Before we examine the principles of these steps, it is necessary to understand what is meant by a market.

Market segmentation
- Identify criteria for segmenting the market
- Develop segment profiles

Market targeting
- Assess segment attractiveness
- Select the target market segments

Market positioning
- Evaluate position for each segment
- Adapt marketing-mix components for each segment

☐ **Fig. 7.1** Relationship between market segmentation, targeting and positioning. (Source: Author's creation)

7.2 What is a Market?

A **market** includes anyone w... chase a tourism and hospitalit... ing consumers, clients, din... tourists, organisations and vi... are made up of buyers who h... and wants, and different buyi... ing frequencies. Some people,... choose to go on holiday th... while others go only once. Ea... tially an individual market, a... feasible for a marketer to de... for each buyer. Most tourism... companies therefore seek grou... share similar needs. It is imper... ers identify their target marke... they understand who the right person is to target for their marketing activities.

> The term "*market*" refers to a group of consumers (actual or potential) with similar needs or wants. In tourism marketing, we refer to a market as a group of actual or potential consumers with similar needs or wants (Gunter & Furnham, 1992: 12).

7.3 Market Research

In general, tourism and hospitality marketers do not spend enough time identifying, segmenting and understanding their markets. They tend to cut corners wherever they can. It is essential to know as much as possible about a target market in a complex society such as the UK or any other country for that matter. At least 50% of marketers' time should be spent identifying and understanding their target market. Market research is required to

...can range from... ample, hiring a... company or... ator to do less... to as dipstick... half-a-dozen... ching the inter-... an be tailored... chers joke that... a certain cate-... usins went on...

7.4 Market Segmentation

Consumer purchases are strongly influenced by the people with whom consumers work, live, and socialise with (see ▶ Chap. 3). Thus, it is possible to target groups of people who share similar behaviour and attitudes towards a particular offering. In other words, they can be distinguished from other groups making up the total market for the offering. This process is known as "**market segmentation**" and is one of the fundamental principles of marketing. The concept of market segmentation is based on the premise that consumers are different. However, this concept is underused in tourism marketing, with many marketers taking a wait-and-see approach and delivering a range of offerings without focusing on the needs of an identified market segment.

> *Market segmentation* is the way in which companies divide a market into clearly defined groups of buyers who share similar needs, characteristics or behaviour patterns and might require separate products or marketing programs (Kotler *et al.*, 2017: 212).

7

Market segmentation is an important analytical tool that forms the basis of the internal analysis stage of the marketing planning process (see ▶ Chap. 5). In recent years, market segmentation has gained considerable importance as a tool used in developing marketing strategies of tourism companies (Font & McCabe, 2017). The purpose of segmentation is to identify and profile segments with varying degrees of buying potential, based on a range of criteria. The objective is then to develop the offering with promotional messages so that it appeals to the segments that it is seeking to serve. It is not feasible to reach all market segments through marketing activities. Similarly, providing each consumer with tailor-made travel services is unrealistic and not economically viable; with the exception of a hand-full of luxury-end markets such as luxury tour operators. Segmentation enables an organisation to discover a particular group or groups whose members become the focus of all of its marketing efforts.

Each segment, or group of buyers, consists of consumers who share one or more similar characteristics, which cause them to have com-

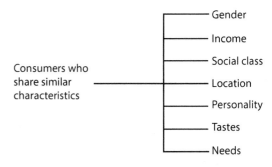

❑ **Fig. 7.2** Examples of market segments. (Source: Author's creation)

parable tourism offering needs. ❑ Figure 7.2 provides examples of market segments.

It is crucial to put the spotlight onto an appropriate segment, then segment it further and, if possible, divide that segment again. Successful marketing campaigns are those where the marketer has identified the market, divided or segmented it as many times as possible, then really got to understand the people within that segment and developed the campaign accordingly. ▶ Industry Insight 7.1 examines the gay tourism market, which comprises of several sub-segments.

Industry Insight 7.1

Gay Tourism Research

Hattingh (2018) argues that the gay traveller, a segment of the lesbian, gay, bisexual, and transgender (LGBT) travel market, is incorrectly perceived to be a homogeneous market segment as a result of the assumption that gay men have a "unique lifestyle". Consequently, the gay traveller is often misunderstood and is segmented in terms of the psychographic (lifestyle) variable. However, Hattingh found that the gay travel segment is actually made up of various sub-segments: The Passive Relaxer, the Wildlife Explorer, the Culinary Enthusiast/Foodie, and the Gay-Centric Traveller. Only a distinct sub-segment, the Gay-Centric Traveller, can be

described as a gay tourist since travellers in this group are specifically motivated by the gay attributes of a destination and are motivated to travel for reasons related to their sexuality. Thus, assuming that all gay travellers are alike is problematic as it conceals many other important variables and may hinder effective destination marketing. Not all gay travellers or activities by these travellers can be labelled as gay tourism.

Source: Hattingh, C. (2018). A typology of gay leisure travellers: An African perspective. Unpublished Doctor of Technology in Tourism and Hospitality Management thesis. Cape Peninsula University of Technology: Cape Town.

7.4.1 Why Segment the Market?

There are several reasons why market segmentation is an important part of the marketing planning process, including the following:
- Marketing segmentation has a role in marketing strategy.
- It helps define consumer needs and wants.
- It helps define marketing objectives.

There are few tourism offerings that can attempt to appeal to an entire market. it is difficult to see how a tourist activity such as bungee-jumping, for instance, would appeal to everyone. So, it is useful for marketers to focus their efforts by segmenting. However, it can be argued that within the restaurant sector of the hospitality industry, segmentation is least evident. Companies such as *Nando's* and *McDonald's* have a standardised service that appeals to almost a total market.

7.4.2 Bases for Segmenting the Market

There is no one way of dividing up a market. A marketer has to experiment with different segmentation variables, depending on the situation. A variable is a characteristic shared by some people and not others. For example, if you and I both live in Madrid, Spain we share the geographic variable of our city. Sometimes it may be appropriate to use one variable. At other times, it is better to use a combination of variables (demographic variables such as age and gender and psychographic such as social class, for instance). These combinations are called "multi-variates". Segmentation is based on the premise that consumers are different. A tour operating company, for instance, might segment the market based on age, gender, occupation, income, and geographic location (using postcodes) to identify attractive market segments.

Five main variables are used to segment markets. The tourism industry uses all of these variables. ◘ Table 7.1 lists and describes these variables.

We will discuss the five main variables listed in ◘ Table 7.1 in more detail below.

7.4.2.1 Profile Criteria

Demographic Segmentation

The word "demographics" is derived from the Greek words *demo* (meaning people) and *graphics* (meaning to write). It is essentially the study of a population of people.

◘ **Table 7.1** Main variables for consumer segmentation linked to chapter section

Base type/criteria	Segmentation variable	Description
1. Profile	1.1. Demographic	Main variables: age and lifecycle, gender, occupation, generational group, education level, social class, income, and religion
	1.2. Geographic	Consumers in one geographic area are often different from those in another area (e.g. based on climate – sun)
	1.3. Geodemographic	The type of housing and location that people live in and their purchasing behaviour
2. Psychological	2.1. Psychographic	AOLs, Lifestyle, Personality
	2.1. Benefits sought	Consumer seek benefits from the purchase and use of an offering
3. Behavioural	3.1. Relationship with the offering	Usage Loyalty to the offering Buyer readiness Media usage

Source: Author's creation

Demographic segmentation involves dividing the market into groups based on variables such as age and life-stage, generation group, education level, social class, income, and religion (Swarbrooke, 2000: 214). This is a popular method of segmenting the market, as consumers' needs, wants, and usage rates are often linked closely with demographic variables. These variables are also relatively easy to measure compared to other variables.

■ **Age and Lifecycle Segments**

Consumer needs and desires change with age. Many tourism organisations provide different offerings and use different marketing strategies to target various age and family lifecycle (or life stage) segments. An example of this is the tourism organisation *Retallack Resort,* situated in Cornwall, south-west England, which is a luxury holiday resort catering for children and teenagers (see ▶ Industry Insight 7.2). Tour operators such as *Saga Holidays* and *Contiki Tours* (formerly *Contiki Holidays for 18–35 s*), specialise by age. *Saga Holidays* specialises in holidays for the over-50s, whereas *Contiki Tours* targets youth and young adult travellers.

Many tour operators, such as *Exodus Travels, Wild Frontiers*, and *Highland Fling Bungee*, target adventure-type holidays (bungee-jumping, cycling and white-water-rafting, for example) aimed at consumers aged between 25 and 45. Similarly, the travel agency chain *Student Flights* targets the under 35 s, the tour operator *Contiki Tours* 18–35 s aims at the 18 to 35 market and the travel company *Topdeck* targets the "18 to 30 southings". Tourism marketers must, however, be careful not to stereotype when using age and life cycle segmentation. Some 75-year-olds might require disabled facilities at service providers such as B&Bs, while other 70-year-olds may take active sporting holidays (such as *Nelson Active Holidays*, which offer tennis, cycling and windsurfing holidays aimed at the older 'grey' market). Similarly, some 40-year-old couples are sending their children off to university while others are beginning new families. Indeed, a marketer's expectation that age equates to a life stage is eroding; the 30-year old of the future may not be forming a family and the 60-year old is as likely to be running a business from their garage. Age should, therefore, not be used as an indicator of a person's life cycle stage, family status, health, or buying power (◘ Image 7.1).

Industry Insight 7.2

Retallack Resort

Retallack Resort is a luxury holiday resort designed for children and teenagers between the ages of seven and 17. The resort is situated just off the north coast of Cornwall, in the southwest of the UK, nestled in 100 acres of beautiful countryside. Retallack Resort is close to the historic market town of St Columb Major, and just a short drive away from the picturesque harbour town of Padstow as well as the popular family and party resort town of Newquay; which boasts seven sandy beaches. The holiday resort runs week-long camps during all school holidays and offers more than 90 leisure activities, including surfing, kayaking, scuba-diving, and has a health and fitness club.

Source: ▶ www.retallackresort.co.uk/resort/

🔲 **Image 7.1**   Grey tourists (group of "grey tourists "/"silver tourists" boarding a coach)

In Westernised developed countries, the over-40s market is an important (and often over-looked) market for travel and other luxury products such as fashion, health items and cruises (see ▶ Industry Insight 7.3). Older travellers now account for over 50% of the global travel market. So-called "Grey Gappers" or "Silver tourists" are emerging middle-class travellers with significant disposable income and time who spend their "silver dollars" on multi-destination holidays to places such as Thailand, Cambodia and the Far East. Figures released by the National Bureau of Statistics of China (NBSC) in 2016 show that the number of Chinese aged 60 or older was 220 million (approximately 16% of the population). By 2050, that number will nearly double to about 400 million (Xinhua, 2016).

🔲 Table 7.2 shows examples of various age and life-stage groups and their profiles.

Table 7.2   Demographic segmentation

Group	Profile	Examples
Young children (4–10)	Parents influenced by desires of young children	Children's activities, parks, jungle gyms, zoos
Young people (11–17)	Adventure	Quick-service restaurants, shopping, camping, beaches, school breaks, theme parks
Young adults (18–30)	Fun, romance, working and backpacking holidays, adventure holidays	Nightlife, hedonistic/party tourism, bungee-jumping
Family (25–50) with children	Children important, activities and relaxation	Butlin's, Alton Towers, Disneyland Paris, aquariums, museums, holiday resorts, surfing holidays
Empty nesters (45–65)	Children have left home, education, discovering new destinations	Cruises, painting holidays, gastronomic adventures, nostalgia holidays
Mature market (55–74)	Older people ("Grey Gappers"), singles, and couples	Bus touring holidays, early-bird specials, Saga holidays, value for money, VFR

Source: Author's creation

Industry Insight 7.3

Full-Time Residents Aboard a Luxury Cruise Liner

A cruise ship company has capitalised on a growing demand from wealthy British pensioners wishing to spend their final days cruising the world. The new way to spend retirement is to buy a permanent home at sea, although at a cost: £1 million (€1.1 million) up front, at least £120,000 (€136,000)a year in service charges, and pocket money. For this, the wealthy retirees can cruise the seven seas eating in Michelin-starred restaurants, watching the sun set, and dancing every night. The World claims to be the only cruise liner on which individuals can purchase a permanent home. It currently has 165 permanent residents and a long waiting-list to get on board. The average owner of The World's cabins is a 65-year-old who wants to see parts of the world he or she could not visit during his or her working lives. The World has a virtual driving range for golfers, a tennis court, and a marina for water sports enthusiasts attached to the ship.

Source: Keate, G. (2016). The Times. 'Sail into the sunset on £1 m cruise to die for'. Monday 21 March, p. 15.

■ **Gender Segmentation**

The differences between the sexes are often used by marketers to develop offerings for the wide variety of physical needs and self-images of men and women. Certain sports offerings (such as golfing holidays), for example, are consumed mainly by men, while shopping holidays are consumed predominantly by women. Women are becoming more dominant in sectors such as nature-based travel and business travel, prompting the tourism industry to respond to the specific needs and preferences of female travellers (see ▶ Industry Insight 7.4). Major hotel groups, for instance, have recognised the increase in the number of businesswomen travellers by providing facilities to meet their needs, such as full-length mirrors, hairdryers, and more feminine décor. Gender market segmentation is not that simplistic; a 'typical;' male or female does not exist. As with some of the other variables, segmentation by gender is most effective when combined with other variables namely demographic and lifestyle.

Industry Insight 7.4

Catering to Female Travellers

Women dominate the adventure travel and eco-tourism market. Industry research suggests that women are increasingly going on holidays by themselves or in the company of other women. A tour operator based in the United States, AdventureWomen, which is a women-owned and women-run adventure travel company, specialises in offering inclusive tours to active women over the age of 30. Since its inception in 1982, AdventureWomen has sent female groups to exotic destinations such as Peru, Alaska, Mexico, Morocco, Uganda, Egypt, and Nepal. The company's holidays are designed for women only. The success of AdventureWomen and similar companies depends largely on their responsiveness to the preferences and needs of women. Women tend to place a high value on physical and psychological security as well as physical comfort. A satisfied female client is more likely than a male to remain loyal to a product and will tell other women about her experiences.

■ **Generational Groups**

An increasingly popular way of segmenting Western market is by generation (similar to the global Generation X or Generation Y concepts). For example, segmenting according to pre- and post-Millennial generations could be an effective way of understanding an organisation's target market better and gaining insight into it (see next section).

A generation is a group of people born around the same time and raised around the same place. People in this "birth cohort" exhibit similar characteristics, preferences, and values over their lifetimes. Generations are not a box; instead, they are powerful clues showing where to begin connecting with and influencing people of different ages.

Most Westernised and developed country's populations can be divided into six generational groups:

Traditionalists or Silent Generation: Born 1945 and before.

– *Baby boomers:* People born after World War Two (between 1946 and 1964). This is an affluent group. The youngest boomers are now in their mid-50's, while the oldest are in their late 70's. 'Boomers' do not see themselves as old and are most likely to postpone retirement. They are active and take part in adventure activities such as cycling, 4 × 4 trips, hiking, snorkelling, and camping holidays. They also like participating in educational tours. Boomers look for value and carry out research on their holiday destinations. Cruises are particularly popular with boomers due to the perceived value of the all-inclusive holiday.

– *Generation X:* Consists of people born between 1965 and 1976. They care about the environment and favour socially responsible companies. Although ambitious, they tend to be less materialistic and strive for a high quality of life. They favour café chains such as *Starbucks* and *Costa Coffee* but also like local restaurants and specialities such as organic restaurants and independent café. 'Gsen-Xers' are environmentally-conscious and prefer more unique holiday destinations far afield. They also like quality hotels with uncomplicated luxury that is timeless and gimmick-free. Gen-Xers are a primary market for business travel. They are an important target market for the tourism industry.

– *Xennials:* Born 1977 to 1983. Not quite as cynical as the 'Xers'. Last generation to grow up before the digital age – they had analogue childhoods and digital adulthoods.

— *Millennials or Generation Y:* Fully computer literate. Born 1997 or 1984 to 1995 (depending on whether the Xennials are accepted), They tend to be an impatient group of people who seek instant gratification, having grown up in the age of the internet and the mobile phone. Members of this group change careers more often than their predecessors. Millennials are the most consistent generation globally. However, there are differences between Millennials raised in an urban environment versus those raised in a rural one or those who move to a new country. Millennials/Generation Yers are an attractive market for marketers, although reaching them requires innovative marketing approaches.

— *iGen or Gen Z:* Born 1993 and later (up to 2000). Also called the "selfie generation". They tend to be more pragmatic, more cautious and more money conscious than Millennials. Growing up amid a global recession, war, and terrorism; Generation Z is expected to take less risks and seek more stability and security than the freedom and flexibility that Millennials seek. They are also more global in their thinking as more of the world is online. The Generation Z is also technology dependent; they are true digital natives since they only know a world with touch-screens, social media, and apps.

■ Social Class Segment

Consumers are strongly influenced by the class to which they belong or aspire to belong. Social class, which is related to income, social standing, and the way in which status evolves from these factors, is widely used by marketers as a way of identifying the spending potential of tourists. In most cases, professionals earn higher incomes and are more likely to take holidays than those in lower social class groups.

In the UK, the most widely used classifications systems are based on data from the national readership survey (NRS) and the Office for National Statistics (ONS). The NRS was developed to profile the readers of British newspapers in the 1960s and has been

◻ **Table 7.3** NRS classification

Social grade	Description
A	High managerial, administrative, or professional
B	Intermediate managerial, administrative, or professional
C1	Supervisory, clerical and junior managerial, administrative, or professional
C2	Skilled manual workers
D	Semi and unskilled workers
E	State pensioners, casual or lower grade workers, unemployed with state benefits only

Source: Adapted from Wilmshurst (1993)

the marketing research industry's main source of social grade/class data. The NRS classifications of social class (A to E) are shown in ◻ Table 7.3.

French Sociologist Pierre Bourdieu argued that the measures of social class ignore social and cultural capital, and focus merely on economic capital. The example given is that of a privately educated, Oxbridge graduate working in the services sector (for example, working at *Starbucks*) shortly after graduating. An occupational measure of class would likely consider this individual to be working class, but this would ignore the social and cultural capital that individual possesses.

In recent years, the traditional social class categories of working, middle and upper class have been considered outdated (Savage, 2015). In response to these criticisms, Savage (2015) developed a new model of seven social classes ranging from the elite at the top to a "precariat" – the poor, precarious proletariat – at the bottom (Savage, 2015: 12). The "BBC UK Lab study" measured economic capital: income, savings, house value, and social capital (the number and status of people someone knows). ◻ Table 7.4 lists and describes the seven social classes.

◘ Table 7.4 Savage's new model of seven social classes (2015)

Class	Characteristics
Elite	This is the wealthiest and most privileged group in the UK. They went to private schools and elite universities and enjoy high cultural activities such as listening to classical music and going to the opera.
Established middle class	This is the most gregarious and the second wealthiest of all the class groups. They work in traditional professions and socialise with a wide variety of people and take part in a wide variety of cultural activities.
Technical middle class	This is a small, distinctive and prosperous new class group. They prefer emerging culture, such as social media, and mix mainly among themselves. They work in science and tech and come from middle-class backgrounds.
New affluent workers	These people are economically secure, without being well-off. This class group is sociable, has lots of cultural interests and sits in the middle of all the groups in terms of wealth. They're likely to come from working class backgrounds.
Traditional working class	This group has the oldest average age, and they're likely to own their own home. They mix among themselves and don't enjoy emerging culture. Jobs in this group include lorry drivers, cleaners and electricians.
Emergent service workers	These young people have high social and cultural capital – so they know people from all different walks of life and enjoy a wide range of cultural activities – but are not financially secure.
Precariat	The poorest and most deprived social group. They tend to mix socially with people like them and don't have a broad range of cultural interests. More than 80% rent their home.

Source: Adapted from Savage (2015)

❓ Questions

Use the social class categories in ◘ Table 7.4 to determine which segment would be the best market for each of the following offerings, a…:

- nine-day Mediterranean cruise
- one-week package holiday in Portugal
- restaurant meal at a fine-dining restaurant
- camping holiday in the south of France.

■ **Income Segment**

Income is a major factor in demographic market segmentation. Income allows or prevents the consumption of many tourism offerings. The major requirements for consuming a holiday are time and money. However, income as a segmentation variable can at times be misleading. It does not always predict which consumers will buy an offering.

Consumers in an upmarket suburb, for example, may not go to an upmarket restaurant because they spend their disposable income on other things, such as the home or cars. Singles (regardless of age) tend to dine out most frequently (and also shop at supermarkets more regularly). Couples with children tend to eat at home and dine out only on special occasions.

Geographic Segmentation

Dividing the market into groups based on where consumers come from is probably the most common form of segmentation. Geographic segmentation divides the market according to different geographical factors (or areas) such as regions, nations/countries, counties/states/provinces, cities, neighbourhoods, or suburbs, city or metro size, and climate (Kotler & Keller, 2016: 122). The needs of potential customers in one geographic area are often different from those of customers in another area, due to climate, custom, or tradition. For example, in some European countries such as Finland and the Netherlands, yet in countries like China, Turkey, and the UK, tea is the preferred beverage.

An example of this is a hotel which segments its market into domestic and interna-

7

tional regions. The main markets for *Ocean View*, a B&B in Brighton, UK might be domestic markets, such as Londoners, and international markets, such as Western Europeans (from France or Germany, for instance). Inbound (or incoming) tour operators often specialise in handling groups of tourists from specific countries. The tour operator *Abercrombie and Kent*, for instance, caters for the North American market, *My Travel* caters for the Scandinavian market and *Crown Travel* caters for the Far Eastern market. Markets can also be divided according to climate. Research has shown that peo-

ple from Northern European climates (such as Sweden) have a preference for warmer destinations (such as Spain and Thailand). In the past, for most national tourism organisations, market segmentation was often limited to attracting international tourism markets. However, since 2001 (the year of the 9/11 terrorist attacks) and more recently the outbreak of coronavirus in 2020), destination marketers have recognised the importance of domestic and regional travel markets. ► Industry Insight 7.5 explains how VisitEngland divides its main domestic tourist markets.

Industry Insight 7.5

VisitEnglands's Visitor Segmentation

VisitEngland recently developed a visitor segmentation, based on a combination of what matters to domestic holidaymakers, their holiday behaviour, and demographics (see ◘ Fig. 7.3). The Visitor Segmentation report identifies five segments of UK domestic holidaymaker:

- Country Loving Traditionalists (30%);
- Fun in the Sun (20%);
- Fuss Free Value Seekers (11%);
- Free and Easy Mini Breakers (26%); and
- Aspirational Family Fun (12%).

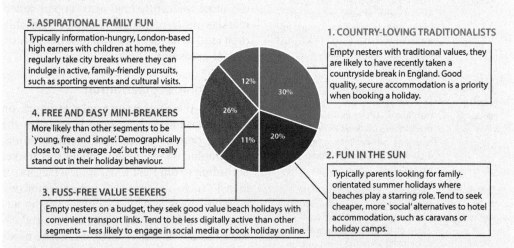

5. ASPIRATIONAL FAMILY FUN
Typically information-hungry, London-based high earners with children at home, they regularly take city breaks where they can indulge in active, family-friendly pursuits, such as sporting events and cultural visits.

4. FREE AND EASY MINI-BREAKERS
More likely than other segments to be 'young, free and single'. Demographically close to 'the average Joe'. but they really stand out in their holiday behaviour.

3. FUSS-FREE VALUE SEEKERS
Empty nesters on a budget, they seek good value beach holidays with convenient transport links. Tend to be less digitally active than other segments – less likely to engage in social media or book holiday online.

1. COUNTRY-LOVING TRADITIONALISTS
Empty nesters with traditional values, they are likely to have recently taken a countryside break in England. Good quality, secure accommodation is a priority when booking a holiday.

2. FUN IN THE SUN
Typically parents looking for family-orientated summer holidays where beaches play a starring role. Tend to seek cheaper, more 'social' alternatives to hotel accommodation, such as caravans or holiday camps.

◘ **Fig. 7.3** VisitEngland's domestic tourism market segments. (Source: VisitBritain. (2016). ► https://www.visitbritain.org/sites/default/files/ vb-corporate/Documents-Library/documents/ England-documents/project_lion_-_overview_-_ for_website.pdf)

Geodemographic Segmentation

Demographic and geographic segmentation are popular methods with which to segment the market, as statistics on these group divisions are readily available and are easy to use. These statistics are available from sources such as the ONS website (▶ www.ons.gov.uk). Marketers also often combine demographic and geographic segmentation variables. This is known as **"geodemographic segmentation"**. It is based on the idea that people are attracted by communities where they will find others with similar lifestyles and characteristics. It does not suggest that all of the people in the defined area have similar characteristics, only that there are common threads that link the community. For example, Kensington in west London, UK is an area of affluence, Greenwich in south-east London has a large number of students, and towns such as Worthing and Eastbourne along the UK South Coast have a high concentration of elderly retired people.

> *Geo-demographic segmentation* is a two-stage market segmentation approach "in which consumers are grouped according to demographic variables, such as income and age, and identified by a geographic variable, such as post code" (Oxford Reference, 2018).

Two of the most popular geo-demographics systems are ACORN and MOSAIC. A Classification of Residential Neighbourhoods (ACORN), which was developed by the market research group CACI, shows how postcode areas are divided into six categories, 18 groups, and 62 types. The six categories are as follows:
1. Affluent achievers
2. Rising prosperity
3. Comfortable communities
4. Financially stretched
5. Urban adversity
6. Not private households

The ACORN geodemographic tool is used to identify the population and its demand for products to help marketers so that they can determine where to conduct marketing communications and social media campaigns. Another popular classification system is MOSAIC which was developed with a global market in mind. MOSAIC classifies the population into 15 main socio-economic groups and, within this, 66 household types to create a three-tier classification that can be used at individual, household, or postcode levels.

Geodemographics as a market analysis tool is becoming increasingly important to the marketer as consumers become more sophisticated and fragmented. This method is frequently used in direct marketing and relationship marketing (see ▶ Chaps. 12 and 13 respectively), enabling marketers to target individual buyers and households with great accuracy (Middleton & Clarke, 1994: 81).

7.4.2.2 Psychological Criteria

The main psychological criteria used for segmenting markets are psychographics (or lifestyles of consumers) and benefits sought.

Psychographic (Lifestyle) Segmentation

Tourism and hospitality consumers can also be divided into different groups based on psychological rather than physical dimensions. This includes variables such as personality, lifestyle and social class characteristics, as shown in ◘ Table 7.5. This division is known as **"psychographic segmentation"**. The reason for segmenting consumers according to psychological attributes is the belief that common values can be found among groups of consumers and that these values tend to determine their purchasing patterns. Furthermore, consumers in the same demographic group can have very different psychographic profiles.

◘ **Table 7.5** Psychographic variables

Variables	Examples of typical breakdowns
Personality	Outgoing, introverted, or ambitious
Lifestyle	Conservative or liberal

Source: Author's creation

> *Psychographic segmentation* divides a market into different groups based on social class, personality or lifestyle factors (Gunter & Furnham, 1992: 133).

❓ Discuss what is meant by the money-rich/time-poor market segment.

■ **Personality**

Markets can be divided according to the personality of consumers. This type of segmentation has been used to distinguish different types of tourist (see the section on consumer typology in ▶ Chap. 3). Originally, tourists were divided into two possible groups namely psychocentrics and allocentrics (Plog, 1984: 113–134). Plog (2001) expanded his original model (see ◘ Fig. 7.4) and renamed allocentrics as venturers, while psychocentrics are now known as "dependables". In the expanded model, Plog identified five personality types ranging from venturers at the one end of the travel continuum through near-venturers, mid-centrics, and near-dependables, to dependables at the extreme end. Venturers are self-assured, risk-taking, energetic and adventurous travellers seeking novel environments, who are sharp-witted and independent decision makers. They are avid and independent travellers to unusual off the beaten track destinations or long-haul destinations who are keen on spending their disposable income and

have a particular desire to experience local customs and cultures. Dependables, at the furthest extreme, are unadventurous, prefer known environments, travel less frequently and for shorter durations, seeking a 'home-from-home' holiday in popular domestic resorts and international mass tourism destinations where they feel safe, and prefer being surrounded by friends, family or other travellers. The 'dependable' is more price-sensitive and prefers an all-inclusive package holiday. Furthermore, as the framework presents primarily two main types of traveller personalities, it is suggested that it will be too limited to place most travellers in either of the personality categories, as most tourists can be plotted somewhere in between the two extremes, and hence more travellers would identify as near-venturer, centric-venturer, centric-dependable, and near-dependable.

While this model in itself is simplistic, it is useful in helping tourism marketers consider the facilities that they should provide to meet these differing needs. A bed and breakfast (B&B), for instance, may cater for both types: tourists seeking the enclave and environmental bubble (familiar home features) of a resort hotel and tourists who may decide to hire a car during their stay in the destination so as to visit areas that are not usually seen by tourists.

■ **Lifestyle**

Lifestyle is a broad term that overlaps with personality characteristics. For instance, is being ambitious a personality trait or a life-

◘ **Fig. 7.4** Psychographic types. (Source: Adapted from Plog (2001, p. 14))

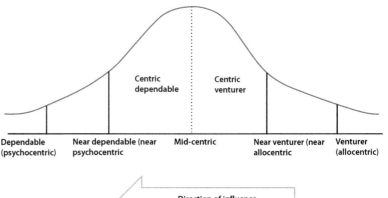

style trait? Lifestyle relates to consumer activities, interests and opinions (see the activities, interests and opinions or AIO analysis discussed in ▶ Chap. 3). It reflects how people spend their time as well as their beliefs on social, economic and political issues. TNS Research Surveys developed a UK Lifestyle typology based on lifestyles and classified the following lifestyle groupings: belonger, survivor, experimentalist, conspicuous consumer, social resistor, self-explorer, and aimless.

Benefits Sought (or Benefits Desired)

Different benefits appeal to different markets. Some people visit a restaurant because it offers quality food. Other people visit that restaurant because it offers value for money, while some people visit it because they like its atmosphere. Still others visit because it has a menu that offers variety or because of its convenient location. The benefits sought approach is based on the principle that marketers should provide consumers with what they want, based on the benefits they seek. From a tourism perspective, some people may stay at a hotel for business, while others go there on holiday. A boutique hotel, for instance, attracts both business people and holidaymakers. However, different markets are attracted at different times. During the shoulder (off-peak) season, for example, a coastal B&B or guesthouse may attract a more upmarket clientele and an older age bracket than it attracts during the peak summer season. Major airlines often segment on the basis of the benefits passengers seek from aircraft by differentiating between first-class passengers (extra luxury benefits such as a flat bed with mattress and duvet) and economy passengers (who get none of the luxury by receiving the same flight). Destination marketers can segment tourists according to the attributes (pull factors) that attract them to a destination. For example, some travellers may wish to visit cultural and historical sites, while others may prefer activities including sunbathing, swimming, adventure (hiking, shark-cage diving, abseiling) or wildlife. Some travellers may be attracted to the destination because of the cost of the trip or value for money received, while others may focus on the

local food and beverages and uniqueness of accommodation available. Furthermore, attributes are perceived differently by different types of travellers, suggesting that different market segments seek different attributes in a destination. Travel agencies, airlines and hotel chains typically divide their markets into these benefit segments:

- Hedonistic
- Education
- Luxury
- Entertainment
- Sun-seeking
- Nostalgia (see ▶ Industry Insight 7.6)
- Scenic
- Activity and adventure
- Social
- Religious
- Health.

People in each benefit segment or group are oriented toward activities and offerings that satisfy them in these areas. Swarbrooke (2000) links the benefits being sought by visitors to various types of tourist attractions, as shown in ☐ Table 7.6.

❓ Collect magazine and newspaper advertisements for five different tourism offerings (for example, a restaurant, a hotel, an airline, a car rental company, and a travel agency). For each advertisement, write a description of the demographic and psychological characteristics of the targeted market.

☐ **Table 7.6**   Benefits sought segmentation

Type of attraction	Main benefits sought
Beach	Suntan, bathing in sea, economy, company of others or solitude
Museum	Learning something new, nostalgia, purchasing souvenirs
Theatre	Entertainment, atmosphere, status
Theme park	Excitement, atmosphere, value for money, fun, entertainment, variety of visitor attractions

Source: Adapted from Swarbrooke (2000). Copyright © Elsevier 2000, p. 211

7

Nostalgia-Craving Baby Boomers are Driving Tourism

In the 1920s, ▶ Route 66 in the US was built to connect Chicago with Los Angeles. Author John Steinbeck dubbed it "the mother road." From Depression-era migrants to returning Government Issues (GIs) to family holiday-makers, motorists on Route 66 rolled past Vegas-style neon lights hovering over low-rise diners, motor courts, and gas stations in designs so distinctive they gave rise to the term "roadside architecture." They are also known as "pueblo-deco", art nouveau lite; and, simply, kitsch. Today, these structures — many of them long vacant — are reopening as trendy hotels, restaurants, microbreweries, and bars along a part of Route 66 through Albuquerque called "Edo", or "East Downtown", that fill with patrons far too young to remember the onetime allure of the highway as a frontier of the freedom of the open road. It is a small but significant example of the way nostalgia increasingly is driving travel, as visitors seek to recapture their own childhoods; or at least a world they recall as, or assume to have been, simpler, safer, and an escape from the conformity of modern-day chain hotels and restaurants.

Source: Jon Marcus Globe Correspondent January 30, 2016 ▶ https://www.bostonglobe.com/lifestyle/travel/2016/01/30/nostalgia-craving-baby-boomers-are-driving-tourism/4eRqFpYF7T7lTToCUFi3oL/story.html Accessed 21 March 2016.

7.4.2.3 Behavioural Criteria

All of the methods of segmentation discussed so far have focused on the type of person the consumer is. The market can also be divided into groups based on the way in which consumers behave (their attitudes toward, use of or response to a tourism offering). This is known as "behavioural segmentation".

Relationship with the Offering

This type of division groups consumers according to their relationship with particular product-offerings. Observing consumers as consumer services and use offerings can be a useful tool for new offering development. In addition, new markets for existing offerings can be identified as well as relevant marketing communications. Offerings such as destinations, car rental companies, airlines, hotels, and visitor attractions may be segmented according to the following variables:

- Usage
- Loyalty to the offering
- Buyer readiness
- Media usage.

◻ Figure 7.5 shows the different types of behavioural segmentation, which we examine below in detail.

- **Usage**

Consumers can also be grouped according to whether they are regular or one-off users (occasion segmentation) (Frochot & Morrison, 2000). Most airlines now have frequent-flyer programs (FFPs) targeted at regular users. Hotels, restaurants and many other tourism and hospitality companies rely on regular users during the off season and one-off holidaymakers during the summer months.

Many restaurants are promoted especially for one-off occasions such as sports events, weddings and parties. For special occasions, consumers are usually prepared to pay more for special treatment. Thus, many restaurants now have special rates for children's parties. Similarly, hotels and cruise lines specialise in the lucrative honeymoon market, providing honeymoon suites and special services to this unique group. Some tour operators offer tours for consumers with a special interest in military history. For example, *Galina International Battlefield Tours* organises tours to Flanders and the Ypres Salinet or to special commemorative events such as anniversaries (for example, in 2017, the 100th anniversary of the Battle of Oppy Wood) (see ▶ Industry Insight 7.7). Travel agencies also specialise in offering

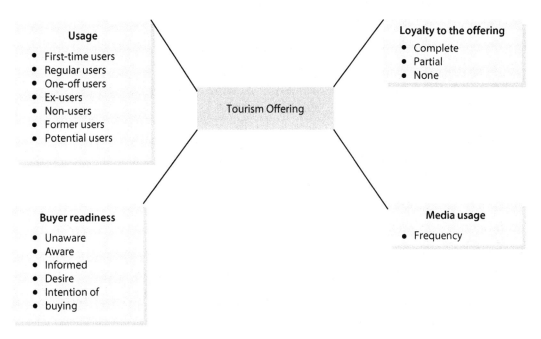

Usage
- First-time users
- Regular users
- One-off users
- Ex-users
- Non-users
- Former users
- Potential users

Loyalty to the offering
- Complete
- Partial
- None

Tourism Offering

Buyer readiness
- Unaware
- Aware
- Informed
- Desire
- Intention of
- buying

Media usage
- Frequency

■ **Fig. 7.5** Different types of behavioral segments. (Source: Author's creation)

religious tours and excursions such as to Mecca in Saudi Arabia. Tourism and hospitality marketers can also prepare special offers and advertising campaigns for holiday occasions. Another example is *Marriott Hotels & Resorts* which promotes a Valentine's weekend package ('Couples Getaways'), including accommodation, his-and-her treatments at their spa, a round of golf, and a dinner and dance.

The rate at which people use or consume tourism and hospitality products provides another segmentation area: former users (or ex-users), non-users, potential users, first-time users, and regular users of a product offering.

Businessmen and -women may be regular users of hotels, for instance, with as many as 20 or more stays in hotels in a year. Regular users very often account for a small percentage of the market, but a high percentage of spending. Included in a potential user group are consumers facing life stage changes, such as new parents and newly married couples, who can be turned into heavy users. For example, restaurants and hotel resorts that cater for families could target new parents.

? Browse this website: ► http://www.wartours.com/anniversaries

---

Industry Insight 7.7

Galina International Battlefield Tours
Since 1989, Galina International Battlefield Tours has organised WWI & WWII battlefield tours in northern Europe. In 1991 the company was committed to providing quality tours for adult groups who wish to visit the battlefields and their environs, either for gen-

eral interest or commemorative purposes. Galina International Battlefield Tours offer executive coach-based travel from the UK to the battlefields of France, the Netherlands, Germany, Belgium, as well as tours within Britain. Its tour itineraries include travel via ferry from Hull, Dover, and Portsmouth, or

7

via Eurotunnel, taking into account the groups' preferred pick-up point, and the route which provides you with the best value for money. The tour company caters for many types of groups: serving or ex-serving military, special interest, educational, corporate or cadet group – as well tours for individuals and small groups.

Source: ▶ http://www.wartours.com/anniversaries

▪ Loyalty to Offering

Some people are particularly loyal to a brand such as a hotel chain or an airline (Uncles, Dowling & Hammond, 2003). Other people are loyal to several brands. For instance, partially loyal consumers will stay only at a *Travelodge* hotel or perhaps a *Premier Inn*, depending on last-minute decisions based on factors such as convenience. Others are not loyal to a brand at all and will buy the cheapest or most convenient tourism offerings (e.g. a low-cost flight). In addition, many people stay in five-star (or six-star) hotels and resorts as much for the status it confers on them as for the additional comfort. Marketers are recognising the importance of brand-loyal consumers more and more, and are using relationship marketing techniques to build and retain relationships with consumers (see ▶ Chap. 13).

The frequent-flyer program *Oneworld* (an alliance of 15 of the world's leading airlines) and the frequent-guest loyalty program of *Hyatt Hotels* (e.g. Hyatt Gold Passport) attempt to make people more enthusiastic about purchasing these organisations' offerings. Consumers who have had a previous negative experience with an offering or who disagree with an organisation's ethics may be completely against purchasing, no matter how much the offering is promoted.

▪ Buyer Readiness

Markets can be divided according to how ready consumers are to purchase tourism product-offerings (Kotler & Keller, 2016: 265). Some people may be completely unaware of the offering, other people may be aware and interested, some people may be informed, while others may desire it and still others are intent on buying it.

▪ Media Usage

Markets are increasingly segmented by frequency of viewership, readership, or patronage of media vehicles. For instance, light and heavy newspaper readers might respond differently to advertisements with different creative appeals (Urban, 1976). This type of segmentation tool can provide insights into whether or not a publisher attracts and retains consumers who are more or less responsive to an advertiser's communication. Such data can provide input when evaluating the efficiency and effectiveness of media.

7.5 Market Targeting

Having identified the different segments of the market, the next stage for the marketer is to decide how many and which segments to target. As we mentioned in the last section, it is not feasible for a company to target all market segments, thus, a company will target the most valuable segments; which in reality for small businesses is one or two segments. Market targeting is the process of evaluating each segment's attractiveness (its size and growth rate), selecting one or more of the market segments and designing different strategies to reach each segment selected. There are three targeting approaches or strategies:

- ▬ Niche marketing
- ▬ Differentiated/customised marketing.
- ▬ Undifferentiated marketing.

These targeting strategies are discussed in more detail below.

7.5.1 Niche Marketing Strategy

Niches cover everything from cruises to pets.

Niche marketing (or "concentrated marketing" as it is sometimes called) is what a tourism organisation does when it focuses on meeting the needs and wants of narrowly defined market segments (a "micro segment"). It is the process of targeting small, readily identifiable sections of a market. Niche marketing is especially appealing to companies with limited resources. It is an approach commonly used in the activity holiday market, where there is an abundance of tourism operators presenting specialist holidays for niche markets (such as medical, health, safari adventure, bird-watching, wine-tasting, heritage, cruise, cycling, skiing, water sports, senior citizen, gay, and even pet travel tourism) (▶ Chap. 3). Niche marketing can be a very effective strategy in tourism since consumers are often willing to pay a premium for a more exclusive offering, for example, a cruise to the Caribbean. A farm, for instance, may wish to target niche market segments such as ramblers, wine fanatics, birdwatchers, or painters. The disadvantage of this approach is that the organisation may become dependent upon the one segment it serves. This may leave the organisation vulnerable should any negative change affect the demand pattern of the segment. The tourism marketing environment is especially volatile and unpredictable.

7.5.2 Differentiated Marketing and Customised Marketing Strategy

Tourism organisations that adopt the differentiated (or 'multi-segment') marketing approach or strategy recognise separate segments of the total market and treat each segment separately (see ▶ Industry Insight 7.8). Targeting for several segments spreads the risk. A game lodge, for instance, may target wildlife tourists as well as tourists who have particular interests in pursuits such as painting, natural history, hiking, military/war, photography, archaeology.

Customised marketing occurs in cases where a market is viewed as being so diverse that a tourism organisation has to focus its marketing efforts on the needs of each individual consumer (as opposed to each market segment). This strategy offers the advantage that the organisation can modify its offering – or the way in which it is delivered, promoted or priced – in order to satisfy individual requirements.

A tourism and hospitality organisation operating with a wide range of offerings in many markets typically uses a multi-segment approach. *TUI* uses this strategy. Its *First Choice* brand focuses on the younger, more family-orientated market, while *Saga Holidays* target wealthier, older empty-nester customers. Multi-segment targeting offers many advantages to companies, including greater sales volumes, larger market shares, and economies of scale in marketing. Before deciding to use this approach, firms should compare the advantages and costs of multi-segment targeting to those of undifferentiated and niche targeting.

7.5.3 Undifferentiated Marketing Strategy (a Mass Market Philosophy)

When using undifferentiated (or 'mass market') marketing, a tourism organisation ignores market segmentation and seeks to communicate to the entire (mass) market with one tourism offering. This strategy focuses on what is common in the needs of consumers, rather than on what is different. Major cities and destinations adopt this strategy because their appeal is very diverse. The market may include groups from school children to business segments. Quick-service restaurants (such as *Nando's)* are another example of tourism offerings that have a wide market appeal. On the whole, however, marketers should be wary of this strategy as there are few offerings that satisfy all or even most consumers.

The effective marketer knows how to combine segmentation and targeting to get the best results for an organisation.

Indonesia Targets Middle Eastern Muslim Tourists

Indonesia has positioned itself as a holiday destination for Muslims worldwide. It has gained a reputation across the world as a destination that caters not only to the Muslim population of Indonesia – which comprise about 95% of the country's population – but also as a place that is accommodative to Muslims from all over the world, who seek to enjoy their holidays without having to make sacrifices in order to cater to their religious needs.

The Halal logo (see below) is the mark of assurance for Muslim tourists, and [having] tourism products and services in line with Islamic beliefs means that a destination is becoming more marketable. The types of accommodation that are available to Muslim travellers vary and can be tailored to the kind of holiday that they prefer.

7.6 Market Positioning

Once the market has been divided and targeted, the product needs to be positioned for the target audience.

Market positioning is the way in which tourism and hospitality organisations want their consumers to perceive their products in relation to the organisations' competitors (Kumar, 2010: 187). Positioning is not about a product or brand's location, it is about the place the brand occupies in a consumer's mind (Ries & Trout, 1972). It is the way an organisation differentiates itself and its products (see ▶ Industry Insight 7.9). Positioning involves an organisation identifying unique selling propositions or points (USPs) and messages to communicate to targeted customers. "Positioning is not something one does to a product or offering. Rather, it is something one does to the minds of consumers" (Pitt, 2013: 58).

7.6.1 Marketing Positioning Strategies

There are several strategies that marketers can take to position tourism and hospitality companies/products in the minds of the consumers and to differentiate themselves from competitors:

- A specific or original product. *Nando's* is known for its original peri-peri chicken sauce recipe.
- Specific benefits that they provide. Theme parks, for instance, advertises the fun and family entertainment that they offer at the theme park. Many marketers use the pronoun "you" in their positioning statements to reflect an association with consumers' needs and desires. For instance, *Sheraton Hotels & Resorts*' tagline is "You don't just stay here, you belong" and "Premier Inn. Premier You" (*Premier Inn*).
- A specific concept, such as boutique hotels – a universal hotel product created for guests who want a more unique and personalised experience than those offered by standardised hotels.
- A specific atmosphere/ambiance. For example, *Henn na Hotel* in Nagasaki, Japan is an innovative robot-themed hotel (customer service desk staffed by robots).
- Against existing competitors. For example, *Avis* versus *Hertz* is a classic example of successful positioning against a competitor. *Avis* sold the travelling public on the idea that because it was the number two company, it had to try harder to satisfy its customers.

7.6.2 The Positioning Steps

Positioning requires three steps, as noted by Kotler et al. (2017: 238). These steps are discussed below.

7.6.2.1 Step 1: Identify a Set of Competitive Advantages

The first step involves the identification of a set of competitive advantages or unique selling propositions upon which to base the gaining of a position in the marketplace. These may include anything that makes the organisation or destination stand out from competitors, including price, a high level of service and particular benefits (see ▶ Industry Insight 7.9). A hotel, for instance, may provide a shuttle service to transport its guests to and from tourist attractions and shopping centres. Similarly, a hotel chambermaid may leave a flower on the pillow of the bed after it has been made. This hotel is providing services that will benefit its target market, which is upmarket leisure tourists.

Industry Insight 7.9

Jet Airways' Positioning Statement

Jet Airways, India's premier international airline, was careful about its positioning. "The whole concept of Jet Airways is to get away from the traditional in India's airline industry," said, Neha Singh, the company's senior brand manager. "To reinforce the fun, easy aspects of the new airline, we have opted for a young, modern look and feel throughout our marketing campaign. The campaign embodies the idea that 'Anyone can fly' and brings in elements of ordinary people becoming superheroes who can fly," added Singh.

Jet Airways' corporate vision is:

» "To be amongst the most innovative and admired brands, renowned for service excellence."

Its corporate mission is:

– Jet Airways will be renowned for reaching out to all our guests with a heart-warming spirit that is our unique Indian hospitality.
– We will delight our guests with genuine care and personalised quality service, along with consistent, reliable and efficient operations.
– We will innovate and deliver service excellence, setting standards for competition to emulate.
– Jet Airways will be the most sought-after place to work.

Jet Airways will achieve these objectives whilst simultaneously ensuring sustainable profitability for all stakeholders.

Source: ▶ http://www.jetairways.com/EN/SA/JetExperience/mission-statement.aspx

---

7.6.2.2 Step 2: Select the Right Competitive Advantages

Once an organisation has identified a set of competitive advantages, the second step calls for the marketer to choose those competitive advantages that will give it a distinctive position in the marketplace. Which advantages should the organisation promote? A marketer may decide to promote one major advantage, such as best price, best value, best location, best quality or best service. However, a marketer may choose to position the organisation or destination on more than one benefit, perhaps by promoting its location as well as quality service delivery.

❓ Analyse the logo and slogan of car-rental company Avis. What does its slogan say about the company's positioning in relation to its competitors?

7.6.2.3 Step 3: Communicate and Deliver the Chosen Position

In the third step of the process, the marketer communicates and delivers the selected position to the target segments by devising a marketing mix.

If a hospitality organisation such as a hotel decides that it wants to position itself as a leader in the marketplace for best quality, then it must employ service-oriented staff and provide training programs for them. In addition, it must advertise and promote a message to consumers that it has quality facilities and service as well as a pricing strategy that reflects that quality.

7.6.3 Points of Parity and Points of Difference

Marketers can define the appropriate points-of-difference and points-of-parity associations. Points of difference (PODs) are attributes or benefits that consumers strongly associate with a brand. Points of parity (POPs) are associations that are not necessarily unique to the brand, but are shared with other brands (in other words, where the firm can at least match the competitors' claimed benefits).

7.6.4 The Product Positioning Map

Marketers can make use of a perceptual or product positioning map that enables them to see where their offerings are positioned in the marketplace in relation to their competitors' offerings. A product positioning map (which is typically two-dimensional) reveals consumer perceptions of the organisation and its products and competitors. Organisations can also use this map to determine the effectiveness of their promotional activities. To make a product positioning map, a survey is conducted among a random sample of consumers who are asked various questions designed to provide an image of the marketplace in which the organisation operates. One such question might be, "How do you perceive our hotel: as leisure oriented or business oriented?" The consumers' images are then plotted on a grid where findings may reveal a gap in the marketplace for developing a new tourism offering.

An example of a product positioning map is given in ◘ Fig. 7.6, which shows consumer images of various travel agencies. The findings in ◘ Fig. 7.6 reveal a gap in the specialist, corporate travel agencies. However, it should be noted that there may also be a gap because there is no demand for such an offering.

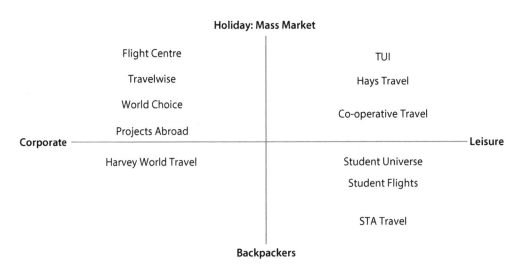

◘ **Fig. 7.6**   Product positioning map. (Source: Author's creation)

Another limitation of a product positioning map is that it is largely reliant on the knowledge of consumers within the target market of the offerings.

Summary

The principles of segmentation, targeting and positioning are interrelated and form part of the analysis stage of the marketing planning process. Successful marketing segmentation is not based on one method alone. A marketer makes use of a blend of different techniques, depending on individual situations. A marketer could combine personality with demographic factors, for example, or social class with geographic factors. Most tourism and hospitality organisations deal with a few or several market segments. In addition, there remains a need for international tourism and hospitality marketers to be aware of the cultural differences that exist in their respective countries, as these contribute to differing brand usage profiles. Marketers will need to communicate with smaller groups of consumers in the future, being sure to address each group as an individual. In addition, they should not over segment the market.

❓ Review Questions

1. Define 'market segmentation' (in your own words) and explain the STP process.
2. Identify five different ways that markets can be segmented.
3. Explain why market segmentation is so important for effective marketing.
4. Discuss the limitations associated with Plog's (2001) typology.
5. Is the tourism industry becoming more or less segmented? Discuss.
6. Provide an example (other than the ones given in this chapter) of the use of generational marketing by a tourism company.
7. Contrast market segmentation and tourist typologies.
8. What factors should be taken into account in deciding whether to target a particular market segment for marketing attention?
9. Explain the concept of a perceptual map. What can it reveal?
10. Visit the website of a major hotel brand, airline, or car hire company. Briefly describe how it appeals to different segments through the website.

In-depth Case Study 1: Segmentation, Targeting and Positioning: Moxy Hotels' Targets Millennials

Objectives

- To understand the meaning of segmentation, targeting and positioning
- To understand target marketing and observe its application to the case study.

During the past 3 years, a growing number of global hotel chains have enterprisingly targeted the Airbnb generation of young urbanites with the launch of sub-brands. A leading player in this emerging market has been the hotel chain Marriott International, which created a new hotel brand called Moxy.

The first Moxy hotel was launched in Milan in 2014 and whilst the Moxy brand franchise has several hotels in the USA, it is largely a European project.

Moxy is a far cry from Marriott International's five star luxurious and conventional design, instead operating within the three-star tier segment with a fresh focus on 24/7 communal living and 'budget is beautiful' mantra. Designed as a boutique hotels, Moxy aims to provide the social heart of a hostel and is marketed by Marriott International as having, 'potency of style, innovation and tech-savviness'.

According to Toni Stoeckl, global brand leader, Moxy is aimed at 'lifestyle-orientated millennial travellers'. Stoeckl describes the launch of Moxy, "As a huge opportunity in the affordable lifestyle segment that was not being addressed". She added "We found a lot of the budget segment, especially in Europe, had stripped the per-

◘ Image 7.2 Moxy Hotels' logo

sonality and fun back and the offer was quite bland, so when designing Moxy we wanted to make sure it was fun, energetic and vibrant".

The Moxy brand is being aimed at a specific age group: the 20 something hipsters who want affordable yet stylish hotel digs. This primary target market is further clarified by a Marriott International executive in the press release announcing the brand as for, 'The next generation traveller, not only Gens X and Y, but people with a younger sensibility.'

As many of the younger generation are living within a global economic slump, the rooms are offered at price points within the economy tier. More youthful consumers are less inclined to pay for services that older generations consider necessities, such as cars, independent living quarters, concierges, and room service. Moxy hotels are designed for value-conscious travellers, which is not to say that all millennials are value conscious, though people in their 20s tend to be more cost conscious. Thus, the Millennials are often a price-sensitive segment yet demanding in terms of features and design.

Ramesh Jackson, former Moxy Hotels vice president and global brand manager describes Moxy consumers as, 'Confident explorers who are wildly self-sufficient, but still wanting a chance to connect with each other in inviting social spaces in person or digitally'. Guests need to engage with a self-service model. Staffing is minimal and self-check-in is available through mobile devices as the initial press release describes creating an overall atmosphere for, 'Savvy travellers who thrive on self-service and embrace new technology'.

Moxy's guestrooms are functional and uncluttered (no more than 183 square feet) and with an emphasis on neutral coloured tones and natural materials. The public spaces have 'art walls', which reflect the local city and surroundings and the traditional reception desk is replaced with a bar. Game arcades and bowling alleys also dominate communal areas. The furnishings are generally industrial chic, and the chain has invested heavily in many tech amenities that younger travellers are more demanding of, such as; flat screen TVs with screencasting features and built in USB ports in rooms, 'Plug and Meet' public areas with state of the art computers, seating areas with large TVs, and free Wi-Fi.

Moxy has been specifically designed to capture the rapidly emerging millennial traveller, with a specific psychographic segment in mind. Its success depends on providing affordable, stylish, and digitally-friendly accommodation. Clearly Moxy targets a specific market that is footloose, free and places socialising in a fun space ahead of spending in a formal setting.

Source: Interview with Erica Flint, Senior Manager, Global Communications, Marriott International Luxury Brands.

1. Describe the profile of a typical Moxy guest.
2. Explain the segmentation variables Moxy has used to segment the market.
3. Briefly explain some of Moxy's key distinguishing characteristics and competitive advantages.
4. List the traits of a 'millennial consumer'.
5. Go online to Moxy Hotels 'website (▶ moxy-hotels.marriott.com). How does the company position itself based upon the images on the website as well as the Moxy brand? Explain the extent to which it appeals to the millennial market.

Image 7.3 Moxy Hotel Tbilisi, Georgia – check-in bar

References

Font, X., & McCabe, S. (2017). Sustainability and marketing in tourism: Its contexts, paradoxes, approaches, challenges, and potential. *Journal of Sustainable Tourism, 25*(7), 869–883.

Frochot, I., & Morrison, A. (2000). Benefit segmentation: A review of its applications to travel and tourism research. *Journal of Travel & Tourism Marketing, 9*(4), 21–45.

Gunter, B., & Furnham, A. (1992). *Consumer profiles: An introduction to psychographics.* London: Routledge.

Hattingh, C. (2018). *A typology of gay leisure travellers: An African perspective.* Unpublished Doctor of Technology in Tourism and Hospitality Management thesis, Cape Peninsula University of Technology, Cape Town, South Africa.

Kotler, P., & Keller, K. (2016). *Marketing management* (15th ed.). New York: Pearson.

Kotler, P., Bowen, J., Makens, J., & Baloglu, S. (2017). *Marketing for hospitality and tourism* (7th ed.). Upper Saddle River, NJ: Prentice Hall.

Kumar, P. (2010). *Marketing of tourism and hospitality services.* New Delhi, India: Tata McGraw-Hill Education.

Middleton, V. T. C., & Clarke, J. (1994). *Marketing in travel and tourism* (2nd ed.). Oxford, UK: Butterworth-Heinemann.

Oxford Reference. (2018). *Geographic segmentation.* Retrieved from http://www.oxfordreference.com/view/10.1093/oi/authority.20110803095848381 [14 September 2018].

Pitt, L. (2013). *Marketing for managers* (3rd ed.). Cape Town, South Africa: Juta & Co, Ltd..

Plog, S. (1984). Why destination areas rise and fall in popularity. *Cornell Hotel and Restaurant Quarterly, 14*(4), 113–134.

Plog, S. (2001). Why destination areas rise and fall in popularity: An update of a classic. *Cornell Hotel and Restaurant Administration Quarterly, 42*(3), 13–24.

Pride, W., Ferrell, O., Lukas, B., Schembri, S., Niininen, O., & Cassidy, R. (2017). *Marketing principles* (3rd ed.). Sydney, Australia: Cengage Learning.

Ries, A., & Trout, J. (1972). The positioning era cometh. *Advertising Age, 24*(April), 35–38.

Savage, M. (2015). *Social class in the 21st century.* London: Penguin.

Swarbrooke, J. (2000). *The development and management of visitor attractions.* London: Elsevier.

Uncles, M., Dowling, G., & Hammond, K. (2003). Customer loyalty and customer loyalty programs. *Journal of Consumer Marketing, 20*(4), 294–316.

Urban, C. (1976). Correlates of magazine readership. *Journal of Advertising Research, 19*(3), 317–337.

Weaver, D., & Lawton, L. (2002). *Tourism management* (2nd ed.). Milton, Australia: Wiley.

Wilmshurst, J. (1993). *Below-the-line promotion*. St. Ives, UK: Butterworth-Heinemann.

Xinhua, B. (2016). 16 per cent of China's population over 60. *China Daily Asia*. Wednesday May 4, 2016.

Further Reading

Hermann, S. (2009). *Hidden champions of the 21st century*. New York: Springer.

Swinyard, W., & Struma, K. (1986). Market segmentation: Finding the heart of your restaurant's market. *Cornell Hotel and Restaurant Administration Quarterly, 27*(1), 88–96.

7

Implementing the Tourism and Hospitality Marketing Mix

Contents

Tourism and Hospitality Products, Branding, and Pricing

Contents

Electronic Supplementary Material The online version of this chapter (https://doi.org/10.1007/978-3-030-64111-5_8) contains supplementary material, which is available to authorized users.

Purpose

This chapter will show you how tourism and hospitality products are designed and managed. Will enable you to understand the role of price as a component of the marketing mix.

🔄 Learning Goals

After reading this chapter, you should be able to:

- Define the terms "product", "offering", and "product mix"
- Explore each of the three levels of a product
- Explain the stages in and uses of the product's life cycle
- Become familiar with the process for the development of new products
- Explain the role of branding in order for businesses to gain a competitive advantage
- Identify the factors that affect pricing decisions
- Describe the role of price in the marketing mix
- Contrast the various pricing strategies that can be used for existing and new tourism and hospitality products
- Explain the importance of evaluating pricing policies
- Apply the principles of principles of pricing as applied to medical tourism company MakeOvertour.

Overview

In this chapter, we talk about the way marketers design and manage tourism and hospitality products, beginning with definitions for the terms "product", "offering", and "product mix". We then explain that the product is a complex concept that should be considered on three levels: the core product, the expected product, and the augmented product. Next, we discuss the product life cycle concept and how it is used by the tourism marketer to assess the development of tourism products. Last, we go over the steps involved in the process of developing a new product.

In the second section we look at the role of branding in the tourism and hospitality industry. Today, travellers are faced with an infinite number of products to choose from, of which they often have limited knowledge, thus, they turn to brands associated with each product for decision-making. The concept of branding serves as a particularly important strategy for tourism and hospitality businesses to differentiate their products from competitors.

In the third section of the chapter we turn our attention to the price component of the marketing mix. Pricing not only determines profitability, but is also a powerful tool for the marketer. We examine the factors that affect the pricing of tourism and hospitality products and compare the various pricing strategies available to the tourism and hospitality marketer. We also look at how price may act as a signal of quality to consumers and influence their buying decisions. We then describe several pricing approaches used in the tourism industry. We conclude by outlining the characteristics of tourism and hospitality products in relation to price.

The chapter's case study demonstrates the principles of pricing as applied to Medical tourism: MakeOvertour, Turkey.

8.1 Introduction

No matter how attractive the price is or how persuasive the promotion is, getting the product right is crucial. So far in this book, we have used the term 'offerings' when referring to tourism products. This has been done to emphasise that tourism and hospitality products include services as well as goods. Whatever we call them, the product or product component of the **marketing mix** is fundamental to an organisation's success. The marketing mix includes all of the components that a tourism organisation controls that can be used to satisfy or communicate with consumers: product, price, place, promotion (McCarthy, 1960). These components can influence a consumer's decision to purchase a product.

The product is at the centre of this mix. It is what provides consumers with the benefits that they are seeking. Its delivery is the key activity of all tourism organisations. Branding tourism and hospitality products is a strategic marketing management tool as competition in the marketplace has become fierce in the contemporary business environment.

Price is the only component of the marketing mix that produces revenue (Kotler & Armstrong, 2019). All of the other components are expenditures. Price represents one of the seven Ps of the tourism marketing mix. The other six Ps include product or offering, promotion, place, people, physical evidence, and process. The nature of the tourism and hospitality market makes price one of the most complicated of all of the elements of the marketing mix.

> The *marketing mix* is a set of tools used by marketers to achieve a strategic position or positions (McCarthy, 1960).

8.2 Tourism Products

In this section, we define a tourism product, product levels, the product lifecycle concept, and new product development.

8.2.1 What is a Tourism Product?

Anything that can be offered for use and consumption in exchange for money or some form of value is referred to as an offering or proposition (Baines, Fill, Rosengren & Antonetti, 2019: 331). Therefore, a tourism product might more accurately be described as a tourism offering because of its composite nature and characteristics. It is made up of products, services, and experiences. This definition implies that there are both tangible and intangible elements involved in the purchase of a tourism product. For example, a hotel's décor, furniture, and staff dress are tangible,

and so too is a travel agency's promotional merchandise, while service levels and atmosphere at a restaurant, a holiday package put together by a tour operator, and a holiday experience are intangible.

In the business of tourism and hospitality, it is almost always the case that the combination of service and benefits that the consumer is seeking is of primary importance. For instance, the manner in which a meal is served at a restaurant, the friendliness of the staff, and the restaurant atmosphere are just as important as the quality of the food. The products provided by the tourism industry are many and varied, ranging from a thousand-room hotel to a car rental company operated by two or three people. So, for our purposes, tourism product offerings are equivalent to manufactured products, with the broader implications of the intangible elements that they also contain. In this book, the terms 'product' and 'offering' may be used to mean the same thing.

8.2.2 Product Levels

Tourism marketers must have a clear notion of what they are really marketing. All products have different features, which can be grouped into three levels: the core level, the expected level, and the augmented level (Levitt, 1983). The tourism product is therefore not just the actual holiday, dining experience or visit to the museum (for example) that is purchased. The product is made up of all of those tangible and intangible elements that make up the experience enjoyed by the consumer. This concept attempts to illustrate the fact that marketers must pay special attention to all the elements of the product to ensure that it lives up to consumers' expectations and leads to repeat purchases. ◘ Figure 8.1 illustrates the three levels of a product, which we shall discuss further.

8.2.2.1 The Core Product

The most basic level is the core product; which is the real core benefit or service (Baines, et al., 2019: 300). According to Levitt (1983), the generic or core product is a material or

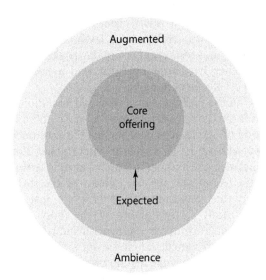

□ **Fig. 8.1** The three levels of a product. (Source: Author's creation)

physical product. As □ Fig. 8.1 illustrates, the core product stands at the centre of the total product-offering. The core product, which is the real core benefit or service is intangible; it is what the consumer is really buying and represents the main benefits that consumers look for to satisfy their needs. For example, for a couple on holiday in Dubai, United Arab Emirates (UAE) staying at the *Radisson Blu Hotel Dubai Waterfront*, a luxurious hotel, the core benefit may be defined as rest and relaxation (i.e. a full service program built around 'staying the night'). The core offering establishes the key message that the hotel aims to communicate. The core product for a theme park such as *Disneyland Resort* in Paris, France is excitement. In Robert Rosenthal's *Optimarketing: Marketing to Electrify your Business*, the author wrote that to be successful, marketers need to think in terms of the benefits of the product, rather than the product's features. Rosenthal added that benefits often have a "psychological component" (Rosenthal, 2014: 22). Going on a holiday and staying at a relaxing holiday resort in a warm climate can help a person's mental well-being.

It is unlikely that a destination or tourism and hospitality organisation's core product-offering will have a competitive advantage. (Most destinations offer relaxation or adventure, most online travel agents have the same booking facilities, airlines generally fly at the same speed, and all hotels have rooms, for example.) Differentiation is more likely to occur at the other two levels of the offering.

8.2.2.2 The Expected Product

The expected product is a combination of the physical good or delivered service which provides the expected core offering (benefit). It includes those specific features that consumers normally expect when purchasing an offering as well as their perceptions of service quality. For example, when staying at a five-star hotel such as *The Radisson Blu Hotel,* guests might normally expect certain features and benefits such as valet service, access to the internet, room service, satellite television, a security safe in the room and privacy. In the context of a theme park, examples of expected offerings include the brand name ("Disneyland"), the various rides, and the quality of service.

> A coffee-making machine, an iron and an ironing board are the two top items travellers look for (and expect) in a hotel.

8.2.2.3 The Augmented Product

Finally, there is the augmented product, which is both tangible and intangible. It is at this level that most of the competition takes place. This refers to the add-ons that are extrinsic to the offering itself, but may influence the decision to purchase. This is where organisations strive for a competitive advantage and to differentiate their product-offerings from those of competitors. For example, The *Radisson Blu Hotel* has a business centre and a health spa, which help attract consumers to the hotel (see ► Industry Insight 8.1).

Business Technology at the Radisson Blu Hotel

The Radisson Blu Hotel Waterfront in Dubai was one of the first hotels in the Middle East to install a facility in its rooms that keeps business travellers in touch by every imaginable means at any time. The Gerber biz-comm system is everything that executives need to communicate instantly across time zones without being constrained by local business hours. It is a five-in-one personal business centre, offering a message centre, printer, photocopier, Wi-Fi, and scanner. This is one example of the non-essential (supporting) offerings that The Radisson Blu Hotel offers.

Source: Based on an interview with Amanda Dietrichsen, receptionist at the business centre, The Radisson Blu Hotel Dubai.

Refer to Industry Insight ► 8.1. Draw a table with 3 columns: Core, Expected and Augmented. Add each of the amenities listed in the Industry Insight box to the correct heading.

The augmented product includes all of the additional features and benefits that the consumer receives. In other words, it includes the add-ons (sometimes up to as many as 20) to the product-offering (see ◘ Fig. 8.2). Some of these add-ons are fairly trivial (for example, a glass of champagne on arrival at the hotel), while others are more significant (for example, hotel guests being given entrance tickets to local visitor attractions or entertainment). Some of the added benefits are tangible, while others are intangible (for example, the quality of service provided, the friendliness of staff and the ambience created). For example, The *Radisson Blu Hotel's* ambience is very upmarket and classy. The city of Dubai and especially the Dubai Waterfront have many so-called high-load elements, such as bright lights, shops, restaurants, nightclubs, crowds, and loud noises, so *The Radisson Blu Hotel* uses a low-load environment with dim lighting and minimalist décor to create a calming atmosphere in which tourists can seek refuge. Atmosphere is an important consideration for tourism marketers when they design products. Marketers must understand what the consumer wants from the purchasing experience and what atmospheric elements consumers are seeking or, in some cases, escaping.

The tourism and hospitality marketer must be aware that augmented benefits soon become

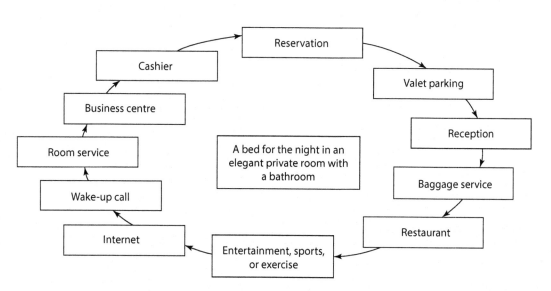

◘ **Fig. 8.2** Luxury hotel core and supplementary services. (Source: Author's creation)

expected benefits. Wi-Fi in cafés, restaurants, hotels, conference centres, and transportation hubs, for example, has become an expected service during the past ten years. Since consumers expect it, it has become a necessity. In recent years, room service or an espresso coffee-making machine in a hotel room.

Similarly, what is contained in the expected offering in one market may be in the augmented offering for another market. Leisure tourists, for instance, may not require access to the internet (a modem), early check-in, or 24-hour gym access while staying at *The Radisson Blu Hotel*. However, these products and services are essential for business travellers.

Conceptualising the product on the three levels we have covered here allows marketers to assess the competitive advantages and consumer appeal of their offering versus the offerings of competitors. To be successful in business, organisations have to review their offerings continually to make sure that they are superior to those of competitors. ◘ Table 8.1 lists some of the ways in which a travel agency and an airline might apply the three-level classification of product features to design and manage their offerings for the market.

❓ Think of an offering from the tourism and hospitality industry (for example, an airline or a theme park). Explain how this offering is marketed using the three levels of features (the core, expected and augmented offerings.

8.2.3 The Product Life Cycle Concept

Tourism and hospitality products (and businesses) are often said to possess life cycles. The concept suggests that all products, like people, have lives, and that it is useful to assess their development so that marketers can plan at various stages. The traditional **product life cycle** suggests that all tourism products have a limited life during which they pass through four stages: introduction, growth, maturity, and decline (Day, 1981). These four stages of the product life cycle can be used to analyse the development path of a tourism product or destination (Vernon, 1979: 256). First the product is introduced. Sales grow as consumers become aware of the product. This success inspires competitors and sales level off. If new alternatives are introduced, the old product is perceived as being dated and sales fall (refer to ◘ Table 8.2).

8.2.3.1 Stages of the Product Life Cycle

Understanding and analysing the various stages, therefore, can be helpful in determining appropriate marketing strategies. The product life cycle concept is also a useful tool for product planning and analysis as well as the prediction of competitive conditions. The S-shaped curve of the product life cycle is illustrated by the graph in ◘ Fig. 8.3 Each

◘ **Table 8.1**   Core, expected and augmented product-offering features for a travel agency and an airline

	Core offering features	**Expected offering features**	**Augmented offering features**
Travel agency	Supply a range of travel service bookings	Brochures Computer technology Ticket delivery Travel agent's travel experience and knowledge	Shop atmosphere Location Hours of operation Refreshments
Airline	Delivering passengers and their luggage safely to their destination	Back-of-seat entertainment systems Punctuality of the flight Clean toilets	Complimentary on-board movies, refreshments, or business facilities WiFi access Extra leg-room

Source: Author's creation

▣ Table 8.2 The characteristics of the stages of the product life cycle

Stage	Characteristics
Introduction stage	The tourism product is new to the market. Typically, the product is bought by 'innovators', a term used to describe a small subset of the eventual market. The marketer must create awareness through extensive advertising and PR activities. There are likely to be high costs associated with the launch and marketing at this stage. Traditionally, profits are low because the product is on trial in the marketplace. Pioneer organisations (those that are first to the market with a particular product) use promotions to get consumers to try the product. The marketer needs to select appropriate pricing strategies carefully when pricing a new product (see section two of this chapter). This is a high-risk stage because the product has not yet proved that it will be successful. Close monitoring is required. However, the risk is counterbalanced by the prospect of building market share in the new product area faster than competitors who enter the market at a later stage.
Growth stage	Sales increase and profit levels begin to improve. The long-term success of the product can be predicted more easily as market penetration advances. However, if the product appears to be profitable, it is likely that competitors will now enter the market with rival products. This is an important time to win market share since it is easier to gain a share of new consumers than to persuade consumers to switch brands later on. Promotional expenditure remains high and may even need to be boosted to maintain the speed of growth. Promotion now focuses on attracting more new consumers as well as repeat purchasers. The organisation may also invest more money in improving the product and distributing it more widely.
Maturity stage	Profits and sales growth slow down. This stage is likely to be the longest but could range from days or weeks to many decades or even centuries. Competition will probably be well established, and it is a question of the survival of the fittest. Tourism organisations must find ways to hold on to their share of the market or to dominate a special niche in the market. Marketers should aim to protect their position in a mature market by modifying target markets, the product and the marketing mix to ensure continued profitability. The organisation should be prepared to reposition the product if need be (see ► Chap. 7).
Decline stage	The popularity of a product inevitably begins to decline. Sales and profits fall steadily as new or modified products are developed and consumers switch allegiance. The decline may be gradual, as in the case of a visitor attraction that lingers for years, or rapid, as in the case of a restaurant that closes within a few months of opening. Sales may drop to zero or they may fall to a low level and stay there for a long time. A decline in sales may be the result of a number of reasons, for example, increased technology, increased competition, loss of strategic direction, changing consumer tastes or as a result of natural disaster or health concern (for example, COVID-19 resulted in the closure of many travel and tourism businesses in 2020). A travel agency, for example, may experience a downturn because technology allows consumers to book directly with airlines much more easily than before. A popular nightclub may simply go out of fashion. After several months in business, the management of a medium-sized tour operator may get bogged down in administrative duties and lose sight of what business it is in. As long as a product is still profitable, the main decision for the marketer is whether to continue to market it or to remove it (delete it) from the marketplace. The organisation may be launching new products that can replace the declining ones and sometimes deletion would enhance their chances of success. Deletion might also reduce the risk of a declining product losing its profitability and becoming a drain on resources. In 2016, *Butlin's* the traditional UK holiday resort with the 'he-de-Hi!' image, launched a series of science festivals aimed at families. The Astonishing Family Science Weekend provided educational fun with activities such as 'Enigma code-breaking' sessions, blowing up microwaves, a walking-on-custard event, computer game programming, and lessons on the science of food.

Source: Adapted from Vernon (1979)

stage of the product life cycle is explained below.

🛈 Apply the concept of the traditional product life cycle to a hotel. What would you as a marketer do at each stage of the life cycle?

8.2.3.2 The Value of the Product Life Cycle Concept to the Tourism and Hospitality Marketer

Managing the tourism and hospitality product through its life cycle is one of the challenges facing marketers. This is a difficult task since there is no way of telling from a sales graph when introduction will become growth, when growth will flatten out to become maturity, or when maturity will begin to decline. It is not always clear which life cycle stage the product offering has reached in the cycle (Baines, et al., 2019: 335). The marketer must consider the market in which the product is. For example, if a product is showing no growth or is declining, it may still be very successful if the market as a whole is declining. Consequently, the life cycle of the market as well as that of the product should be taken into account.

One limitation of the product life cycle (PLC) is that while some products follow the pattern of the S-shaped curve illustrated in 🔲 Fig. 8.3, many products appear to stay in the maturity stage permanently. Some

products, such as *Raffles Hotel* in Singapore (opened in 1887), have been in the maturity stage for many years. These products rejuvenate themselves continuously and remain successful. Some products do not make it through the introduction stage, while other products enter the decline stage and are then cycled back into the growth stage through strong advertising or repositioning (Moon, 2005).

Cowell (1984: 15) suggests a degree of caution in using the concept of the PLC for portfolio approaches to marketing planning for services. This is because most service organisations have a small number of core products. The PLC cannot be used to predict when a product will move from stage to stage, so it has limited use for the tourism marketing planner. However, it can be viewed as a useful diagnostic tool that can help in making decisions relating to the marketing mix for different stages of a PLC.

8.2.4 Innovation and New Tourism and Hospitality Products

The concept of the product life cycle discussed in the preceding section has shown that most tourism and hospitality products eventually enter maturity and decline. It is important to note that changes in society, markets, and economies have led to a

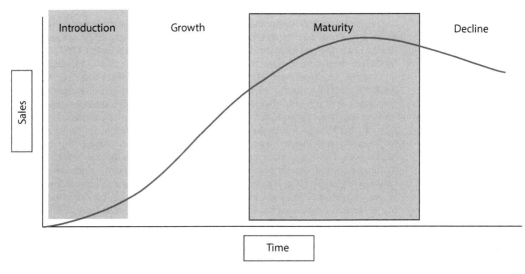

🔲 **Fig. 8.3** The PLC. (Source: Adapted from Vernon (1979))

shortening of life cycles. This has increased the need for organisations to be more innovative in terms of the products that they provide. These 'new' products include everything from restyling or minor modifications to a restaurant menu or a brochure, the development of a new hotel or resort, and the promotion of a destination that is 'new' (repositioned) to the international tourism market (for example, Rwanda). It is essential that the marketer replace those products that have reached the end of their life cycles with new products (Hjalager, 2010).

The risks of new product development (NPD) are exceptionally high. Take, for example, the building of a high-quality hotel, for which the costs are substantial. If the hotel remains half-empty, it is considered a failure. However, the chances of failure can be reduced by using screening in the development process.

8.2.4.1 Stages in New-Product Development

Starting the product life cycle again and again is a necessary part of marketing. The traditional NPD model comprising of steps (see Dibb, Simkin, Pride & Ferrell, 1994: 14) is now considered outdated and has been replaced with the stage-gate process. The stage-gate process places more emphasis on risk control at each development stage. There are five stages in the process of NPD. In the model (see ◨ Fig. 8.4), the gates are used to make decisions to move forward or to return

to the previous stage to improve the product. These stages of the NPD process are discussed below.

- **Stage 1: Preliminary (Idea Stage)**

The marketer must look for ideas to develop a new product. The sources for these ideas can come from consumers, competitors, internal sources (for example, a customer via a staff member), intermediaries, suppliers, and other sources. The greater the range of sources used, the more likely it is that a wide range and a large number of ideas will be produced (Sowrey, 1990: 24). In this stage, the NPD team tries to identify whether the idea is viable and can present a market opportunity. This can be achieved through tools, such as the SWOT analysis (see ► Chap. 5) that help the team to evaluate the idea based on strengths, weaknesses, opportunities, and threats (Cooper, 2014).

- **Stage 2: Detail (Building a Business Case)**

After an idea for developing a new product has been formed, the NPD team should carry out a business analysis to determine whether the idea is commercially viable. A business analysis involves devising a product definition and analysis, a business case, a project plan, and a feasibility review. Essentially this means assessing the size of the market and potential sales against the costs of development. The NPD team can then decide whether the organisation should proceed with the development process.

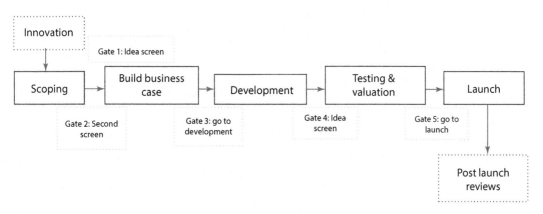

◨ **Fig. 8.4** The stage-gate process of NPD. (Source: Adapted from Cooper (1986))

■ **Stage 3: Development**

The aim of this stage of the process is to bring the product to the market. This is achieved by producing a prototype of the product. For example, a large hotel group might build a replica of a hotel room (i.e. a showroom). Similarly, a restaurant might design the logo for its staff uniform.

■ **Stage 4: Test and Validation**

The next stage is to test-market the product or idea. This involves partially launching the product in the marketplace for a limited period of time to assess the level of consumer demand. If the idea is not well accepted, the NPD team knows that it is not worth investing large amounts of money in the next stage of the process.

■ **Stage 5: Launch**

The last stage of the process – officially introducing the product to the market – involves high costs. The marketer has to spend large amounts of money on promotions to create consumer awareness.

8.2.4.2 What is Meant by a New Product?

In practice, many tourism and hospitality marketers do not have the time or resources to go through all of the stages of the NPD process outlined above. With increasing competition, reducing the time it takes to get a new product into the market has become extremely important in the tourism industry. Similarly, talking about developing new products is somewhat misleading, since few products are actually new. They are usually modifications of existing products or a repackaging of core brands. Several years ago, *Emirates* offered wireless headphones to all its business-class passengers. This is an example of service modification rather than an entirely new product. In addition, many organisations promote so-called new-and-improved products. In reality, it is difficult to see how a product can be both new and improved.

Lovelock (1984: 11) identified five types of new product. These five types are described in ◘ Table 8.3.

Industry Insight 8.2

A younger, Slimmer Mascot for Air India's Logo

After calls from the Prime Minister Narendra Modi to redesign the logo, Air India launched a younger, slimmer Maharajah on its emblem in 2014. The new-look mascot has traded in his traditional turban and sherwani for a vest, blue jeans, trainers, and a low-slung satchel. His trademark swirling moustache remains, although it has been trimmed. Since the Air India Maharajah could not be retired for contractual reasons, the airline decided to tweak his image to bring him more in line with modern times, hence the leaner, younger, sporty, and more dynamic look. Air India will be using 27 different pictures of the new Maharajah to showcase the destinations to which the airline flies. One version sees him dressed as a cricketer for the national team.

Industry Insight 8.3

World's Largest Holiday Inn Built In Makkah, Saudi Arabia

The world's largest Holiday Inn was built in Makkah, Saudi Arabia in 2016. The 5154-room hotel was built in response to the boom in religious tourism to Saudi Arabia. More than three million pilgrims took part in the Hajj in 2018. International tourist numbers to Saudi Arabia are expected to top 20 million by 2020. This will be the first InterContinental Hotel Group Holiday Inn on the pilgrimage route.

Source: Staff writer. (2015). Saudi's Makkah to host world's largest Holiday Inn hotel. Arabian Business. ► https://www.arabianbusiness.com/saudi-s-makkah-host-world-s-largest-holiday-inn-hotel-594930.html [19 October 2018].

Table 8.3 Types of new product: Descriptions and examples

Types of new product	Description
Style changes	This includes changes or makeovers in décor or changes to an organisation's logo (for example, *Air India* has a new logo; see ▸ Industry Insight 8.2).
Product improvements	This involves an actual change to a feature of a product that is already available to an established market. For example, theme parks and visitor attractions often improve or develop new attractions. In 2020, *Air New Zealand* introduced flat beds in economy class for some long-haul flights (its trademark name is *Economy Skynest* (Taylor & Blackall, 2020: 3).
Product line extensions	These are additions to the existing product or service product range, for example, international airlines regularly introduce new airline routes.
New products	These are new products that an organisation makes available to its existing consumers (see ▸ Industry Insight 8.3), although they may currently be available from its competitors.
Major innovations	Innovation is defined as "all the activities that a firm carries out having a research and development objective with the aim of launching new products" (Fyall et al., 2019: 412). Innovations are entirely new products for new markets. For example, the opening of a convention centre in Panama in 2015 attracted local and international business tourists to Panama City (see ▸ Industry Insight 8.4).

Source: Author's creation

Industry Insight 8.4

Panama City – Ideal Convention Centre Destination

According to the International Congress and Convention Association (ICCA), Panama registered an impressive leap in world rankings, climbing eight spots by number of association meetings, from 54th in 2012 to 46th in 2016. In 2016, 46 meetings were held, 60 of them in Panama City. Similarly, the capital city climbed 10 places on ICCA's 2016 ranking of cities in Latin and North America, ahead of all other Central American cities. Panama's strategic location in the heart of the Americas, its regional connectivity, and the presence of one of the region's largest international financial centres have contributed to the steady flow of business tourists to the capital and, more generally, to the development of the meetings industry market. According to the Tourism Authority of Panama (Autoridad de Turismo de Panamá, ATP), business and convention tourists accounted for 11.1 of total tourists in 2016. In 2016, the World Economic Forum (WEF) named Panama the most competitive country in Central America. That same year, Panama was named "best destination for business in Central America" at the World Travel Awards (WTA).

Source: ▸ https://www.iccaworld.org/dcps/doc.cfm?docid=2082

8.3 Branding Tourism and Hospitality Products

8.3.1 What is Branding?

Branding was first used as a marketing tool by tourism and hospitality organisations such as the UK-based *Thomas Cook* (now re-branded as *Hays Travel*), which, back in the 1930s, started one of the first international package tours to the south of France (Holloway, 2006: 14). The concept of branding tourism products has since become a common marketing practice. Branding has developed to such a level that brand names are sometimes more valuable than the products that they represent. Some tourism and hospitality products have strong brand identities. Examples are *TUI, Airbnb, British Airways* (see ▶ Industry Insight 8.5), *Emirates, Avis Rent a Car, Expedia, Hilton Hotels,* and *Premier Inn.* These leading brands have a huge advantage over other brands because consumers are busy and it is always easier to go with the company that is perceived to be the market leader. The rationale underlying branding is that a product's image is as important as its tangible attributes.

> A *brand* is a name, logo and slogan designed to differentiate a product, company, or destination from competitors (Pike, 2018: 109).

BA – A Very British Airline

British Airways (BA) is one of the UKs most visible brands. It sells Britishness as a mark of quality. Some passengers pay close to small fortunes to fly first-class. A one-way fare flying economy class can cost around £765 (€875/$1000). A first-class one-way fare New York to London costs just over £7650 ($10,000/€8750) (the cost of a brand new small car!). Customer service must have a critical eye; ask staff to walk around with a critical eye. As a manager (by walkabout) you have to look at everything that customers are going to see and experience. Every little detail counts in an operation so valuable to BA.

Source: British Airways. ▶ www.ba.com

name and a registered trademark (to give the company legal protection stipulating its exclusive right to use that name). The brand name can be in the form of letters (for example, *BA*), words (for example, *Travelbag* or *Wow Air*) and/or numbers (for example, *Jet2Holidays*). The trademark (or brand mark) is the feature of the brand that can be recognised. It might be a symbol or a design, such as *Expedia's* yellow airplane and blue globe, *Airtours'* bird, *TUI's* red smiley face and dot, *TripAdvisor's* owl eyes (see ◙ Image 8.1), or *Club Med's* trident insignia. Branding adds value by giving a product a personality. A travel agency becomes, for example, *Blue Planet Travel* or *Southall Travel.*

Branding is about creating trust and making an emotional link with customers. Key elements of a branded product or service are trust, confidence, quality, and availability. Trust is particularly important in today's competitive world; people want to know that they can trust brands. Creating a distinctive brand image is one of the ways in which tourism and hospitality organisations signal their positioning and competitive advantage. This principle applies whether the target travel business is a small local visitor information centre or a multinational online travel agent.

8.3.1.1 The Benefits of Branding in Tourism

Assigning a brand name or trademark to a product provides a number of advantages (see ▶ Industry Insight 8.5). Some of the reasons for its importance are discussed below.

◙ **Image 8.1**   TripAdvisor logo

■ **Reducing Perceived Purchase Risk**

Given the intangible nature of tourism, a strong brand can reduce the uncertainty associated with the purchase of a tourism and hospitality product. There are a number of perceived risks when purchasing different products. These can be financial risks ("Can I afford to go on holiday?"), functional risks ("Will this travel app work?"), or social risks ("What will other people think if I go on a luxury cruise holiday?"). Branding helps reduce these risks so that buyers can make a purchase without fear or uncertainty (Baines, et al., 2019: 513). In addition, a product is more recognisable if it has a brand name. For example, *Marriott International* hotels has developed a name and a logo that are recognised internationally. Consumers are confident of what they will get. A brand cuts across countries, classes, and cultural backgrounds.

■ **Achieving Differentiation**

Given the intangible nature of tourism and hospitality products and the inherent difficulty of distinguishing one product from another, branding provides a significant way for achieving differentiation. In other words, branding helps an organisation to stand out from its competitors. Quality and depth of experience are important in tourism. This is reflected in marketing campaigns. For example, the advertising campaign of *InterContinental Hotels & Resorts* promotes the hotel group as a lifestyle.

■ ■ **Simplifying Decision-Making**

Tourism and hospitality consumers are faced with an overwhelming number of choices of products offering similar features and benefits. Recognising a brand name can help simplify their decision-making, especially when they are unfamiliar with a particular market or category. When people travel overseas or are first-time visitors to a city, many of them stay at hotels such as *Holiday Inn* or *Marriott International* because the brand indicates something about the standard of service that they can expect. Branding shapes consumer expectations and can lead to them making rapid purchase decisions.

■ **Creating Expectations**

Brand names, logos, and trademarks encourage consumers to purchase particular products because of the unstated promise that these products provide consumers with the benefits that they are seeking. These benefits vary from familiarity and safety to status and self-esteem. For example, *Relax Inn* located in Male, capital of the Maldives demotes a tranquil place for visitors. Similarly, the name *Comfort Stay Group* (a portfolio of B&Bs) implies that its B&Bs have rooms that are cosy and comfortable, while the *Ocean View* guesthouse clearly overlooks the sea. Similarly, *Sleep Easy* hotels offer guests a comfortable night's sleep. Quick-service restaurants sell *Giant Pizzas* and *Budget Car Rental* means just that: inexpensive car rentals. The tour operator *Contiki* attracts certain segments of the British youth holiday market while it discourages others (consumers who are older than 35/Millenials!). The tour company now uses the slogan "TRAVEL WITH NO REGRETS".

■ **To Sell a Line of Products**

Branding can be used to sell a product or a line of products. This technique is known as "brand stretching". For example, a well-established brand such as *TUI Group* is stretched to include new ranges of cruise or skiing holidays. *The Virgin Group* uses the power of the *Virgin* brand to 'stretch' and diversify the brand into other products such as music products, soft drinks, rail services, mobile phone services, and airline seats. Some of these have been very successful, for example, *Virgin Atlantic, Virgin Holidays, Virgin Hotels, Virgin Holiday Cruises, Virgin Money, Virgin Holiday Hip Hotels,* and *Virgin Galactic*; while others have failed, these include *Virgin Clothing, Virgin Flowers, Virgin Cola, Virgin Cars,* and *Virgin Vodka* (Russell, 2012).

The Virgin brand began as a retail company selling records by post. It then became a vinyl record shop in London, in the United Kingdom. Today, there are more than 60 Virgin companies worldwide, employing approximately 71,000 people in 35 countries (Virgin, n.d.).

8.3.1.2 Co-branding

Co-branding is the strategy of presenting two or more independent brands jointly on the same product or service (Abratt & Motlana, 2002). It means providing two or more brands at one business location. It is a strategy in which a company puts more than one of its brands into the same location with the aim of increasing sales and efficiency. For example, café chains such as *Costa Coffee* have units (or pods or kiosks) in airports, pizza restaurants (such as *Pizza Hut*), cinemas, railway stations, bookshops, hotels (namely *Marriott International*, and *Premier Inn Hotels*), clothing shops, supermarkets, hospitals, motorway service stations, pubs, health and fitness clubs, petrol stations, universities, and theme parks across the UK and Europe. Co-branding has been referred to by many different terms, including multi-branding, brand partnership, co-marketing, joint branding, brand alliances, and symbiotic marketing.

8.3.1.3 Brand Equity

Brand equity is the measure of the value and strength of a brand (Baines, et al., 2019: 533). Also referred to as "goodwill value", brand equity is an estimated intangible asset value on the balance sheet (Pike, 2018: 108). Tourism brands are more than just names and logos. They are a vital element in the firm's relationships with customers. Brands represent customers' expectations and feelings about a product, encapsulating everything that the product means to customers. A brand with strong equity is more likely to be able to maintain its customer loyalty and fight off competition.

Brands vary in the amount of power and value they hold in the marketplace. Some brands such as *Marriott International, British Airways, Holiday Inn* (owned by IHG), and *McDonald's* sustain their power in the market for decades. Fresh and funky brands in the marketplace include *Trivago, Kayak. com, Nando's, Moxy Hotels*, and *Airbnb* (see ► Industry Insight 8.6).

Lasser, Mittal & Sharma (1995) state that there are two main perspectives about how brand equity should be valued: from a financial viewpoint and from a marketing viewpoint. The *financial view* is established on a

Industry Insight 8.6

New Brand Logo and Slogan for Airbnb

In 2014, Airbnb revamped its logo and introduced a squiggly shape called the "Bélo". The Bélo was designed to resemble a heart, a location pin, and the "A" in Airbnb. The logo was intended to be simple, so that anyone could draw it. Indeed, the holiday accommodation rental site invited people to draw their own versions of the logo, which, it was announced, would stand for four things: people, places, love, and Airbnb. In addition, the phrase "Belong anywhere" from AirBnB's mission statement was incorporated into the company's official tagline.

Source: Gallagher, L. (2016). How Airbnb found a mission – and a brand. Retrieved from ► http://fortune.com/airbnb-travel-mission-brand/ [19 September 2018].

consideration of a brand's asset value that is based on the net value of all the cash the brand is expected to generate over its lifetime. The *marketing view* is based on the images, beliefs, and core associations that consumers have about particular brands as well as the degree of loyalty or retention a brand is able to sustain (Lasser, Mittal & Sharma, 1995).

There are two main aims of branding (Pike, 2018: 109):
1. Ensuring that the brand comes to mind immediately when consumers are considering a purchase situation
2. Ensuring that when the brand (for example, a hotel) comes to mind, the consumer associates it favourably with various features (such as exceptional rooms and service) and benefits (for instance, the hotel lounge's relaxing atmosphere).

8.3.1.4 The Power of Branding

The value of established brand names is closely related to perceptions of quality and consistent standards. For tourism and hospitality businesses, a strong brand is developed through real-time interactions and actual involvement between the tourism company and consumers. Branding offers either an implicit or an explicit guarantee to the consumer. For example, firms such as *Hays Travel* have developed an image of quality that consumers expect to experience at all of their outlets and online. Some tourism consumers are loyal to a brand if they can get it (availability) and if it is affordable. Availability refers to the ease of purchase of the product as well as its design (physical evidence), and has the potential to persuade consumers, even at the last moment of decision-making. The greater the availability, the greater the power of the brand name. Affordability is also an obvious reason why people go with the brands that they love.

For large hotel groups that have a wide variety of properties, grouping these properties into brands can enable each branded group to be targeted at defined market segments. For example, *Marriott International's* luxury hotel products *Ritz-Carlton, Bulgari,* and *JW Marriott* target business travellers and upmarket guests, while its *Aloft Hotels* and *Moxy Hotels* cater for the new generation of Millennial (or Gen Y) or 'next generation of mobile travellers'. *Marriott* developed specific slogans or payoff lines (also known as "strap lines" or "tag lines") for each hotel product: *JW Marriott* "Quiet Luxury", *Aloft Hotels* "Style at a steal", and *Moxy Hotels* "Less is more". Sometimes it is necessary for a company to be rebranded in order to reach particular markets (see ► Industry Insight 8.7).

Industry Insight 8.7

Hays Travel Undergoes a Rebrand
John Hays (Owner and Chair of the Hays Travel Group) said: "Thomas Cook was a much-loved brand and a pillar of the UK and the global travel industry. We will build on the good things Thomas Cook had – not least its people – and that will put us in even better stead for the future."

John Hays (Owner and Managing Director) said: "I'm very proud of the fantastic team who have helped me build Hays Travel

over almost 40 years and they have worked tirelessly over the last couple of weeks to bring this about. It is a game-changer for us, almost trebling the number of shops we have and doubling our workforce - and for the industry, which will get to keep some of its most talented people. We are delighted to have a presence in Northern Ireland for the first time. It's a wonderful opportunity for all of us and we can't wait to come over and meet everyone soon!"

In times of economic hardship, consumers tend to opt for tried and trusted brands.

8.3.1.5 Building a Brand
According to Keller (2009), the development of a successful brand is achieved by adhering to a series of three brand-building stages:
1. Building a brand identity: This is the image aspired to by the tourism company.
2. Establishing a brand image: This refers to the actual perceptions of the brand held by consumers.
3. Brand positioning. This is the attempt by marketers to achieve congruence between

the image aspired to in the brand (brand identity) and the actual perceptions held in the market (brand image).

Brand Identity
The first stage of developing a brand is to build a brand identity that will differentiate the product and company from competitors.

The vision, core values, and brand promise (or mantra) of the company underpin the name, logo, and slogan used in all the company's marketing and branding communications. Research has shown that the strength of a name, the style of a slogan, and the design of a logo can greatly affect people's perception of an organisation's products (Keller, 2012). A good brand says "use me!".

There are three aspects to consider when developing a brand identity:

1. The brand name
2. The brand slogan
3. The brand logo.

While logos are visual representations of a brand, slogans are audible representations of a brand. Both formats grab consumers' attention more readily than the name a company or product might.

■ **Brand Names**

Choosing a brand name is critical as it should take several considerations into account. It should be (Baines, et al., 2019: 512):

- Easily recalled, spelled, and spoken
- Strategically consistent with the organisation's branding policies
- Distinctive
- Meaningful to the customer
- Capable of registration and protection.

Names should also be easy to pronounce and remember. According to Jeremy Sampson, brand consultant and group executive chairman of Interbrand (▶ www.interbrand.com), "A name is a brand ... they should be pronounceable, memorable, and distinctive!" The name of a product should help to convey its benefits. The name may be descriptive or abstract. In the long term, the decision to choose a distinctive name pays off. For example, Icelandic airline company uses the name "*Wow Air*". Names associated with an organisation's founder remain popular brand names. An example is *Hays Travel* (John Hays).

■ **Brand Slogans**

A **slogan** (also called a "payoff line", "tag line", "strap line", "byline", or "motto") is a short phrase that communicates descriptive information about the brand (Keller, 2003). In many ways, slogans are like mini mission statements. Companies have slogans for the same reason they have logos: advertising (Zwart, 2017). In addition, they are simpler to understand and remember. Godin (2003: 18) sug-

gests that a slogan is a type of script that reminds the user, "Here's why it's worth recommending us; here's why your friends and family will be happy you told them about us." Slogans function as useful hooks or handles to help consumers grasp the meaning of a brand in terms of what the brand is and what makes it special (Keller, 2012: 188). A slogan can be described as a brand promise or mantra. It makes a promise of what consumers can expect from the brand. For example, *Sandals Resorts'* slogan is "The Luxury Included Holiday". ◘ Table 8.4 lists examples of the slogans of various international tourism businesses.

According to Aaker (1996: 232), an effective slogan has the power to capture the essence of a brand identity, yet it can be changed, replaced, or augmented more easily than a brand name. A good slogan should resonate with internal and external stakeholders as well as consumers. Staff members and the company's target market should be involved in the process of formulating a slogan. It is better to consult stakeholders and consumers during the process rather than finalising a slogan and testing it on them after the fact. This will ensure internal buy-in and allow the organisation to determine if the proposed slogan is appropriate for consumers. In addition, a slogan should be memorable and should create instant recall. The best taglines use words that are positive and upbeat. For example, *TUI*'s slogan, "Discover your smile," gives consumers a good feeling about *TUI* (see ◘ Image 8.2). *Avis's* "We try harder", which was the company's motto for over

◘ **Image 8.2**   TUI logo

◻ Table 8.4 Examples of various tourism and hospitality organisations' slogans

Organisation	Slogan
Travelodge	"Sleep tight"
Chessington World of Adventures	"Britain's Wildest Adventure"
Contiki Tours	"NO REGRETS"
Emirates Airline	"Hello Tomorrow"
Hyatt Hotels and Resorts	"Feel the Hyatt Touch"
STA Travel	"Start the Adventure"
Club Méditerranée	"Where happiness means the world"
Association of British Travel Agents	"Travel with Confidence"
Jet2Holidays	"Package Holidays you can Trust"
Best Western Hotels & Resorts	"Wherever Life Takes You, Best Western Is"
Ryanair	"The Low Fares Airline"
Europcar	"We will Impress You"
Premier Inn	"Premier Inn. Premier You"
Hotel Boehler (Germany)	"Your Home away from Home"
Southall Travel	"The Future of Travel"
Grand Hotel Bonavia (Croatia)	"Five-star quality in a hotel of four stars"
East Coast Car Rentals (Sydney, Australia)	"Pay less. Get more"

Source: Author's creation

50 years, and *British Airways'* "The World's Favourite Airline" are examples of easy-to-remember slogans.

❓ Clearly, the brand image of a product is closely related to that product's brand characteristics. Look at the two lists of brand characteristics below. They describe two separate tourism products (A and B). Can you suggest what each product might be?

Tourism product A:	Tourism product B:
Colourful	For older people
Young	Scenic
Heart-stopping	Educational
Fun for the family	Healthy
Exciting	Relaxing.

■ **Brand Logos**

A logo is a name, symbol, sign, colour, or design. Logos should be distinctive. Their design and colour should support the product concept (Holloway, 2006: 134). The colours used in an organisation's logo should be chosen carefully. It is useful to remember that the colour green signifies the environment, the colours red and yellow signify fast and speedy service, and the colour blue signifies water or the ocean. The use of pastels and bright colours attracts attention (see ◻ Image 8.3). The logo of *TUI* is a good example. (See the logos of various tourism organisations in this chapter.) Some organisations choose to include a slogan or strapline as well as their website address incorporated into the logo.

Image 8.3   Emirates' logo

Establishing a Brand Image

The next stage of developing a brand is to establish a brand image. A brand's image represents the actual market perceptions held of the product or organisation (Pike, 2018: 111). In some cases, the actual brand image in the market is not always similar to the brand identity. In fact, it might not even exist. The tourism marketer needs to be aware that brand images are formed from many sources of information. There are three main sources of image formation and the level of influence of the tourism and hospitality marketer varies greatly between the them (Gunn, 1988):

— *Induced* (forced) *agents* designed in the form of advertisements. Today's consumers are the most sophisticated in history, having been exposed to more marketing communications than previous generations, and do not always believe everything they see in advertising.

— *Organic* (natural) *agents* developed from exposure to a wide range of stimuli including our own travel experiences and WoM publicity (via reference groups, including, friends and members of associations, neighbours, relatives, and colleagues). Organic images are more influential in overcoming intangibility and risk because they are more credible than induced image sources.

— *Autonomous agents* such as media editorials, television and movies, fiction and non-fiction books, museums, school geography lessons, art galleries, sporting events, festivals, the internet (such as websites, social media platforms, marketing influencers, online travel reviews and ratings), and education. Most of these sources are beyond the control of the marketer.

Brand Positioning

The third stage of the brand development process is concerned with brand positioning. Brand positioning represents the attempt by marketers to achieve congruence between the image aspired to by the brand (brand identity) and the actual perceptions held in the market (brand image) (Pike, 2018: 112). In ▶ Chap. 7 – we discussed how an effective positioning of a product offering is one that successfully differentiates the brand in the minds of consumers on the basis of its attributes and benefits.

Not all attributes of a brand differentiate an organisation from its competitors. Neither are all of them important to the consumer (Pike, 2018: 112). ☐ Figure 8.5 shows how the distinction between attribute importance, salience, and determinance in the context of a guesthouse. When a consumer considers a purchase, there are usually numerous important attributes. However, as most competing guesthouses offer some, if not all, of these important attributes (for example, cleanliness and a quality breakfast), they will not all be considered during the decision-making process. Instead, there will be a subset of important attributes that are salient (top-of-mind) (for example, parking and a good view). Of the attributes that are salient, one or more will determine the choice of guesthouse (for example, price and location). Thus, it is crucial to be positioned on the basis of the determinant attribute (Pike, 2018: 212).

8.4 Pricing Tourism and Hospitality Products

Marketers often underestimate the importance of price as a strategic marketing tool (Lumsdon, 1997: 157). Price can be used to defend an existing market from new entrants,

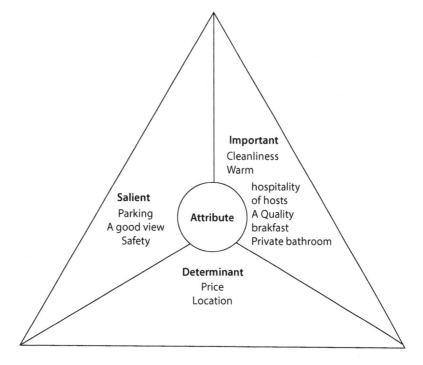

■ **Fig. 8.5** Keller's (2012) Brand Equity Model. (Source: Adapted from Keller (2012))

to increase market share within a market, or to enter a new market (Gregson, 2008). As a crucial component of the marketing mix, the price of a product must be acceptable to target consumers. Ultimately, consumers decide whether the product-offering was good value for money (VFM). This decision depends on their wants and expectations, their level of satisfaction in terms of whether the benefits of the product met their expectations, and the price they paid for the product (Pike, 2018).

Pricing is important for organisations in the public sector, where profit is not always the main objective. For example, museums and national parks may have other objectives, such as increasing participation, education, and conservation.

Many tourism and hospitality organisations have a range of offerings at various price levels designed to meet the needs of target segments that may have different levels of spending power. For example, *Virgin Atlantic* offers business-class seats at a higher price (up to three or four times higher) than economy-class seats. Similarly, hotels offer rooms at different prices according to the location of the rooms. For instance, rooms with a sea view are

usually priced higher than rooms without a view. Airlines and hotels also offer different prices to consumers who purchase offerings at certain times. For example, lower prices are charged during off-peak (less busy) periods.

8.4.1 Factors That Affect Pricing Decisions

The tourism and hospitality marketer must be aware of internal factors and external forces that affect an organisation's pricing decisions. As was the case in the SWOT analysis in ▶ Chap. 5, the marketer has some degree of control over internal factors. However, he or she has little, if any, control over external forces that affect pricing. These factors are shown in ■ Fig. 8.6. The internal and external factors that affect pricing decisions are discussed below.

8.4.1.1 Internal Factors Influencing Pricing Decisions

The internal factors that influence pricing decisions include the organisation's objectives, the other components of the marketing mix, and the overall costs of providing and promoting the offering.

■ **Organisation and Marketing Objectives**

The decisions that a tourism organisation makes about the pricing of its offerings are taken in the context of the organisation's overall objectives (McCarthy, Cannon & Perreault, 2015: 4).

Managers develop a set of objectives and policies in the context of the company's overall objectives. The policy explains how flexible prices are to be, the level at which they will be set over the life cycle of the service, and to whom and when discounts will be allowed.

The objectives of organisations can be closely linked to specific pricing approaches and strategies. Tourism and hospitality organisations may have different objectives when prices are set. Examples of possible objectives include survival, increased market share, offering quality leadership, and other objectives McCarthy, Cannon & Perreault (2015: 4), as outlined below.

— To generate immediate cash flow (for the sake of the company's survival): If a company is burdened by high levels of competition, an economic recession or slump, an endemic (such as COVID-19), or changing consumer tastes, then generating immediate cash flow may be about survival. The organisation usually lowers prices to try to generate as much money as possible.

— To achieve market share: A new firm, in particular, will aim to increase market share or get more buyers. Usually, lowering prices will achieve this on the premise that in the long term, the organisation will enjoy sustained profit. International airlines such as *Emirates* and other multinational corporations use this strategy to out-price competitors.

— To achieve product quality leadership: Organisations that have the objective of being a quality leader with their offerings must charge more for their offerings in order to cover their costs. Luxury providers such as *One&Only Resorts*, for example, have high operating costs as a result of its high staff–consumer ratio, and its luxury facilities require maintenance (see ► Industry Insight 8.8).

— Other objectives: There may be legal and regulatory issues that control the way in which an organisation sets prices. A public sector or voluntary (non-profit) tourism organisation may want to entice new users. For example, museums and national parks in India, which are subsidised by the government, aim to keep prices affordable to encourage India citizens as well as foreign tourists to visit. Non-profit organisations

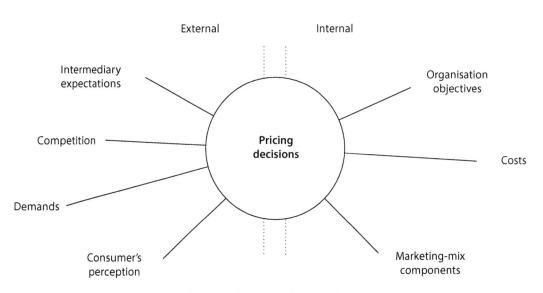

□ **Fig. 8.6** Factors that affect pricing decisions. (Source: Author's creation)

often use different pricing strategies, in which different prices are charged for different market segments (see ▶ Industry Insight 8.8). For example, a museum will charge reduced prices to encourage students, unemployed people, and senior citizens to visit the museum. Pricing can also be used to help an organisation achieve other objectives, such as preventing competition. An airline, for instance, may reduce prices to prevent competitors from entering the market.

Industry Insight 8.8

One&Only Luxury Resorts

The One&Only portfolio consists of Reethi Rah in the Maldives, Le Saint Géran in Mauritius, Royal Mirage and The Palm in Dubai, Ocean Club in the Bahamas, Palmilla in Los Cabos, Mexico, Nyungwe House in Rwanda, Wolgan Valley in Australia, Sanya in China, The Only&Only in Cape Town, Portonovi in Montenegro, Jeddah in Saudi Arabia and Desaru Coast in Malaysia. Each One&Only property offers guests a unique experience where luxurious accommodation is complemented by personalised and friendly service, award-winning spas, lively entertainment and a host of activities as well as unforgettable culinary experiences from some of the world's most accomplished chefs.

Source: Based on information at One&Only. (2019). One&Only. For more information, go to ▶ https://wwwoneandonlyresorts.com/ [2 May 2019].

■ **Other Components of the Marketing Mix**

The components of the marketing mix are interdependently linked (McCarthy, 1960). Price must interact with the design of the product-offering as well as the costs of distribution and promotion of the product-offering. For instance, the high price of a luxury hotel room reflects the higher costs of design, furnishing, and building it as well as operating and marketing it. Price must therefore be consistent with the company's brand identity (Pike, 2018: 121).

Price must accurately reflect the value of the offering. Many tourism organisations have a range of offerings at varying prices to target as many consumers as possible. It is crucial that the quality of the offering meets the expectations that the price has generated in consumers' minds. Price gives consumers the first indication of how to determine the quality of an offering.

Where an offering is sold depends on what kind of offering it is. This is the place factor of the mix. For example, the marketer of a luxury hotel such as the *One&Only Royal Mirage* in Dubai may decide to distribute most of the rooms through a reputable and exclusive tour operator or travel agency in order to reflect the hotel's status, high-quality image, and high price. In addition, consumers expect to pay more for accommodation at a conveniently located hotel in the central business district of a city centre, for instance.

An organisation's promotional mix also reflects the quality and prices of offerings. Price may be a feature of the promotional message when a discount or voucher is offered. If price is referred to in the message, it must accurately reflect the service quality and value that match consumers' expectations. The type of promotional tool must also reflect the cost of an offering. For example, the *One&Only Royal Mirage is* promoted in quality newspapers and magazines.

Service quality should never be compromised by price within the people factor of the services marketing mix ('the 7Ps'). The different levels of service that are offered are also reflected in the price charged for various offerings. For example, the *One&Only Royal Mirage* must have qualified and experienced staff, and so requires regular staff training. An upmarket travel agency will possess knowledgeable or specialist staff. In both

8

cases, the higher costs of staffing will be reflected in the higher price of the organisation's offerings.

Physical evidence is a crucial factor that consumers consider when determining what constitutes value for money (VFM) in the tourism industry. The facilities, the décor and the physical environment of an offering should reflect the price. For example, the *One&Only Royal Mirage* offers a variety of physical evidence that attracts consumers: well-trained staff dressed in smart uniforms, relaxing décor, elegant furnishing, well-kept gardens, and the latest technological check-in and in-room facilities.

- Costs

When setting prices, marketers should consider how much it costs the tourism and hospitality organisation:

- To produce the product offering (i.e. the cost of expenses such as meals and overheads)
- To distribute the offering (payment of commission to a travel agency)
- To promote the offering (e.g. the cost of advertising in a national newspaper, brochure design, and production)
- To staff the organisation (staffing costs).

A profit-oriented organisation will charge a price that covers these costs of the marketing mix and brings in a return for investors. Organisations such as airlines may sell below cost for a period of time to match competitors or to undercut the competition with the aim of increasing sales and gaining market share (referred to as "tactical pricing"). Selling below cost might hurt short-term profits but improve long-term ones. Organisations must manage costs and prices carefully in order to profit overall.

8.4.1.2 External Forces Influencing Pricing Decisions

The external forces that marketers should consider when making pricing decisions include the nature of the demand for the offering and price elasticity as well as the competition and consumers' perceptions (Tanner & Raymond, 2012).

- Nature of Demand and Price Elasticity

While costs set the lower limits of prices, the market and demand set the upper limits (Kotler & Armstrong, 2019). Both consumers and distribution channels such as travel agents and tour operators are considered part of the market, and their beliefs about the value of an offering create a demand for it and a ceiling for its price. As a result, before setting prices, a marketer must understand the relationship between price and demand. Tourism and hospitality organisations must adapt their pricing strategies according to the economic health of the country or region. For example, if the economic climate of the region is in recession, then the demand by the domestic tourism market for a luxury hotel room may well be affected. An increase in prices would reduce the size of the market able to afford the hotel's prices. The marketer must adapt pricing tactics to suit the recession in order to continue to attract customers.

Tourism and hospitality products are often not essential for consumers and many alternatives are available (staying or eating at home, or visiting a shopping centre, for example). Price, therefore, has a powerful influence on demand. The key task for the marketer is to forecast levels of demand and potential demand, taking price into account. Marketers also need to know about price elasticity: how much demand will grow or shrink when there is a change in price. **Price elasticity** is the sensitivity of consumer demand to changes in the prices of offerings (Tanner & Raymond, 2012).

If demand hardly changes with a small change in price, the demand is inelastic. If demand changes greatly, the demand is elastic.

Demand levels may vary for a number of reasons:

- Economic conditions and trends in consumer spending
- The stage in the product life cycle of an offering
- Seasonal variations (different seasons of the year, holidays)
- Busier times of the day/week
- Level of marketing and promotional effort.

Consumers are usually less price sensitive when an offering is unique (the Taj Mahal, India, for example) or when it is high in quality, prestige or exclusiveness (for example, The *Set Hotels* – H*otel Café Royal London, Lvtetia Paris,* and *Conservatorium Amsterdam.* Hotel chains attempt to differentiate their brands to create a perception of uniqueness. Price elasticity can be seen clearly in the tourism industry, where transport technology has made destinations more affordable and accessible. Countries such as Brazil, Turkey, Croatia, Mexico, Kenya, Bulgaria, Myanmar, and Vietnam are tourism destination offerings that have become more affordable and accessible to the international tourism market over the last decade.

■ Competition

Tourism and hospitality marketers need information about competitors' prices in order to make pricing decisions. If a consumer thinks that the *Travelodge* is similar to a *Premier Inn* hotel, *Travelodge* must set prices close to those of Premier Inn or lose that consumer. In addition, *Travelodge* should charge less than more luxurious hotels and more than those that are not as good. Travelodge uses price to position its offer relative to competitors' offers. Similarly, low-cost airlines *EasyJet* and *Ryanair* have used the strategy of offering fares costing up to 50% less than the lowest fares of *British Airways* on various UK and European flight routes. *Norwegian Airlines* offers low-cost long-haul travel flying from UK cities to the likes of Buenos Aries, Singapore, and a number of US cities. (The airline charges for luggage and on-board meals).

However, marketers must be aware of who their competitors are and consider indirect competition as well as direct competition. For example, a restaurant may compare its prices with those of other restaurants in the locality, but in reality, there are also other options available to prospective consumers for spending their leisure time and money. Marketers may want to consider how the price of a meal at the restaurant they are marketing compares with the price of a trip to the cinema or theatre because this is how broadly consumers may think about their choices.

» In the tourism and hospitality industry, consumers vote with their feet ... and any provider who overcharges is ultimately going to pay the penalty.
— Moeketsi Mosola, former chief executive officer, SA Tourism

■ Consumer Perceptions

The most crucial external factor affecting price is consumer perceptions of price (Zeithaml, 1988). Ultimately, it is the consumer who decides whether the price of an offering is affordable. Consumers often use price as an indication of quality when purchasing tourism offerings (Zeithaml, 1988). If the offering is priced too high in relation to what consumers think it is worth (in other words, consumers do not feel that it offers value for money), then they will not buy it. However, if the price is too low, the product may be perceived as inferior in quality. Again, consumers will not buy it. It is essential that marketers strike a balance between too high and too low when making pricing decisions. They must try to understand consumers' reasons for choosing an offering and set the price according to consumers' ideas about its value. Consumers will, for example, expect different prices at different kinds of restaurants, so even similar menu items can be priced differently. For example, a hamburger may cost £2.49 (€2.90/$3.40) at a quick-service restaurant (QSR), £5.95 (€6.80/$8) at a sit-down restaurant, and £12.50 (€14.30/$16.80) at a fine-dining restaurant.

Consumers associate price with quality (Zeithaml, 1988). Some hotels offer consumers the opportunity to 'pay for what you want' bid to fill-up rooms. Several hotels in Paris started the trend in 2014 when they allowed guests to pay only what they think their stay was worth (Orr, 2014). In the airline sector, where high prices are charged for first-class seats, consumers know that they receive extra comfort and room on the aeroplane, extra personal service, first-class check-in facilities, a waiting lounge, and benefits such as free drinks and an *à la carte* menu on board in return for the higher ticket price. Similarly, in the accommodation sector, facilities at a five-

8

star *Michelangelo Hotel* are going to be far superior to those offered at *SUN1* budget hotels. Relative prices may act as an indicator of quality to consumers and influence their purchasing decisions (Laws, 2002). Consumers expect a normal level of service if they are paying a standard price, but they expect better service when paying a premium (above-the-going-rate price). Consumers who buy an offering at a low or discounted price and receive high or normal levels of service will be delighted. In contrast, consumers who buy an expensive offering and receive low levels of service are likely to be dissatisfied (Laws, 2002). ◘ Fig. 8.7 illustrates the fact that consumers who receive low levels of service are likely to feel unhappy and exploited, regardless of the price they paid.

> The most expensive hamburger – the 'Glamburger' dish – costs £1100 (€1256/$1480) and is served in a golden bun. The dish is served at the Honky Tonk restaurant in Chelsea, London, UK.

■ Intermediary Expectations

The prices set for tourism offerings must also reflect the intermediaries in the distribution channel. Travel agents, for instance, expect to earn a commission for selling offerings.

Various tourism providers such as airlines, tour operators, car rental companies, and hotel groups are now cutting out the middle-man and selling directly to consumers via the internet.

Depending on the internal factors and external forces, tourism companies have a range of pricing options available at their disposal.

8.4.2 Approaches to Pricing

Revenue management is the strategy of selling the right product to the right customer at the right time for the right price. This includes reducing prices to stimulate demand when sales are low, as well as increasing prices to maximise income when demand is strong (Withiam, 2001). There are many different pricing approaches and techniques available to the tourism marketer. As with all marketing principles and tools, some of these approaches have more relevance to tourism and hospitality organisations than others. Many of these approaches may be combined with others. The pricing techniques that are considered the most effective for an organisation fall into four main groups: cost-based pricing, demand-based pricing, going-rate pricing, and value-based pricing (Kotler & Armstrong, 2019).

Service quality levels

	High	Normal	Low
High	Pleased	☹	☹
Normal	☺	Pleased	☹
Low	Delighted	Pleased	☹

Price (vertical axis label)

◘ **Fig. 8.7** Different price-service quality combinations. (Source: Adapted from Laws (2011))

8.4.2.1 Cost-Plus Pricing

Many tourism and hospitality tourism organisations calculate prices using what may be the simplest method: cost-plus pricing (also known as "cost-based pricing"). This concept is based on the costs of producing or providing the offering, for instance, overhead costs such as staffing or food. The total costs are calculated, and the price is then determined by adding on some required margin or mark-up. This form of pricing is often used for the retail outlets of tourist attractions and for restaurants. It offers the marketer a flexible tool for pricing. Once costs are covered, however, the mark-up may not be set in an effective way. A restaurateur might quite simply mark up a bottle of wine by 200%. In other words, a bottle of wine that costs £8 (€9.14/$10.78) would sell for £26 (€29.70/$35), no matter what consumer demand might be. The profit would be £18 (€21/$24.25) and the costs for serving each bottle of wine would be the same. If the marketer does not take into account the competitive situation or the market demand, prices may be set too high to attract consumers or may not be set high enough to exploit demand, especially if an offering is new or differs in some way from competing offerings.

The break-even-point is a function of the fixed costs divided by the contribution, which is the proposed selling price minus the variable cost per sale (see ◘ Fig. 8.8).

8.4.2.2 Demand-Based Pricing

This approach to pricing allows the marketer to charge higher prices when demand is up and lower prices when demand is down, regardless of the costs of producing the offer-

Fixed costs

_____

Contribution (selling price – variable cost) per sale

Source: Author's creation

◘ **Fig. 8.8** Break-even point. (Source: Author's creation)

ing. An example of this is a seaside B&B accommodation, which tends to be more expensive during the summer (when there is more demand) than during the winter. This approach results in greater profits as long as consumers value the offerings enough to pay the price. The success of demand-based pricing depends on the ability of marketers to analyse the demand. Airlines often use this approach, with passengers paying different amounts for seats with varying levels of service attached. Many airlines offer three types of cabin service: first class, business class, and economy class. *Qatar Airways,* for example, offers Economy, Business, and First classes. These classes have varying benefits on the seat pitch, excess baggage allowance, priority check-in, lounge access, and reservation benefits according to the price paid.

❓ Some airlines offer a "two airlines in one" strategy with two classes of travel: premier class (at the front of its aircraft) and economy or "no-frills" class (at the rear of its aircraft). Discuss this strategy.

8.4.2.3 Going-Rate Pricing

In the case of going-rate pricing, marketers set the price of offerings according to competitors' prices. This is known as "the going rate". This approach has the advantage of giving an organisation the opportunity to increase sales or market share because it is based mainly on competitors' prices rather than costs or market demand. This approach is also known as "me-too pricing". It is frequently used in markets that are very price sensitive and where the core benefits are similar (for example, backpacker hostels and budget accommodation). Marketers who use this strategy usually attempt to influence consumer preference through other components of the marketing mix, such as service excellence. A disadvantage of this strategy is that it is not always easy to identify who competitors are since there are indirect competitors as well as direct competitors. For instance, a restaurant may set prices according to other restaurants in the area, but there are other choices available to prospective consumers in terms of how they spend their money and leisure time (for example, home entertainment or going to the theatre).

8.4.2.4 Value-Based Pricing

With the value-based approach, price is based on what consumers perceive a product or service to be worth, not the cost of the offering. Value-based pricing (also called "consumer-based pricing") is very different from cost-plus pricing, which is product driven. Value-based pricing is the opposite. The organisation sets its prices based on customer perceptions of the product service value.

When marketers use the value-based approach, it is important that they find out what consumers think of different competitive offers. They can do this by carrying out research. The researcher should ask consumers how much they are willing to pay for an offering with or without certain benefits. It is not enough to ask, "Would you rather pay £75 or £90 for a hotel room?" Consumers want to know what they are getting for their money. Instead, researchers might ask, "How much are you willing to pay for a hotel room without air conditioning, a flat screen television, or room service?" or "How much are you willing to pay for a hotel room with air conditioning, a plasma screen television, and room service?"

It is important to note that good value is not the same as low price. For example, some consumers consider taking a seven-day cruise on the luxurious cruise liner the Cunard *Queen Elizabeth* as good value, even at a very high cost of £1500 upwards.

❓ Identify a tourism local small business whom you know. Ask the owner how the prices for his or her offerings are set. What pricing approaches do you think this tourism business uses?

Although the four main pricing approaches have been discussed, there are in fact several different possible pricing tactics within these approaches that could be used (Baines et al., 2019: 368). These include:

- List pricing: A single price is set for an offering, for example, hotels charge "rack rates" for hotel conferencing facilities.
- Pay-what-you-want pricing: The price is determined by the customer. Tourist guides and taxi drivers (at least those who are part of the "black market" or "underground economy") allow customers to pay whatever they want. In some cases, with this pricing approach, customers may pay more than if firms set the price (Kim, Natter & Spann, 2009).
- Promotional pricing: Tourism and hospitality firms reduce prices below the usual rates to raise awareness, boost sales and encourage first-time users. This approach incorporates the use of loss leaders, sales discounts, and other price-based promotional incentives. For example, in 2020, many tourism and hospitality companies - hotels, airlines, tour operators, car hire companies, cruise liners - restaurants, lowered prices and bargains to encourage travel bookings.
- Segmentation pricing: Different prices are set for different groups of consumers (Belobaba, Odoni & Barnhart, 2009). Visitor attractions (particularly the likes of zoos, theme parks, and royal gardens) sometimes use this approach where foreign tourists may be charged more than locals, or when students are charged less than working adults (see ◘ Image 8.4). (This approach, which is also known as "discriminatory pricing", is discussed in more detail later in this chapter.)

8.4.3 Tourism and Hospitality Pricing Strategies

The tourism and hospitality marketer uses different pricing strategies when pricing new or existing offerings. As we noted in the first section of this chapter, the pricing of offerings usually changes as they pass through their life cycles. The introduction stage is perhaps the most important and challenging stage for the

🔲 **Image 8.4** Discriminatory pricing sign. (Source: Joseph Bird, CEO, Reality Tours and Travel)

marketer, as it determines whether or not the offering will continue to exist (Lumsdon, 1997: 160–161).

The various pricing strategies used in the tourism and hospitality sector are described in 🔲 Table 8.5.

Psychological Pricing: The Difference of a Cent

Retailers' beliefs that customers like a price ending in a nine rather than a rounded-up zero – £99 instead of £100, for instance – is borne out by scientific research on a restaurant menu. Researchers carried out a field study at a 22-seat restaurant in Brittany, western France, where customers were given a limited choice of dishes. The team singled out the restaurant's most popular pizza to see what happened over six weeks when customers had the option of a rounded-up price ending in a zero or a price ending in a nine. For the first two weeks, all of the items on the menu had prices that ended in a zero. For the following fortnight, the price of the target pizza was brought down by one centime of a euro so that it ended in a nine, while the prices of the other dishes still ended in a zero. For the last two weeks, all of the dishes had prices that ended in a nine. The popularity of the target pizza rose by around 15% during the test's second phase. It was ordered by 49.5% of customers who ordered a pizza. However, when all of the dishes had prices that ended in a nine, the target pizza was preferred by only 34–36% of customers.

Source: Guéguen, Jacob, Legohérel, and NGobo (2008).

Industry Insight 8.10

Foreign Tourists Pay More than Locals to Eat in Restaurants and Stay in Hotels

Cafés in Bruges, Belgium charge tourists 10% more than locals for chips. The disgruntled tourists were informed that there is a "discount for customer loyalty".

The practice of charging tourists more to use facilities is widespread in countries such as Thailand, Italy and India as well as in numerous Central and South American and African countries. In some hotels in Sofia, Bulgaria, foreign tourists are charged more for hotel rooms than locals despite legislation banning the practice. Dual (or differential) pricing is com-

mon practice for travellers in certain parts of Asia and Africa, where foreigners are charged more than locals for food and tourist visits.

Source: Mowat, L. (2017). Belgian rip off revealed: Food in Bruges restaurants costs more for tourists than locals. Retrieved from ▶ http://www.express.co.uk/news/world/822516/Bruges-dual-pricing-Belgium-tourists-pay-more-locals. [21 August 2018]; Everett, S. (2017). Expecting tourists to pay more than locals can be controversial – but it's the right thing to do. Retrieved from ▶ https://qz.com/1021270/expecting-tourists-to-pay-more-than-locals-can-be-controversial-but-its-the-right-thing-to-do/ [6 November 2018].

Table 8.5 Pricing strategies used in tourism and hospitality

Pricing strategy	Description	Examples
Premium	Involves setting high prices to position a product-offering at the upper or luxury end of the market (Hardy, Macrury & Powell, 2018).	New and exclusive tour operators, hotels, restaurants and resorts. Luxury cruises (*Cunard Cruises*, for instance), airlines offering first class travel (i.e. *Cathay Pacific, Emirates*), special interest tour operators, upmarket holiday resorts (e.g. *One&Only Luxury Resorts*), and destinations such as Botswana in southern Africa.
Psychological	There are five main psychological pricing strategies (Boachie, 2016): **Charm pricing** A finishing-touch pricing strategy in which a price that has been set using another pricing method is adjusted slightly to attract consumers. **Prestige pricing** Making all numerical values into rounded figures. In other words, £999,95 is converted to £1000. Buy one, get one free (BOGOF) **Comparative pricing** Promoting two similar products simultaneously, but making one product's price much more attractive than the other. Visually highlight the different prices A new sale is more attractive when offered side-by-side with the previous price. The font, size, and colour of the sale price should be changed.	Instead of using prices rounded off to the pound or in £10 increments, a marketer uses rates such as £19,95 or £99 (see ▶ Industry Insight 8.9). A cruise liner holiday package is more attractive at a price of £1500 than £1495,50. "Buy one and get 20% off your next purchase".

◘ Table 8.5   (continued)

Pricing strategy	Description	Examples
Market skimming	Setting a relatively high price for a product or service at first, then lowers the price over time (Dean, 1976). Market-skimming strategies seek to gain the highest possible price from the early users (also called "early adopters") (Marn, Roegner & Zawada, 2003).	The proprietor of the only hotel in a small village in the countryside, for example, could charge high prices until competitors recognised the lucrative business opportunity and entered the market. Space tourism operators are currently utilising this strategy, as are offerings which anticipate a short life cycle such as global sporting events such as the FIFA World Cup, UEFA Champions League Final, and the Olympic Games.
Market penetration	Rather than setting a high price to start, the marketer may set a low price in order to penetrate the market rapidly and to gain market share (Tellis, 1986).	A newly opened restaurant on the main tourist avenues of the Costa Brava or Santa Cruz in Tenerife might use this strategy to attempt to penetrate the market.
Package	Combining several of their products or offerings in a package or bundle at a reduced rate The bundled price and extras might be enough to convince consumers to purchase the package, even if these benefits are minimal in terms of cost (Stremersch & Tellis, 2002).	Package tours are a prime example of package pricing (Tanford, Baloglu & Erdem, 2012). The "Sydney Attraction Pass: One card, three adventures" includes a city sightseeing bus trip, a ticket for Taronga Zoo, and a ticket for Sydney Opera House.
Discriminatory (or differential)	Identical or largely similar goods or services are transacted at different prices by the same provider in different markets (Belobaba, Odoni & Barnhart, 2009).	Visitor attractions in some countries charge higher prices to foreign/overseas visitors than locals, as foreign tourists are willing to pay more to make the most of their time on holiday (see ► Industry Insight 8.10). The Taj Mahal, in Agra, India charges 600 rupees for domestic tourists and 3000 rupees for foreign visitors. Museums, zoos, royal gardens, and theme parks often charge different rates for families and students (see ◘ Table 8.6).
Yield management	A system that allows a sector to predict consumer behaviour and adjust its pricing strategies accordingly to maximise profits (Witham, 2001)	Hotel chains installing sophisticated computerised systems to track data (Lundberg, Krishnamoorthy & Stavenga, 1995)
Dynamic	Charging different prices for the same product (or ticket) at different times in response to demand (Baker, 2017). This strategy is well-suited to meet the fluctuating levels of demand and to maximise yield (return on investment) (Pike, 2018: 134).	When booking a holiday on the internet; prices for flights, hotels, cruise liners, and rental cars fluctuate during a single day; the cost of a flight for example, may increase by as much as £100 (£114/$135) over a 24-hour period.
Personalised	specific consumers being asked to pay different prices for the same product or service, tailored to what the retailer thinks they can and will spend according to their personal data (Walker, 2017)	Airlines and travel companies to collect passengers' data to present with "personalised offerings" based on their marital status, their birthday, and their travel history

(continued)

□ Table 8.5   (continued)

Pricing strategy	Description	Examples
All-inclusive	charging consumers just one fee for the use of the facilities (Hudson & Hudson, 2017)	Club Mediterranean and Saga Holidays, which offer "total all-inclusive" holidays.
Promo-tional	Temporary price reductions on some items to attract consumers in the hope that they will purchase other offerings at normal prices	Hotels in casino resorts such as Las Vegas, United States, for example, offer reduced room rates to attract consumers who are likely to spend a lot of money gambling in the casino

Source: Author's creation

□ Table 8.6   Pricing Panel for the London Toy Museum. London Toy Museum admission prices 2021

Individual	
Adults	£12
Over 60/students	£8
Under 17	£6.50
Family ticket	£31
Under 5	Free
Group	
Adults	£10.50
Over 60/students	£7
Under 17	£5.50

8.4.3.1 Evaluating Pricing Strategies

Prices are not set just once. They must be evaluated and adjusted whenever the need arises. The marketer needs to ask the question, "How did the selected pricing strategy affect sales?"

While price and sales are measurable, it is difficult to measure other factors, such as changes in consumer tastes, competition and macroenvironmental factors (for example, climate, health issues and political issues), which also have an impact on sales. The most effective way of evaluating the success of pricing strategies is through marketing research (see ► Chap. 4). Research can determine if consumers were attracted by price or whether other factors such as quality, location, service levels, and accessibility were more important.

❓ Collect a range of tourist brochures and newspaper or magazine advertisements selling similar offerings to similar markets (two-star B&Bs or guesthouses, for example). Explain the differences and similarities between the prices offered.

Summary

In this chapter, we discussed the tourism product, branding and the role of price in tourism and hospitality marketing. When managing and designing products, marketers need to understand branding, the product life cycle, and the five stages involved in the development of a new product. The product life cycle is a useful tool to diagnose which stage a product is in. It forms an integral part of the internal situational analysis done during marketing planning (see ► Chap. 5). This enables the marketer to develop new products while other products are at their peak, rather than waiting until those products decline. The five stages in the process of developing new products act as a guide to tourism marketers, although in reality, few organisations have the resources to adhere to all these stages. The concepts of the product life cycle and branding will be revisited in the context of destination marketing in ► Chap. 14.

In the second section we discussed the concept of branding applied to the tourism and hospitality industry. Branding has become increasingly important to the marketer, as a strong brand name signals the advantages of a product and creates a personality that consumers recognise immediately.

In the third section of the chapter we looked at pricing of tourism and hospitality products. We discussed the numerous pricing approaches (and also the fact that a combination of approaches is often used) as well as the fact that price must also reflect the other components of the marketing mix, such as costs of promotion and distribution. Pricing is a key marketing function. Price is ultimately determined by the market, by what consumers are willing to pay, and by the prices of competitors. For tourism and hospitality businesses, pricing is one of the most flexible components of the marketing mix. It plays a crucial role in the marketing strategy by allowing the positioning of an offering to a target market to gain competitive advantage. Pricing decisions should be monitored and evaluated continuously to allow for adjustment when required. In closing, it is important to note that tourism and hospitality products, especially restaurants and visitor attractions, should not out-price the local market in a bid to capitalise on tourist spending because tourism organisations need both markets if they are to survive.

? **Review Questions**

1. Apply a product from the tourism and hospitality industry to explain these terms:
   - Core product
   - Expected product
   - Augmented product.
2. As a hotel marketer, briefly explain would you generate ideas for new products?
3. Identify five distinguished global tourism and hospitality brand names and explain why each brand name has been included in your list.
4. Explain this phrase, coined by Baines, Fill, Rosengren & Antonetti (2019: 511): "tourism brands are more than just names and logos".
5. Briefly explain why many consumers are willing to pay more for branded tourism products than for unbranded products.
6. "Most consumers will buy whatever is cheapest." Discuss this statement.
7. Explain the concepts of price elasticity of demand. Provide examples of tourism offerings that are both price elastic and price inelastic.
8. When would a newly opened hotel introduce a new product with premium pricing?
9. Discuss what is meant by cost-based pricing and consumer-based pricing. Why is it important for tourism marketers to understand these concepts?
10. Explain and give an example of tourism package pricing.
11. Conduct a price comparison of several B&Bs or hotels in your local area. What price differences did you discover?

In-depth Case Study 8: MakeOver Tour: A Cut Above the Rest

Objectives
- To understand the concept of pricing applied to a tourism business
- To comprehend pricing and observe its application to the case study example.

Medical tourism is not a new phenomenon. In ancient times, people travelled to other countries for health-related purposes (Bookman & Bookman, 2007). The ancient Greeks and Egyptians went to hot springs and baths to improve their health and the first recorded case of medical tourism describes Greek pilgrims travelling from the Mediterranean Sea to Epidaurus, a small territory in the Sardonic Gulf (Ben-Natan, Ben-Sefer & Ehrenfeld, 2009).

Contemporary travel for the purpose of obtaining modern medical treatments, such as dental and cosmetic surgery is a relatively new phenomenon. In the 1980s and 1990s, medical tourism tended to mainly incorporate those who travelled from less-developed countries abroad to major medical centres in developed countries for treatment unavailable at home (Horowitz, Rosensweig, and Jones, 2007). In recent years, medical tourism now also includes those from developed countries who travel to developing countries for lower-priced medical treatments.

Medical tourists are able to combine treatment and tourism activities at the same time. Popular medical tourism destinations include the likes of India, Hungary, South Africa, Thailand, and Turkey, which offer the twin pull of major tourist attractions and modern hospital facilities (Saleh et al., 2015; Piazolo and Zanca, 2011). This has led to medical tourism companies and operators advertising their services, not only in their own countries, but now also in the global marketplace.

Turkey is now considered to be one of the top ten medical tourism destinations in the world and has experienced an influx of medical tourists over the last decade. According to the Istanbul International Health Tourism Association (IIHTA), there were 75,000 medical tourists visiting Turkey in 2007, increasing to more than 551,000 (from over 120 countries) in 2018. Inbound medical tourism in Turkey continues to be on the rise with the nation's healthcare facilities having treated 264,138 medical tourists in the first six months of 2019. The Turkish cities of Istanbul, Ankara, Antalya, Izmir, Yalova, and Adana are the hotspots for medical tourism and receive the highest number of medical tourists each year. Most of these medical tourists travel from Gulf Cooperation Council (GCC) nations, including the UAE, Saudi Arabia, Kuwait, Bahrain, and Qatar. There is also a growing number of medical tourists visiting Turkey from the likes of Germany, Russia, the USA, Iraq, and the UK. Foreign medical tourists often visit Turkey for cosmetic treatments combined with a holiday experience. Faced with soaring healthcare costs at home, tourists from Europe, the USA,

Russia are choosing to fly thousands of miles, saving up to 90 percent on the cost of treatments and incorporating a summer holiday into their trip.

Turkey is well known for its scenic beauty and cultural history and has a number of other competitive advantages such as climate, cuisine, and historical attractions. A study showed that the main factors of attracting tourists to Turkey are easily accessible locations, high quality medical care, and affordable prices. The cost of medical services in Turkey is significantly lower than in advanced economies found in the USA and Europe (Kilavuz, 2018). The low cost of treatment remains the most attractive factor for the majority of medical tourists, particularly those from countries with a no paid-for state medical system such as in the USA, where healthcare costs are extremely expensive even for those with medical insurance.

MakeOver Tour is an Istanbul-based medical tourism company which started in 1995 and is situated in one of Istanbul's busiest business hubs. The company offers a range of surgical and non-surgical procedures coupled with the opportunity for clients to partake in tours around the city. MakeOverTour also provides airport transfer, sightseeing tours, luxury accommodation, private translation, and personal and medical assistance during recuperation for its clients. The recuperation facilities are located in an up-market residential area and offer exclusive and private secluded grounds for recuperation and relaxation.

The most common cosmetic procedures include hair transplants, dental treatments, breast augmentation, face lifts, lip augmentation, liposuction, and nose surgery. Hip, knee and shoulder replacements are also offered as part of packages. MakeOver Tour's clients are predominantly international clients. They tend to come from the UK, Canada, USA, Saudi Arabia, and Jordan, and have high levels of disposable income. They also tend to be middle-aged, as older people are more likely to require and want surgery than young people, but cosmetic surgery is currently becoming increasingly popular amongst the younger 24–44 years age group.

Premium pricing is defined as a product or service being sold at a higher rate than that of competing brands to give it a certain appeal through an aura of exclusivity. The increased price being attached to the product or service allows for the perception of a superior nature or superior quality. MakeOver Tour's premium pricing emphasises the uniqueness of the package, attracting clients who want to be associated with the provision of bespoke and exclusive offerings. MakeOver Tour has a standard global cost for their services and offers no seasonal rates or specials.

MakeOver Tour has been accredited by the Medical Travel Quality Alliance and Health on the internet as well as the Turkish Healthcare Tourism Development Council member establishment. It has adopted the Code of Practice for Medical Tourism launched by Treatment Abroad.

Various packages are available. The fees include the following costs:
- Specialist (qualified, certified and registered) surgeon with adequate malpractice insurance
- Anaesthesiologist
- One to two nights' stay in a fully certified private hospital
- 24-hour nurse facility
- Operation (operating theatre charges)
- Medication whilst in the clinic
- Pre- and post-operative consultations

- Administration
- Follow-up consultation in the home country.

The future for the cosmetic/medical tourism business looks promising. Research suggests a growing influx of medical tourists to Turkey over the coming years. MakeOver Tour provides a premium service to a unique set of tourists. The company also offers a competitive range of prices with high-quality, certified service and equipment. The pricing of the service places Turkey on the global medical tourism map, attracting clientele who in turn bring in foreign currency and invest in the Turkish economy.

Questions and Activities

1. What pricing strategy is MakeOver Tour using for medical tourists? Analyse any disadvantages of this strategy.
2. Briefly describe what other product offerings could MakeOver Tour include as part of a package. What type of pricing strategy is this called?
3. Describe whether the demand for medical tourism product product-offerings is price elastic or price inelastic.
4. Is the medical tourism sector growing? Justify your answer.
5. MakeOver Tour's slogan is "Best way for your health & travel". Describe what this slogan implies.

References

Aaker, D. A. (1996). *Building strong brands.* New York: The Free Press.

Baines, P., Fill, C., Rosengren, S., & Antonetti, P. (2019). *Marketing* (5th ed.). Oxford: Oxford University Press.

Baker, T. (2017). *Dynamic pricing: an introduction.* www.theaudienceagency.org/insight/dynamic-pricing-an-introduction. Accessed 20 November 2017.

Belobaba, P., Odoni, A. & Barnhart. C. (2009). *The global airline industry.* New Jersey: Wiley.

Ben-Natan, M., Ben-Sefer, E., & Ehrenfeld, M. (2009). Medical tourism: A new role for nursing? *Journal of Issues in Nursing, 14*(3).

Boachie, P. (2016). *Five strategies of psychological pricing.* https://www.entrepreneur.com/article/279464. Accessed 3 May 2018.

Bookman, M. Z., & Bookman, K. R. (2007). *Medical tourism in developing countries.* New York: Palgrave MacMillian.

Cooper, R. (1986). *Winning at new products.* Reading, MA: Addison-Wesley.

Cooper, R. (2014). What's next?: After stage-gate. *Research-Technology Management, 57*(1), 20–31.

Cowell, D. (1984). *The marketing of services.* London: Butterworth-Heinemann.

Day, G. (1981). The product life cycle: Analysis and applications issues. *Journal of Marketing, 45*(Autumn), 60–67.

Dean, J. (1976). Pricing policies for new products. *Harvard Business Review, 54*(6), 141–153.

Dibb, S., Simkin, L., Pride, W., & Ferrell, O. C. (1994). *Marketing: Concepts and strategies* (2nd ed.). London: Houghton-Mifflin.

Fyall, A., Legoherel, P., Frochot, I., & Wang, Y. (2019). *Marketing for tourism and hospitality*. London: Routledge.

Godin, S. (2003). *Purple cow*. London: Penguin.

Gregson, A. (2008). *Pricing strategies for small business*. Vancouver, BC: Self Counsel Press.

Guéguen, N., Jacob, C., Legohérel, P., & NGobo, P. (2008). Nine-ending prices and consumer behaviour in a restaurant. *International Journal of Hospitality Management, 28*(1), 170–172.

Gunn, C. (1988). *Vacationscape: Designing tourist regions* (2nd ed.). Austin, TX: Bureau of Business Research University of Texas.

Hardy, J., Macrury, I., & Powell, H. (2018). *The advertising handbook* (4th ed.). New York: Routledge.

Hjalager, A. (2010). A review of innovation research in tourism. *Tourism Management, 31*, 1–12.

Holloway, J. C. (2006). *Marketing for tourism* (4th ed.). Harlow, Essex: Prentice-Hall.

Horowitz, M., Rosensweig, J., & Jones, C. (2007). Medical tourism: Globalization of the healthcare marketplace. *Medscape General Medicine, 9*(4), 33.

Hudson, S., & Hudson, L. (2017). *Marketing for tourism, hospitality & events* (2nd ed.). London: Sage.

Keller, K. (2009). Building strong brands in a modern marketing communications environment. *Journal of Marketing Communications, 15*(2/3), 139–155.

Keller, K. L. (2003). *Strategic brand management: building, measuring, and managing brand equity* (2nd ed.). Upper Saddle River, NJ: Prentice-Hall.

Keller, K. L. (2012). *Strategic brand management: Building, measuring, and managing brand equity* (4th ed.). Upper Saddle River, NJ: Prentice-Hall.

Kilavuz, E. (2018). Medical tourism competition: The case of Turkey. *International Journal of Health Management and Tourism, 3*(1), 42–58.

Kim, J. Y., Natter, M., & Spann, M. (2009). Pay what you want: A new participatory pricing mechanism. *Journal of Marketing, 73*(1), 44–58.

Kotler, P., & Armstrong, G. (2019). *Principles of marketing* (17th ed.). London: Pearson Education.

Lasser, W., Mittal, B., & Sharma, A. (1995). Measuring customer-based brand equity. *Journal of Consumer Marketing, 12*(4), 11–19.

Laws, E. (2011). *Tourism marketing: Quality and service management perspectives* (p. 124). London: Continuum International Publishing.

Laws, E. (2002). *Tourism marketing: Quality and service management perspectives*. London: Continuum.

Levitt, T. (1983). After the sale is over. *Harvard Business Review, 61*(5), 87–93.

Lovelock, C. H. (1984). Developing and implementing new services. In W. R. George & C. E. Marshall (Eds.), *Developing new services*. Chicago, IL: American Marketing Association.

Lumsdon, L. (1997). *Tourism marketing*. London: International Thomson Press.

Lundberg, D., Krishnamoorthy, M., & Stavenga, M. (1995). *Tourism economics*. New York: Wiley.

Marn, M., Roegner, E. & Zawada, C. (2003, July). Pricing new products. *The McKinsey Quarterly, 3*: 40–49.

McCarthy, E. J. (1960). *Basic marketing: A managerial approach*. Homewood, IL: Irwin.

McCarthy, E. J., Cannon, J., & Perreault, W. (2015). *Essentials of marketing* (14th ed.). Homewood, IL: Irwin.

Moon, Y. (2005). Break free from the product life cycle. *Harvard Business Review, 83*(5), 86–94.

Orr, G. (2014, 22 July). Honestybox hotels: You decide how much you pay'. *Independent*. http://www.independent.co.uk/travel/hotels/honesty-box-hotels-you-decide-how-much-you-pay-9622062.html. Accessed 24 Aug 2017.

Piazolo, M., & Zanca, N.A. (2011). Medical tourism: A case study for the USA and India, Germany, and Hungary, *Acta Polytechnica Hungarica, 8*(1), 136–160.

Pike, S. (2018). *Tourism marketing for small businesses*. Oxford: Goodfellow Publishers.

Rosenthal, R. (2014). *Optimarketing: Marketing to electrify your business*. Seattle, WA: Amazon Create Space Publishing.

Russell, M. (2012, 21 April). Richard Branson fails: 14 Virgin companies that went bust. *Business Insider*. www.businessinsider.com/richard-branson-fails-virgin-companies-that-went-bust-2012-4. Accessed 7 Dec 2016.

Saleh, S., Husain, F., Saud, M., & Isa, M. (2015). Strategic marketing and competitive analysis of Malaysian medical tourism industry. *Proceeding-Kuala Lumpur International Business, Economics and Law Conference 6*, Vol.2. Kuala Lumpa.

Sowrey, T. (1990). Idea generation: Identifying the most useful techniques. *European Journal of Marketing, 42*(5).

Stremersch, S., & Tellis, G. (2002). Strategic bundling of products and prices: A new synthesis for marketing. *Journal of Marketing, 66*(1), 55–72.

Tanford, S., Baloglu, S., & Erdem, M. (2012). Travel packing on the internet: The impact of pricing information and perceived value on consumer choice. *Journal of Travel Research, 51*(1), 68–80.

Tanner, J., & Raymond, M. (2012). *Principles of marketing*. Boston, MA: Flat World Knowledge.

Taylor, J. & Blackall, M. (2020, February 27). Bunking up: Airline unveils sleep pods for economy passengers. *The Guardian*, 3.

Tellis, G. (1986, October). Beyond the many faces of price: An integration of pricing strategies. Journal of Marketing, 50: 146–160.

Vernon, R. (1979). The product life cycle hypothesis in a new international environment. *Oxford Bulletin of Economics and Statistics, 41*.

Walker, T. (2017, November). The price is…right? 20 *The Guardian G2*: 10–11.

Withiam, G. (2001). A"4-C" strategy for yield management. *Cornell Hospitality Report, 1*, 4–17.

Zeithaml, V.A. (1988, July). Consumer perceptions of price, quality, and value. *Journal of Marketing, 52*:2–22.

Zwart, E. (2017). *Commercial TV slogans*. Retrieved from www.edwinno.com/edwinno-publications/my-writings/commercial-tv-slogans-1. Accessed 21 Aug 2018.

Further Reading

Burgess, C. (2014). *Essential financial techniques for hospitality managers*. Oxford: Goodfellow.

Slade-Brooking, C. (2017). *Creating a brand identity: A guide for designers*. London: Laurence King.

Trott, P. (2017). *Innovation management and new product development* (6th ed.). London: Pearson.

Tourism Distribution

Contents

Electronic Supplementary Material The online version of this chapter (https://doi.
org/10.1007/978-3-030-64111-5_9) contains supplementary material, which is available to
authorized users.

Purpose

This chapter will provide you with an under-standing of distribution channels and their role in the international tourism industry.

🔍 Learning Goals

After reading this chapter, you should be able to:

- Explain the role of distribution chan-nels within the industry
- Describe the concepts of commission and horizontal integration
- Explore the roles played by tour opera-tors, travel agents, online retailers, desti-nation management companies, and other marketing intermediaries
- Understand the impact of information and communications technology on marketing intermediaries
- Explain the factors that influence the choices of distribution channels in vari-ous sectors of the international tourism industry
- Apply tourism distribution principles to Reality Tours and Travel.

Overview

Distribution channels are involved in the process of making tourism and hospitality products available and accessible to con-sumers. We begin the chapter with a defini-tion of the role of distribution channels in the tourism industry. We then outline the benefits of using marketing intermediaries (the middlemen who sell offerings within the tourism industry). We explain the con-cepts of commission and horizontal inte-gration. The chapter then focuses on the activities of key marketing intermediaries such as the tour operator, the travel agent, and the online travel retailer. Next, we dis-cuss various direct intermediaries such as the multi-media kiosks, video conferencing, virtual reality, and global distribution sys-tems. This technology is changing the role of distribution channels in the industry. We conclude with a discussion of the factors that influence the selection of an appropri-ate distribution channel.

The chapter's in-depth case study applies the principles of distribution (or place) to *Reality Tours and Travel*: Slum Tours, Mumbai, India.

9.1 Introduction

Tourism products are intangible (Rathmell, 1974). This means that they cannot be deliv-ered from point A to point B, as physical goods can. Tourism organisations must get consumers to come to them by selling their offerings directly or indirectly through one or more distribution channels. The industry's distribution channels are unique because they have an influence on travellers' itineraries and consumers also participate in the distribution process. In addition, distribution is based on a tourism provider paying a commission to an intermediary (such as a travel agent) who sup-plies a customer; for many tourism firms, this can affect pricing, competitiveness, and prof-its (Pike, 2018: 207) (see ▶ Chap. 8). Intermediaries also play an important role in providing both information and services to tourism consumer markets. These channels are sometimes referred to as the "travel indus-try".

The value of place within the marketing mix must not be underestimated, as it is where tourism businesses can gain a competitive advantage. It is the battleground of strategic tourism marketing (Evans, Campbell & Stonehouse, 2003). Consumers may have heard of a particular offering. They may also desire the offering and may even be willing to pay its price, but if it is not accessible or avail-able, then they cannot purchase it.

9.2 Distribution Channels in Tourism

Distribution is regarded as the place of sale in the traditional marketing mix, along with product, price, and promotion (Borden, 1964). It describes the location and availabil-ity of the product-offering and the method by which it is distributed to consumers. The term "distribution channels" (also known as "the chain of distribution") describes the system by which an offering is distributed from a tourism provider to a consumer (Holloway & Humphreys, 2020).

In the manufacturing industry, distribution channels are used to move tangible goods from the manufacturer to the customer. In the tourism industry, they are used to move the consumer to the supplier (see ◻ Fig. 9.1). A supplier (or principal) is any individual or corporate entity in the travel industry contracting with consumers to organise or provide a facility or service directly rather than acting as an intermediary (Beaver, 2012). The term "principal" is meant to differentiate agents from tour operators (wholesalers). However, as we will discuss later, this is not always a clear-cut distinction; in some cases, depending on the circumstances, a tour operator can take the role of a supplier.

Tourism products are traditionally distributed through a number of intermediaries that link tourism businesses with consumers. These intermediaries are either wholesalers, such as tour operators, who consolidate products into packages, or retailers, such as travel agents, which form the link in the chain of distribution and sell bundled packages or individual offerings to end-consumers. However, even before the internet changed everything, this concise description was never that simple. As shown by the dotted lines in ◻ Fig. 9.2, travel agents did not always go through tour operators, and consumers have always been able to book airline tickets, hotel accommodation, and car rental directly, but many chose not to because it was always too much trouble to make bookings themselves. Similarly, tourism providers are not obliged to sell their offerings

through the chain of distribution. Indeed, many of these providers choose to sell directly to the consumer or retailer, thereby cutting out some or all of the middlemen. The latter method is referred to as "disintermediation".

A retailer is another term for an agent who provides a downstream link between providers and users (Baines et al., 2019: 539).

The role of intermediaries is to bring consumers (buyers) and providers (sellers) together. Intermediaries improve the flow of information and offerings (termed "distribution channels") between suppliers or principals and consumers.

9.2.1 Levels of Distribution in Tourism and Hospitality

Tourism products can be sold to the consumer in a number of ways. In other words, there are several types of distribution (or marketing) channels that can be used to access tourism product offerings and information about services. A marketing channel is a chain of organisations that are concerned with the management of the processes and activities involved in creating and moving products from suppliers to end-user consumers (Kotler et al., 2016). These channels range from one-level direct access to more complex three-level arrangements involving several intermediaries. In general, the longer the distribution channel, the higher the cost of the tourism and hospitality offering is to consumers. ◻ Figure 9.3 shows one-, two- and three-level distribution channels for tourism organisations.

The simplest form of distribution is to sell directly to the consumer. This single-level

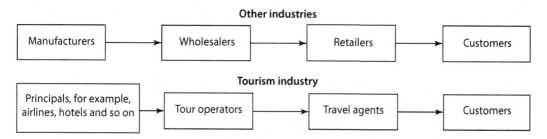

◻ **Fig. 9.1** Distribution channels: other industries versus the tourism industry. (Source: Author's creation)

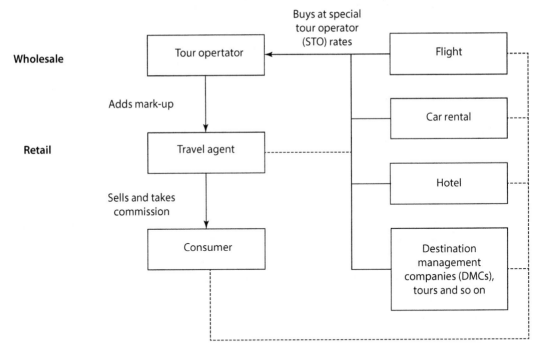

◻ Fig. 9.2   The theoretical travel supply chain. (Source: Author's creation)

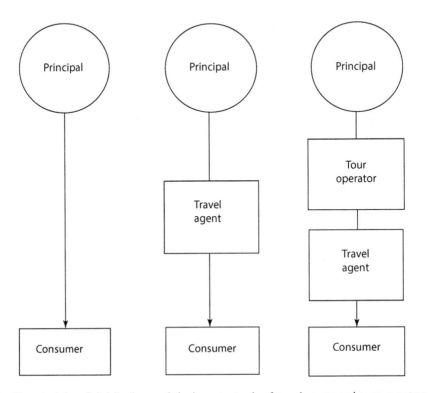

◻ Fig. 9.3   The principles of distribution, and the important role of travel agents and tour operators. (Source: Author's creation)

channel or unbroken chain is represented by the first arrow in ◫ Fig. 9.3. This might be a hotel selling a room directly to the person who will stay in it, for example. (In the manufacturing industry, the parallel would be the customer going directly to the factory.) A principal or a tour operator can also sell directly to the consumer. However, in each case, staff will need to process and administer the bookings.

The second form of distribution is indirect, with longer multi-level channels or broken chains. This is known as a "multi-channel distribution system". A multi-channel distribution system is a system in which a single tourism organisation sets up two or more marketing channels to reach one or more consumer segments (Teltzrow, Berendt & Günther, 2003). A single tourism firm may set up two or more direct or indirect marketing channels to reach one or more consumer segments. A tourism principal (or supplier, such as a hotel, a resort, an airline, or a cruise-liner company) can choose to sell through intermediaries such as travel agents (for example, *The Co-operative Travel*) or tour operators (for example, *Jet2holidays*). Tour operators sometimes use travel agents as intermediaries. A simplified example of distribution in tourism is when tour operators liaise with hoteliers and airlines to buy hotel bed spaces and airline seats. They then produce a travel brochure of their holiday packages. Travel agents stock the brochures and sell the packages for a commission from tour operators. In this way, the tour operator acts as a wholesaler and the travel agent acts as a retailer.

The number and types of links in the chain of distribution vary, depending on the nature of the tourism offering to be distributed, the type of customer, and the type tourism organisation. For example, smaller tourism businesses may sell directly and through one type of intermediary to one type of customer. Most of the larger tourism organisations and multinational corporations (MNCs) have more complex distribution strategies. They use a variety of distribution methods, which reflects the different market segments that the organisation aims to target. The different levels in the travel industry are therefore becom-

ing less defined, as many of the bigger companies fill every link in the supply chain.

9.2.2 Issues in Distribution in Tourism

Two trends that impacted on tourism distribution over the last couple of decades are commission and horizontal integration.

9.2.2.1 Commission

A commission is a rate paid to a third party for a sale on behalf of a business (Pike, 2018: 208). A commission is only paid when a sale is made. It is a cost of getting a sale through a distributor, much in the same way as advertising is a cost to achieve direct sales (Pike, 2018: 209). When a **commission** is payable, the range of product offerings that a travel agency chooses to provide varies depending on the commission rates (also known as "commercial agreements") as well as the demand from the consumer marketplace. Services range from accommodation bookings and transportation arrangements (air, rail, coach and cruise tickets, and car rental) to hotel and tour packages. Different commission rates are paid by different subsectors and commission levels vary around the world. Usually the commission rate is whatever was agreed to between the tourism supplier and the intermediary. Car hire commission, for example, is generally higher than rail or cruise commission. Travel agents can expect in the region of 10–20%, concierge services 10–20%, inbound tour operators 25–30%, airlines 25–30%, and visitor information centres 10% (Pike, 2018: 209). Most of the leisure travel agent's revenue comes from selling package tours and holidays. Over the last decade, airlines have reduced the amount of commission paid to travel agents for international flights, under international agreement, to as low as 5%. Commission paid by hotels to online sites (such as ▶ Booking.com and ▶ Expedia.com) is usually at least 15 per cent, but hotels can pay extra for more "visibility"; in other words, given a higher profile in search engine results (Calder, 2019). In some cases, if tourism businesses are unable to absorb this fee (which can in fact be as high as 25% of the overall cost) they may be forced to increase prices.

9.2.2.2 Horizontal Integration

Horizontal integration is where a business forms an alliance with other businesses that are at the same level in the supply chain (Lafferty & van Fossen, 2012). This integration allows one organisation to offer various elements of the holiday product to consumers because it owns the travel agency, the tour operator, the transport providers, and sometimes the accommodation provider too. The extent of integration in the global tourism industry has been such that there are large tour operators now linked with travel agency chains, yet these linkages are not always recognised by consumers.

> *Horizontal integration* is where an organisation owns two or more companies, on the same level of the buying chain (Holloway & Humphreys, 2020).

9.2.3 Intermediaries in Tourism

As we saw earlier, an intermediary refers to any dealer – a business or a person – in the chain of distribution that acts as a link, go-between, or middleman between the tourism principal or supplier and its consumers (see ◻ Fig. 9.4). An intermediary, therefore, is a person or an organisation that liaises between the tourist and the tourism supplier or provider. The best-known intermediaries in the tourism industry are travel agents, who mainly transact with tourism principals such as airlines, hotel groups, car hire companies, coach operators, destination management companies (DMCs), and tour operators. Intermediaries such as tour operators, wholesalers, travel agents, and online travel agents (OTAs) play a significant role in attracting international visitors to tourist destinations. While consumers are increasingly organising and planning their own trips directly, intermediaries remain effective in reaching large numbers of potential tourists in several markets, particularly long-haul ones. The travel trade can help open up new markets, attract more visitors to a destination, and encourage tourists to spend more time exploring what the destination has to offer.

Nowadays, both tourism principals and consumers have a great deal of choice of distribution methods, from travel agencies and call centres to sales representatives and supermarkets. Distribution channels influence consumer behaviour and determine the ability of the industry to respond efficiently to consumers' requests (Cooper, 2016: 422).

In tourism, the concept of intermediation is complex as principals and intermediaries are able to switch roles in the chain of distribution (see ▶ Industry Insight 9.1). An intermediary,

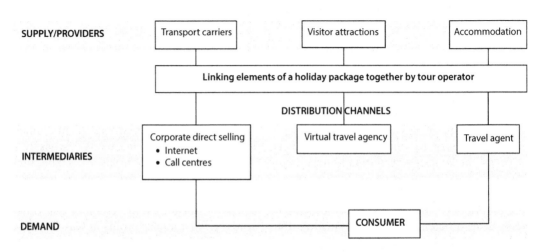

◻ **Fig. 9.4** The elements of a holiday package. (Source: Author's creation)

such as a tour operator may act as a principal and vice versa. is A hotel that becomes a tour operator by packaging its surplus capacity to offer midweek breaks aimed at the domestic leisure tourism market, and sells airline tickets and admissions to visitor attractions is an in an all-inclusive package is an example of a principal acting as an intermediary. Similarly, airlines entice consumers to book flights online, and in doing so, encourage them to access a range of third-party services such as car rental and hotels. Some travel companies take on the role of several companies. Indeed, several of the bigger companies or multi-national companies (MNCs) fill every link on the supply chain. For example, *TUI Group* owns travel agencies, hotels, airlines (see ◘ Image 9.1), cruise ships, and retail stores (see ◘ Image 9.2). The company owns *TUI Airways*, which is the largest charter airline in the world with a fleet of 64 aircraft, and was formed by the merger of *Thomsonfly* (formerly *Britannia Airways*) and *First Choice Airways*.

Integration also takes place within smaller travel trade businesses. *Flamingo Tours & Disabled Ventures*, for example, functions as a tour operator, a travel agency, and a DMC in that it also runs tours aimed at travellers with special needs. While this integration has the advantage of maximising revenue, it may also be done to ensure service quality.

Retail travel agents not only compete with other travel agents, but also with the internet, with OTAs, and with tour operators that are encroaching into the retail sector by selling directly to end-consumers. Tour operators are also feeling vertically threatened as product owners take advantage of the numerous channels that enable them to sell at the same prices that they give tour operators while retaining a bigger profit margin.

While tourism consists of a number of different sectors, including accommodation and transportation, it is the travel agencies and tour operators that drive the industry and enable it to continue to grow.

◘ **Image 9.1** A TUI aircraft. (Source: TUI)

TUI Group is the world's largest tourism business with 1600 travel agencies, six airlines with around 150 aircraft, over 380 hotels with 250,000 beds, 17 cruise liners.

The *TUI Group* is listed on the LSE (London Stock Exchange).

Source: ► https://www.tuigroup.com/en-en/about-us/about-tui-group.

Industry Insight 9.1

Back to Basics! Ryanair Selling 'No-Frills' Holidays

Ryanair, the low-cost airline, moved into the tour operating sector and is not only selling no-frills flights but is selling no-frills holidays. It is offering flight, hotel, and transfer packages on its website, for example, a fully-inclusive seven days' holiday in Costa Brava at £176 (€200). The strategy was met with ambiguous reactions online; with one person asking: "I wonder if consumers will have to pay for extras such as adding a bed in their hotel room?" Some of the hotels on the website appear to have only basic facilities and some even lack that, according to online reviews. The Aquarium II in Benidorm, for example, has been deemed on TripAdvisor as "the worst hotel", with many guests saying that they had to bring their own toilet paper and were asked to pay to use sun loungers at the pool. Another guest wrote that "the sofa bed was a disgrace, we got eaten alive every time we slept on it."

Source: Ellson, Andrew. (2017). 'Ryanair starts selling budget holiday deals'. *The Times*, Monday 27 February, p.9.

9.2.4 Marketing to Tourism Intermediaries

Tourism businesses need to work with travel trade intermediaries to access consumers. There are several tools that can be utilised.

- Sales calls: Making appointments with intermediaries such as visitor information centres (VICs), travel agents, tour operators, and professional conference organisers (PCOs) are a useful way promoting travel trade services.
- Brochure distribution: Professionally produced brochures should be displayed in VICs, travel agency stands, and hotel foyers to target consumers.
- Educationals: Also known as "familiarisations", educationals entail hosting intermediaries on a visit to the business or destination to experience what is offered first-hand (Pike, 2018: 13).
- Travel trade shows: Participating in travel trade shows is an excellent sales tool for tourism businesses, particularly SMEs. There are two types of travel trade events: travel trade expos and travel industry exchanges.

Examples of a travel trade expo include the World Travel Market (WTM), hosted in London annually in November, and the Tourism Indaba, hosted in Durban, South Africa annually in the month of May.

9.3 The Range of Tourism and Hospitality Intermediaries

There is a wide range of intermediaries between tourism suppliers and consumer markets at various levels in the distribution system. Some of these channels are indirect, while others are direct. Indirect channels tend to be more personal than direct distribution channels. Direct channels tend to be technological in nature.

We begin by looking at indirect marketing channels, and then discuss direct marketing channels.

9.3.1 Indirect Marketing Channels

There are a number of indirect marketing channels or intermediaries in tourism. These intermediaries are usually referred to as the travel trade (or travel industry).

9.3.1.1 Tour Operators

The primary function of a **tour operator** is to assemble the main elements of a holiday (transport, accommodation, ancillary services, and so on) into a single product (or package) and sell this to consumers through a travel agent, airline sales office, or other intermediary (Page & Connell, 2020). Tour operators have played a significant role in the growth of international tourism over the last 40 years. For many tourism principals, especially those with limited resources, tour operators have been the only means of reaching international markets (although the internet has changed this). The business of tour operating is an important and dynamic subsector of the tourism industry. It is highly competitive, and is characterised by expansion, mergers, and acquisitions.

> A *tour operator* is any bulk buyer and seller of a single travel and tourism service (for example, acting as a broker in the sector of air transport or hotel accommodation) (Dwyer & Forsyth, 2006).

Essentially, tour operators negotiate prices called "special tour operator" (STO) rates from tourism providers, add a mark-up, and consolidate them into packages. In the chain of distribution, tour operators are the wholesalers (or middlemen) of the tourism industry, buying in bulk from principals (for example, airlines, hotels, and car rental companies) and reselling through retail travel agencies. In the tourism industry, tour operators take on the role of wholesalers, since they buy their different tourism offerings (for example, airline seats or hotel bed spaces) in bulk for subsequent sale to travel agents or directly to the tourist. The terms "tour operator" and "wholesaler" are often used interchangeably; however, wholesalers generally develop and market inclusive tours to sell to other elements of the travel trade (via travel agents) rather than to the public.

Inbound tour operators (ITOs) are companies that package individual travel services within their own destination and act on behalf of international tour operators in coordinating components of an independent itinerary or package. Tour operators also carry out several functions, including conducting research, contracting suppliers, costing the package, and marketing and selling the holiday package.

The components of a typical inclusive tour might include transport (for example, a return flight from London Heathrow to JFK Airport in New York with *Virgin Atlantic*), a transfer from the airport to the hotel (with a local ground handling agent), accommodation (for example, seven nights' half board at *Holiday Inn Times Square* in New York), and optional travel services, such as car hire (see ◘ Table 9.1).

■ **The Specialised Roles of Tour Operators**

When people think of tour operators, they almost always tend to think of them as outbound tour operators (transporting tourists

◘ **Table 9.1** Components of a package holiday (inclusive tour)

Core elements	Add-ons
Aircraft seat	Car hire
Transfer from airport to accommodation establishment and back to airport (transfer companies)	Excursions or tours (excursion providers)
Accommodation at destination	Activities, for example, paragliding
Restaurant meals	Tourist guide services
Insurance	
Services of a representative of a tour operator	
Source: Adapted from Page (2019)	

out of a country). However, tour operators fulfil several different roles. They may organise holidays domestically (within a country), handle incoming foreign tourists (inbound tour operators), arrange holidays in other countries (outbound tour operators), or specialise in an aspect of operating. At one extreme, for instance, there are the mass market operators – the larger integrated tour operators – such as German-owned *TUI Travel Group*, which owns over 100 brands. *TUI* owns the UK sun-and-sand operations *Thomson Holidays* and *First Choice* (although these band names have been phased out in recent years and been replaced by '*TUI*'), the ski operator *Crystal,* and the Italy specialist *Citalia*, as well as *Hayes & Jarvis, Sovereign, Sunsail, Exodus, Le Boat*, and hotel booking online portal ► LateRooms.com. Other examples of mass operators are *Jet2holidays* (the sister company of ► Jet2.com), *Trailfinders*; all offer a range of holiday brands to appeal to very broad market segments. Then there are the specialist tour operators that target particular niche markets and special interest tourism activities. Each of these kinds of tour operators is briefly examined below.

■■ Domestic Tour Operators

Operators that organise package holidays and tours in a particular country form a much smaller component of the tourism industry than operators who organise tours beyond its borders. The reason for this is that it is relatively easy nowadays for tourists to organise their travel arrangements within their own home country. An example of one of the leading domestic tour operators in the UK is *Abercrombie & Kent.*

■■ Outbound Tour Operators

Outbound tour operators (OTOs) offer holidays abroad. They sell a package tour to an individual or a group of people of his/her own country to another country or a number of countries for a specific time period.

Outbound tour operators arrange travel documents, transportation to a central point where the tour starts and contracts with inbound tour operators or destination management companies (DMCs) and ground handlers to provide accommodation, transportation, local sightseeing, and other services as needed throughout the tour. Generally, OTOs work in liaison with the inbound tour operators/ground handlers and offer services involving meeting the inbound tour group at the airport, transferring the tour group from the airport to the arranged accommodation in a town or city hotel, arranging or organising local sightseeing that may be a single day or multi days tour of the home county, region or area. These may be in the form of business or leisure-oriented tours.

■■ Inbound Tour Operators

Inbound tour operators (ITOs) specialise in handling incoming foreign (or overseas) tourists and have a different role from that of outbound operators. Some are ground-handling agents, ranging from agents who organise hotel accommodation on behalf of an overseas tour operator to agents who offer a comprehensive range of services, including coach tours (and other modes of transportation), booking of theatre tickets, currency exchange, arranging sightseeing tours and other trips to visitor attractions as well as study tours, and special interest tourism holidays. Various tour-operating companies also specialise according to the markets they service, for example, the UK tour operator *Abercrombie & Kent Safaris* works with inbound North American tourists.

■■ Specialist Tour Operators

Specialist (or independent) tour operators cater for niche tourism markets (domestic, inbound, or outbound). Tour operators may specialise in terms of the activities that they offer, by destination or by the markets that they serve. Some outbound operators even choose to specialise according to the mode of transport by which their customers travel, for example, coach travel, cruise liners or railway companies.

Specialist tour operators target particular niche markets and special interest tourism (SIT) activities, for example, sports enthusiasts (golf, angling and so on), single travellers, female travellers, pink tourists (gay and lesbian travellers), cruisers, hobby tourists (tourists who are interested in activities such as bird-watching, antique-collecting, painting, photography, naturism, cycling, wine-tasting, and gastronomy), adventure tourists, and marine tourists (see ▶ Industry Insight 9.2).

Industry Insight 9.2

Specialist Marine Tourism Operator

Specialist tourism company Marine Travel is an independent marine travel specialist. It caters for the individual traveller as well as servicing larger maritime organisations from its UK and Manila (Philippines) offices. Marine Travel provides a bespoke travel service including flights, hotels, and car hire and many other ancillary products for a cross section of marine-related businesses throughout the UK and worldwide. Marine Travel is the founding partner of mta7 Global Alliance, an alliance of Marine travel companies.

Source: ▶ http://www.themarinetravel.co.uk/our-company/

❓ Carry out research into one of your country's major tour operators. Describe the scale and structure of the organisation and the offerings it provides.

9.3.1.2 Destination Management Companies

Destination management companies (DMCs) manage/handle all tourists' (or delegates') travel arrangements when they arrive in the country (Pike, 2016: 122). The DMC manages all of the visitors' ground arrangements from booking accommodation, restaurants, and golf tee-off times to arranging transportation, tourist guides, entertainment and adventure activities, and tours. According to the website of a Mexican DMC, "a DMC is a service professional company with a wide-range of knowledge and experience over the conditions and touristic resources of a region" (Tropical Incentives DMC, 2018).

DMCs are usually based in the destination and create and manage an infrastructure that allows the various products of that destination to be marketed effectively, and to be sold to tour operators and end-users. Knowledge of the destination (for example, amenities, activities, and attractions) and information about clients (for example, knowing whether clients have been on a safari before) are key to successful destination marketing. For instance, *Nomad Africa Adventure Tours* puts together trans-Africa expeditions, camping tours, and dive tours.

DMCs are essential agents that work on behalf of international and inbound and domestic tour operators, travel agents, and suppliers. They are also referred to as "ground handlers", "ground operators", "reception operators" (in the United States), and "handling agencies" (in India). A DMC works with an outbound agency who gives it a budget within which to design a suitable programme or itinerary on behalf of the client. Partnerships with airlines, car hire companies, hotel groups, and international tour operators enable the DMC to offer its clients competitive deals. The DMC may also be expected to manage corporate branding on behalf of the organisation. This may include items such as signage, gifting, and t-shirts. In addition, the DMC manages everything at the destination, including conferencing arrangements. Some DMCs own all the travel products along the chain of distribution.

9.3.1.3 Tour Brokers

A tour broker is an individual or a firm that sells coach tours, which are attractive to a variety of markets (Holloway & Humphreys, 2020). Tour brokers assemble tour packages for groups and clubs (for example, a religious group, a group of pensioners, or a sports club). These tours are usually organised by a tour leader, who may charter a coach. The tour leader arranges details of the travel itinerary, including booking tickets to visitor attractions, making restaurant reservations, and hiring the services of a tourist guide. These intermediaries play an important role in transporting tourists to hotels and visitor attractions.

9.3.1.4 Air Brokers

An air broker (also known as a "consolidator") is a person or organisation that specialises in selling airline seats in bulk to other tour operators. Air brokers can also arrange charter planes or executive jets for individuals, groups, or people who need to transport people or goods by air.

9.3.1.5 Coach Operators

Coach operators range from small driver-owned companies to large operators that publish their own brochures offering various coaching holidays.

9.3.1.6 Retail Travel Agents

Travel agents are perhaps the best-known intermediaries. They act as the retailing arm of the tourism industry and are key intermediaries in the distribution chain (Holloway & Humphreys, 2020: 321). Essentially, they function as convenient outlets at which holidays and other travel-related offerings can be purchased. The first travel agency appeared in the mid-1700s; with the inception *Cox & Kings* in 1758. The company is still in business and is the longest-established travel agency in the world; it celebrated 250 years of being in business in 2018 (▶ www.coxandkings.com/about-us/index.shtml). Travel agents organise personal travel and accommodation for travellers. Travel agents generally act on behalf of principals (such as hotels, airline companies, railways, and cruise-lines) as well as other intermediaries (including package tour operators, DMCs, and tour brokers). Therefore, (unlike tour operators and principals) they do not purchase tourism offerings or hold stock of any travel product offerings. (This is sometimes referred to as consignment sales, which involve no actual transfer of ownership.) Only when a consumer has decided on a purchase do travel agents approach the principal on the consumer's behalf to make the purchase. This has an important implication for the business of tourism distribution, as travel agents do not carry any financial risk in terms of unsold stock or sales (unused bed spaces, empty seats on aircraft or unused places on tours) because they do not purchase offerings in advance.

This means that any financial risk lies with the principal or tour operator. Nonetheless, when there is high demand for a particular offering and supply is short, the travel agent can only make the sale if the tour operator provides sufficient availability. Thus, travel agents cannot adjust supply for popular destinations. They do, however, have to have a guarantee for the value of their air-ticket sales, which is often a substantial amount.

In many ways travel agents are similar to tour operators. The main difference is that a travel agent builds the business around their retail space. Tour operators are less likely to have retail space - as they sell via travel agents - they place more emphasis on selling tailor holiday packers to suit individual groups of customers.

The main task of a travel agency is to supply the public with travel services. Most travel agents handle some leisure and some corporate travel. Besides their main role of selling holidays and business travel, travel agents act as a source of information and advice on travel services. For example, they offer advice on visa applications (nowadays, visa procedures and applications are outsourced to companies appointed by consulates in order to facilitate the process), make reservations for visitor attractions and entertainment venues, and plan itineraries (see ▶ Industry Insight 9.3). Many full-service travel agents have evolved into more specialised holiday shops, which are one-stop travel shops where consumers can purchase a variety of travel-related products and services ranging from selling travel insurance, coffee, and luggage to exchanging money and arranging visas. Customers pay an additional fee for some of these value-added services.

■ **Characteristics of Travel Agents**
Most travel agents charge a service (or "management") fee (built into the cost price). Some travel agents charge a percentage while others charge a flat fee. A travel agency company, for example, may charge a standard fee of £10 (€12) for a domestic holiday booking and £15 (€18) for international travel. However, the fee is only payable if the client actually buys from

the agent. Some travel agencies charge for giving information and charge for brochures (usually refunding when a booking is made). Travel agencies earn their income mainly from the commission that they receive from each sale involving principals, tour operators and other intermediaries. Up until about fifteen years ago, commission from airlines was the main source of income for travel agents, but only a few airlines continue to pay commission.

Industry Insight 9.3

Southall Travel Ltd

Southall Travel is a privately-owned UK-based travel agency located in the Municipal Borough of Southall, Middlesex. The company is part of Southall Travel Group and operates both physical retail outlets and online booking. Formed in 1984, Southall Travel Ltd. has over 40 years' experience in the air travel business. The company provides air booking services, hotels, and package deals to clients throughout the UK. Southall Travel Ltd. has an ever-increasing network of customers in the entire UK including individual travellers, small, and medium enterprises as well as major businesses. The company's high degree of customer orientation is the key for their exponential growth in the past. The company arranges airline reservations, hotel bookings, visa services, car rentals, and holiday package deals. Efficient and knowledgeable travel consultants are available 24 hours-a-day, 7 days-a-week to help clients with planning and scheduling of their travel.

Source: ► http://www.southalltravel.co.uk / ► www.holidayhypermarket.co.uk/operators

---

❓ Browse this website to view Virgin Atlantic's Fares & Ticketing courses: ► www.gsmlondon.ac.uk/professional/travel-and-tourism/virgin-atlantic-fares-and-ticketing

Quality customer service (QCS) is paramount if an agency is to succeed in the competitive retail travel business. Travel agents are expected to be on call 24/7 in order to make last-minute changes to itineraries in response to delayed flights, airlines strikes, or natural disasters (for example, severe weather conditions). QCS ensures that the needs and wants of an agency's customers are satisfied, helps gain repeat business, and gives the agency a competitive advantage. Travel agency managers need good interpersonal skills to be able to manage a team of people as well as the technical skills required for financial management of accounts and cash flows, the invoicing of customers, and the control and running of a business. Most travel agencies have an online presence – these are known as "hybrid" agencies – offering both online and brick-and-mortar retail stores; OTAs, however, generally do not have a so-called "bricks-and-mortar" presence.

Travel agencies have responded to technological advances such as the internet as well as to adjustments to earning levels (caused by a reduction in commission rates) by offering value-added services (or "add-ons"), charging fees for various professional services (itinerary planning, for example), and providing QCS. In essence, travel agents are becoming agents for the traveller instead of for the tour operator or principal.

There are three several ways of categorising travel agencies: multiples, miniples, and independent agencies, discussed below.

▪▪ Multiples

Multiple travel agencies are private companies that usually have a presence on the main high street of all of a country's major cities and most large towns. Many of these, for example, *American Express* (USA), *The Flight Centre* (Australia), *Going Places* (UK), *TUI Holiday Store* (Europe) (see ◘ Image 9.2), ► Yatra.com (India) are household names in the international tourism industry. Multiples comprises a number of national chains, often part of large (or parent) organisations.

9

■ **Image 9.2**   A TUI high street/shopping mall store. (Source: TUI)

Airtours, for example, are owned by *Thomas Cook* (now *Hays Travel*), while *Student Flights is* part of the *Flight Centre Limited* group. These types of agencies deal with high volumes of clients and are equipped to sell all types of leisure and business travel to individuals or groups. As with tour operators. Some multiple travel agencies such as *Student Universe and Trailfinders cater* specifically to the Higher Education (HE) student market and list exclusive airfare deals and travel products. *STA Travel*, a travel agency specialising in student travel since 1971, ceased trading in August 2020 due to the coronavirus pandemic.

■■ Miniples

Miniple travel agencies have a number of branches located in particular parts of a district or area, meeting a regional demand. For example, *Althams Travel* (established in 1874) has most of its branches in Lancashire in the North West of the UK. Miniples do not benefit from economies of scale to the same extent as multiple travel agents, but they are able to build close relationships with business and leisure tourists. However, their success often makes them prime targets for takeovers, mergers, or acquisitions by the multiple travel agencies.

■■ Independents

Most independent travel agencies are small, family-run businesses. The owner usually acts as manager and employs two or three members of staff. The independent travel agency market in many countries is extremely competitive, and thus is making increasing use of marketing tools and modes of distribution to maintain its presence. Some travel agents employ independent travel consultants (ITCs) who work from home while the head office plays a supportive role. Many are specialist agencies focussing on a specific market, destination, or activity, such as birding or golf. *Birdfinders,* for example, sells only specialist products to a niche market (avitourism) and is therefore a niche travel agency.

9.3.1.7 Online Travel Agents

Online travel agents (OTAs) are electronic retailers. They provide a convenient booking mechanism for consumers and are therefore an integral part of the distribution system for some tourism businesses, such as hotels (Pike, 2018: 13). OTAs conduct business via the internet and do not have any bricks-and-mortar presence (that is, stores or locations). One of the features of an OTA is that consumers often search online through hotel choices, and then visit the .com to book the reservation. It is for this reason that hotels and other travel companies aim to have a good presence in terms of photographs and descriptions on OTA sites (Kotler et al., 2017). Traditional travel agencies now have to compete with OTAs, such as *Travel Supermarket,* ▶ Yatra.com, ▶ Lastminute. com, ▶ Expedia.com (*Expedia* acquired *Trivago* in 2013), *Holiday Hypermarket, Travel Republic*, and *Travelocity.*

▶ Booking.com, ▶ Priceline.com, ▶ Agoda.com, ▶ Kayak.com, fare aggregator and travel metasearch engines where consumers can search for best prices for flights, hotel rooms, and holidays. These website platforms offer consumers the ability to choose between thousands of hotels from around the world. But contrary to popular belief, they do not always have the lowest prices available. In some cases, it may in fact be less expensive for consumers to telephone and e-mail directly to the hotel to make a booking. Some of the large OTAs enforce rate-parity clauses which ban hotels from offering cheaper rates anywhere else online (Hern, 2020). This, however, does not exclude consumers booking using e-mail, telephone, or walk-in visits.

According to the ABTA's Holiday Habits Report 2019 there has been a drop in the number of UK consumers using a PC to book a holiday from 92% to 85%. Tablet bookings have remained steady, being used by 23% of people. Mobile bookings, however, have seen a significant jump from 13% to 20%.

OTA: On the Beach

On the Beach is an online travel agency/retailer, which sells beach holidays to places including the Canaries, the Balearic Islands, the Algarve, Turkey, and Greece. The company is one of the UK's leading OTAs of beach holidays. From humble beginnings in 2004, as a start-up business in a terraced house in Macclesfield, England, to a listing on the London Stock Exchange (LSE) in 2015, the company sends over one million holidaymakers away on beach holidays each year.

▶ https://www.onthebeach.co.uk/about-us

9.3.1.8 General Sales Agents (GSAs)

GSAs are business to business (B2B) entities that represent the interests of a group of independent tourism businesses (such as an airline or hotel group) in a particular market (Pike, 2018: 216). The GSA acts as a local agent in a country in which the tourism product has no presence. An example is *Aviareps,* an international company with offices on every continent that acts as a local agent for a number of airlines and other tourism providers.

9.3.1.9 Alliances or Consortia

Tourism intermediaries and suppliers can also market themselves by becoming part of an alliance or consortium. An alliance is a partnership formed when two or more organisations combine resources and work together to achieve a common objective (Kogut, 1988). An example of this affiliation is the marketing consortium, which allows independent organisations to carry out mass marketing or compile a joint brochure *Indian Hotels Company Limited* (IHCL) *Taj Hotels* is an example of a hotel consortium operating, across South Asia, such as the *Taj Mahal Palace*, in Mumbai, India.

Organisations can combine their resources into a partnership in order to promote their respective tourism offerings. An example of this is the *BestCities Alliance*, a global convention bureau alliance that includes the cities Berlin, Cape Town, Chicago, Copenhagen, Dubai, Edinburgh, Houston, Melbourne, Singapore, and Vancouver. The alliance enables these cities to align international marketing campaigns and to share knowledge as well as to collaborate on information distribution, online campaigns, events, and travel trade shows.

Consortia are widely used in the marketing of visitor attractions, tour operators, travel agents, hotels (see ◘ Image 9.3), B&Bs, and destinations. For example, a marketer of a number of visitor attractions and tour destinations (such as a city walking tour, a trip to a museum, and a visit to an art gallery) can combine resources (also known as "clustering") to produce marketing collateral, such as a brochures and an online portal (website) and (see ▶ Industry Insight 9.5). Tour operator and travel agency consortia (for example *Carlson Wagonlit Travel* in the USA) enable a number of smaller businesses to join together to gain market share in a region, compete with major operators, and provide competitive rates. *&Beyond,* for example, is an upmarket tour operator consortium that organises conservation wildlife holidays in Africa, Asia, and South America.

The Vanilla Islands

The "Vanilla Islands" is an alliance of Mauritius, Reunion, Seychelles, Madagascar, and Comoros Island with the aim of boosting tourism to the islands of the Indian Ocean. The tourism sector, which is the backbone of the economies of most of these countries, is facing competition from emerging tourism products. In order to tackle this threat and to increase their attractiveness to tourists, the countries are working together on a shared marketing strategy and a common selling point to promote their different cultures. The Vanilla Islands Organisation's objective is to position the

Indian Ocean region as a quality world-class holiday destination that offers unparalleled diversity and one of the last frontiers of sustainable tourism.

Source: International Coalition of Tourism Partners. (2019). Vanilla Islands Organisation. [Online], Available: ▶ http://ictp.travel/vanilla-islands-organization/ Accessed 31 May 2019.

9.3.1.10 Franchises

Franchises are businesses in which a franchiser permits a franchisee the right to engage in selling, offering or distributing its offerings using its trademark, name and advertising. Typically, a firm must be large enough to offer management support, a good business concept and finance. Franchising has become popular in the tourism industry, particularly in the hotel sector. Some popular hotel franchises include *Best Western Hotels* and *Holiday Inn Hotels*. Examples of travel agency franchises that have proliferated throughout Europe and the USA include *Flight Centre* and *Travel Leaders* (USA). Likewise, in the car rental business *Thrifty Car Rentals* have global franchising operations as do *Costa Coffee* in the restaurant sector.

◻ **Image 9.3** The Red Carnation Hotel Collection – an example of a consortia

9.3.1.11 Sales Representatives

Sales representatives are hired by principals or intermediaries to develop existing business and to generate new business in a region or country. It is often more cost effective for a large tourism organisation to hire a sales representative than to use its own sales staff, especially when the market is overseas and there are cultural differences.

The main functions of sales representatives (also known as "contractors") are to call on and make deals with existing and potential contacts (such as hotels), advise and update travel agents about the services they offer, support them with merchandising material, and to provide their agents with suitable marketing collateral. (This is a similar arrangement to that of representatives of pharmaceutical companies who service medical doctors.) Multi-national companies such as *Kuoni Travel* has sales representatives who conduct business in the Maldives, Mexico, Dubai, Switzerland, and so on. Smaller travel companies such as *Bike Tours Portugal* have sales representatives in the UK, USA, and Canada. Sales representatives receive a commission on the bookings that they make.

9.3.1.12 Professional Conference Organisers

Professional conference organisers (PCOs) specialised companies that plan and co-ordinate external conferences on behalf of organisations. They are employed by corporations, associations, government agencies, educational institutions and large non-profit organisations. PCOs play an important role in the meetings industry. The term 'professional conference organiser' is used interchangeably with a range of other titles such as meeting planner, conference co-ordinator and meetings executive (see ▶ Industry Insight 9.6).

Events Plus: A One-Stop Service

Events Plus Egypt, a professional conference organiser (PCO) based in Cairo, Egypt, started operations in 2004. Events Plus Egypt (EPE)is a full-service events management company. It has the advantage that an in-house network of services, including public relations, advertising and design, investor relations and client services, is at its disposal. This sets the company apart in the marketplace. According to Omar Mohamed., manager of EPE, "The role of a professional conference organiser is to act as a conductor, bringing all the variety of services and suppliers to order. It is also to act as a conduit between the client and all the subcontractors involved with the conference." EPE offers a one-stop service that provides a very tailored and detailed offering for its clients. Omar says, "We take buying behaviour extremely seriously … we carry out market research to help us identify potential clients, specifically corporates, and to make sure that we know everything about a potential client's buying behaviour before we approach it to promote our services." Omar adds, "If our client's delegates play golf, we want to know whether they need to hire golf clubs and if so, should the golf clubs be right- or left-handed?"

9.3.1.13 Incentive Travel Planners

Incentive travel planners (ITPs) are specialised tour operators that primarily serve corporate clients. They arrange and put together tailor-made packages that include accommodation, meals, transportation, special functions, and tours (Holloway & Humphreys, 2020: 325). The packages that they assemble are given to certain of their clients' employees or dealers as a reward for outstanding sales or work performance. Romania's unique locations, (see ▶ Industry Insight 9.7) and the wide range of leisure activities on offer (i.e. adventure tourism, mountains, beaches, Dracula tours, and Gothic architecture) make it a leading player in the incentive travel market.

Industry Insight 9.7

Bucharest: One of the World's Top Ten Incentive Travel Destinations

Over the last decade, Romania's capital city Bucharest has become one of the most popular tourist destinations for executives. According to the International Congress and Convention Association (ICCA), in 2017 Bucharest was placed among the world's top ten incentive travel destinations.. The largest of the Balkan countries, Romania offers outstanding mountain scenery and a coastline on the Black Sea. The capital, Bucharest, is known as "Little

◘ **Image 9.4** Bucharest – a popular incentive travel destination. (Source: Unsplash)

Paris", featuring beautiful architecture and the second largest building in the world – the Palace of Parliament – with over 3000 rooms. The Balkan City is competing against the likes of New York, Dubai, and Barcelona. Businesses in the UK, the USA, Germany, France, and Italy are finding that Bucharest and a Romanian

holiday with mountains and beaches are terrific ways of motivating and rewarding their best executives (◻ Image 9.4).

Source: ▶ http://incentiveandmotivation. com/the-worlds-10-best-incentive-travel-ideas-for-2016-incentive-motivation/

9.3.1.14 Visitor Information Centres

Local tourism offices (or organisations), visitor (or tourist) information centres representing villages, towns and cities are often the first contact or point of entry for domestic and international tourists seeking accommodation, transport, and tours in these regions. The purpose of a visitor information centre (VIC) or a local tourism office is to provide tourist information that is accessible to all. These organisations have the responsibility of selling their destinations' unique selling propositions or points (USPs). VICs are intermediaries between tourism suppliers or destinations and tourists. Besides handling visitor enquiries, local tourism organisations and visitor information centres also make bookings on behalf of visitors. Communication facilities such as multi-media kiosks (discussed in the next section) are often available at these information centres. Visitor information centres are increasingly under threat from technology as more and more tourists make use of smartphones and tablets to access travel information.

9.3.1.15 Destination Marketing Organisations and Convention and Visitor Bureaux

The term "destination marketing organisation (DMO)" is generally used to refer to a convention and visitor bureau (CVB), a provincial office, a regional tourism organisation, a local tourism organisation or a national tourism organisation. Most DMOs are information brokers in the tourism distribution system (Pike, 2018: 214). ▶ Chapter 14 discusses DMOs in more detail.

Convention and visitor bureaux (CVBs) are located in cities that have the appropriate meetings products and services to meet the demands of the meetings industry. The prime function of these bureaux is to promote these cities to the national and international tourism industry. CVBs play an important role in positioning the destination in the tourism industry as a conference and meetings destination. Meetings and events provide important economic benefits to the host destination, city or country.

9.3.1.16 Accommodation Booking Agents

Accommodation (hotel) booking agencies specialise in procuring accommodation facilities and services on behalf of their clients. They range from large organisations run by global hotel brands, to independent properties. Perhaps the best-known accommodation booking agency is Airbnb whose members can use the service to arrange or offer lodging, primarily homestays, or tourism experiences. The broker, which is considered part of the "sharing economy" offers you someone's home to stay in, instead of a hotel. *Airbnb* has caused controversy in many destinations around the world because it is perceived as taking business away from hotels and traditional accommodation providers (Zervas et al., 2017).

9.3.1.17 Tour Guides

Tour (or tourist) guides and couriers travel with tourists, working to ensure travellers' needs are met and that their visit runs smoothly. Their work often involves researching on behalf of the traveller, making travel arrangements for accommodation and sightseeing, and organising excursions. Many tour guides and travel couriers are freelance, and work for tour operators.

9.3.1.18 Concierge Services

Most upmarket hotels, resorts, and cruise liners offer a concierge service. A concierge essentially provides information and bookings for local services (Pike, 2018: 214). In the hospitality industry, a concierge is a person who is employed in a hotel or resort to help guests by performing various tasks, such as booking theatre tickets, making restaurant reservations, booking hotels, arranging for spa services, recommending nightlife hot spots, booking transportation (including taxis, limousines, airplanes, and boats), and co-ordinating porter service (luggage assistance requests). Concierges are usually well-informed on where to go and what to do in the local area.

9.3.2 Direct Marketing Channels

Having considered the various indirect marketing channels, we will now consider direct marketing channels. Direct booking systems are growing rapidly with developments in digital technology, enabling consumers to book a tourism product from the comfort of their homes, workplaces, or while on the move (accessing the internet via a mobile phone or iPad/tablet). In addition, technology provides consumers with all of the information that they need to make a decision about travel.

There has been a surge in the provision of information and booking using online communication systems over the last decade. The same technology that renewed the role of the travel agency is now available to the consumer (see ▶ Industry Insight 9.8). Digital technology – in particular the internet and call centres – has been the driving force behind disintermediation, a term that refers to the way in which consumers bypass traditional intermediaries to deal directly with principals and suppliers of tourism offerings (Middleton & Clarke, 2001: 293). Disintermediation can provide market access for sole traders and tourism SMEs in developed and developing countries. For example, tourism and hospitality brands such as *Uber*, the global taxi firm where customers can request a taxi using an app on their mobile phones, has provided opportunities for people with cars to earn income by providing personalised transport at prices lower than established operators. The likes of *Uber* and *Airbnb* are considered part of the "shared economy" and have changed the rules of the competitive environment in the sector where existing companies are bypassed entirely through the use of apps and mobile technology.

Industry Insight 9.8

Travel Agents Versus the Internet
With the arrival of the internet in the early 1990s, travel changed for good. Many people were concerned that the high street travel agency would become obsolete. However, traditional travel agencies are fighting back against the internet. Why? Firstly, consumers are becoming confused by the overwhelming amount of information that is available on the internet. There are more than 50 million holidays available on offer on the internet. Type in the word "travel" and you'll get five billon responses on Google! Secondly, a travel agent provides travellers with a personal touch (especially if there are travel disruptions) not afforded by the internet. Thirdly, a travel consultant at a travel agency can give personal knowledge and experience. That said, the online travel market is still expected to grow. Booking travel via the internet is convenient. Consumers can book in the comfort of their own homes or on the move via their mobile phones. In addition, consumers booking travel online can shop around and know what they are paying for.

Source: Adapted from information on the BBC programme *The Travel Show*, 13 October 2018.

Direct marketing channels include information and communications technology and the internet, global distribution systems, electronic point-of-sale systems, multi-media kiosks, virtual reality (VR), and call centres.

> According to research carried out by ▶ compareholidays.com 80% of tourists book their holidays online (▶ www.travelweekly.co.uk/articles/41280/80-booking-holidays-online-finds-study).

9.3.2.1 Digital Technology

Travel distribution has been affected most by digital technology. Internet-based (online) booking systems are increasingly being used, and in doing so, are eliminating traditional travel agents from the distribution chain (Buhalis & Jun, 2011). It is becoming ever easier for leisure tourists to search for travel information and to make their own bookings, buying individual elements of the holiday package from different providers. In addition, the growth of OTAs, such as ▶ Expedia.com and *Travelocity*, has decimated traditional "bricks and mortar" travel agents and as such they are rethinking their roles as "specialist" travel agents (Cooper & Hall, 2019: 116). Nevertheless, tour operators appear to have benefited; internet technology has enabled tour operators to provide flexible packages ("dynamic packaging" – see ▶ Chap. 8) and deal directly with consumers (travel agents again be at a loss).

The use of mobile devices used to access travel websites has proliferated. A mobile phone, which is essentially a "smart computer", is a single point of contact for people (Wang, Park, & Fesenmaier, 2012). Mobile phones and other mobile devices, such as tablets and iPads enable consumers to search for travel information, shop around for travel services, and access travel apps (24 hours a day, 7 days a week while on the move or in the comfort of their own homes.).

Consumers, travel agents, or tour operators can use a fare aggregator or meta-search engines, such as Google Flights, Google Hotel Finder, TravelFusion, ▶ Booking.com, or ▶ Kayak.com. These tools utilise powerful search functions and redirect users to airline, cruise liner, hotel, car rental websites, or OTAs for the final purchase of an e-ticket. For instance, Google's Hotel Finder allows users to find hotel prices with Google. However, it does not offer to book hotels; it merely compares rates. Unlike global distribution systems (GDSs), meta-search engines have no capacity to analyse the information, but merely find it and make it available to the user. Aggregators generate revenues through advertising and charging OTAs for referring clients. The difference between a 'fare aggregator' and 'metasearch engine' is unclear, although different terms may imply different levels of cooperation between the companies involved. ▶ Orbitz.com is a travel fare aggregator website, and travel metasearch engine. The website is owned by *Orbitz Worldwide, Inc.*, a subsidiary of Expedia Inc.

Airlines, especially low-cost carriers, tour operators, travel agents, and hotels (particularly small hotels) are controlling distribution and driving down costs by using the internet. Even companies that are not typically associated with tourism or travel distribution such as supermarkets, retail shops (e.g. in the UK: *WH Smiths*), post offices, petrol stations, universities, and car rental companies. Are offering travel bookings. ▶ Chapter 12 examines the role of the internet in tourism marketing in more detail.

New innovations offering "seamless" travel arrangements as practical solutions to travellers include artificial intelligence (AI), virtual reality (VR), and speech recognition technologies Examples of these include keyless hotel room-access using a mobile phone, a robotic multi-lingual concierge, real-time luggage tracking through a mobile app, and having a single app for all travel planning, booking, and travel needs. Research conducted by the travel fare aggregator ▶ Booking.com shows that almost a third (31%) of global travellers like the idea of a "virtual travel agent" in their homes (similar to virtual assistants, such as "Siri" and "Alexa"), using voice-activated assistants to answer travel queries, and 20% of "new travellers" want to see technology such as augmented reality (AR) helping them to familiarise themselves with a holiday before they arrive at the destination (Booking.com, 2019).

Global Distribution Systems

While it is easy enough for a consumer to book a flight and/or accommodation via the internet, travel agents have access to global distributions systems (GDSs) that give them real-time access to a vast range of travel products and services, including flights, accommodation, and car rental services. It is impossible for the end-consumer to replicate this usability on the internet because these global distributions systems utilise highly sophisticated software to access and analyse all available flights in order to build an itinerary to specified criteria, for example, by price, by routing or by preferred airlines. When a booking has been made through a global distribution system, payment is made for the booking through a billing and settlement plan (BSP). A BSP is a unified worldwide system that facilitates billing and payments between travel agents and approximately 400 IATA-affiliated airlines (IATA, 2018). The three biggest global distributions systems are *Amadeus, Sabre,* and *Travelport.* These systems are dominated by American and European airlines, since they developed the systems.

Electronic Point-of-Sale Systems

Electronic point-of-sale (EPOS) systems allow consumers to buy tickets directly at supermarkets, petrol stations, shops, and travel departure points such as airports and train stations. In most countries, self-ticketing machines can be found at airports and train stations, enabling consumers to avoid long queues. Electronic point-of-sale systems are particularly convenient for business people who are frequent travellers and need to purchase tickets at the last moment (see  Image 9.5).

Multi-media Kiosks

Multi-media kiosks provide educational information, information directories, and point-of-sale systems. Multi-media kiosks are alternatives to traditional printed travel literature and brochures, which take up a lot of space, and can quickly become disorganised and out of date (Fesenmaier & Kingsley, 2010). Kiosks provide an interactive guide to a variety of tourist attractions, activities, and offerings and promote tourist destinations.

Call Centres

Call centres are sophisticated telephone information and booking companies. The purpose of a call centre is to establish a single point of contact for people wanting to communicate with an organisation. In recent years, call centres have been one of the fastest-growing industries in countries such as the Philippines (coined 'the call centre capital of the world') and India. They enable larger tourism organisations such as airlines and budget hotel chains to process consumers' telephone calls more efficiently. Call centres were developed

■ **Image 9.5**   An electronic point-of-sale system (EPOS) in action. (Source: Unsplash)

to cater for trends such as increased usage of telephones, demand for services 24 hours-a-day, and expansion of the use of mobile phones. Online booking site *SafariNow*, which has over 100 staff, utilises call centre agents. However, call centres are becoming increasingly automated, which may well result in fewer jobs in the sector, particularly in countries such as India and the Philippines (The Economist, 2016).

- Online Video Conferencing

Virtual conferencing is now widely available and has significantly increased in popularity over the last few years largely due to the outbreak of the coronavirus pandemic in 2020. It is really an extension of the telephone system, with video cameras and television screens linked by high-speed telecommunication lines to enable users to hold discussions. Speed is a key factor in video conferencing (VC); A meeting may be conducted without the need for travel. Participants in the average virtual conference meeting (also known as "virtual meetings") need to invest only 4 hours of their time. Videoconferencing provides cost savings for firms. Costs are saved on flights, hotel rooms, car-rental services, food, and employee time. An example is Zoom Meetings, a video-conferencing company based in the USA that specialises in video and audio conferencing, webinars and wireless communication across electronic devices and room systems. Microsoft Team, Slack, and GoToMeeting are other video-conferencing offerings.

❓ What do you think are the advantages of travelling to meet someone face-to-face rather than talking by video conference?

- Virtual Reality

Virtual reality (VR) is defined as the use of a computer-generated three-dimensional environment that allows the user to experience a virtual world, resulting in real-time simulation of one or more of the user's five senses (Guttentag, 2009: 638). Nowadays, many tourism organisations and products make use of VR or VR-type technologies to attract tourists. For instance, consumers can find hotels, DMOs, theme parks, museums, national parks, wine farms, and other destinations offering 360-degree virtual tours on the internet. VR allows the user to experience a situation visually and audibly. (Flight simulators are examples of more advanced and interactive forms of virtual reality.) With this type of VR programme, the user wears a visual headset with earphones (see ◪ Image 9.6). The machine provides a simulated travel experience. Although it is a very recent technological addition, VR may affect demand for tourism destinations in the future (see ▶ Industry Insight 9.9).

VR can give users a taste of what a particular resort is like, including the weather, the beach, and so on. It also allows consumers to go to places that are inaccessible (such as the planet Mars) or even to places that do not exist except in the imagination. The internet provides opportunities for browsers to take virtual tours of key visitor attractions around the world. For example, on the Open Heritage website, it is possible to view detailed 3D models of unique heritage sites such as Pompeii in Naples, Italy, the Brandenburg Gate in Berlin, Germany, and a WWI one battlefield at Flanders Field in Belgium using a web browser and VR interface developed by Google.

Industry Insight 9.9

VR at the National Archaeological Museum, Madrid, Spain

In 2017, the National Archaeological Museum (Spanish: Museo Arqueológico Nacional) in Madrid, Spain teamed-up with the technology company Samsung to transform cultural experiences inside and outside the Museum by using the latest mobile devices and VR technology to enrich visitor experiences. The "Living in..." (in Spanish: Vivir en...) offers visitors a virtual journey through the history of Spain. The collaboration between the National Archaeological Museum and Samsung included the installation of a large video wall in the Museum's main lobby, made up of 12 LED panels with Samsung's most advanced visual display technology. In addition, Samsung supplied 80 new tablets to the Museum for use as multimedia guides for visitors. The VR experience includes five scenarios of the History of Spain (Prehistory, Protohistory, Roman Hispania, the Middle Ages, and the Modern Age), which form part of the permanent exhibition. A virtual guide narrates visitors through time; visitors pass through spaces such as the caves inhabited in the Palaeolithic period, the streets of a Celtiberian village, the forum of a city in Roman Hispania, a market from the age of the caliphates, and a home from the Golden Age. The virtual journey has been designed with the scientific input from the Museum's history and archaeology team. To ensure visitors enjoy the experience to the fullest and discover more about the past, each of the Museum's rooms corresponding to each historical scenario has a station with Gear VR goggles, Samsung Galaxy S9 smartphones, and headphones. The VR experience in the National Archaeological Museum was designed by Magoga Piñas Azpitarte, a specialist in historical digital recreation and animation. Magoga, who is the Museum's Director of the 'Living in...' has worked on major exhibitions, audio-visual productions and film projects such as the HBO's Game of Thrones, National Geographic's Cosmos, a Spacetime Odyssey, and Alejandro Amenábar's Ágora. In 2018, a multi-platform virtual visit, accessible via smartphone, tablet, or laptop was devised allowing users from outside the Museum – anywhere around the world – to visit the rooms of the National Archaeological Museum remotely was launched.

- **Augmented Reality**

Augmented reality (AR) allows travellers to experience three-dimensional models of destinations and 'meet' tour guides. AR also helps with navigation in unfamiliar places and destinations. Details about local destinations and visitor attractions can also be displayed as a tourist points his/her smartphone at them,

□ **Image 9.6**   VR being used at a travel trade show. (Source: SA Tourism)

providing information at the exact time that it is most relevant. Over recent times, AR has become increasingly popular within the travel industry. This is primarily because it enables hotels and other tourism and hospitality businesses to enhance the physical environments that they are trying to encourage customers to visit, including local attractions and hotel rooms. Mobile augmented reality (MAR) can help tourists in the process of obtaining such information in a simplified way. MobiAR is an Android service platform for tourist information based on AR, which allows users to browse information and multimedia content about a city through their own mobile devices (Marimon, 2010).

9.3.3 Selecting Marketing Intermediaries

Tourism marketers must choose the intermediary that is most effective and appropriate in reaching their target markets. They must take care when selecting intermediaries. Since they make direct contact with consumers, intermediaries can influence levels of quality and satisfaction. The choice of intermediary also depends on the size and type of the organisation. For example, a large organisation such as *Emirates Airline* uses several distribution channels to reach different target markets. A small business, such as a B&B, in contrast, deals directly with consumers, many of whom will purchase at the location of the business. (These consumers are known as "walk-ins".) Three factors that may influence a tourism and hospitality organisation's intermediary selec-tion are cost, control and level of service, and efficiency (Holloway & Humphreys, 2020: 240).

Summary

Distribution channels (the place component of the marketing mix) deal primarily with two main issues: accessibility and availability. The channels of distribution in the tourism industry are vastly different from the ones used by all other industries. The consumer has to be enticed or attracted to travel to the offering. In this chapter, we examined the role of distribution in tourism, and then discussed the concepts of commission and horizontal integration, two trends that have impacted the sector in the last couple of decades. We then discussed the functions of tour operators, travel agents, online retailers, and other marketing intermediaries We also looked at how the recent pace of technological advances has affected the role of intermediaries in tourism. The growing importance of digital technology in giving participants in the tourism industry a competitive advantage is clear, although the human interface will always remain a crucial element. Technological developments have revolutionised the travel trade affecting all tourism enterprises, from small to medium enterprises (SMEs) to multinational corporations (MNCs). Technology, in particular the internet and online booking, has created a digital form of distribution for SMEs bound by limited resources for reaching customers. Product distribution and markets no longer have to be dictated by location. However, this same digital technology can pose a threat to traditional travel agents and other traditional intermediaries, since consumers can book flights and hotel rooms directly at a lower cost (in most cases) than they would pay through an intermediary. In addition, there are concerns over the security of financial data and personal identity as online fraud increases and consumers lose confidence in online business transactions (Mills & Law, 2015).

For many tourism businesses, distribution is an important facet of strategic management. Tourism marketers need to be familiar with the diversity of distribution channels now available as well as how best to manage them.

? Review Questions

1. Explain why place (distribution) is such a key component of the tourism and hospitality marketing mix.
2. Briefly explain Why might a supplier or principal choose to sell directly to the consumer?
3. Explain the major differences between a distribution channel for a manufacturing company and a distribution channel for a tourism organisation.
4. Why do companies use marketing intermediaries?
5. Discuss how you think technology will affect distribution channels in the tourism industry over the next five years.
6. What is the difference between a tour operator and a travel agent?
7. Can a business have too many distribution channel members?
8. Select two channels of distribution for these tourism principals:
   - A low-cost airline
   - A hotel group
   - A mass-market tour operator.
   Compare the two distribution channels and explain why they are best suited for these companies.
9. Explain the advantages and disadvantages of tourism companies forming an alliance.
10. Go online to find a tourism or hospitality company that allows consumers to make a booking directly through its website. Is the design of the site effective? What market segment is the company and this functionality targeting?

In-depth Case Study 9: Distribution Strategies: Reality Tours & Travel, Mumbai, India: A Slum Tour Operator

Objectives

- To understand the role of intermediaries in tourism
- To apply the principles of distribution to the case study.

If you visit Dharavi slum, as many tourists do, the weather may be hot and the locals friendly, but there will be no golden sands, museums, or luxury hotels. So why does Dharavi, a locality in Maharashtra, India, attract such high numbers of inquisitive tourists? It is because Dharavi, the second-largest slum in the continent of Asia, and the third-largest slum in the world, is a renowned location which forms part of the growing tourism sector known as 'slum tourism', which falls under the broader umbrella concept of 'dark tourism'.

It is useful to make the distinction between slum tourism and dark tourism. Dark tourism grew from the 1990s and is so named as it involves travel to sites of death, disaster, and the seemingly macabre (Lennon & Foley, 2000). Examples of dark tourism sites include Robben Island in Cape Town, Auschwitz in Poland, the Killing Fields of Cambodia, and the Fukushima in Japan. Slum tourism is a type of tourism that involves tourists visiting impoverished areas. It entails the arrangement of tours in poor areas which do not have death as its main theme. Indeed, slum tourism can be a richly rewarding experience as it can offer an exchange of culture with local inhabitants and a more real, authentic representation of society and the host people.

These tours combine history with social issues and are usually frequented by Western tourists. The concept of 'slum tourism' was first coined back in the Victorian era (the 1880s), when wealthy UK citizens visited poor areas in London's East End to observe the conditions in which poor people lived. Contemporary slum tourism emerged in developing countries in the 1990s in the inner-city slums of India, the crowded favelas of Brazil, and the bustling townships of South Africa. The international tourism industry is today embracing the concept; other countries where slum tourism is

9

on the rise are Kenya, Egypt, Mexico, and Indonesia (George & Booyens, 2014).

Slums generally have negative connotations and are typically characterised by urban decay, fed by high rates of poverty, illiteracy, ill-health, and unemployment. With a population of over one million citizens in an area of just over 2.1 square kilometres, Dharavi is one of the densest areas in the world. It is a city within a city; one unending stretch of narrow lanes, open sewers, and cramped huts. Dharavi has a large number of thriving small-scale industries that produce embroidered garments, export quality leather goods, pottery and plastic. It is essentially a recycling centre for the Maharashtra state, where literally anything can and is recycled from car batteries and computer parts to plastic bags and wire hangers. The state government has plans to redevelop Dharavi and transform it into a modern township, complete with proper housing, and shopping complexes, hospitals, and schools.

Due to changing social conditions and the growth of international tourism, slum tourism has become increasingly popular and organised tours have generally replaced the initial gang-run provision of unlicensed visits. A slum tourist is often seeking an emotional response by experiencing 'reality' and a taste of others' lives, which may tie in with ethical sentiments. Slum tours in Dharavi are provided by a handful of tour operators; the longest-running is Reality Tours and Travel (RTT): a company based in Dharavi and set-up in 2005 with the twin objectives of using walking tours to challenge the negative stereotypes about slum life, and at the same time, raise funds for local community projects. The 'Dharavi Tour' and the concept behind Reality Tours was originally inspired by the favela tours in Rio de Janeiro, Brazil.

RTT's mission statement is "to provide authentic and thought-provoking local experiences through our tours and to use the profits to create change in our communities". RTT's modus operandi is that tourism can and should be a force for local development. RTT is a social enterprise with a profit-sharing model which funds its sister non-governmental organisation (NGO): Reality Gives. Eighty-percent of RTT's post-tax profits and 100 per cent of merchandise sales go to Reality Gives, who in turn, provide quality educational programs for young people from under resourced communities.

The walking tours of Dharavi were launched in 2005/6 and quickly grew from 367 visitors to 677 the following year. In 2017, RTT escorted over 16,000 tourists on its slum tours and over 4000 tourists on its city tours. On RTT's signature Dharavi Tours, visitors see on foot why Dharavi is at the heart of small scale industrial landscape in Mumbai. The educational walking tours offer the opportunity to visit a wide range of business activities including recycling, pottery-making, embroidery, bakery, soap factory, leather tanning, and poppadom-making. Dharavi boasts two community centres and a school, which RTT supports with teachers, materials, and a syllabus. Other tours of Mumbai have been added in recent years including bicycle, car (with a stop off at Dhobi Ghat, the largest open-air laundry in the world), street food, night, and family lunch tours. The company has also expanded into Delhi offering both slum and city tours.

Initially, a distribution strategy was difficult for RTT as hotels and backpacker hostels wouldn't work with them for fear of endorsing slum tours and tarnishing their reputation. RTT'S big break came when it was included in the Lonely Planet India 2007 travel guidebook (regarded by many as 'the travellers' bible'). A decade later, business has moved on for RTT. Today, it is internationally recognised for its positive social and economic impact it provides as an 'ethical slum tour operator'. Domestic and international agents and operators feature and promote its tours, including industry leaders such as tour operator Trailfinders in the UK. RTT has been invited to speak at the annual World Travel Market (WTM) in London, where they were awarded the WTM Community Award in 2015. RTT entertains multinational corporations such as Facebook and Google who have visited

Dharavi to seek inspiration by understanding this unique community.

Today, RTT employs 19 tour guides in Mumbai and six in Delhi and has an office team of around 10 in management, sales, accounts and marketing. It promotes itself via tour operators, sales agents, hotels, and backpacker hostels. RTT has since expanded its offerings and now promotes tour packages around Rajasthan, South India, and Delhi.

■ **Image 9.7** Reality Tours and Travel. (Source: Joseph Bird, former CEO, Reality Tours and Travel)

In a chaotic, challenging location and in a busy, competitive marketplace, RTT stands out by providing responsible, authentic and fun tours. RTT is a shining example of mining the curiosity of certain tourists to visit a challenging environment and transforming it into a meaningful and beneficial experience for all involved (◘ Images 9.7 and 9.8).

Source: Interview with Krishna Pujari, Founder, RTT

Website: ► http://realitytoursandtravel.com/about.php

Questions and Activities

1. What type of tour operator is RTT?
2. Do you think slum tourism is ethical? Is it a force for the good? Does it have a beneficial impact on the host destination? Discuss.
3. Why is quality customer service so important in the retail travel agency sector? What are the benefits of quality customer service to retail travel agents?
4. Visit RTT's website (► http://realitytoursandtravel.com/about.php) and compare it with the websites of other dark tourism websites such as

◘ **Image 9.8**   A Reality Tours and Travel tour of Dharavi in Mumbai. (Source: Joseph Bird, former CEO, Reality Tours and Travel)

References

Baines, P., Fill, C., Rosengren, S., Rossenetti, P., & Antonetti, P. (2019). *Marketing* (5th ed.). Oxford: Oxford University Press.

Beaver, A. (2012). *Oxford dictionary of travel and tourism*. Oxford: Oxford University Press.

Booking.com. (2019). *Booking.com reveals eight travel predictions for 2019*. Retrieved from https://globalnews.booking.com/bookingcom-reveals-8-travel-predictions-for-2019/. Accessed 21 May 2019.

Borden, N. (1964). The concept of the marketing mix. *Journal of Advertising Research, 4*, 2–7.

Buhalis, D., & Jun, X. (2011). *E-tourism: Contemporary tourism reviews*. Oxford: Goodfellow Publishers.

Calder, S. (2019). Trivago, Expedia, and other hotel booking websites agree to clean up their act. Retrieved from *Independent*. https://www.independent.co.uk/travel/news-and-advice/booking-com-expedia-trivago-cma-hotel-booking-websites-discount-claims-hidden-charges-a8765241.html. Accessed 21 May 2019.

Cooper, C. (2016). *Essentials of tourism* (2nd ed.). London: Pearson.

Cooper, C., & Hall, M. (2019). *Contemporary tourism: An international approach* (4th ed.). London: Goodfellow.

Dwyer, L., & Forsyth, P. (Eds.). (2006). *International handbook on the economics of tourism*. Cheltenham: Edward Elgar.

Evans, N., Campbell, D., & Stonehouse, G. (2003). *Strategic management for travel and tourism* (2nd ed.). Oxford: Butterworth-Heinemann.

Fesenmaier, D., & Kingsley, I. (2010). Travel information kiosks: An emerging communications channel for the tourism industry. *Journal of Travel & Tourism Marketing, 4*(1), 57–70.

George, R., & Booyens, I. (2014). Township tourism demand: Tourists' perceptions of safety and security. *Urban Forum, 2*(3), 49.

Guttentag, D. A. (2009). Virtual reality: Application and implications for tourism. *Tourism Management, 31*(5).

Hern, A. (2020, March 5). Hotel guests often pay less if they book by phone rather than online. *The Guardian*, Thursday, p. 5.

Holloway, J. C., & Humphreys, C. (2020). *The business of tourism* (11th ed.). Harlow, Essex: Prentice-Hall.

Kogut, B. (1988). Joint ventures: Theoretical and empirical perspectives. *Strategic Management Journal, 9*.

Kotler, P., Bowen, J., Makens, J., & Baloglu, S. (2017). *Marketing for hospitality and tourism* (7th ed.). Upper Saddle River, NJ: Prentice Hall.

Kotler, P., Keller, K., Brady, M., Goodman, M., & Hansen, T. (2016). *Marketing management* (4th ed.). Englewood Cliffs, NJ: Prentice-Hall.

Lafferty, G., & van Fossen, A. (2012). Integrating the tourism industry: Problems and strategies. *Tourism Management, 22*(1), 11–19.

Lennon, J., & Foley, M. (2000). *Dark tourism: The attraction of death and disaster*. London: Continuum.

Marimon, D., Sarasua, C., Alvarez, R., Montesa, J., Adameh, T., Romero, T., Ortega, M. & Gasco, P. (2010, January). Tourist experiences through mobile augmented reality. Journal of *Information and Communication Technologies in Tourism*. pp. 1–6

Middleton, V. T. C., & Clarke, J. (2001). *Marketing in travel and tourism* (3rd ed.). Oxford: Butterworth-Heinemann.

Mills, J., & Law, R. (2015). *Handbook of marketing in travel and tourism, consumer behaviour, tourism, and the internet*. London: Routledge.

Page, S., & Connell, J. (2020). *Tourism: A modern synthesis* (5th ed.). Andover: Cengage.

Page, S. J. (2019). *Tourism management* (6th ed.p. 118). Oxford: Routledge.

Pike, S. (2016). *Destination marketing essentials* (2nd ed.). Oxford: Routledge.

Pike, S. (2018). *Tourism marketing for small businesses*. Oxford: Goodfellow Publishers.

Rathmell, J. M. (1974). *Marketing in the service sector*. Cambridge, MA: Winthrop.

Teltzrow, M., Berendt, B. & Günther, O. (2003). *Consumer behaviour at multi-channel retailers*. Proceedings of the 4th IBM eBusiness conference, University of Surrey, School of Management, UK.

Tropical Incentives DMC. (2018). *What is a DMC?* Retrieved from http://www.tropicalincentives.com/what-is-a-dmc. Accessed 17 July 2018.

Wang, D., Park, S., & Fesenmaier, D. (2012). The role of smartphones in mediating the touristic experience. *Journal of the Academy of Marketing Science, 44*(1), 5–23.

Zervas, G., Proserpio, D., & Byers, J.W. (2017). The rise of the sharing economy: Estimating the impact of Airbnb on the hotel industry. *Journal of Marketing Research, 54*(5), 687–705.

Further Reading

Buhalis, D., & Jun, X. (2011). *E-tourism: Contemporary tourism reviews*. Oxford: Goodfellow Publishers.

Cooper, C. (2016). *Essentials of tourism* (2nd ed.). London: Pearson.

Promoting and Advertising Tourism and Hospitality Products

Contents

Electronic Supplementary Material The online version of this chapter (https://doi.org/10.1007/978-3-030-64111-5_10) contains supplementary material, which is available to authorized users.

10

Purpose

This chapter will give you an understanding of the communication methods that are used to promote tourism and hospitality offerings.

🏠 Learning Goals

After reading this chapter, you should be able to:

- Explain the relationship between promotion and marketing communications
- Understand the role of promotion within tourism and hospitality marketing
- Briefly describe the various promotional techniques available to marketers
- Define the terms "promotions mix" and "advertising"
- Explain the major decisions to be made when designing an advertising campaign
- Discuss advertising as a promotional tool in tourism
- Understand the role of media agencies in marketing
- Apply the principles of marketing communication and advertising in the context of Matchbox Hostel.

Overview

In the last three chapters, we have looked at the management and branding, pricing, and distribution of tourism products.

Marketers must communicate these offerings to consumers (including the travel trade). Promotion is used to communicate information about offerings to target markets. A tourism and hospitality marketer has to be an effective communicator as well as an effective promoter.

We begin by explaining the relationship between promotion and marketing communications. Then we discuss each of the seven stages of the promotional campaign, from determining the marketing objectives through to assessing the impact of the promotional techniques. We look briefly at the concepts of integrated marketing communications (which involves the use of the promotional tools in combination with each other), convergence, and below-, above-, and through-the-line marketing.

In the second half of the chapter, we discuss the role of advertising, which is considered to be the most dominant tool of the promotions mix. We discuss what advertising entails, and then look at an explanation of major advertising decisions such as assigning objectives and a budget, designing, and evaluating an advertisement, and selecting various types of media. Then we review the advantages and disadvantages of advertising. Finally, we turn to the role of media agencies in tourism and hospitality marketing.

The chapter's in-depth case study examines the principles of marketing communication and advertising in the context of *Matchbox Hostel*, a backpacker hostel located in Singapore.

10.1 Introduction

Of all the components of the marketing mix, promotion receives the most attention in tourism and hospitality marketing. Indeed, for some marketers, promotion is perceived as the only marketing activity. Promotion is used to communicate information about offerings to target markets. It also plays an important role in informing, educating, persuading, and reminding consumers. The intangible nature of tourism offerings makes this role even more crucial since there is no physical product or packaging to attract the attention of potential consumers.

The aim of promotion is to stimulate demand and generate customers (Pike, 2018: 136). Thus, promotional activities include any actions designed to encourage or advance the sales of a tourism offering. Promotion achieves these objectives by communicating a message about the product offering to the target market (both consumers and the travel trade). The marketer can choose from a number of tools to communicate the message: advertising, digital marketing and social media, sales promotion, public relations (PR), personal selling, sponsorship, and marketing collateral. These techniques are otherwise referred to as the promotions mix. The message must then be carried to prospective consumers through word of mouth, some form of display, or the media (television, radio, the internet, and the press). The choice of media is sometimes referred to as the marketing communications mix.

The marketer's task is to tell target consumers that the right tourism offering is available at the right place at the right price. The main objective of marketing communications is to convert initial awareness and interest in product offerings into actual sales (Kotler & Armstrong, 2017: 222).

10.2 Communications Theory

Communication theory explains why certain marketing communication actions take place. If they are to design effective promotional messages, tourism marketers must understand the theory of communication: how and why certain marketing activities take place. Communication that travels from the source (or sender) is a one-way process and involves nine key components, as depicted in ◘ Fig. 10.1.

Schramm (1954) developed the three-step linear model of mass communications in which a message is produced by a source and is then transmitted to the receiver. However, each of three process were unexplained (e.g. "How does the recipient receive the message?") The Schramm was further developed by Shannon and Weaver (1962) to include four major communication elements: encoding, decoding, response, and feedback. The fifth element of the marketing communications process is noise which can disturb the communication process (McCabe, 2012).

We will use television and newspaper advertisements for *Emirates Airline* to help us define these elements.

10.2.1 Source

The marketing communications process begins with the source (or sender) of information: the person or organisation with a message to deliver to consumers. In this case, *Emirates Airline* has different messages that it wants to deliver to different target markets. To families, for example, it wants to communicate the message of family-oriented entertainment and low all-inclusive prices. And to

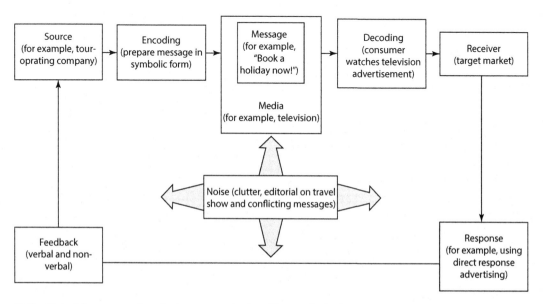

◘ Fig. 10.1   The process of marketing communication. (Source: Author's creation)

business travellers it wants to convey a message of superior quality and comfort.

10.2.2 Encoding

Encoding is the process of arranging the message into a symbolic form that will be clearly understood by the target market. *Emirates'* marketing department assembles the advertisements (television and radio) into suitable words, pictures, use of celebrities, symbols, music and sounds (of passengers having fun and an upbeat song, for example) to convey the message.

10.2.3 Message

The message is what the source wants to communicate and hopes the receiver understands. For *Emirates'* TV commercials, the message is that the airline is a high-quality passenger airline with superior service and that while first-class cabins are luxurious, economy class seating is very comfortable too with a large selection of in-flight entertainment. It is evident from the airline's advertisements that it wants to move away from the perception of many consumers that it is an airline for business and first-class passengers only. The message should be clear and unambiguous. It is vital that the message says the right thing to the right people.

10.2.4 Noise

The major concern for the marketer is that the message should not be distorted during the marketing communications process. This noise can result in the consumer receiving no message or a different message from the one that the source intended. For example, a television advertisement for *Emirates* shown just after a news item referring to an aircraft crash or a terrorist incident at an international airport would fail to convey a convincing message. Similarly, the message might be distorted by clutter, which means that the audience may be exposed to an excessive number of commercial messages that get in the way of the advertiser's intended message. Even the most expensive and carefully plotted newspaper advertisement can fall flat. For example, an advertisement for a theme park will not have the desired impact on consumers if there is a negative news story about a terrible accident involving a tourist at the theme park on the next page.

10.2.5 Media

The media are the communication channels through which the message moves from source to receiver. In the case of *Emirates*, television advertising, sports sponsorship, cinema advertising, newspaper advertising, out-of-home advertising (billboards, transport, etc.), and social media are the message channels.

10.2.6 Decoding

Decoding a message means that receivers interpret it for themselves. An *Emirates'* advertisement may be decoded or interpreted in such a way that it takes on a personal meaning to the consumer who watches or hears the message.

10.2.7 Receiver

Receivers are the people who notice or hear the source's message: that is, consumers who watch or listen to the *Emirates'* advertisement.

10.2.8 Response

The ultimate objective of all promotion is to affect consumers' buying behaviour by stimulating demand to generate sales. The receiver then responds and reacts. This might range from basic thoughts and feelings about the message to action response. *Emirates'* advertisements include an *Emirates'* website address, Twitter handle, LinkedIn, Google+,

Instagram, and Facebook addresses and links, and the telephone number of its call centre so that consumers can obtain further information about the airline, such as booking information and details about other Emirates' services (i.e. car hire and hotel booking, holidays, visitor attractions).

> *Integrated marketing communication* is the co-ordinated development and delivery of a consistent marketing communications message(s) with a target audience (Kitchen & Burgmann, 2015).

10.2.9 Feedback

Feedback is the response message that the receiver sends back to the source. Feedback between two individuals is relatively easy to judge. However, it becomes more difficult to evaluate feedback when several promotional techniques are used with a group of receivers. Ultimately, feedback is expressed in the promotion's impact on the number of consumers who use *Emirates Airline*. Research must also be carried out to determine if consumers like or remember *Emirates'* television and newspaper advertisements. Nowadays, marketers have a lot less control over the message being communicated due to electronic word-of-mouth (e-WoM) and both positive and negative consumer feedback being posted online in mediums such as *TripAdvisor* and Facebook.

The communications model is simplistic, yet it is the quality of the linkages between the various elements in the process that determines whether the communications will be successful (Baines et al., 2019: 390).

10.3 The Promotional Campaign

It is important that the tourism marketer choose the correct blend of the different promotions mix techniques (see ◙ Fig. 10.3) to achieve an effective promotional campaign. A marketer may choose to employ only one of these techniques or a combination of all of them, which is called "**integrated marketing communication**" (IMC). It is important to consider a number of factors when choosing the most appropriate promotional technique or techniques. We discuss IMC in more detail later in this chapter.

In a similar way to any other marketing activity (such as pricing or marketing planning), promotion starts from an analysis of objectives, which includes these decisions made about the promotional campaign:

1. Determining the marketing objective or task
2. Identifying the target segment
3. Determining the desired response
4. Designing the message
5. Considering the promotional budget
6. Selecting the type of promotion
7. Monitoring the impact.

10.3.1 Determining the Marketing Objective or Task

The first stage of designing the promotion is to determine which marketing objective is being addressed. There are four main objectives to choose from: differentiating, reminding, informing, and persuading. This is referred to as the DRIP model by Fill (2002).

10.3.1.1 Differentiating

In many markets, there is little to separate brands (for example, guesthouses, airlines, and rental-car companies). The images created by marketing communications help differentiate one brand from another.

10.3.1.2 Reminding

Reminder promotions are used primarily when offerings have matured to remind consumers of their existence. For example, Emirates Airlines continually runs advertisements to remind the international public to fly with *Emirates*. Reminder promotions and advertising are also used to remind consumers about where and when they can purchase the offering.

10.3.1.3 Informing

Informative promotions are used to make potential consumers aware of the features and benefits of a tourism offering, in other words, when the objective is to create new demand. It Is used to inform consumers of a price change (for example, "£30/€34 off per person on weekdays"), to appeal to new target markets (for instance, school children) and to build or enhance an organisation's image (for example, *Legoland Dubai* in the United Arab Emirates ran a series of television advertisements informing the public about its opening).

10.3.1.4 Persuading

Persuasive promotions are important to improve consumer loyalty as competition increases, to alter consumers' perceptions, and to encourage consumers who are using a competitor's offering to change their brand. This type of promotions often involves the use of comparative advertising, when two organisations or offerings are contrasted in an advertisement. For example, R*amada Inn* in the US ran an advertising campaign directed at *Holiday Inn*. The advertisement's theme was "Ramada's in, Holiday's out". This type of advertising is illegal in some countries. Its effectiveness has been questioned by marketers who believe that the consumer's attention is directed towards the competitor rather than the offering. In addition, some people argue that the old adage "Any advertising is good advertising" applies.

10.3.2 Identifying the Target Segment

The first factor that needs to be considered is the target audience as well as the benefits that this audience is seeking. Most tourism businesses target more than one market segment (defined as a group of consumers who share similar needs and/or characteristics). The market segment may include current and potential users, category and brand users (for example, "people who go on holiday" or "people who go on overseas holidays"), individuals, and groups. The target audience greatly affects the marketer's decision on what the message will say, how it will be said, where it will be said, and who will say it. For example, hotels groups such as *Travelodge* and airlines such as *British Airways* target business travellers. To do this, it advertises in business magazines such as *Forbes* and *The Business Times*. Decisions about the details of the message and which media channel to use are made based on marketing research (for example, the use of secondary data; see ▶ Chap. 4).

10.3.3 Determining the Desired Response

Having defined the target audience, the marketer must determine the desired response (also known as "call to action"). Different objectives related to the (AIDA) process require different promotional techniques to create **A**wareness, stimulate **I**nterest, and create a **D**esire, leading to **A**ction (Lavidge & Steiner, 1961). Thus, the desired response to any promotional activity is linked to the marketing objective. For example, a travel editorial in *Condé Nast Traveler* magazine (an example of a PR technique) featuring an upmarket game reserve and lodge in Kenya enhances the awareness of a potential consumer. This awareness is achieved by the use of colour photographs of wild game and the lodge, or by a good story, or both. The consumer is prompted to visit the website address provided in the feature. When the consumer receives a digital brochure (e-brochure) about the safari, his or her interest is maintained and he or she makes a direct online enquiry. This leads to a desire for the safari and the action of an online booking being made.

If the promotional activity achieves the desired response, the task of the marketer is to reassure consumers that they have made the right choice in a holiday, provide them with a quality experience to secure a repeat visit, and continue promotion to attract new users.

Apply the principles of the AIDA communications model (see paragraph above) to a tourism and hospitality organisation's promotional message.

Competition among low-cost airlines is fierce and most of the companies rely heavily on national press advertising. Examine several press advertisements for these airlines. Compare them in terms of their success in using the awareness, interest, desire, and action (AIDA) communications model.

10.3.4 Designing the Message

When designing a message, marketers should take a couple of factors into consideration:
- The source of the message
- The media channel to be used.

The credibility of the message depends on who is supplying it. A friend or relative would be a strong source, for example, whereas a stranger would need credentials to strengthen the reliability of the information. For example, an experienced travel writer who has written a travel feature on a Kenyan game reserve and lodge in *Condé Nast Traveler* would be extremely credible because he or she is an expert delivering a message in a reputable magazine.

The marketer must then select a media channel through which to deliver the message to the target audience. Media channels include broadcast (television, radio, cinema) print (press, posters, monthly and weekly consumer magazines, trade magazines), digital (including e-mail, websites, billboards, apps, and social media), and OOH (billboards, street furniture).

Another factor in the choice of promotional techniques is whether a tourism organisation chooses a push strategy or a pull strategy (Kotler & Armstrong, 2017: 307). Figure 10.2 shows a comparison of the two strategies.

A **push strategy** is a technique by which an organisation pushes sales by promoting directly to the intermediaries who stock the offering and who then, in turn, push it to their consumers. The principal (for example, a hotel, a visitor attraction, or a cruise line) uses promotional techniques such as personal selling and sales promotion to encourage intermediaries (in other words, tour operators or wholesalers, who then promote the offering to retailers or travel agents) to order, stock, and promote the offering to consumers. For example, *Avis Rent a Car* might offer travel agents a commission of 15% instead of the usual 10% to give them an incentive to use Avis rather than another car rental organisation.

> A *push strategy* is a promotional strategy that uses sales techniques to push the product offering forward.

In contrast, a tourism organisation using a **pull strategy** directs its promotional techniques (mainly advertising and some sales promotion) towards consumers to encourage them to buy offerings. This strategy is designed to generate consumer demand and pull consumers into travel agencies, forcing intermediaries to stock the offering owing to demand. *Virgin Holidays,* for example, might advertise its overseas package holidays directly to the consumer via television, radio, the Internet, and the press, hoping that the consumer will then demand holidays from a travel agency

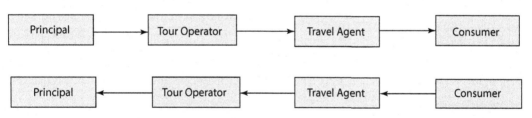

◘ Fig. 10.2 Push and pull strategies. (Source: Author's creation)

such as *Flight Centre*, who in turn will ask tour operators and producers (in other words, *Virgin Holidays*) for the product offering.

A *pull strategy* is a promotional strategy in which money is spent on advertising to build up consumer demand for a product offering.

10.3.5 Considering the Promotional Budget

Another factor that the marketer should consider when choosing which promotional tool to use is the amount of money to be spent on the promotional campaign. Setting a budget for a new product can be problematic for the marketer since there are no established levels of sales and profitability. A promotional budget may be calculated using one or more of the methods outlined below.

10.3.5.1 Affordability or Ad Hoc Basis

The simplest method is to set a promotional budget based on what the company can afford. In reality, most small businesses operate with an uncertain cash flow. One downfall of this method of setting a budget is that it completely ignores the effect of promotion on sales volume.

10.3.5.2 Industry Average

This approach is based on an analysis of the promotional budgets of competitors. As with the going-rate pricing strategy (see ▶ Chap. 8), where prices are set to match those of competitors, this method sets the promotional budget at the level needed to achieve parity, or match competitors' outlays. Companies observe competitors' advertising or carry out research into industry spending estimates from trade associations, and then set their budgets based on the industry average.

10.3.5.3 Percentage-of-Sales Method

In this method, the promotional budget is calculated as a percentage of past or pro-

jected sales. (In the hotel sector, the estimated advertising expenditure is 1% of sales for an average hotel and 2% of sales for a limited service or budget hotel.) The problem with this method is that it does not take into account a decrease in sales or revenue owing to an unforeseen event such as a recession, or loss of market share as a result of competitive activity.

10.3.5.4 Marketing Objectives

In this method, the budget is based on the tasks required to fulfil the specific marketing objectives. These tasks are then costed. For example, the objective might be to increase sales by 15%, so the marketer constructs a budget to achieve this.

10.3.5.5 Share-of-Voice Method

Products and brands are assessed according to the share of voice they have in the marketplace. This is worked out according to the value (based on cost) of the exposure that they receive during monthly periods in promotional material, including advertisements in print, in cinemas, on television and radio, in **out-of-home media** (OOHM) (such as transport), on flyers, and on the Internet. A tool called "AdEX measures advertising expenditure" in different categories based on the standard rate cards of media owners.

> *Out-of-home media* refers to any advertising that reaches consumers outside the home. It includes billboards, displays in shopping centres, and washroom advertising as well as signs on buses, taxis, and other forms of transport.

Selecting the Type of Promotion

The role of promotion is to convince potential consumers of the benefits of purchasing or using the tourism product-offerings of a particular organisation. The tourism and hospitality marketer has eight distinct ways (tools) of communicating promotional messages (the promotions mix) to the public:

— *Advertising* the offering through a selected medium, such as digital/broadcast (television, radio, cinema, Internet, mobile), print media (newspapers, travel, trade magazines, and consumer magazines), or OOHM (billboards, transit posters).

— Using *digital marketing*, Creating website content (e.g. video, photographs, text, apps, newsletters, e-brochures, press releases, and newsletters), social media (e.g. Facebook, Instagram, Tik Tok, Twitter, SnapChat, Linked-In, and Flickr), and e-mail to communicate with consumers and promote tourism and hospitality products.

— Carrying out *direct marketing* activities to evoke a direct response from the targeted market via mobile phone (telemarketing), direct e-mail or mail (postal), SMS/ text, and travel trade exhibitions and events.

— Engaging in *sales promotion* activities such as point-of-sale merchandising, sampling, flyers, in-store (travel agency) window displays, coupons or pounds- or euros-off deals, contests, and sweepstakes (these short-term activities may be aimed at salespeople, intermediaries such as travel agents or consumers).

— Generating publicity about the offering through *public relations (PR)*, for example, by inviting travel writers or sales reps from the travel trade to experience the offering (known as "educationals" or "fam" trips).

— Persuading consumers to purchase offerings in face-to-face situations using *personal selling* techniques (e.g. up-selling).

— Using various forms of *marketing collateral*, such as e-brochures, guidebooks, business cards, and posters, to convert an enquiry into a sale.

— Engaging in *sponsorship* of sports events and teams, festivals, and causes.

All of these promotional techniques except advertising (which is covered in this chapter) are discussed in greater detail in other ▶ Chaps. 10 and 12. Some of these tools overlap with one another, for example, mar-keting collateral such as brochures and newsletters are also digital marketing tools when accessible on a business's website).

In addition to these promotional techniques, marketers should remember the power of word-of-mouth (WoM) advertising and electronic (eWoM), such as online ratings and reviews (e.g. *TripAdvisor*, Google Reviews and individual business's ratings). This so-called hidden sales force may be the most effective of all the marketing communications techniques. However, we will not discuss it in great detail in this chapter because it is not a technique that the marketer performs. The benefits of having a satisfied consumer recommending an offering to another potential consumer can never be overestimated. This form of advertising costs the organisation nothing. An experienced consumer convinces a potential consumer of the value of the tourism organisation's product offering.

The components that serve to achieve a marketer's communication campaign are called the "promotions mix". This is the marketer's tool kit (see ◘ Fig. 10.3).

The marketer adjusts the promotions mix according to the organisation's current situation (situational analysis) and marketing objectives (where the organisation wants to get to) (see ▶ Chap. 5: Tourism and hospitality

◘ **Fig. 10.3** The tourism and hospitality promotions mix. (Source: Author's creation)

marketing planning). As we saw earlier, a marketer may choose one of these tools or a combination of tools. In the case of integrated marketing communications (IMC), a marketer can achieve a sales target with varied mixes of advertising, personal selling, sales promotion, digital marketing and social media, direct marketing, marketing collateral, sponsorship, and PR. Integrated marketing communications is also known as "platform convergence" because different communication channels work together to enhance the customer experience. For example, mobile marketing could be combined with print media.

The tourism and hospitality marketer must alternate the use of these tools to improve promotion and reduce costs to the organisation. For example, a marketer may choose to replace advertising activities temporarily with PR, or to increase advertising expenditure in relation to sales promotion to gain faster sales.

Each promotional tool has its own features. Tourism and hospitality marketers must understand these features if they are to select their tools wisely (see ▶ Industry Insight 10.1). We discuss each of these tools in more detail in the two chapters that follow.

Industry Insight 10.1

Integrated Marketing Communications

Zhang Chan, the owner of a small tourism business specialising in airport shuttle runs and ground handling, often complained that he spent too much on marketing without any results. "I bought some radio ads and got a few calls," he says. "A few weeks later, I put an ad in the newspaper and set up a page on Twitter. Then I got a call from a guy doing a flyer campaign and thought I'd go with that for a week or two. Not much came from any of it."

Zhang was spending a lot of money, but it is not surprising that he got poor results. In today's world, prospective consumers are bombarded with countless marketing messages. While Zhang was right to use diverse media, his communication strategies were wrong because they had no sense of continuity, targeting, consistency, integration, frequency, or brand building. To see results, John needs to get his marketing efforts organised and integrated.

10.3.5.6 Integrated Marketing Communications

Integrated marketing communications (IMC) involves using the promotions mix tools (see ◘ Fig. 10.3) in a co-ordinated manner (Gronroos, 2004). For example, a marketer could use advertising to create awareness and public relations to provoke media comment, and then reinforce the messages through personal selling and direct marketing.

Mobile marketing is often used to reinforce messages and to persuade consumers to make repeat purchases of offerings. According to Baines et al. (2019: 386), the growth in the use of digital marketing presents problems for utilising IMC. These include issues such as measuring the effectiveness of a promotions

campaign (called "metrics") and the budget to do this, and developing content (gathering, writing, and editing promotional information).

If marketers use more than one method of marketing, it must be co-ordinated. Their advertisements, commercials, telemarketing, a website, and social media strategies must be integrated in a way that creates a unified message.

10.3.5.7 Above-, Below- and Through-the-Line Promotional Activities

All activities within the promotions mix generally fall within one of three categories: above-, below- or through-the-line marketing.

■ **Above-the-Line Marketing**

Above-the-line (ATL) promotion refers to marketing exposure on media space that is paid for and may attract a commission (a fee) for the advertising agency (also called a "media agency"). This includes television, radio, print advertising, billboard advertising, online banners, and any other promotional activity where space has been purchased according to time, frequency, or size.

■ **Below-the-Line Marketing**

Below-the-line (BTL) promotion refers to any activity in which a message is exposed via channels where the media space has not been purchased. This includes anything from the use of merchandising or press releases in a local newspaper to attending a travel trade expo, telemarketing, and direct (e-)mail marketing (discussed in ▶ Chaps. 11 and 12 respectively).

■ **Through-the-Line Marketing**

Through-the-line (TTL) promotion refers to a marketing campaign that includes elements of both above- and below-the-line promotional activities. A through-the-line campaign is also referred to as a "360-degree approach".

> The term "above-the-line (ATL) marketing" was coined at *Proctor & Gamble* in 1954 when accountants differentiated between payments made to advertising agencies who undertook promotional activities other than advertising for fixed fees and payments made to agencies who were involved with advertising for fixed fees only. Gradually, marketers started to differentiate activities other than advertisements as a separate marketing practice called "below-the-line" (BTL) marketing.

10.3.6 Convergence

In recent years, there have been several developments in the digital media sector, most notably convergence. The term "convergence" refers to the combination of two or more technologies in one device (Stokes, 2018). For example, mobile phones are no longer simply a device for communication; they also have the properties of a computer, a gaming device, and a television. Thus, various types of media have become more interactive and more portable. A convergence marketing strategy is when digital marketing is utilised to ensure an integrated and consistent message across all the deployed media. The customer is at the centre of this strategy, where he or she is targeted through every possible means of communication, including blogs, social media, news sites, video sites, and forums.

10.3.7 Monitoring the Impact

The last step in the promotional campaign is to attempt to quantify the impact made. Have marketing objectives been met? It is easier to monitor the results of some promotional tools than others. For example, the success of sales promotions such as coupons is relatively easy to evaluate compared to outdoor advertising (it is almost impossible to assess how many people notice an outdoor advertisement).

[line space].

Market research is required before, during, and after any promotion campaign. It is used to identify the target audience and the message needed. In ▶ Chap. 4, we discussed the importance of conducting market research to help identify the market segment at which the promotions activity will be targeted. There are several market research instruments that can be used such as focus group interviews and hiring the services of a professional market research company.

10.4 Advertising

Advertising is the most widely recognised tool of the promotions mix. It is a paid media placement of a message designed to influence consumers (Pike, 2018: 140). **Advertising** enables tourism and hospitality principals (for example, hotels, car-hire companies, visitor attractions, and airlines) and intermediaries (for instance, tour operators, travel agents, and online travel agencies) to reach people (target markets) in their own homes, in other

10

places, or on the move and to communicate messages intended to influence their buying behaviour. Thus, the difference between advertising and other promotional tools is that organisations pay for advertising. This fact allows a marketer to have control over the advertising message: what is to be said, when and how it is to be transmitted, and by which means. For example, a marketer of a travel agency decides that a budget of £2000 (€22,400) will be spent on an advertisement. The marketer also decides where the advertisement will be placed (for example, in a local newspaper), when the advertisement will appear (Thursdays to Sundays, for example), the size and quality of the advertisement (half-page size), and whether it will be a full-colour or a black-and-white advertisement.

> *Advertising* is a paid, mediated form of communication from an identifiable source, designed to persuade the receiver to take some action, now or in the future (Richard & Curran, 2002).

Advertising is probably the first promotional tool to come to mind when people think about promotion or marketing. It is an above-the-line marketing activity, whereas the other promotional tools (sales promotion, digital marketing and social media, direct marketing, personal selling, marketing collateral, PR, and sponsorship) are all considered to be below-the-line marketing activities.

Advertising is a one-way activity and is thus different from personal selling, which is a two-way activity (Baines et al., 2019: 430). In the case of personal selling, a salesperson has direct contact with potential consumers, and can answer questions and attempt to persuade them to buy a product offering. In other words, the salesperson and the potential customer(s) have a dialogue or two-way conversation. In the case of advertising, however, mass media (including newspapers, radio, online, television, and OOHM media such as billboards) are used.

Advertising is used when it is not possible to go and see a consumer. This means that marketing communication only goes one way: out to the consumer. In addition, advertising is paid for, making it different from PR, which is free in most cases. The Advertising Association is the trade organisation representing the advertising media industries in the UK (see ▶ Industry Insight 10.2).

Industry Insight 10.2

The Advertising Association

The Advertising Association (AA) is a trade association that represents all sides of the advertising industry in the UK: advertisers, agencies, media, and research services. An 'umbrella organisation', the AA represents industry associations including ISBA, IPA, IAB, DMA and a number of media owners such as ITV, Channel 4, and Five. The AA promotes the role, rights and responsibilities of advertising and its impact on individuals, the economy and society. It is the only organisation that brings together agencies, brands and media to combine strengths and seek consensus on the issues and opportunities that affect them. Through engagement and evidence-based debate the AA aims to build trust and maximise the value of advertising for all concerned. According to the Marketing Agencies Association (MAA), the Advertising Association is 'the only body that speaks for all sides of an industry.

Source: ▶ http://www.adassoc.org.uk/about-us/

10.4.1 The Advertising Campaign

When planning an advertising campaign (or media plan), the tourism marketer must make five important decisions (Kotler, Bowen, Makens & Baloglu, 2017). These decisions are discussed below.

10.4.1.1 Objective Setting

As with all marketing plans, the best way to start planning an advertising campaign is by setting objectives. As you learnt above, there are four main objectives to choose from: differentiating, informing, persuading, or reminding the target market (Fill, 2002).

10.4.1.2 Budget Decisions

Once the marketer has decided on the advertising objectives, a budget for the campaign must be determined. In the first section of this chapter, which addressed communications theory, we discussed these methods for developing a promotional budget:

- Affordability or *ad hoc* basis
- Industry average
- Percentage-of-sales method
- Marketing objectives
- Share-of-voice method.

These methods may also be applied to determine the advertising budget.

10.4.1.3 Message Decisions

The third step in developing an advertising campaign is to decide on the message that the advertisement is to communicate. No matter how much money is spent on advertising, the advertisement will only succeed if the message gains attention and communicates effectively. The message should be creative, entertaining, and rewarding to consumers (Kotler et al., 2017: 414). The three steps that marketers should follow to develop a creative advertising message (Kotler et al., 2017: 399) are outlined below.

i. Message generation

An idea for a message must be created. The intangible nature of tourism offerings makes choosing a message difficult for the tourism marketer. How do you illustrate a stay at a hotel, a holiday, or a dining experience? However, with some creativity, it is possible to do this. ◘ Image 10.1 shows an advertisement for *Hamilton Princess Hotel* in Bermuda.

ii. Message evaluation and selection

The tourism marketer must evaluate possible messages based on criteria such as meaningfulness, credibility, and distinctiveness. For example, *Ferrari Land* in Barcelona, Spain advertises that it has the fastest and highest roller coaster ride in Europe, pointing out its distinctions.

iii. Message execution

The message has to be put across in a format that will gain the target market's attention and interest. The marketer must find an appropriate style, tone, words, and format in which to execute the advertising message.

This list includes some of the commonly used styles of message executed in the tourism industry and gives an example of each type.

- Special effects: The television advertisement of *Celebrity Cruises* uses trick photography and a special-effects format.
- Fantasy: The slogan of *Titan Holidays* ("See the world differently") attempts to create a mood of fantasy.
- Slice-of-life. Used in TV, YouTube, and radio adverts, that offer a mini-drama, involving fictitious but realistic characters, experiencing a product's uses/benefits. *TUI* uses pictures of families and groups of friends having fun whilst on a beach in what is called "slice-of-life" advertising because it depicts a scene from everyday life.
- Lifestyle: The advertisement for *British Airways* featuring a businessperson sitting in an upholstered leather high-backed chair reading a newspaper is used to show viewers that a product (business class) fits with a particular lifestyle.
- Humour: *Travel Lodge's* television advertisement featuring a male guest in underwear making himself coffee combines humour and lifestyle. *Disneyland Paris* used dark humour with its "Get Rid of your Bad Dreams."

10

— Fantasy and surrealism: *Royal Caribbean Cruises'* advertisement showing a sunbather floating in the ocean and being served a cocktail by a waiter creates a fantasy for viewers and appeals to their desire to escape from their humdrum lives.

— Testimonials: Selling a product through the testimony of satisfied customers. It may be the testimony of an individual, a number of people or a famous celebrity (e.g. *P&O Cruises* media advertising is endorsed by Rob Brydon. This is an example of testimonial evidence). Avoid irrelevant celebrities whose fame has no natural connection with the offering.

- Animation: Cartoon and animation techniques can work well, particularly with offerings targeted at young consumers. *Disneyland Paris.* Animation can be effective when you are talking to children.
- Presenter(s): Used in TV and radio, the use of a presenter to deliver the story. The presenter may be anonymous or a celebrity. easyJet launched a series of TV adverts targeting business travellers with TV celebrity Hugh Laurie narrating a scene in which features a rabbit and businessmen and women rush to catch a flight.

Marketers must be sure to give careful thought to what consumers will think of an advertising message and how they will respond.

❓ Collect five or six advertisements for a tourism offering. Critically evaluate them in terms of the following criteria:
- Objectives achieved
- Message execution
- Target market.

❓ Find an example of a television or cinema advertisement for a tourism and hospitality offering. What style of execution does it use (for example, humour)? Do you think that the advertisement is effective? How would you improve it?

10.4.1.4 Media Decisions

The medium carries the message. Thus, the next step in the advertising campaign is to choose the type of media on which to spend the advertising budget. There is an enormous range of advertising media available to the tourism marketer.

There are three stages in making media decisions:
- Choosing among media types
- Deciding on reach, frequency, and impact
- Deciding on timing.

Each of these stages is discussed below.

- **Choosing Among Media Types**

This is often a difficult decision to make because of the variety of media vehicles available, including newspapers, the Internet, magazines, television and radio stations, digital, and out-of-home media (OOHM). The main classes of media are print media, broadcast media.

Print media contain all advertisements that appear in print: newspapers (local and national), magazines (consumer and specialist trade journals), posters, maps, brochures and guidebooks, outdoor or out-of-home advertising, circulars, and inserts in free press and magazines.

Consumers use local community newspapers and magazines for bargain hunting (for example, weekend getaways and restaurant specials). Consumers read and respond to local media advertising; local print media (e.g. community newspapers) offer an ideal platform on which to connect with consumers.

There are two options in newspaper advertising: local or national newspapers. The quality of local newspapers can vary greatly. Local newspaper advertising is less generic and more personalised than other forms of advertising. In addition, magazines are able to obtain the undivided attention of consumers in their homes. Magazines also play an educational role during the conversation between brand and consumers.

Advertisers use **broadcast media**, namely television and radio. Broadcast media enables advertisers to add visual and/or sound dimensions to their messages. Broadcast media generally reaches a mass audience. Television advertising is generally expensive for companies with modest marketing budgets. For small companies, national coverage on television coverage is viewed as taking a big step up. Companies that are seen on television by the public are viewed in a different light to those that aren't. Television advertising is excellent for smaller companies aiming to build brand awareness. Radio (public broadcasting) is the most widely used medium in many developing countries. It has the advantage over other mediums of being interactive (listeners can telephone, e-mail, tweet, or text into the broadcaster). Increasingly radio listeners are using mobile devices (in particular mobile phones) and accessing the internet to listen to their favourite radio stations (but mostly from home) (BR, 2018). Radio can be extremely effective as an advertising medium. However, radio advertisements should not be longer than about twenty to thirty seconds. In this short time, the advertisement must grab the attention of listeners. A radio advertisement should be engaging and should prompt action on the part of the consumer (Pike, 2018).

Digital media enables two-way interactive communication. For example, banner ads provide a click, which takes the user to a new website and receives information and makes choices, and possibly registers at the site. It includes the internet, social media, e-mail, and apps. Digital advertising reaches far beyond the Internet, delivering several forms of digital content (including text, video, audio, and graphics) to numerous information-receiving appliances other than personal computers. Advertising on social media has proliferated in recent years. It is expected to eclipse TV advertising by 2020 (Sweney, 2018). The digital marketplace has put a lot of buying power back into the hands of buyers and consumers, forcing many marketers to get more creative, more genuine, and more helpful. Marketing online has the distinct advantage over other mediums of being targetable and measurable. It is immediate, and messages can be customised to target audiences. The internet's vast reach can allow advertisers to reach significantly more people than traditional advertising media at a fraction of the cost. Internet advertising is ideal for businesses with a national or international target market and large-scale distribution capabilities.

In addition to advertising, the internet offers opportunities to leverage word-of-mouth marketing and generate "buzz" about a tourism offering. Product or service review websites (such as *TripAdvisor*) and social media (for example, Facebook), among other online communities, allow customers to praise or condemn your company based on their personal experiences. Thus, the internet ties the customer service component directly to advertising. A digital advertisement has the potential to reach a large audience (a big reach and is well-suited to mobile (phone and tablet) engagement.

Print, broadcast, and digital media all form part of the media mix. The media mix is created by media planners who select the most effective combination of traditional, non-traditional, and marketing communications tools to reach the target audience. The selection of media is based on considerations that include factors such as the size of readership or viewership of various media.

Media types are sometimes referred to as traditional media or new media. The term "traditional media" incorporates print, television, radio, and outdoor media. The term "new media" refers to digital, texting/SMS, online, and other types of promotions activities.

Media research organisations publish **rate cards** showing the regular prices of advertising space for all types of media. (A rate card is a document containing prices and descriptions for the various advertising placement options available from a media outlet.) Information on most popular TV programmes, OHHM advertising trends (such as billboard advertising, shopping centre displays, signs on buses and bus shelters, and cinema advertising), radio listenership, magazine readership (for weekly, fortnightly, and monthly magazines), and newspaper readership (for local and national daily and weekly newspapers) can be obtained from various websites and companies. Usually prices reflect the size of the advertisement and the number of viewers or readers that the media vehicle reaches.

> A *rate card* is a printed list of advertising rates charged by print and broadcast media.

Advertisers and companies looking to make a profit turn to these rate cards to see how much they will need to spend to get their message across to consumers.

Image 10.2 OOHM media on a London black cab (taxi). (Source: RG's own photograph)

Rate cards usually include details regarding demographics, policies, additional fees, and artwork requirements. Most national newspapers have rate cards for particular kinds of advertisement. They may have their rates broken down into classified advertisements, retail advertisements, and even national advertisements. When choosing a newspaper or print media, marketers can use rate cards to compare advertising rates based on circulation before buying advertising space.

OOHM have a high impact, they are cost effective (when compared with the reach and frequency of television, radio, and print), and they can be broad or focused. Examples of OOHM include transit or public transport media (taxis - see  Image 10.2), underground stations, hot-air balloons), trailers, washroom advertising (known as "toilet talkers"), building wraps, airports, advertising on street poles and bus shelters (known as "street furniture"), posters, billboards (electronic and fixed face), and television monitors in train and bus sta-

Image 10.3 The Agency logo. (Source: The Agency)

tions and airports. Out-of-home media is a cost-effective form of outdoor advertising. Consumers spend an average of six seconds when reading a billboard. Thus, around six words should get the message across (Suggett, 2019).

It is important that the marketer consider all types of promotions mix activities. The final selection must be based on market research and should not simply be the easiest mix for the company or media/advertising agency to implement. The choice of medium depends on the target market. To select the appropriate media tool, the tourism marketer must decide what reach, frequency, and impact are required to achieve the organisation's objectives. The reach is the number of potential consumers who are exposed to the advertising campaign at least once. Frequency refers to the average number of times that potential consumers are exposed to the advertising message. For example, the marketer might want an average exposure frequency of three. The impact is how effective and believable the advertising message is. Television is a more effective media vehicle for making an offering tangible. For example, an exotic island destination can be given shape by using images of deserted golden beaches along with sounds of seagulls and crashing waves. What stirs more emotion: an image of a tropical paradise or the words "tropical paradise"? Similarly, a message in *The Economist* magazine may be more believable than the same one in *OK* or *NOW*, simply because *The Economist* has a higher profile than these gossip magazines.

The advantages and disadvantages of various types of media are listed in ▢ Table 10.1.

10

▢ **Table 10.1**   Advantages and disadvantages of major types of media

Media type	Advantages	Disadvantages
Broadcast media		
Television	Combines sound, colour, and movement Ability to reach a mass consumer audience (high reach) High attention-gaining medium (high persuasive impact) Opportunity for creativity Good for the image of a company or brand.	High production and airtime costs Fleeting exposure Short life span Lots of advertising clutter The use of advertisement-skipping technology, which prevents the viewing of advertisements The display of company details is difficult, which limits the possibility of a transaction.
Cinema	Good for reaching specific markets (for example, youth or professionals) High-quality audio and visual dimensions Very high attention-gaining medium.	Fleeting exposure Limited reach (the majority of cinema goers are 18–35) High production and airtime costs.
Commercial radio	High reach Target different segments (e.g. domestic), socio-demographic (e.g. youth), lifestyle (e.g. sports), and religious markets Low cost Good local acceptance Short lead times possible Loyal listeners.	Audio presentation only, so difficult to tangibilise offerings Fleeting exposure (short shelf life) Advertising clutter Low attention-gaining medium.
Print media		
Local newspapers	Effective for delivering messages to target audience High degree of consumer trust Less expensive than television Relatively inexpensive, so allows for repetition of advertisements.	Poor reproduction quality Media clutter Short shelf life Small pass-along audience.

◻ Table 10.1 (continued)

Media type	Advantages	Disadvantages
National newspapers	Large circulation (high reach) Appeals to most income levels Frequency allows repetition Consumers have more time to read print advertisements than digital advertisements Tangible (ideal for coupons and can prove contact details) A short lead time is possible.	Audience reads selectively Advertising clutter Low attention-gaining medium Can be expensive.
Posters	Targets specific markets (for example, shoppers) Low cost Longevity (especially on public transport)	Limited audience selectivity Creative limitations Poor brand image Short exposure time.
Specialist trade magazines and journals	Good for specific target markets Short lead times High information-content advertisements High credibility Good pass-along readership.	Clutter Competitors' advertisements may be featured Long advertisement purchase lead time.
Monthly and weekly consumer magazines	Good for reaching specific target markets Tend to be read more than once and good pass-along readership High credibility Large circulations High information-content advertisements Long shelf life.	Long advertisement purchase or contract time No guarantee of position Expensive (a high cost per contact and expensive production costs) Clutter.
Digital media		
Online advertising (for example, banner advertisements and e-mail)	Wide coverage Targeted audience Easy to track and measure High user engagement.	Marketing materials can easily be copied Advertising clutter.
Social media	Low cost Personalisation Immediacy Interactive capabilities.	Potentially low impact Short attention span High audience control of content and exposure.
Out-of-home (OHH) media		
Billboards	High reach in high-profile locations Longevity (long life span) Low cost High visual impact through size High repeat exposure.	Cannot use detailed message Fleeting consumer attention Difficult to measure effectiveness.
Transit media	Targets specific markets with high frequency.	Brief exposure Brand image problems.

Source: Adapted from Baines et al. (2019), p. 429; Middleton et al. (2009), p. 212; Pike (2018), p. 122

■ **Deciding on Timing**

The marketer must also decide when and how often to place advertisements. Three types of scheduling approach are available: pulsing, concentrated, and continuity scheduling.

- Pulsing refers to scheduling advertisements intermittently or unevenly over a certain time period. For example, a cruise-line company such as *MSC Starlight Cruises* might use a two-month burst of advertising for cruises from Mozambique to the Mediterranean in national daily newspapers over the Christmas period.
- A concentrated approach concentrates advertisements in a specific part of the planning period and not at other times. For example, a theme park, which is open for only five or six months of the year, might concentrate its advertising during the months leading up to busy operating periods.
- Continuity scheduling means that advertisements are scheduled evenly and continually throughout a given time period. Hotels, restaurants, and airlines require a steady number of consumers throughout the year, so they use this approach.

❓ Collect examples of tourism and hospitality advertisements from newspapers or magazines.
  1. Identify the objectives of the messages.
  2. Identify the market or markets at which the advertisements are aimed.
  3. Decide whether the advertisements achieve their objectives.
  4. Assess whether the advertisements are imaginative and whether it is possible to improve them. If so, how would you improve them?

10.4.1.5 Evaluation of Advertising Campaigns

Perhaps the best way to assess the effectiveness of an advertising campaign is to note the amount by which sales increase. However, advertising as a promotional tool is rarely used in isolation, which makes it difficult for the marketer to evaluate its impact accurately. In addition, the aims of advertising are usually long term. They are not immediate, like the aims of sales promotion and other below-

the-line promotional tools. There are many factors that are capable of influencing the relationship between advertising and sales (Kotler & Armstrong, 2017: 309). These factors, which were considered in ► Chap. 3, may include anything from the weather to a change in exchange rates. According to Pike (2018: 227), the most practical ways of evaluating advertising effectiveness for small tourism businesses are:

- Tracking the number of enquiries within a given time period
- Estimating the cost per enquiry
- Surveying the level of advertising recall and purchase intent
- Conversion studies.

Two types of conversion studies are available to the marketer (Kotler et al., 2017):

- Response measurement
- Pre- and post-testing.

■ **Response Measurement**

In the case of advertisements that provide a telephone number, e-mail address, or Twitter handle, it is possible to quantify responses against expenditure. Advertisements can also be coded with letters or numbers so that they can be tracked and measured. In addition, people who respond can be asked how they heard about the advertisement or offering.

■ **Pre- and Post-testing**

Personal interviews with a sample of the target market may be conducted before or after an advertising campaign to evaluate how a specific advertisement affected consumers. For example, a panel of consumers exposed to a series of advertisements can be asked how they rate them. Alternatively, a percentage of consumers can be asked what they remember about the message after an advertisement has been released. Visitors to hotels and attractions can be asked how they heard about the offering and what advertising they have seen.

In addition to advertising, the internet offers opportunities to leverage electronic word-of-mouth (e-WoM) marketing and generate "buzz" about a tourism offering. Product or service review websites (such as

TripAdvisor) and social media (for example, Facebook), among other online communities, allow customers to praise or condemn your company based on their personal experiences. Thus, the Internet ties the customer service component directly to advertising. A digital advertisement has the potential to reach a large audience (a big reach and is well-suited to mobile (phone and tablet) engagement.

One of the disadvantages of advertising on the Internet is that marketing material is automatically available for anyone – anywhere in the world – to copy, regardless of the legal ramifications. Brand logos, images, and slogans can be copied and used for commercial purposes. This is not the case with television and magazine advertising: here, images must be replicated rather than simply copied electronically. Another disadvantage of online advertising is that the Internet-advertising gold rush has begun to introduce advertising clutter to the Internet. Internet users are generally so inundated with banner advertisements and spam e-mail that they have begun to ignore Internet advertising just as much as advertisements on traditional media.

10.4.2 The Role of Media Agencies

Most medium-sized and large tourism organisations (for example, *BA, TUI, Trailfinders, MSC Starlight Cruises,* and *Avis*) use the services of media agencies to develop and place their advertisements. The term "media agency" (or sometimes called "advertising agency") is generally applied to a company whose main role is to conceive and create large-scale marketing concepts for its clients.

Traditionally, media agencies come up with the core idea for a marketing campaign, and then create a series of advertisements that communicate that idea across different media. They tend to specialise in above-the-line (ATL) marketing. In the past, media agencies offered a variety of different marketing services under one roof. Nowadays, most large agencies outsource their more specialised in-house departments as separate agencies in their own right. Some media agencies buy ads, some do both: plan and buy.

There are five distinct functions of media agencies:

- Advertising planning: Most agencies can put together a complete advertising campaign, making all necessary decisions on behalf of the tourism organisation.
- Creative services: A media agency has the advantage of creating imaginative messages as well as selecting the advertising media and media vehicles.
- Media services: Agencies select the media and buy airtime or space. They earn commission from the media companies that place the advertisements.
- Research services: Most media agencies offer research facilities for evaluating pre- and post-advertising campaigns, as shown in Industry Insight ▶ 10.3.
- Sales promotion and marketing of collateral services: Media agencies also provide services related to sales promotion and sales literature materials such as coupons and brochures.

Industry Insight 10.3

The Agency.io, Barcelona, Spain

The Agency is a 360° media company that offers tailored-solutions to big and small companies. What best defines The Agency and sets them apart from others is leadership, versatility, and unconventionality. The Agency handles a wide variety of projects: from representing the comedian Jim Gaffigan for three 3 tours in Spain, to carrying out online marketing campaigns for BCN Beer Festival and developing the Biovène cosmetics marketplace. The role of a media agency is to understand the essence of the businesses and industry it is representing, and choosing the correct timing and channels to deliver their message. The Agency's cosmopolitan and diverse staff is reflected in every single strategy and project they carry out. Coming from different backgrounds gives the

10

firm the opportunity to create projects from scratch and to come up with alternative solutions and strategy consulting for companies from very different industries. Chris Rowan, managing director of TheAgency.io says "We love to think outside the box, experiment with new technologies and trends; and mix the traditional with the pioneer." Chris added: "In fact, recently we went through a challenging situation which proved us strong. Despite the restrictions imposed by quarantine in Spain during COVID-19 in 2020, that cut most of our income from events and activities going on that time, we managed to carry on working from home efficiently: taking in new clients and help-

ing our existing clients to make effective decisions in difficult times". Since lockdown started the Agency have taken on three new projects in the health, cosmetics, and the food industries, and successfully ran a marketing giveaway to give support to Coronavirus-affected companies; mostly related to hospitality and tourism ("Project COVI▶ D-19 Marketing help"). "We understood from the start that helping the surrounding businesses is what keeps the economy going" concluded Chris.

Source: Based on a June 2020 interview with Chris Rowan, managing director, The Agency, Barcelona, Spain.

Visit this website: ▶ www.theagency.io

10.4.2.1 Advantages of Using a Media Agency

The advantages of using a media or advertising agency to create and place advertising for a tourism organisation include the following:
- Media agencies have employees who are trained to be creative.
- They have a great deal of experience in advertising and tend to be objective.
- Agencies can save the marketer money by costing less than it would to employ a full-time staff advertising specialist.
- Media agencies are more likely to be familiar with the media and media vehicles than tourism marketers.
- Media agencies are usually able to obtain better advertising rates than individuals.

10.4.2.2 Selecting a Media Agency

It is advisable that marketers select a media agency carefully. Many organisations ask a number of agencies to tender for business, and then select one. Tourism marketers should, however, be careful of this approach. Some agencies today are reluctant to spend time producing proposals that may not be accepted, particularly for smaller accounts. In addition, many of the larger media or adver-

tising agencies do not tender for business unless it is a really large account simply because they do not need to. Likewise, agencies that do tender for business may need to because they are not very effective.

Smaller tourism organisations should also be wary of using large media agencies that send relatively inexperienced junior staff to work on smaller accounts. It is advisable to contact clients of an agency and ask them what it is like to work with the agency.

All media agencies essentially plan and/or buy advertising media space. Some agencies are better-equipped to be able to buy media more cheaply and effectively than others.

Another important consideration when selecting a media agency is that there should be agreement on the objectives of the advertising campaign. This should be set out beforehand, otherwise it will be difficult to call the agency to task if the objectives are not achieved. Similarly, there must be an agreement between the marketer and the agency on how the success of the campaign is going to be measured. Depending on the budget, it may be worthwhile to evaluate the effectiveness of the advertising campaign independently.

Summary

Promotion involves all communication between a tourism organisation and its consumers. Marketers have to be acquainted with the elements of the marketing communications process. Selecting a promotional campaign that is going to be effective requires research and planning. Although defining the promotional objectives and the target market provide the basis for selecting a promotional technique, other factors also need to be considered. These include the company's marketing objectives, competitors, push or pull strategies, message design, and the available promotional budget.

Advertising is the most powerful and perhaps the most expensive – component of the promotions mix. It is used by all tourism marketers, no matter the size of the organisation. According to *Marketing Week*, on average, more than 50% of a marketer's budget is spent on advertising, and yet it is estimated that as little as 20% of his or her time is allocated to this activity (Vizard, 2018). Nevertheless, it is a very effective promotional tool if marketers adhere to the guidelines discussed here.

In today's Information Age (also known as the "Digital Age"), consumers are bombarded with advertisements and information (Hilbert, 2015). This makes it even more important for the marketer to get the attention of the consumer, and then to get the right message across in a way that will be well received and not misinterpreted or misunderstood.

If the marketer decides that the design and placement of advertisements is best left to a media agency, then careful selection of an agency is required. The objectives of advertising campaigns should be clearly defined and set within a realistic and affordable budget.

❓ Review Questions

1. Discuss the role that marketing communication plays in the marketing mix.
2. What is the purpose of promotion?
3. List three disadvantages of advertising.
4. Discuss the importance of the concept of integrated marketing communications (IMC). Provide some examples of tourism organisations that are practising integrated marketing.
5. Contrast advertising with public relations. Use examples from the tourism and hospitality industry.
6. What are the advantages of the percentage-of-sales method when setting an advertising budget?
7. Apply five of the eight tools of the promotions mix to a tourism company by showing how it could use all of these tools.
8. Briefly explain why it is difficult to quantify the direct impact of the entire promotions mix to sales.
9. Discuss some of the limitations of online advertising?
10. Explain the role of media agencies in tourism and hospitality marketing. What are the advantages of using a media agency when buying advertising space?

In-depth Case Study 10: Promoting and Advertising Tourism and Hospitality Products: Matchbox Student Hostel, Singapore

Objectives

- To understand the communications mix
- To understand the concept of advertising.

For people whose minimum accommodation needs involve an en-suite bathroom, room service, parking, and transfers, then a stay in a hostel could feel less like a trip away and more

10

like a prison term. Hostels can carry grim images of bare dormitories, one bathroom-for-all, and a kettle and a toaster for sustenance; basic living at a basic price. It would probably come as a surprise to the wealthier traveller that many of their essential and non-essential requirements can be catered for by certain hostels. One such hostel, which has evolved into a hotel-like experience for its guests is the ground-breaking Matchbox student hostel in Singapore.

Matchbox, located on Pandan Road, in the Pioneer district, Singapore, started as a pod-style boutique hostel for backpackers, and then evolved into a lavish student hostel. Matchbox aims to create a" home away from home" for students, who provide the main source of the residents. Most of its residents are foreign students, who are below 30 years old and tend to be studying at nearby higher education institutions such as Singapore Institute of Management and Ngee Ann Polytechnic.

Matchbox focuses on providing a cosy home, facilities for a balanced lifestyle, ample socialising areas, a thorough maintenance regime, and stringent pest control and security. The design of Matchbox is contemporary and minimal, lit up by vibrant orange and turquoise signature colours. Surrounded by lush green spaces, Matchbox has an "out-of-town" feel about it, whilst retaining excellent links to transport, shops, and local services. Every room is furnished with a comfortable mattress. Furniture is in the form of a well-designed wardrobe, and each room has a study desk. If the room accommodates two persons or more, the pod-like beds have curtains, creating a private space.

The backbone of any hostel's marketing strategy is a successful website. Matchbox chose to work with an online hostel marketing specialist to help with their website in order to bring the property to life before the guest arrives. The marketing specialist has utilised tools such as e-mail marketing, remarketing, social media campaigns, blogs and content marketing, and search engine optimisation (SEO) to create a brand personality and ultimately increase revenue and bookings.

Matchbox has utilised its interesting story: growing from a run-of-the-mill hostel to providing a bespoke accommodation experience for international students and travellers. Matchbox has strategised like a publisher by generating regular news and securing media coverage in target publications such as *The Smart Local* and *Time Out Singapore*. The Smart Local is the most visited travel and lifestyle portal in Singapore and Time Out Singapore visits and reviews the many local attractions and venues. Matchbox has also advertised in both those publications. Matchbox has also been featured and advertises in *About Blog Campus Magazine*, which is a bi-monthly publication for tertiary students distributed free across all of Singapore's major universities, polytechnics, private schools, art schools, and junior colleges.

Matchbox also promotes via their own online media platforms, website, social media pages, and e-newsletters. Matchbox has paid particular attention to Instagram, which as a platform targets their audience without requiring a huge budget. Recently, Matchbox has shared how they have improved their on-site social mediums and by disclosing what is going on gives a fresh and contemporary insight into life at the hostel. Good blog content can increase traffic and leads.

The hostel has explored the opportunities to form partnerships with those who can influence the customer journey. They have forged working relationships with the numerous nearby higher and further educational institutions. Digitally, Matchbox now has added exposure via these institutions who have access to thousands of monthly web visitors, active social media communities, and vast e-mail subscriptions including current students and alumni. Matchbox also attends the educational institutions open days and hosts a stand promoting in person and distributing flyers and brochures.

Slogans can help businesses attract more customers and in the case of Matchbox draw more students. Matchbox employed a PR company to help with various aspects of their business and one of which was to develop the slogan; 'More than housing we're home'. By using a catchy slogan, a desired image of the hostel can be impressed in the minds of people. Slogans being short and catchy can stick in the mind of people for a long time.

Most travellers much prefer local information from people who actually live in the destination and possess the most current information on what to do. Upon arrival at a hostel, asking the staff what to do is often the first thing travellers do, and they usually have great respect for this local, insider perspective. If a hostel takes the time to execute an online marketing strategy that conveys this local information on their website, before a visitor arrives, they have a much higher likelihood of obtaining a new guest. Also, by simply providing relevant travel information about their city, a hostel has the opportunity to reach a far broader audience online. If someone is doing research for a trip and ends up finding the information they need on the blog of a hostel, there is a good chance they will evaluate that accommodation outlet to see if they would like to stay there.

Singapore has a lot to offer budget-conscious travellers, up-market tourists and long-term students from visitor attractions such as island-hopping to cultural heritage products allied with a fantastic climate. Matchbox has successfully crossed the divide between different travel markets, by offering an inclusive facility.

By successfully using a rich and varied promotions mix to attract international travellers and at the same time support the local market, Matchbox student hostel has developed a flourishing business.

Questions and Activities

1. Which type of advertising (informative, persuasive, electronic or reminder) does Matchbox make use of? Justify your answer.
2. If you were the marketing manager of Matchbox, explain how you would go about promoting the company internationally?
3. Briefly discuss why Matchbox targets much of its promotional activity on international marketing channels.
4. Explain what Matchbox could do to attract more SE Asian backpackers.
5. Go online to the Matchbox website (▶ https://matchbox.sg/hostels/100up/about-us/). Identify which tours would appeal to you. Briefly explain why.

References

Baines, P., Fill, C., Rosengren, S., & Antonetti, P. (2019). *Marketing* (5th ed.). Oxford: Oxford University Press.

Fill, C. (2002). *Marketing communications: Contexts, strategies, and applications* (3rd ed.). Harlow, Essex: FT/Prentice-Hall.

Gronroos, C. (2004). The relationship marketing process: Communication, interaction, dialogue, value. *Journal of Business & Industrial Marketing, 19*(2), 99–103.

Hilbert, M. (2015). *Digital technology and social change.* Retrieved from https://canvas.instructure.com/courses/949415 [18 July 2018].

Kitchen, P., & Burgmann, I. (2015). Integrated marketing communications: Making it work at a strategic level. *Journal of Business Strategy, 36*, 34–39.

Kotler, P., & Armstrong, G. (2017). *Principles of marketing* (17th ed.). London: Pearson Education.

Kotler, P., Bowen, J., Makens, J., & Baloglu, S. (2017). *Marketing for Hospitality and Tourism* (7th ed.). Upper Saddle River, NJ: Prentice Hall.

Lavidge, R., & Steiner, G. (1961). A model for predictive measurements of advertising effectiveness. *Journal of Marketing*, 2559–2562.

McCabe, S. (2012). *Marketing communications in tourism and hospitality: Concept, strategies and cases.* Abingdon: Routledge.

Middleton, V., Fyall, A., Morgan, M., & Ranchhod, A. (2009). *Marketing in travel and tourism* (4th ed). Oxford: Butterworth-Heinemann.

Pike, S. (2018). *Tourism marketing for small businesses.* Oxford: Goodfellow Publishers.

Richard, J., & Curran, C. (2002). Oracles on advertising: Searching for a definition. *Journal of Advertising, 31*(2), 63–77.

Schramm, W. (1954). How communication works. In W. Schramm (Ed.), *The process and effects of communication* (pp. 3–426). Urbana, Illinois: University of Illinois Press.

Shannon, C. & Weaver, W. (1962). *The mathematical theory of communication.* Urbana, IL.: University of Illinois.

Stokes, R. (2018). *eMarketing: The essential guide to online marketing* (6th ed.). Cape Town: Quirk eMarketing.

Suggett, P. (2019). *Steps to making a great billboard ad.* https://www.thebalancecareers.com/six-steps-to-making-a-great-billboard-ad-38479

Sweney, M. (2018). Social media ad spend to overtake TV's in spite of Facebook woes. *The Guardian.* Monday 2 April, p. 13.

Vizard, S. (2018). *Marketing budget slows as marketers face challenging 12 months.* https://www. marketingweek.com/2018/01/17/marketing-budget-growth-slows-ipa-bellwether/ [12 June 2018].

Further Reading

Luxton, S., Reid, M., & Mavondo, F. (2015). Integrated marketing communication capability and brand performance. *Journal of Advertising, 44*(1), 37–46.

10

Designing the Tourism and Hospitality Promotions Mix

Contents

Electronic Supplementary Material The online version of this chapter (https://doi.org/10.1007/978-3-030-64111-5_11) contains supplementary material, which is available to authorized users.

Purpose

This chapter will give you the knowledge and skills you need to understand the various communications mix tools to promote tourism offerings.

🔖 Learning Goals

After reading this chapter, you should be able to:

- Explain the characteristics of each of the promotional tools used in tourism and hospitality
- Understand the concept of integrated marketing communications
- Set out the criteria that should be used to select the right promotions tool
- Consider the advantages and disadvantages of each promotional tool.

There's much more to marketing and promotions than advertising. The five promotional tools discussed in this chapter are known as the "promotions mix". We start with an explanation of the role of sales promotion in the promotions mix and discuss the objectives and the various techniques of this promotions tool. In the next section, we then look at the various types of personal selling techniques. We then outline the various types of marketing collateral and travel brochures used in the tourism industry. Next, we explain the various public relations (PR) techniques available to the tourism marketer. PR provides an excellent opportunity for tourism businesses to gain free media publicity. In the last section, we look at the role of sponsorship in tourism and hospitality marketing.

The chapter's in-depth case study applies the principles of PR and sponsorship to *Isandlwana Lodge* in South Africa.

▪ Introduction

Tourism businesses use a variety of promotional tools and media to engage with their target markets. The main marketing communications mix tools used in tourism are advertising, sales promotion, personal selling, marketing collateral, public relations (PR), direct marketing, and digital marketing. These promotional tools are very rarely used in isolation and usually complement advertising or one another (this is known as "integrated marketing communications"). These promotions mix techniques should not be underestimated, as they can be highly effective ways of getting a message across to consumers. A quirky and attention-grabbing pamphlet can be as powerful and clever a communication tool as any of the latest social media marketing tools.

The previous chapter discussed how advertising messages are used to communicate with a target audience away from the places where tourism offerings are sold. Sales promotion, personal selling, marketing collateral, PR, and sponsorship are all marketing activities used to promote offerings. This chapter starts by discussing how tactical promotional techniques are used to communicate special offers to motivate potential buyers.

11.1 Sales Promotion

Sales promotion is an activity that acts as an extra incentive for consumers, sales representatives, and intermediaries to purchase (Blattberg & Neslin, 1990: 3). It is a term that is frequently confused by marketers, who interpret it to mean anything that encourages or promotes sales (advertising, marketing collateral and so on). However, its most common usage refers to the promotion of additional sales through incentives and discounts (Baines et al., 2019: 428).

Sales promotion is to do with special offers. It is usually a short-term incentive offered to a consumer or intermediary to induce a booking. The main aim of this activity is to encourage people to make a buying decision at the point of sale (see ◘ Image 11.1). Most tourism and hospitality marketers use sales promotion tools at one time or another. Sales promotion involves two approaches: intermediary push or consumer pull (see page 323). However, it should not merely be viewed as an alternative to advertising. Instead, sales promotion and advertising should be used to complement

■ Image 11.1   Sales promotion - happy hour at a restaurant. (Source: ▶ Pexels.com)

11

each other. For example, advertising creates awareness of the offering, in-store merchandising (a special display, perhaps) reminds the consumer about the offering and sales promotion induces the sale (Morrison, 1996: 405). Sales promotion requires advertising support through the media (for example, internet, television, or radio) or at the point of purchase. There is no point in running a special offer if nobody knows about it.

11.1.1   The Role of Sales Promotion

Sales promotion has had a significant role in tourism and hospitality marketing, largely owing to the fact that most offerings are perishable. Marketers can use sales promotion techniques when there is a need for a quick increase in sales, such as with the introduction of a new product-offering or when there is a need to sell excess capacity or stock (Pike, 2018: 145). However, marketers often misuse sales promotion because they tend to employ it as a quick-fix solution for situations that

need longer-term solutions. For instance, if a restaurant has serious problems (such as a poor reputation for food or service, an ineffective marketing strategy or incorrect positioning), sales promotion will rapidly increase the number of visitors for a short period of time, but conceal the underlying management problems, making the restaurateur appear efficient. When management finally uncovers the real problems, it may be too late to repair the damage.

Sales promotion should be used for short-run adjustments to bottom-line results on an as-needed basis (*ad-hoc*) rather than a continuous basis. In this respect, it is vastly different from advertising, personal selling, or public relations. It should be used at irregular intervals, particularly if the market is seasonal (which it tends to be in the tourism industry). For example, hotels may boost initial sales of rooms at the beginning of the holiday season by offering discounts for families with children. Sales promotion can also add value to an offering by retaining the standard price, but giving the consumer more value for

Table 11.1 Sales promotion objectives and examples in the tourism industry

Objectives	Example and techniques
To gain consumer awareness or attract new users	*Flybe* airline used a £1 special promotion when it first began operating Gifts
To increase off-peak sales	An airline may offer early-bird flight specials A city hotel may offer weekend specials targeting leisure tourists Visitor attractions offer off-peak entry fees Discount vouchers or coupons
To encourage repeat visits by loyal consumers	IHG, the loyalty club scheme of *InterContinental Hotels & Resorts, Crowne Plaza, Hualuze Hotels & Resorts, Holiday Inn*, and several other leading travel and tourism brands. Additional products or services
To combat or pre-empt competition	Airlines and tour operators may reduce prices to match or undercut the competition Contests and games Prize draws Point-of-sale displays
To encourage early bookings	Hotels and tour operators offer discounts at the start of the season to generate immediate bookings (for example, *Virgin Holidays* promises the following: "Early booking offers: Book by 28 October 2023")

Source: Author's creation

money. For instance, a restaurant may offer a free glass of wine with a meal.

11.1.2 The Objectives of Sales Promotion

The objectives of sales promotion are outlined in Table 11.1, which includes an example for each objective.

11.1.3 Activities Associated with Sales Promotion

"Sales promotion" is a term covering a variety of techniques or incentives, including cut-price offers or discounts (used by a variety of offerings such as holidays, hotel rooms, rental cars, cruises or theme parks), competitions ("Win a 10-day holiday in Mauritius"), personality promotions (having a sports star or Hollywood actor visit), and so on. Sales promotion techniques work well for producing activity and interest at the point of sale. Discounts, for example, induce consumers to purchase a particular offering rather than purchasing an alternative offering.

A number of sales promotion techniques are available to the tourism and hospitality marketer to achieve the objectives outlined in Table 11.1. When choosing which technique to use, the marketer must take the following into account:
- The type of market
- The competition
- The cost and effectiveness of each technique.

The main sales promotion techniques are shown in Table 11.2.

❓ Select two patronage award schemes offered by tourism and hospitality organisations in your country. Compile information about both schemes (for example, by contacting the organisation or visiting its website).

11

Industry Insight 11.1

Trade Fairs and Shows: Important for Networking

According to Bogden Dimitrova, director of Wagon Trails, a tour operator based in Bucharest, Romania, trade fairs are extremely important for networking. "It's good to be seen at travel trade fairs," says Bogden. "It's important for overseas agents to see you again and again." Wagon Trails attends all of the major travel trade fairs, including the ITB Berlin, the World Travel Market (WTM) and the

Independent Travellers World (ITW) (the latter two both in London). "Travel fairs are good for networking, making contacts and getting business," adds Bogden. "It is said that 90% of new business comes from focused, proactive networking and word-of-mouth referrals. The WTM is really just one big sales pitch; it is a talking shop for people in the world tourism industry."

Source: Based on an interview with Bogden Dimitrova, director, Wagon Trails

Industry Insight 11.2

The Cape Town International Boat Show

According to Dana Whiting of Impact Exhibitions, the owner of various trade and consumer exhibitions, exhibitions are the most valuable and cost-effective marketing tool that there is. Whiting says, "No other marketing medium brings your customers directly to you. When last did you do a radio spot that put between 10,000 and 30,000 customers in your shop over three days, seeing and feeling your product, in direct contact with your best sales and marketing staff? When last did a print media campaign allow you to demonstrate your product, answer questions and overcome objections, and extol the virtues of your product over that of your competitors?"

Whiting adds, "What would a radio, print, billboard or television campaign that brought 30,000 potential customers to you cost? How would that cost compare with the cost of an exhibition?"

The Cape Town International Boat Show is an example of an annual event that brings the entire South African boating and water sports industry together in one venue over a period of 3 days. This gives international buying agents

and domestic buyers the opportunity to view the latest models as well as the newest boats and related products in one venue, all during one visit to Cape Town. The exhibitors know that, over the course of 3 days, they will see buying agents for international retailers and charter fleets, domestic and international individual buyers, trade and general media, existing customers, suppliers and the general public at their stands. Over the course of the 3 days, exhibitors will:

- Launch new products
- Generate sales leads
- Build brand awareness
- Generate media exposure
- Educate the market
- Extend relationships with existing customers
- Build a prospect database
- Entertain suppliers and customers
- Position their company as a market leader.

"There is no other marketing medium that can achieve these goals at the cost and in the time that exhibitions do," says Whiting.

Source: Based on an interview with Dana Whiting, chief executive officer, Impact Exhibitions, 2017

The use of sales promotion by tourism marketers is increasing. It is less expensive than advertising and its effectiveness can be verified. It is also effective when external (macroenvironmental) events affect consumer

demand. For example, poor weather, a terrorism incident, a global health issue (such as the 2020/21 Coronavirus), or an economic downturn can all result in a reduction in consumers. Such events require tactical promotional

◘ Table 11.2 Sales promotion techniques examples in the tourism and hospitality industry

Sales promotion technique	Description	Examples
Merchandising and point-of-sale material	Wall displays, posters, counter cards, brochure dispensers, menus, wine lists, pens, banners, signs and tent cards destination-branded souvenirs, caps, t-shirts, and pens	Airlines' in-flight magazines and in-flight bags
Samples	Free samples of items to encourage sales or arranging in some way for people to try all or part of a tourism offering (Morrison, 1996: 410).	Samples or taster sessions are often used at exhibitions Familiarisation trips (or 'educationals'
Coupons (vouchers) and gift certificates	Coupons are vouchers or certificates that give consumers savings when they buy specific offerings (Kotler, Bowen, Makens, & Baloglu, 2017: 426)	Online coupon "15% discount off the admission price to a visitor attraction"
Discounts and special offers	Advertised reductions in price that does not involve a coupon or voucher (see ◘ Image 11.1)	Two-for-the-price-of-one offers, children-eat-for-free or children-stay-for-free offers and volume discount. Hotels' "Stay four, pay three" promotion Buy-one-get-one-free (BOGOF)
Patronage awards (also known as "loyalty incentives", club memberships or passport schemes)	Aimed at rewarding and promoting loyalty and frequency of purchase by identified existing consumers (Kotler et al., 2017)	Airline may offer free air miles or frequent-flyer points to regular users Restaurants, hotels, car rental companies, and airlines offer club (or 'privilege') cards, giveaways, and further discounts.
Competitions, sweepstakes, and prizes	Give consumers a chance to win money, a gift, or a holiday. They provide tourism organisations with useful information to add to a consumer database (e.g. e-mail addresses, postal addresses, mobile phone numbers)	Intrepid Travel, in partnership with Babbel (an online language learning company) offers a chance to win a holiday, including flights to South America by completing information online. Prize draw (or lucky draw) is collecting business cards (perhaps in a large glass bowl) and then offering a prize such as a backpack. Sales contests, scratch-and-win cards, sweepstakes.
Free gifts, premiums, and incentives	Items offered either free or at a low cost as an incentive to purchase an offering.	Quick-service restaurants, for example, sometimes give away children's toys and Hollywood movie merchandise. Gifts: balloons, golf balls, pends, USB-drives, diaries, and calendars that endorse the name of an organisation and are usually presented to clients or regular consumers.
Exhibitions	Draw together all sectors of the tourism industry, including suppliers, intermediaries, carriers and DMOs. They allow marketers to network among industry players and gain marketing ideas as well as to promote and sell offerings	India International Travel & Tourism fair (IITT) – a networking and marketing platform for the travel and tourism industry (see ► Industry Insight 11.1). The Cape Town International Boat Show (see ► Industry Insight 11.2).

Source: Author's creation

11

responses. Sales promotion yields short-term results and can be effective in supporting other promotional tools.

> ❓ Collect a sample (for example, a newspaper voucher or coupon) of a sales promotion activity by a tourism organisation, and then answer the following questions:
> - What is the sales promotion's objective?
> - Do you think it will achieve its objective?
> - How could the sales promotion be improved?
> - What might the disadvantages of this sales promotion be?

11.2 Personal Selling

As we discussed in ▶ Chap. 2, one of the characteristics of tourism and hospitality offerings is that they are inseparable; both the service provider and the consumer have to be present. Personal selling is the process of person-to-person communication between a salesperson and a prospective customer in which the former learns about the latter's needs and seeks to satisfy those needs by offering the prospective customer the opportunity to buy something of value, such as a good or service (Futrell, 2014: 3). It entails persuading consumers to buy offerings in a face-to-face encounter and therefore must be viewed as an important and highly effective promotional tool for the marketer. Personal selling is an activity carried out by an individual representing a company, or collectively in the form of a sales force.

Personal selling is perhaps one of the most underrated promotional tools. It has both a strategic and a tactical role in marketing. It should not be viewed merely as a tool that is employed from time to time, but rather as a tool to be used at all times by all of the staff. This communication tool is directly related to sales promotion and merchandising techniques. It is the direct contact between buyer and seller, face-to-face, by mobile phone or through video conferencing. Personal selling enables a dialogue to take place. It is this two-way communication (during which the consumer can ask questions and the sales representative can react to the particular situation) that is more effective than one-way communication such as advertising (Wilmshurst, 1993: 38). It differs from advertising, sales promotion, marketing collateral, and direct marketing in that there is personal interaction between two or more people. However, this unique quality comes at a price. Personal selling requires a lot of time and expense compared to other promotional tools. Personal selling should be integrated with other tools of the promotions mix so that it is supported by the likes of advertising and public relations in creating an awareness of the organisation and its products. This tool of the promotions mix is the driving force behind specific sectors, particularly the meetings and events industry.

11.2.1 Types of Personal Selling in Tourism

There are four main methods of personal selling in marketing tourism and hospitality: internal selling, external selling, telephone sales, and personal skills (Blem, 2008). ◻ Table 11.3 describes these methods and provides examples of each.

Industry Insight 11.3

Up-selling Fuels Obesity

Consumers are choosing to buy larger coffees, more fries, or extra cream because of up-selling, which experts warn is fueling the obesity epidemic. A study conducted in the UK found that 78% of respondents said they are asked in restau- rants, fast food outlets, and stores at least once a week if they would like to upgrade their orders. According to the study's report, 'up-selling' is defined as the act of persuading customers to buy something additional or more expensive. The report added that studies have shown that when people are presented with larger portion sizes, they consume more and increase their calorie intake. At some restaurants and fast-food outlets staff are trained to and incentivised to up-sell and are incentivised for upselling in the form of team competitions, with a prize for the winning team.

Source: Boseley, S. (2017). 'Up-selling' fuels obesity. *The Guardian*. 7 September. Page 9.

Table 11.3 Personal selling methods

Personal selling technique	Description	Examples
Internal selling	Face-to-face transaction efforts made within an organisation to obtain a sale. Upselling (or suggestive selling) (see ► Industry Insight 11.3) Cross-selling	A travel agent selling a holiday A tour operator recommending a tour or activity packaged with the accommodation and transport options A receptionist describing the hotel facilities An airline salesperson negotiating a bulk contract to supply 50,000 seats to a tour operator
External selling	Face-to-face presentations of the offering to prospective consumers outside the organisation or in the field. Sales representatives/teams	Hotel chains and airlines' sales representatives and sales teams/forces to sell seats and beds to tour operators, corporate travel buyers and conference organisers. Visitor attractions such as theme parks and museums sell facilities to event organisers and educational trips to schools and colleges.
Telephone	Telesales method involves using the telephone to promote offerings.	A travel agency consultant carrying out personal selling over the telephone
Personal skills	The appearance, presentation, and hospitality of employees. A friendly smile, eye contact, confidence, and a listening ear are all attributes.	Waiters and waitresses providing a polite, efficient service so that consumers go away happy and come back again.

Source: Author's creation

? Conduct an interview with a salesperson for a tourism company. Find out what their typical day is like: what they do, what they like and dislike about the job. Ask some other questions that are of interest to you. Write-up your findings in a report.

11.2.2 The Advantages and Disadvantages of Personal Selling

The advantages and disadvantages of personal selling as a promotional tool (compared to other tools) are outlined in Table 11.6.

11.3 Marketing Collateral

Marketing collateral is one of the most widely used promotions mix tools for tourism organisations. It refers to printed information about offerings, including flyers, brochures, maps, business cards, leaflets, sales or fact sheets, postcards, posters, and videos (Kotler, Rackman, & Krishnaswamy, 2006). A hotel needs a brochure that includes its tariff, a theme park or visitor attraction requires a guide or pamphlet, a tour operator promotes itself using a brochure offering various types of holidays and destinations, and a holiday resort uses a guide or pamphlet.

11

Therefore, we will look closely at the brochure, which may fulfil the function of selling as well as providing information.

In the tourism and hospitality industry, marketing collateral is partly advertising, partly sales promotion, and partly distribution. For example, a theme park's brochure contains an advertisement promoting attractions at the park and discount coupons for certain rides, and it is distributed to the consumer upon entering the park. Because of the characteristics of tourism offerings (see ▶ Chap. 2), printed sales literature is far more extensively used to market these offerings than is the case in the marketing of manufactured products. The design, distribution and mass use of sales literature, particularly the brochure, are major distinguishing features of marketing in tourism (Middleton & Clarke, 2001: 189). In the late 1990s, there were expectations that CD-ROMs would replace printed brochures. However, this has not happened largely because nowadays electronic brochures are sent to prospective customers or made available on a company's website – in the form of e-brochures – whereby consumers can read them 'online'. Indeed, for many potential visitors the brochure they possess actually represents the product or destination they are purchasing (Molina, Gómez, & Martín-Consuegra, 2010).

Consumers expect companies to have printed sales literature such as business cards and letterheads. A brochure lets everyone know that the company means business. People want material to take home or whilst on the move and read at their leisure. While it may be true that consumers who make enquiries can be directed to a company's website, a brochure adds a personal touch, informing prospective consumers what the offering can do for them and why they should buy it. In the digital online era hard copy brochures still have their place as a tangible part of the tourism decision-making, and as a souvenir of an experience that can be passed on to others (Pike, 2018: 148). Brochures should be used in support of other elements of the promotions mix.

11.3.1 Types of Marketing Collateral

There are several types of collateral that can function to promote and provide information about offerings, including guidebooks, posters, holiday brochures, leaflets, flyers, in-house magazines (see ▶ Industry Insight 11.4) and booklets, and tourist information packs (consisting of newsletters, discount leaflets, tariffs and travel brochures).

11.3.2 Objectives of Marketing Collateral

Marketing collateral and travel brochures have several functions: to create awareness, to make the offering tangible, to provide education, and to promote the offering.

11.3.2.1 To Create Awareness

The main function of a travel brochure is to create awareness among prospective consumers. Many first-time consumers become aware of products through marketing collateral first seen at a hotel, at an airport, in a tourism information centre or travel agency, or passed on by friends and family. The design of the brochure, particularly the front cover, is crucial in getting the attention of consumers because once this has been achieved, the chances of a booking being made are greatly increased. We will discuss good design in the next section.

11.3.2.2 To Provide Information

A travel brochure is an important tool given the intangible nature of tourism offerings (Andereck, 2005). Brochures provide information about an organisation's benefits, style and strengths. Brochures also enable potential consumers to read about what they want to purchase. A brochure promoting an upmarket game lodge such as *MalaMala* near the Kruger National Park shows photographs of its well-furnished bedrooms, its restaurant and meals, scenic views, wildlife, and 4 × 4 game-viewing vehicles, and includes maps. However, it is important that the destination or offering live up to the image portrayed in the pictures in the brochure. How often do tourists complain about a particular destination or offering not being what they expected on arrival at the destination or offering?

11.3.2.3 To Provide Education

Besides creating consumer awareness and making the offering tangible, another function of marketing collateral and travel brochures is to educate consumers. In the 2020s, responsible tourism marketers have the duty of educating consumers about the impacts of tourism on the environment. The brochure is an effective medium for achieving this.

Brochures for national parks and game lodges, museum leaflets, destination guides, and maps are examples of literature that often contain information to raise awareness about environmental issues. For example, the UNWTO, in conjunction with the World Committee on Tourism Ethics (WCTE) and several environmental organisations and non-governmental organisations, produced an educational brochure on responsible tourism guidelines for tourists called *Tips for a Responsible Traveller*. Educating tourists is an effective measure for reducing damage to the environment. Hotel marketers can also use brochures to educate consumers about ways of conserving the environment (such as recycling and water conservation) and codes of conduct for behaving in a way that is environmentally responsible.

11.3.2.4 To Promote the Offering

Another objective of printed material and brochures is to promote the organisation and its offerings. Tour operators rely heavily on their brochures as their main communications and promotion tool. In many instances, potential customers contact a tour operator (via e-mail, telephone or from a company's website link) and request a brochure for information on specific holidays and tours. A brochure is designed to entice consumers and motivate them to purchase, and to portray the image and positioning of the organisation through the use of photographs and words.

Brochures are mailed (and e-mailed) by some tour operators to targeted consumers, using information obtained from client databases (see ▶ Chap. 12). For example, many tour operators have established through marketing research that the highest percentage of their customers are women, since they choose and book the family's holidays. They therefore take great care to select an image for the brochure cover that will attract the attention of women.

11.3.3 Producing Successful Brochures

In order to produce an informative and persuasive brochure, marketers should apply the AIDA principle in their design (see ▢ Table 11.4).

❓ Collect several brochures from tourism businesses. Analyse the brochures in terms of their strengths and weaknesses. Make suggestions as to how they could be improved to ensure that they meet the needs of customers better.

Industry Insight 11.4

The Four Seasons Magazine

The Four Seasons, the luxury hotel group, has its own printed magazine title. The Four Seasons Magazine (published by Pace Communications) is very important to the hotel group brand name. According to Jason Friedman, general manager of The Four Seasons Siam, a luxury resort in Bangkok "the glossy printed magazine helps keep guests connected to the luxury experience even when they are not there". That said, a printed magazine or brochure cannot provide the kind of immediacy that many tourists demand.

11.3.4 E-Brochures and Other Forms of Technology

Advances in technology are challenging the role of print materials. Digitalisation has offered alternatives that can replace printed maps, guidebooks, and brochures. Tourists can download travel guides apps (such as

□ Table 11.4   The AIDA principle applied to a tourism brochure

AIDA	The brochure should…:
Awareness	grab the reader's attention – with use of colour, imagery, and position in the brochure rack – and get him or her to pick up the brochure make the reader keep reading the brochure until all of the information has been absorbed.
Interest	look interesting to the reader be interesting to the reader (maintain his or her interest) be easy to read and understand.
Desire	distinguish the offering from other product-offerings demonstrate why the offering is good persuade the reader to agree that it is the only offering for him or her.
Action	Make it easy for the reader to take action and make a booking or purchase (include a telephone number, e-mail address, website).

Source: Author's creation

□ Image 11.2   Interactive maps are replacing traditional maps. (Source: ▶ Pexels.com)

▶ LonelyPlanet.com), and electronic (digital) maps on their mobile phones rather than using travel guidebooks and audio guides or printed maps respectively (see □ Image 11.2). The social networking site Facebook is replacing the traditional holiday postcard as a way of letting peers know that they are travelling (Cooper & Hall, 2019: 105). Prospective consumers can visit websites on the internet and view information about the offerings of various tourism businesses (usually accompanied by photographs, maps, and the company logo). If they wish, they can even print the pages.

The information found in brochures can be made available to prospective consumers via downloadable and printable e-brochures from internet sites, on social media apps, and portable navigation devices (PNDs).

11.3.4.1 E-Brochures (Digital Brochures)

An e-brochure is a brochure in electronic format. An e-brochure (also called a "digital brochure" or "electronic brochure") can be downloaded, and then printed out in colour. It is easy to distribute (can be e-mailed to customers) and can deliver rich multimedia content blending text, images, sound, and video. It can be accessed when needed and is easy to translate. It is also measurable. (A company can measure how many people have seen it.) Special offers can also be loaded easily in an e-brochure. Photos, videos, virtual tours, photo galleries, information, 360-degree images, interactive maps (see ◘ Image 11.2), and electronic travel itineraries are all features that can easily be added to e-brochures. They are in direct contrast to traditional paper brochures, which are expensive to print and distribute, date quickly and are expensive to translate into different languages. It is important that brochures be printable.

11.4 Public Relations

Public relations (PR) refers to communications that a tourism or hospitality organisation carries out to improve or maintain favourable relations with other organisations and individuals (Field, 1997). There are various definitions of PR because it encompasses a broad set of communication activities. These range from managing consumer perceptions of an organisation's offerings to its employees, its corporate identity, and its promotional activities (French, 1994: 2). In short, PR is concerned with everything that contributes to an organisation's public image.

The definition adopted by the Chartered Institute of Public Relations (CIPR) states that "Public Relations is the discipline which looks after reputation, with the aim of earning understanding and support and influencing opinion and behaviour. It is the planned and sustained effort to establish and maintain goodwill and mutual understanding between an organisation and its publics" (CIPR, 2017).

❓ Obtain a selection of tour operators' brochures and compare the way in which they present the information. In a group, discuss which brochures you think are the most effective promotional techniques. In other words, which brochures would be most likely to persuade you to book a holiday?

❓ Browse the website of the Chartered Institute of Public Relations: ► https://www.cipr.co.uk/

Many people confuse PR with publicity. The two are most definitely not the same thing. According to the *Blackwell Encyclopedia of Management*, publicity refers to a non-aid and non-personal form of communication from a specific source with the aim of providing Information about the organisation, its offerings and Its position on different Issues (Cooper & Argyris, 1997). Public relations is about reputation, which is the result of all you say, all you do and what others say about you. An organisation is continually communicating messages to the public, whether it wants to or not. ◘ Figure 11.1 illustrates the various publics that may influence a tourism organisation. In reality, most

◘ **Fig. 11.1** Various publics in the tourism industry. (Source: Author's creation)

11

small tourism businesses will have fewer publics than larger tourism organisations; although there is still a need for maintaining positive mutually beneficial relationships with employees, customers, and the local community (Pike, 2018: 175).

In recent years, tourism marketers have increasingly begun using PR rather than other, more expensive promotional tools, such as advertising and sales promotion, because PR is essentially free advertising. For example, an editorial feature on Swaziland in a travel magazine such as *Condé Nast Travel* magazine or a write-up or recommendation of a hotel or holiday resort in a Lonely Planet travel guidebook does not cost the marketer anything except time. In addition, PR is likely to be more far effective than any other promotional tool. However, PR should not always be considered free or inexpensive. It is often costly to arrange a press reception for the opening of a new offering. The contracting-out of PR activities to a media agency can also be quite expensive. However, PR does not require the purchase of airtime or space in media vehicles, such as TV or online (Baines et al., 2019: 444).

11.4.1 The Differences Between Public Relations and the Other Promotional Tools

The major difference between PR and the other promotional tools is that it involves messages to the general public rather than to one or a few target market segments. PR is aimed at consumers, the travel trade, suppliers, tourist associations, business communities, local communities, politicians, and employees. Another major difference is that tourism marketers do not always pay for media space, as with other promotional tools. Instead, they invest their time in providing news items or stories that the media consider of interest to their readers, listeners, or

viewers, ultimately hoping to make a good impression on the public and develop a strong image. Consequently, when using PR as a promotional tool, marketers have no guarantee that the message will be transmitted. While the company has control over its advertising, sales promotions, and personal selling, marketers must take into account the fact that it has little control over its PR (Field, 1997: 32).

Increasingly, businesses are demanding greater proof of the impact of their PR campaigns. The unit known as advertising value equivalent (AVE) is traditionally used to measure the media exposure of public relations activities. Research has, however, found that it is in fact the impact of the PR activity that is the absolute measure. The CIPR has established criteria to calculate the impact of media publicity and public relations. (These criteria can be found at a link on the organisation's homepage: ▶ www.cipra. co.uk).

PR is a part of marketing and should be integrated with the other promotional tools. As discussed earlier, this is known as integrated marketing communications (IMC) and includes the use of any promotions mix tools such as advertising, sales promotion, digital marketing, social media marketing, direct marketing, and personal selling in a coordinated manner (Gronroos, 2004). (See ▶ Chap. 10).

In large tourism and hospitality organisations, the marketing department (and its PR division) usually carried out its own PR activities or contracts them out to a PR/media agency or PR consultant. Destination marketing organisations (DMOs) and other organisations focusing on destinations tend to have separate PR departments.

11.4.2 Public Relations Techniques

PR is perhaps more useful to the tourism and hospitality marketer than to the manufacturing goods marketer. An exotic location, for example, is far more interesting and glamorous to the general public than a bottle of household bleach. Similarly, a review of an upmarket restaurant or an international airline makes interesting newspaper and magazine reading. At the same time, a negative occurrence at a tourism destination (such as pollution at a beach location, for example) or hospitality business (an outbreak of food poisoning at a hotel resort) can make a dramatic and interesting news (but negative) item for the public (see ▶ Industry Insight 11.5). This type of publicity must be managed by companies and their PR teams.

The main techniques used in PR are media relations, feature stories, corporate communications, lobbying, counselling, crisis management, community relations, networking, travel trade events, memberships, product placement, and educational trips (see ◘ Table 11.5).

Editorial coverage has, on average, a credibility rating that is three times higher than advertising.

Industry Insight 11.5

United Airlines: Another Day, Another PR Disaster for United Airlines

In March 2017, United Airlines CEO Oscar Munoz was named USA Communicator of the Year by the magazine PR Week. Just one month later, his company's poor response to a customer incident has turned into a PR disaster, caused its stock to dramatically drop $1bn in value and has placed the entire airline industry under the microscope.

America's third biggest carrier was slammed online for violently dragging a passenger - a 69-year-old Asian man, believed to be a doctor - off an overbooked flight. This came just weeks after the company, whose slogan is "Fly the Friendly Skies", was ridiculed for refusing to allow two teenage girls to board a flight because they were wearing leggings. The CEO added more fuel to the fire with his response, which didn't mention the use of force. "This is an upsetting event to all of us here at United. I apologise for having to re-accommodate these passengers," he said in a statement. But Mr Munoz also sent an e-mail to employees calling the passenger, who was pictured with a bloodied face, "disruptive and belligerent". United Airlines, which made $2.3bn (£1.85bn) in profit last year, isn't alone in the PR disasters club. Delta Airlines has cancelled thousands of flights since Wednesday because of severe weather. It's not the first time.

Delta chief executive Ed Bastian was forced to apologise after thousands of flights were delayed and cancelled due to a computer bug and power failure in August 2016.

Source: ▶ http://www.bbc.co.uk/news/business-39562182

❓ In a group, draft a communications plan to deal with negative publicity - a terrorist incident - that has recently occurred at a local tourism attraction.

11

WTM: A Great Networking Opportunity

The World Travel Market (WTM) is an excellent way to network with industry professionals and learn about the latest trends in the tourism industry. All major players in the industry, from every continent and country, have representation at the WTM exhibition, and it almost feels like travelling the entire world without leaving your own city. It can take a couple of days to "visit" the whole exhibition, which includes seminars and workshops.

Source: World Travel Market. (2019). 3–6 November 2019/ExCel London. [Online], Available: ► www.wtmlondon.com/ Accessed 1 December 1 2019.

■ **Image 11.3**   The WTM travel trade show - an excellent event for networking with fellow tourism professionals

The Tourism Society

The Tourism Society is the professional membership body for people working in the international travel and tourism industry. The Tourism Society has over 11,000 members drawn from tour operators, hotel chains, PR, marketing and representation companies, tourist attractions, national, regional, and local tourist boards, restaurants, trade media, charities, consultants, academics, students, and educational establishments.

Since its inception in 1977, the Tourism Society has provided tourism professionals with a forum to debate and exchange views, expertise, and opinion through meetings, conferences, and its own journal. Within the Tourism Society, there is the *Tourism Consultants Network (TCN)*, the largest association of consultant tourism experts in the United Kingdom. Collectively, they provide expertise in most areas of Britain's thriving and highly diversified tourism sector and take their skills to developing markets all over the world. Members are listed on the TCN website, where they can increase their exposure to companies and organisations looking for high-quality expertise in specific areas of tourism work. With over 15,000 follow-ers of @tourismsociety on Twitter and more than 5000 followers of the Tourism Society group on LinkedIn, the society has a very active social media profile, which helps it achieve its aim of educating and informing members about developments in all areas of the visitor economy and enabling its extensive network of profession-als to exchange information, experience, and expertise.

Table 11.5 PR tools used in tourism

Type of PR toole	Objectives/description	Example/s
Community relations	Maintaining a good relationship with the local community.	A visitor attraction offering free guided tours to school groups or providing support to various communities in local events.
Corporate communications	To promote understanding and a good image of the organisation among the internal and external publics.	(i). Sending out newsletters and magazines to employees, holding staff briefing presentations and meetings. (ii). A logo and brand name of the organisation which is consistent with the image that the organisation portrays.
Counselling	Advising management about issues, brand image, and public policies that affect the image of the organisation during times of crisis.	Waiting staff might hear that consumers are not happy about prices of offerings on a hotel menu. Management needs to be informed about such issues so that they can be addressed.
Crisis management/ communications	To handle negative events as they occur	Addressing issues such as overcoming negative publicity because of violent incidents, natural disasters, strikes, and so o
Digital content and social media	PR agencies are increasingly generating their own video- and text-based digital content on behalf of their clients. A tourism company has to be a media company in its own right, telling its own stories through video and mobile applications.	PR officers can provide the editorial content to websites and digital media. A company has to engage with consumers about its brand.
Editorials (or feature stories)	To draw attention to a product offering's selling points. Articles of human interest that entertain, inform or educate listeners, viewers or readers.	A feature or write-up (a short article) about a restaurant in the local newspaper by the paper's food editor.
Educational trips (or familiarisation trip or fam trip)	A tour that provides travel agents, tour operators, travel writers, and other members of the tourism industry with the opportunity of trying out facilities and services first-hand, so that they are in the best position to advise clients on their holiday choices.	Inviting travel agents and other publics such as journalists (also known as "journos"), television crews and trade delegates

(continued)

◘ Table 11.5 (continued)

Type of PR toole	Objectives/description	Example/s
Lobbying	To deal with government primarily for the purpose of influencing legislation and regulation (Broom & Sha, 2012: 4).	Tourism trade associations, airlines and other suppliers might lobby government to reduce or eliminate tourism tax (VAT) or to encourage acceptance of an airport development
Media/Press relations	To present a positive image of a company or event by creating newsworthy stories to the press, radio, and television	Media releases and press conferences A meeting or contacting travel writers and journalists face-to-face or calling a press conference to brief a larger number of people at one time.
Memberships	Taking out memberships should also be part of a tourism business's networking strategy.	Association of British Travel Agents (ABTA), European Tour Operators Association (ETOA), World Youth Student and Educational Travel Confederation (WYSE).
Networking	The art of mingling with potential customers and other tourism providers at an event. Obtaining information that can lead to opportunities and result in new marketing strategies.	Attending all tourism offering-related launches, local business clubs, tourism industry forums, and tourism industry association meetings, seminars, awards events, talks, and conferences. They should also consider attending local and regional tourism boards meetings.
Product placement	A form of sponsorship which entails the incorporation of branded products into movies and television shows.	Placing a destination in a film is a prime example of product placement. *Skyfall* (Scotland), *The Beach* (Thailand), *The Hangover* (Las Vegas), Life of Pi (India), *Long Walk to Freedom* (South Africa), *365* (Romania), *La Dolce Vita* (Rome, Italy), and *Tampopo* (Japan).
Travel trade events	(i). Travel trade expos (ii). Travel exchanges involve a DMO inviting key international intermediaries to a 2–3-day expo where they typically have a series of 50 fifteen-minute meetings with tourism businesses who have paid for display space (Pike, 2018: 218). Events are usually targeted at the travel trade, while some shows are also aimed at consumers. Provide excellent intimate and interactive direct-selling opportunities.	Travel trade expos are either general leisure trade shows (for example, the annual Travel Expo), or those that specialise in adventure, backpacking, luxury travel and so on. Tourism Indaba (Africa), International Trade Bourse (ITB) in Berlin, World Travel Market (WTM) in London (see ▶ Industry Insight 11.6).

Source: Author's creation

? Access a good example of publicity in a newspaper or magazine that has been linked to a social media site such as Facebook or Twitter. Explain how the print and digital media complement one another. Before we look at a suggested definition of marketing, how would you define it? Write down what you think marketing entails, and then compare your definition with the definitions offered in this chapter. Browse the AMA website: ▶ www.ama.org

11.4.3 **Public Relations Strategies for Small Tourism Businesses**

Since advertising and some of the other promotional tools are costly, PR can be extremely effective for small tourism businesses such as cafés, restaurants, guesthouses, and boutique hotels. The PR strategies described below, can be useful to entrepreneurs who pay close attention to this aspect of the business.

11.4.3.1 **Construct PR Around an Individual**

An individual or the owner of an offering may be the centrepiece around which to construct public relations. Individuals who are successful at promoting themselves have charisma and often use some form of theatrical prop (perhaps a costume, for instance). Tourist destinations use PR around an individual, usually a celebrity, to great effect. For example, the city of Adipur in the state of Gujarat in northwest India hosts an annual Charlie Chaplin parade in which hundreds of locals dress-up like Charlie Chaplin and parade through the city to celebrate his birthday. Several cafés and bars in Madrid are named after the novelist Ernest Hemmingway who frequented the haunts in the 1920s and 930s.

Some offerings are named after individuals, such as Nelson Mandela Bay in Port Elizabeth in South Africa. Richard Branson (*Virgin Group*), Conrad Hilton (*Hilton Hotels*), Tony Ryan (*Ryanair*), Thomas Carlyle (*Carlyle Hotels*), Stelios Haji-Ioannou (*Easy Jet, Easy Group*), and John Hays (*Hays Travel*) are strong personalities who turned their travel and hospitality brands into household names in the UK and internationally.

Encouraging celebrities to use tourism and hospitality offerings or visit destinations can result in considerable media attention and thus help promote the offering. Prince Harry, model Elle McPherson, golfer Tiger Woods and Hollywood actors Johnny Depp Smith and Gwyneth Paltrow take frequent holidays in the Bahamas. Celebrities are effective PR ambassadors for environmental protection and social responsibility (See ▶ Industry Insight 11.8).

Industry Insight 11.8

Uganda PR Campaign Uses Celebrities to Promote Environmental Cause

In 2018, Uganda ran a PR campaign to promote its tourism industry through local and international celebrities. Through a partnership with the Uganda Conservation Foundation, the Uganda Wildlife Authority, the international conservation group WildAid launched a campaign titled "Poaching Steals from Us All." The three-year PR campaign was officially rolled out in Kampala with funding from charitable foundations and the private sector. The campaign was aimed at raising the profile of wildlife conservation in Uganda, emphasising its cultural and economic importance. A combination of local and international celebrity ambassadors was deployed, and the campaign was rolled out in several Ugandan languages in the form of TV documentaries and short public announcements, billboards, social media, events, and other outreaches aimed at instilling a sense of pride in the country's wildlife heritage and entrenching a desire to protect it. During the last few years, WildAid has been using celebrities to speak to people about conservation. They have worked with the likes of football star David Beckham, actors Jackie Chan, Leonardo Dicaprio, Yang Ming, and Lupita Nyongo, and Britain's Prince William and DJ Fresh. They have targeted different parts of the world under the global theme: "When the buying stops, the killing can too." "In Uganda, the ambassadors include comedians Anne Kansiime and Salvador, singers Irene Ntale and Maurice Kirya, the Uganda Cranes football team, the Rugby Sevens team, and the Inter-Religious Council of Uganda," says Ms. Nayantara Kilachand, WildAid's Africa manager. "The celebrities have been chosen because they are trendsetters, admired, and followed by many people" she added.

Source: ▶ http://www.theeastafrican.co.ke/business/Celebrities-to-promote-tourism-Uganda/2560-4164904-ymp331z/index.html

11

11.4.3.2 Construct PR Around a Unique Product-Offering

A unique offering can serve as a PR focal point. Restaurants and hotels may build a long-lasting image around a specially concocted cocktail, unique service (ironically, the service may be very bad, while the food is good), their histories, or a unique destination. For example, a hotel or B&B may highlight the fact that it is situated in or near a unique site such as a natural reserve, a cave, a rainforest, a park, an area of outstanding beauty, a visitor attraction, or a UNESCO site. These unique offerings may get the attention of local or international media, which in turn generate publicity for the organisations offering them.

11.4.3.3 Construct PR Around a Unique Location

A tourism offering in a unique location may also attract the attention of the media, for example, a game lodge that visitors cannot locate without a topographical map. A DMO in Queensland, Australia created an enormous amount of PR and media buzz around a job offer (see in-depth case study at the end of chapter).

11.4.3.4 Construct PR in the Neighbourhood

Providing a tour to local schools and colleges through a tourism organisation (such as a visitor attraction, hotel) can be an effective PR strategy for creating business and goodwill. Students are also likely to tell others about their visit. Getting a free write-up in a local newspaper as well as some exposure on social media sites are other ways of gaining publicity and reaching a target market. These types of PR activities do not cost anything other than a little time and creativity.

11.5 Sponsorship

Sponsorship is the provision of financial support by an organisation to another organisation to gain prestige and status from its association with the other organisation (Deuschl, 2006: 4).

It is often included in an organisation's public relations activities since it indirectly enhances the customer's perceptions of the organisation or its offerings. An organisation might sponsor a television programme, a sporting event, a hallmark event, a cultural event or even an individual. Sponsorship is a high-profile form of collaborative marketing between organisations that have only a market in common.

11.5.1 Sponsorship Versus Advertising

Sponsorship is vastly different from advertising. The main function of advertising is the promotion of an organisation and its offerings. In sponsorship, the organisation's name plays a supportive or secondary role to the event, activity or person being sponsored. It is regarded as 'a commercial activity whereby one party permits another an opportunity to exploit an association with a target audience in return for funds, services, or resources' (Fill, 2009). Sponsorship is less overtly commercial than advertising, which has a greater impact.

11.5.2 The Role of Sponsorship in Tourism and Hospitality Marketing

The two main areas of sponsorship in tourism and hospitality marketing are discussed below.

11.5.2.1 Sponsorship of an Event or a Tourism Activity By a Non-tourism Organisation

Examples of tourism events that are sponsored by non-tourism firms include the logistics company DHL which sponsors the *Red Bull Air Race*. In addition to the promotional exposure and publicity, *DHL* also provides transport services for the event. An example of a tourism activity sponsored by a non-tourism firm is bungee-jumping at Storms River, South Africa, which is sponsored by *Hunter's Gold* cider.

11.5.2.2 Sponsorship of a Non-tourism Event By a Tourism Organisation

Examples of non-tourism events that are sponsored by a tourism and hospitality organisation include the sponsorship of the annual South African Open golf championships and the ATP World Tour, which are both sponsored by the city of Johannesburg (Johannesburg)

Other types of sponsorship include financial or material support for the arts (for example, *Emirates Airline* sponsors the Festival of Literature hosted annually in Dubai, UAE), fine arts, concerts, educational trips and courses, television programmes, and sporting events. Sponsorship has been a major part of the promotional activity of major sporting events, with sponsors (ranging from soft drink companies to newspapers) supporting football, rugby, cycling, cricket and so on. Sporting events attract a significant share of sponsorship revenue. For example, the FIFA 2018 World Cup™ hosted in Russia secured over US$1.65 billion (£1,3 billion) in sponsorship revenue (Badenhausen, 2018). The sponsorship of events is an effective way of gaining publicity. It enables the sponsor to invite and host suppliers, journalists and customers, and attracts the public's attention to the firm's name and offerings. Event sponsorship is defined as the financial support of an event by a sponsor in return for advertising privileges associated with the event. *Emirates Airline* sponsors several European football clubs including real Madrid, Arsenal, Paris Saint Germain (PSG), and Arsenal. The DMO *VisitFlorida* sponsors Fulham FC, and *Etihad Airways* sponsors Manchester City FC and New York City FC.

11.5.3 The Advantages and Disadvantages of Sponsorship

The advantages and disadvantages of sponsorship, along with other below-the-line (BTL) promotional tools, are outlined in ◘ Table 11.6 below.

Summary

Sales promotion, personal selling marketing collateral, PR, and sponsorship are all below-the-line promotional tools that can be used either in isolation or as an integrated approach by marketers. Rather than regarding them as separate tools, the marketer should use an integrated approach and see them as different ways of delivering the same message. Sales promotion is a powerful tool of the promotions mix, but it is often misused. As for personal selling, when executed properly, it is one of the most effective promotions mix tools available to the tourism marketer.

Marketing collateral and travel brochures are important communications tools. They are almost a necessity for all tourism organisations and destinations. The design of travel brochures is especially important as it reflects the image and nature of the offering. Public relations can be a cheaper alternative to advertising, although this is not always the case. Public relations also includes the management of crises and negative publicity. Gaining free media publicity (media releases) and DMO educationals are effective PR techniques for small tourism businesses. Sponsorship is increasingly being recognised as an effective promotional tool in tourism marketing. It has the advantages of increasing brand awareness and promoting the image of an organisation.

? Review Questions
1. Briefly explain why a tourism and hospitality marketer should not overuse sales promotion.
2. Explain how sales promotion can be used to enhance other elements of the communications mix.
3. What are the benefits of exhibitions as a promotional tool?
4. Contrast the concept of up-selling with cross-selling. Provide some practical examples from the hospitality sector.

5. Explain why personal selling is important to tourism organisations.
6. Discuss the role of brochures in the promotion of package holidays by tour operators.
7. What are the primary objectives of a brochure? Critically evaluate several tourism and hospitality brochures to see how well they meet these objectives.
8. What are some of the advantages of PR over the other promotions mix tools?
9. Is public relations always free? Justify your answer.
10. Compare and contrast sponsorship with advertising.

Table 11.6 The advantages and disadvantages of each below-the-line promotional tool

Promotional tool	Advantages	Disadvantages
Sales promotions	Short-term results (quick increase in sales) Flexible; can be used at any stage of the product life cycle Can shift slow-moving tourism and hospitality offerings (excess capacity/inventory) Ability to measure responses Increases awareness of new offerings or price	Does not provide investment in long-term sales Provides little information about the market If sale is run for too long, consumers expect a discount (it is a short-term tactic) Promotion and perceived quality may be lowered May conceal management problems
Personal selling	Aimed at specific target markets (external selling) Gets far more information across to the consumer than an advertisement (more persuasive) The process is interactive Builds consumer relationships (repeat business) Passive sales are inexpensive; it doesn't cost anything to smile and be polite	Limited target audience Expensive to set up and train a sales force Telephone selling viewed as irritating and intrusive by consumers
Marketing collateral	e-brochures is that they can be embedded into a company's website, quickly and easily making a website more interactive.	
Public relations	High credibility Low cost	Low level of control
Sponsorship	Enhances the image and reputation of the company. Sales and merchandising opportunities. generates goodwill Costs can be offset against taxes. Increasing brand awareness and publicity	Can be expensive and is not always effective. Difficult to evaluate the impact of sponsorship activity. There is no guarantee that the sponsored team or individual will live up to expectations.

Source: Author's creation

Objectives

- To understand the communications mix in tourism and hospitality marketing
- To understand and apply the tools of the promotions mix to a tourism and hospitality organisation.

Isandlwana Lodge in KwaZulu-Natal, South Africa is unique in many ways. It was built by two American women who met by chance on an aeroplane in 1996. Their common interest in southern Africa was the springboard from which a partnership was formed that led them to the heart of Zululand.

The two enterprising women visited Isandlwana together for the first time in 1997. After discussing the possibilities with the tribal councillors, the women and the councillors walked the site. Then a simple handshake with the Inkosi of the tribe created a partnership that has brought jobs to the local community and revenue (to be used for building schools and clinics, and generally enhancing the lives of the villagers) to the tribal trust.

Another unique part of the story is that the lodge was purposely designed to look as though it grew out of the rock formations on which it was built. The distinctive shape of a shield can be seen from above. The lodge has a thatched roof and is built with rock from the area to resemble native kraals. In addition, most of the furniture in the lodge is made locally from indigenous wood. The columns that support the roof are from the old West Street Pier in Durban. Each column is named after a Zulu commander or significant person in the chain of command during the South African War of 1879. Isandlwana Lodge is believed to be one of the few tourism facilities built on an historical site in southern Africa.

Isandlwana Lodge was officially opened in May 1999. Many of its overseas visitors come from the UK, the USA, Germany, and Switzerland. Although Isandlwana is a niche tourism destination, it does not appeal to only one defined market, but rather to the following specific markets:

- International travellers (the accommodation rack rate in 2020 is R2 995 (£144/€168) per person per night, with a 50% single supplement)
- Special interest groups (located near to the battlefields of KwaZulu-Natal, Isandlwana attracts people and study groups interested in the historical, military, and cultural aspects of the area)
- The local corporate market (with small but exclusive conference facilities, the lodge accommodates exclusive corporate groups).

According to Anita Foxcroft, Director of Southern Spoor, a public relations and marketing agency which includes Isandlwana Lodge on its account: "We also target cycle and walking groups as the surrounding terrain is perfect for enthusiastic cyclists or walkers. Birdwatching is another albeit small potential target market. Other popular pursuits include climbing and mountain biking". The lodge's target market can be further divided according to its geographical markets. For instance, to most of the UK market, Isandlwana is a battlefield destination. The German tourists, in contrast, are attracted to the lodge for cultural reasons such as visits to nearby Zulu villages. Anita says that many of the UK tourists spend their days touring the battlefields and listening to lectures on the Anglo-Zulu and Anglo-Boer wars by well-known historian and guide Dalton Ngobese. Dalton is a local Zulu descendent of one of the impi warriors at The Battle of Isandlwana. Visitors interested in the history of the area and the country will be mesmerised by the storytelling of Dalton. In the evening, all guests enjoy an authentic South African dinner cooked by a local chef. There is always time to relax in a pool built among the rocks or simply to enjoy the panoramic view of the Isandlwana Valley.

A unique characteristic of Isandlwana Lodge is its marketing activities. Isandlwana Lodge has made excellent use of various elements of the promotions mix to communicate its unique offering and carve a niche for itself in the tourism market. The entire staff complement, from

11

kitchen workers to receptionists, is trained in personal selling skills. Isandlwana Lodge carries out public relations activities (for example, online press releases, newsletters, and social media) through local and international organisations.

Isandlwana Lodge has produced a landscape DL-size full-colour brochure for international and local distribution. In addition, it has printed flyers featuring details of the guided tours of the battlefield. It also uses printed and online flyers to promote various seasonal and special interest tourism campaigns (for example, astronomy). Isandlwana is also promoted via various tour operator programs (along with other lodges and resorts in the region) in several tourist brochures that highlight the attractions of KwaZulu-Natal in a six- or nine-day package as well as by agencies that promote tailor-made packages. As much as 80% of Isandlwana's business is driven through its travel trade partners: overseas tour operators and its local destination management companies (DMCs). This is a cost-effective way for small tourism and hospitality businesses such

as Isandlwana to market themselves. By working with other offerings in the area, Isandlwana also creates an itinerary that appeals to international travellers and assists with the increase in bed night occupancy. Physical evidence and merchandising at the lodge are all of the highest quality. This begins with the design of the building and the Zulu theme, which is carried through in staff uniforms and interior design. The lodge's colourful menu is an example of an excellent merchandising tool.

Naturally, the Lodge has also been successful in getting Isandlwana included in a number of South African tour itineraries. A limited amount of advertising has been carried out. The focus remains on PR communications in various national and international publications that are aimed at consumers who are interested in travelling in South Africa. Isandlwana communicates its brand in special interest magazines nationally and internationally, constantly creating top-of-mind awareness. It also relies on receiving bookings and enquiries via wholesalers (tour operators) and retailers (travel

□ **Image 11.4**   Isandlwana Lodge located by the site of the famous Anglo-Zulu War of 1879 in Isandlwana, KwaZulu-Natal, South Africa. (Source: Dionne Collett, Take Note Repustation Management)

agents). "We attend a number of international trade fairs and exhibitions. This provides us with a good platform to engage with key customers and to source new ones", says Anita.

Marketing a product/property like Isandlwana Lodge requires a good mix between brand awareness, which is achieved through its newsletters, social media activity, some advertising, and our sales activities. Of particular importance is the relationships with the travel trade and their individual consumers. Through these relationships Southern Spoor is not only able to gain more business for Isandlwana but many of its trade partners also add additional marketing through their own activities.

Isandlwana Lodge is a good example of how to use a promotions mix to attract international travellers and still support the local market.

Source: Based on an interview with Anita Foxcroft, Director of Southern Spoor.

Case Study Questions and Activities

1. Isandlwana's marketing campaign combines marketing collateral, sales promotions, and personal selling. Analyse the mix and discuss its effectiveness.
2. Which promotional tool do you think Isandlwana Lodge should use to target special interest tourism groups?
3. Explain what could be done to encourage Isandlwana staff to engage in more up-selling. Provide examples.
4. Identify other special interest tourism groups that Isandlwana could target.

□ **Image 11.5** Isandlwana Lodge. (Source: Dionne Collett, Take Note Repustation Management)

References

Andereck, K. (2005). Evaluation of a tourist brochure. *Journal of Travel & Tourism Marketing, 18*(2), 1–13.

Badenhausen, K. (2018). FIFA world cup 2018: The money behind the biggest event in: Sports'. *Forbes.* [Online]. Available: https://www.forbes.com/sites/kurtbadenhausen/2018/06/14/world-cup-2018-the-money-behind-the-biggest-event-in-sports/#3c5aa6fb6973. Accessed 11 May 2019.

Baines, P., Fill, C., Rosengren, S., & Antonetti, P. (2019). *Marketing* (5th ed.). Oxford, UK: Oxford University Press.

Blattberg, R., & Neslin, S. (1990). *Sales promotion: Concepts, methods, and strategies*. Englewood Cliffs, New Jersey: Prentice-Hall.

Blem, N. (2008). *Achieving excellence in selling* (3rd ed.). Cape Town, South Africa: Oxford University Press.

Boseley, S. (2017). "Up-selling" fuels obesity. *The Guardian.* 7 September, Page 9.

Broom, G. M., & Sha, B.-L. (2012). *Cutlip and center's effective public relations* (11th ed.). Upper Saddle River, NJ: Prentice Hall.

Chartered Institute of Public Relations (CIPR). (2017). *'About PR'.* [Online]. Available: https://www.cipr.co.uk/content/about-us/about-pr. Accessed 1 Apr 2017.

Cooper, C., & Hall, M. (2019). *Contemporary tourism: An international approach* (4th ed.). London: Goodfellow.

Cooper, C. L., & Argyris, C. (1997). The Blackwell encyclopaedia of management. In *Marketing* (Vol. IV). Oxford, UK: Blackwell.

Deuschl, D. E. (2006). *Travel and tourism public relations*. Oxford, UK: Elsevier Butterworth-Heinemann.

Field, D. (1997). *Marketing for leisure and tourism.* London: Hodder & Stoughton.

Fill, C. (2009). *Marketing communications: Interactivity communications and content* (5th ed.). Essex, UK: Prentice-Hall.

French, Y. (1994). *Public relations for leisure and tourism*. Exeter, UK: Longman.

Futrell, C. M. (2014). *Fundamentals of selling: Customers for life through service* (13th ed.). Boston: Irwin McGraw-Hill.

Gronroos, C. (2004). The relationship marketing process: Communication, interaction, dialogue, value. *Journal of Business & Industrial Marketing, 19*(2), 99–113.

Kotler, P., Bowen, J., Makens, J., & Baloglu, S. (2017). *Marketing for hospitality and tourism* (7th ed.). Upper Saddle River, NJ: Prentice Hall.

Kotler, P., Rackman, N., & Krishnaswamy, S. (2006). Ending the war between sales and marketing. *Harvard Business Review*, July–August, 68–78.

Middleton, V. T. C., & Clarke, J. (2001). *Marketing in travel and tourism* (3rd ed.). Oxford, UK: Butterworth-Heinemann.

Molina, A., Gómez, M., & Martín-Consuegra, D. (2010). Tourism marketing information and destination image. *African Journal of Business Management, 4*(5), 722–728.

Morrison, A. M. (1996). *Hospitality and travel marketing* (2nd ed.). New York: Delmar Publishers.

Pike, S. (2018). *Tourism marketing for small businesses.* Oxford, UK: Goodfellow Publishers.

Wilmshurst, J. (1993). *Below-the-line promotion.* St. Ives, UK: Butterworth-Heinemann.

Further Reading

Futrell, C. M. (2014). *Fundamentals of selling: Customers for life through service* (13th ed.). Boston: Irwin McGraw-Hill.

Granville, F., Mehta, A., & Pike, S. (2016). Destinations, disasters and public relations: Stakeholder engagement in multi-phase disaster management. *Journal of Hospitality Management, 28*(September), 73–79.

Digital Marketing in Tourism and Hospitality

Contents

Electronic Supplementary Material The online version of this chapter (https://doi.org/10.1007/978-3-030-64111-5_12) contains supplementary material, which is available to authorized users.

Purpose

This chapter will give you an understanding of how digital marketing and social media marketing are used to promote tourism and hospitality product-offerings.

🌐 Learning Goals

After reading this chapter, you should be able to:

- Define the terms "digital marketing" and "social media marketing"
- Identify the various functions of the internet
- Explain the advantages of digital marketing
- Describe the three types of media used in digital marketing: paid, owned, and earned
- Explore the techniques used in digital marketing and social media marketing (SMM)
- Explain how to evaluate digital and social media in the practice of tourism
- Understand how to promote a website using various offline and online techniques
- Apply the concept of influencer marketing to a case study in tourism and hospitality marketing.

Overview

We begin this chapter by looking at definitions of digital marketing, and then discuss how the internet and social media have transformed tourism marketing practice. Next, we look at the main areas of digital marketing with respect to three types of media: paid, owned, and earned.

The chapter's case study examines the role of travel influencers in tourism and hospitality marketing.

12.1 Introduction

In this fast-paced, competitive, technology-driven world, people are bombarded by between 3000 and 5000 messages daily, via numerous channels (Janabi, 2017). New digital technologies and channels have multiplied and will continue to do so. Through e-mail, social media, web banners, direct mail, short message service (SMS or text messaging), and mobile apps, people are using a multitude of different devices to research, review, and ultimately purchase accommodation, tours, and holiday activities. All these touch points present opportunities and challenges for travel companies to add value with personalised engagement and to attract consumers. Holidays are no longer simply about a consumer going into a travel agent and booking a holiday; they are about engagement, offline and online. Travel companies must find new ways to understand, engage with, and provide value during every single customer interaction to remain top-of-mind, retain market share, and ultimately meet revenue targets in this noisy, technology-obsessed world in which we now live. With the explosion of channels and choice, the successful operator will build a combination of specialist knowledge and advanced technology – a customer-centric marketing ecosystem – that uses every digital touch point and adds value where customers expect it least (Mapp Corporation, 2017).

Digital marketing is the new marketing. The internet and increasingly mobile communication as well as other digital technologies now impact on almost every organisation in some form or another. For some time now, the internet and mobile communication have opened up new and comparatively inexpensive ways to reach consumers, offering a myriad of options. The internet encompasses a new marketspace (the digital version of a marketplace) and a new sales channel as well as a new method of advertising. It allows innovative ways of communication and customer relationship management (CRM). Hundreds of millions of people use the internet on a daily basis, and thus provide a potential target market for the products and services of tourism and hospitality businesses. The internet has resulted in one of the most fundamental changes in marketing: it has shifted the balance of power to individual consumers and even entire communities through social networking sites (Pitt, Berthon, Watson. & Zinkhan, 2002).

We will begin this chapter by looking at a definition of digital marketing as well as some of the terms associated with digital marketing.

12.2 Digital Marketing

Digital marketing is defined as "Achieving marketing objectives through applying digital technologies and media" (Chaffey & Ellis-Chadwick, 2019: 4). Digital marketing is the marketing of products or services using digital electronic devices or channels such as the internet, social media, e-mail, digital television, search engines, and wireless media. It differs from traditional marketing in that it involves the use of channels and methods that enable an organisation to analyse marketing campaigns to gain an understanding of what is working and what is not, typically in real time.

> *Digital marketing* is the marketing of products or services using digital electronic technologies and channels such as the internet, e-mail, digital TV, and wireless media (Strauss & Frost, 2013: 3).

Over time, digital marketing has been referred to as internet marketing, e-marketing, and web marketing. ◩ Table 12.1 introduces some digital marketing concepts that we will use throughout this chapter.

12.2.1 Advantages of Digital Marketing

One of the main advantages of digital marketing as a marketing tool is that it has made tourism organisations of all sizes much more equal in their competition for the consumer's attention (UNWTO, 2008). In other words, it has levelled the playing field. For small tourism businesses, digital marketing offers the advantages of lower costs and better efficiency than traditional marketing tools and provides opportunities to enhance consumer experience and relationships with customers.

The internet allows organisations to have a worldwide market. For example, a prospective traveller from Brazil to Maputo, Mozambique can access information about a hotel, including prices, availability, graphics and photographs of rooms, details about meals and amenities, and photographs of scenic views. This online information can be accessed from a number of devices, sent via the internet, and used across a tourism business's various online promotional platforms.

Digital marketing is a two-way communication channel. It has more of an impact than traditional communication channels as a result of its use of media content: text, audio, photographs, graphics, and video clips can all be used to deliver a message. The information that digital marketing conveys can be changed and updated relatively easily. Travellers can also post online reviews of destinations and tourism offerings as they experience them.

Another advantage of digital marketing is that it can provide consumers with fast and immediate responses. With a few taps of a touchpad, keyboard, or screen, consumers can book a flight or a hotel room, or download a holiday brochure or newsletter online. In addition, digital marketing and social media make it possible to do business 24 hours a day, 7 days a week for every week of the year (also known as the "24/7 economy").

12.2.2 The 5Ds of Digital Marketing

The 5Ds of digital marketing outline the opportunities for consumers to interact with brands and for tourism and hospitality businesses to reach consumers:

1. Digital devices – users experience brands as they interact with business websites and mobile apps typically through a combination of connected devices including smartphones, tablets, desktop computers, TVs, and gaming devices.

2. Digital platforms – most interactions on these devices are through a browser or apps from the major platforms or services, namely Facebook, Instagram, Google,

◘ Table 12.1   Digital marketing definitions

Digital marketing	The marketing of products or services using digital electronic devices (for example, e-mail, internet, digital television, and wireless media) and digital data about consumers' characteristics and behaviour (Strauss & Frost, 2013).
SEO	Involves designing website content to improve a business's ranking on internet search engines for popular travel search terms (Pike, 2018: 164).
SEM	The paid-for advertising that usually appears alongside, above, and occasionally below the organic listings on the search engine results pages (SERPS), or on a partner site
Pay-per-click (PPC)	The way of using search engine advertising to generate clicks to your website, rather than "earning" those clicks organically.
Social media marketing (SMM)	A type of digital marketing using social media and social web (that is, social networks, online communities, blogs, and wikis) or any other online collaborative technology for marketing activities (Stokes, 2018).
E-marketing	The promotion of products or brands via one or more forms of electronic media (Stokes, 2018).
Mobile marketing	A multi-channel, multi-channel *online marketing* technique focused at reaching a target audience on their *smartphones*, *tablets*, or any other related devices through websites, E-mail, SMS and MMS, social media, or mobile application (Karjaluoto & Leppäniemi, 2005).
Direct marketing	The term used to describe the various techniques that an organisation can use to sell its offerings on a personalised basis directly to the consumer, without the use of an intermediary (middleman); direct marketing via digital means generally involves e-mail, and to some extent, mobile channels (DMA, 2019).
Interactive marketing	Using interactive media to enable a situation or mechanism through which a tourism marketer and a customer interact, usually in real time (Baines, et al., 2019)
Viral marketing	Electronic word-of-mouth whereby some form of marketing message related to a company, brand, or product is transmitted in an exponentially growing way—often through the use of social media applications (Kaplan & Haenlein, 2011).

Source: Author's creation

YouTube, Twitter, SnapChat, TikTok/Douyin, and LinkedIn.

3. Digital media – paid, owned, and earned media channels for reaching and engaging consumers including advertising, e-mail and messaging, search engines, and social network sites (refer to section 1.4).

4. Digital data – the insight businesses collect about their user profiles and their interactions with businesses, which now needs to be protected by law in most countries.

5. Digital technology – the marketing technology that businesses use to create interactive experiences from websites and mobile apps to in-store kiosks and e-mail campaigns.

The internet (also referred to as the Information Superhighway or the Net) is a powerful global network of millions of computers linked via broadband backbone networks, telephone lines and satellite links (Strauss & Frost, 2013: 4).

12.2.3   Digital Marketing Domains

There are four digital marketing domains, as illustrated in ◘ Fig. 12.1.

The four digital marketing domains, which are classified according to the type of buyer and seller in the transaction, are described below.

	Targeting consumers	Targeting businesses
Initiated by business	B2C (Business to consumer)	B2B (Business to business)
Initiated by consumer	C2C (Consumer to consumer)	C2B (Consumer to business)

Fig. 12.1 The four digital marketing domains. (Source: Strauss, El-Ansary, & Frost, 2008. © 2008 Reprinted by permission of Pearson Inc.)

12.2.3.1 Business to Consumer

Business to consumer (B2C) e-commerce involves selling products and services online to final consumers. Nowadays, just about anything can be purchased online, for example, cars, flowers, Viagra, education, houses, books, food, music, and airline e-tickets. These highly publicised e-businesses are typically online retail stores. Examples include airline tickets and holidays from online travel companies such as *Travel Republic*, *Trivago*, *Booking.com*, *FlightSite*, and *Expedia*. Almost all travel and tourism companies have an online presence, with their own websites selling offerings.

12.2.3.2 Business to Business

Business to business (B2B) e-commerce involves online transactions between businesses (known as "group buying"), such as between a tour operator and a travel agency, or between a professional conference organiser (PCO) and a conference centre. It can also include business-related services such as printing services, outsourced marketing, hiring, and selling of office equipment, and so on. Like B2C, the same benefits of lowered inventory management costs as well as a more streamlined procurement and distribution process make e-commerce an efficient and attractive model for companies selling to other businesses (Stokes, 2018: 235).

12.2.3.3 Consumer to Consumer

The consumer to consumer (C2C) domain has been one of the fastest-growing digital marketing domains. The internet provides an ideal medium by which consumers can exchange or purchase products or information with or from each other. Examples include classified advertising sites such as *Gumtree* as well as auction sites such as *eBay* and *BidorBuy*. A recent large-scale example of C2C e-commerce is *Uber*, the business simply provides a transactional platform where consumers offer other consumers a lifting service based on location and cost preference (Stokes, 2018: 236). Another popular example of C2C is *Airbnb*, an online marketspace that connects travellers seeking authentic experiences with hosts offering unique accommodation and experiences around the world (see **Fig. 12.2**).

C2C includes online forums and social networking sites, enabling consumers to offer their opinions to other consumers, which, in turn, affects their purchasing decisions. Blogs (web journals) are also a C2C medium in which consumers share information. *TripAdvisor* is an example of an affiliate marketing website that collects user testimonials on recommended destinations, hotels, restaurants, and things to do (see **Image 12.1**).

12.2.3.4 Consumer to Business

The fourth online marketing domain is consumer to business (C2B), in which consumers communicate with organisations by sending in suggestions and questions via business websites. Alternatively, consumers can search for sellers on the internet, gather information, initiate purchases, and give feedback. In this way, consumers initiate transactions with firms, as opposed to the other way around (B2C). ▶ Priceline.com, for example, allows potential buyers to bid for airline tickets, rental cars, hotel rooms, and cruise and holiday packages, leaving the seller to decide whether to accept their offers (**Image 12.1**).

Visit these websites: ▶ www.tripadvisor.com and ▶ www.priceline.com.

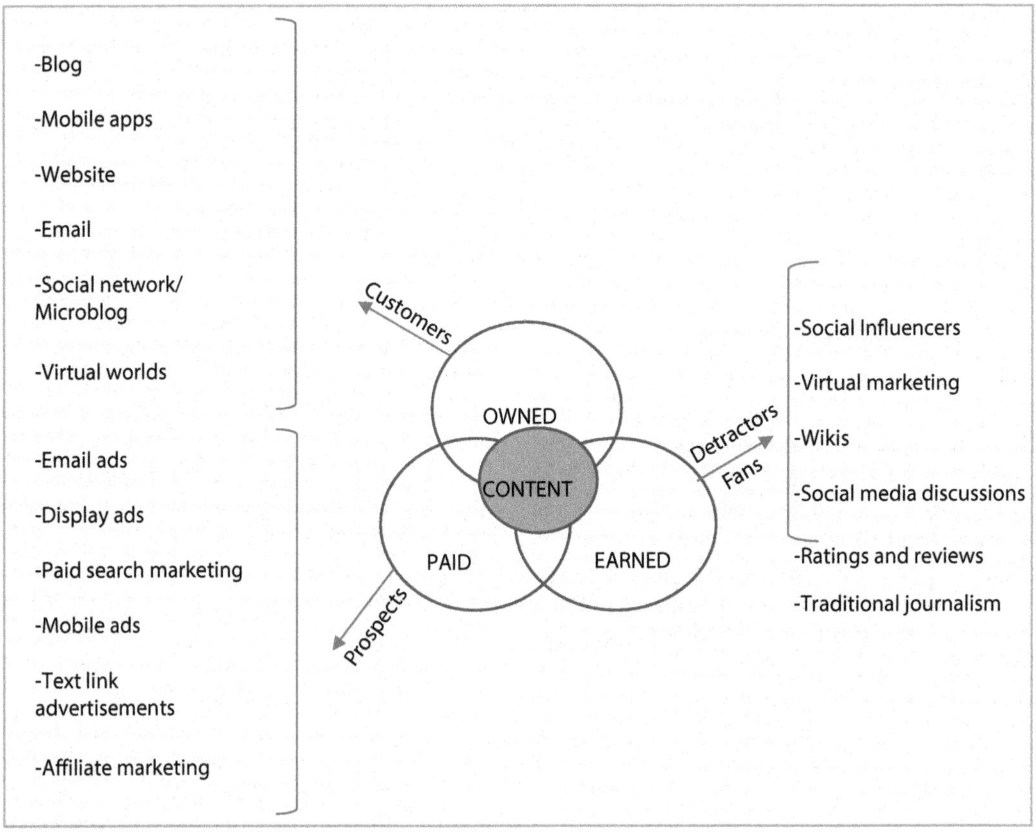

-Blog
-Mobile apps
-Website
-Email
-Social network/ Microblog
-Virtual worlds
-Email ads
-Display ads
-Paid search marketing
-Mobile ads
-Text link advertisements
-Affiliate marketing
Customers
OWNED
CONTENT
PAID
EARNED
Prospects
Detractors
Fans
-Social Influencers
-Virtual marketing
-Wikis
-Social media discussions
-Ratings and reviews
-Traditional journalism

12

Fig. 12.2 Various forms of digital content in digital marketing

TRAVEL NOTICE: Learn more about COVID-19
Tripadvisor
Post
Alerts
Trips
Sign in
Hotels
Holiday Rentals
Things to Do
Restaurants
Write a review
Travel Forums
More
Find the good out there.
Where to?
Support the Good Out There

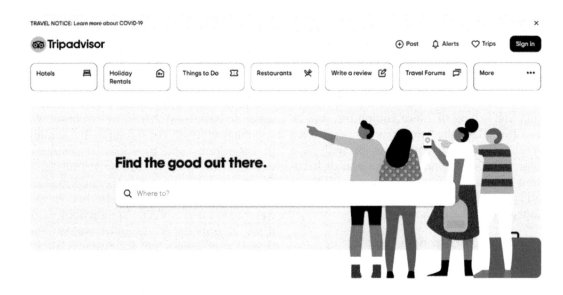

Image 12.1 Trip Advisor's homepage

The average user looks at 40 offers before booking travel on the internet.

12.2.4 Digital Media: Content Marketing, and Owned, Paid, and Earned Media

The most common way of thinking about digital marketing is to think in terms of the three types of media available to marketers: owned, paid, and earned (Strauss, El-Ansary & Frost, 2013: 333). Each of these three media options act as a type of online communication channel that advertisers can use to reach their target audiences. A good online marketing strategy requires a mix of all three types. The remainder of the digital marketing section of this chapter is based on this figure and is divided into these three types of media, with content marketing running as a thread through all types of media.

Content marketing is the process of creating and distributing relevant and valuable content to attract, acquire, and engage a clearly defined target audience with the objective of driving profitable customer action (Pulizzi, 2012). It is a strategy involving the creation and publication of content on websites and in social media.

For many years, tourism and hospitality marketers have created content offline in the form of paper flyers, newsletters, brochures, catalogues, posters, and so on. This content in the pre-digital age was distributed by direct mail. Many mail order customers wanted to read this content, which took the form of ideas, product information, and reviews. In the days before Google, consumers needed information in order to make their purchases. Millions of these purchases were based on branded content that consumers read via direct mail marketing material (Ryan, 2014: 299). What is new is that tourism marketers now use digital content as inbound marketing that attracts customers and prospects (Strauss & Frost, 2013: 334).

Content is at the heart and soul of any digital marketing campaign; it is the foundation on which a company's search, social, e-mail, and paid traffic campaigns are built. Without content, Google has nothing to discover on a company or personal website, Facebook fans have nothing to share, newsletters have no news, and paid traffic campaigns become one-dimensional sales pitches (Deiss & Henneberry, 2017: 61).

At its core, the internet is a place where people gather to discover, interact with, and share content. Engaging with valuable content is a natural, or "native", experience on the internet. People are drawn to content that teaches them something, inspires them, or makes them laugh or cry, and people share and talk about content that has provided them with some form of value. Content marketing works and will always work because it offers value to a potential customer; in addition, it fulfils his or her immediate requirement for information, it engages the customer, and it does not use coercive methods to "sell" to him or her. Done right, it is a powerful brand-building and business-building tool (Ryan, 2014: 299). Well-executed content marketing includes planning what content you will produce, for what audience, and for what purpose.

— *Owned media* carry communication messages from the organisation to internet users on channels that are owned and thus, at least partially controlled by the company. Owned media offline include company brochures, catalogues, signs, and promotional items (for example, branded pens) (Strauss & Frost, 2013: 332).

— *Paid media* are properties owned by others who are paid by the organisation to carry its promotional messages (for example, advertising). The company controls the content; however, the media have content and technical requirements to which the advertisers must adhere (thus, advertisers have less control than when using owned media). Paid media offline include traditional advertising in magazines, in newspapers, on television, on radio, outdoor, in cinemas, and in stores (Strauss & Frost, 2013: 332).

— *Earned media* are messages about a company that are generated by social media authors (such as bloggers), by traditional journalists on media websites, and by internet users who share opinions, experiences, insights, and perceptions on websites and mobile applications. This is when individual conversations become the channel. Offline, earned media (also known as "user-generated media" [UGM] or "user-generated content" [UGC]) include word-of-mouth (WoM) and stories about the company or brands in traditional media. Companies have the least amount of control over this media channel; however, they can respond to customer conversations and attempt to guide these conversations towards their positive brand messages. For instance, companies can use the brand website, blogs (owned media), and display advertisements on websites (paid media) as well as various forms of social media to tell the company story; they must then monitor the internet for conversations about their brands (earned media), responding when appropriate (Strauss & Frost, 2013: 331).

Now that we have introduced the concepts of owned, paid, and earned media as well as that of content marketing, we will discuss each concept in more detail.

12.2.4.1 Content Marketing

Most of the content consumed online has a specific purpose: to get consumers to buy something, to sign up for something, or to learn more about a product. Even seemingly banal articles such as "The 10 best visitor attractions in Bulgaria" have been crafted to influence a specific response. The content should be unique and not plagiarised for better reach and ranking. Most of the content that consumers read and with which they interact on a daily basis is part of the content marketing funnel, which visualises the journey that potential customers go through when considering a purchase (see ◘ Fig. 12.3).

Tourism and hospitality marketers need to consider what they are doing to attract those people who are not familiar with their brand. They also need to consider what they are doing to reach consumers who are familiar

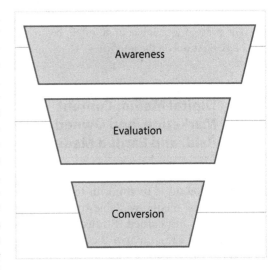

◘ **Fig. 12.3**   Content marketing funnel. (Source: Deiss & Henneberry 2017, p. 65)

with their brand as well as those customers who have purchased the brand in the past and have some intention of returning. All these groups need to be pushed through the content marketing funnel and moved toward making a purchase (for example, buying a flight ticket or booking a hotel room). Marketing campaigns that reach audience members at each level or stage of the funnel will help them take soft travel leads (people who have shown interest in a brand, product, or service who could be converted into customers) from the awareness stage to conversion (Stokes, 2018: 446). Conversion refers to the completion of an action by the user that a website wants that user to take. Usually a conversion results in revenue for the brand in some way and includes, for instance, signing up to a newsletter or purchasing an offering (Stokes, 2018: 530). The content in the different stages of the funnel supports the customer journey, and good content pushes the tourism marketer's lead's closer to a travel purchase.

Before a prospective consumer can become a paying customer, he or she goes through three stages: awareness, evaluation, and conversion (see ◘ Fig. 12.3).

▪ Awareness

When potential customers (prospects) first enter into the content marketing funnel, it can be assumed that they are unaware of the tourism product offering and the needs, wants, and desires that the offering could fulfil. During this stage, the tourism marketer needs to make these potential customers aware of the product offering. Content generated at this stage of the funnel should be of high value, and may be in the form of entertainment, education, or inspiration. The various content types to consider include the following (Deiss & Henneberry, 2017: 66–67):

- Blog posts: Arguably the most recognised form of online content, blogging platforms (for instance, WordPress) are an excellent way of raising awareness.
- Social media updates: As with blogs, social media platforms such as Facebook, Twitter, LinkedIn, TikTok, Snapchat, and Instagram are effective avenues for tourism marketing and driving demand.
- Infographics: Infographics are an interesting and engaging way to display content and typically contain fun images with contrasting, eye-catching colours. The way in which infographics break up text makes this form of content easily readable for the viewer.
- Photographs: Pictures are powerful because they can explain a great deal in a single image. With the increasing popularity of platforms such as Instagram, Facebook, Snapchat, Flickr, and Pinterest, more digital marketers are turning their attention to the creation of photographic content.
- Video: Video content is increasingly important for digital marketing. YouTube, TikTok, Vimeo, Twitch, are examples of video-sharing social media sites and apps.
- Digital magazines and books: Digital magazines and books are popular, and excellent ways to distribute content and raise brand awareness.
- Audio and video podcasts: Another form of content that may be used at the top of the funnel is a podcast, which runs on services such as Spotify, SoundCloud, and GooglePlay. A podcast delivers consumable content "on the go", with users usually subscribing to an online channel.
- Features, guides, and interviews: Interviews with key members of a tourism company,

for example, can work well to highlight business strengths and tell the story behind the brand.

It might not be possible to curate all these content types at the top of the funnel (◻ Fig. 12.3). Thus, most small tourism businesses post content to a blog as well as to social media channels such as Facebook, Instagram, Snapchat, TikTok, Twitter, LinkedIn, Pinterest, and Flickr. Once they have mastered these two content types, they should add more top-of-funnel content to the mix (for instance, a podcast or an infographic). Unfortunately, the top of the funnel is where many tourism businesses begin and end their content marketing efforts. Smart content marketers know that with more effort, they can move prospects from awareness to evaluation at the middle of the funnel.

- **Evaluation**

Those prospects who move through the awareness stage must now evaluate the various choices available to them, including the competitor's product offerings. Now that these prospective customers have become aware of the tourism offering and are interested in learning more, the goal at the middle of the funnel should be to convert those prospective customers into leads with whom the organisation can follow up. Tourism businesses should, for instance, be looking at growing their e-mail lists and gaining more leads at this point of the funnel. Free content is often used to incentivise prospects to submit their contact information (such as their e-mail address) and opt in to receive future marketing messages in exchange for valuable content. This type of content is referred to as a "gated offer" or a "lead magnet" (Stokes, 2018: 320). By ensuring that gated offers are created in a downloadable format, the business can request anyone who wants to download the content to supply his or her contact details. This allows the tourism business to compile a list of new contacts that are pre-vetted as being interested in the tourism offering since they gave the business permission to e-mail content and offers to them in the future.

Examples of content that can be used as a gated offer include the following:

- Educational resources (case studies, newsletters, and so on)
- Useful resources (for example, handouts, resource lists, templates, and checklists)
- Software downloads (for instance, travel applications)
- Blogs
- Discount or coupon offers
- Quizzes or surveys
- Webinars.

It is important to provide the audience with content or other marketing tactics that give them something to "walk away with". Tourism businesses often create a dedicated landing page for every gated offer and use social media, e-mail marketing, search engine optimisation (SEO), and search engine marketing (SEM) (discussed in detail later in this chapter) to drive traffic directly to that page. A landing page is the first page a visitor sees on a website; it is also referred to as an "entrance page" (Stokes, 2018: 532). It is a single web page that appears in response to a website visitor clicking on a search engine optimised search result or an online advertisement (Ash, 2012). Any page of a website could be a landing page, especially if users are coming to the website via search engines.

- Conversion

Prospective customers who move through the evaluation stage are at the "moment of truth", or the travel purchase decision. The goal at this stage is to convert leads into buyers.

Once tourism businesses have prospects' e-mail addresses, it is important to consider the types of content that will result in these new leads making an informed travel purchase decision. Conversion content answers these questions for the potential customer: "Why should I buy?", "Why should I buy now?", and "What's in it for me?" In this stage, the content should create a sense of urgency to purchase in the prospective customer. The content should also include a call-to-action that guides the reader into making the travel purchase, such as an enticement to "Book flights today", which usually appears as a clickable link or a brightly coloured button. Content that works well at the bottom of the funnel includes, for instance,

showing the prospective customer how superb the overall holiday experience is with a quick video gallery, or calculating how much he or she could save on the holiday package if the prospective customer books through a particular company and not a competitor. For example, *Student Flights* aims to convince would-be travellers that they are unlikely to find a Contiki European tour cheaper at any other travel company and offering a 10% discount, thereby saving them money. In addition, *Student Flights* creates a sense of urgency by making the offer available for a limited time only and providing a telephone number through which prospective travellers can contact the business (the call-to-action). Content could also be shared via e-mail marketing since a business at this stage of the funnel has acquired leads or the e-mail addresses of prospective travellers. It would be easy to create a sense of urgency by using an e-mail subject such as "Contiki Europe sale: 10% discount until 11 June. Save more than £250".

After "funneling" through the previous steps, the travellers go on their trip and walk away with an experience. At the core of that experience is the tourism business brand (the website, the content that educated them, the offer they purchased, and the fun or enjoyment they had). This is where customers can become advocates for a tourism brand and voice their opinions on their overall experience. Content in a testimonial or review form is pivotal when the time comes for other would-be travellers to make their own purchase from that brand. These testimonials or reviews have a huge impact on how the brand is portrayed. The better the reviews on websites such as TripAdvisor, Google Maps, and social media pages such as Facebook, the more people will view the tourism business's content and be converted into travel leads/advertisements.

According to findings from the 2018 Digital Marketing Plan Survey, 8% of respondents cited increased lead generation and sales revenue as their most important objectives for 2018 (Tourism Tattler, 2019). Conversely, the most critical challenge to the success of a digital marketing plan for 2018 was data quality, with 15% of respondents citing lead generation and user experience as a critical challenge. The study found that research reports, videos, social media, and webinars generate the highest rate of lead-to-customer conversions, while websites, blogs, case studies, and infographics also contribute to effective conversions (Tourism Tattler, 2019).

12.2.4.2 Owned Media

Digital media channels are fully or partially controlled by the organisations that create the majority of multimedia content (referred to as "owned media") (Stokes, 2018: 412). For example, a company's website and e-mail are totally controlled by the company itself; however, its Facebook page and many other media channels that it uses are conducted on "borrowed space". This means that some company-owned media are operationalised on another person or organisation's site, so there are various rules and requirements to which the company must adhere. Nevertheless, the primary goals are to achieve the following:

- Engage consumers with positive brand content
- Entice them to pass this content along to others (earned media)
- Exercise CRM.

These goals are all aimed at increasing business (initial and repeat consumer purchases).

We will now consider several owned media channels, including company websites, blogs, search engine optimisation (SEO), social media and micro blogging, e-mail marketing, SMS marketing, augmented reality (AR) and virtual reality (VR), gaming and gamification, mobile travel apps (see ◘ Image 12.3), quick response codes, location-based marketing, and search engine optimisation (SEO).

- **Company Websites**

In digital marketing, a tourism company's website is its place of business (see ◘ Image 12.2). A company may have all types of marketing campaigns, but ultimately everything is channelled back through a single point: the company's website. That makes a website incredibly valuable (Ryan, 2014: 44). Thus, the first step in conducting a digital marketing campaign is to create a website. The main aim of a website is to engage consumers (move them closer to a direct purchase) and create consumer-branded loyalty (Kotler, Bowen, Makens. & Baloglu, 2017: 478). A website should primarily be considered as a conversion engine for the traffic that is garnered through all other digital marketing tactics. Conversion could, for instance, include an actual online purchase (for example, a hotel booking transaction), an online query (lead generation), or a subscription to an online newsletter (opt in for future marketing). Conversion is the key to digital marketing success; a company's website and the user experience delivered through it, are what ultimately drive that conversion (Ryan, 2014: 44). Certain domain names are highly sought after (see ▶ Industry Insight 12.1).

◘ **Image 12.2** Marine Dynamics' website

Industry Insight 12.1 ▶ Holiday.com: The most Sought-After Dot-Com Domain Name

The website "▶ holiday.com" may be worth as much as $20 million (R297 million) or even more: the word "holiday" is one of the most searched-for terms online. Even though new domains (such as ".uk") are being released all the time, single-name dotcoms are still the most sought-after domain names.

The domain name regarded as setting the record is "▶ sex.com", which sold for $13 million (R193 million) in 2010, although the founder of one holiday site has said he paid $35 million (R520 million) for the name "▶ VacationRentals.com".

Who registered the domain name "▶ holiday.com"? More than two decades ago, the name was not registered. The person or organisation that bought it probably paid as little as $50 (R744) to $100 (R1 490) or the name.

Some of the domain names that now sell for an ultra-high premium were once active businesses back in the dot-com days. Many companies that built businesses around one-word dotcoms ran into financial trouble during the global economic crash. The companies collapsed and, in some cases, did not even hold on to the domain names. In other cases, domain names were lost through oversight or technical incompetence. About 15 years ago, a generation of domain speculators scooped up those names when they expired. Today, there are very few one-word dot-com domains left to be registered.

Source: Saner, E. (2014). ▶ Holiday.com worth $20-million? Get away! Retrieved from ▶ https://www.theguardian.com/technology/shortcuts/2014/nov/03/holiday-dot-com-20-million-pounds-domain-name-sale-desirable [8 August 2018].

▪▪ Designing an Effective Website

A website needs to be attractive so that consumers visit the site, stay around, and return at a later stage. (The degree to which a website has this quality is referred to as the "stickiness" of the site.) The web design process starts with the user in mind: what is he or she looking for and at what stage did he or she enter the buying process?

> A website has approximately 8 seconds to grab a user's attention.

The key aspects in website design (Gay, Charlesworth & Esen, 2007: 281–296) are discussed in ❑ Table 12.2. This is a high-level overview of the important elements to consider when designing your website from a digital marketing perspective. It is not meant to be an exhaustive guide. Most of the topics we touch on here would warrant an entire book to themselves.

TO DO

Visit the websites of two similar tourism organisations, for example, two destination marketing organisations (DMOs), two tour operators, or two travel agents. Using the information from this chapter, critically evaluate the websites.

▪ Blogs

The rise of the internet and social media has seen an explosion in the number of blogs on the Web, and increasingly tourism businesses are using blogs as part of their digital marketing plans. Blogging is now seen as an efficient method of sharing expertise and building a rapport between a business and its consumer. If executed correctly, it can significantly increase traffic to the business.

A blog (derived from the words "web log") is a public comment website (Business Dictionary, 2018). It is a medium typically driven by a content management system that features short articles (blog posts) and comments on those blog posts. Blogging is one of the earliest forms of social media or "citizen journalism", as it is sometimes called. The world of blogs, bloggers, and blog posts is commonly known as "the blogosphere".

Blogging is essentially writing a story or article on your own website. Other forms of blog include wikis (publicly edited knowledge bases that resemble an encyclopaedia; for example, Wikitravel is an online, interactive, and free travel guide), podcasts (audio-blogging), vodcasts (video files), vlogs (video blogging), and moblogs (mobile phone blogging).

Travel blogs are one of the most recent trends in travel decision-making. They offer consumers credible guides to tourism do's and don'ts. Blogs provide a trusted and often more personal source of information for tourists than other traditional sources of information, such as travel brochures and travel guide-books. They help tourists to become informed about travelling. They also help reduce some of the anxiety that many tourists experience about making arrangements to travel, including booking accommodation and transport options (as well as giving information about driving and flying times), planning itineraries, and finding good restaurants. With travel blogs, travellers are able to access travel tips, up-to-date prices, exchange rates, weather reports, and so on quickly at any time of the day by reading the stories and experiences of other travellers.

◘ Table 12.2 A website design process	
Navigation	This is how users make their way through a website by clicking on various hypertext links built into the site. Users should be guided comfortably through the website pages step by step. Unlike brochures, which allow a consumer to see the front page of the brochure first, websites can be accessed through any page. No matter what page of the website a consumer sees first, the navigation should be able to orientate the user in the website and provide clear signals on what to do next. Navigation is usually aided by a site map and easy-to-use search functions. A small text menu should be included at the bottom of every page. "Breadcrumbs" are a useful navigation device. This refers to text that shows where the user is currently located in the site, for example, Home > About us > History. Thus, if a user wishes to go straight to the website's home page, he or she can click on the Home section in the breadcrumbs.
Usability	Usability is a measure of how easy it is for a user to complete a desired task. Internet usability is about making a user-friendly website. A website should be simple in design and should keep users interested; otherwise people will leave that site and visit a competitor's site. The longer visitors stay on the site, the more likely they are to make a booking or purchase. Websites with excellent usability fare far better than sites that are difficult to use. It is also important to offer users transaction tools to ensure that the process of booking and payment is as user friendly as possible.
Design guides	A number of well-researched design guides are available. They suggest the following: Keep it short and simple (for example, use brief paragraphs). Do not launch a website with Flash technology or heavily laden multi-media pages. Avoid overusing pronouns such as "we", "us", "our", "me", and "mine". Avoid typographical and grammatical errors. Be consistent. Use either British English or American spelling. Never leave the visitor stranded on the site (in other words, in a situation where he or she does not know where to go next). Make sure that all images have captions (The spiders used by search engines cannot search images, but can track the text accompanying images. Spiders are programs that crawl the web and fetch web pages in order for them to be indexed against keywords. They are used by search engines to formulate search result pages [Ryan, 2014: 395].) Avoid "under construction" notices or missing graphics. It is important for all brands to be accessible on mobile devices. This means that websites need to be responsive (that is, designed to be accessible, and optimised for a variety of screen sizes and devices).

(continued)

⬛ Table 12.2   (continued)

Credibility	From a marketing perspective, the design of a website can add to or detract from an organisation's credibility. Visitors form first impressions about a company based on their visit to its website. Nothing will erode your online credibility or your search engine ranking more than a website that does not work. Before making your site "live", test it exhaustively to make sure that everything works as it should and that it achieves your original goals. If possible, test it on different platforms (operating systems, browsers, and so on.) to ensure consistency.

These are some of the indicators that visitors use to determine the credibility of a website (Stokes, 2018: 97–98):

Looks: Does the website look professional?

Genuine telephone numbers and addresses are easy to locate – this assures the visitor that there are real people behind the website, and that they are easily reachable.

Informative and personal "About us" page: Some customers want to see the inner workings of a company and may be interested in who runs it. Consider including employees' pictures and profiles to add personality to the site.

Genuine testimonials: Testimonials are a great way to show potential customers what the company's current customers have to say about the organisation. Video testimonials can be particularly effective, assuming the company's audience does not face data restrictions.

E-commerce: Using a reputable sales channel helps your website's credibility.

Social media: Having a social media presence often goes further towards establishing credibility than testimonials.

Logos of associations and awards: If you belong to any relevant industry trade associations or have won any awards, feature them prominently.

Links to credible third-party references or endorsements: These are useful for asserting credibility.

Up-to-date content: A news section that was last updated a year ago implies that nothing has happened since or that no one cares enough to update it.

No editorial errors: Spelling and grammar mistakes are unprofessional, and while the large majority of readers may not pick them up, the one or two readers who do will question your credibility. This extends to broken links, malfunctioning tools, and interactive elements that do not work as advertised.

Widgets	Widgets are browser extensions or small applications that usually sit on the sidebars or at the bottom of the company's website. A widget is a small piece of code, often provided by a third party, which allows companies to display self-contained content on any HTML webpage (Stokes, 2018: 314). Widgets usually have some special functionality, such as automatically updating with fresh content pulled from another website or allowing users to perform specific actions. Other terms used to describe Web widgets include "gadget", "badge", "module", "webjit", "capsule", "snippet", "mini", and "flake". Web widgets usually (but not always) use DHTML, JavaScript or Adobe Flash. Widgets often take the form of on-screen tools such as currency converters, clocks, event countdowns and auction tickets (bidding countdown clocks), and information about flight arrivals and daily weather. Live chat widgets, or "chat bots", allow for a live conversation with visitors on a website. Another example is TripAdvisor's widget, a simple web application that enables hotels, attractions, restaurants, destination marketers, and bloggers to add TripAdvisor content such as reviews, awards, and local area attractions to their website.

Source: Author's creation

Travel blogs may cover every aspect of a tourist's holiday trip, from the overall experience of travelling, the anticipation, planning, packing, departure, driving, flying, and delays en route. They are also a useful tool for monitoring how a destination fares against its competitors and can provide valuable feedback for DMOs and suppliers. They can give news about upgrades to a tourism business (for example, a new hotel dining area), guests' stories, and recipes from the hotel's chef. Remember that a blog is a place to interact and encourage guests to interact. It provides an opportunity to ask guests what they want to hear and talk about.

However, not all blogs can be regarded as social media. It is reported that half of all internet blogs are in fact spam (Corbett, 2015). They exist to benefit other commercial sites and are not seen as useful to internet users.

Browse these travel blog sites: ► www.grumpytraveller.com, ► www.adventurous-kate.com, ► www.nomadicmatt.com, and ► www.gobackpacking.com (◘ Image 12.3).

■ **Search Engine Optimisation**

Search engine optimisation (SEO) involves designing website content to improve a business's ranking on internet search engines for popular travel search terms (Pike, 2018: 164). Examples of some of the most popular search engines include Google (which has approximately 80% of the share of searches worldwide), Bing, Yahoo!, Baidu, ► Ask.com, and Yandex. In recent years, Google's travel tools (Google Flights and Google Hotel Finder) have been popular search engines used by consumers in online travel planning.

SEO is a topic that requires its own chapter; in fact, it could fill an entire book. Thus, we will only discuss a few principles in this section.

There are three main elements to search engines (Stokes, 2018: 323):

1. The spider, or crawler (called a "web crawler"), is the part that visits sites to read them and follow links.
2. The index or catalogue contains the information found by the spider.
3. Each search engine uses special software to sift through the index and determine the rank of websites in its listings. For example, a Portuguese golf tour operator will be ranked differently by different search engines. Some search engines also index pages more frequently than others.

Over the last few years, SEO has become one of the most important online (digital marketing) tools. SEO (also known as "organic optimisation" or "natural optimisation") plays a key role in acquisition (gaining new customers) as it ensures that an organisation's website appears in search results (Pike, 2018: 164). A search is usually the first port of call for anyone looking for anything online. People enter a search term that is relevant to the information or business they are looking for (for example, "safari", "golf", or "London"). Thus, ensuring that an organisation's website can be found easily by means of search engines increases the traffic to its website significantly.

Travel aggregators are search engine sites that pull together information from many sources to give consumers various travel options that are available on the internet. Examples of travel aggregators include Travelocity, ▶ hotels.com, ▶ Expedia.com, Google Hotel Finder, and Google Flights.

With millions of people performing billions of searches each day to find content on the internet, Google alone processes more than 40,000 searches per second, which translates to over 3,5 billion searches per day and 1,2 trillion searches per year worldwide (internet Live Stats, 2018). Thus, it makes sense that marketers want their products to be findable online. Search engines, the channels through which these searches happen, use closely guarded algorithms to determine the results displayed. Determining what factors these algorithms take into account has led to a growing practice known as SEO: the practice of optimising a website to achieve the highest possible ranking on the search engine results pages (SERPs) (Ortiz-Cordova & Jansen, 2012). A person who practices SEO professionally is known as a "search engine optimiser" (Stokes, 2018: 182).

Rowett (2017) likens SEO to real estate and argues: "If you don't optimise your web pages for search engines, you are literally building a house in the middle of nowhere, and expecting people to find you without a map." Thus, there is little point investing in a website unless you are committed to drawing a "map" so that your ideal customers can find you when they are looking for travel inspiration or undertaking research online.

SEO should be a main component of any industry's marketing plan; for the travel industry, it is absolutely essential. According to a study, worldwide e-WoM - in the form of travel review sites - is the most popular online planning source for travellers (69%), and (see ▫ Fig. 12.4). The internet has revolutionised the tourism industry by giving travellers access to greater choices, better deals, more flexible plans, and a wealth of media designed to immerse them in the destination before they even get there (Bearne, 2016). It is thus recommended that all tourism brands invest in SEO in order to leverage these opportunities.

SEO involves optimising websites to achieve high rankings on search engines for certain selected keywords. SEO can be divided into two main strategies (Stokes, 2018: 188):
1. On-page optimisation refers to the creation of great content (unique, informative, original, not copied from other websites, well-researched, and in-depth). It also refers to doing the basics right, such as including the right words (keywords for which you would like the website to be found by search engines) inside your website text. For example, if you would like the website to be found for the keywords "Kruger National Park birding guide", all of these words (or at least some of them) need to appear in the website.

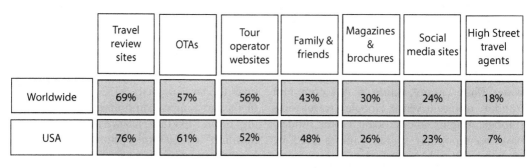

	Travel review sites	OTAs	Tour operator websites	Family & friends	Magazines & brochures	Social media sites	High Street travel agents
Worldwide	69%	57%	56%	43%	30%	24%	18%
USA	76%	61%	52%	48%	26%	23%	7%

▫ Fig. 12.4   Sources used in travel planning. (Source: Zaui 2019)

2. Off-page optimisation refers to the process of obtaining backlinks. (Each link from an external domain to a specific page is known as an "inbound link" or a "backlink".) The number of backlinks influences a company's SEO ranking. Thus, the more backlinks there are, the better (Stokes, 2018: 187). For example, you could ensure there are backlinks linking your business Facebook page or your "Google My Business" listing to your business website. Having great content makes it more likely that other websites will link to your website. In turn, your "Google My Business", page which is vetted or verified by Google, will include your precise geographical location. If your business is indeed situated inside or adjacent to the Kruger National Park and you are a birding guide, then it follows that people doing online searches will be able to find your website.

3. Technical optimisation refers to the process of completing activities on your site that are designed to improve SEO but are not related to content. It often happens behind the scenes. It is a technical procedure to enhance search visibility by optimising the website for a better crawling and indexing experience (Kumar, 2013).

Keywords are the very foundation of search. When users enter a query on a search engine, they use the words that they think are relevant to the search. The search engine then returns the pages that it has calculated to be most relevant to those keywords and, increasingly, the implied meaning of the search. Developers of search engines have built a sophisticated understanding of semantics and the way in which we use language. So, if a user does a search using the keywords "car rental", the search engine will look for pages that are relevant to these keywords as well as synonyms such as "car hire", "vehicle hire", and so forth. Search engines have also built up knowledge around common misspellings, typos, synonyms, and related searches. It is crucial that tourism marketers implement keywords that are likely to be used by target audiences. Websites need to appear when potential customers are searching for them.

A large part of keyword research is understanding search psychology. When we build our keyword listswe are tapping into the mental process of searchers and putting together the right mix of keywords to target. There are four aspects to consider when choosing a keyword (Stokes 2018: 186–188)

I. *Search volume*

How many searchers are using that phrase to find what they want? For example, there is an estimated monthly search volume of more than 338 million for the keyword "hotel", but only an estimated 6600 searches per month for a keyword combination such as "Rio de Janeiro waterfront hotel".

II. *Competition*

How many other websites are targeting the same phrase? For example, Google lists more than 7,000,000,000 results for the keyword "hotel", but only 320,000 for the keyword combination "Copacabana waterfront hotel".

III. *Propensity to convert*

What is the likelihood that the searcher using that keyword is going to convert on your website? (A conversion is a desired action taken by the visitor to your website.) Related to propensity to convert is the relevance of the selected term to what you are offering. If you are selling rooms at a hotel at the Rio de Janeiro Waterfront, which of the two terms, "hotel" or "Rio de Janeiro waterfront hotel", do you think will lead to a higher rate of conversions?

IV. *Value per lead*

What is the average value per prospect attracted by the keyword? Depending on the nature of your website, the average value per lead varies. Using the hotel example again, consider these two terms: "luxury Rio de Janeiro hotel" and "budget Rio de Janeiro hotel". Both are terms used by people wanting to book a hotel in Rio de Janeiro, but it is expected that a person looking for a lux-

□ Table 12.3   Aspects to consider when choosing keywords or phrases

Keyword or phrase	Search volume	Competition	Propensity to convert	Value of lead
Hotel	3870	90%	2%	$18 (R241)
Luxury hotel	345	80%	35%	$35 (R470)

Source: Stokes (2018), p. 189

ury hotel is intending to spend more. That means that this specific lead has a higher value, particularly if you have a hotel booking website that offers a range of accommodation.

□ Table 12.3 illustrates these four aspects.

■ ■ Optimising Content for Keywords

Once keywords and keyword phrases have been selected, the tourism marketer will need to optimise web pages and web content with these validated keywords and search query phrases, so that search engines have the best opportunity of ranking the business's pages positively. Before placing keywords in the business website, it is important to be aware of the different types of content that search engines rank, as this will determine all the potential content needed to optimise the website (Rowett, 2017).

There are three types of content:

1. Standard web pages: Any page on a business website can be made available to search engines.
2. Videos: Google includes YouTube and Vimeo video matches in its search results.
3. Images: Sometimes images appear in the main body of the search results, although this is not the case for all searches. There is a tab for "Images" in the top menu on Google, which enables people to search specifically for images that are relevant to their search keywords.

■ ■ Optimising Standard Web Pages

Once the tourism marketer has chosen the keywords or search phrases for each of the website pages, then it is a matter of working them into the content of the website.

■ ■ Optimising off-Page Elements

Tourism marketers need to ensure that keywords are placed in the URL of the web page. Most content management systems offer the option to personalise URLs, except for home pages.

It is important to ensure that keywords are placed once in the page title and once in the meta description. Search engines no longer use the meta description for ranking purposes, but it is still advisable to place the keywords here for user relevance. If possible, keep the page title to fewer than 55 characters, and the meta description to fewer than 150 characters.

It is recommended that businesses include the selected keywords or search phrases in the heading tags, the first 100 words in the body copy, and then two or three times as variations within the rest of the body copy. Heading tags (H1, H2, H3, and so on) are standard elements used to define headings and subheadings on a webpage. The number indicates the importance, so H1 tags are viewed by spiders as being more important than H3 tags. Using targeted keywords in the H tags is essential for effective SEO (Stokes, 2018: 183).

■ ■ Optimise Images for Image Search Results Pages

Before uploading images into a business web page, the file should be saved using certain keywords or search phrases. Then, when the image is uploaded into the website gallery, the keyword or search phrase should be added into the "Alt Attribute Tag" in the image details section. This strengthens the keyword density for the page and supports the ranking of the images for keywords when people use the image search function in search engines (Stokes, 2018: 183).

■ ■ **Optimise Videos for Video Search Results Pages**

Finally, as a Google product, YouTube gains a great deal of traction in Google's search engine results. Thus, where possible, a tourism business should publish its video content on YouTube, and then embed the content on its website.

When uploading videos to YouTube, there are several optimisation opportunities that businesses can take advantage of to ensure that the videos leverage Google's search engine results:

- Optimise the video file name for relevant keywords.
- Ensure the video title includes relevant keywords or phrases.
- Write detailed, keyword-rich video descriptions. Use the first 22 words strategically, as these are seen in the search page.
- Add relevant keyword tags to the video (but do not add too many).
- Choose the most relevant category for the video.

As with any digital marketing practice, SEO should not be the only focus of digital marketing efforts. It works best when used as part of a holistic online marketing strategy (Stokes, 2018: 201).

■ **Social Media**

Social media marketing (SMM) is a form of digital marketing that utilises social networking platforms to increase brand or product exposure and cultivate relationships with consumers. Social media are media (in the form of text, visuals, and audio files) that can be shared online (Stokes, 2018: 19). These online platforms include social media websites, blogs, chat rooms, moblogs, or mobile bloggings (sites consisting of images, movies, digital audio, or photographs), and consumer product or service rating forums and websites (Mangold & Faulds, 2009). In their most basic form, social media are online tools that allow consumers to collaborate and share information, content, and ideas with each other.

■ **Table 12.4** Most popular social media sites in July 2020

Social networking site	Number of active users per month (millions)
Facebook	2603
YouTube	2000
Instagram	1082
WhatsApp	2000
Facebook Messenger	1300
Weixin/WeChat	1203
TikTok	800
Snapchat	301
Reddit	274
Pinterest	330
LinkedIn	200

Source: ▶ statista.com/statistics/272014/global-social-networks-ranked-by-number-of-users/

Social media (also known as "social networking") has changed the face of marketing by allowing collaboration and connection in a way that no other channel has been able to offer. Social networks can be general (for example, Facebook) or niche (for example, LinkedIn). Mobile social networking – using mobile phones for social networking – is growing in popularity.

The most popular social media websites, which are listed in ■ Table 12.4, have millions of members globally. Increasingly, tourism and hospitality businesses have their own social media pages (such as 'Instagram Business Account', 'Facebook Business Page', 'Company Page' on LinkedIn); users accessing the page can click on the "Like" icon, post photos and videos, post comments, and are able to interact with other users of the company concerned.

A research study found that users of social networking sites fall into one of five distinct categories (see ▶ Industry Insight 12.2).

Industry Insight 12.2 A Typology of Social Networking Users

Research conducted by Ofcam found that users of social networking sites fall into one of five categories:

- "Alpha socialisers" are mostly males younger than 25 who use sites in intense short bursts to flirt, meet new people, and be entertained.
- "Attention seekers" are mostly female users who crave attention and comments from others. They often post photos and customise their profiles.
- "Followers" are males and females of all ages who join sites to keep up with what their peers are doing.
- "Faithfuls" are older males and females (generally older than twenty) who typically use social networking sites to rekindle old friendships, often from school or university.
- "Functionals" are mostly older males who tend to be single-minded in using sites for a particular use.

Source: Adapted from Ofcom Office of Communications. Annex 3.

Social media refers to online discussion forums and boards, including blogs and microblogs, as well as consumer rating websites (such as *TripAdvisor*), and online forums, wikis, social, and business networking sites (for example, Facebook, LinkedIn, and Twitter), and multi-media (e.g. videos, photography) sharing websites (such as YouTube, Tik Tok, Pinterest, Instagram, Snapchat, and Flickr). In contrast to content provided by marketers and suppliers, the content generated by many social media sites is produced by consumers to be shared among themselves. Travellers are increasingly tapping into the collective intelligence that is available on the internet (for instance, by sharing their travel experiences on Twitter or Instagram, or reading about the experiences of other travellers and 'influencers' (such as celebrities, bloggers, activists, and personalities). This challenges the marketing practices of many tourism businesses and DMOs. For example, tourism and hospitality businesses are increasingly utilising YouTube and Instagram travel influencers - through advertising - to help promote their products and brands.

Social networking is still somewhat less understood than other marketing tools and does not enjoy the same level of confidence from tourism product owners, tour operators, travel agents, and DMOs. This is because it is virtually impossible to measure the effect of social-networking sites on actual booking or visitor numbers. Travel review information sites such as *TripAdvisor* and ► Lonelyplanet.com, which offer reviews of tourism product offerings by people who have experience of them, have been shown to enjoy more credibility than official or marketing websites. However, recent online activity suggests that many potential travellers now want the opinion of people whom they know or with whom they have a Facebook connection. As a result, online travel agencies (OTAs), such as *Expedia* and *Trivago* are using Facebook connections (for example, via Facebook's "Friends of Friends Travel" link) to create this sense of personal recommendation and the element of trust that used to be produced by the presence of an actual travel agent developing a relationship with his or her client.

A click-through is a click on a link that leads to another website.

If Facebook were a country, it would be substantially bigger than China. The size of Facebook's user base translates to almost two in seven of the global population using it each month - around 1.9 billion people. By comparison, China's 2018 population is estimated to be 1.4 billion (World Economic

Forum, 2016). ► https://www.weforum.org/agenda/2016/04/facebook-is-bigger-than-the-worlds-largest-country/

Micro blogging is a form of blogging that allows users to write brief text updates about their lives and experiences while on the go and send them to friends and interested observers via SMS marketing, instant messaging, e-mail, or the Web (Stokes, 2018: 198). The most popular micro-blogging platform is Twitter. Micro blogging fulfils a need for an even faster mode of communication than regular blogging. For example, a blogger might update his or her blog once every few days, while a micro blogger might post several updates on the same day. Micro blogging offers users a fast and easy way to share information in real time. While a person is experiencing a travel product, he or she can post a comment on a micro-blogging platform and express his or her opinion immediately. Micro blogging is mainly used for four purposes: daily chatter, conversation, sharing information, and reporting news (Java, Song, Finn & Tseng, 2010). Twitter is commonly used for daily chatter. Users frequently write messages about their daily routine, including messages describing their travel experiences and their opinions about travel products.

Twitter has become popular with travellers seeking travel advice and special offers. This unique approach to communication and social networking is a combination of instant messaging and e-mail. Messages are limited to 280 characters (called "tweets") that answer the set questions: "What are you doing?" or "What are your friends doing right now?" Twitter is a network with several million registered users (users active every month) who can choose from whom they wish to receive messages or tweets (Statista.com, 2018). The system is intended primarily for friends, family, and colleagues to communicate and stay connected.

Twitter has been used as a platform to spread travel advice and share holiday photos. Thousands of travel experts and travel firms, such as airlines, cruise lines, hotels, and tour operators, as well as bloggers and other travellers post messages on Twitter. Many travel companies use Twitter to deliver news and special offers or deals, from flights to discounts (known as "twiscounts"). Twitter is also used to advertise last-minute availability. It has become an instant, bottomless resource for savvy travel advice and a mobile coupon book with deals from hotels, tour operators, and airlines. Increasingly, travel companies are building long-lasting relationships with their customers, largely because they are engaged in conversation. For example, travel firms tweet special deals such as airfares (*United Airlines* coined the term "twares") and room rates. Increasingly, travel companies are using Twitter to offer customer service facilities as an alternative to call centres. Airlines and airports use Twitter to inform passengers about flight information.

▪ **Database Marketing**

Database marketing is a collection of data, such as customers' names, addresses and purchases, which provides marketers with information that enables them to make better decisions in working toward accomplishing the company's objectives (Schoenbachler, Gordon, Foley & Spellman 1997).

Many tourism companies confuse a customer mailing list with a customer database. A customer mailing list is simply a set of names, addresses, and telephone numbers. A customer database contains much more information, gathered through customer transactions, telephone and online queries, registration information, cookies, and every contact with customers. Ideally, a customer database contains information such as buying behaviour (for example, the value of customers' past purchases and their buying preferences), demographics (for example, age, income, family members, and dates of birthdays), psychographics (activities, interests, and opinions), media graphics (preferred media), and other useful information. A good database is essential for successful direct marketing and for successful e-mail campaigns.

In order to use database marketing effectively, organisations need to store customer enquiries and sales information electronically along with each transactional record. This data should be kept up to date, preferably in real time.

A company's information systems' (IS) team is often responsible for database management and the marketing team is responsible for driving the campaign itself (in other words, developing the offering and computing numbers).

The effectiveness of direct marketing is largely dependent on the development of a marketer's database. A database is a record of information on past or present consumers. In Chap. 7 (Market segmentation, targeting, and positioning), we discussed the role of marketing segmentation and the creation of databases or mailing lists, which represent invaluable information for the marketer.

There are four possible sources of information for databases:

- Purchasing a database from a direct marketing company (or mailing house)
- Using government statistics such as UNWTO for international travel flows and statistics (see ► Chap. 4: Tourism and hospitality marketing research)
- Encouraging end-users, visitors, competition entrants, and especially website users to register information for the database
- Collecting information held within the organisation, for example, consumer records, till receipts, consumer service questionnaires, consumer bookings, and enquiries.

One of the major problems with database marketing is that it can be extremely complex if there are several databases that are not linked to each other within a company. It could be expensive to integrate the databases. This problem is common within the hospitality industry, where there may be various databases, for example, a sales database, an accounting database, a reservations database, and so on (Kotler, Bowen, Makens & Baloglu, 2017: 473). As with other tools of the promotional mix, database marketing requires investment. Tourism and hospitality organisations need to invest in computer hardware, database software, analytical programmes, and trained staff. An example of this is HubSpot, an "► all-in-one marketing software"that provides tools that can help a company with SEO, blogging, social media, e-mail, landing pages, and web analytics. Hubspot acts as a content management system (CMS). The database system should also be user-friendly and must be accessible to other departments, such as advertising, customer service, sales, product offering development, and brand management.

Today, many companies combine the use of the internet and databases to gain greater benefits from their marketing. Several of the larger tourism and hospitality organisations capture information every time a customer comes into contact with any of their departments. They therefore know a great deal about their customers, including contact details, transactions, demographic data, and income. This data is periodically dumped into a data warehouse (a repository for large amounts of information) where it is stored indefinitely. Company researchers can then analyse the mass of data and draw inferences about individual customers, trends, and segments. This is known as "data mining" and involves the use of sophisticated statistical techniques such as cluster analysis to uncover patterns and other useful information about customers and market segments.

The tourism and hospitality marketer may convert this information into a comprehensive database in order to create a profile on individual consumers: name (surname and title), date of birth, last booking, country, preferred destinations and travel dates, the ages of family members and the dates of their birthdays, frequency (how often they like to hear from you), and so on. This consumer information, which should be updated regularly, is then used to target responsive consumers through a variety of online and offline direct marketing techniques.

■ **E-mail Marketing**

E-mailing is an extremely versatile digital marketing tool. It includes "opt-in" or "opt-out" mailing lists, e-mail (for example, a newsletter e-mailed by a travel agency to its existing clients), and discussion list subscriptions (Baines, et al., 2019). Bulk e-mails can also be sent out to prospective consumers. This technique involves sending out the same message to groups of people (up to as many as 1000 people at a time). The consumer does not always proactively visit a company's website or find a business on Google. However, e-mail marketing is the channel that allows you to reach out to subscribed consumers who want to hear from you.

In most countries it is against the law to send out unsolicited and untargeted e-mails to a list of people. (Unsolicited e-mails are referred to as **spam**.) Permission must be granted by the intended recipient. Some internet service providers cancel their services to known spammers. Any e-mail sent to a list of subscribers needs to include an easy and accessible "unsubscribe" link.

> *Spam* is unsolicited, unwanted commercial e-mail advertisements.

Tourism and hospitality businesses should attempt to build up a database of interested people to whom they can send marketing e-mails by, for example:

- Including users who request information from the organisation;
- People who have already used the service;
- Newsletter sign-ups;
- Running an online survey; and
- Giving away a gift such as a free guidebook and asking users to complete a form with their details.

Direct e-mail marketing can be a most effective business tool with which to market a tourism business and special offers, and to maintain long-term relationships with the company's existing customers. It is one of the most powerful digital marketing tools. It is an excellent way of communicating with consumers and suppliers. Additional advantages for the tourism marketer are that e-mail is more eco-friendly than direct mail (there is no wastage of paper). It is immediate, has a high response rate, and is cost effective. It is useful for building virtual relationships with consumers and creating brand or image awareness. It takes advantage of consumers' most prolific touch point with the internet: their inbox.

One disadvantage of e-mail marketing is that it is easy for the receiver to discard the mail, perhaps without even opening it, at the click of a button. In addition, direct e-mail can be expensive when contact lists need to be purchased (Pike, 2018: 147).

With the adoption rate of smartphones increasing, more and more people are viewing their e-mails on mobile phones. When designing a direct e-mail for mobile phones, you need to keep the following in mind:

- The screen is much smaller.
- Mobile users are often checking their mail on the run.

Very few people view an e-mail on only one device; they switch from their smartphones to their laptops to their tablets and back to their smartphones during the course of a day.

■ **SMS Marketing**

Short message services (SMSs) or texting are electronic messages sent on a wireless network. Mobile phones are a mass market medium. The mobile phone market (SMS and MMS) is a huge marketing opportunity, especially in developing countries; texting, or SMSing, is an effective medium with which to reach the youth market.

Once prospective customers have granted permission for a firm to communicate with them via their mobile numbers, messages can be sent to their mobile phones. These can be promotional or sales-orientated messages, such as special offers or information about upcoming events. On most mobile phones, prospects need to at least open a text (SMS) message in order to delete it. Mobile phones are generally kept on one's person at all times, meaning that their messages are likely to be read shortly after being broadcast. Mobile technology is about connectivity, just as the internet is about interactivity. However, in general, mobile phone users have proved reluctant to hand over their phone numbers for marketing messages, perhaps fearing a similar deluge of spam for which e-mail has such a poor reputation.

As with e-mail marketing, consumer consent is required to receive an SMS from a specific firm. This is known as "permission marketing". A text sent to a person who has not requested this communication is a form of spam and is illegal.

Multi-media messaging service (MMS) is the next generation of mobile messaging. It allows for images, sound bites, and even short video clips to be incorporated into a message. It is argued that it is more conducive to digital marketing than texting. However, texting is still utilised to a greater degree than the sending of MMSs, as it is more cost effective and not all mobile phones support MMS functionality.

■ **Augmented Reality and Virtual Reality**

Augmented reality (AR) is defined as "an enhanced version of reality created by the use of technology to add digital information on an image of something" (Mohr, 2017). With AR technology, computer-generated layers in the form of graphics, sound, and videos are stacked on to real-life objects so as to enable users to interact with that environment. The user can experience an artificial environment while being present in the real world without getting detached from their surroundings. Instead of replacing things, AR adds modifications in real time that can be experienced through an app and a mobile device (Rastogi, 2018). Mobile apps can use AR for fun, such as the game "Pokémon GO", or for information, such as the app "Layar". The Layar app uses AR to show people interesting information about places that they visit. Users can open the app when they visit a site and read information that appears in a layer over their view. (See ▶ Industry Insight 12.3 on how Cape Town's Sea Point Promenade came alive with Layar AR (Mohr, 2017).

Industry Insight 12.3 Sea Point Promenade AR Exhibits

Artists and storytellers are now able to use AR technology to display digital content behind their artworks and increase the impact of their work on an artistic and interactive level. Content of all forms can be layered on top of print media that can only be viewed by consumers through their smartphones or tablets.

Cape Town's Sea Point Promenade was host to one of Cape Town's most exciting exhibitions that used AR technology. The Sea-Change exhibition was a multi-media project that told the story of the birth of humanity and the ancient relationship that humans have with the sea. Large-format photographs were displayed along the sea wall on the Promenade. A selection of these panels could be transformed into perfect HD videos using the free Layar mobile app.

Source: Walters, Johan. (2014).

Virtual reality (VR) takes AR a step further in an attempt to create an even more immersive interaction (Stokes, 2018: 162). VR is the simulation of a real-life environment that stimulates the vision and hearing of users, allowing them to experience a simulated reality (Guttentag, 2009). It makes use of VRML (virtual reality modelling language), a coding language that creates a series of images and enables various kinds of possible interactions.

The user usually has to put on a VR headset, known as "a head-mounted display", after which he or she is able to look around, hear, touch, and (possibly even) smell objects arranged in an artificial world.

VR isolates the user and takes him or her to a digital world, while AR users continue to dwell in the real world during their interaction with virtual objects. VR is more immersive and offers a digital recreation of real life,

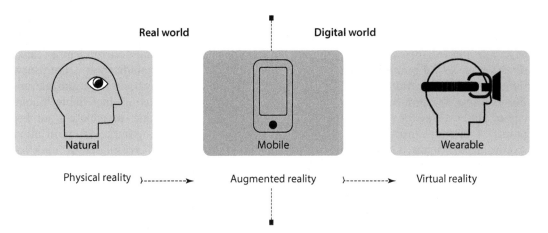

Real world   **Digital world**

Natural   Mobile   Wearable

Physical reality ⟩----------→   Augmented reality   ⟩----------→   Virtual reality

Fig. 12.5 The difference between physical reality, augmented reality, and virtual reality. (Source: Rastogi 2018)

while AR delivers virtual elements as an overlay to the real world and gives more freedom (see ☐ Fig. 12.5). Both technologies are primarily used to create an exciting experience for their consumers that makes them want to engage with the brand (Stokes, 2018: 162).

VR allows users to move around and look in every direction (up, down, sideways, and behind them) as if they were physically there. With VR apps, users can explore any place in the world (from anywhere in the world), including "walking" in the streets of Paris, "gliding" down Venetian canals, and even "swimming" to areas deep under the sea. VR is therefore increasingly used in the tourism industry to enhance travellers' experiences.

Immersive videos, more recently known as 360° videos (or 360-degree videos), are video recordings of a real-world scene, where the view in every direction is recorded at the same time. During playback, the viewer has control of the viewing direction. These videos are frequently used by the hospitality sector to create all-round (360°) room tours to give travellers the opportunity to view rooms prior to booking. Tourist destinations and attractions can also offer 360° views of their offerings. For example, the official website for Australia's tourism agency has created a series of stunningly realistic 360-degree scrolling videos that simulate an action-packed holiday experience at some of the country's iconic adventure spots. From swimming with a pod of playful dolphins in Tasmania, snorkelling along the Great Barrier Reef, and feeding marsupials on the shores of Kangaroo Island, each video is designed to entice tourists to explore Australia's exotic shores for themselves: virtually first, and then in person.

■ **Gaming and Gamification**

Gaming and gamification are two technological developments increasingly being used in tourism (Xu, Tian, Buhalis, Weber & Zhang, 2016). The travel and tourism industry is dominated by two kinds of games: online/offline games and location-based mobile games. Games can be used by the tourism Industry to stimulate tourists' engagement with a destination and to enhance their on-site experiences with the destination in a fun and informative manner (Corrêaa & Kitanoa, 2015).

■■ **Gaming**

Gaming, or electronic games (often simply called "games"), provide players with an immersive and interactive entertainment experience, often through dynamic and real-time interaction with their context, local organisations, and fellow players (Xu et al., 2016) (1) Gaming refers to electronic games, often played on mobile devices and smartphones.

Gaming is emerging as a useful tool that is being used by some tourism organisations for marketing purposes as well as to establish dynamic engagement with users. As a new approach to promoting tourism destinations, gaming provides tourism organisations and destination marketers with the opportunity to create informative and entertaining settings for successful brand awareness, interaction, and communication (Xu et al., 2016. (2) For example, location-based games and AR games can be a way for tourists to experience points of interests through a treasure hunt. According to Linaza, Gutierrez and Garcia, "tourists can follow a list of recommendations given by a mobile game and can learn something about their environment by solving mini games related to their experiences" (2014: 498).

The current use of gaming by the tourism industry can be divided into two types: social games and location-based or AR games (Xu et al., 2016: 5):

— Social games are used as an innovative way to create brand awareness for a destination and are played prior to travelling to a destination. These games are often made available on social media, such as Facebook, with the aim of attracting the attention of potential tourists and building up the image of a destination or a tourism business.

— Location-based AR mobile games are mainly used to encourage more engagement at the destination, and to enhance tourists' on-site experiences in a fun and informative way. Most of the existing location-based AR mobile games are constructed on the game principles of the classic treasure hunt. One of the most well-known location-based AR games is Pokémon Go, a global positioning system (GPS) and AR exploration game inspired by the popular television show that allows users to catch Pokémon in the real world by using a smartphone's GPS features to find areas that are populated with Pokémon. A smartphone's camera is used to find virtual Pokémon in reality (Goel, 2018).

▪▪ Gamification

In addition to the progress made in the mobile game market, game design elements (for example, teamwork, competitions, achievements,

challenges, and rewards) have been used lately in non-gaming contexts. This is known as "gamification" (Digital Tourism Think Tank, 2014: 3). Although gamification is not a new concept, it is currently becoming more relevant to the topic of marketing since the technique can use game mechanics to achieve a number of outcomes, including improving motivation and concentration, increasing effort, and fostering customer loyalty.

Game design elements are already being applied in the marketing of tourism but may not have been recognised or named as gamification. Every loyalty card or frequent-flyer programme, for instance, is a gamification approach as points are collected to be redeemed for a bonus (Xu, Weber & Buhalis, 2014: 526). Although gamification uses game mechanics, it does not necessarily involve creating whole games. Gamification can be differentiated from whole games as it uses game design elements in a different context and for a different purpose (Xu et al., 2014: 527).

Gamification can be used by tourism organisations for the purposes of marketing, sales, and customer engagement (external applications), or in human resources, training, productivity enhancement, and crowdsourcing (internal applications). ◘ Table 12.5 lists and describes some of the ways in which gamification is applied in different tourism industries. Compared with other fields, the use of gamification in tourism is still in its infancy (Xu et al., 2014: 531).

▪ Mobile Travel Apps

A mobile app (short for 'mobile application') is ► application software designed to run on ► smartphones, ► tablet computers, and other ► mobile devices. Some travel apps are free, while others must be purchased. They are usually downloaded from the platform to a target device such as a smartphone (see ► Industry Insight 12.4 for information about the *WeTravelSolo* travel app). Examples of travel-related apps include ► Booking.com, *Airbnb*, and *Trivago* (for travel booking), *TipAdvisor* (for recommendations), *Expedia (OTA)*, Google Trips (for holiday organising), Maps.me (for maps), City Souks,

◨ **Table 12.5** Applications of gamification in the tourism industry

Gamification in hospitality	Sharing-economy websites such as AirBnB that offer holiday-rental options for travellers are becoming increasingly popular. However, guest experiences with the hosts are often a concern. In response to this issue, AirBnB implemented gamification by awarding "Superhost" badges to deserving hosts. The website sets clear targets for hosts who want to be awarded this badge. For instance, hosts must have hosted at least ten trips, should maintain a 90% e-mail response rate or higher, must receive five-star ratings for at least 80% of their reviews, and should not cancel confirmed reservations. Accommodation that has been awarded the "Superhost" badge is more likely to receive positive reviews and high ratings, and guests are willing to spend more on "Superhost" accommodation. In addition, AirBnB awards various prizes to superhosts, ranging from $100 credit to new mattresses.
Gamification in the car rental industry	SmartDriver is a mobile application that monitors and assesses an individual's driving behaviour. Car rental agencies can reward drivers who score well by providing a discount on car rental premiums when users return their cars.
Gamification in the airline industry	The Dutch airline, *KLM*, launched the "Meet & Seat" feature, enabling passengers to find out who else is on a specific flight and to connect with that person via his or her Facebook, Google+, or LinkedIn profiles. The value for passengers of sharing their personal details with other customers is to find interesting people or passengers who are attending the same event at the destination. *Virgin Atlantic* introduced the "Seat-to-Seat" delivery feature, which launched the first social network for meeting and collaborating in the sky. The idea was to facilitate connecting people who want to treat a companion or break the ice by sending another passenger a drink or snack. The communication, which also delivers text messages (SMS) to other passengers, works over the built-in touchscreen in-flight entertainment system.
Gamification in the restaurant industry	The mobile application Guests Engine allows restaurants and bars to engage teams of employees and locations in competitions and give them feedback to increase sales. Employees receive missions and feedback via SMS or e-mail, and through a website application. The technology also integrates a learning management system for training employees.

Source: Author's creation

Marrakesh (for destination guides), *Uber* (for ride sharing), App in the Air (flight status), LiveTrekker (travel journals), and XE Currency (currency conversions). There are many innovative smartphone travel apps, including the following:

— A real-time currency converter
— A destination-based listing of world customs, taboos, dress codes, etiquette, laws, and so on
— Phrasebooks
— Google Goggles, which can pull information about almost anything from a photograph submitted on a smartphone
— National Geographic Atlas, with associated location-specific information
— GPS-based guides to service providers such as accommodation and restaurants
— A facility for booking flights from a mobile phone
— Real-time flight updates for a range of airlines.

12

Industry Insight 12.4 Wetravelsolo Travel App

WeTravelSolo is India's first Solo Traveller's community app. The mobile app offers options such as "take a trip", "find your soulmate", and "unique trip ideas". It is ideal for travel lovers who feel reluctant to travel because of lack of an ideal partner for a trip. Solo travellers can find and help users meet like-minded travellers anywhere in the world.

WeTravelSolo can be downloaded on all Android-enabled platforms. The app has a feature where users can search for and "Find your true travel soulmate". In addition, users can share holiday photographs and travel stories and experiences with other users. The app offers limitless options to travel and meet like-minded people as well as expert advice, guidance, and company of experienced travellers. It enables users to take trips, explore the world, connect with people you never knew existed and share travel stories with the whole wide world. With this app, you not merely travel solo, but you travel solo, together.

Source: WeTravelSolo launches mobile app for travellers. Financial Express. ► https://www.financialexpress.com/industry/technology/wetravelsolo-launches-mobile-app-for-travellers/202897/

► https://www.financialexpress.com/industry/technology/wetravelsolo-launches-mobile-app-for-travellers/202897/

■ **Quick Response Codes**

A quick response (QR) code is a machine-readable code, such as a barcode, that can be used to store information (for example, URLs) and can be read by an app through the camera of a smartphone (Stokes, 2018: 154). Travellers who have a mobile tag reader application can, for instance, scan a QR code appearing in a print or outdoor advertisement by taking a picture of it or scanning it with their phones. This immediately takes the user to a Web or social media site for more information on the offering, competitions, or other information provided by the offering online (Strauss & Frost, 2013: 352).

There are two main uses of QR codes in tourism: to inform consumers and to receive payments.

■■ **Informing Guests or Visitors**

A website is the perfect platform to share the volume and types of content that would not be accessible on signage boards or in printed material. A large resort could, for instance, add QR codes around the property linking to a resort map on its website, helping guests find their way around attractions and food points. In the same way, a museum could educate visitors by placing QR codes at artefacts or installations, directing them to additional audio or video content, or encouraging them to share an interesting snippet of information via their social media accounts. QR codes can easily be incorporated into self-guided walking tours. For example, a QR code could be placed at the entrance to or the start of the route. When visitors use their smartphones to scan the code, useful information to guide them on their walk is displayed on their smartphones. QR codes could also be placed at strategic points along the route where travellers might require additional information about a specific attraction.

■■ **Receiving Payments**

By using their smartphones to scan a QR code linked to a mobile payment application, guests can conveniently pay their hotel or restaurant bill, or pay for access to any attraction at a destination. The most popular mobile payment applications working with QR codes in Apple Pay, Paypal, mVisa, and Snapscan.

■ **Location-Based Marketing**

Location-based marketing (LBS) is defined as "services connected with the location of the customer or any application or service that receives a customer's location and provides that customer with information or services tailored to that location" (Pedrana, 2014: 755).

Research carried out by Google found that 85% of leisure travellers only decide which activities they are going to participate in after they have arrived at their destination, and 50% of travellers use smartphones to search for things to do once they have arrived there (White, 2017). This presents a huge opportunity for all locally based tourism experiences: visitor attractions, restaurants and cafés, wine farms, tours, rental companies, accommodation, events, and visitor information centres. Below, we discuss some location-based marketing concepts that tourism businesses can implement to help reach browsers and convert them into actual customers.

■ ■ Optimising for Local Mobile Search

Up to 82% of smartphone users use a search engine when looking for a local business (Jeffs, 2018). Thus, it is important to ensure that the tourism company's website appears in the smartphone search results of potential customers. Tourism businesses need to consider the questions their prospective customers have about the type of tourism experience they are researching when they are already in a destination (White, 2017). In other words, what questions do they have that will prompt the use of specific keywords in their search? They may, for example, search using the keywords "best tourism experience/breakfast/coffee/pizza in Goa", or "wine tours in Seville" or "kitesurfing Morocco". This information should be included on the company's website, either on a standard web page or as a blog post and optimised for key search phrases (keywords) that travellers are likely to use.

In addition to optimising its website for local searches, a tourism business must optimise its Google Maps listing. Google Maps has over a billion users worldwide (Rowett, 2017) and is used widely by domestic tourists travelling in the country as well as international tourists visiting the country. These tourists use it to access map information while planning and booking travel as well as during the journey itself.

The main benefits of optimising a tourism business on Google Maps listings include the following (Rowett, 2017):

- It is an excellent way of being "found" by travellers who are using search engines to find local products, whether that is by typing in search queries or by using the "Near me" function
- Businesses can easily share their blog or event listing content, which extends the reach of the content far beyond a website
- It is an additional outlet to gather product reviews, which influences the business' ranking of its map listing in search results
- It is a distribution promotion point for online travel retailers such as *Wotif*, *Expedia*, and ▶ Booking.com who sell tourism products and services online
- It provides a relevant backlink to the company's website, which improves the website's optimisation in search engine results.

Google Maps listings are managed by business owners via "Google My Business", which is simply a management portal solely for this purpose. It allows businesses to claim and optimise their listings, encourage reviews, and post articles (Rowett, 2017). "Google My Business" populates Google Maps and Google Trips, and also ranks high in smartphone search results, especially when people choose the suggested "Near me" search query (White, 2017).

■ ■ Optimising the TripAdvisor "near me"
      Function and Facebook's "Nearby Places"

Seventy-three per cent of travellers voted *TripAdvisor* as the most influential source of information for holidays, ahead of WoM, content, and official hotel ratings (White, 2017). The *TripAdvisor* mobile app has an incredibly useful "Near me" search function that is used by many travellers when researching their visit once they are already in a destination. Tourism businesses need to ensure their product offerings are included in this search by selecting the category in which their offering is most likely to show up and confirming that their listing is showing up by adjusting the business' address until it reflects on the map. Equally important is improving the ranking of a business's listing on the *TripAdvisor* website. An algorithm factors in the quantity and quality of reviews over a year for various service categories (SiteMinder, 2016).

Similar to *TripAdvisor*, Facebook has a "Nearby places" search function on its smartphone app. It works in a similar way to *TripAdvisor's* "Near me" function, allowing people to find local businesses such as accommodation providers, restaurants, attractions, shopping facilities, and nightlife activities. Tourism businesses need to ensure that their Facebook page category is set to "Local business", otherwise the page will not be displayed on the map. Tourism companies must also check that their contact information is correctly updated, including their opening hours, contact details, and physical address. Guests should be encouraged to "check in" online and/or leave a review as, according to Facebook, this helps strengthen the chances of their Facebook page being shared in the Facebook "Nearby places" search.

12.2.4.3 Paid Media

Paid media refers to the second of the three elements of content marketing used to communicate with customers and prospects (see ■ Fig. 12.2). As the name suggests, paid media takes the form of advertisements that promote content and help it gain reach, or exposure (Deiss & Henneberry, 2017: 80). Paid media can engage target markets, moving them to owned media (for example, a tourism business's website) and resulting in social media conversation (earned media).

Paid media is available in many forms, such as display advertisements, online classified advertisements, text link advertisements, e-mail advertisements, social media advertisements, affiliate marketing, mobile advertisements, and pay-per-click or search engine marketing using platforms such as *Google Ads* (formerly Google AdWords).

▪ Display Advertisements

Online display advertisements are embedded in web pages, allowing users to click through to the advertiser's site, and may include text, graphics, video, and animation. There are many different ways to display advertisements in digital marketing. The most common options include banner advertisements, interstitial banners, pop-ups and pop-unders,

floating advertisements, video advertisements, native content, and sponsored content (Stokes, 2018: 294–297).

▪▪ Banner Advertisements

A banner advertisement is a graphic image or animation displayed on a website for advertising purposes. Banner advertisements usually include interactive technologies that allow the viewer to interact and transact with the banner. For instance, some banners expand when the user moves his or her mouse over them or clicks on them, while some can even capture data within the banner.

▪▪ Interstitial Banners

Interstitial banners are banners shown between pages on a website or, more often, between screens on a mobile app. As a user clicks from one page to another, he or she is shown the advertisement before the next page is displayed.

▪▪ Pop-Ups and Pop-Unders

As the name suggests, these are advertisements that pop up or pop under the webpage being viewed. They open in a new, smaller window. Browsers see pop-ups immediately, but probably only become aware of pop-unders once they have closed their browser window. Pop-ups and pop-unders were very prominent in the early days of online advertising, but audience annoyance means that most web browsers today have built-in pop-up blockers. This can be problematic as websites sometimes use pop-ups legitimately to display information to the user.

▪▪ Floating Advertisements

This type of advertisement appears in a layer over the content but is not in a separate window. Best practice dictates that a prominent close button should be included on the advertisement, usually in the top right-hand corner. Floating advertisements are created with DHTML or Flash, and float in a layer above a site's content for a few seconds. Often, the animation ends by disappearing into a banner advertisement on the page. Many sites use floating advertisements to encourage newsletter sign-ups or social media "likes" rather than to advertise products.

▪▪ Video Advertisements

This is a video advertisement in one of the formats discussed above. It starts to play when the user arrives at a site or moves his or her mouse over the advertisement.

▪▪ Native Content

Native content advertising is the online version of advertorials. This is where the advertiser produces content that is in line with the editorial style of the website, but it is sponsored, or the product is in some way endorsed by the brand. Video is an increasingly popular method used for of native advertising. Essentially, it is paid advertising that works hard not to disrupt the user experience. In its ideal form, the user is presented with useful, engaging content, which is much more engaging than a banner advertisement. Native content can look like paid search advertisements on a search engine, sponsored content on LinkedIn or Facebook, or promoted listings, such as on Twitter. However, it looks much more like content than advertising.

▪▪ Sponsored Content

Sponsored content advertising exists at the bottom of many online articles. This is where the "suggested articles" posts appear and, in most cases, this is paid-for promotion. Advertisers pay to have their content promoted under certain categories of websites or articles.

▪ E-mail Advertising

One of the least expensive types of online advertising is e-mail advertising, where paid content is embedded in another company's e-mail. Advertisers purchase space in the e-mail sponsored by others, often an e-mail newsletter. For example, ▸ eMarketer.com sends "eMarketer FYI" e-mails to its regular newsletter subscribers that include graphical advertisements and links to white papers (a white paper is an authoritative report or guide that solves a reader's problem, answers their question, or helps a reader make a decision) from other companies (and is paid for this). Note that e-mail messages sent from a company directly to internet users are owned content, not paid media.

▪ Text Link Advertisements

These advertisements take the form of a hyperlink placed in specific text in a blog post or other owned media content (including content downloaded by mobile phone users). In a hypothetical example, a South African travel agency selling European destinations (for example, Spain, the UK, and Italy) might buy a specified number of links for the words "Spain", "United Kingdom", and "Italy" on many travel blogger sites, with hyperlinks to the travel agency's website.

▪ Online Classified Advertisements

Online classified advertisements are placed by individual consumers as well as by businesses. They usually use text but may also include photographs. The advertisements are advertisements according to classification (for example, cars, sport, travel, and so on.) and tend to be an inexpensive format. Online classified advertisements can be found on dedicated sites (for example, ▸ www.gumtree.co.za) as well as online newspapers, exchanges, and web portals. In many cases, posting a regular-size classified advertisement is free, but placement of a larger advertisement in colour, or with some other feature that attracts attention, is done for a fee.

▪ Affiliate Marketing

Affiliate marketing is the online version of rewarding referrers for business or leads generated as a result of their efforts. Referrers are given a "finder's fee" for every referral that they give (Gregori, Daniele & Altinay, 2013). The difference between affiliate marketing and other online marketing or advertising is that affiliates are only paid when they refer business to the organisation. For an affiliate programme to work successfully, the affiliated organisation (the organisation publishing the sites containing the links) must be proactive and promote the offering aggressively (Gay, Charlesworth & Esen, 2007: 419). Affiliate marketing can be used to complement other campaigns, whether they are online or offline. Online affiliate marketing is widely used to promote websites, with referrers being rewarded for every visitor, subscriber, or customer provided through their efforts. It is thus a useful tool for branding and acquisition. Affiliate marketing allows for targeted traffic from niche websites (Gregori, Daniele & Altinay, 2013).

■ Mobile Advertising

Mobile advertising is a form of paid advertising that appears on mobile phones and tablets that have wireless devices connections (but not on laptops) (Yang, Kim & Yoo, 2013) This type of mobile advertising can take place as text advertisements via SMS, or banner advertisements that appear embedded in a business's website, in downloaded apps, or in mobile games (Investopedia, 2018).

■ Search Engine Marketing

Paid search marketing, commonly referred to as "pay-per-click" (PPC) advertising or search engine marketing (SEM), is the paid-for advertising that usually appears alongside, above, and occasionally below the organic listings on the search engine results pages (SERPS), or on a partner site. These are usually labelled "Sponsored link", "Sponsored result", or "Ad" in order to make it clear to users that they are, in fact, paid-for advertisements and not part of the search engine's organic (natural or not-paid-for) listing. Typically, website owners pay each time their advertisement is clicked on, hence the name "pay-per-click". PPC is the most common form of paid search marketing, but advertisements may also be bought on a "cost-per-thousand" (CPT) basis. The biggest player in the PPC arena is also the leading search engine: Google Ads (Ryan, 2014: 128). SEM is mainly Google Ads to promote a web-site and obtain a good ranking on search engine sites. It is similar to paid ads only whereas PPC is a part of Google Ads.

■ ■ How Does Paid Search Advertising Work?

When a user enters a search query into a search engine, the engine returns a list of organic search results. It also determines which advertisements to show that are relevant to the search query. These advertisements, which sit adjacent to or above the organic listings, used to be small, unobtrusive text-based advertisements, but now come with enhanced listings that include images and other data, such as price and merchant name. While a high ranking in the organic listing is what most webmasters are striving for (because it is free and because users see organic results as impartial: they trust, and therefore click on, organic listings in preference to paid advertisements), optimising a page to rank in organic search results can be difficult, and getting a consistently high and sustainable ranking takes a substantial amount of effort and time.

Time without web traffic is, of course, a missed opportunity. That is where paid search advertising comes in. By agreeing to pay the search engine a fee per click for an advertisement to show up as a sponsored result when a user types in the keywords or phrases chosen by the tourism marketer, a business can put its website in the SERPs in front of its competitors almost immediately. It works like this: when a user clicks on one of the advertisements placed by a tourism business, that business gets a new visitor and the search engine bills the business for the click.

PPC keywords are bid on by advertisers in an auction-style system. Generally, the higher the bid per click, the higher the advertisement's placement in the SERPs. Most PPC systems also work a quality quotient (for example, Google's Ads Quality Score) into their advertisement placement rankings. This is based on the popularity of the advertisement (its click-through rate, or CTR) as well as the perceived quality of both the content of the advertisement and the landing page to which it points (Ryan, 2014: 129).

Why Use Paid Search Marketing?

Here are two of the many reasons to use PPC search marketing (Ryan, 2014: 130):

- PPC generates traffic while waiting for the SEO to kick in. It can take months to get a website to the top half of the first page of organic search results through SEO. PPC advertisements can get a website in front of a targeted audience almost immediately.
- Highly targeted advertisements mean a better chance of conversion. The tourism business is not broadcasting its message to the masses as it would be with a display advertisement. The search marketing advertisement will only appear in front of users who have prequalified themselves by typing the business' chosen keywords into a search engine in the geographical regions selected by the tourism business.

Targeting Options

Search advertisements are targeted in a variety of ways, depending on how the business wants to reach its intended audience. Three of these targeting options are listed and described in ◘ Table 12.6.

Social Media Advertising

Social media advertisements can be recognised by labels such as "Suggested post", "Promoted", "Sponsored", and so on, depending on the platform. The advertising formats available are continuously evolving, which means that tourism marketers need to keep up with what is available to them. It also means that there are ever-increasing opportunities to reach travellers on a platform and in a format that suits them (Stokes, 2018: 314).

Social media advertising should be considered as part of an overall social media strategy. While brands can start a Facebook page and share engaging posts, those posts would be seen only by a fraction of the possible audience (those who have "liked" the business's Facebook page, for example). Paying to promote posts is necessary to ensure that a tourism business reaches a much larger percentage of a target audience.

Social media advertising is a form of online advertising that takes place on social media networks. Many platforms offer extraordinarily detailed targeting options that match users whom advertisers have identified as belonging to specific purchasing groups, making it a great way to reach exactly the right group of users with targeted advertisements. While more traditional forms of advertising are arguably somewhat inefficient, the targeting offered by social media platforms make it stand out even from other forms of online advertising, such as display advertisements. Social media advertising also tends to have higher click-through and engagement rates at a lower cost (Stokes, 2018: 315).

Platforms

One of the core principles to keep in mind when choosing a social media platform on which to advertise is that tourism marketers need to go where their audience is. We will consider three of the most popular social media platforms: Facebook, Twitter, Snapchat, and Instagram.

Facebook

Facebook offers several paid-for advertising solutions based on the action the advertiser wants the audience to take (the purpose of the advertisement). The core objectives are usually awareness, consideration, or conversions (see ◘ Table 12.7), which Facebook has broken down further into more specific objectives on which tourism marketers can base their creation of advertisements.

Once the tourism marketer has chosen an objective, Facebook offers a number of advertisement formats to choose from that will help the marketer meet his or her objective.

- Format 1: Single image. A single image advertisement is one of the simplest advertisements available because it is easy to set up; it does not take a lot of time to make.
- Format 2: Single video. If the marketing objective is to get traffic to a website, then a video advertisement is one way to grab the attention of potential site visitors.
- Format 3: Carousel. marketer can upload between two and ten images that the advertisement will scroll through.

■ Table 12.6   Three options for targeting search advertisements

Keywords and match types	Keywords are the foundation blocks for any successful PPC account. To ensure maximum return on investment, a list of relevant keywords must be researched that correctly represents the products and services offered by the website. The presence of these keywords will ensure that when a user enters his or her search query into the search engine, a quality advertisement will be triggered, and a sale captured. Advertisers can assign as many keywords as they want to an advertisement, but only one advertisement will be shown for each URL. If two advertisers are bidding to show advertisements for the same domain, only one will be displayed. The selection of this advertisement is based on the bids placed and the quality of the advertisements.
	As search advertisements are charged on a per-click basis, the cost for every click is determined by a variety of factors and is based on a bidding system. The different advertising platforms offer advanced bidding options, all aimed at helping tourism marketers to improve their advertising campaigns. Marketers can bid for placement on the SERP or they can bid based on how much they are willing to pay-per-click. Tourism marketers are also able to tailor their approach to, for example, bidding for advertisements during certain times of the day only.
	The search engine takes a number of factors into account in addition to the bid an advertiser places on a keyword. In the case of Google Ads, this is known as "Quality Score". Quality Score is applied on keyword, advertising group, and account level. It is important that the entire Google Ads account has a good Quality Score, as it affects ranking and the cost-per-click (Stokes, 2018: 202–203). The Quality Score is determined by, among other factors, the relevance of the keyword to the search term, the relevance of the advertising copy to the search term, and the relevance of the landing page to the search term.
Language and location targeting	Search engines have versions customised for specific regions and languages, based on the user's settings and where in the world he or she is searching from. Tourism marketers can choose the language and the location they wish to target. This is known as "geotargeting". For example, a tourism marketer may want an advertisement to be displayed only to English searchers in Brazil or to German searchers in Johannesburg. Targeting the advertisement means that users outside the target area will not see a specific advertisement and the business does not pay for traffic that it cannot convert into customers.
Behavioural and demographic targeting	Search advertising can also be targeted based on personal behaviour. Using Ads, a tourism business can retarget visitors who came to its website via an Ads advertisement based on actions that they took. This means that if users came to a website, but did not complete a purchase, the tourism business can target advertisements to them in the SERPs or through other online advertising channels, such as the Google Display Network. This is called "remarketing" or retargeting and can be very effective for remaining top-of-mind until the user is ready to convert. It is usually advisable to cap the number of times a remarketing advertisement is shown to an individual to avoid annoying the person.
Psychographic targeting	Psychographics is a qualitative method used to depict the characteristics of people based on their psychological qualities. The psychographic target is segmenting people based on values, personalities, interests, and opinions. It aids in better customer understanding, repositioning the brand, and developing new segments (Plog, 2002).

Source: Author's creation

- Format 4: Slideshow (video-like advertisements). Slideshow advertisements are a hybrid of videos and image advertisements. If the objective is "conversions", but the tourism marketer is working with a limited budget, a slideshow is a good option.
- Format 5: Collection. With this format, marketers can use a combination of images

■ Table 12.7 Facebook advertising objectives

Awareness	Consider-ation	Conversion
Brand awareness	Traffic (sending users to your website or app)	Conversions (encourage valuable actions on your website or app)
Local awareness (promoting to users nearby)	App installations	Product catalogue sales (create advertise-ments that automatically show your offerings from your catalogue based on your target audience)
Reach (show an advertise-ment to the maximum possible number of users)	Engagement (encourage comments, shares, and page "likes")	Store visits (promote multiple business locations to users nearby)
	Video views	
	Lead generation (collect lead information from interested parties)	

Source: Stokes (2018), p. 327

and video to make their advertisements more versatile and engaging. Start with a short video highlighting the tourism offering's main selling features.

These advertising formats have several options for placement in the feeds of Facebook users. They can appear on the RHS (right-hand-side) desktop, in the news feed on desktop, or in the news feed on mobile. Since Facebook owns Instagram, tourism marketers also have the option of showing certain types of advertisement on that platform.

Once the tourism marketer has chosen an objective and advertisement type, he or she needs to look at Facebook's targeting options, which also gather user data from Instagram and WhatsApp. Facebook offers marketers three audience options:

1. Core audiences, where an audience is selected manually based on demographics such as age and location, interests, and behaviours
2. Custom audiences, where a contact list is uploaded to connect with customers on Facebook
3. Lookalike audiences, where customer information is used to find people similar to them on Facebook.

■■ Instagram

Instagram is a mobile application with an engaged mobile audience, making it a good option for some tourism businesses. It allows users to take, edit, and share photographs and videos. Since Facebook owns Instagram, it offers almost identical core objectives to Facebook; that is: awareness, consideration, or conversions (see ■ Table 12.7).

Instagram was founded in 2010 and became an Instant success acquiring over 1 million members in the first couple months of operation. In May 2020 it has over 1 billion users. Along with Instagram came the new phenomenon of 'Instagram Influencers' - people who have a strong influence on Instagram and have the power to influence consumers. These could be celebrities, blog-gers, activists, and personalities - anyone with credibility and a fan base. Some influencers popular are demanding thousands of US dol-lars/euros - depending on where they are from - for a mention on their posts. Those influencers with a large social media following have been able to introduce tourism and hos-pitality brands to tens of thousands of con-sumers. For tourism and hospitality businesses interested In increasing their brand awareness with the right Influencers on Instagram can be an effective marketing strategy.

In 2018, over U$ 2 billion was spent on advertising with 'Instagrammers'. A signifi-

12

cant portion of this money Is dedicated to inspiring audiences to travel to new locations. Marketers can specify their target audience's demographics, interests, and behaviours, just as with Facebook. They can even target users who have used their services before or engaged with the business' Instagram page by commenting on or liking [♥] content on the page.

■■ Twitter

Twitter offers a self-service advertising platform with several options and allows a degree of specific targeting. As with Facebook and Instagram, the platform tends to change frequently, and not all options may be available to all regions or user accounts. Like Facebook, Twitter's priority is the mobile marketplace and the ad formats match the actions businesses want users to take.

Twitter targeting options are nearly as detailed as those of Facebook. Audiences can be chosen based on the following criteria: location (country, province, region, metro area, or postal code), gender, language, device, platform, carrier, keywords, followers, interests, tailored audiences (a list of e-mails or Twitter IDs can be uploaded, or businesses can put a code snipped on its website to collect visitors, purchasers, or downloaders, and then target them), TV targeting (targeting users who engage with television programmes in a specific market or by show), behaviours, and events (users interested in global or regional events).

12.2.4.4 **Earned Media**

Earned media is exactly what the name suggests; media where a marketer's presence is not determined by what he or she spends, but by how interesting people think the company and its products and services are (Ryan, 2014: 83). Earned media is the digital version of WoM marketing (see ▫ Fig. 12.3). For instance, when someone posts a positive comment about a product on his or her Facebook wall, it serves as a recommendation to friends. Earned media occur when "individual conversations become the channel" on blogs, product review sites, news sites, and in comments

on owned media pages and everywhere else they are allowed (Strauss & Frost, 2013: 394).

The next section examines this third element of the online content strategy and discusses these types of earned media:
■ Social media influencers
■ Viral marketing
■ Travel and content communities
■ Wikis
■ User reviews and ratings
■ Social media discussion platforms.

■ Social Media Influencers

Influencer marketing is a type of social media marketing involving endorsements and product placement from influencers, people, and organisations who have a purported expert level of knowledge or social influence in their field (Brown & Hayes, 2008). The tourism industry is heavily dependent on the internet because people look for feedback from others to find out about the best places to visit when they travel. Social media influencers can play an important role in a tourism and hospitality business's marketing efforts (Marchante, 2016). Influencers are people who can change opinions and behaviours among an audience, driving measurable outcomes for a tourism brand. Depending on the business, influencers might include popular authors, celebrities, personalities, speakers, bloggers, analysts, journalists, and so on. They are people who make their opinions known, and whom consumers respect and listen to (Marketo, 2014: 62).

For the tourism industry – as with other industries – social media is utilised for the purpose of marketing, drive engagement, brand exposure, and ultimately to increase sales. At times, companies and influencers might have a similar target market. In this case, tourism businesses can reach out to those influencers. Relevant social media influencers, such as travel bloggers, share the story of their journeys via marketing channels (see ▫ Table 12.8) Travel influencers gain feedback from their followers (readers), who admire their work, and thus followers who are inspired by the blog may book a similar trip

◻ Table 12.8 Influencer marketing channels

Influencer marketing channels	Influencer content types
Facebook	Blog posts
Instagram	Instagram posts/stories
LinkedIn	LinkedIn posts/videos
Snapchat	Sponsored Facebook Live
Twitter	Twitter posts/videos
Blogs	Snapchat videos/photos
YouTube	E-mails
E-mail	LinkedIn posts
Newsletter	YouTube videos
Digital/print ads	Magazine/newspaper articles
Television	Television appearances/videos

Source: Author's creation

for similar experiences (see ◻ Image 12.4). Thus, travel bloggers influence consumers' purchase decisions. An example of a travel influencer is Shivya Nath from India, going by the alias "Shooting Star", who has more than 70,000 followers on Instagram and 10,000 followers on Facebook.

Social media influencer Callum Snape's Instagram post to increase the brand awareness of Sun Peaks Resort, a ski resort in British Columbia, Canada. This post achieved 200,000+ article views in 3 minutes, generating great Interest in Sun peaks' target market (◻ Image 12.4).

■ Viral Marketing

Viral marketing is the mutual sharing and spreading of marketing-relevant information, initially distributed deliberately by marketers to stimulate and capitalise on WoM behaviours (Van der Ians & van Bruggen, 2010). An example of viral marketing is a person forwarding an e-mail message, the address of a website, or other information about a special offer for a tour or an airfare to his or her friends.

Viral marketing, which is unpaid communication, was given its name because of its similarities to a virus: users pass on the message to each other and growth is exponential. Examples of effective viral content include short video clips or jokes (also known as "memes") that get forwarded around the world.

Marketers use the power of viral marketing to encourage people to use their products and services. The goal of viral marketing is to create potential for exponential growth through the message's exposure and influence. Viral marketing is effective as long as the recipient's friends are in the target market of the company.

■ Travel and Content Communities

Virtual communities started in the mid-1990s. In tourism, consumers use online travel communities to seek travel information and tips, make travel transactions, foster relationships with people from far away, and find travel companions. Content on online (virtual) communities is autonomously generated by its users. They post reviews, comments, and ratings on a destination, a hotel, an attraction, or any other tourism-related product or service. In addition, users can add multi-media elements (photos and/or videos) and travel maps or take part in discussion forums.

■■ Travel Communities

▶ TripAdvisor.com is an example of an online travel community. It is a website based on the notion that travellers rely on other travellers' reviews to plan their trips or that they can at least be helped in their decision-making by reading these reviews. The assumption is that because the people writing these reviews do not have a financial interest in the product reviewed, their opinions are objective. The site, which began operations in 2000, operates in 47 countries worldwide, including China (under the domain name ▶ daodao.com).

Gogobot (▶ www.gogobot.com) recently rebranded as Trip by Skyscanner (▶ www.trip.skyscanner.com), is a social networking

Image 12.4 Travel influencer Melanie Sutrathada

12

site for frequent travellers. Members can share information about their trips and make plans to meet up when their schedules overlap.

Other examples of travel communities include ▶ Lonelyplanet.com, VirtualTourist, tripwolf, and IgoUgo. Other more specific tourism sector sites include ▶ Hotelchatter. com, which reports on boutique hotels around the world, and ▶ CruiseDiva.com, which focuses on the cruise liner industry. TravelPod allows users to create free travel blogs (travelogues or travel journals). Users can chart trips on a map and share photos and videos.

■■ Content Communities

The main aim of content communities is the sharing of media content between internet users. They exist for a wide range of media types, including text, photos (for example, Flickr), and videos (for example, YouTube). The high popularity of content communities makes them an extremely attractive contact channel for many tourism companies.

YouTube is a site where users can upload and watch videos. It is the global leader in the video streaming market, with more than a billion videos viewed every day. In May 2019, YouTube had over one billion (monthly) users; 70% of YouTube traffic is from mobile phones (Smith, 2019). Thus, it is not surprising that marketers are investigating YouTube as a tourism marketing tool. However, very few companies have fully realised the potential of this platform; most brands have been left behind. The success of utilising this platform largely depends on publishing refreshing content and images online consistently and frequently (see ▶ Industry Insight 12.5).

A YouTube video (▶ https://www.youtube.com/watch?v=HyB8sTiKcQQ) tells travellers what to do if they are caught up in a terrorist attack. The police and government ministers are supporting the effort and encouraging holidaymakers to take heed of the "Run, hide, tell" safety procedure.

The four-minute film explains the message by depicting a gun attack at a hotel and the action guests should take. The video advises people to run to a place of safety if there is a safe option, leaving their belongings behind, and insisting that others go with them. If there is nowhere to go, then they should hide by barricading themselves into a room and turning their mobile phones to silent. Then, only when it is safe to do so, should they attempt to alert the authorities by calling the local emergency number, which holidaymakers should find out in advance.

Source: ▶ https://www.youtube.com/watch?v=HyB8sTiKcQQ

Flickr is a popular image- and video-hosting website and online community. It enables users to organise photographs using tags that, in turn, enable searchers to find images related to particular topics, such as place names or subject matter.

■ **Wikis**

Wikis are knowledge-sharing sites. They can be open to all (for example, Wikipedia and Wikitravel), they can be aimed at certain communities only, or they can be private and open only to individuals within an organisation. Essentially, a wiki is a piece of software that allows users to create and edit content online, using simple mark-up language via a web browser.

> *Wiki* means "rapidly" in the Hawaiian language.

■ **Online User Reviews and Ratings**

Online user product reviews are playing an increasingly important role in consumer decision making. Consumer reviews serve two distinct purposes:
- L They provide information about products and services.
- L They serve as recommendations.

Research has shown that online reviews (and ratings) have a significant effect on the sales of various products, including books, cinema movies, restaurants, hair salons, and holidays (see Hu, Koh & Reddy, 2014). In tourism, most travellers look for reviews during the beginning and middle stages of the holiday planning process as a way of narrowing down their choices. Online review and travel advice sites (such as *TripAdvisor*, Google Review, and ▶ Lonelyplanet.com) have a considerable impact on consumers' choice of accommodation for holidays. Research shows that more than 85% of travellers use the internet during travel planning (Leung, Law, van Hoof & Buhalis, 2013).

■ **Social Media Discussion Platforms**

Tourism companies and DMOs are recognising the marketing potential of image-sharing applications such as Flickr and Instagram, which allow users to share holiday photographs on various social media platforms. Once an image has been posted, other users can comment on both the image and the destination, creating a comment–review–query snowball effect.

A significant number of people use social networks as their first choice for queries about holiday destinations. Sites such as Trippy, Gtrot, FlyMuch, and Trippy SkyScanner offer platforms for individuals to discuss and review a range of products. Users can then connect these network sites as well as other reviews to their social media platforms (for example, Facebook, Instagram, LinkedIn, Google+, and Twitter), while Pinterest and the "like" button have turned the travel product landscape into a popularity contest.

TripAdvisor reports that more than 60 million users have logged onto its review site (which enables users to access recommendations from people in their network) from Facebook. (These reviews then appear on users' Facebook pages and possibly also on other social media, such as Twitter.) Thus, social media sites are full of comments from users, and many of these comments relate to tourism products, companies, brands, and destinations.

Blog conversations occur with lengthy lists of comments, especially in the B2B market, where professionals share information on various topics. The way to engage users on business blogs is to write timely, interesting, and current content, and to include buttons so users can easily "like" content on Facebook, tweet about it on Twitter, recommend it on Google+, and share it on LinkedIn (Strauss & Frost, 2013: 406–407).

Social media and networking sites are extremely conducive to the distribution of travel reviews because both activities involve a great deal of interaction. As a result, tourism companies have a lot to gain from social networking sites, as long as they offer an exceptional product and service. Conversely, tourism companies stand to lose business if reports of poor service and other complaints are posted on social media sites (highlighting the importance of online reputation management, discussed below). Increasingly, consumers are using social media platforms such as Facebook and Twitter to voice their complaints. Consumers feel that their voices are more likely to be heard and that they will receive a rapid response when using social media. Social media platforms such as Snapchat, WhatsApp, and Instagram are particularly popular among the 18–24 years market (Smith & Anderson, 2018).

■ **Evaluating Digital and Social Media**

Website analytics (or Web analytics) involves the tracking, measurement, collection, analysis, and reporting of data in order to understand and optimise the performance of a website (Web Analytics Association, 2007).

Web analytics provide a tourism marketer with extensive information as to how a website is performing. A range of information is gathered, such as the websites that referred traffic, including search engines, the pages that users visited on the website, and the entry and exit pages for website visits and activity interaction on the site. This information is collected through analysis of the website's server logs or through page tagging. Web analytics help to identify what areas of the website are performing well and what areas need attention. Successful analytics rely on determining the goals of a website to optimise Web usage in line with business objectives. Metrics that are key performance indicators (KPIs) are then measured and analysed. KPIs used in digital marketing measurement include the following (Pike, 2018: 228):

- A count (in other words, the number of visitors to the website)
- A ratio (the ratio of visitors to the website who made bookings to all of the visitors to the website)
- The conversion rate (the number of visitors to the website who made a booking)
- The bounce rate (the percentage of visitors who left the website after looking at only one page)
- Tweets
- Posts
- Comments
- The click-through rate (CTR)
- Shares (for example, on Facebook)
- Page visits
- Viewable impressions
- Time spent.

It should be noted that while these metrics may be impressive to owners and shareholders, they are not necessarily related to sales. Steps should be taken to improve the KPIs that affect the business's marketing objectives.

Facebook Analytics allows businesses to undertake real-time and social media analyses for their Facebook pages, and to track the effectiveness of paid and owned content. Google Ads offers conversion tracking tags, which allow marketers to report on Google

Ads campaigns from impression through to conversion. If you are sending traffic to a website that uses Google Analytics, you can use campaign tracking to track and report on campaigns that are driving traffic to the site. A free online "Google Analytics for Beginners" course is available. It shows users how to set up an account, implement tracking code, set up metrics dashboards, and generate audience and campaign tracking reports.

■ Online Reputation Management

A company's reputation is present on the internet for all to see. Online reputation management (ORM) refers to a tool in which a company monitors and manages what is being said about it and responds to let its customers know that they are being heard (Kotler & Keller, 2016: 192). This is also known as "monitoring the chatter online" or "social listening". Social media listening (measurement or monitoring) is the process of discovering and evaluating what is being said about a brand, company, individual, or product offering on social media channels (including blogs, logs, wikis, news sites, micro blogs such as Twitter, social networking sites, video or photo sharing websites, forums, message boards, and user-generated content) (Financial Times, 2018).

ORM can have a huge impact on a brand's reputation and its bottom line. It is only through listening to conversations involving its customers and potential customers that an organisation can respond adequately and manage its situation in the marketplace. Effective ORM tools such as Google Alerts, Trackur, Reputology, Chatmeter, and Social Mention can help a tourism and hospitality company in engaging with its customers where relevant and providing better service by responding to queries and complaints.

Social media monitoring is a critical tool for finding out (Stokes, 2018):
- Who is talking about your brand and what they are saying
- Where your audience is and what they are interested in
- The hot topics and trends
- The current thought leaders and influencers

■ Digital Marketing Issues

Tourism marketers must also understand and respond to several problems associated with the internet as a marketing tool, including the following:
- High costs of and/or slow broadband connections, which deter high-speed take-up, particularly in developing countries and in rural areas
- The internet's secondary boundaries (these boundaries limit the use of senses such as taste and touch, which influence buyers' decisions)
- Concerns over security issues (some online consumers are reluctant to provide personal details such as credit card information that are required when performing online transactions)
- Consumers' concerns over privacy issues, for example, spam and chat rooms
- The possible obsolescence of information displayed on a tourism company's website
- Lack of trust of unknown virtual traders (there are fraudulent companies on the Web, so consumers may be concerned that a company might not actually exist, or that the company and its offerings might not live up to their expectations or the images portrayed on the company's website).

12.3 Summary

The internet is one of the most exciting developments in the tourism industry in recent years. Tourism organisations are increasingly using the Net to communicate with and reach consumers. In this chapter, we analysed three types of media used in digital marketing: paid, owned, and earned media. We considered how organisations use the internet and looked at how to establish a website, including developing and designing a website. We discussed several digital marketing tools, including affiliate marketing, social networking, search engine marketing, and blogging. The internet provides an untapped opportunity for many small and medium-sized tourism businesses. It is, however, a marketing tool, not a magic formula to business success.

Tourism businesses need to advance their digital marketing strategies by embracing a more innovative approach. This could include utilising applications such as video and mapping facilities.

❓ Discussion Questions

1. The internet offers a number of benefits to buyers and sellers. Describe some of the benefits gained by both the consumer and the firm. Use an example of a tourism or hospitality company to illustrate your answer.
2. Discuss how an internet website can be used to collect information about consumers.
3. Briefly explain why website content is so important.
4. Describe some of the ways of getting consumers to revisit a website.
5. What is 'conversion rate'? And explain why is it important in monitoring Web traffic?
6. Explain what is SEO? Provide examples in the context of tourism and hospitality marketing.
7. A local guesthouse/B&B requires advice on setting up a customer database for direct marketing purposes. Describe the qualities it should consider in order to create an effective database?
8. Provide one example each of paid, owned, and earned media used in tourism digital marketing.
9. What are the main reasons why small tourism and hospitality businesses should engage with consumers through digital marketing and social media?
10. Outline two ways in which a holiday resort or upmarket restaurant could recruit satisfied customers as social media travel influencers.

Visit this website for information about a digital marketing aptitude test and certify your digital marketing knowledge with Red & Yellow Creative Business School:
► https://dmat.ac/

Vouchers for a 100% discount voucher on the Digital Marketing Aptitude Test. Your voucher code is: Tourism1000 (Limited to the first 1000 students).

The Red & Yellow Creative School of Business is a leader in digital marketing education and have been teaching business leaders to think creatively since 1994.

In-Depth Case Study 12: Travel Influencers Driving Tourism Marketing

Objectives

- To understand the concept of influencer marketing
- To understand the increasing role of travel influencers in tourism marketing

Instagram, perhaps more so than any other social media platform, has created a wave of social media-driven tourism particularly amongst millennials (Generation Y) and the "follow-me too" generation. Instagram was founded in 2010 and became an instant success acquiring over 1 million members in its first couple months of operation. By February 2020, it had over 1 billion monthly users (► https://www.omnicoreagency.com/instagram-statistics/) meaning an estimated that one out of every seven people in the world regularly access the photo and video-sharing social networking site.

Along with Instagram came a rising phenomenon of Instagram Influencers - people who have a strong presence on Instagram and have the power to influence consumers - these could be celebrities, bloggers, activists, and personalities, anyone with credibility and a fan base. Influencers can have a major sway when it comes to fashion, political beliefs, brand loyalty, and even travel and hospitality purchasing habits. Have you ever purchased something because a well-known person you admire used the product or service? Do you ever check-out Instagram for inspiration when planning a trip or a holiday? If you answered "yes" to either of these questions - did it lead you to a purchase of a product or service?

Social influencer marketing has become big business over the last few years with some influencers demanding thousands of US dollars or Euros for a mention on their Instagram postings. In turn, Instagram is looking to turn their followers into actual business and have monetised everything from parenting to baking. Not only is influencer marketing driving business to relatively 'unknown' companies and destinations it is creating new roles in the industry. One area which has seen the biggest growth over the last few years by Instagrammers has been tourism and hospitality marketing.

Simply put, travel influencers are people who can persuade others to take action. The action might be a website visit, travel guide or e-brochure download, social media engagement, or sales conversion; depending on what the tourism business wants to achieve with a campaign. Essentially, travel influencers experience a travel product-offering and then present a rave review to their audience in a bid to prompt the desired action. The key point here is that the audience trusts the influencer or blogger. They see them as a reputable peer and because of this, are open to their suggestions.

By default, travel influencers need a large following. A good NTO will have millions and millions of followers. An influencer may have less (though of course not always). More importantly though, is that the travel influencer's content should be relevant to the audience it reaches. Most travel influencers on Instagram usually work on other social media platforms too and share content to their profiles on Facebook, Snapchat, LinkedIn, Pinterest, YouTube, TikTok, Flickr, or Twitter, for example. It is the unique reach they provide to certain audiences that is key. For example, a travel influencer who is known for visiting luxury spas and retreats may have a unique group who follow her that a destination may want to tap into.

Ultimately, partnering with a top influencer should be a mutually beneficial relationship that adds value for everyone. A tourism business should either have great travel content or a product and a suitable and interested audience to market it to. Instagram travel influencers are obsessed with capturing perfect photographs to get maximum likes and comments. A social media platform is a 'digital scrapbook and slideshow for the modern-day traveller' but on a much grander scale. Travel influencing has inspired and energised a new generation of travellers, particularly the millennial generation (Generation Y) as well as niche groups they provide reach into. Those with a large social media following have been able to introduce travel and hospitality brands to tens of thousands of consumers. For tourism and hospitality businesses interested in increasing their brand awareness, working with the right travel influencer on Instagram or YouTube can be an effective as part of a tourism company's marketing strategy that includes content marketing at its core and employing influencers to share that content Typically, those influencers who are interested in partnering-up with a brand will have the contact information visible on their social media page.

When considering which influencer to work with, a tourism business should be mindful of those who call themselves 'influential'. A large following is not necessarily the most important measurement metric, instead, the business should consider if the content is reaching the right audiences. Which channels you employ is also dependent on whom you want to reach and how you want to land your content. In addition, the business should consider those influencers who have accounts across several social media platforms. For example, is the influencer actively engaged on YouTube, TikTok, Snapchat, and Twitter platforms? (e.g. a LinkedIn account may not be the best for a tourism marketing campaign targeting millennials).

For the right tourism and hospitality organisation building a business strategy that incorporates Instagram is a useful effective tool. The platform is used by tens of millions of potential consumers which means it is a great medium to keep track of travel trends. However, as with any marketing platform there are certain pitfalls to be aware of. It is expensive, there are brand-fit issues, and it relies on content management. Further, make sure the partner influencer is focussed on travel and tourism and keeps engagement levels high. Additionally, it is helpful to work with the partner influencer to find a payment policy that both parties are comfortable with whether it is an affiliate fee or a one-off fee; that way both parties' benefit. And be honest with the consumer that this is paid. Instagram is a very versatile platform. Instagram now insists that when there is a paid partnership that it is labelled as so.

Melaine Sutrathada is a New York-based actor, host, and travel content creator with a love for hamming it up and laughing entirely too loudly. As a multi-media powerhouse, Melaine is making waves online and on-camera with her signature brand of personality and lifestyle expertise. Her approachable attitude, outgoing personality, and feminine style have made her an in-demand host in New York City. Melanie got her start in travel by documenting her own trips and when she's not on-camera, Melanie is often found planning her next excursion. After sharing her initial experiences in Iceland and Spain, she started getting requests from several DMOs, tourism boards and agencies about visiting different destinations domestically and internationally. Melanie hasn't looked back! She currently has over 195,000 followers on Instagram. Melanie provides the following advice: "Picking the right partners makes all the difference. It's all about finding tourism boards and hotels that make sense and provide the most value for your audience".

When asked "What is a typical day in the life of a travel influencer?" She responded: "Every day is a little different, but one non-negotiable is several hours spent on my laptop; whether it's e-mails about ongoing campaigns, organising details for upcoming travels, or editing images from the day and pitching tourism boards." She adds: "I am pretty much attached to a screen throughout the day. That being said, creating content surrounding travel is an absolute dream - there are so many beautiful experiences on trips that take my breath away and I could not be more grateful for the opportunities". However, it's not all sunshine, beaches and cocktails. Melanie says that there's a lot of work that's gone on behind-the-scenes. "I can't even count the number of all-nighters on press trips or the 4am wake-up calls to get to a location first-thing in the morning to make sure you get a great shot". She concluded: "One of the many wonderful things about being a travel influencer and content creator though is how incredibly worth it the job is. I worked in an office job for years and nothing compares to the freedom of being able to chase sunsets and add stamps to your passport" (◼ Image 12.5).

Case Study Questions and Activities

1. Why is it important for a travel influencer to build a good relationship with a tourism business?

2. Discuss the value and risk of a NTO working with travel influencers.

3. Besides the number of followers, what are the other useful metrics for measuring the popularity of a travel influencer and travel influencer campaign?

4. How are travel influencers usually rewarded?

5. Travel influencers have been accused of creating a fake perception of travel that cannot be replicated by the average travellers". Discuss this statement.

6. Go online to Melanie's official website (▶ melaniesutrathada.com) and at Instagram: @melaniesutra. Evaluate these two digital marketing platforms in terms of content. Describe the quality of the video and photography materials. Which audiences do they appeal to?

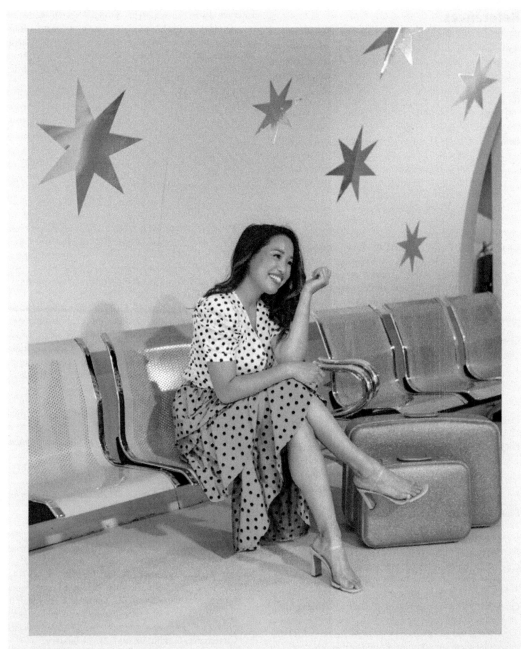

◻ **Image 12.5** Travel influencer @melaniesutra

References

Ash, T. (2012). *Landing page optimization: The definitive guide to testing and tuning for conversions* (2nd ed.). New York: Wiley Publishing. https://www.omnicore-agency.com/youtube-statistics [10 July 2018].

Baines, P., Fill, C., Rosengren, S., & Antonnetti, P. (2019). *Marketing* (5th ed.). Oxford, UK: Oxford University Press.

Bearne, S. (2016). How technology has transformed the travel industry. *The Guardian Online*. Retrieved from: https://www.theguardian.com/media-network/2016/feb/29/technology-internet-transformed-travel-industry-airbnb [22 August 2018].

Brown, D., & Hayes, N. (2008). *Influencer marketing: Who really influences your customers?* Oxford, UK: Butterworth-Heinemann.

Chaffey, D., & Ellis-Chadwick, F. (2019). *Digital marketing* (7th ed.). Harlow, Essex: Pearson.

Corbett, T. (2015). What is spam? A quick history of email spam and why you should avoid it. Experian. Retrieved from: https://www.experian.co.uk/blogs/latest-thinking/marketing/spam-origin-email-marketing/ [8 July 2018].

Corrêaa, C.& Kitanoa, C. (2015). Gamification in tourism: Analysis of Brazil quest game. In: Proceedings of ENTER 2015, The National Council for Scientific and Technological Development. Retrieved from https://agrilifecdn.tamu.edu/ertr/files/2015/02/SP05_MobileSession_Correa.pdf [22 August 2018].

Deiss, R., & Henneberry, R. (2017). *Digital marketing for dummies.* Hoboken, NJ: Wiley.

Digital Tourism Think Tank. (2014). Gaming and gamification in tourism. Retrieved from https://thinkdigital.travel/wp-content/uploadvertisements/2014/05/Gamification-in-Tourism-Best-Practice.pdf [5 May 2018].

Financial Times. Ft.com/lexicon Definition of social media monitoring. Retrieved from. http://lexicon.ft.com/Term?term=social-media-monitoring [31 July 2018].

Gay, R., Charlesworth, A., & Esen, R. (2007). *Online marketing: A customer-led approach.* Oxford, UK: Oxford University Press.

Goel, A. (2018). Augmented reality in social media, marketing, mobile apps and more. Retrieved from https://www.gc-solutions.net/blog/augmented-reality-in-social-media-marketing-mobile-apps-and-more/ [6 May 2018].

Gregori, N., Daniele, R., & Altinay, L. (2013). Affiliate marketing in tourism: Determinants of consumer trust. *Journal of Travel Research, 53*(2), 196–210.

Guttentag, D. A. (2009). Virtual reality: Application and implications for tourism. *Tourism Management, 31*(5).

Hu, N., Koh, N. S., & Reddy, S. (2014). Ratings lead you to the product, reviews help you clinch it? The mediating role of online review sentiments on product sales. *Decision Support Systems, 57*(January).

Internet Live Stats (2018). Google search statistics. [Online], Available: http://www.internetlivestats.com/google-search-statistics/ Accessed 23 July 2018.

Investopedia. (2018). Mobile advertising. Retrieved from https://www.investopedia.com/terms/m/mobile-advertising.asp [14 July 2018].

Janabi, O. (2017). Creating the ultimate digital retail experience for your customers. Retrieved from https://www.marketingtechnews.net/news/2017/may/04/creating-ultimate-digital-retail-experience-your-customers/ [14 June 2018].

Java, A., Song, X., Finin, T. & Tseng, B. (2010). Why we twitter: understanding microblogging usage and communities. In K. Ehrlich & S. Shami. Microblogging inside and outside the workplace. *Association for the Advancement of Artificial.* Retrieved from *Intelligence.* https://www.cs.cornell.edu/~sadats/icwsm2010.pdf [12 September 2018].

Jeffs, M. (2018). The di blog. Local search marketing statistics – show me stats nearby. Retrieved from https://edit.co.uk/blog/local-search-marketing-stats-show-me-stats-nearby/.

Kaplan, A., & Haenlein, M. (2011). Two hearts in three-quarter time: How to waltz the social media/viral marketing dance. *Business Horizons, 54*(3).

Karjaluoto, H., & Leppäniemi, M. (2005). Factors influencing consumers' willingness to accept mobile advertising: A conceptual model. *International Journal of Mobile Communications, 3*(3).

Kotler, P., Bowen, J., Makens, J., & Baloglu, S. (2017). *Marketing for hospitality and tourism* (7th ed.). Upper Saddle River, NJ: Prentice Hall.

Kotler, P., & Keller, K. L. (2016). *Marketing management* (15th ed.). Upper Saddle River, NJ: Prentice Hall.

Kumar, A. (2013). Search engine optimization (SEO): Technical analysis concepts. *International Journal of Emerging Technology and Advanced Engineering (IJETAE), 3.*

Leung, D., Law, R., van Hoof, H., & Buhalis, D. (2013). Social media in tourism and hospitality: A literature review. *Journal of Travel & Tourism Marketing, 30*(1/2), 3–22.

Linaza, M.T., Gutierrez, A. & Garcia, A. (2014). Pervasive augmented reality games to experience tourism destinations. In Z. Xiang & I. Tussyadiah (Eds.), *Information and communication technologies in tourism 2014.* Proceedings of the International Conference, Dublin, Ireland, 21–24 January.

Mangold, W., & Faulds, D. (2009). Social media: The new hybrid of the promotion mix. *Business Horizons, 52*(4), 357–365.

Mapp Corporation. (2017). The secret recipe to create the ultimate digital travel experience. Retrieved from https://mapp.com/resources/the-secret-recipe-to-create-the-ultimate-digital-travel-experience/ [30 April 2018].

Marchante, E. (2016). The use of social media influencers by the tourism industry. Retrieved from https://www.linkedin.com/pulse/use-social-influencers-tourism-industry-eliecer-marchante/ [21 May 2018].

Marketo. (2014). The definitive guide to engaging content marketing. Retrieved from http://www.marketo.com/definitive-guides/definitive-guide-to-engaging-content-marketing/ [12 May 2018].

Mohr, C.N. (2017). Augmented reality vs. virtual reality – what's the difference? Retrieved from https://learningenglish.voanews.com/a/augmented-reality-versus-virtual-reality/3844772.html [25 April 2018].

Ortiz-Cordova, A., & Jansen, B. (2012). Classifying web search queries in order to identify high revenue generating customers. *Journal of the American Society for Information Science and Technology, 63*(7), 1426–1441.

Oxford Dictionary of Business and Management (2016). Oxford: Oxford University Press.

Pedrana, M. (2014). Location-based services and tourism: Possible implications for destination. *Current Issues in Tourism, 17*(9), 753–762.

Pike, S. (2018). *Tourism marketing for small businesses.* Oxford, UK: Goodfellow Publishers.

Pitt, L., Berthon, P., Watson, R., & Zinkhan, G. (2002). The internet and the birth of real consumer power. *Business Horizons, 45*(4), 7–14.

Plog, S. C. (2002). The power of psychographics and the concept of Venturesomeness. *Journal of Travel Research, 40*(February).

Pulizzi, J. (2012). Six useful content marketing definitions. Retrieved from https://contentmarketinginstitute.com/2012/06/content-marketing-definition/ [28 April 2018].

Rastogi, N. (2018). 'Virtual reality vs. augmented reality: A comparative analysis'. Retrieved from https://www.engineersgarage.com/blog/virtual-reality-vs-augmented-reality-comparative-analysis [1 May 2018].

Rowett, P. (2017). 'How to optimise your Google Maps listing in Google My Business'. Retrieved from https://tourismeschool.com/how-to-optimise-google-maps-listing-google-my-business/ [17 May 2018].

Ryan, D. (2014). *Understanding digital marketing: Marketing strategies for engaging the digital generation.* London, UK: Kogan Page Limited.

Schoenbachler, D., Gordon, G., Foley, D., & Spellman, L. (1997). Understanding consumer database marketing. *Journal of Consumer Marketing, 14*(1), 5–19.

SiteMinder. (2016). Nine interesting things we learned about TripAdvisor's new method for ranking hotels. Retrieved from https://bit.ly/2ISX0nJ [14 May 2018].

Smith, K. (2019). 48 Fascinating and Incredible YouTube statistics. Retrieved from Smith, A. & Anderson, M. 2018. Social media use in 2018. Pew Research Center. Retrieved from https://www.brandwatch.com/blog/youtube-stats/ [10 June 2019]

Statista.com (2018). Number of monthly active Twitter users worldwide from 1st quarter 2010 to 2nd quarter 2018 (in millions). https://www.statista.com/statistics/282087/number-of-monthly-active-twitter-users/. 14 June 2018.

Stokes, R. (2018). *eMarketing: The essential guide to online marketing* (6th ed.). Cape Town, South Africa: Quirk eMarketing.

Strauss, J., El-Ansary, A., & Frost, R. (2008). *E-marketing* (5th ed.). Upper Saddle River, NJ: Pearson.

Strauss, J., El-Ansary, A., & Frost, R. (2013). *E-marketing* (7th ed.). Upper Saddle River, NJ: Pearson.

Strauss, J., & Frost, R. (2013). *E-marketing* (7th ed.). Upper Saddle River, NJ: Pearson.

Tourism Tattler. (2019). Why content marketing will remain king in 2020. Retrieved from https://www.tourismtattler.com/articles/marketing/content-marketing-2020/ November. [25 May 2021].

UNWTO. (2008). *Handbook on E-marketing for tourism destinations.* Madrid, Spain: UNWTO.

Van der Ians, R., & van Bruggen, G. (2010). *Viral marketing: What is it and what are the components of viral success?* New York: Routledge.

Web Analytics Association. (2007). Getting started with Google Analytics. Retrieved from http://www.webanalyticsassociation.com [24 June 2018].

White, R. (2017). Six location marketing ideas for tourism businesses and destinations. Retrieved from https://tourismeschool.com/location-marketing-for-tourism/ [15 May 2018].

World Economic Forum. (2016). If social networks were countries, which would they be? Retrieved from https://www.weforum.org/agenda/2016/04/facebook-is-bigger-than-the-worlds-largest-country/. [26 January 2021].

Xu, F., Tian, F., Buhalis, D., Weber, J., & Zhang, H. (2016). Tourists as mobile gamers: Gamification for tourism marketing. *Journal of Travel & Tourism Marketing, 33*(8), 1–19.

Xu, F., Weber, J. & Buhalis, D. (2014). Gamification in tourism. In Z. Xiang & I. Tussyadiah (Eds.), *Information and communication technologies in tourism* (2014). Proceedings of the International Conference, Dublin, Ireland, 21–24 January.

Yang, B., Kim, Y., & Yoo, C. (2013). The integrated mobile advertising model: The effects of technology- and emotion-based evaluations. *Journal of Business Research, 66*(9).

Zaui. (2019). Why you need to leverage TripAdvisor. Retrieved from https://www.zaui.com/why-you-need-to-leverage-tripadvisor/. 14 July 2020.

Further Reading

Chaffey, D., & Ellis-Chadwick, F. (2019). *Digital Marketing* (7th ed.). Harlow, Essex: Pearson (ISBN: 978-1292241579).

Hollensen, S., Kotler, P., & Opresnik, M. O. (2020). *Social media marketing: A practitioner guide* (2nd ed.). London, UK: Prentice Hall.

Stokes, R. (2018). *eMarketing: The essential guide to online marketing* (6th ed.). Cape Town, South Africa: Quirk eMarketing.

Understanding Tourism and Hospitality Marketing Issues

Contents

Quality Service Experiences Through Internal and Relationship Marketing

Contents

Electronic Supplementary Material The online version of this chapter (https://doi.org/10.1007/978-3-030-64111-5_13) contains supplementary material, which is available to authorized users.

Purpose

This chapter will give you the information and skills necessary to understand the role and importance of internal marketing and relationship marketing programmes in tourism and hospitality marketing.

🎓 Learning Goals

After reading this chapter, you should be able to:

- Identify the components of an internal marketing programme
- Understand the link between service quality and customer satisfaction
- Become familiar with the relationship marketing process
- Understand the importance of relationship marketing
- Explore the connection between relationship marketing and service quality
- Explain how technology enhances relationship marketing
- Outline the benefits of quality service delivery
- Identify the various techniques used to measure service quality
- Apply the concepts of internal marketing and relationship marketing to *Hays Travel*.

13

Overview

The chapter begins with a discussion of why internal marketing (marketing that addresses employees inside the organisation) is important. We then discuss the role of internal marketing and the components of the internal marketing programme. We consider each of these components in detail and address strategies for implementing a programme.

The next section discusses relationship marketing. We outline the different levels of relationships and discuss the importance of relationship marketing.

In the third section of the chapter, we focus on service quality delivery, and discuss the link between service quality and customer satisfaction. We also examine various techniques used to measure service

quality, including the SERVQUAL model and the importance–performance analysis (IPA) model.

The chapter's case study examines the customer service policy and internal marketing activities of *Hays Travel*.

■ Introduction

In ▶ Chap. 2, we introduced the services marketing triangle (see page 52) and noted that this marketing activity needs to be carried out in order for a tourism organisation to be successful.

The tourism and hospitality industry is unique in that employees are part of the offering. In an industry where there are extremely high levels of consumer service, an organisation depends heavily on the personnel who interact with consumers. Marketers must therefore have an understanding of all employees and develop a programme that brings out their best level of performance. This can be achieved by getting employees to understand their role in the marketing process.

13.1 Internal Marketing

Internal marketing is a marketing concept aimed at employees (who constitute the internal market within a tourism organisation), whose participation and role are essential to ensure satisfactory levels of quality service and delivery (Williams & Curtis, 2008). If employees are not content, then it is unlikely that consumers will be satisfied. Internal marketing can be described as the strategy of looking at jobs as products and looking at employees as internal customers. Therefore, businesses must shape the "products" to satisfy the needs of "customers" (Ahmed & Rafiq, 2003: 1177).

Internal marketing is concerned not only with treating employees as consumers, but also with developing programmes for enhancing employee satisfaction in much the same way that external marketing aims to meet and satisfy consumers' needs and wants. *Marriott International* uses the mantra "The customer is number 2, our employees are number 1". This company philosophy suggests that employees are brand ambassadors for the hotel group, and that if their employees are happy, so are customers.

Employees deliver the offering to consumers. In doing so, they become part of the product-offering. This is particularly evident in the hospitality sector, where employees carry out most of the marketing activities that take place outside the marketing department. For instance, a restaurant meal includes the food as well as the manner in which it is served. Similarly, hotel staff – from the receptionist to housekeeping staff – all have to perform well and must help to get consumers to return to the hotel.

13.1.1 The Internal Marketing Programme

Marketers must devise an internal marketing programme to ensure that employees are both willing and able to deliver first-rate service. According to Kotler, Bowen, Makens & Baloglu (2017), an internal marketing programme consists of the following components:

- Creating a service-oriented culture
- Developing recruitment and training schemes
- Informing and communicating with employees
- Rewarding and honouring employees who perform well.

These four components of the internal marketing programme are discussed below.

13.1.1.1 Creating a Service-Oriented Culture

The first component of an internal marketing programme is the creation of a service-oriented culture among the workforce. The programme will not work unless the organisation has a culture of focusing on satisfying consumers. All staff must be service-oriented, including staff members who do not have a great deal of consumer contact (such as management). To be service-oriented, employees must have a sense of purpose and motivation in their jobs. They must feel that they are a part of the organisation and feel good about it, just as the organisation wants them to make consumers feel good about buying its offerings.

Understanding the organisation that they are working for and feeling that they have a good dialogue with management is only part of what it takes to make employees service oriented. Remuneration and benefit levels, decent working conditions, and opportunities for job satisfaction also play a big role in having happy, first-rate staff. For example, if a coffee shop offers its staff free meals, but what they really want is better wages, it will not help service delivery.

One of the reasons that internal marketing programmes fail is that tourism and hospitality managers themselves do not recognise the importance of service orientation because they are pressured into reaching sales targets and profits. For example, think of the member of a hotel restaurant's floor staff who is not permitted to spend time chatting to guests or tourists, or the hotel receptionist answering the telephone who continually has to place guests on hold because the reception desk is understaffed. These scenarios are all too familiar in the international travel and tourism industry.

A service-oriented culture within an organisation is achieved through a commitment from management to time and financial resources so that the other components of the internal marketing programme can be implemented. Managers should spend time talking to consumers and should encourage employees who have consumer contact to do so. In addition, dealing with complaints from both consumers and staff requires dedication from managers (see ► Industry Insight 13.1). Remember, if staff are not content, it is unlikely that consumers will be satisfied.

At large tourism organisations such as *Costa Coffee*, *Avis*, *Nando's*, and *Holiday Inn*, it is not unusual to see managers serving consumers alongside consumer-contact employees (staff working at the frontline, or the "coal face", as it is sometimes called). This creates a good service-oriented atmosphere as well as an opportunity for managers to appreciate consumers and employees. Managers cannot expect employees to be service oriented if they themselves are not. Internal marketing programmes attempt to ensure that employees at all levels of the organisation understand the business in which they work. An internal marketing programme that does not have management support will not succeed.

13.1.1.2 Developing Recruitment and Training Schemes

The second component of the internal marketing programme involves the recruitment and training of employees. The main focus of a tourism organisation wishing to improve its service levels must be to develop a human resources management scheme. Human resources management (HRM)

Industry Insight 13.1 the Falcon Rock Hotel's Service-Oriented Approach

A waiter at The Falcon Rock Hotel in Kerak in Jordan received a complaint from a guest who was served a meat dish after requesting a vegetarian meal. The waiter told his manager about the complaint. The manager apologised to the upset diner, replaced the dish with a vegetarian one and delivered a bottle of champagne to the table. The manager then noted in the lodge's computer records that the guest had experienced a problem. When the woman checked out at reception, she received another apology. After returning home, the guest received a letter of apology stating that the management had made a note of her dietary requirements and that she should rest assured that the next time she returned to *The Falcon Rock Hotel,* the mistake would not be repeated.

However, the waiter would not have informed management about the complaint if

the incident had occurred in a hotel with a traditional organisational structure. Instead, he would have kept quiet and hoped that his manager wouldn't find out about the mistake. In turn, the guest would not have received the extra apology, the champagne, or the letter. The waiter was concerned about the guest and knew that the manager would take action that would allow the lodge to recover from the error. The waiter did not think about pleasing his boss or covering up a mistake. He was working to give the consumer the best possible service.

Source: Based on an interview with Jamila Jaffal, manager and owner, The Falcon Rock Hotel, 2020.

(also called "talent management") refers to the effective management, or training and use of, an organisation's employees. An effective scheme consists of recruiting and training the best people for the organisation.

■ **Staff recruitment**

If an organisation wants to maintain or improve levels of service delivery, the first place to begin is when it recruits new employees. The hospitality sector is notorious for being an industry with a high rate of employee turnover. Organisations that have a high staff turnover find it difficult to have the service-oriented culture that we discussed above. One

of the reasons for high rates of staff turnover is inadequate recruitment (or selection) of staff. The tourism industry is a people industry where there is a lot of interpersonal contact (Grobler, 2007: 206). Therefore, the first rule is to recruit employees who are friendly and polite, and who possess good people skills. It is difficult to train staff to acquire these attributes. They either have them or they do not.

It is better to spend money carefully selecting the right employees than to try to train employees who perform inadequately. For example, *Sun City* resort in South Africa carefully screens its applicants, selects candidates for personal interviews, and puts them through a five- to six-hour selection process (see ► Industry Insight 13.2). The resort then puts successful applicants on trial for a three-month period. This organisation understands the importance of recruiting the right employees.

Industry Insight 13.2 Sun City's Staff Selection Process

The staff selection process at Sun City in the North West province of South Africa can take from one to three days, depending on the position for which applicants are being screened. The basic requirements for entry-level staff include enthusiasm and the ability to read, write, and speak English.

Applicants for gaming jobs at Sun City are placed in a workshop for two to three days and assessed to ensure that they are going to fit in with the Sun City culture. Their basic competency levels as well as their ability to understand what needs to be done and how it must be done are also assessed.

During this period, the applicants are tested and interviewed rigorously. Applicants must be competent in maths and must speak English. Sun City employs more than 4500 staff. Human resources staff at Sun City use a targeted selection procedure whereby all candidates applying for each kind or level of job are asked a standard set of questions.

Applicants applying for management-level posts undergo a two- or three-day selection process. They are given a competency assessment on the first day. Applicants are assessed on their ability to work in a team (they are given tasks to complete in a group situation), their technical ability (they are given a case study with a problematical situation that they must resolve), and their creativity (they have to introduce themselves using only some crayons, scissors, and paper). Finally, they are given a financial problem to work out as a group activity. They are then interviewed over the next few days. At least two Sun City human resources staff are present at each interview.

Source: Based on an interview with Kaita Graca, human resources manager, Sun City.

■ **Training of newly appointed staff**

Training is another vital aspect of preparing new service-oriented employees. Newly appointed staff members need to buy into the vision and the values of the organisation. They should be informed about the organisation for which they are working, including the organisation's mission, vision, history, and offerings. All this information can be included in an orientation programme for new employees, which can last anywhere from one day to a couple of weeks. In this time, new employees are familiarised with their work environment and their roles in the organisation. In the travel and tourism industry, it is common to come across staff who lack basic knowledge about the organisation for which they are working. Hotel staff, for example, should know about the hotel's restaurant menu, what the hotel's website address is, what leisure facilities are available, and even what tourist activities are offered in the area.

Inadequate staff training is particularly apparent when members of staff are filling in for colleagues who perform different roles. For instance, if a member of the waiting staff has to cover for the hotel receptionist, he or she should be informed about front-desk procedures, including how to answer the telephone and respond to enquiries. He or she should also know basic information such as the prices of rooms.

Newly appointed staff should never be thrown in at the deep end, so to speak, or left to learn the job by themselves. Staff should be given several days or weeks of supervised first-hand training. For example, a newly appointed travel agent might shadow another member of staff for a week and waiting staff at a hotel restaurant could sample every item on the menu as part of the orientation pro-gramme.

Another strategy is to ensure that new employees spend time in every department of the organisation. (This practice is also known as "job rotation".) For instance, a newly appointed hotel receptionist might spend one day in the hotel's dining room, another day in the kitchen, the third day in housekeeping, the fourth day in the hotel's sales department, and so on. This practice provides employ-ees with insight into the importance of each department and helps to create team spirit. *The Holiday Inn* is known for its effective staff training programme (see ▶ Industry Insight 13.3).

Industry Insight 13.3 E-training for Holiday Inn Express Staff

Holiday Inn Express uses e-learning program called "Smart Service University" as part of its staff training. The franchise company of 2470 hotels (with about 300,000 employees) is part of the InterContinental Hotels Group (IHG). Holiday Inn Express designed a cur-riculum delivery system to train people 24/7 in delivering the Holiday Inn Express brand experience. The e-training modules offer the benefits of being easy to update and are accessible at all hotels. They are also self-paced and can be used In English or Spanish.

A unique element of the e-training modules is that they are scenario-based, so that learn-ers can go through the same module many times and always learn something new. The modules incorporate 3-D technology and innovative design to create an engaging, impressive learning environment.

Source: Holiday Inn Express Hotels. (2019). About Us. [Online], Available: www. ▶ https://www.ihg.com/content/gb/en/about/brands#scmisc=nav_brands_6c Accessed 15 July 2019.

■ Ongoing staff training

The three cornerstones for preparing service-oriented staff are selection, orientation, and training. After staff members have received an orientation to the organisation, training should not come to an end. Training schemes should be an ongoing part of the internal mar-keting programme. All staff members need to be updated continually on offerings that the organisation has recently introduced (for example, new items on a restaurant menu, a new leisure facility at a hotel, or a new attrac-tion at a theme park). Restaurants should have sampling sessions during which the floor staff sample items on the menu. (This could even take place as part of a shift meal. Staff members will enjoy the experience and get to know the menu.) Hotels should provide tours of the hotel and its facilities for all members of staff so that they know exactly what is available.

From time to time, staff members need to brush up on their service skills. Receptionists should go on training courses, perhaps to improve communication and telephone-answering skills, for example. Floor staff of restaurants should receive training sessions in specialised areas such as wine serv-ing. Senior staff such as managers and super-visors should attend courses to improve their leadership skills, management, and marketing practices, and so on.

Many tourism managers are reluctant to provide training schemes for employees. They believe that training is a waste of time and money since staff turnover is so high. However, tourism marketers who implement the service-oriented policy discussed in the last section understand that training helps to retain staff. In addition, employees who are not adequately trained are not capable of delivering first-rate service. In a restaurant, for example, this might mean that consum-ers are not motivated to leave a tip or gratu-ity. The better the service, the more likely it is that the server will receive a good tip. Not being able to deliver good service means that employees do not receive adequate financial and emotional rewards for their efforts. They become discouraged and leave the organisation. A high staff turnover means that an organisation's employees are not happy. This is a sure sign that the organisation's consumers are also not satisfied.

13.1.1.3 Disseminating Marketing Information to Employees

» *Communicate, communicate, communicate!*

The third component of the internal marketing programme is effective communication with employees. Frontline staff members are often not informed about the organisation's advertising campaigns or new promotions, forthcoming events, and so on. A communication gap between management and frontline staff often exists. Managers and marketers must communicate with employees about promotions. They cannot wait for staff members to hear about promotions through consumers or external advertisements. For example, imagine a situation in which a consumer asks about a special offer that the employee does not know is available. The consumer is forced to wait while the embarrassed employee tries to find out the details of the promotion.

Internal marketing is sometimes called "behind-the-line marketing" since it involves developing promotional activities aimed at employees of the organisation (the internal target market). Employees are, after all, the primary brand ambassadors of any firm, and therefore of its products and services. Talking to staff requires a promotions mix that is specific and as personalised as possible. Examples include handouts, office posters, and personalised mail.

Another way of improving communications with employees is to produce an electronic newsletter. Newsletters can be used to inform employees about new offerings and promotions, forthcoming events (such as fundraising, sports and leisure events, and meetings), the vision of the organisation, and sales figures. Regular internal newsletters keep staff members informed. They also contribute to staff motivation, and improve morale and team spirit.

Group and individual meetings are also crucial for continuous communication between managers and employees. Meetings provide a dialogue (two-way communication) and should be held on a weekly, fortnightly, or monthly basis. Frontline employees may be aware of problems that managers do not encounter. Managers should utilise these meetings to make it easier for employees to serve consumers better. For example, managers should ask staff about new stationery or equipment that might be needed.

13.1.1.4 Rewarding and Honouring Employees

The last component of the internal marketing programme focuses on making employees feel important by honouring staff members who perform well. Managers should talk to employees about their performance in order to ensure that they provide first-rate service. This is known as "feedback". There are two ways of producing feedback: either through consumers or via staff. Consumers may complete consumer comment cards or in-house surveys (see ▶ Chap. 4), or they may communicate with managers or supervisors.

This type of feedback may be positive or negative. For example, a consumer may tell a manager about a member of staff who has performed well or may complain about service levels. In the first instance, managers should inform the employee that he or she has performed well and commend the employee for good work. In the second instance, managers should view consumer complaints as constructive criticism and must seek to rectify the problem.

Staff members can also be a source of feedback concerning levels of service in an organisation. Employees should inform managers about consumers who are satisfied or dissatisfied with the service or the offering. For instance, a consumer might complain to a waiter about a menu item that is too expensive. The waiter should inform the manager on duty so that the complaint can be reviewed.

Employees who perform well should be honoured. The most popular reward system used in the tourism industry bases rewards on achieving sales goals. For example, a restaurant may offer a reward for the waiter who sells the most bottles of a particular wine in one month or a travel agent who sells a certain number of holiday packages in a set time. Organisations are increasingly devising imaginative ways of honouring employees who provide high levels of service. Examples include letting an employee be "CEO of the day" or have "Lunch with the boss", or taking staff members on a "team shopping spree".

TO DO

A tourism/hospitality organisation that has a reputation for below-average service has hired you. Your task is to upgrade the service orientation of staff members significantly. Draw on examples of successful tourism organisations. Use the internal marketing programme outlined in this chapter to help you and add some creative ideas of your own.

13.2 Relationship Marketing

Relationship marketing is one of the oldest approaches to marketing, yet it is one of the least understood approaches (Zineldin & Philipson, 2007). In the last few years, it has become a popular marketing technique as marketers have recognised the importance of focusing on a relationship with consumers in today's competitive tourism business environment. For example, airlines offer frequent-flyer programmes (for example, *Emirates' Skywards*), restaurants have frequent-diner programmes (e.g *Starbucks Rewards*), and hotels provide special benefits to regular guests (for example, *Accor Le Club*).

In relationship marketing, or "customer relationship management" (CRM) as it is sometimes called, the sale is not viewed as the end of the marketing process, but as the beginning of a relationship between the marketer and the consumer. The purpose of relationship marketing is not solely to secure a sale, but to maintain long-term relationships between the organisation, current and potential consumers, employees, business partners, and all other parties associated with the organisation, including marketing intermediaries, principals, and destination market-

ing organisations. The key to implementing a relationship marketing programme is delivering a quality service offering upon which to build and maintain a relationship with all consumers.

13.2.1 What is Relationship Marketing?

Relationship marketing is about attracting and retaining customers, and enhancing their satisfaction (Berry, 1983). It is based on the premise that getting new consumers is much more expensive than keeping existing consumers. Today's marketers are discovering that relationship marketing is vital to success in the highly competitive tourism industry. Relationship marketing is another marketing term that may be defined in several ways depending on the marketer using it. In tourism marketing, one of the most effective ways of defining any concept is in the context of how an organisation's consumers perceive that concept. Therefore, relationship marketing could be described as the way in which an organisation:

- Identifies the consumer
- Gets to know the consumer
- Keeps in touch with the consumer
- Tries to satisfy the needs and wants of the consumer
- Ensures that the organisation keeps all promises made to the consumer.

In essence, relationship marketing is about treating different consumers differently.

Relationship marketing is not a new concept. Rather, it is a refocusing of traditional marketing with a greater emphasis on the creation of customer value (Payne, Christopher, Clark & Peck, 1999: vii). However, there are certain marketing activities that do not constitute relationship marketing. Sending out unsolicited e-mails or making unwanted telephone calls, for example, cannot be classified as relationship marketing strategies as they are not long-term oriented and are merely direct marketing or personal selling activities that are sales oriented (see ▶ Chap. 11 as well as ▶ Chap. 12).

13.2.2 Importance of Relationship Marketing

Relationship marketing is crucial to a tourism organisation because acquiring new consumers is much more expensive than keeping existing consumers. The four main reasons for this are explored below.

13.2.2.1 Revenue from Repeat Business

Marketers only have to estimate the total value of orders or bookings that a single consumer may place in his or her lifetime with an organisation to realise the importance of maintaining a good relationship with each and every consumer (Chang, Yen, Ku, & Young, 2002). Over a long period of time, a tourism business may generate large amounts of money from a regular customer. Thus, for example, a restaurant that loses a regular consumer can lose thousands of rands. The same applies to hotels and travel agencies. In addition, when an organisation loses a consumer, it also loses the potential revenue from WoM recommendations to new consumers that might otherwise have been made by that consumer.

13.2.2.2 The Costs of Acquiring New Consumers

An organisation that has a good relationship with its consumers and retains them needs to spend less on marketing activities to create new consumers. Repeat business and turning prospective consumers into advocates of the organisation are the long-term aims of relationship marketing. Since it costs between four and five times as much to attract consumers as it does to keep them, relationship marketing makes economic sense (Ozgener & Iraz, 2006).

13.2.2.3 Increase in Employee Satisfaction

The third benefit derived from relationship marketing is that employees, who are central to building and maintaining a relationship with regular consumers, are also more satisfied. This reduces the costs of hiring and

training for management, and results in an increase in levels of service. As with internal marketing, satisfied employees mean a lower staff turnover, which means satisfied consumers.

13.2.2.4 Regular Consumers Spend More Money than Non-regular Consumers

The old adage that 80% of revenue is derived from 20% of an organisation's consumers applies to one of the benefits of relationship marketing. Research has shown that regular consumers spend more money than non-regular consumers.

13.2.3 The Principles of Relationship Marketing

The principles of relationship marketing include the following:
- Identifying consumer markets
- Devising a relationship marketing planning strategy
- Focusing on quality
- Maintaining consumer retention and loyalty
- Using relationship marketing strategies.

These principles are outlined below.

13.2.3.1 Identifying Consumer Markets

The first principle of relationship marketing involves identifying the organisation's various markets (see ◙ Fig. 13.1). The concept of relationship marketing is not only concerned with consumers, but with all of the people who help the organisation serve its consumers, from employees to marketing intermediaries. The aim of relationship marketing, therefore, is to build and maintain relationships with all of a tourism organisation's internal and external markets. Organisations should focus on their relationships with consumers (internally and externally) as well as their relationships with other elements within the tourism industry and in society, all of which can impact on the

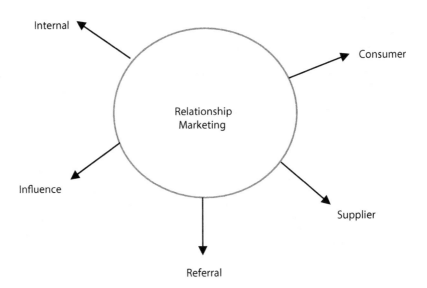

Fig. 13.1   Various consumer markets. (Source: Author's creation)

organisation's long-term success (Woodruffe, 1995: 95).

■ **Relationships with consumers**

Consumers are the most crucial market that organisations need to retain. After a sale has been achieved, contact with consumers should be kept up since it is cheaper to retain consumers than to attract new ones. Customer relationship marketing enables organisations to recognise repeat consumers and address them individually by name.

A marketer may not, however, want a relationship with every consumer. Occasionally, there are so-called "bad" consumers. The relationship marketer must select the best consumers – the ones worth cultivating – and attempt to satisfy their needs more effectively than competitors.

■ **Supplier markets**

Suppliers are organisations that interact directly with a tourism organisation. Suppliers co-operate in an organisation's business activity and it is important to build relationships with them. Organisations that develop good relationships with their suppliers gain a competitive advantage through benefits such as improved service. Tour operators such as *TUI Group*, for example, must have positive relationships with their suppliers (for example,

airlines and hotels) and with their distributors (travel agencies), as they are all dependent on the same consumer markets.

■ **Referral markets**

Referrals are intermediaries who influence an organisation's performance. These referrals will not send consumers to an organisation with a bad reputation, so this market can be especially detrimental since WoM and eWoM recommendations (also known as "referral marketing") strongly influence consumer buying behaviour. Referrals may come from friends or family, satisfied consumers, or marketing intermediaries such as sales representatives, concierges, and travel agents. For instance, a city hotel concierge receives commission and other incentives for sending guests to restaurants, visitor attractions, theatres, and theme parks, and on tours. Most tourism and hospitality organisations find that many of their consumers come to them directly as a result of recommendations. Travel review websites and social media platforms such as *TripAdvisor*, Facebook, ▶ Lonelyplanet. com, and Google Reviews provide reviews and are used by travellers during pre-travel, travel, and post-travel. Increasing numbers of consumers seek recommendations from virtual communities, and deviate from their original plans based on information on digital and social media (Pike, 2018: 161). Customer reviews have a significant influence over consumer spending. Three-quarters of consumers read the reviews posted about products and services (Thornhill, 2019). For hotel reviews, for example, consumers tend to focus on the hotel room space and cleanliness, guest service delivery, and hotel food.

Marketers therefore need to attempt to measure the value of customer referrals. This involves analysing a customer's previous purchasing patterns and referrals, and projecting forward. In this way, the company can begin to understand that customer's referral value. This relatively new approach requires gathering data on how new customers chose the service to make a connection between existing customers and new customers. It also requires that marketers distinguish between cases of referral in which the customer would have joined without the referral and cases in which the customer would not have joined without the referral. For example, a new customer who had a long-standing plan to spend a holiday at a game lodge in Botswana would not be as valuable a referral as the undecided family swayed from a beach holiday in Thailand to the wildlife Big Five experience. A research study carried out in the financial services sector in the United States found a gap between customers who were most loyal (with high

customer lifetime values) and customers who were the strongest advocates (with high customer referral values) (Petersen, Kumar & Leone, 2007: 140). The results suggest that the best referrers may have low purchasing values and vice versa. To account for both the purchasing and referring dimensions, the researchers clustered their sample of customers into segments, separating customer lifetime value and customer referral value. Petersen et al. (2007) devised a matrix of four quadrants (see ◱ Fig. 13.2) based on the two dimensions.

1. Champions are customers who have high lifetime value and high referral value.
2. Affluents are customers with high lifetime value, but low referral value.
3. Advocates are customers with high referral value, but low lifetime value.
4. Misers are the customers who add the least value on both dimensions.

Analysing existing customers' lifetime and referral values thus helps marketers target consumers.

■ **Internal markets**
Another task for the marketer is to build and maintain a relationship with the organisation's internal or employee markets. As we saw in the first section of this chapter, satisfying the

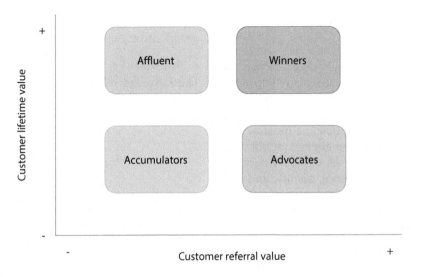

◱ **Fig. 13.2** Customer referral value matrix. (Source: Adapted from Petersen et al. (2007))

workforce is paramount to the success of an organisation. The tourism industry is a people industry in which service quality depends a great deal on the people who are delivering the offerings. Building long-term relationships with employees is as important as building long-term relationships with consumers.

■ Influence markets

Influence markets are those individuals, institutions, and organisations that have the ability to influence (positively or negatively) the macroenvironment in which the tourism and hospitality organisation operates. It is important that the organisation have a good relationship with the sources of influence that are relevant to its markets. For instance, a destination marketer should maintain a good relationship with the press and the media.

13.2.3.2 Devising a Relationship Marketing Planning Strategy

Relationship marketing strategies are similar to regular marketing strategies except that they focus more on relationship building throughout the formulation of strategic plans. These plans still begin with a mission statement, an analysis of the firm's strengths, weaknesses, opportunities, and threats (SWOT), market segmentation research, and strategy formulation. They also still include the seven Ps.

■ Mission statement

A tourism organisation that is committed to a relationship marketing programme devises a mission statement that focuses on treating individual consumers as people, rather than as statistics. A well-devised mission statement provides employees with a shared sense of purpose and direction for achieving people-oriented goals. Goals that the mission statement should mention might include consumer and employee loyalty as well as striving for service delivery excellence, quality, and value for all.

■ SWOT analysis

A SWOT analysis is the next step of the relationship marketing strategy. The four consumer markets form part of this analysis. The strengths and weaknesses of these markets are highlighted so that the relationship marketer can decide with which consumer markets to create and manage a relationship.

The external marketing environment should also be analysed to identify opportunities and threats. In particular, the marketer should consider developing a relationship with certain competitors, focusing on co-operation in order to develop markets.

■ Market segmentation

The next stage in the relationship marketing planning strategy is market segmentation. The identified consumer markets should be divided into groups so that the tourism marketer can tailor a relationship to suit their needs, behaviours, and perceptions. For instance, internal markets (employees) of a hotel might be divided into frontline and behind-the-scenes staff. These groups should then be listed in order of their relative importance. Some of the groups may not need to be targeted via traditional marketing activities, but may be approached through informal communication to build and maintain a relationship.

■ Strategy formulation

After the marketer has defined the mission statement and conducted a SWOT analysis, the next step is to set objectives. The relationship marketer then needs to select the strategic options that will achieve the organisation's goals (see the Ansoff matrix or Porter's generic strategies in ▶ Chap. 5).

■ The seven Ps

The next step of the relationship marketing planning process is to tailor the tourism marketing mix (the seven Ps) to each of the identified markets. Some of the components have more significance to particular markets than others. For example, the product offering will be most significant to the consumer market, while the promotional mix will be used to target each market segment.

Relationship marketing can also be used to differentiate a tourism offering. A tourism business that has a successful relationship marketing programme through interpersonal relationships with its consumers will be able to publicise that it has achieved this.

13.2.3.3 Focusing on Quality

Another principle of relationship marketing is that the organisation focuses on the role of quality management. Relationships with consumer markets cannot be sustained if there are problems with the quality of the product-offering. The quality of the offering must live up to the claims made by marketers.

Tourism and hospitality businesses can apply management techniques such as benchmarking to measure and improve service quality. In order for an organisation to evaluate service quality, it is important for that organisation to establish its performance relative to that of its competitors (Payne, 1993: 223). Benchmarking enables tourism organisations to find out how well they are doing compared with competitors. However, benchmarking does not have to be confined to competitors. It can extend to other organisations or strategic business units within a group. Marriott *International*, for example, distributes the results from its in-house surveys among the hotel group as a way of benchmarking its service quality.

13.2.3.4 Maintaining Customer Retention and Loyalty

Many tourism and hospitality businesses have placed too much emphasis on gaining new consumers and too little emphasis on retaining existing consumers. This is evident in the try-us-or-you'll-miss-out type of marketing activities conducted by some tourism organisations (Payne, 1993: 229). Retaining loyal, repeat consumers is especially difficult in the tourism industry because it is easy for consumers to switch between airlines, travel agencies, hotels, and other offerings. According to Tearfund (2002: 2), fostering loyalty is especially difficult within a tourism context. It has been shown that loyalty towards tour operators is exceptionally low. Loyal consumers who repurchase tourism offerings are extremely valuable. Research suggests that there is a high correlation between consumer retention and organisation profitability (Payne, 1993: 230). Loyalty programmes

offering economic incentives can have a positive effect on customer satisfaction, customer retention, and market share (Verhoef, 2003).

Trauer and Ryan's (2005: 481) intimacy theory postulates that tourists are more likely to return to a destination where they have formed meaningful relationships and had meaningful experiences, making them loyal customers.

13.2.3.5 Using Relationship Marketing Strategies

The key to a successful relationship marketing strategy is to make consumers feel special and to make them feel that the organisation has chosen to provide them with attention. This consumerisation or individualisation can be achieved through increased consumer contact, providing consumer incentives, communicating with consumers, providing special extras, and developing pricing strategies.

Industry Insight 13.4 Hyatt gives away miles

In 2012, members of Hyatt's Gold Passport loyalty programme were offered the chance to win 365 nights at its hotels around the world along with a million free air miles. A further 30,000 Hyatt customers were eligible to win one free night each. The hotel group also launched a survey among members of its loyalty programme, who, in order to enter the competition, had to write a 250-word essay on how they would spend "365 free nights at Hyatt to create an unforgettable experience".

Source: Hyatt. (2014). Hyatt Gold Passport. Retrieved from ► www.hyatt.com/hyatt/about/our-company/hyatt-gold-passport.jsp [15 April 2014].

■ **Developing pricing strategies**
Repeat consumers should be offered special prices or discounts. For example, the National Arts Festival loyalty club, Artbucks, offers regular festival goers several benefits (see ► Industry Insight 13.5).

Industry Insight 13.5 The National Arts Festival's Artbucks Loyalty Club

Artbucks is a loyalty club for regular visitors to the annual National Arts Festival (NAF). Members receive the following benefits:
- Earn 10% credit spent on Festival tickets
- Preferential booking
- 'Sneek peeks' of up-and-coming shows
- Regular newsletters.

When Artbucks members have accumulated currency they can use it to purchase tickets at the following year's Festival, or donate it to the Festival's development projects: Arts Encounter, ArtReach, and the Remix Lab. The Arts Encounter project distributes Festival tickets to community groups who would otherwise be unable to attend; ArtReach takes Festival performances to prisons, clinics, hospitals, orphanages and care homes; and the Remix Lab offers a two-week experience to community-based theatre groups during the Festival, giving workshops, masterclasses, and hands-on experience to participants.

Source: ▶ https://www.nationalartsfestival. co.za 2018. Artbucks. Retrieved from ▶ https:// www.nationalartsfestival.co.za/artbucks/   [15 September 2018].

■ **Loyalty awards programmes**

The aim of loyalty rewards programmes (sometimes referred to as relationship marketing programmes) is to build long-term, mutually beneficial relationships between an organisation and its regular customers (Pike, 2018: 194). There are many examples of travel and tourism businesses that have used relationship marketing programmes to develop consumer loyalty. Car rental companies, hotels, and other tourism-related businesses offer frequent-user programmes, thus encouraging a feeling of membership and an opportunity to build loyalty (see ▶ Industry Insight 13.6).

Industry Insight 13.6 Avis Preferred® Loyalty programme

The Avis Preferred® Loyalty card programme is a free loyalty club scheme that entitles its members to a number of benefits and privileges, including fast-track service at counter, pre-prepared rental paperwork, cars parked in convenient locations, exclusive Avis Preferred® telephone and e-mail contacts, and free upgrades and free rentals. The scheme offers three levels of membership:
1. Avis Preferred member (requires signing-up)
2. Avis Preferred Plus (hire 5+ vehicles and spend €1000); and
3. Avis President's Club tiers (hire 10+ vehicles and spend €2000) – with each tier rise valid for one year. A little bonus to get you started (helping you reach Avis Preferred Plus status even faster): the 'loyalty value' of your rental

Source: Avis. (2020). Avis Preferred® Loyalty. Retrieved from ▶ https://www. avis.co.uk/your-avis/avis-loyalty? kpid=site-google_camp-1372086895_ adgroup-56255490153_target-kwd-306293993971_creative-300406911978_ device-c_feed-&gclid=Cj0KCQjwu6fz-BRC6ARIsAJUwa2RSX3Wy-iqe5NoyaWDoMA6ewEmZnD9hyd-sxp5nIr8Z7GDol1nz6uTaAaAqI-yEALw_wcB [12 March 2020].

Loyalty schemes have become increasingly important in recent years, with advances in information and communications technology as well as the widespread use of database marketing techniques. As tourism marketers adopt the principles of relationship marketing, loyalty schemes are becoming more popular in the retail industry. The development of swipe cards and smart cards has allowed stores to monitor what individual consumers are buying.

South African National Parks (SANParks) operates a loyalty programme called the "Wild Card" that gives discounts, special offers, and rewards to all members over a twelve-month period and access to over 80 National Parks, Reserves and Resorts around Southern Africa (▶ SANParks.org).

13.2.4 Relationship Marketing and Technology

The internet is an ideal tourism marketer's tool for building customer relationships. In particular, e-mail marketing has emerged as a key tool in developing relationships. Many organisations send their customers regular personalised and customised e-mail messages (see ▶ Chap. 12).

The internet and various digital technologies (for example, social media, cookies, and website logs) help organisations collect information about consumer behaviour and characteristics. Some companies have dedicated customer service accounts on Twitter (for example, @easyjetcare). Databases and data warehouses store and distribute this data from online and offline points, enabling tourism marketers to develop better strategies through which to meet the needs and wants of their customers.

Electronic customer relationship management (e-CRM) refers to the efficient handling of all customer relations by web-based methods integrated into an organisation's back-office system.

We will now look at three customer relationship marketing techniques that are technology based: affiliate marketing, permission marketing, and social media.

13.2.4.1 Affiliate Marketing

Affiliate marketing is the online version of rewarding referrers for business or leads generated as a result of their efforts. Revenue is generated by promoting and linking one site to another site. With one click, the consumer is directed to the associate's site. Income is usually calculated on the basis of sales or leads generated in one month.

13.2.4.2 Permission Marketing

Permission marketing is about building an ongoing relationship of increasing depth with customers. According to Seth Godin, who coined and popularised the term, permission marketing is "turning strangers into friends, and friends into customers" (1999: 43).

13.2.4.3 Social Media

One of the best tools for building customer relationships is social media. In many ways, social media epitomises what the internet is about: collaborating and sharing content, ideas, and information. *TripAdvisor* is one of the most popular social media networks for travellers to share reviews and experiences of tourism businesses (see ▶ Industry Insight 13.7).

Industry Insight 13.7 TripAdvisor: The world's Most Popular Travel Website

▶ TripAdvisor.com is a travel website that compiles millions of holidaymakers' star ratings. The world's most popular travel website helps customers gather travel information, post reviews and opinions of travel-related content, and engage in interactive travel forums. TripAdvisor was an early adopter of ▶ user-generated content. Research carried out in 2016 shows that 85% of leisure travellers find user reviews important when determining which hotel to stay at during their trip and nearly half will not book a hotel or accommodation provider if it doesn't have reviews on sites such as TripAdvisor. Online customer reviews provide an excellent source of customer feedback for tourism companies.

Source: Schaalk, D. (2018). ComScore study claims TripAdvisor is top-visited site before booking. Skift. For more information, see ▶ https://skift.com/2018/04/12/comscore-study-claims-tripadvisor-is-top-visited-travel-site-before-booking/ Retrieved from https:// [5 May 2019].

Did you know?

» Increasingly, companies are now rating customers as good or bad. Restaurants, for instance, blacklist customers if they do not show up.

These three e-CRM marketing tools are discussed in more detail in ▶ Chap. 12.

13.3 Delivering Service Quality/a Quality Experience

» *A guest never forgets the host who had treated him kindly.*

  HOMER, THE ODYSSEY, 9TH CENTURY B.C.

Tourism and hospitality firms that implement internal marketing and relationship marketing programmes are more likely to deliver a quality customer experience. Research indicates that the perceived quality of an organisation's offerings is the most important factor for success. Firms that are perceived as being quality experience/service providers are likely to show improved results in terms of profitability and market share. Quality is therefore one of the keys to success. It has become a tool that can be used by tourism and hospitality organisations to gain a competitive advantage in the marketplace.

13.3.1 What is Quality?

Quality is believed to be instrumental in achieving customer satisfaction. Quality can be viewed in two ways:

1. *Technical* quality refers to what the consumer is left with after the employee interactions have been completed. For example, technical quality relates to the room in a hotel, the meal at a restaurant, and the car from a car rental agency.
2. *Functional* quality refers to the process of delivering the product or service (Palmer, 2011: 280). This includes all the interactions that occur between consumers and employees. We will examine functional quality in greater detail in the last section of this chapter.

Customers perceive services in terms of the quality of service provided and the satisfaction level attained. These two concepts, service quality and customer satisfaction, should be the focus of attention of tourism organisations so that they can differentiate themselves by means of providing better quality service and overall customer satisfaction. The relationship between service quality and customer satisfaction is illustrated in ▣ Fig. 13.3.

Service quality is defined as customers' perceptions of the service component of an offering (Parasuraman, Zeithaml & Berry, 1985). Service quality in tourism is far more complex than in the manufacturing industry, where products can be standardised. In tourism, customers want tailor-made experiences to match their needs and desires. Quality is not always guaranteed, as all customers are different. Quality is a perception in the minds of customers. Indeed, quality is very much in the eye of the beholder. It is often assumed that quality means charging a premium price for an offering. This is

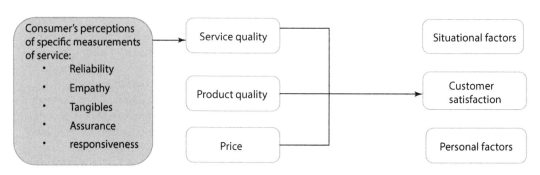

▣ **Fig. 13.3** The relationship between service quality and customer satisfaction. (Source: Adapted from Zeithaml and Bitner (2003))

certainly not true in the tourism industry, where a backpacker hostel could be a quality product for a young backpacker on a budget holiday. Whether or not tourists perceive an offering to be a quality offering depends on a number of factors:

- Their individual attitudes, expectations, and previous experience
- The benefits that they are seeking from the particular holiday.

13.3.2 Benefits of Quality Customer Service

Satisfying tourists and providing QCS is important for the reasons discussed below.

13.3.2.1 Retaining Consumers

A quality product and service create loyal consumers and increase WoM and eWoM advertising. Remember that it costs five times more to create a new consumer than it does to keep a consumer.

13.3.2.2 Retaining Good Employees

Staff are more content working for a tourism organisation that provides high-quality service.

13.3.2.3 Avoidance of Price Competition

A tourism organisation that provides a quality offering does not need to use price discounting and special offers to attract consumers, as it relies on repeat visitors and WoM advertising.

13.3.2.4 Reducing Complaints

Dealing with complaints is expensive, time consuming, and harmful to the organisation's reputation. Restaurant managers, for instance, no longer have to give away free items to compensate for poor service if they provide QCS. Similarly, hotels, airlines, and visitor attractions can reduce the number of freebies that they give away to make up for consumer complaints about inadequate service if they improve their service (▢ Image 13.1).

13.3.3 The Gaps Model of Service Quality

The gaps model of service quality is a tool that can be used to identify areas for service quality improvement within tourism organisations. The gaps model, which was devised by Parasuraman, Zeithaml and Berry (1985), provides a method of illustrating consumer needs and expectations diagrammatically. The conceptual model helps marketers identify the gaps between the service quality that consumers think they receive and what they expect. It enables a structured thought process for evaluating customer satisfaction. The five gaps postulated in the model are explained below.

13.3.3.1 Gap 1: Consumer Expectations–Management Perception

The first gap is the difference between consumer expectations and management's perception of consumer expectations. This gap may be the result of a lack of understanding of what consumers expect from a service. What consumers consider to be important might not be the same things that management considers to be important. For instance, guests at a hotel may value a newspaper being delivered to the room, but management might decide that this is not necessary.

13.3.3.2 Gap 2: Management Perceptions–Service Quality Specifications

The second gap occurs where managers are unaware of both consumer expectations and service quality standards. Managers tend to set standards for service quality based on what they believe consumers require. These standards may not be very clear, they may be unrealistic, or they may simply not be enforced.

13.3.3.3 Gap 3: Service Quality Specifications–Service Delivery

The third gap results where guidelines exist for performing a quality service, yet the staff involved deliver the service inadequately. This

13

◻ **Image 13.1**   Quality customer service delivery gives tourism and hospitality businesses many competitive advantages

is especially important in the tourism industry, where the service delivery system relies heavily on people. The difficulty for the tourism marketer is to ensure that quality specifications are met when a service relies on the performance of employees interacting with consumers.

13.3.3.4   Gap 4: Service Delivery–External Communications

A gap exists when there is a difference between intended service delivery and what is promised about the service to consumers. Promises may establish expectations for consumers, which may not be met. For example, a hotel that mentions in its brochures that it offers silver restaurant service must keep its promise with properly trained employees to deliver that service.

13.3.3.5   Gap 5: Perceived Service–Delivered Service

The fifth gap represents the difference between actual performance and consumers' perceptions of the service. This is also known as the "service gap". It results when one or more of the preceding gaps occurs. It provides a clear indication of the level of service quality in a tourism organisation.

The tourism and hospitality marketer's aim is to try to close the first four gaps of the model and keep them closed. The gaps model provides the marketer with a framework for developing a better understanding of service quality problems within an organisation. Ultimately, it serves as a model to help the marketer improve service quality. The conceptual model assumes that consumer expectations of a service are influenced by four factors:

- WoM communication
- The personal needs of consumers
- Consumers' previous experience
- External communication (in other words, information provided and promised by the organisation).

In general, service expectations are formed at the beginning of the service encounter, whereas service perceptions are formed during and after exposure to the service.

The various techniques for measuring service quality that we have examined need to be adapted to the firm's business environment. The marketer needs to recognise that the service culture in Indua is different from the service culture in the United States, which is the service culture on which these models are based.

The five gaps can potentially cause dissatisfaction with a holiday, as indicated in ▢ Fig. 13.4. Gap 1 relates to a mismatch between managers' perceptions of what customers want and what consumers actually want from their holiday. Gap 2 is the result of problems in the technical specifications for a holiday (for example, the tour operator may schedule a departure at 6 a.m., which could inconvenience the consumer). Gap 3 can arise from circumstances such as departure delays

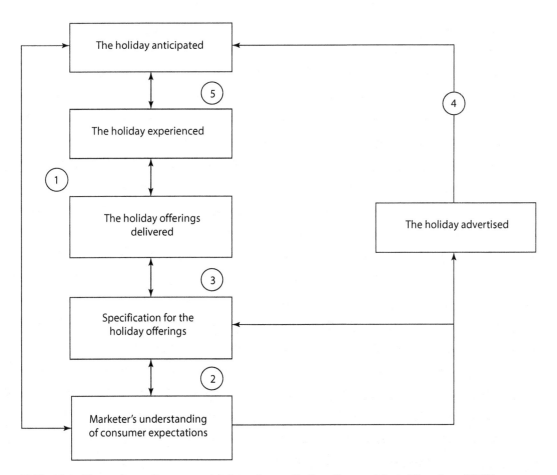

▢ **Fig. 13.4** The service quality gaps model: A tourism application. (Source: Adapted from Laws (2011))

that sometimes occur. Gap 4 may be a result of exaggerated advertising promises. Any or all of these four gaps contribute to Gap 5.

To do

» Imagine that you are the manager of a visitor attraction. You decide to apply the gaps model to improve customer service. Which gap would you start with? Why? Which gaps would you then proceed to close?

13.4 Service Blueprinting

The approach of blueprinting was proposed by Shostack to help marketers design complex processes (1984: 135). Zeithaml et al. (2017: 211) describe a **service blueprint** as "a map that accurately portrays the service system, so that the different people involved in providing it can understand and deal with it objectively." A critical incident point (CIP) is an encounter between consumers and tourism providers. The aim of a service blueprint or flow chart is to make improvements to the service delivery process. Essentially, blueprinting represents diagrammatically how organisations can break the service process down into separate critical incident points and who holds responsibility for each service encounter. The principles of a service blueprint are shown in ◘ Table 13.1. As an example, the model is applied to the purchase of a cup of coffee in a restaurant. The blueprint must consist of all the steps in a service process: that is, all the tasks that are carried out to meet consumers' needs. In this case – the process of the making and the delivery of a cup of coffee – the steps are shown in time-sequential order, from left to right on the diagram. The diagram is also divided into two regions: a region of visibility (processes that are visible to the consumer) and a region of invisibility (processes that are necessary, but are not seen by the consumer).

Consumers of a restaurant are deeply affected by the manner in which staff members serve them and the amount of waiting time involved during the production process. The blueprint ultimately allows the tourism

◘ **Table 13.1**   Example of a consumer service blueprint applied to the purchase of a cup of coffee

Stage in production process	Obtain seat	Take order	Make coffee	Deliver coffee	Pay for order
			(Repeat if coffee is unsatisfactory)		
Target time (minutes)	One	One	Three	One	
Critical time (minutes)	Five	Five	Eight		Three
Is the incident critical?	Yes	Yes	No	Yes	No
Participants	Customer	Customer and waitron	Barperson	Customer and waitron	Customer and cashier
Visible evidence	Furnishings and décor	Staff appearance	Coffee and service delivery		Payment process
Line of visibility					
Invisible processes	Cleaning of restaurant		Preparation of coffee		Accounting

Source: Adapted from Shostack, G.L. (1984). Designing services that deliver. *Harvard Business Review*, 41: April

13

marketer to identify a process problem and possible steps to be taken to resolve it. For example, a blueprint can be used to identify what employees should do in any of the following circumstances:

- A restaurant consumer complains of a badly cooked meal. Who should have the authority to decide whether any compensation (for example, the choice of an alternative meal or a meal voucher) is to be made?
- An airline overbooks its seats. Which alternative airlines should it approach first to try to obtain alternative air travel for its passengers? Should it buy off intended passengers with free travel vouchers for use on future occasions? How will the value of these vouchers be calculated?

It does not matter how a blueprint is expressed (for example, in a diagrammatic form or in words). The important thing is that it should form a shared and agreed basis for action that is focused on meeting consumers' needs effectively and efficiently.

13.4.1 Building a Service Blueprint

This requires teamwork. According to Zeithaml et al. (2017: 245), these are basic steps in building a service blueprint:

- Step 1: Identify the service to be blueprinted.
- Step 2: Identify the consumer or consumer market segment.
- Step 3: Map the process from the consumer's point of view (charting the actions that the customer performs or experiences in the service process).
- Step 4: Draw the lines of interaction and visibility (front- and backstage activities).
- Step 5: Draw the link between consumer and frontline staff activities (the interaction).
- Step 6: Add evidence of service to show each consumer action step (what the customer sees and receives as tangible evidence at each step in the customer experience).

Lovelock and Wirtz (2010) provide examples of strategies used to reduce the negative impacts of queuing, including redesigning the servicescape to accommodate high numbers of customers and to facilitate their movement. Lovelock and Wirtz propose that customers be given accurate forecasts of time to be spent in queues, a way of understanding that progress is being made along the queue, and some form of distraction from the boredom of waiting. This distraction could even present a sales opportunity for the services organisation.

The ten principles of waiting time (Lovelock & Wirtz, 2010: 442) are listed below.

1. Unoccupied time feels longer than occupied time.
2. Pre- and post-service process waits feel longer than in-process waits.
3. Anxiety makes waits seem longer.
4. Uncertain waits seem longer than finite waits.
5. Unexplained waits seem longer than explained waits.
6. Unfair waits seem longer than equitable waits.
7. The more valuable the service, the longer people are prepared to wait.
8. Lone waits feel longer than group waits.
9. Physically uncomfortable waits feel longer than comfortable waits.
10. Unfamiliar waits seem longer than familiar ones.

13.4.2 Consumers' Journey Map

A consumer journey map is a useful mapping tool that helps a hospitality and tourism business to visualise the different steps of the consumer experience; it represents all the interactions (or "touch points") that consumers have with a business. These interactions include the indirect contacts that took place before the actual experience (both physically and online) and post-experience (such as after-sales service, online review ratings, etc.). A consumer journey map looks at the frequency of the touch points and provides marketers with a powerful tool indicating areas for managing them and improving the consumer experience.

13.5 Measuring and Controlling Service Quality in Tourism

It is important that the quality of product and service delivery be measured and controlled. This can be achieved in a number of ways using a number of quantitative and qualitative research techniques, including customer surveys, comment cards, employee surveys, focus group interviews, mystery shopping, and observation (see ► Chap. 4). The two research tools that are used to evaluate quality and consumer satisfaction in the services industry (including the tourism and hospitality sectors) are **SERVQUAL** and the importance–performance analysis model.

13.5.1 SERVQUAL

The SERVQUAL model has dominated the process of measuring service quality in services and tourism marketing for several decades. SERVQUAL, which was developed by Parasuraman, Zeithaml and Berry (1988: 12–40), is an instrument measuring the difference between consumers' expectations and perceptions of service quality. The model has been widely used to measure service quality across a range of services organisations, including diverse organisations such as banks, call centres, television repair companies, airlines, and hotels. The SERVQUAL scale involves a survey containing 22 service attributes, grouped into five service quality dimensions: reliability, assurance, tangibles, empathy, and responsiveness (also known by the acronym "RATER"). These dimensions, which provide the basic skeleton underlying service quality, are described below.

13.5.1.1 Reliability

This involves the consistency and dependability of the service. It means that the organisation's employees should perform the desired service correctly the first time. It also means

that the organisation honours its promises, such as accuracy in charging, performing the service at designated times, and so on.

13.5.1.2 Assurance

This refers to employees' knowledge and courtesy. It refers to the assurance that employees have the ability to convey trustworthiness and evoke a feeling of confidence in consumers. For example, hotel staff dealing with a guest's financial and personal security must be trusted by that guest.

13.5.1.3 Tangibles

This refers to the physical aspects of the service, for example, hotel bedrooms and facilities, the presentation of staff uniforms, and the physical representation of the organisation in items such as brochures and frequent-guest cards.

13.5.1.4 Empathy

This relates to consumers being given caring, individual attention. Employees need to treat consumers as individuals. They can do this by addressing consumers by their names, knowing their preferences and interests, and so on.

13.5.1.5 Responsiveness

This means that the service is delivered promptly, and that the staff are willing and ready to serve and help consumers. Examples include responding to a consumer request promptly, and dealing with consumer problems and queries rapidly.

The SERVQUAL survey asks customers to provide two different ratings on each dimension: one reflecting the level of service they would expect from excellent companies in a sector and the other reflecting their perception of the service delivered by a specific company within that sector. The results from the two sections are then compared to arrive at gap scores for each of the five service quality dimensions listed above. Service quality is determined as the difference between customers' expectations and their perceptions.

Data gathered through a SERVQUAL survey can be used for a variety of purposes:

- To determine the average gap score (between customers' perceptions and expectations) for each service quality attribute
- To assess a company's service quality along each of the five SERVQUAL dimensions
- To track customers' expectations and perceptions (on individual service attributes and/or on the SERVQUAL dimensions) over time
- To compare a company's SERVQUAL scores against those of competitors (benchmarking)
- To identify and examine customer segments that differ significantly in their assessments of a company's service performance.

Research into the importance of the five dimensions found that reliability was regarded as the most important aspect of service quality. This dimension is thus very important in services. It largely concerns the service outcome: that is, whether the promised service is delivered.

Criticisms of SERVQUAL include the length of the questionnaire: there are 44 questions (two sections of 22 items each) in all. Another major criticism of the model pertains to the validity of the five service quality dimensions. It is argued that the dimensions are interrelated and that the importance assigned to each dimension depends on the extent of intangibility of the service offered.

The SERVQUAL instrument is, however, a valuable diagnostic tool for measuring customer service. It can be used to reveal an organisation's strengths and weaknesses in the area of service quality, but it requires modification to suit the specific service environment of the organisation, for example, an airline, restaurant, or hotel. Knutson, Stevens, Wullaert, Patton and Yokoyama (1990), for instance, devised LODSERV, which measures the five dimensions of service quality prescribed in the SERVQUAL model, but is based on 26 lodging-specific items. Similarly, Stevens, Knutson and Patton (1995) created the DINESERV instrument, made up of 29 items based on the five dimensions of service quality, specifically for the restaurant industry.

13.5.2 Importance–Performance Analysis

An importance–performance analysis (IPA) is a simple approach that compares the performance of elements of a service with the importance of each of these elements to the consumer. Martilla and James (1977) originally applied the IPA framework to develop organisations' management strategies. It has been widely used in tourism for several years and has grown in popularity among researchers in service quality. In essence, the IPA model helps managers identify areas in which service quality delivery could be improved. The IPA model generates four different suggestions based on importance–performance measures. The results are plotted on a two-dimensional grid (see ◘ Fig. 13.5).

The first quadrant, "Concentrate here", includes attributes that are perceived to be important to consumers' purchase decisions, but on which the company does not perform well. The company needs to focus on improving its performance on these attributes. The second quadrant, "Keep up the good work", concerns attributes that are perceived to be extremely important to customers and their purchase decisions. The company seems to have high levels of performance in these activities. Some attributes may fall in the third quadrant, "Low priority", as both the importance and the performance ratings of these attributes are lower than average. (These items are thus likely to receive a low priority in resource allocation decisions.) The fourth quadrant, "Possible overkill", contains attributes that are of relatively low importance, but where the company performs well. It is not necessary for the company to focus on improving its performance in these attributes.

Through simple analysis of the matrix, tourism managers can make decisions about where future resources need to be allocated. The instrument provides a snapshot of how well a tourism company is meeting customers' important concerns on selected attributes.

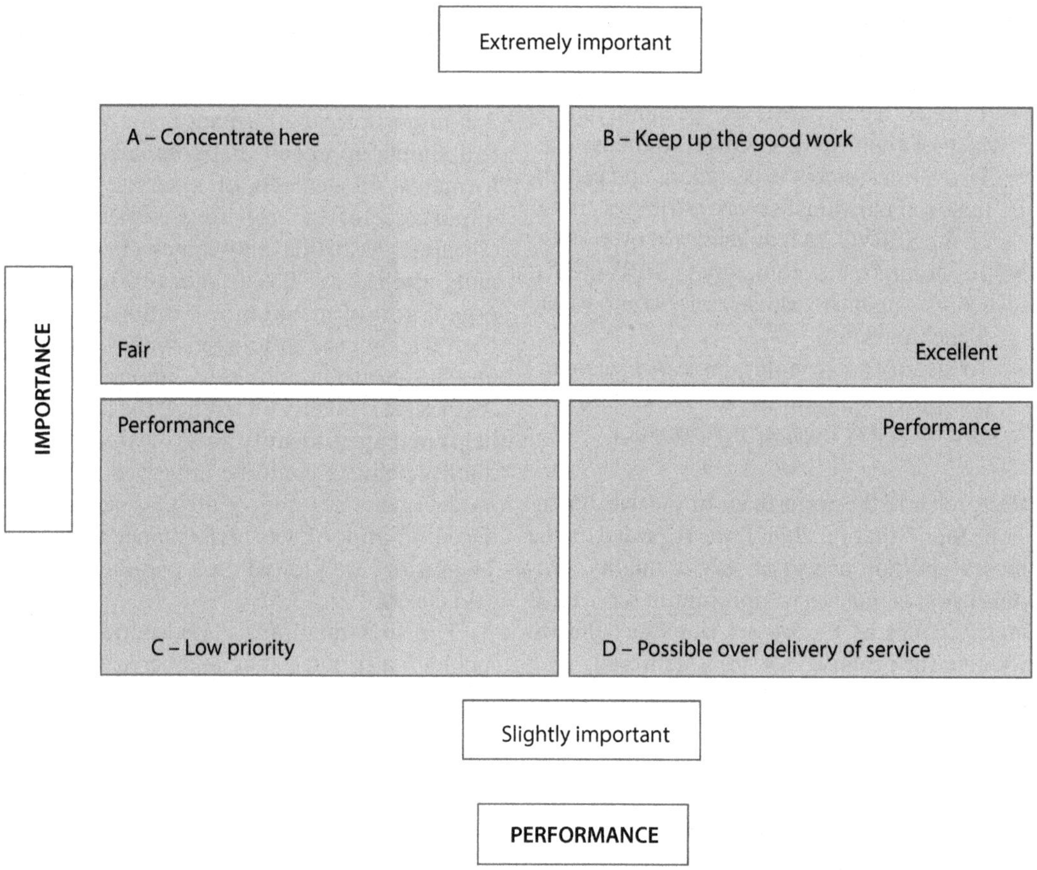

Extremely important

A – Concentrate here	B – Keep up the good work
Fair	Excellent
Performance	Performance
C – Low priority	D – Possible over delivery of service

IMPORTANCE

Slightly important

PERFORMANCE

■ **Fig. 13.5** IPA model. (Source: Adapted from Martilla and James (1977), p. 78)

13

13.5.3 Online Customer Satisfaction Research

Another method of conducting research into customer satisfaction is to use electronic surveys that ask consumers questions, and immediately record and tabulate the results. In ▶ Chap. 4, we discussed the role of technology used in research: online surveys and virtual focus groups used to gather consumer insights that help tourism businesses and improve customer service delivery. Analysing a tourism and hospitality business's feedback and product/service ratings on social media sites such as *TripAdvisor* and online postings and blogs is an excellent way of responding to and improving customer service.

■ Summary

Internal marketing is the concept of treating employees like consumers, bringing the marketing concept into the organisation. It is about communicating with internal markets as well as external markets. The importance of internal marketing should not be underestimated. An internal marketing programme consists of a number of components, all of which help contribute towards first-rate consumer service. Traditionally, marketing, and human resources management have been treated as two separate functions. However, the two are closely linked in the tourism industry. Firms with outstanding internal marketing programmes are usually more successful than organisations that do not have them.

Relationship marketing is concerned with building long-term relationships with present consumers rather than with attracting new ones. Tourism and hospitality marketers are finding that employing a relationship marketing strategy is vital to the success of tourism organisations. Relationship marketing is not a set of marketing tools, but a way of doing business and building relationships with consumer markets. It allows marketers to get to know their consumers. Relationship marketing is becoming an increasingly important marketing tool to the tourism marketer.

In the last section of the chapter, we looked at the issue of service quality delivery. We discussed the benefits of quality customer service and analysed two instruments for evaluating consumer satisfaction with quality: SERVQUAL and the importance–performance analysis model. Well-trained and motivated staff are more likely to build relationships with consumers and deliver quality consumer service.

? Discussion Questions

1. Explain why employees are called "internal consumers".
2. Briefly describe what is meant by a service-oriented policy.
3. Identify four components that are essential for an internal marketing programme.
4. Explain why it is important for management to communicate with employees.
5. Compare and contrast relationship marketing with traditional marketing.
6. Critically evaluate the value of frequent-flyer programmes in terms of the following:
   - Tactical marketing
   - Achieving brand loyalty
   - Relationship marketing.
7. Describe how an airline could seek to differentiate its frequent-flyer programme from the programmes offered by its competitors. Use examples from the airline sector.
8. Explain what is meant by a critical incident point (CIP) during the service process? Use an example of a hotel or guesthouse.
9. In what ways could a tourism organisation (for example, an airline, a car rental company, or a hotel) attempt to measure service quality?)
10. Describe some of the limitations of the SERVQUAL model?

Case Study 13 Quality Service Experiences: Hays Travel: Looking after Employees Looking after Customers

Objectives

- To understand the importance of internal marketing and service quality delivery
- To apply the principles of internal marketing to the case study.

In 1980, John Hays opened a small retail shop at the back of his mother's children's clothing store in Durham, North-East of England. Known as Hays Travel, a couple of years later John opened a second shop in Sunderland, where the firm has its headquarters today and where John still works as Managing Director. By 1987, the company expanded to seven shops in the North-East and Hays Travel has since become well established within the UK and has won tourism awards on a global stage.

In October 2019, Hays Travel purchased all stores of Thomas Cook Group in the UK which were all assumed to be closing due to the travel agency entering liquidation during the previous month. The company took over the 550 existing retail locations across the UK, saving more than 2330 jobs and by the end of the year, had hired an extra 1500 staff. The total number of Hays Travel employees totals 5700 people, which makes the company the UK's largest independent travel agent with 675 retail branches and three call centres across the UK, with a turnover of more than £1 billion.

Irene Hays, Chair of the Hays Travel Group reflected on the new position the company finds itself in. "Thomas Cook was a much-loved brand and a pillar of the UK and the global travel industry. We will build on the good things Thomas Cook had – not least its people – and that will put us in even better stead for the future. We all share a passion for the travel industry and we want to continue to build the company's reputation for first class service and being a great place to work and develop a career."

Hays Travel has garnered a burgeoning reputation for being an excellent employer, by embedding a culture of recognising and valuing employees and offering development and progression through training and coaching. The firm also aims to maximise job satisfaction by ensuring staff feel engaged and motivated in a friendly and supportive environment.

The effort Hays Travel has put in to ensure a flourishing employee experience was recognised in 2006, when it was first included in the prestigious Sunday Times 100 best Companies to work for and was included again in 2016. Further recognition came in 2018, when the company was awarded the Investors in People Apprentice Employer of the Year title.

The company has a flourishing apprenticeship scheme, which recruits new apprentice travel consultants in its branches all around the UK as well as for other roles at its head office in Sunderland. Since 2015, over 860 apprentices have been taken on in shop and head office roles. The apprenticeships offer the opportunity to earn a salary, gain valuable on-the-job experience and achieve a nationally recognised certificate.

With regard to the apprenticeships, Victoria Hill, Hays Travel's Head of Recruitment, says, "We are looking for individuals who have passion, drive, and enthusiasm. We aim to develop our apprentices to their full potential, both during the apprenticeship and afterwards." Apprentices benefit from experienced learning and development coaches who offer expert advice, one-to-one support and award-winning

training. It appears that Hays Travel is an excellent company for career progression as over 150 current managers started their career as apprentices and then graduated from an expert management development scheme.

Hays Travel has a culture of training which is life-long and not solely centred around the apprenticeship programme. All staff are given the opportunity to attend a variety of training courses throughout their careers. They also get the chance to travel the world on educational trips. The company has an in-house training team who provide a wide range of opportunities such as expert management development training through its Rising Stars programme, to specific skills training for individuals in head office departments. A well-trained and rewarded staff group translates into Hays Travel employees providing excellent customer service. "The most distinctive signature of Hays Travel is its people. We require staff that reflect our brand," says Victoria.

Investors in People further recognised Hays Travel by awarding them Gold status in response to staff getting involved in local community partnership projects on a regular basis. The company are investing £360,000 (U$450,000/€400,000) to kick start fundraising in local communities all over the UK and extending its Community Partnership scheme, which provides every branch manager with £500 (U$624/€555) cash, to its newly expanded portfolio of 745 shops. The managers and their teams can use the money to raise further funds for good causes of their choice in their local area. The innovative scheme has been running since the opening of the first Hays Travel store in Seaham, nearly 40 years ago. By integrating employees into community projects, it would appear that Hays Travel is aiming to convince staff of the company's vision and worth.

As an independent company, Hays have access to a wide choice of tour operators and airlines. As well as finding people their ideal holiday, Hays can arrange all the extras like car hire, transfers, and insurance. A further additional service offered by the company is a foreign exchange bureau in the branches across the North East of the UK, where customers can pick up commission free currency.

Employees are taught to do everything they can never to lose a customer. "We never say no, but always find a way to help. We never skimp and share everything we have," says Victoria. "Employees learn that anyone who receives a guest complaint owns that complaint until it has been resolved. They are trained to drop whatever they're doing to help a guest, no matter what department they belong to. Hays Travel employees are empowered to handle problems on the spot without consulting higher-up staff" added Victoria.

The business's motto states, "Our purpose is to deliver world-class products and services to the activity-based tourism and leisure markets. To achieve financial objectives that ensure long-term benefit to our guests, customers, shareholders, and employees. To ensure the fair treatment and ongoing personal development of all our employees. To ensure the ongoing preservation of our natural heritage and wildlife. To support the efforts of our neighbours within local communities to enhance their quality of life." Hays Travel tries to apply this motto to every aspect of the organisation. Staff are trained to never lose sight of their core purpose: to make every guest's stay as enjoyable and trouble free as possible, and to address and put right any problems guests might encounter during their visit.

Under its "employee of the month" program, outstanding performers are nominated by peers and managers on an annual basis, and

winners receive a fully paid trip for two to an exclusive hotel in Cape Town. Hays Travel further motivates its employees with five-, ten- and fifteen-year service awards in which a celebration is held, service certificates and badges are handed out, and a gift is presented. As a result, Hays Travel employees appear to be just as satisfied as its guests.

Hays Travel's success is based on a simple philosophy: to take care of guests, you must first take care of the people who take care of guests. Satisfied employees deliver high service value, which then creates satisfied guests. Satisfied guests, in turn, create sales and profits for the firm.

Source: Based on information found on the website of Hays Travel (haystravel.co.uk) and an interview with Victoria Hill, Hays Travel's Head of Recruitment, Hays Travel, 2020.

Case Study Questions and Activities

1. Explain why it is important for a tourism organisation such as Hays Travel to have well-trained staff.
2. Hays Travel has a comprehensive recruitment policy. With reference to this chapter, explain the advantages of such a policy.
3. What can other tourism and hospitality organisations learn from Hays Travel internal marketing program?
4. Go online and find Hays Travel's website (haystravel.co.uk). What accolades has Hays Travel received? What do these accolades say about Hays Travel employees and service delivery?

References

Ahmed, P. K., & Rafiq, M. (2003). Internal marketing issues and challenges. *European Journal of Marketing, 37*(9), 1177–1186.

Berry, L. (1983). Relationship marketing. In L. Berry, G. Shostack, & G. Upah (Eds.), *Emerging perspectives on services marketing* (pp. 25–28). Chicago, IL: American Marketing Association (AMA).

Chang, J., Yen, D., Ku, C.-Y., & Young, D. (2002). Critical issues in CRM adoption and implementation. *International Journal of Services and Technology Management, 3*(3), 311–324.

Godin, S. (1999). *Permission marketing: Turning strangers into friends and friends into customers.* New York, NY: Simon & Schuster Ltd..

Grobler, P. (2007). Managing human resources in tourism. In R. George (Ed.), *Managing tourism in South Africa.* Cape Town: Oxford University Press.

Knutson, B., Stevens, P., Wullaert, C., Patton, M., & Yokoyama, F. (1990). LODSERV: A service quality index for the lodging industry. *Hospitality Research Journal, 14*(2), 277–284.

Kotler, P., Bowen, J., Makens, J., & Baloglu, S. (2017). *Marketing for Hospitality and Tourism* (7th ed.). Upper Saddle River, New Jersey: Prentice Hall.

Laws, E. (2011). *Tourism marketing: Quality and service management perspectives* (p. 33). London: Continuum International Publishing.

Lovelock, C., & Wirtz, J. (2010). Services marketing: People, technology. In *Strategy* (7th ed.). Upper Saddle River, New Jersey: Prentice-Hall.

Martilla, J., & James, J. (1977). Importance–performance analysis. *Journal of Marketing, 41*(1), 13–17.

Ozgener, S., & Iraz, R. (2006). Customer relationship management in small-medium enterprises: The case of Turkish tourism industry. *Tourism Management, 27*(6), 1356–1363.

Palmer, A. (2011). *Principles of services marketing* (6th ed.). Maidenhead, Berkshire: McGraw-Hill.

Parasuraman, A., Zeithaml, V. A., & Berry, L. L. (1985). A conceptual model of service quality and its implications for future research. *Journal of Marketing, 49*(4), 41–50.

Parasuraman, A., Zeithaml, V.A. & Berry, L.L. (1988, Spring). SERVQUAL: Multiple item scale for measuring consumer perceptions of service quality. *Journal of Retailing, 64*(1).

Payne, A. (1993). *The essence of services marketing.* New York, NY: Prentice Hall.

Payne, A., Christopher, M., Clark, M., & Peck, H. (1999). *Relationship marketing for competitive advantage.* Oxford: Butterworth-Heinemann.

Petersen, A., Kumar, V. & Leone, R.P. (2007). How valuable is the word of mouth? *Harvard Business Review*, October.

Pike, S. (2018). *Tourism Marketing for Small Businesses.* Oxford: Goodfellow Publishers.

Shostack, G.L. (1984, April). Designing services that deliver. *Harvard Business Review, 41*

Stevens, P., Knutson, B., & Patton, M. (1995). DINSERV: A tool for measuring service quality in restaurants. *Cornell Hotel and Restaurant Administration Quarterly, 12*(2), 25–37.

Tearfund. (2002). *Worlds apart: A call to responsible global tourism.* London: Tearfund.

Thornhill, J. (2019, July 14). Five stars or fake? How to avoid the threat of fraudulent online reviews. *The Observer.* p. 58.

Trauer, B., & Ryan, C. (2005). Destination image, romance and place experience: An application of intimacy theory in tourism. *Tourism Management, 26*(4), 481–491.

Verhoef, P. (2003). Understanding the effect of customer relationship management efforts on customer retention and customer share development. *Journal of Marketing, 67*(October), 30–45.

Williams, J., & Curtis, T. (2008). *CIM coursebook 08/09 handbook: Marketing management in practice.* Butterworth-Heinemann.

Woodruffe, H. (1995). *Services Marketing.* Cornwall: Pitman.

Zeithaml, V., & Bitner, M. (2003). *Services marketing* (3rd ed.p. 85). New York: McGraw-Hill.

Zeithaml, V., Bitner, M., & Gremler, D. (2017). *Services marketing: Integrating customer focus across the firm* (7th ed.). New York, NY: McGraw-Hill.

Zineldin, M., & Philipson, S. (2007). Kotler and Borden are not dead: Myth of relationship marketing and truth of the 4Ps. *Journal of Consumer Marketing, 24*(4), 229–241.

Further Reading

Chen, L.-F. (2013). A novel framework for customer-driven service strategies: A case study of a restaurant chain. *Tourism Management, 41*(April 2014), 119–128.

Hudson, S., & Hudson, L. (2017). *Customer service for hospitality and tourism* (2nd ed.). Oxford: Goodfellow Publishers Limited.

Kumar, C. (2016). *Relationship management in hospitality and tourism: A professional approach of RM for hospitality and tourism professionals.* Self-published.

Marketing Tourism Destinations

Contents

Electronic Supplementary Material The online version of this chapter (https://doi.
org/10.1007/978-3-030-64111-5_14) contains supplementary material, which is available to
authorized users.

Purpose

This chapter will give you the skills necessary to understand some of the key issues in the marketing of tourism destinations.

🔄 Learning Goals

After reading this chapter, you should be able to:

- Explain why destination marketing is a complex activity
- Understand the role of destination marketing organisations
- Set out the main components and stages of the destination marketing campaign
- Explain the role and importance of destination image and branding
- Become familiar with the tourism area lifecycle model
- Explain various destination promotional activities
- Understand the importance of marketing of events to attract visitors to destinations
- Apply the concepts of destination marketing and branding to the country Rwanda.

Overview

The concept of destination marketing is an exciting one. In this chapter, we examine the key issues involved in the marketing of tourist destinations, beginning with why this concept is more complicated than the marketing of individual tourism product offerings. We follow with a definition of a destination. We then describe the role of destination marketing organisations (DMOs) and discuss the challenges they face. We then briefly look at the various stages of the destination marketing campaign and the components of a destination marketing plan. Next, we discuss the concept of destination image, one of the crucial factors that prospective visitors take into account when choosing a holiday. Then we consider the concept destination branding. We discuss the tourism area lifecycle model as well as the various promotional techniques used by DMOs such as social media and other digital marketing tools.

Finally, we look at the role of events to attract visitors to destinations.

The chapter's in-depth case study applies the concept of destination branding to the central African country Rwanda.

14.1 Introduction

» The destination is not really the point. The true desire is to get away, to go. Anywhere! Anywhere! So long as it is out of this world. Charles Baudelaire

The marketing of destinations brings together all aspects of tourism: marketing, transport, attractions, accommodation, and hospitality services as well as the host community. The destination is, after all, where the most significant elements of tourism.

occur and where the inbound tourism industry is located. Quite simply, it is the place where the attractions and all of the other amenities required by visitors are found (Pike, 2020). Notwithstanding, the marketing of destinations is perhaps the most complicated marketing activity in the business of tourism.

14.2 The Concept of Destination Marketing

Destination marketing is not a new activity. Destinations began to engage in adopting the principles of marketing in the 1970s when the advent of mass international tourism enhanced competition between destinations (Cooper & Hall, 2019: 261). The concept has continued to evolve, and destination marketing has emerged as a central element of tourism research (Fyall, Garrod & Wang, 2012; Wang & Pizam 2011). Destination marketing is thus associated with the operational activities undertaken in the highly competitive business of attracting visitors to places. Destination marketing is both a process (dealing with stakeholders) and an outcome (formulating a brand) (Pike, 2020). A good destination marketer, thus, will focus on two key operations: first, managing the destinations' many stakeholders and networks; and second, devising and managing the destination brand (Copper & Hall, 2019: 261). Destination marketing operates at a variety of scales ranging from countries and states or provinces to cities, rural villages, and purpose-built resort areas. Increasingly the term 'destination branding' and 'destination marketing' are used interchangeably.

The principles of marketing destinations are not too different from the principles of marketing tourism offerings (Morgan & Pritchard, 2004). Indeed, many references have been made throughout this book to destinations as offerings. However, destinations are far more complex than fast moving consumer goods (FMCGs) and other types of services in that they are multi-faceted (Pike, 2005). In other words, a destination is made-up of countless private, public-sector, and voluntary tourism organisations including visitor attractions and amenities (such as hotels and restaurants), as well as the local residents, and the tourists themselves. Therefore, the principles of tourism marketing need to be adapted for destination marketing activity.

In the next section we define what is meant by a destination.

14.2.1 What is a Destination?

Destinations are physical spaces where tourists and suppliers interact, and where communities live and work (Cooper & Hall, 2019: 262). According to Bierman a destination is a place, including a physical or perceived location, consisting of primary and secondary attractions, and supporting amenities that entice people to visit. It is where products designed to meet tourists' needs are located (Beirman, 2003: 2). What is important to note in Beirman's (2003) definition is that a destination is often a perceived location. This refers to the image (a mental map or picture) that the prospective visitor has of the destination. The prospective visitor might have a mental picture of a physical boundary of the destination (such as an island), political boundaries, or even market-created boundaries (such as the

boundary provided by an online travel agent who might define a southern African tour solely as Zimbabwe or Victoria Falls). A tourism destination may mean different things to different people. To some people, India may be about culture and historical and religious sites or a cross-country trip on train; to others, it may be about its desert, bustling cities, the highest mountain range in the world, while to some people, it is a beach-and-sun destination. In all, this makes the marketing of destinations quite different from the marketing of physical goods. Later in this chapter, we discuss the importance of destination image in more detail. Destinations can be local, regional, or even national; we can speak of the Dharavi or Mumbai or Maharashtra, or India as destinations. They rely on tourism as a major tool in the creation of economic development and support for the local population. ▶ Industry Insight 14.1 provides an example of a holiday resort brand (◘ Fig. 14.1).

> *Destination marketing* is "the process of communicating with potential visitors to influence their destination preference, their intention to travel, and ultimately their final destination and product choices" (Pike, 2020: 11).

14.3 The Role of Destination Marketing Organisations

Destination marketing organisations (DMOs) coordinate the efforts of many stakeholders to achieve the destination's vision and goals for tourism (Morrison, 2019: 5). DMOs coordinate planning, developing, and marketing tourism destinations. According to Pike, a DMO is "the entity officially recognised by stakeholders as being responsible for coordinating the tourism marketing communications for a geographic boundary" (2020: 25). This therefore excludes separate government departments that are responsible for planning and policy, for example, a country's Department of Tourism. A DMO represents

Fig. 14.1 Maharashtra Tourism train in the India state of Maharashtra

Table 14.1 Levels of DMOs: England and Brazil

Destination	NTO/DMO	
Country	Visit England	Brazil Tourist Board (Embratu)
Region	West Midlands	South Eastern
County/ state (estados)	Warwickshire	São Paulo State
City	Birmingham	São Paulo
Town	Stratford-Upon-Avon	Parati

Source: Author's creation

a destination and is tasked with increasing its competitiveness, building a brand identity, and devising and implementing a marketing campaign. A DMO is (which used to be called a 'Tourism Board' such as Jamaica Tourist Board or Croatian National Tourist Board) or in some countries and regions referred to as a 'Tourist Office' (e.g. Bahamas Tourist Office), 'Convention and Visitors Bureau (CVB)' (e.g. New York CVB/NYCVB), or a 'Tourism Authority' (e.g. Malta Tourism Authority). pre-fix 'Visit' (e.g. VisitCopenhagen), or simply 'Tourism' e.g. Tourism Australia or 'Romania Tourism '.

The term "destination marketing organisation" is used for an organisation marketing a region whether that be a country, region, city, or town. The terms "national tourism organisation" (NTO) or "national tourism administration/agency" (NTA) are generally used for organisations marketing a country as a whole.

For example, Romania Tourism is Romania's national tourism organisation (NTO). It is considered to be the destination marketing arm of the Romania government. Its main aim is to market the country to international and domestic tourists. State tourism offices (STOs) have the task of marketing and branding their region (for example, Muntenia), province, state, territory, or county (e.g. Ilfov), or city (e.g. Bucharest), or town (for example, Otopeni in the region of Muntenia. Table 14.1 provides examples of various levels of DMOs for England and Brazil.

DMOs at a country level (these are called national tourism organisations/associations) usually have offices in major source markets. These tourism offices (or branch offices) promote the country within the market. They act as shop windows for potential visitors who are able to obtain travel information about the country. Examples of promotional activities carried out by these offices include billboards, road shows, websites, attending travel trade shows, toll-free telephone numbers and e-mail addresses that interested parties can contact for information, and advertisements in consumer travel (such e.g. *National Geographic*) and travel trade magazines. Increasingly, in the last few years largely due to external factors such as the global financial crisis of 2008 and the Coronavirus pandemic in 2020, NTOs have been promoting domestic tourism to encourage citizens to travel within their own country.

DMOs need to understand their role in the consumer journey cycle - from awareness to post-holiday sharing the holiday experience (see consumer decision-making process – ▶ Chap. 3) and how to create interest to convince consumers to visit a destination. However, a DMO's role is not only about the consumer journey, but it is also about cooperation and collaboration with different role-players such as partners (e.g. travel influencers and investors), the local community as well as creating and publishing content across different promotional channels and storytelling about the destination at each stage of the consumer journey cycle.

Industry Insight 14.1

COVID-19 DMOs Asking Tourists to Stay Away!

In May 2020, some DMOs actually took measures to ask tourists to stay away and not visit as opposed to encouraging people to visit. This reversal in fortune strategy was taken in light of the outbreak of the Coronavirus (COVID-19) to protect tourists and local communities. Facebook page with the heading "Wish you weren't here" (UK seaside resorts traditionally use the "Wish you were here" caption printed on holiday postcards). Weston Super-Mare in Somerset Council.

DMOs and NTOs are public sector (government-funded) organisations; they are not private operators or providers. Their role is to market and sell places to tourism intermediaries (the travel trade) and individual travellers (consumers). They have the task of selling the unique selling propositions or points of a place in a way that appeals to visitors. Quite simply, destinations need tourists so that their commercial providers (such as attractions and accommodation establishments) are financially viable, thereby delivering the employment and income impacts promised by governments. Generally, these organisations do not sell products directly to visitors or the travel trade and they are not solely responsible for the quality of products and services delivered. The term 'regional tourism organisation' (RTO) tends to be used to represent a concentrated area such as a coastal resort area, island, or rural area (Fyall et al., 2019: 396). ▶ Industry Insight 14.2 explains the role of the DMO 'Tourism & Events Queensland.'

Industry Insight 14.2

Tourism & Events Queensland

The DMO for the state of Queensland in Australia is Tourism and Events Queensland (TEQ) aims are as follows:

- Marketing Queensland as a world-class destination
- Building unique and appealing tourism experiences
- Identifying, attracting, developing, and marketing major events for the state
- Researching and analysing tourism in Queensland
- *Source:* TEQ, 2020

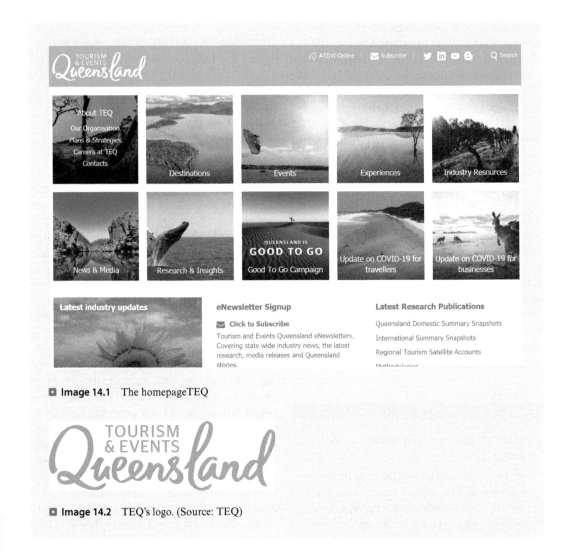

■ **Image 14.1**   The homepageTEQ

■ **Image 14.2**   TEQ's logo. (Source: TEQ)

14

❓ Do you think Bhutan, which is considered the happiest country in the world, should push 'happiness' as a unique selling point when marketing the country?

14.3.1 Challenges Facing DMOs

Destination marketing is unique and thus present DMOs face a number of challenges, including:

14.3.1.1 Lack of Control Over the Marketing Mix

The destination product comprises a multitude of elements, including accommodation, transport providers, tourist activities, visitor attractions, and the natural environment. Marketers of DMOs have no direct control over the product offerings they represent nor the packaged offerings of intermediaries such as airlines, tour operators, and travel agencies (Pike, 2020: 41). The only aspect of the product 'p' of the marketing mix is branding, referring to the branding of the destination in its entirety; no control of the branding of individual businesses). The 'Place' component is irrelevant as DMOs have relatively little, if any, control over access to the destination (this is left to governments, transportation companies, and trade associations such as IATA). Furthermore, DMOs have no control over the prices that individual businesses such as amenities and visitor attractions charge, although they are concerned with the price levels set and the quality of service delivery which affect the image of their destination. The most relevant of the marketing mix model is the 'Promotions' variable. This is where the promotional activities, such as digital marketing, advertising, and PR are carried out (see ▶ Sect. 3.3.2.1).

14.3.1.2 Access to Funding

DMOs have relatively limited budgets with which to promote their destinations. Even the budget of the largest DMO pales in comparison with the budgets of the major corporate brands with which it competes for discretionary consumer spend (Pike, 2005: 265). Funding is a challenge for DMOs and many have to work from lower budgets than they have been accustomed to (because of government budget deficits in recent years) (Morrison, 2019: 667).

14.3.1.3 Politics and Diverse Needs of Stakeholders

DMOs are constrained by political pressures. In particular, the politics of decisions regarding controversial issues (for example, who decides on the brand theme, who is appointed to the tourism board, and how the DMO is held accountable to taxpayers' money) are issues for DMOs.

14.3.1.4 Fragmentation of the Industry

DMOs have many stakeholders or constituencies that they serve and service ranging from small tourism businesses (SMEs - souvenir vendors, tourist guides), MNCs. and government agencies to local community residents. The tourism industry within a destination is fragmented, comprising hundreds, if not thousands, of tourism businesses: providers, support facilities, the travel trade, and visitor attractions. DMOs should be objective and aim to balance the varying needs of these role-players. Branding and marketing a destination is more of a collective activity than is found in the marketing of FMCGs (Cooper & Hall, 2019: 285).

14.3.1.5 Creating Differentiation

DMOs are also faced with the challenge of creating differentiation (Buhalis, 2000). Many destinations have points of parity (PoP), such as beaches, waterfront developments, culture, and heritage, climate, ski resorts, and natural attractions. It is, thus, crucial for DMOs to build brands based on unique aspects of their destinations – points of difference – (PoD) that appeal to consumers. There are four main elements to gaining a unique selling point (USP): authenticity, passionate citizens (locals must live the brand), an emotional pull (visitors must have an emotional connection with the place), and a story (the destination's visitors and locals must have a story to tell about it. - i.e. posting on social media platforms). Travel is social; people share experiences when they travel, for example, by using social media and enabling and encouraging visitors to share content online (such as reviews, stories, tweets, blog posts, comments, videos, and photographs).

14.3.1.6 Applying the Principles of Branding to a Destination

Associating a brand with a destination is difficult (Morgan & Pritchard, 2004: 9). There are several problems with treating destinations as brands:

1. A destination is a multi-dimensional composite featuring several regional levels of brands, for example at country, city, town, resort, and visitor attractions levels. India, for example, has various brands: the Taj Mahal, Mumbai, The Red Fort, Varanasi, Rajasthan, deserts, wildlife, Gandhi, Goa, and The Gateway of India. Similarly, Rajasthan possesses numerous brands: The Golden City (Jaisalmer), The "Pink City" (Jaipur), the "Blue City" (Jodhpur), Jaisalmer Fort, Hawa Mahal (Palace of Winds), and so on.

2. It is difficult to develop a brand personality based on a physical space where there is a diverse community where people live and work.

3. Promoting and branding a destination requires different approaches for the different segments of a heterogeneous market regarding the content of the message and the use of communication channels (Buhalis, 2000). Typically, product or business branding, thus, involves promoting different products to particular market

segments (for example, a city hotel targeting business people), whereas destination marketers must brand destinations to many types of consumers often through a single marketing campaign. Consequently, it is difficult to see how one branded destination might appeal to all consumers.

14.3.1.7 Safety, Security, Public Health Issues

Safety, security, and public health issues have become key challenges facing DMOs in recent years. These macro environmental factors are out of the DMO's control. Negative perceptions of safety and security issues such as crime and political stability negatively affect the image of a destination. Health issues such as food poisoning, sexually transmitted disease, the outbreak of an infectious disease or virus (in 2020 the travel, tourism and hospitality industries were decimated by the impact of COVID-19).

14.3.1.8 Lack of a Database

One of the challenges for DMOs is the difficulty in obtaining customer data from the tourism providers which they have no direct control of. The DMO rarely comes into contact with actual visitors, except through their TICs, how are they to obtain contact details to be able to keep in touch? (Pike, 2020: 67). Thus, the development of a database by DMOs is rare. Even with access to contact details, another challenging question has been how is it possible for the DMO to engage with so many visitors with meaningful messages? Several DMOs have attempted to track and measure repeat visitation with the use of a visitor monitor programme (Pike, 2005).

14.3.2 The Activities of DMOs

The activities of DMOs are often more complicated than those of private sector tourism

Image 14.3 Some tourist destinations (e.g. Istanbul) employ 'tourism police' to help protect tourists from crime. (Source: RG's own)

organisations (businesses) because they are carried out by public sector or public–private partnership (PPP) DMOs. The only way in which genuine sustainable tourism development can be achieved is through a solid partnership between government and the private sector (Neto, 2003). National and regional DMOs predominantly target travel trade/ Intermediaries, consumers, investors, and business travellers. The main activities of DMOs include:

We will now discuss the following destination DMO marketing activities:
- Devising a marketing campaign;
- Building a brand identity;
- Positioning the destination;
- Visitor relationship marketing
- Education, organising workshops, and attending travel trade shows; and
- Conducting destination marketing research.

These activities are discussed in more detail below.

14.3.2.1 Devising a Destination Marketing Campaign

The aim of a destination marketing campaign is to drive business; to get people to visit the destination (Morrison, 2019: 4). This is achieved through marketing planning – the systematic (step-by-step) approach – in developing marketing strategies and marketing plans (see ▶ Sect. 3.3 in this chapter). It is important that marketing strategies/plans are implemented (i.e. to move from planning to implementation); it is no use having an excellent plan that has been drafted for national and local destinations lying idly on a shelf. A typical table of contents for a DMO's marketing plan generally includes the stages of the marketing planning process: analysis, planning, implementation, and monitoring (see ◘ Table 14.2). And this process leads to the development of a marketing plan. One of the tasks of the planning stage is for the DMO to devise a mission statement, ◘ Table 14.3 provides examples of three DMO's missions statements.

Industry Insight 14.3

Dubai Tourism's Vision and Strategic Objectives

Dubai's Tourism Vision for 2020 is a strategic road map with the key objective of attracting 20 million visitors per year by 2020, doubling the number received in 2012. The strategy outlines what needs to be delivered for the city to drive and serve visitor growth effectively, with multiple initiatives covering regulatory policy, infrastructure development, product offering enhancement, and destination marketing investments. The overall aim is to position Dubai as the "first choice" for the international leisure and business traveller.

Tourism is a central pillar of Dubai's economic growth and diversification. The tourism vision for 2020 will further leverage the sector by broadening Dubai's offering across events, attractions, infrastructure, services, and packages. Part of this strategy involves adapting a marketing approach to showcase Dubai to a wider audience and increasing awareness of Dubai as a preferred tourist destination. To accomplish these goals, the Department of Tourism and Commerce Marketing (DTCM) will harness the collective power of key stakeholders, both in the public and private sectors in Dubai and abroad, and will focus on three key objectives:

1. Maintaining market share in existing source markets
2. Increasing market share in markets that it has identified as having high growth potential
3. Increasing the number of repeat visits.

The DTCM's 'Visit Dubai' and '#BeMyGuest' digital marketing campaigns have been very successful across several social media platforms. Its Visit Dubai on Instagram has over 1.5 million followers. In 2018, 15.9 million international tourists visited the UAE city.

Source: Dubai Tourism. (2018). Tourism vision 2020. Retrieved from ▶ http://www.visitdubai.com/en/department-of-tourism/about-dtcm/tourism-vision-202v0 [17 August 2018].

□ Table 14.2   Contents of a DMO marketing plan

I. Analysis

Situation analysis:

Environmental scan	PESTLE analysis	An analysis of the macroenvironmental factors. These are uncontrollable. The Coronavirus (COVID-19) pandemic of 2020 is a prime example of an 'Ecological' factor that impacted upon the global tourism industry as well as other interconnected factors such as global and local economies.
Destination analysis	TALC analysis	Apply the TALC model to assess the stage of evolution of the destination and appropriate marketing and development strategies. See ▶ Sect. 3.4 of this chapter.
	SWOT analysis	Identify and assess the SWOT as they relate to the DMO's marketing goals (strengths such as the brand, weaknesses-such as limited visitor attractions or waterfront hotels).
Competitive analysis	Porter's (1979) 5 Forces model	Competitors by target market (e.g. business market, wedding tourists, sports, family) Research into visitors' destination sets/competitors.
Positioning analysis	Destination image research	Tourists take image into account when choosing a destination All destinations have images, be they positive or negative
Unique selling propositions (USPs)	USPs identification and branding analysis	How is the destination different compared to competitor destinations? Differences = USPs.

II. Planning

Destination vision	A DMO mission statement	The destination vision usually states its desired positioning (e.g. tourism markets such as adventure, cultural, or wildlife tourism) and its priorities (for example, authenticity, responsible tourism). The DMO vision is what the marketing action the organisation intends to achieve. (see □ Table 14.3)
Destination marketing goals	Longer-term (3–5 years) Measurable results that the DMO wants to achieve Target market and time specific.	Usually expressed in numerical terms (#s of visitors, total income or % of GDP). For example, Korea Tourism −230 million domestic tourist trips and 17 million foreign tourists by 2025
Destination marketing objectives	Set as part of an annual marketing plan (sometimes called actions or tactics) Short-term (1–3 years).SMART (criteria for setting objectives) Measurable results that the DMO wants to achieve Based on the marketing goals Target market and time specific	The Ministry of Culture & Tourism, Turkey has set a number of objectives for 2025: Increase the number of international arrivals to Turkey to 70 million Increase revenue to $70 billion Promote niche tourism markets, including gastronomy, faith, medical, thermal, and health tourism Spread tourism across 12 months Increase per capita spending Offer visitors a quality experience (Ministry of Culture & Tourism, 2019).

◘ Table 14.2 (continued)

III. Implementation

Action plan timelines		
Promotions mix selection	Advertising Sales (personal selling) PR and publicity Sales promotion and merchandising Product placement (film-induced tourism) Digital marketing	Promotional mix and destination integrated marketing communications (IMC).
Destination/4As mix	Attractions Amenities Accessibility Ambiance	Theme park, convention centre, shopping mall, culture, and heritage Hotels, resorts, restaurants Airports, railways hub Climate, palm trees.
Marketing budget	Develop a marketing budget	Objective-and-task budgeting method (estimating costs of each activity).

IV. Monitoring

Performance measures/indicators KPIs	Tourist volumes Tourist revenue Profit of each visitor Reduce seasonality Geographical spread	SEO - Click-through rate (CTR), keywords performance, impressions, traffic Social media - CTR, clicks, sign-ups, conversions, reach, impressions, traffic, 'likes', comments, follower growth, App downloads Website - log-file analyser programmes to analyse all the traffic to a DMO's website, views, time spent on each page and the website in general, favourite pages, app downloads, newsletter sign-ups, etc. Facebook Insights - a powerful tool for those wanting to track user interaction on their Facebook Fan Page. Facebook Can be seen by all the administrators of your page and it can help you track the number of active users to better understand page performance. Instagram how many people are commenting on a given post? Twitter Analytics shows you how your audience is responding to your content, what is working, and what is not.

Source: Author's creation

❓ Questions

Romania's USPs are:

— Dracula tourism (Transylvania)
— Mountains (Ratezat)
— Wine regions
— Biggest castle in E. Europe (Corvin Castle)
— The Black Sea

What are the USPs of your country?

14.3.2.2 Building a Brand Identity

In the highly competitive tourism destination marketplace (there are quite literally a million and one destinations around the world), DMOs must build and communicate a unique destination brand identity that embodies the values and uniqueness (the unique selling point or pièce de résistance) of the destination. The right brand identity provides a

◨ Table 14.3 Examples of various DMOs' mission statements

DMO	Vision/missions statement
Kenya Tourism Board	"To inspire the world to visit Kenya through effective marketing of Kenya's tourism products while enriching the lives of Kenyans and visitors alike." Source: ▶ http://ktb.go.ke/about-ktb/vision-mission/
Singapore Tourism Board	"Our vision is to shape a dynamic tourism landscape for Singapore in partnership with industry and community".
Tourism Northern Ireland	"Mission is to build the value of tourism to the local economy. Our Vision is to confidently and passionately champion the development and promotion of the Northern Ireland experience". Source: ▶ https://tourismni.com/

Source: Author's creation

destination with a sustainable point of differentiation from the competition (Pike, 2018: 110). A brand identity is the enduring set of destination attributes and associations that the DMO wants tourists to perceive about a place (Morgan & Pritchard, 2012: 181). We discuss brand identity.
in more detail in ▶ Sect. 3.5 of this chapter.

❓ There is vast potential to reinvent and redefine Africa. Discuss how you would brand Africa. What captures the brand essence of the African continent?

14.3.2.3 Positioning the Destination

Positioning is a form of communication that plays an important role in enhancing the attractiveness of a destination (Pike, 2005: 120). The destination positioning (DP) process is a link between the brand identity crafted by the DMO and the actual image that people have of a destination (Morrison, 2019). The objective of DP is to create a distinctive place in the minds of potential tourists (Pike, 2020: 184). This is achieved by communicating a focused and consistent message, and by promoting benefits associated with the destination that differentiate it from competitors. DP requires that DMOs create a lasting, favourable, and competitive image or perception of the things for which a destination stands in the marketplace. As most tourism destinations are easily substitutable (for example, hundreds of destinations around the world have become indistinguishable because they offer similar products, such as golf courses, convention centres, beaches, and mountains, history, culture), positioning should emphasise destination attributes that are unique, salient, and of importance to the targeted tourists (Pike, 2018: 28). For example, the city of London in the UK markets its USPs which differentiates the destination from competitors, namely, theatres, art galleries, entertainment, events, and museums.

Positioning can therefore be based on physical attributes (for example, the iconic statue of Christ the Redeemer in Rio de Janeiro, Brazil). In addition, subjective positioning can be used on any other part of the brand identity. For example, when using subjective positioning to advertise the destination of Brazil, the destination marketer would emphasise the feelings of awe that tourists can expect to experience when visiting natural attractions such as the beaches of Rio and the Iguazu Falls.

Other positioning approaches may be based on price value (for example, "Malaysia gives more natural value"), positioning by featuring the targeted user (for example, Thailand positions itself as appealing to

☐ **Image 14.4** Uganda and Rwanda promote and position themselves as Gorilla tourism destinations. (Source: Unsplash)

youth travellers, while New York and Singapore appeal to shopping tourists, and Dubrovnik in Croatia is synonymous with cruise tourism). Positioning can also be based on emphasising strengths compared to competing destinations (this is known as "points of difference"). For example, destinations such as Uganda and Rwanda promote Gorilla tourism (see ☐ Image 14.4).

The positioning is then implemented through the consistent use of DP elements. These elements include anything that represents the destination in the target markets, including the place name, its logo, its symbol, its design, and its positioning slogan. Destination positioning elements should appear consistently in television advertising as well as in print and all online media.

14.3.2.4 Visitor Relationship Marketing

Customer relationship marketing (CRM) initiatives are increasingly being adopted by DMOs in the attempt to enhance brand loyalty and stimulate repeat purchases. A study by Murdy and Pike (2012) found that maintaining meaningful dialogue with previous visitors in some markets represents a more efficient use of resources than above the line advertising to attract new visitors. Effective visitor relationship marketing (VRM) strategies include the likes of e-mail and e-newsletters; although developing a database is problematic for DMOs.

14.3.2.5 Education, Organising Workshops, and Attending Travel Trade Shows

DMOs and NTOs participate in major travel trade shows such as the World Travel Market (WTM) in London and the International Travel Exchange (ITB) in Berlin, which are the two largest travel trade shows in the world. These international exhibitions provide exposure to consumers, tour operators, wholesalers, and travel agents who may wish to visit the destination.

DMOs also facilitate the interaction of tourists with members and industry stakeholders, including other DMOs, emerging small businesses, tour operators, transport providers, and so on. Trade shows and road shows provide intimate and interactive direct selling opportunities. Many DMOs now have a greater presence at roadshows where specific markets and interest groups can be targeted. Niche tourism trade shows such as golf tourism, adventure, backpacking, safari, luxury travel, as well as industry education workshops, and trend workshops (virtual and on-site) are important elements of travel trade shows.

14.3.2.6 Conducting Destination Marketing Research

DMOs have the responsibility of coordinating marketing research and gathering market intelligence on the existing and potential markets of their destinations. Marketing research is a traditionally neglected aspect of destination marketing and is increasingly regarded as a fundamental basis for the following purposes (Pike, 2020: 38):

- Success at all levels of destination marketing
- Justifying marketing spend
- Harnessing future partnerships.

Information on international and domestic tourist arrivals should be collected, analysed, presented and then disseminated to members of the DMO as well as to role-players. Market research data (marketing intelligence) is important - in the form of reports - for local businesses to enhance what they are doing and their marketing plans. Mechanisms increasingly utilised by DMOs include collating statistics on visitors (domestic and inbound) involving the following information:

- Volume
- Origin
- Length of stay
- Geographical spread
- Seasonal spread
- Most visited attractions
- Type of accommodation used
- Expenditure on tourism activities
- Perceptions of safety, security, and service levels
- Spending patterns within a destination.

This data is collected through secondary and primary research methods such as interviews and destination exit surveys (see ▶ Chap. 4). The data ('marketing intelligence') is then usually disseminated on the NTO's official website via links (e.g. 'Research') to annual and quarterly research reports and marketing plans and strategies. Research data assists the DMO to evaluate performance against key competitors (known as "destination benchmarking"), assess best practices (for example, branding, advertising, funding, technology, and website), evaluate trends and forecasts in the travel and tourism industry, and develop a comprehensive marketing strategy. Destination benchmarking is a management technique that enables DMOs to compare how well they are performing relative to their main competitors (Kozak & Rimmington, 1995: 185). Identifying the important attributes that visitors perceive in the destination and understanding how tourists select a destination are clearly important, as are the specific aspects

Romania's Ministry of Tourism Marketing Research Activities

Romania's Strategic Research Unit produces a range of research documents, including quarterly reports on international tourist arrivals, monthly tourist statistics, tourism marketing strategies, and annual statistical reports.

The Ministry of Tourism's research activities over the past few years have focused on gaining a broad understanding of its consumer markets. The Ministry of Tourism has identified core markets and pinpointed the needs of each market segment. The research is in line with achieving the objectives of the National Tourism Development Strategy (2021–2026) 5-year strategy. The strategy aims to monitor data on four international and domestic tourism key performance indicators:

- Tourist volumes;
- Tourist spend;
- Seasonality; and
- Geographical spread.

Source: Romania Tourism. (2019). Visit Romania's 5-year NTDS. Retrieved from ▶ https://www.oecd-ilibrary.org/sites/721999bd-en/index.html?itemId=/content/component/721999bd-en [13 September 2019].

explore the Carpathian garden

☐ **Image 14.5** Romania Ministry of Tourism's logo

of destination image and promotion. Research into measuring residents' attitudes and maintaining databases or marketing information systems are also important research activities. Information collected from studying the behaviour of different types of destination visitor (for example, business, leisure, and event tourists) is vital marketing intelligence. Destination marketers need to understand how tourists select the destinations that they visit ("value propositions") so that they can decide which marketing strategies to use to influence consumer behaviour. Website link dedicated to research activities/research SA Touros reports strategies.

14.4 Destination Image

While the importance of a destination's attractions and amenities cannot be underestimated, research has shown that the **image** of a destination is of equal importance (Choy, 1992). Indeed, it has been found that prospective consumers are influenced as much by their perceptions of the particular destination as they are by the destination's potential for performance (Kim, 1998: 341). Tourist destination image (TDI) is defined as the result of a person's beliefs, ideas, feelings, expectations, or impressions about a tourist destination (Sussmann & Űnel, 1999: 223). A destination image is the visual or mental impression that a person has of a place. Mental images of places are often coloured by the works of impressionist artists, as in the case of Gauguin and the Pacific Islands, Van Gogh and the south of France, and Monet and the French village of Giverny. The image of a destination is one of the main factors that prospective visitors take into account when choosing a holiday destination.

Image is often taken for reality in the tourism industry (Avraham & Ketter, 2013). For instance, a tourist might perceive that a destination has the image of being unsafe and a dangerous place to visit. For example, in recent years, the Central American country Mexico's drug-related crime has affected its image. The reality may well be that Mexico is no more dangerous than any other destination. Notwithstanding, the prospective visitor might change his or her plans as a result of these negative perceptions (George, 2003). Place images can be very influential in destination choice decision-making (see ▶ Chap. 3). It is for this reason why analysing, understanding, and measuring the projected Image is a necessary step for every marketer and is crucial for every marketing initiative (Khan, 2013). If a destination is portrayed in a particular way (perhaps through popular culture media such as television programmes or movies), there may be an immediate effect on the destination. For example, small-scale destinations that receive positive media coverage may find themselves besieged by visitors in the peak tourist season (Connell, 2005: 763). Movies and television series, in particular, can influence the image of destinations (this is known as 'film-induced tourism' (see page 85). *Games of Thrones* enticed film tourists to various film locations in Northern Ireland and the HBO/Sky television series *Chernobyl* has inspired an influx of tourists to the site of the former Soviet-era power plant in Ukraine (Addley & Convery, 2019).

All destinations have images. Some of these images are based on the destination's geography, standard of living, people, infrastructure, climate, wildlife, and other natural attractions. Other images are based on the cost, ambience, history, cleanliness, and safety and security of the destination. Images may be good, bad or indifferent. Generally speaking, images can be either descriptive (for example, the perception that Las Vegas is a family-holiday coastal resort) or evaluative (for example, the perception that Las Vegas is tacky, dirty, and unsafe). The PESTLE factors (see ▶ Chap. 6) affect the image of destinations. For example, a destination that has an image of being unsafe (socio-cultural factor) is likely to deter people from travelling to that destination.

> "Perception is reality" is one of the best-known marketing axioms. This is based on Thomas and Thomas's theory (1928) (in Patton, 2002), which suggested that what people believe to be true will be real in its consequences. In essence, whether an individual's perceptions about a destination brand are correct or incorrect, those perceptions will influence his or her purchase decision.

Industry Insight 14.5

Bermuda Tourism Given a Kiss of Life

Bermuda is known for its pink sand beaches, azure seas, history and heritage buildings, snorkelling, sailing, golf courses, and unique authentic experiences (carnivals, local food, and culture). The 1970s and 1980s were the heyday for tourism in the country, but its success made it complacent and it slipped off holidaymakers' radars, earning a reputation as a destination for the "newlywed and nearly dead". The Bermuda Tourism Authority (BTA) has recently started to rebuild the brand, coming up with creative ideas to promote the destination that suit all tastes and ages. With a newly opened spa in a cave, adventure tours that include cliff jumping and jungle treks, and a $100-million (R1.4-billion) renovation of its best-known hotel, Bermuda is regaining lost ground and planning to re-establish itself as a leading tourist destination. The BTA is hoping that the new initiatives will give a substantial boost to a tourism market that has been in decline.

Source: Dawe, T. (2016). Tourism given overdue kiss of life. The Times, Thursday 21 July, p.13.

14.5 The Tourism Area Life Cycle

Destinations, just like tourism offerings, manufactured products, and people, have a lifespan. Butler (1980: 5) applied the traditional product life cycle (PLC) concept (discussed in ► Chap. 8) to destinations and devised the tourism area life cycle (TALC) model. The tourism area life cycle model is a model for understanding how destinations evolve over time and pass through a series of stages (from exploration to involvement to development to consolidation to stagnation to decline or rejuvenation) (Butler, 1980: 2). Destinations go through a similar evolution to that of products, but visitor numbers are substituted for tangible product sales. Butler (1980) classified the stages of tourism destination development as shown in ■ Table 14.4 and ■ Fig. 14.2).

Using the TALC (also known as the "tourism destination life cycle model") provides a framework for understanding how

destinations and their markets evolve. Each stage of the TALC needs its own strategies adopted by the DMO. The model helps to identify where the destination is positioned within the life cycle at a given point in time and what implications this has if measures are not taken. The TALC model also suggests that a destination will appeal to different markets as it matures. In addition, the concept can be applied to the various tourist typologies discussed in ► Chap. 3. The destination life cycle will attract different types of travellers and for different lengths of stay (Plog, 1974). For instance, mature destinations are more likely to attract short-break holiday tourists rather than longer stay tourists (Pike, 2020). Similarly, Plog (2004: 55–59) suggested that adventurous and outgoing tourists (allocentrics) are going to seek unspoilt destinations, while less adventurous tourists (psychocentric) prefer more popular destinations.

◻ Table 14.4 TALC destinations: Characteristics and examples

PLC stage	Characteristics	Examples
Exploration	The number of tourists is very low. Visitation patterns are irregular. There are no tourist facilities This is the stage when a resort or destination is discovered by independent travellers or explorer-type tourists (see ▶ Chap. 3).	The Comoros Islands in the Indian Ocean, Atacama Desert in Chile, Corn Island in Nicaragua, Papua New Guinea, Leiden in the Netherlands, North Korea, areas of Columbia, and northern Mozambique. Some parts of the Canadian Arctic and Latin America (such as the Amazon basin).
Involvement	Locals begin to participate in tourism activities. Regular patterns of visitors start to emerge. Locals begin to participate in tourism activities. The transition from exploration to involvement is triggered by several factors. For example, e entrepreneurial activity (for example, the opening of a guesthouse, restaurant, hiking trail) or a visit by a well-known personality).	Panama, Iran, Columbia, Laos, Ecuador, Bhutan and Myanmar (formerly Burma), Lhasa in Tibet, the Atlantic Ocean island of St Helena, and Calabria along the south coast of Italy. Areas in Mexico, Turkey, India, Philippines, Maldives, and Indonesia.
Development	Increased advertising and promotions. Transformed from relatively unknown, quiet or undiscovered destinations into fully fledged or developed resorts. Visitor attractions are developed. The number of visitors grows exponentially.	Costa Rica, the west coast of Scotland, Cuba, Buenos Aires, Guam, Vietnam, and regions of the North African coast. Areas in Mexico, Turkey, India, Philippines, Maldives, Indonesia, north and west African coasts, and many other places.
Consolidation	The consolidation stage is marked by a drop in the rate of increase in visitor arrivals. The destination has lost its exclusivity and uniqueness and joins the ranks of many other similar destinations. Development is slowing down.	Several Mediterranean and Caribbean resorts. Some areas in Barcelona (Spain), Goa (India), Marina Bay Sands and Resorts World Sentosa (Singapore), St. Kitts and Nevis island (the Caribbean).
Stagnation	Tourist arrivals to the destination reach maximum capacity. The destination may no longer be fashionable. Signs of negative impacts of tourism (such as traffic congestions, increase in crime rate, price increase for locals). It relies heavily on repeat visitors.	Areas of Florida in the USA, Venice, Barcelona, some areas in the Balearic Islands – Majorca, Minorca, and Ibiza. Coastal resorts in Kenya, Machu Picchu in Peru, and some beach destinations In Mexico and Singapore.
Decline	The destination loses visitors to more exciting competition. Repeat visitors are no longer satisfied with the available destination and new competitors emerge. The destination now becomes more reliant on day excursionists and weekend visitors. Many of the existing tourism developments and facilities may be converted into other businesses (for example, retirement homes).	Zimbabwe, Guaíra Falls (Paraguay, Brazil), Sutra Baths (San Francisco), Porcelain Tower of Nanjing (China), Chacaltaya Glacier (Bolivia), and Royal Opera House of Valletta (Malta).
Relaunch or rejuvenation	(i) Product-led rejuvenation: Investment is made in new product offerings, attractions, resorts, and accommodation providers. Efforts are made to reposition and market the destination based on these improvements. (ii) Market-led rejuvenation: introducing the offering to new markets and consumers. This concept involves giving the destination a new image (or rebranding it) in order to attract a new target market.	Santiago (Chile) has experienced a major transformation in the last few years. Dubai (UAE) reinvented itself from a sleepy town in the 1970s to a thriving city and tourist destination. Las Vegas in Nevada in the United States has moved away from a glitzy, gaudy gambling destination to rebranding itself as a family, shopping, golf, and convention destination. Varosha beach resort in Northern Cyprus.

Source: Adapted from Butler (1980)

14

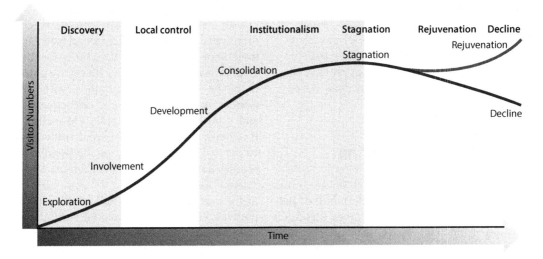

● **Fig. 14.2** Butler's (1980) TALC model. (Source: Adapted from Butler (1980))

Industry Insight 14.6

Italians Tell Tourists to Stay Away'
Most tourist destinations try to attract visitors but officials in Italy's picturesque Cinque Terre want to curb them. The park authority responsible for the pastel-coloured villages, vineyards and coastal trails along the rugged northwest coast says that visitor numbers need to be reduced by a million and it will introduce a quota system this summer. Officials agreed that the move was eccentric but Vittorio Alessandro, president of the national park, said "Arrivals have to be rationalised otherwise the overwhelmed villages will lose their original inhabitants. The Cinque Terre is a string of fishing villages that date back to the medieval period, connected by narrow Cliffside paths. Mr. Alessandro said that the trails risk being swamped by a mass of tourists brought in by train, coach and boat and that their numbers had to be cut from 2. Million a year to 1.5 million. Electronic people counters have been introduced to control the flow.

Source: Willan, Phillip. (2019). The Times. 'Italians tell tourists to stay away'. Thursday 18 February, p. 13.

The model does not work well when applied to large-scale countries, large cities, or even regions such as Eastern Europe because of the tendency of large-scale tourism to concentrate in certain areas of countries. The tourism area life cycle model is best applied to individual resorts or small-scale destinations and areas such as Margate, waterfront developments, *Alton Towers,* Cornwall, and Jersey in the Channel Islands. Caution is still required, however, when marketers apply the TALC model to these destinations, as significant internal variations often occur even at these destinations. (For instance, 'The French Riviera' (or Côte d'Azur) along the Mediterranean coast of south-eastern France includes (beach resort) destinations such as Saint-Tropez and Cannes, as well as the capital of the region Nice and the sovereign state of Monaco; each of these vary in evolution/development.) Similarly, the resort of Malaga, along the Costa del Sol, in the Andalucia area of Spain varies significantly as the west is well-developed with tourist towns Marbella and Torremolinos as well as golf courses and ceramic shops; while the east is quieter, less-developed undiscovered land.

❓ Apply the concept of the TALC model to a destination or large-scale resort (such as Alton Towers in Staffordshire UK, Europa-Park in Germany, or Paris Disneyland in France) in your state/province/county. How would you keep the offering from going into the decline stage?

14.6 Destination Branding

One of the functions of DMOs is to position or brand their destination in the minds of prospective visitors and so differentiate that destination from all others (Pike, 2018: 26). Destination branding (also known as "place marketing") is a process that is similar to destination image management. Ashworth and Voogd (1988: 68) define place marketing as the process of identifying a place as a place product and developing and promoting it to meet the needs of identified users. It requires the development of a destination image that is well positioned in relation to the needs and wants of the target market, the images of competitor destinations, and, of course, the deliverable attributes of the destination (Laws, 2002: 63).

The question of whether or not destinations can be branded has been the subject of much discussion by tourism researchers, who have assumed that the branding concept (see ▶ Chap. 8) is as applicable to destinations as it is to hotels, restaurants, attractions, and airlines. Morgan and Pritchard (2004: 61) noted a general agreement that branding can be applied to destinations, but added that there is "less certainty about how the concept translates into practical marketing activity". Similarly, as Pike notes "There is a dearth of tourism destination branding research in the academic literature with which to guide DMOs" (2005: 258; 2016: 193).

Famous and successful cities are usually associated in people's minds with a single quality, promise, story, or attribute. Milan, for example, has the reputation of being the fashion capital of Europe and Paris has the repu-

tation of being a romantic city. Barcelona is known for its art and culture, Rio de Janeiro for its parties, fun, and beaches, and New York for its shopping, energy, and vibrancy. London is renowned for its museums. Places are potentially the world's biggest brands, with high degrees of conversational and celebrity value, and great emotional pull (Morgan & Pritchard, 2004: 49). Cities are considered to be the new "super brands" of the twenty-first century and are crucial destination marketing "hooks" (to draw visitors) for countries and regions. With more than half of the world's population living in cities and the number expected to reach almost five billion by 2030, the scope for city tourism is growing rapidly (United Nations, 2018).

Branding provides information about a destination that consumers have not visited previously (Keller, 2012). For example, while people may not have travelled on the *Orient Express* or visited the Israeli city of Haifa, they may know a lot about these products and this influences their decision-making. The main advantage of branding is that it creates a favourable position for the destination and allows consumers to distinguish it from competitors according to attributes that are significant to their motivations. As Plog points out, "A strong brand helps establish an identity for an offering to help consumers call to mind its essential qualities and its position in the marketplace ... Without good branding, even the best positioning strategies can fail" (Plog, 2004: 130). The source of this position is known as the "destination's brand identity".

A destination brand identity usually consists of the following components:

- The *brand essence* is the heart and soul of the destination brand. It is the main quality that is inherent to that brand. This is what the destination brand wants to portray as its core. The brand essence is what makes it different from other destination brands. It is the DMO's essential and central promise for the tourism experience. Paris's brand essence is described as follows: "Be refreshed, inspired and revital-

Fig. 14.3 Brand
pyramid. (Source:
Adapted from Morgan
and Pritchard (2004))

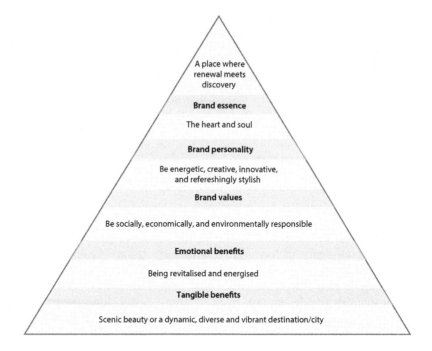

A place where
renewal meets
discovery

Brand essence

The heart and soul

Brand personality

Be energetic, creative, innovative,
and refereshingly stylish

Brand values

Be socially, economically, and environmentally responsible

Emotional benefits

Being revitalised and energised

Tangible benefits

Scenic beauty or a dynamic, diverse and vibrant destination/city

ised, and discover new experiences and opportunities." The city's brand also provides a vision (see ◻ Fig. 14.3).

- The *brand personality* is how a brand looks and acts within the marketplace. It should be built directly from the brand essence. It is made up of the human characteristics that tourists would use to describe a place (for example, Paris could be described as energetic, creative, innovative, and refreshingly stylish). The destination brand personality is about the promise that the DMO makes to visitors.

- Destination *brand values* are the values represented by the brand. For example, a destination could be perceived as being socially, economically, and environmentally responsible.

- The *brand benefits* are what visitors actually take away from their experience. They can be emotional benefits (such as feeling revitalised and energised) as well as tangible benefits (such as scenic beauty or a dynamic and vibrant city).

14.6.1 Brand Elements

Some countries (for example, Israel, Turkey, Spain, Malaysia, Australia, and Ireland) have developed strong national brand images in the marketplace, while Sydney, Dubai, Paris, Belfast, London, and San Francisco have all acquired strong brands as cities. These destinations have used the power of brand elements to gain specific identities. Keller defines **brand elements** as those trademarkable devices that serve to identify and differentiate the brand, of which the main elements are brand names, logos, slogans, symbols, characters, spokespeople, packages, jingles, and signage (2012: 197). These elements function independently and collectively as brand equity creators (or brand builders). Brand elements also involve the use of icons to enhance brand memorability. Building a destination brand identity is a complicated and lengthy process involving many role-players, but it is crucial for the sustained success of any destination marketing campaign.

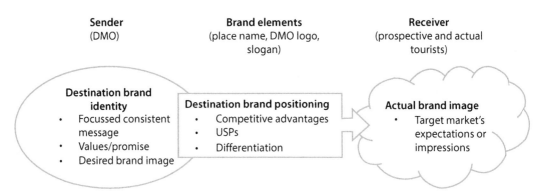

Fig. 14.4   The destination positioning process. (Source: Adapted from Pike (2012))

Brand elements include the destination name, the destination logo, and the destination slogan. These elements, which may help to distinguish the destination from its competitors, are discussed below.

14.6.1.1   Destination Name

The destination's brand name is its core indicator and is a component of its image (Avraham & Ketter, 2016: 55). It evokes certain images in people's minds and so can be expected to contribute to the destination brand (Tasci, 2011). The brand name (or "word mark") captures the theme of the destination (for example, regional names such as the '#Mediterranean Live' (Benidorm, Costa Blanca, and Valencia), the Sapphire Coast, the Golden Mile, the West Coast, and the Wild Coast). In general, most place names are changed very rarely (Araham & Ketter, 2016: 55). Destinations are not like products or organisations, whose names can be changed regularly. However, in recent years, several names of towns and cities have changed to more politically and historically correct names. For example, the Indian city of Bombay was renamed "Mumbai" in 1995. Today, the former Yugoslavia is the six nations of Serbia, Montenegro, Slovenia, Croatia, Macedonia, and Kosovo.

14.6.1.2   Destination Logo

Logos (also called "symbols" or "emblems") are part of a destination sign system. Logos can range from a name to an abstract logo that is unrelated to the destination (such as a swirl, a circle, or an arc). A logo is a visual shorthand that carries a desirable meaning and association for products, services, and organisations (Pimental, 1997). Logos play an important role in destination brand awareness, recognition, and recall (Keller, 2012: 14). They are a key differentiating characteristic of a brand and are effective for tangibilising the abstract nature of the destination offering. In recent years, it has become quite fashionable for DMOs and national tourism organisations to feature their website addresses in their logos. Many destinations, particularly at a national level, have both a corporate logo (representing the DMO) and a destination logo.

Destination logos often include icons representing the city or country. Here are some examples:

- France (flag-coloured woman)
- Greece (spots to represent islands)
- Holland (tulips)
- Incredible!ndia (! for the I)
- Monaco (winding roads)
- Mozambique (shell spiral)
- Panama (butterfly)
- Cape Town (heart). (see ▪ Image 14.7)

14.6.1.3   Destination Slogan

Slogans for destinations should focus on some of the most important associations of the desirable image, and try to increase the strength and distinctiveness (uniqueness) of these core associations (Supphellen &

Inspiring new ways

■ **Image 14.7** South African Tourism's logo. (Source: SA Tourism)

Nygaardsvik, 2002: 387). Destination slogans add more meaning than the meaning that is achieved by the brand name or symbol (Pike, 2004: 8). **Slogans** (sometimes called "mottos", "taglines", "brandlines", or "straplines") and logos are integral elements of a destination branding initiative. Slogans are short phrases that communicate descriptive information about the brand (Keller, 2012: 207). They should tie together the complete value chain of people, resources, wildlife, and even the weather of the destination. They should convey powerful ideas and resonate with consumers. Powerful destination slogans have several benefits (Morgan and Pritchard, 2004: 95):

- Desired association
- Reinforcement of the name or symbol
- Reinforcement of positioning
- Development of an identity.

Many destination slogans attempt to appeal to tourists' emotions rather than providing information. Examples include "Malaysia – Truly Asia", "There's no place in the world like Sydney", "Argentina beats to your rhythm", "Paraguay – You have to feel it!", "100% pure New Zealand", and Croatia "Full of Life" (see ■ Image 14.8). The Department of Tourism, Philippines, says, "It's more fun in the Philippines" and InterContinental Hotels & Resorts asks, "Are you living an InterContinental life?"

Destination marketers should avoid duplicating slogans that are used by other destination marketing organisations. For example, Hong Kong's slogan "Hong Kong, Live it, Love it" is also used by the city of Leeds ("Leeds, Live it, Love it") in the UK.

Developing a successful destination brand is a complex task that requires the input of destination stakeholders as well as support from research (in other words, finding out what the unique selling points of the destination are) and marketing specialists to help determine the destination's attributes. This role is usually undertaken by the national tourism organisation or DMO as an integral part of its marketing strategy.

New Logo for Rajasthan Tourism
Rajasthan Tourism has relaunched themselves with a new look. The land of deserts, camels and colours - Rajasthan - is wooing tourists with a brand new logo and marketing campaign. According to recent media reports, all of this is a part of a new tourism campaign that has been launched by the state government in a bid to double the annual footfall of international tourists from 1.5 million to 3 million by the year 2020. Even though the larger objective is to draw foreign tourists, the Government of

Rajasthan is also aiming to increase domestic visits from 33 million to 50 million tourists on an annual basis. The campaign was designed by Ogilvy and Mather, the same ad agency that devised the 'Hindustan ka Dli Dekho' campaign for Madhya Pradesh tourism. One of the major messages that this campaign is trying to send out to is that the state of Rajasthan is an ideal travel destination for any time of the year. Besides, it is also trying to spread awareness about the lesser-known destinations of the state.

14.7 Destination Promotional Mix

The primary marketing function of a DMO is to increase awareness of attractions and activities at the destination. For example, Abu Dhabi Tourism & Culture Authority (ADTCA) promotes attractions and activities throughout the UAE capital, including its islands, beaches, theme parks, convention centres, culture, and heritage, Emirates Palace, and other human-made attractions.

Many of the tools of the promotional mix that we covered in Part IV can be applied to the marketing of tourist destinations. As a result of budget restraints, DMOs at state/regional/provincial level (sometimes referred to as the 'state tourism office') and at local level generally carry out below-the-line promotional activities aimed at key source markets. Tourism Western Australia is an example of a DMO at this level. Advertising in existing and new markets is extremely expensive. The promotional mix includes integrated marketing communications (IMC), which is defined as "the coordination and integration of all a DMO's external communications and promotions to increase their effectiveness and consistency" (Morrison, 2019: 411).

A DMO should have a coordinated promotional campaign that may include above-the-line activities such as advertising to develop the destination brand. NTOs direct their advertising at key market segments. (For example, Visit Norway targets key markets such as Sweden, Denmark, UK, Germany, and the USA.) Destination advertising tools may use media advertising such as television and cinema, press advertisements, billboards, and digital marketing activities such as internet advertising and social media marketing (YouTube, Facebook site). Undertaking advertising is, however, expensive. It is also difficult to assess its effectiveness unless costly tracking and conversion studies are deployed (Kotler & Armstrong, 2017). DMOs also conduct below-the-line activities, including attending trade shows or fairs, distributing brochures and other marketing collateral, and sponsorship. For example, in 2019/20, VisitMalta sponsored the premier football league team Manchester United FC. In addition, DMOs handle media enquiries, organise familiarisation trips (or 'educationals') for travel writers, the media, overseas travel agents, airlines and inbound tour operators, and co-ordinate press releases. They also participate in joint marketing campaigns and co-ordinate destination quality schemes to maintain and raise standards for visitor well-being.

We now discuss each of the following destination promotions mix tools:

- Advertising
- Sales (personal selling)
- PR and publicity
- Sales promotion and merchandising
- Product placement (film-induced tourism)
- Digital marketing

14.7.1 Advertising

Destination advertising is defined as "the placing of messages by a DMO in any mass media to remind, inform, persuade potential tourists, and travel trade to consider the destination for future travel". One of the main objectives of both broadcast and print advertising is to direct traffic to a DMO's website. Television advertising is an effective medium for creating a greater degree of awareness about a country or destination (Avraham & Ketter, 2016: 59). In recent years, many national tourism organisations and DMOs have advertised on national and international television. For example, during the run-up to the 2018 FIFA World Cup™, the Russian Federation National Tourist Office ran a series of fifteen-second commercials showcasing various Russian Federation icons and attractions (for instance, shots of architecture, mountains and wildlife and cities, such as Moscow, St. Petersburg, and Vladimir) as well as the organisation's logo (incorporating the address of its website) on SKY News, a global satellite television channel. However, television advertising is expensive, and most destinations' advertisements are placed in print media (newspaper, magazines, especially weekend editions). Advertising in trade maga-

🞏 **Image 14.8** Cape Tourism Tourism's logo. (Source: Leigh Dawber, Marketing Executive, Cape Town Tourism)

zines and newspapers is also an effective way of targeting the travel trade, including conference organisers, meeting planners, tour operators, and travel agents.

14.7.2 Sales (Personal Selling)

This involves communications between DMO sales staff and prospective customers (via video such as Zoom, SMS, telephone, e-mail or social media messaging programmes: WhatsApp, Skype, WeChat, etc.).

Many DMOs use travel trade shows (also referred to as "trade fairs") and exhibitions to promote their attractions to the travel trade as well as the general public. These events, which are usually annual, bring together all elements of the tourism industry. For example, Tourism Rwanda has stands that promote the country's attractions and destinations at the World Travel Market (WTM) in London, England and the ITB Berlin, Germany. Likewise, various international backpacking associations and role-players attend the annual World Youth and Student Travel Conference (WYSTC). The Tourism Indaba, which is held at the International Convention Centre in Durban, South Africa annually, provides a networking platform for the promotion of southern African destinations. The World Travel Expo, which is held annually in five Australian cities, promotes tourist regions and destinations (the 2019 show for example,

featured the Americas) to the travel trade as well as to consumers.

14.7.3 PR and Publicity

Public relations (PR) is one of the main activities for DMOs. As a result of the high costs involved in advertising, travel journalists, travel agents, and inbound tour operators (ITOs) are frequently invited to destinations at the expense of the DMO in the hope that this will result in promoting it or favourable article or feature about the destination. (These trips are known as "familiarisation trips" or "educational trips"). Similarly, PR techniques are used to improve a destination's image with the general public, especially if the destination has received negative publicity as a result of high levels of crime, occurrences such as natural disasters or political instability. Publicity is a non-paid communications technique about the destination.

Industry Insight 14.8

Welcome to Bland, Dull, and Boring

Bland in Australia has turned a negative into a positive by establishing links with Dull in Scotland and Boring in the United States. Bland in New South Wales, population just short of 6000, was named after William Bland, a doctor in the colonial era. The towns of Dull in Perthshire and Boring in Oregon have joined forces with Bland to draw in tourists and forge closer links.

Source: Squires, N. (2013). Bland's plan to link with Dull and Boring. *The Daily Telegraph*, 31 May.

PR and publicity include the activities that a DMO initiates in with the aim of maintaining and improving its relationship with other stakeholders. Marketing collateral such as postcards are an effective destination marketing tool for building relationships. In 2017, the Bulgarian Ministry of Tourism sent out 400,000 postcards to foreign tourists who had visited Bulgaria that year with a "Thank you" message from its Minister. In addition, celebrity visits, and press releases are effective PR techniques used to promote and improve the image of a destination (see ► Industry Insight 14.9 and the section on public relations in ► Chap. 12). For example, regular visits to Africa during 2019 by the Duke and Duchess of Sussex (Prince Harry and Meghan Markle) had the effect of promoting the likes of Angola and Malawi worldwide.

14.7.4 Sales Promotion and Merchandising

Sales promotion involves techniques used by a DMO to give short-term inducements for people to visit and special communication methods not included in other promotional elements. Examples include posters and special offers such as competitions (see ◨ Image 14.9), sweepstakes, which are usually incorporated into a DMO's social media campaign (such as Facebook).

Retail merchandising materials and point-of-purchase (POP) advertising carried out by DMOs in locations such as visitor information centres, transport hubs, and visitor attractions. Examples of merchandise, usually handed-out at travel trade shows include t-shirts, USB drives, beer mats, caps, key rings, pens, logo bags, calendars, and even customised hand-sanitizer bottles.

◨ **Image 14.9**   The Croatian National Tourist Board's (CNTB) logo

◨ **Image 14.10**   South African Tourism's stand at the 2018 WTM travel trade show hosted in London. (Source: SA Tourism)

14.7.5 **Product Placement**

Placing a destination featured in movies and TV series is a prime example of product placement. Film-induced tourism is defined as tourist visits to the destination featured on television, video, or cinema screen (Hudson & Ritchie 2006). Placing a destination in a film is a prime example of product placement. Examples of film-induced tourism include *Lord of the Rings* (New Zealand), and *Girl with the Dragon Tattoo* (Sweden), and *Hanna* (Romania), and *Extraction* (Bangladesh). Consumers are induced to such destinations due to fascination and/or dramatic scenery.

> *Digital marketing* is the use of digital-format information and communication technologies by DMOs to liaise with various audiences, to provide information and to promote the destination (Morrison, 2019: 442).

☐ **Image 14.11** SA Tourism's competition at a travel trade show. (Source: SA Tourism)

14.7.6 **Digital Marketing**

Destinations are increasingly using **digital marketing** and social media to promote their services and reach consumers in a more interactive and instant way. Today's tourists use digital media and social media sites or information-sharing sites at all stages on the holiday decision-making process (or customer journey). For example, consumers may view Instagram Influencers posts and stories during the anticipation stage, write and post blogs and photos of their holiday on WordPress during the engagement stage, and finally recommend destinations to friends and relatives via Facebook (review stage). The internet and social media have become major information dissemination and marketing tools for DMOs. All DMOs have their own websites ('official website') which are important 'shop widows' for showcasing a destination's attractions and activities, and most have their own sites and social media networks and sites. DMOs utilise digital (online) marketing techniques, include the following:

- A website serving as an interactive portal that conveys the image of the destination
- A DMO database with e-mails and social media (such as LinkedIn, Facebook, Instagram, Snapchat, and YouTube) tactics to invite tourists to interact and engage with the destination
- Engagement of the destination community in dialogue via social media so that they become active advocates of the destination. Communicating and interacting with local communities is paramount. This is a type of PR activity (see ▶ Chap. 11).

The main functions/tools of digital marketing in destination marketing are as follows:
- Content creation
- A DMO website

- SEM and SEO
- Social media campaigns
- Develop DMOs and travel itinerary Apps
- E-mail
- Other functions of digital marketing

We will now discuss each of these functions.

14.7.6.1 Creating Content

Content is at the centre of DMO digital marketing activity. There are three major sources of digital content: DMO-developed, user-generated (UGC), and co-created content.

- Photographs are also important visual communication for DMOs. Photographs

---

Industry Insight 14.9

New Zealand's Website: A Benchmark for National Tourism Organisations

The destination marketing website for New Zealand, ▶ www.newzealand.com, has won numerous awards (it was voted the best destination website in the Asia Pacific region at the International Tourismus Borse (ITB) Asia in 2017) and can be considered a benchmark for national tourism organisations. People were encouraged to cast their vote based on the content, layout, ease of navigation, and innovation of the website, rather than the organisation behind it. Not only is the ▶ newzealand.com website very user-friendly, with clear navigation, but it also provides a number of interactive tools. The aim of newzealand.com is to connect consumers with travel sellers. Forty-one million people visit the site each year which results in 3.2 million referrals to the tourism industry. Research also shows that 50 per cent of travellers who visit ▶ newzealand.com before they arrive in New Zealand stay longer and visit more regions than those who don't visit the site. The site offers interactive itinerary planning tools, special travel deals, operator listings and information about New Zealand. After planning a trip, users can send the planner directly to a travel agent who can assist with booking the trip.

Source: Winning website collects another award. ▶ https://www.tourismnewzealand.com/news/winning-website-collects-another-award/

◘ **Image 14.12**   Location for the movie *The Hobbit* in New Zealand. (Source: Unsplash)

14

Visit Dubai

The "Visit Dubai" website attempts to position Dubai as a cultural melting pot celebrating all races and religions, a family-friendly destination, and a luxurious, modern, and safe holiday destination by the sea. It includes links to a currency converter, an events calendar, an app, a Dubai map, visa and entry information, and an accommodation directory. It also offers press releases, news, travel planning (itineraries, accommodation, getting around Dubai, neighbourhoods, and landmarks, and a distance calculator), information about weather, including temperatures and forecasts, a Dubai video, media contacts, a section on careers, education, and training, website feedback, and a "what's on" section consisting of information on cultural and hallmark events in Dubai.

☑ **Image 14.13**   Visit Dubai's website homepage

taken by visitors (for e.g. Instagram "selfies"), professional photographers for DMOs, commissioned travel influencers' posts on Instagram, and community residents and are then shared on social media and DMO sites.

- Video is particularly important as It tangibilises bringing the destination to life. Most popular destination videos will be shared on video-sharing sites such as YouTube, Instagram, LinkedIn, Tumblr, and Twitter.

- Text - storytelling and local news are growing in importance for DMOs. Text could also include interesting facts ('Factsheets'), Did you knows?, historical facts, and digital press releases and newsletters.
- Online press releases and announcements
- Blog posts & vlogs - about destinations. Four sources of blogs and vlogs: DMO developed, consumer-developed (by visitors), travel/social influencer-developed (see chapter 12 case study), and tourism industry-developed.

- User-generated content. DMOs utilise (by the visitors) for eWoM and research and feedback
- Co-created - content created by both the DMO, the community, and visitor (travel experience).

14.7.6.2 A DMO Website

The internet is a natural medium for DMOs. It enables a country or destination to create an encyclopedia of information. Internet search engines (such as Google) are a valuable tool connecting prospecting tourists with DMO websites (Pan et al., 2010). A DMO's website is not only an information service it is also an important promotional and communications tool for the destination marketer. The success of a website depends upon the DMO's ability to design an effective and interactive website. A well-designed website assists in travellers' planning, helping to ensure that they make the right decisions, and have an enjoyable experience. A DMO's website also serves as a one-stop-shop for accessing information, research, and direct booking for visitor attractions, travel passes, amenities, transport providers, tours, events news, and activities that visitors to the destination require (see ▶ Industry Insights 14.10).

The functions of a DMO website are to:
- Provide information on the destination
- Promote and 'showcase' the destination
- Communicate positioning and branding
- Collate visitor database statistics and research
- Allow bookings and reservations (e-commerce)
- Engage travellers in discussion on social media (information sharing such as Instagram Geotags)
- Disseminate important news (for example, in 2020 many DMOs provided 'COVID-10 updates' and funding advice)
- Build relationships with the travel trade (separate link for the travel trade).

14.7.6.3 SEM and SEO

The majority of consumers use a search engine to find a DMO website. The most popular search engine is Google; as many as three-quarters (73%) of consumers use it to search for websites (Carter, 2020). Other popular search engines include Baidu, Bing (Microsoft), Pinterest, and Yahoo! Search engine marketing (SEM) involves DMOs promoting the visibility of their websites on search engines. Search engine optimisation (SEO) entails the steps that DMOs take to ensure that their sites are relevant and important to potential visitors. Websites that rank better than the others are because of a powerful web marketing technique called search engine optimisation (SEO).The aim of SEO is to get destinations listed early (ranked) and frequently in Google and other search engines sites. Whenever consumers enter a query in a search engine and hit 'enter' they receive a list of web results that contain that query term (For example, "Romania tourism travel"). Users normally tend to visit websites that are at the top of this list as they perceive those to be more relevant to the query.

14.7.6.4 Social Media

Social media marketing is a major influence on DMOs and destinations. Popularity of the social media networks varies by country in the world (for example, VK is popular in Russia; Renren in China). Popular social media networks include, Facebook, Twitter, Instagram, YouTube, Google+, Pinterest, Tumblr, TikTok, Bing, Hi5, Flickr, LinkedIn, Snapchat, and WeChat. For example, the DMO VisitMalta have photos on its Flickr group page "Memories of Malta", an official page on YouTube for visitors to download and share videos of Malta, as well as a VisitMalta Twitter account (@VisitMalta). DMOs are increasingly using YouTube video clips to shape a destination's image and to counter any negative perceptions that consumers may have of it (see ◻ Image 14.11). Besides showcasing tourist destinations, these social media sites can also drive traffic to DMOs' websites.

DMOs can measure the results of their social media campaigns. Measurement tools include metrics such as reach, views, referrals, members (people who participate in an ongoing relationship as fans or followers and engagement, for example: referrals, sharing, 'tags', clicks, and comments).

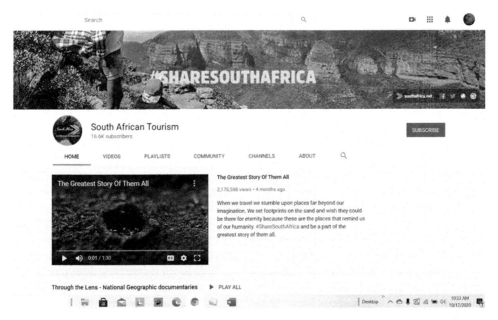

The main functions of social media in destination marketing are to:

- Collect user-generated content (UGC), such as tourist 'selfies' (self-photographs)
- To drive web traffic to the DMO's official website (for example, a link to the DMO URL - web address - on the DMO's Instagram site)
- Display videos and photography
- Disseminate topical news stories (for example, an upcoming cultural event)
- Display upcoming events
- Encourage word-of-mouse referrals (e.g. Facebook "likes", and Instagram "Geotags")
- Request and gather feedback (about the social media site)

14.7.6.5 Apps

Mobile phone apps are extremely popular. In 2020, there were over 5.5 million apps and 5 billion mobile phone users. Many DMOs have developed their own apps. That can be accessed from their homepage and social media sites. These apps incorporate travel itineraries, virtual travel guides, and AR. For example, the DMO VisitMalta has a downloadable mobile app 'VisitMalta Plus' for holiday planning and practical information on the Maltese Island.

14.7.6.6 E-mail

E-mailing is essentially direct mail via the internet. E-mails are inexpensive, environmentally-friendly, and an easy-to-use destination promotional tool. Most people who use the internet have an e-mail account. DMOs use apps such as WhatsApp, Facebook Messenger, WeChat, and others in conjunction with e-mail. Destination e-brochures, newsletters, e-flyers, e-surveys, and virtual guides can all be e-mailed to prospective tourists.

14.7.6.7 Other Tools

Other digital marketing tools include:

- Travel reviews sites: assessments made by consumers who have visited destinations, hotels, attractions, and restaurants (e.g. *TripAdvisor*, travel guide sites such as Lonely Plant and Thorn Tree)
- Podcasts – digital audio or video files made available on social media platforms and DMOs websites which can be downloaded onto users' smartphones and/or touchscreen tablet
- Webcams – for streaming live views of attractions at the destination, use of drones for aerial shots

- Texting/SMS – consumers use it to request information and newsletters from DMOs and DMO social media sites
- Virtual guides and e-brochures (interactive guides) – print-outs in PDF format, links to a DMO's website and social media sites
- Virtual reality – 360-degree panorama video (allows consumers to sample destinations). It has a great deal of potential to promote and sell tourism offerings and destinations as a result of its ability to provide sensory information to prospective tourists (Guttentag, 2009). Incorporated into the DMO's website.
- Augmented Reality (AR) allows travellers to enjoy three-dimensional models of places, and "meet" tour guides. AR also helps with navigation in unfamiliar places and destinations. Details about local destinations and visitor attractions can also be displayed as a customer points his/her smartphone at them, providing information at the exact time that it is most relevant.

Several of these tools might be located on the DMO's homepage reached through a 'media gallery' link.

Japan Tourism Wins Social Media Awards for Social Media Campaign

Encouraging people to consider Japan as a ski/snowboard destination, Japan Tourism launched a Facebook game called "Powder Dash". Allowing players to experience the 'powder' that Japan has to offer, the game saw players race down mountains, hit jumps, do tricks, in a bid to score high points and unlock advanced snowboards. Users can also challenge friends.

14.8 Marketing Events to Attract Visitors

Key events, conferences, and festivals are also being used more and more as strategic marketing tools to leverage destination awareness and to enhance competitive positioning opportunities for destinations (Getz, 2010). The staging of an event can contribute to a country's political identity and the type of event can affect the image of the destination. An event can be used to showcase a country; it can provide a snapshot of why tourists should visit, work, or live in the destination. Events and festivals, for instance, are often hosted by destinations to counter seasonality and increase tourism revenue during quiet times of the year (Connell, Page & Meyer, 2015). For example, a number of events in Italy such as the Euro Chocolate in Perugia, the White Truffle Festival in Alba, and the Palio in, are held in September in order to increase tourist arrivals at the end of the tourist season.

Events can showcase a destination. DMOs, along with other government agencies, bid for the right to host various types of events. Even the process of bidding for large events such as the Olympic Games can increase the exposure of the bidding destination. Events range from local community events, which attract local visitors, to mega events such as the FIFA World Cup™, which attract people from all over the world, and gain significant global media attention before, during, and after the event. Sport has the potential to have a significant impact on a country or city's brand. Google searches for "Russia" peaked during the FIFA 2018 World Cup™ finals. Sport inspires more interest in host countries than politics, economics, or other events.

Summary
In this chapter, we have highlighted the fact that destination marketing is perhaps the most complex form of marketing in tourism. Destination marketing is about selling a dream and translating it into a first-class visitor experience. It is predominantly carried out by DMOs in the public sector, whose task is to promote an extremely diverse range of private and public tourist attractions and amenities. As consumers become more demanding, the global competition for visitors among destinations is becoming greater. In turn, the approaches employed by destination marketers are becoming more sophisticated.

We have also applied various marketing concepts to destinations, and emphasised the importance of tourist destination image and branding. Branding a destination is a slow process. Research suggests that it can take up to 2 years to brand a destination successfully (Ekinci & Hosany, 2006). DMO marketers should be as concerned about the perceptions that prospective visitors have of a destination as they are about its visitor attractions, service delivery, safety and security, transport and infrastructure, and amenities.

❓ Review Questions

1. Briefly explain why destination marketing is a complex activity. Discuss how the marketing of a destination differs from that of the marketing of a FMCG or a tourism business/product.
2. Outline the challenges facing destination marketing organisations (DMOs).

3. Identify and briefly explain five activities carried out by DMOs to market a destination?
4. Discuss Butler's (1980) tourism area life cycle model in terms of examples of destinations and resorts in your country, and types of tourist associated with the different stages.
5. Explain why it is important for DMOs to undertake marketing research.
6. "Image is reality in the tourism industry." Discuss this statement.
7. Why is the branding of a destination problematic? Use industry examples to explain your answer.
8. Suggest ways in which your county/province/state/territory could market itself to attract more domestic tourists.
9. Go online to find three destination slogans. Critique each one. What makes a good slogan?
10. Explain why it is important for small tourism and hospitality businesses to understand the key challenges facing DMOs?

In-depth Case Study 14: Marketing Tourism Destinations: Marketing and Branding Rwanda: Rwanda Opens Up Its Doors

Objectives

- To understand the concept of destination marketing
- To examine the concept of branding tourist destinations.

Rwanda may be one of the smallest countries on the African continent but is home to a vast and stunning range of mountains, giving rise to it affectionately being known as 'Le Pays des Mille Collines' (Land of a Thousand Hills). This mountainous country, officially known as the Republic of Rwanda, is located a few degrees south of the equator in Central Africa and is bordered by Uganda, Tanzania, Burundi, and the Democratic Republic of the Congo (DRC).

Despite its beautiful scenery, associations of Rwanda for many people will sadly not conjure up inspiring images of a thousand hills,

but horrifying television footage of many thousands' dead from the Rwandan Genocide of 1994. The genocide resulted in up to 800,000 people slaughtered by ethnic Hutu extremists, shocking the world with one hundred days of brutal violence (BBC News, April 7, 2014). The civil war (the Rwandan Civil War) tore the country apart and lasted from October 1990 to July 1994.

Rwanda has made a concerted effort to move on from its darkest and bloodiest years towards the end of the last century. As part of the long road to recovery, the Rwanda Development Board (RDB) implemented a tourism marketing campaign in the mid-2000s using the slogan, "Discover a New African Dawn" (Tasci, 2011). By implementing this slogan and campaign, Rwanda tourism marketers acknowledged the long stretch of darkness and troubled period that the country had undergone. In Kigali, Rwanda's capital city, a Genocide Memorial Centre has been built to acknowledge the remains of over 25,000 victims. Today, the African dawn represents that a new day is on the horizon along with opportunities for peace and prosperity (Avraham & Ketter, 2016: 116).

Rwanda has started to move on from being a 'war-torn' nation and has a burgeoning reputation for its 480-strong mountain gorilla population, attracting 'gorilla tourists' from all over the world to see. Home for the endangered mountain gorillas is the Volcanoes National Park, situated in the far northwest of Rwanda. The Volcanoes National Park is named after the chain of dormant volcanoes making up the Virunga Massif: Karisimbi – the highest at 4507 m, Bisoke with its verdant crater lake, Sabinyo, Gahinga, and Muhabura. Dian Fossey, the esteemed primatologist and conservationist, wrote: "In the heart of Central Africa, so high up that you shiver more than you sweat are great, old volcanoes towering almost 15 000 feet, and nearly covered with rich, green rainforest – the Virungas". This magnificent mountain range is a rich mosaic of montane ecosystems, which embrace evergreen and bamboo forest, open grassland, swamp, and heath.

Making the most of its natural advantage, Rwanda is an up-and-coming safari destination, with central Africa's largest protected wetland in the Akagera National Park on the country's eastern border with Tanzania. The Akagera National Park hosts the Big Five (lion, leopard, elephant, black rhino, and buffalo) and along with safaris, offers other popular tourist activities, including gorilla tracking, birdwatching, and primate tracking. The west of Rwanda forms a branch of the Great Rift Valley known as the Albertine Rift. It has many unique, endemic species and is bursting with life. Chimpanzees, golden monkeys and other primates live alongside hundreds of brightly coloured birds, orchids and butterflies.

With such a rich and diverse natural habitat, it is no surprise that tourism is Rwanda's largest foreign exchange earner and contributes about 13 per cent of the country's GDP, supporting over 130,000 jobs. A gorilla tourism permit costs $1500 (£1150) each, which equates to more than $50 (£38 million) million a year in total. Ten per cent of the income derived from gorilla, safari, and other tourist permits, as well as park fees, is spent in partnership with local communities to change lives for the better.

Visit Rwanda' is the nation's tourist board and destination marketing organisation (DMO). The DMO is a subsidiary of the Rwanda Development Board (RDB), a government department that facilitates various agencies in the national economy; one of these being the tourism sector. The RDB was established in 2009 to coordinate and promote Rwanda's economic development. Visit Rwanda devised a marketing strategy, Vision 2050, which identified several long-term tourism development and conservation initiatives. As part of the strategy, the Rwandan government upgraded its conference and hospitality infrastructure, transport networks, visitor attractions, and conservation policies.

Tourism in Rwanda is an important component of the Rwandan economy. Rwanda is today ranked third most popular destination country in Africa for hosting international meetings and events by the International Congress and Convention Association (ICCA). The Kigali Convention Centre, which opened in 2016, is the first and largest convention centre in the region.

Another Visit Rwanda initiative was to increase routes of Rwanda's national airline; RwandAir. The airline now flies to 26 destinations globally. In June 2017, it began services between Kigali and Gatwick Airport in the UK and now offers three direct flights-a-week. As a consequence, the number of UK tourists increased by 21 per cent in 2017 to more than 16,000 out of a total 1.2 million global tourist

VISIT RWANDA

⬛ Image 14.15 Visit Rwanda's logo. (Source: Communications Division, Rwanda Development Board (RDB))

arrivals. Rwanda is hoping to continue to take advantage of growing commercial links with the UK, especially among coffee traders, to market the capital city Kigali as a regional hub for connecting flights and to encourage tourism.

The RDB's aim is to double tourism receipts from U$404 million (£310 million) to U$800 million (£614 million) by 2024. This ambitious goal is only possible by marketing Rwanda as a tourist destination in innovative ways. In 2017, Visit Rwanda signed a sponsorship deal to have its brand name 'Visit Rwanda' displayed on the shirt sleeves of London based UK Premier League football team, Arsenal Football Club. The three-year sponsorship deal cost approximately £30 million ($39 million) and benefits to Rwanda are hoped to be gleaned by the global reach of Arsenal as they are watched by millions of television viewers around the world whenever they play.

Tourism has also played a major role in helping the local community. One of the major tourism initiatives has been the Revenue Share Program. Initiated in 2005 by the Government of Rwanda, the Revenue Share program aims to guide investment in the areas surrounding the Akagera National Park, Nyungwe National Park and Volcanoes National Park. Over U$1.28 million (£984,000) has been distributed by the RDB to more than 158 community-based projects. These projects have provided clean drinking water, health centres, classrooms, and housing to members of the communities living around the three national parks.

As a testament to Rwanda's tourism revival, in 2018, luxury holiday resort brand *One&Only* opened Nyungwe House to appeal to travellers who "have been everywhere and wanted something that is different, unique, customised and provides a once-in-a-lifetime experience". Such a facility illustrates how Rwanda has progressed from a recent war- ravaged country to avoid, to a place offering wonderful holiday experiences to compare favourably with its more established tourist-friendly African neighbours.

Source: The Times (2017). Monday 15 May 2017 page 40. Business. Business news reporter.

Visit Rwanda (2020). ▶ https://www. visitrwanda.com/

Questions and Activities

1. The case study raises the issue of a brand as a concept applied to a destination. Consider the issue in the context of the discussion contained in ▶ Chap. 14.
2. Is the £30 million paid by Rwanda Tourism for sponsoring UK premiership football club Arsenal FC justified given Rwanda is one of the poorest countries in the world? Discuss.
3. Explain why branding is considered important to countries such as Rwanda?
4. Devise a new slogan for Rwanda Tourism.
5. At what stage is Rwanda currently in the tourism area life cycle model?
6. Go online and find Rwanda Tourism's website (▶ visitrwanda.com). Critically evaluate the website's homepage in terms of the following:
   - Information and content provided
   - Ease of navigation
   - Graphics
   - Organisation of information
   - Level of interaction.

◪ **Image 14.16**   Nyanza King's Palace, Rwanda. (Source: Communications Division, Rwanda Development Board (RDB))

◪ **Image 14.17**   Volcanoes National Park, Rwanda. (Source: Communications Division, Rwanda Development Board (RDB))

References

Addley, E., & Convery, S. (2019). Chernobyl writer begs Instagram tourists to respect site of disaster. *The Guardian*, 13 June. p. 3.

Ashworth, G., & Voogd, H. (1988). Marketing the city: Concepts, processes and Dutch applications. *Town Planning Review, 59*, 65.

Avraham, E., & Ketter, E. (2013). Marketing destinations with prolonged negative images: Towards a theoretical model. *Tourism Geographies, 15*(1), 145–164.

Avraham, E., & Ketter, E. (2016). *Tourism marketing for developing countries*. London: Palgrave Macmillan.

BBC News. (2014). Rwanda genocide: 100 days of slaughter. Retrieved from https://www.bbc.co.uk/news/world-africa-26875506 [12 January 2020].

Beirman, D. (2003). *Restoring Destinations in Crisis*. Crows Nest, NSW: Allen & Unwin.

Buhalis, D. (2000). Marketing the competitive destination of the future. *Tourism Management, 21*(1), 97–116.

Butler, R. W. (1980). The concept of a tourist area lifecycle of evolution: Implications for management resources. *Canadian Geographer, XXIV, 1*(5).

Carter, J. (2020). Search engine marketing statistics 2020. *Smart Insights*. Retrieved from: https://www.smartinsights.com/search-engine-marketing/search-engine-statistics/ [13 March 2020].

Choy, D. J. L. (1992). Life cycle models of Pacific island destinations. *Journal of Tourism Research, 30*(3).

Connell, J. (2005). Toddler, tourism and Tobermory: Destination marketing issues and television-induced tourism. *Tourism Management, 26*(5), 763.

Connell, J., Page, S. J., & Meyer, D. (2015). Visitor attractions: Responding to events. *Tourism Management, 46*(4), 283–298.

Cooper, C., & Hall, M. (2019). *Contemporary tourism: An international approach* (4th ed.). Oxford, UK: Goodfellow Publishers.

Ekinci, Y., & Hosany, S. (2006). Destination personality: An application of brand personality to tourism destinations. *Journal of Travel Research, 45*(2), 127.

Fyall, A., Garrod, B., & Wang, Y. (2012). Destination collaboration: A critical review of theoretical approaches to a multi-dimensional phenomenon, *Journal of Destination Marketing & Management, 1*(1–2), 10–26,

Fyall, A., Legoherel, P., Frochot, I., & Wang, Y. (2019). *Marketing for tourism and hospitality*. London: Routledge.

George, R. (2003). Tourists' perceptions of safety and security while visiting Cape Town. *Tourism Management, 24*(5), 575–585.

Getz, D. (2010). The nature and scope of festival studies. *International Journal of Event Management Research, 5*(1), 1–47.

Guttentag, D. A. (2009). Virtual reality: Application and implications for tourism. *Tourism Management, 31*(5).

Hudson, S., & Ritchie, J. (2006). Promoting destinations via film tourism: An empirical identification of supporting marketing initiatives. *Journal of Travel Research, 44*(4), 387–396.

Inskeep, E. (1991). *Tourism planning: An integrated planning and development approach*. New York: Wiley.

Keller, K. L. (2012). *Strategic brand management: Building, measuring, and managing brand equity* (4th ed.). Upper Saddle River, NJ: Prentice-Hall.

Khan, S. (2013). An insight into stereotypical images and encountered reality of south Asia as a tourism destination. *Asia-Pacific Journal of Innovation in Hospitality and Tourism, 2*(1), 17–36.

Kim, H. (1998). Perceived attractiveness of Korean destinations. *Annals of Tourism Research, 25*(2).

Kotler, P., & Armstrong, G. (2017). *Principles of marketing* (17th ed.). London: Pearson Education.

Kozak, M., & Rimmington, M. (1995). Benchmarking: Destination attractiveness and small hospitality business performance. *International Journal of Contemporary Hospitality Management, 10*(5), 184–188.

Laws, E. (2002). *Tourism marketing: Quality and service management perspectives*. London: Continuum.

Ministry of Culture & Tourism. (2019). *Tourism strategy of Turkey – 2023*. Ministry of Culture & Tourism, Ankara. Retrieved from: http://www.kultur.gov.tr/Eklenti/43537,turkeytourismstrategy2023pdf.pdf?0&_tag1=796689BB12A540BE0672E65E48D10C07D6DAE291 [15 June 2019].

Morgan, N., & Pritchard, A. (2004). Meeting the destination branding challenge. In N. Morgan, A. Pritchard, & R. Pride (Eds.), *Destination branding: Creating the unique destination proposition* (2nd ed.). Oxford, UK: Elsevier Butterworth-Heinemann.

Morgan, N., Pritchard, A., & Pride, R. (2012). Destination brands: Managing place reputation (3rd ed.). Oxford, UK: Butterworth-Heinemann.

Morrison, A. (2019). *Marketing and managing tourism destinations* (2nd ed.). London: Routledge.

Murdy, S., & Pike, S. (2012). Perceptions of visitor relationship marketing opportunities by destination marketers: An importance-performance analysis. *Tourism Managemnet, 33*(5), 1281–1285.

Neto, F. (2003). A new approach to sustainable tourism development: Moving beyond environmental protection. *Natural Resources Forum, 27*, 212–222.

Pan, B., Xiang, Z., Laws, E., & Fessenmaier, D. (2010). The dynamics of search engine marketing for tourist destinations. *Journal of Travel Research, 46*, 46–63.

Pike, S. (2004). *Destination marketing organisations*. London: Elsevier.

Pike, S. (2005). Tourism destination branding complexity. *Journal of Product and Brand Management, 14*(4), 258–259.

Pike, S. (2012). Destination positioning opportunities using personal values: Elicited through the repertory test with laddering analysis. *Tourism Management, 33*(1), 100–107.

Pike, S. (2020). *Destination marketing essentials* (3rd ed.). Oxford: Routledge.

Pike, S. (2018). *Tourism marketing for small businesses*. Oxford: Goodfellow Publishers.

Pimental, R. (1997). *Consumer preference for logo designs: Visual design and meaning*. Tucson, AZ: The University of Arizona.

Plog, S. C. (1974). Why destinations areas rise and fall in popularity. *Cornell Hotel and Restaurant Administration Quarterly,* November 13–16.

Plog, S. C. (2004). *Leisure travel.* Upper Saddle River, NJ: Prentice-Hall.

Porter, M. E. (1979). How competitive forces shape strategy. *Harvard Business Review, 57*(2), 137–145.

Supphellen, M., & Nygaardsvik, I. (2002). Testing country brand slogans: Conceptual development and empirical illustration of a simple normative model. *Journal of Brand Management, 9,* 4–5.

Sussmann, S., & Ünel, A. (1999). Destination image and its modification after travel: An empirical study on Turkey. In A. Pizam & Y. Mansfeld (Eds.), *Consumer behaviour in travel and tourism.* New York: Haworth Hospitality Press.

Tasci, A. (2011). Destination branding and positioning. In Y. Wang & A. Pizam (Eds.), *Destination marketing and management: Theories and applications* (pp. 113–129). Oxfordshire: CABI.

Thomas, W., & Thomas, D. (1928). The Thomas theorem. In M. Patton (Ed.). (2002). *Qualitative research and evaluation methods* (3rd ed.). Thousand Oaks, CA: Sage.

United Nations. (2018). *World's population increasingly urban with more than half living in urban areas.* Retrieved from: http://www.un.org/en/development/desa/news/population/world-urbanization-prospects-2014.html [6 September 2018].

Wang, Y., & A. Pizam, A. (Eds.). *Destination marketing and management: Theories and applications.* Oxfordshire: CABI.

Further Reading

Avraham, E., & Ketter, E. (2016). *Tourism marketing for developing countries.* London: Palgrave Macmillan.

Campelo, A. (Ed.). (2017). *Handbook on place branding and marketing.* Gloucester, UK: Edward Elgar Publishing Ltd..

Morrison, A. (2019). *Managing and marketing tourism destinations* (2nd ed.). Oxford, UK: Routledge.

Pike, S., & Page, S. (2014). Destination marketing organisations and destination marketing: A narrative analysis of the literature. *Tourism Management, 1,* 202–227.

14

Supplementary Information

Index

Printed by Printforce, United Kingdom